Cisco® Internetworking and Troubleshooting

Cormac S. Long
MSEE, CCNP™, CCNA™

McGraw-Hill
New York San Francisco Washington, D.C.
Auckland Bogotá Caracas Lisbon London
Madrid Mexico City Milan Montreal New Delhi
San Juan Singapore Sydney Tokyo Toronto

Library of Congress Cataloging-in-Publication Data

Long, Cormac
CISCO internetworking and troubleshooting / Cormac Long.
p. cm. — (McGraw-Hill technical expert series)
ISBN 0-07-135598-7
1. Routers (Computer networks) 2. Internetworking (Telecommunication)
3. Computer network protocols I. Title. II. Cisco technical expert
TK5105.543.L66 1999
004.6'2—dc21

99-051994

McGraw-Hill

*A Division of The **McGraw-Hill** Companies*

1 2 3 4 5 6 7 8 9 0 AGM/AGM 9 0 4 3 2 1 0 9

ISBN 0-07-135598-7

The sponsoring editor for this book was Steven Elliot, the managing editor was Jennifer Perillo, the editing supervisor was Ruth W. Mannino, and the production supervisor was Claire Stanley. It was set in New Century Schoolbook by Don Feldman of McGraw-Hill's desktop composition unit in cooperation with Spring Point Publishing Services.

Printed and bound by Quebecor / Martinsburg.

This book is printed on recycled, acid-free paper containing a minimum of 50% recycled de-inked fiber.

CONTENTS

PREFACE

Some Background

Troubleshooting is the ultimate internetworking skill. No aspect of the technology tests the internetworking engineer more than having to apply a comprehensive skill set to resolve a complex and critical problem in a timely manner. It is equally a fact of life in this industry that such skills are in extremely short supply. Internetworking is a fascinating discipline, but it is also complex and very broad in subject matter. It pertains not just to one technology but to several. Each of these technologies needs to be understood in depth in order to perform network troubleshooting, but it is even more important to clearly understand how these different technologies relate to one another. Proficiency in internetworking technology is built up with experience over time. There are no short cuts. Almost all high-caliber professionals whom I know in this area have attained their positions by having a keen interest in the technology coupled with a love of learning. Although there are many people in this industry who can "talk the talk," there are significantly fewer who can apply themselves in practical situations when it is most required. This, of course, presents enormous opportunity for those who will eventually master the technology.

This is the backdrop against which I wrote this book. The greatest challenge I faced was in deciding how the book's structure and content could be best tailored to meet the reader's needs. I decided on a predominantly practical approach in presenting the subject matter. Each chapter contains a certain amount of theory; however the main focus is a practical one in terms of working with Cisco® networks. If I were to provide a "from the ground up" theoretical explanation of each technology and also include extensive practical examples, the book could have run into several volumes. In fact, many of the chapters have sufficient scope for a dedicated book of their own. This is not to say that there is a lack of detail in the material. In many cases I ensure that there is enough room to go into each subject to an advanced level of detail by assuming that the reader already has at least a basic understanding of the technology in question. I think this is a valid assumption since troubleshooting is not an area that you should enter into before having a grasp of the technology fundamentals. The exception to this is so-called first-level support, which is both an important and undervalued function.

A more compelling reason for providing a practical focus is that this type of information is far more difficult for readers to obtain. In the information age that we live in, the theory of most LAN and WAN protocols can be found either in existing texts or via the Internet. However, it is far more difficult to find information that is of a practical nature. One of my goals in writing this book was to help fill that void.

Who Should Read This Book and Why

This book is aimed at internetworking professionals who wish to further develop their skills. The material has a sufficient level of detail and complexity to provide a useful on-the-job reference for established networking professionals, particularly those who frequently operate in a hands-on environment. I assume that the reader has at least one year of experience, preferably practical, in a Cisco internetworking environment. The reader should also understand the concept of protocol layering and have a reasonable grasp of the first four layers of the OSI model.

All of the troubleshooting scenarios are of CCIE standard. Many of the issues addressed in each chapter and the tips that are provided should be extremely helpful for CCIE candidates. However, my main focus is on the real world rather than any particular certification. Thus, for example, a tool such as debug ipx packet and the concept of OSPF virtual links are really only mentioned in passing in this book. This is because they are of limited use and significance in most networking environments; however they do need to be part of your arsenal if you are preparing for the CCIE. On the other side of the coin, topics such as IP and IPX client-server connectivity are covered in more detail than is required for most industrial certifications.

So what else can you expect to get out of this book? I would not be so naïve or dishonest as to claim that this book will teach you everything you need to know about Cisco internetworking and troubleshooting. No book will. But I have made every effort to share my technical experience with the reader in order to convey an appreciation of the level of knowledge required for success in the area of Cisco internetworking. I would like to think that this book would open your mind to the use of the different Cisco tools, and also teach you as many of the internetworking "gotchas" as possible.

Another fundamental point that you will notice recurring throughout this book is that network design, configuration, and troubleshooting are all interrelated and can never be fully isolated as purely autonomous disciplines. Although there is a clear focus on troubleshooting, this is really a book about Cisco internetworking.

In writing this book I aspired to a high standard of quality. For that reason I would appreciate feedback on any errors that are found in the text. I will maintain a log of any such errors on my Web page. This page also includes a selection of router configurations, internetworking tips and more network scenarios, which you can feel free to download.

—Cormac Long
www.cormaclong.com

ACKNOWLEDGMENTS

Breakfast with a stranger in a San Francisco hotel was an unlikely start to St. Valentine's Day 1999, but that meeting with Steve Elliot of McGraw-Hill made this book possible. I would like to thank Steve for making the leap of faith and believing in this project.

Other people at McGraw-Hill provided assistance during the various stages of production. These include Jennifer Perillo and Ruth Mannino. A special mention has to be made of Franny Kelly if for no other reason than the fact that he grew up a couple of miles away from me in Ireland!

I want to express gratitude to the number of top class engineers that I was fortunate enough to work with over the last few years. I also want to thank the people that I trained who asked the tough questions of me. These experiences combined to provide stimulating and enjoyable environments in which I gained much of the knowledge that I am imparting in this book.

Finally, I would like to again thank Sarah for her support and understanding during the most demanding months that were spent writing this book at the expense of much needed leisure time for both of us. Hopefully some of this time will have been made up before the book got to press.

CHAPTER 1

A Structured Approach to Cisco Troubleshooting

Introduction

The objectives of this chapter are

- To emphasize the need for a structured approach to troubleshooting
- To demonstrate the application of a problem-solving model to internetwork troubleshooting
- To summarize the support resources that are available from Cisco Systems

To become successful at internetwork troubleshooting, an engineer must possess two fundamental skills. The first of these is a solid knowledge and understanding of internetworking technology and protocols. This is the foundation on which all other troubleshooting skills are built. Without appropriate knowledge and experience, troubleshooting tools such as router diagnostic commands and network analyzer traces cannot be applied or interpreted intelligently. The greater part of this book will concentrate on building up this knowledge in support of your current skills and experience to date. This is intended to help you in applying a variety of diagnostic tools, including but not limited to those available on Cisco devices.

The second basic requisite skill is the ability to apply this internetworking knowledge in a methodical and structured manner when troubleshooting a network problem. This chapter will discuss the issue of planning your approach to troubleshooting, why it is so important, and how it can be done. There is often a natural tendency on the part of technologists to consider planning to be more mundane than studying and applying the technology itself. Perhaps it is, but with regard to troubleshooting and problem solving in general, proper planning is a mandatory element of the process. The spontaneous actions of a group of network support personnel are no substitute for a structured troubleshooting process, however capable these individuals may be. A small number of problems can be solved in such a manner, but think honestly about network problems you have encountered that have resulted in excessive downtime. Now ask yourself whether or not there was a well-planned and well-structured approach to troubleshooting in these situations.

Troubleshooting Methodology

The Complexity of Internetworks

Internetworking is an extremely broad and complex area of communications technology. For the foreseeable future its scope will expand in conjunction with a continuous increase in complexity. This presents both increased opportunities and challenges for the internetworking engineer who is designing, installing, and maintaining such networks.

In the case of troubleshooting, the network engineer must have a detailed, hands-on understanding of the technology and protocols implemented on the network, and also must be able to apply this knowledge in a structured manner when confronted with network problems. A greater level of knowledge is required to support a network as it becomes more complex. Modern networks support a broader array of applications than ever before. Applications are also being supported in an increasingly integrated manner, with data, voice, and multimedia applications frequently being run on the same network infrastructure. The development of new applications is fueling a need for higher bandwidth, which in turn drives the development of new technology. For example, the transition from shared 10-Mbps Ethernet to switched Gigabit Ethernet happened in a remarkably short time frame. Yet it is not all about new technology; legacy systems also must be understood and supported. Systems Network Architecture (SNA), for example, is still alive and well, and technologies such as Data Link Switching (DLSW) are being used for more efficient integration into modern network infrastructures. The coexistence of legacy systems alongside state-of-the-art client-server applications ensures that the internetwork is a complex melting pot of different local-area network (LAN) and wide-area network (WAN) media-types and multiple desktop and routing protocols supporting a diversity of applications.

People often fail when faced with increased complexity because they stop following the fundamental steps that they would not be afraid to apply in a seemingly less challenging scenario. Consider the situation of an adolescent learning to drive a car. When practicing in a quiet suburban area, the adolescent operates the controls carefully and checks the mirrors frequently. However, on his or her first visit to the city, the adolescent nervously operates the controls and does not check the mirrors at all, almost causing a crash in the process. Although we may not like to admit it, people working in the technology sector sometimes can behave like this too. When faced with a problem that at first appears to be very complex, do not think that a structured approach no longer applies. It is all the more critical to use a methodical troubleshooting approach when dealing with apparently complex problems. You will often find that if the problem is broken down and analyzed in a structured, rational manner, using an approach such as the one we are about to discuss, the solution may not be so complex after all.

The Problem-Solving Model

Figure 1-1 displays a flowchart for a problem-solving model that can be applied in internetworking problem resolution. Each of the individual steps will now be discussed in the context of Cisco-based internetworks.

Problem Definition For any problem, particularly a complex network problem, this is probably the single most important element of the problem-solving process. It is also the part that is most frequently overlooked and dealt with inadequately. Too often there is a natural tendency on the part of the network engineer to "jump in" and start troubleshooting without first understanding exactly what the issue is that needs to be resolved. This is especially true and understandable in the case of a time-critical problem that is affecting essential networking resources. In such a situation, it is important that both engineers and managers are capable of remaining calm and realizing that in the case of a high-severity problem it is even more critical that a rational troubleshooting methodology is followed.

When defining an internetworking problem, one should attempt to answer most, if not all, of the following questions where applicable:

- Is the problem constant or intermittent?
- Does the problem relate to degraded service or complete loss of service?
- What LAN servers are affected, and what is their addressing information?
- What clients have problems accessing these servers, and are these clients local or remote to the servers?

The following is an example of a well-defined problem:

No users on the 204.210.10.0 network can connect to the mail server 208.11.1.18.

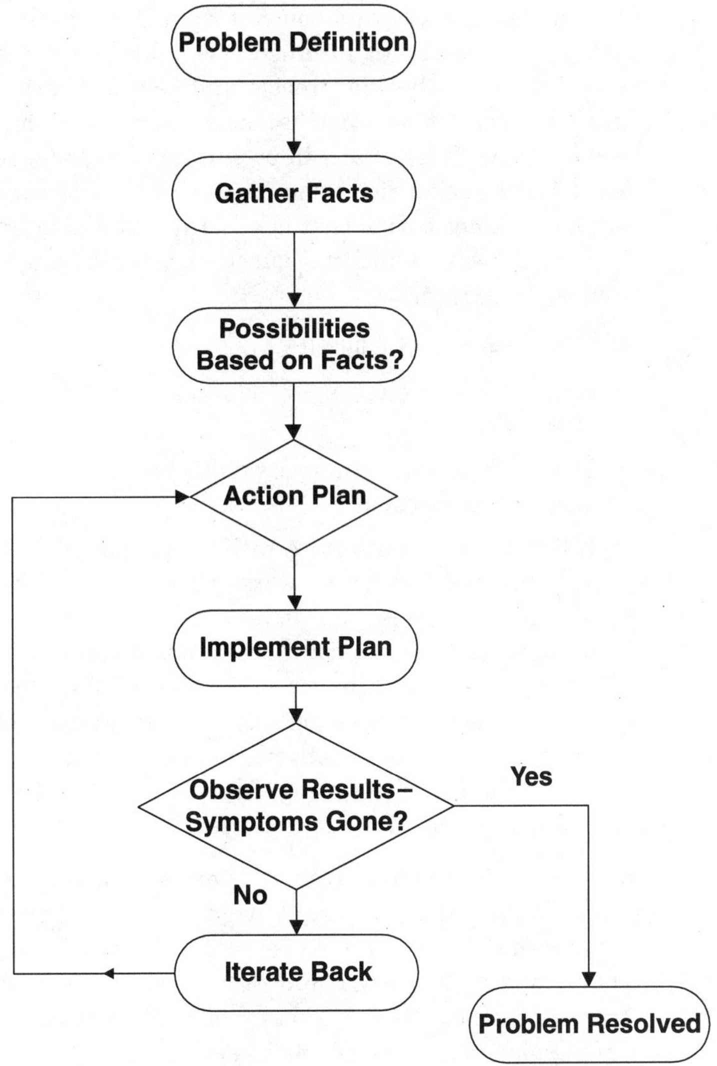

Figure 1-1 Problem-solving flow-chart.

An inadequately defined version could be

A lot of users are having problems with their email.

Gather the Facts This is the stage where the problem definition is built on with more facts and information. A number of methods should be used to gather this information, and you should always start with the simplest and quickest sources. Ask the users who report the problem as many questions as possible, but bear in mind that there is a possibility that not all the answers you receive will be absolutely accurate. This is extremely important because the information-gathering stage is all about *facts*. Gathering precise and relevant facts is critical. You also must be clear about distinguishing facts from mere possibilities and assumptions. It is equally important to be capable of distinguishing relevant information from the irrelevant, particularly considering the amount of information that is generally available from different sources.

The following additional questions should be asked of network users and administrators:

- When was the problem first noticed?
- Are there any clients who do *not* have problems attaching to the affected servers?
- Have any network changes taken place that coincide with the appearance of this problem?
- If this is degraded service rather than complete loss of service, can it be estimated how much worse than usual the service is? What I am alluding to here is what is known as the *network baseline*, and it will be discussed in more detail later in this chapter. The network baseline essentially defines the actual level of performance on the network on a daily basis. Network performance should be assessed and a baseline defined as part of a network manager's periodic tasks. The baseline allows the troubleshooting engineer to assess the extent to which the problem is disabling the network.

After gathering facts from network administrators and users, the network diagnostic tools can be used to obtain more information. Again, start with the simplest tools, e.g., the Network Management Station, the router and switch `show` and `debug` commands, and possible analyzer traces if the need arises. These tools will be discussed and demonstrated throughout the course of this book.

One very important task that should be completed during the information-gathering stage is to build an accurate network diagram using the tools on the routers and switches. This is particularly relevant in the case of a network with which you are unfamiliar or one that you do not normally manage. A detailed physical and logical network diagram can be of great assistance when analyzing network connectivity, traffic flow, and routing issues. Do not assume that you can trust the available documentation or the information sources (human or other). On a well-administered network, up-to-date copies of all device configurations and network diagrams will be maintained. Unfortunately, many real-life networks fall short of this ideal, so you may have to personally verify such information.

Following through on the sample problem definition, the following further information could have been gathered:

- Users on the 209.21.11.0 network have no problems obtaining mail from the 208.11.1.18 server.
- Users on the 204.210.10.0 network had some work done on the LAN operating system the previous night. However, this was not expected to affect service.
- The network topology diagram shown in Figure 1-2 has been built using the appropriate Cisco router commands (that you will learn about in subsequent chapters).

Consider Possibilities Based on Facts The most important word again is *facts*. You must act on facts, not assumptions! A complex problem sometimes occurs on an intermittent basis because an assumption that is true 95 percent of the time is now no longer valid. I call this the *100 percent rule*. If you are not 100 percent sure of something, then that piece of information must be treated as an assumption rather than a fact. Another point to add here is that a full set of facts is a luxury that is not always afforded the network engineer. In some cases, there are no users or network administrators available to report information. There also may be no means to gather information using management or diagnostic tools.

Returning to the sample problem, the following are some possibilities based on the facts:

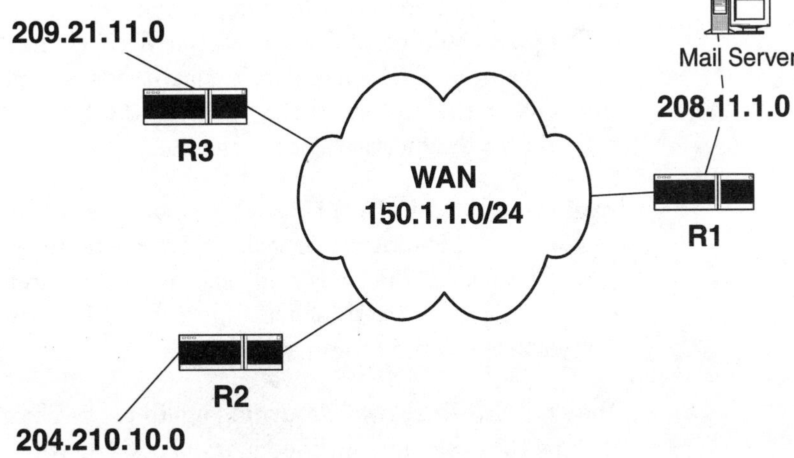

Figure 1-2 Network topology diagram.

1. It is possible that the server or R1 has a problem routing to the 204.210.10.0 network. However, I think that there are more distinct possibilities to be considered first.
2. The router R2 could have its WAN access or LAN connectivity down.
3. Users on the 204.210.10.0 network may not be able to route off their own network.

Form an Action Plan From the flowchart in Figure 1-1 you will notice an iterative feedback loop to this particular step if the first effort does not isolate the problem. For this reason, among others, part of a plan may entail simulating the problem in a laboratory environment. The implementation stage, along with observing the results, also would then take place in a laboratory. This approach may not always be practical because of time and resource constraints. However, it is often the most satisfactory method because it allows the use of such tools as processor-intensive debug commands that may not be viable in a production environment.

You should clearly understand the time frame required for resolving the fault. This is particularly significant when the problem may be a symptom of poor network design. In the case of a time- and mission-critical application failing because of poor design, there may be no time for a redesign. Conversely, if the time frame allows a bad design to be rectified, then the redesign should be implemented rather than an interim "patch" solution.

From the possibilities compiled to solve our sample problem, the one that is easiest to check, along with being a realistic possibility, is number two. In any case, it is a good idea to check R2, since the diagnostic tools are likely to provide relevant information.

The plan could be to first check the WAN connectivity from R1 to R2. While examining R1, also check that it has a route to 204.210.10.0. If this is okay, then telnet to R2, examine the LAN interface, and perform other router diagnostics as appropriate.

Implement Plan In this stage, the plan is implemented using a combination of Cisco diagnostic tools, network management tools, and other test methods. All the tools and techniques required for implementing a fault-isolation or troubleshooting plan will be described and demonstrated through the course of this book.

Observe the Results Returning again to the sample network problem. Assume that the plan outlined is implemented with the following results:

- The WAN link from R1 to R2 is operating satisfactorily. R1 also has a route to 204.210.10.0.
- When R2 is accessed via telnet, all interfaces are seen to have line protocol up. No significant errors have been observed in relation to the interfaces or the router's general operation. The router is also seen to have a route to 208.11.1.0/24.

Thus the plan failed to isolate the problem, but it did eliminate a lot of possibilities. Now iteration must be performed and a new plan created.

The Iterative Process A new plan must be created based on the updated set of facts. Given that it has been established that R1 and R2 have LAN and WAN access as well as appropriate Internet Protocol (IP) routing working, it may be prudent to now consider the third possibility that was documented. That is, can it be verified that users on 204.210.10.0/24 can route to other networks? It is possible that the LAN operating system work performed could have altered the IP configuration on the local workstations. They may have lost their static routes or default gateway information, for example. It was stated that the change was not *expected* to affect service, but this is an assumption, not a fact, and it should be treated as such.

The next step in the iterative process is to put a plan in place to check the IP routing capabilities of local users on the 204.210.10.0 network. This plan then has to be implemented and the results observed, as before. This type of iterative process is repeated until the problem is isolated and resolved.

The model described here is a standard problem-solving model, variations of which are to be found in many business and technology textbooks. It is nothing new or novel, and it is certainly not proverbial rocket science. It is, however, firmly rooted in common sense. While it is not essential to follow any model or methodology to the letter of the law, it is very important to have a structured approach that roughly matches this model at least in principle. Of course, a model such as this is applicable to a design project just as equally as to a troubleshooting problem.

Information and Documentation Checklist

Before troubleshooting any serious or even moderately complex network problem, the following items of information and documentation should be compiled.

Detailed and Accurate Network Diagram The importance of having a detailed physical and logical network diagram has been stressed already. If you manage the network on a daily basis, then there is no excuse for waiting until a problem presents itself to complete this task. Device configurations and network diagrams should be backed up for the entire network and updated as changes are made. I will revisit this subject when discussing network management in Chapter 2. In other chapters throughout this book I will be working through network troubleshooting scenarios. In most cases, a network diagram will be provided along with a description of the problem. Please bear in mind that in the real world you are not always so fortunate, and you may have to compile this information yourself.

Understand the Fundamental Network Technology You cannot hope to resolve problems on a network without having a good understanding of the network technology and the protocols being implemented. The following is a summary of the most fundamental issues, which should be understood in as much detail as possible. This list can be treated as a good starting point, but it is by no means exhaustive. Experience and intuition teach you how to drill down in more detail as necessary and appropriate.

- What LAN and WAN media are in use?
- What are the desktop protocols, and on what LAN and WAN segments are they being implemented?
- What are the routing protocols?
- Are any protocols being bridged or switched?
- What are the specifics of the applications and the client-server traffic flow?
- What security policy is being implemented? Perhaps a client cannot connect to a server because the client is not permitted access rather than because of a network fault.

Document External Connections to Business Partners Most networks do not operate as autonomous units because they have connections to different business partners as well as to the Internet. Technologies that are not implemented elsewhere in the network often are used in the domain that interconnects to other businesses and the Internet. This must not be overlooked when gathering fundamental network technology information. For example, the location and configuration of firewalls must be understood. Frequently, an engineer may think that there is a problem because the firewall router does not respond to Internet Control Message Protocol (ICMP) ping packets. This may be part of the security policy implemented on the firewall, however. Another example could be use of the Border Gateway Protocol (BGP) to connect to a business partner when this protocol is not used elsewhere in the network. Issues such as default routes also must be understood to avoid resolving a problem using a default route that potentially could cause a routing loop.

A point to bear in mind is that problems with connectivity to the Internet or other business partners often require access to routers that may be beyond your normal scope of network administration. When the cooperation of a third party is required, it is even more essential that your own information is compiled and documented correctly.

The Network Baseline The formulation of a network performance baseline is a task that should be performed regularly by the network manager. Of course, it is too late to attempt to establish a network baseline when a fault arises on the network. The whole point of baselining is to establish a normal network performance benchmark against which a fault scenario can be compared in order to assess its severity.

There are many baselining methods of varying sophistication. They can range from very fancy features that are included in network management applications to measuring ICMP ping response times across LAN segments and through the WAN.

It is important to have a clear idea of the level of service that can be expected under normal network traffic conditions. For example, a slow response problem may be reported that is simply a symptom of poor network design rather than the result of any particular fault. Consider a situation where clients are performing file transfers across a 56-kbps link from multiple servers that are all located on a single shared Ethernet segment. If the users report slow response, then it is likely that there is no particular problem to troubleshoot here. The design has been severely underdimensioned in terms of both LAN and WAN resources. Baselining will confirm that normal performance is poor and will not improve until the network is redesigned. A further benefit of baselining is that it confirms that the troubleshooting engineer does not have to waste time trying to fix a problem that is outside his or her scope.

In the case of network performance that is degraded beyond the normal level, the baseline provides a reference for determining severity.

Cisco Troubleshooting Resources

Now I will briefly outline the main support and troubleshooting facilities that Cisco Systems provides for its customers. These resources will be referred to during the course of this book.

Cisco Connection Online

Cisco Connection Online (CCO) is Cisco's Web page at *www.cisco.com*. Above and beyond troubleshooting support, it provides an excellent range of technical internetworking information, albeit with an understandably proprietary slant.

CCO is best explored by entering the Web site yourself because it is being updated continuously in both content and structure. At the time of this writing, the sections that are most relevant to troubleshooting are

- *Service and support*, which includes
  - A complete hardware and software documentation suite for Cisco routers and switches
  - Sample configurations
  - Technical tips relating to design, configuration, and troubleshooting
  - The Cisco IOS™ bug search facility
  - Software Center (This allows the downloading of Cisco IOS and switch software for Cisco customers.)
- *Partners and resellers* provides a range of services relating to troubleshooting, support, upgrades, and training. It is intended for Cisco customers as well as value-added resellers who have a particular relationship with Cisco Systems such as a gold or silver partnership. Some of the resources in this section require a login ID to be accessed. This login ID can have different privilege levels depending on the nature of your company's relationship with Cisco.

Technical Assistance Center

The Cisco Technical Assistance Center (TAC) can be contacted via telephone or the Web. Cisco customers who have maintenance contracts on their Cisco equipment can open trouble tickets with the TAC. Different priority levels are assigned to the tickets depending on the severity of the problem and the terms of the maintenance contract.

Other Cisco Resources

- *The device manuals that ship with all products*. This is such an obvious source of information that it is sometimes overlooked and literally left in the box. Much of the information in the manuals is available on CCO; however, the manuals can be particularly useful for the following reasons:
  - They provide a step-by-step guide for the basic initial device configuration. This is important if you have never configured the particular type of router or switch before.
  - They provide a detailed illustration of how various pieces of hardware should be installed or removed. This is very important not only for new installations but also for hardware upgrades and during hardware replacement to resolve a fault.
  - They provide useful hardware troubleshooting information that is difficult to find elsewhere. For example, they document what the color and status of the different light-emitting diodes (LEDs) indicate. With this information, the basic health of the device and its individual cards can be evaluated.
- *UniverCD*. This can be loosely described as a snapshot of CCO in CD form.
- *Hardcopy documentation*. The complete IOS documentation suite is also available in hardcopy form. Cisco Press also publishes a variety of technical literature relating to the design and configuration of Cisco-based networks.

CHAPTER 2

Network Testing, Management, and Analysis

Introduction

There is an extensive array of fault diagnosis and troubleshooting tools available on Cisco routers, but this chapter focuses on the aspects of the network that these tools cannot analyze. This ranges from the testing of physical layer problems in the wide-area network (WAN) or in the local-area network (LAN) wiring up to sophisticated higher-layer protocol and packet analysis.

The employment of the different types of testing tools will be discussed. The topic of network management and how it can be used to diagnose, resolve, and avert network problems will be addressed. How network monitoring is distinguished from network management will be explained. In particular, the chapter will examine the Simple Network Management Protocol (SNMP), as well as some popular network management software packages and platforms that are based on this protocol.

Much of the subject matter of this chapter pertains to very broad areas such as network management and network analysis. The different topics are dealt with in the form of an overview intended to give the reader an introduction to the subject and an understanding of its key issues. It is beyond the scope of this book to impart detailed information on issues such as cable testing, network management, and network analysis because these subjects are ancillary to the core objectives of this book.

The objectives of this chapter are to

- Introduce the physical layer test equipment for different LAN and WAN media types.
- Learn how SNMP and Remote Monitoring (RMON) can be used to monitor and diagnose network faults.
- Understand how to gather detailed packet-level troubleshooting information by capturing and interpreting data with a third-party network analyzer.

Physical Layer Test Equipment

Cable Testers

Copper Cable Testers Cable testers can range from simple hand-held meters to more sophisticated discrete or modular pieces of equipment. Consider the simplest type of cable tester, a digital multimeter. This measures cable parameters such as electrical resistance, capacitance, and inductance. A picture of a typical cable tester is shown in Figure 2-1.

A multimeter also can be used to test physical layer connectivity. For example, the multimeter probes could be attached to each end of the wiring connection, either directly or via patch extensions. The electrical resistance between the two probe leads is then tested. If the electrical resistance reading is zero ohms (a short circuit), then the two ends are connected. A resistance reading of infinity (an open circuit) indicates that there is no metal connectivity between the end points.

There are a wide variety of cable testers on the market that can be used for testing unshielded twisted-pair (UTP), shielded twisted-pair (STP), and coaxial cables. Other cable parameters apart from simple connectivity also can be tested, including

- *Attenuation*. The amount of signal loss, or *attenuation*, can be measured in decibels (dB). The decibel attenuation loss is a logarithmic representation of the ratio of output signal to input signal, which indi-

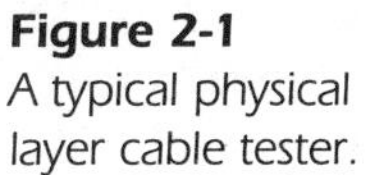

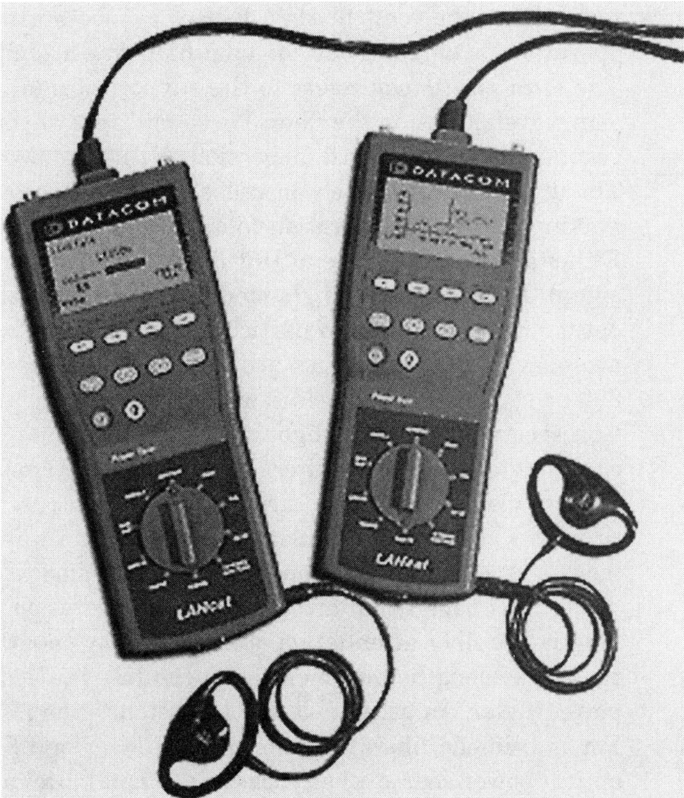

Figure 2-1 A typical physical layer cable tester.

cates how much of the signal has been lost along the transmission path.

- *Noise.* Any unwanted component in the line signal is termed *noise.* The level of noise is quantified in the *signal-to-noise ratio* (SNR). This parameter, which should be as high as possible, has an acceptable value of the order of 10^8.
- *Crosstalk. Crosstalk* is interference between the signals on different cable pairs sharing the same cable. A certain level of crosstalk interference is inherent to the electromagnetic nature of line signals. By measuring the near-end crosstalk (NEXT), it can be determined whether or not the level of interference is acceptable.

Some cable testers also incorporate limited test functionality for layers 2 and 3. This can include the identification of MAC addresses and Internet Protocol (IP) ping tests.

Fiberoptic Testers Most fundamental fiber testing is carried out at the manufacturing stage due to the high cost of fiberoptic cable. This is termed "on the reel" testing. Fibers can be multimode for short-haul operation or single mode for long-haul low-attenuation requirements. The term *multimode* refers to the support of multiple optical transmission wavelengths on the fiber. These multiple wavelengths will exhibit a certain amount of optical dispersion as the signal travels along the fiber. The dispersion ultimately increases the signal attenuation on the fiber, making multimode operation more suitable for short-haul applications. Either a laser or a light-emitting diode (LED) can produce the multimode signal. In contrast, a single-mode fiberoptic cable is manufactured for optimal performance at a particular transmission wavelength where the attenuation characteristics are minimized. This wavelength is usually 800 or 1500 nm and coincides with the strictly defined narrow transmission spectrum of a laser light source. The manner in which the narrow-core single-mode fiber filters out all other transmission wavelengths reduces dispersion and in turn minimizes attenuation. This characteristic makes single-mode transmission, which is always synonymous with a laser source, suitable for long-haul transmission.

For fiber cables that are optimized for operation at a particular wavelength, the fiber attenuation is measured by generating laser signals at these wavelengths and measuring the loss in decibels using an optical power meter. An acceptable level of attenuation is less than 0.1 dB/km. For multimode fibers, a lower-quality laser or LED can suffice as the optical power source when measuring signal attenuation.

Digital Interface Testing

Two of the most commonly used tools for testing the physical layer status and quality of digital circuits are

- *A breakout box.* This piece of equipment is used to check the integrity of the connection between the DTE and the DCE. A breakout box (BOB) has two connections that can be extended to the DTE and DCE. It is capable of providing status information on the circuit as well as any data that are presently being carried. The device typically displays real-time status information on mark, space, data, clocking, and inactivity using status LEDs. A standard type of breakout box is shown in Figure 2-2. The BOB is usually compact and battery-powered. It contains buffered electrical circuitry so that it does not interfere with the actual line signal while measuring it. It is also capable of verifying line voltage and electrical resistance.
- *A bit-error-rate tester (BERT).* A BERT is a more sophisticated piece of equipment that can accurately measure the error rate in a digital signal. The bit error rate can be measured on the entire end-to-end circuit or on a portion of the circuit for fault isolation. BER tests typically are done at the commissioning stage of a new circuit in order to verify circuit integrity and also to provide a baseline for future performance. A BERT measures error rates on different bit patterns that it generates. This can be used to assess any timing or noise problems

Figure 2-2
A breakout box.

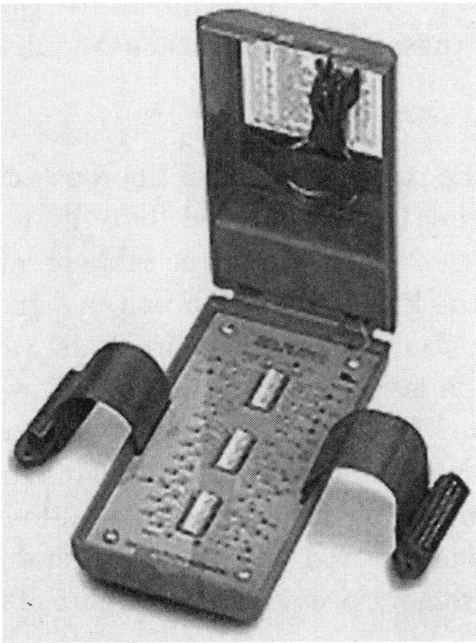

on the circuit. The line can be monitored for a configurable period of time, and traffic and error analysis can be performed. A satisfactory bit error rate on a digital signal is less than 10^{-9}. A BERT also can measure the line's signal-to-noise ratio.

Time Domain Reflectometry (TDR)

TDR is a more sophisticated form of cable testing that exploits the electromagnetic characteristics and transmission-line model that can be applied to both copper and fiberoptic cables. In the case of a copper cable, TDR uses the principle that a cable break results in an impedance mismatch on the transmission line. The impedance mismatch causes at least part of the signal to be reflected back to the source.

The test signals are sent by the time domain reflectometer at a known and constant velocity; thus the exact location of the cable break can be identified by measuring the time taken for the signals to reflect back to the source. This principle also can be used to measure the cable length. Cable attenuation can be measured by comparing the amplitude of the transmitted and reflected signals. Apart from troubleshooting, attenuation is usually measured on a new installation in order to establish a baseline for future performance.

Those of you with skills in a discipline such as electrical engineering will already have a good understanding of transmission-line theory and electromagnetic wave motion. Readers without such a background should be relieved to know that they can survive quite well simply using devices that employ these principles without requiring an understanding of the relevant physics.

Optical TDR In the particular case of fiberoptic cables, an optical time domain reflectometer (OTDR) is used, but the principle is the same. Optical signals also get reflected back at cable breaks due to a change in refractive index at the location of the break. A signal of known propagation velocity can be used to locate the break as well as verify the cable length. Attenuation is measured by comparing power in the transmitted and reflected signals. The measurement of optical backscatter, which occurs uniformly along the fiber, also can provide information on attenuation. It is important to measure the total end-to-end attenuation on a fiber cable that is spliced and coupled to other fibers along the cable path. Such a measurement provides an estimate of splicing and coupling loss, which is often the most significant contributor to the attenuation on a fiberoptic cable.

Network Management and Why It Is Useful

Some level of network management is performed on all networks no matter how small. In its simplest form, network management can entail attaching to the console port of network devices in order to configure them. A telnet session is often used to communicate with network devices in order to execute a number of possible management functions. These tasks may include the troubleshooting of network problems, the verification of different performance parameters such as device utilization, or to configure network security. This type of unsophisticated network management may suffice on very small networks and in an environment where the network manager is in close contact with the users. However, as a network grows, it is usually necessary to replace this reactive approach with a more systematic means of managing the network. We will now take a panoramic overview of the extremely broad area of network management. I emphasize that this is an overview, because this book deals primarily with the subject of troubleshooting, which relates to just one or possibly two of the subsets (fault management and performance management) into which network management is segmented.

Network management traditionally is broken down into five distinct areas:

- *Fault management.* This relates to the detection, reporting, and resolution of network faults. A successful fault management strategy means that these tasks are performed in an efficient, timely, and effective manner. A proactive fault reporting mechanism is usually necessary on medium to large networks. It is equally important to ensure that adequate technical support resources are continuously available to provide fault resolution services.
- *Configuration management.* This entails the ability to monitor and control the configuration of all network devices from anywhere within the network. Effective configuration management eliminates the need to dispatch technical support personnel to solve configuration-related issues that can be resolved remotely.

- *Accounting management*. This is the ability to collate information on what network stations were communicating with whom and for how long. Accounting information also may include the application that was employed in the communication along with the medium over which it took place. This is important for network auditing as well as for assessing the cost-effectiveness of network communications.
- *Performance management*. This entails the ability to collect, store, and analyze performance statistics on a designated set of network performance parameters. Examples of such parameters are utilization statistics on a WAN link and the percentage of collisions on an Ethernet segment. This analysis can be performed on both a real-time and historical basis. Performance management can be used to predict the impact of any moves, adds, or changes to network elements or applications. For example, it can assess the effect of a growth in network traffic as a network grows or as new applications are implemented and more users are added to the network.
- *Security management*. A security policy must be implemented that not only refers to the access to network devices but also to access to network resources and applications. Access to network devices is controlled using either static passwords restricting console and telnet access to these devices or, alternatively, a centralized security server such as TACACS. If static passwords are used, then they should be changed on a periodic basis. The policy for controlling access to the different network resources is implemented in the device configurations using, for example, access lists on a router.

SNMP Overview

The Simple Network Management Protocol (SNMP) has become the de facto industry standard for network management. Some of the key components and principles of SNMP are as follows:

- *Managed devices*. These devices have SNMP enabled and therefore are capable of being managed. A managed device could be a router, switch, hub, or server, for example.
- *Agent*. The SNMP software that runs on a managed device is termed the *SNMP agent*. An SNMP agent can collect, store, and communicate management information.
- *MIB*. The management information base (MIB) is a collection of *managed objects*. A managed object is a particular parameter about which

management information is to be gathered. An example of a managed object would be a list of routes in an IP routing table. A particular instance of a managed object (e.g., a single IP route) is termed a *managed variable*.

- *Network management station (NMS)*. The main SNMP network management application resides on an SNMP server, which usually also acts as the network management station. Managed devices relay information to the SNMP server about managed objects using the SNMP. The NMS typically includes a management application package that is capable of customizing the information provided by SNMP and displaying it via a graphical user interface (GUI).

The interaction of the different elements of SNMP is displayed schematically in Figure 2-3.

The major types of SNMP communications that take place between the managed objects and the NMS can be summarized as follows:

- *Reads*. Read messages are exchanged between the NMS and the managed object so that the NMS can gather information on managed variables. An SNMP Read operation usually entails the sending of a Get-

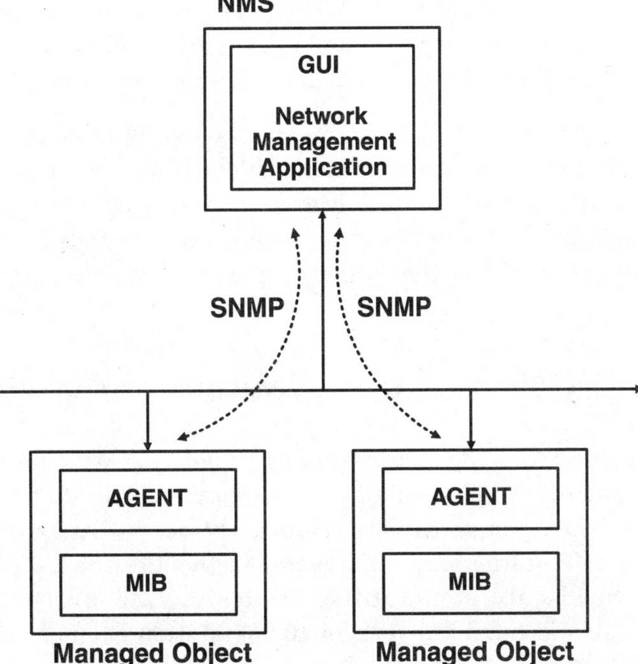

Figure 2-3 Schematic diagram for SNMP operation.

Request message by the NMS with the managed objects responding with a Get-Reply. Get-Next messages are used to sequentially compile information on a list of variables such as a router's IP routing table. An SNMP NMS console that can only perform Reads is said to belong to the *read-only community*. This community is password-protected with a *read-only community string* that must agree between the object and the SNMP server.

- *Writes*. SNMP Write messages take the form of Set-Request messages sent by the NMS server to the managed object. These Set messages are used to modify the value or status of managed variables. For example, a Set message could be used to change icons on the NMS GUI map such as removing an icon for a router port that has been decommissioned. An NMS station console that is capable of executing SNMP Sets is said to belong to the *read-write community*. It is configured with a *read-write community string* that must agree with that of the managed object.
- *Traversal operations*. The NMS uses this type of operation to determine what variables are being managed on an object and to gather information about them. An example is the sequential gathering of the entries in a router's IP routing table.
- *Traps*. SNMP traps are generated by managed objects to report a particular event to the NMS. An example of such an event could be a predefined alarm threshold being exceeded on a managed variable, such as the number of collisions on an Ethernet segment.

The communications messages just described relate to SNMP version 1 rather than version 2. SNMP v.2 is an enhancement of SNMP v.1 that will gradually replace it over time. It is by no means dissimilar from its predecessor. I will simply note in passing that these enhancements pertain mainly to the security features of the protocol.

SNMP on Cisco Routers and Switches

The following is a standard type of SNMP configuration that is frequently implemented on a Cisco router. Both the read-only and read-write communities are protected by access-list 9, which specifies two host NMS stations. In this example, the 192.168.2.6 station belongs to the read-only community, as designated by the community string "JoeCooney." The 172.24.10.235 station belongs to the read-write community, meaning that it can implement SNMP Writes or Set messages on the router's managed variables.

```
access-list 9 permit 172.24.10.235
access-list 9 permit 192.168.2.6
!
snmp-server community JoeCooney RO 9
snmp-server community CyrilFarl RW 9
snmp-server host 192.168.2.6 JoeCooney
snmp-server host 172.24.10.235 CyrilFarl
!
```

The SNMP options on a router also allow the inclusion of useful reference information such as site contact information and device chassis ID.

Now let's look at SNMP on the Catalyst 5000 switch. Along with the read-only and read-write communities, there is a read-write-all community that has the power to modify the actual SNMP parameter settings rather than just the managed variables. In this example, module and chassis traps are being sent to the SNMP server at 133.1.1.9 as part of the read-only community. Port traps are not enabled by default; this is to prevent the SNMP server or monitoring station from being overloaded with traps simply due to stations being powered on and off. As is the case on a router, the SNMP configuration also can be verified using the `show snmp` command (see Listing 2-1).

Network Monitoring

It is important to be able to distinguish between network monitoring and network management. *Network monitoring* entails the gathering, collation, and reporting of network information. How this information is handled to resolve existing network faults, anticipate future network problems, enhance performance, tighten security, and make accounting decisions pertains to the area of *network management*.

In any area of management, the reporting of information is an essential tool, and network management is no different. Rather than confusing the two areas, network monitoring should be thought of as a fundamental tool that facilitates network management. Apart from fault reporting, one of the most important uses of a network monitor is baselining, a concept that is integral to fault and performance management.

In the next chapter you will learn how to configure a Cisco router to send logging information to a Syslog server and to limit the error and event information based on severity level.

Listing 2-1

```
#snmp
set snmp community read-only       sam98
set snmp community read-write      maguire
set snmp community read-write-all secret
set snmp rmon enable
set snmp trap enable  module
set snmp trap enable  chassis
set snmp trap disable bridge
set snmp trap disable repeater
set snmp trap disable vtp
set snmp trap disable auth
set snmp trap disable ippermit
set snmp trap 133.1.1.9   sam98

Galway-C5500> (enable) sh snmp
RMON: Enabled
Traps Enabled: Module,Chassis
Port Traps Enabled: None

Community-Access     Community-String
----------------     ----------------
read-only             sam98
read-write           maguire
read-write-all       secret

Trap-Rec-Address                                      Trap-Rec-Community
----------------------------------------             ------------------
133.1.1.9                                                sam98
Galway-C5500> (enable)
```

Remote Monitoring (RMON)

RMON is an extension of SNMP. It differs in that SNMP gathers network information from a single type of MIB, whereas RMON defines nine additional MIBs or RMON groups. All or a combination of these RMON groups can be implemented on a network. The remote monitoring capability of RMON exploits the intelligent manageable properties of modern network devices, and this monitoring and data gathering can be executed on a single remote device or station, often referred to as an *RMON probe*. In the next section the topic of network analysis will be visited. The first stage of network analysis is the gathering and collation of data, and RMON is a feature that provides this service. The RMON probe will observe and capture each packet that it detects to be within its monitoring specification on the remote network segment on which the probe resides.

I will now summarize the nine different RMON groups. Network problems can be analyzed using a combination of some or all of these groups.

Note that many of the devices on the market that support RMON do not necessarily support all nine groups. This may or may not be an issue for your network, but it is important to be very clear about what RMON services are provided.

1. *The Statistics Group*. This group maintains low-level statistics on parameters such as number of packets sent, packet size, broadcasts, multicasts, and errors detected.
2. *The History Group*. This group uses information obtained in the Statistics Group to provide trend analysis. A set of counters relating to different network parameters is incremented for specific time intervals, providing historical trend analysis.
3. *The Alarms Group*. This group allows the user to define a sampling interval and error threshold for any managed variable that is being viewed by the RMON probe.
4. *The Events Group*. This provides for three basic types of events: rising threshold, falling threshold, and packet match. A rising threshold could be set for the number of CRC errors on a LAN segment. An example of packet match is the identification of a Token Ring beacon frame.
5. *The Host Group*. Statistics relating to the different MAC addresses present on the network segment is provided by this group. Information on incoming and outgoing packets, packet sizes, errors, broadcasts, and multicasts is included.
6. *The Top N Hosts Group*. This facility enables the user to reduce the amount of management traffic being reported on the network by limiting the activity of the Host Group to, for example, the *N* busiest hosts on the monitored network segment.
7. *The Packet Capture Group*. This group allows the network manager to configure and manipulate the buffer sizes used for packet capture. The conditions under which packet capture should commence or stop also can be set.
8. *The Traffic Matrix Group*. Traffic information based on pairs of stations that are in conversation is available using the Traffic Matrix Group. The idea of measuring what station is talking to whom and for how long is part of accounting management.
9. *The Filter Group*. This allows the user to predefine a number of different filter types that will provide more focus to the data being captured. Filters can be defined based on address or protocol type or a combination of each.

Network Analysis

Network analysis takes the area of network monitoring one step further. Once data have been captured, they must be collated and analyzed to resolve faults, avert future network problems, and enhance performance. You will have noticed from the discussion on RMON that some of its groups start to go beyond simple data capture in that they provide the capability for analyzing the data.

There is a principle of network analysis that nobody should ever lose sight of. The single most important and essential analysis tool is a knowledgeable network engineer. Without such a resource, the investment in any other network analysis capabilities is a complete waste of money. This probably sounds very obvious, but from my experience in the industry, there are a lot of people, particularly in management, who have yet to get this point. With a broad array of data being reported by a network monitoring station or network analyzer, it is first of all critical that you are capable of deciding what data are relevant to the issue in question. This data first must be processed (e.g., what two parameters should be graphed against each other?). The collated data then must be interpreted. This is the part that demands the most skill. As you will see when protocol and packet analysis is discussed, a detailed understanding of the network protocols is essential if the captured data on a protocol analyzer are to be interpreted competently. Despite what some vendors will claim, network management and analysis tools are not magic devices that will proactively solve all network problems. Ultimately, the engineer must resolve all problems. I emphasize this point because I have seen too many instances where companies think that an investment in network analyzers coupled with training their support personnel in the basic use of such instruments is an adequate network support strategy.

Protocol Analysis

Network analysis can be broken roughly into two areas: protocol analysis and packet analysis. *Protocol analysis* relates to the collection and collation of summary information on what protocols are running on the various segments of the network and what the corresponding traffic and error levels are. Protocol analysis is typically used for performance baselining, capacity planning, and network redesign. In terms of troubleshooting, it is usually only suitable for a very high level approach. When troubleshooting a complex network problem, packet analysis is often required.

To illustrate the use of protocol analysis, Figure 2-4 shows a graphic display of data that were captured on an Ethernet segment using a Network Associates Sniffer for Windows. The capture ran for less than 2 minutes, collecting approximately 30,000 bytes of data. All the data are IP traffic, with the large majority of it being NetBios over UDP. The protocol distribution breakdown is shown in tabular form in Figure 2-5.

Packet Analysis and the Sniffer

The ability to examine captured data down to the packet and frame level is termed *packet analysis*. With this type of analysis, the different components from the physical, data link, network, and transport layers can be examined for each captured packet. The more sophisticated packet

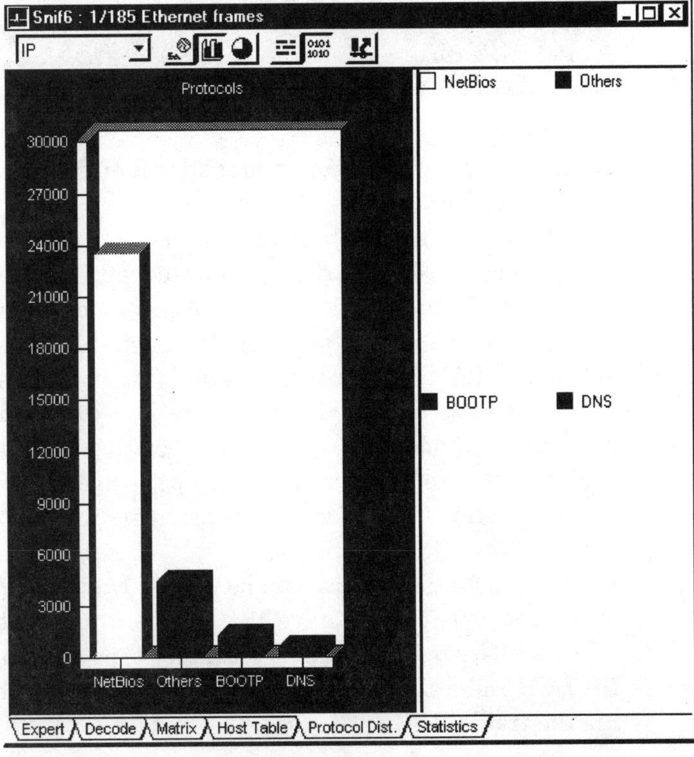

Figure 2-4 Protocol distribution for a simple trace.

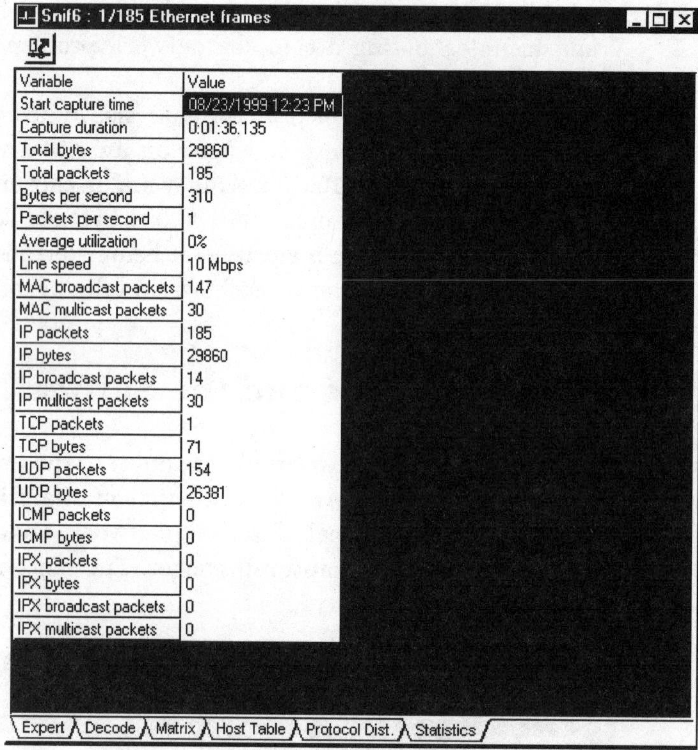

Variable	Value
Start capture time	08/23/1999 12:23 PM
Capture duration	0:01:36.135
Total bytes	29860
Total packets	185
Bytes per second	310
Packets per second	1
Average utilization	0%
Line speed	10 Mbps
MAC broadcast packets	147
MAC multicast packets	30
IP packets	185
IP bytes	29860
IP broadcast packets	14
IP multicast packets	30
TCP packets	1
TCP bytes	71
UDP packets	154
UDP bytes	26381
ICMP packets	0
ICMP bytes	0
IPX packets	0
IPX bytes	0
IPX broadcast packets	0
IPX multicast packets	0

Figure 2-5 Summary statistics for a simple trace.

analyzers also will provide a breakdown of the data up to and including the application layer.

A LAN analyzer in the form of a modular box can have its Ethernet, Token Ring, or FDDI port plugged into a port on the hub or switch where it "listens" to the traffic on the LAN segment. Alternatively, the LAN analyzer can be run as an application on a station that is already present on the LAN segment in question. Many modular analyzers support remote management, whereby there is a communications port with a configured IP address and another port used for data capture. Remote access to the analyzer then can be performed via telnet. Note that the communications port does not necessarily need to be on the same segment as the data-capture port.

Network analyzers also can be used to capture WAN traffic. To achieve this, it obviously must have the appropriate interface type, e.g., frame relay, ISDN, etc. The analyzer usually taps into the WAN line between the DTE and DCE, using a three-way breakout cable, without interrupting the traffic flow.

There are a wide variety of network analyzers of varying specification on the market. In order to demonstrate the use of packet analyzers, I will use the example of the Network Associates Sniffer product. The more traditional version of this product is DOS-based, but the product used in this demonstration runs on a Windows platform. I will use a very simple example to demonstrate the capability and power of a network analyzer. It is required to test the IP connectivity between the workstation 159.249.105.19 and its local router 159.249.105.253 and also to examine the traffic being sent and received by each station. A capture filter is defined in order to avoid overflowing the Sniffer's buffer with unnecessary data; choosing "Capture" followed by "Define Filter" does this. A filter can be defined based on the following parameters

- *Network layer address*
- *MAC address*
- *Data pattern* (e.g., a sequence of As or 5s can denote a late collision)
- *Protocol* (e.g., IP, IPX, NetBEUI, LAT, etc.). A single protocol or multiple protocols can be defined in the capture filter.
- *Packet type*. The categories of packet type include normal packets as well as packets that signify an error condition such as CRCs, runts, collisions, etc. It is often useful when troubleshooting a problem to configure the Sniffer to only capture certain error packets that may be symptomatic of the problem.

Figure 2-6 demonstrates a simple capture filter based on IP address. Any traffic to or from the 159.249.105.19 and 159.249.105.253 stations will be captured. The first statement, which defines any broadcasts being sent or received by 159.249.105.19, is actually unnecessary because this is just a special case of the second statement. How specific the capture filter is depends on how well the problem has been defined and how much information has been gathered on it. For example, if a fault is reported that "most users cannot attach to a number of different servers at different times of the day," this is a problem that has not really been defined at all. At a minimum, information would have to be gathered to specify client and server addresses along with protocol information on the applications. In fact, a network analyzer should never be used until an adequate definition of the problem has been formulated (remember the model in Chapter 1?). Sometimes the initial problem definition is itself quite broad, in which case the Sniffer may be used to gather data and "zoom in" to a better understanding of the nature of the problem. An

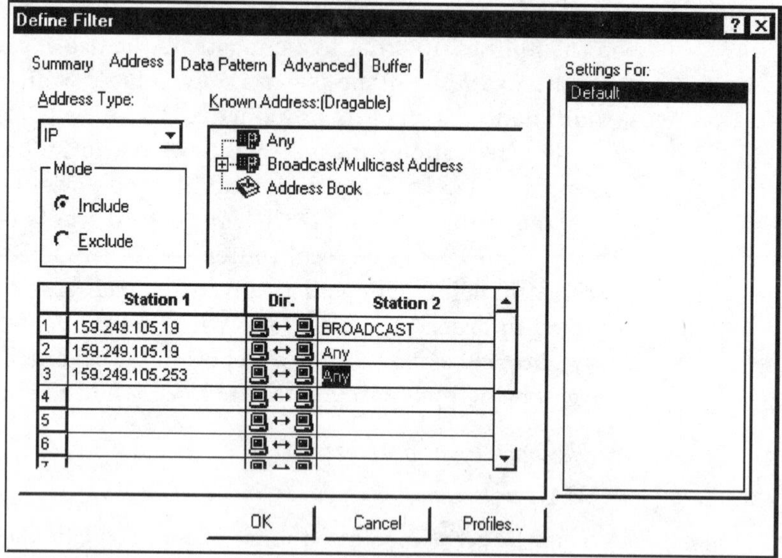

Figure 2-6 Defining a capture filter based on IP address.

understanding of when and how to use capture filters is built up with pure networking experience more than any other factor.

After the capture filter has been defined, the data capture process, frequently called a *trace*, can commence. Simply choosing "Capture" and "Start" does this. An appropriate duration for a trace varies depending on the nature of the problem being investigated. If the problem is constant and very stark, such as a complete connectivity failure, then a short-duration trace may provide the required data. In contrast, an intermittent problem that is characterized by, for example, slow response may well require a longer-duration trace to capture relevant data.

During the trace, a summary is provided of frames observed and frames captured (these will be equal if no capture filters were defined). A summary of serious errors is also provided. In certain situations, this can act as a prompt to stop or pause the trace.

When it is decided to stop the trace, the data then have to be displayed. A display filter can be defined just as in the case of a capture filter. Alternatively, all captured data can be displayed.

Figure 2-7 shows the capture display with the "Decode" option selected. The activity that occurred during this brief trace was a telnet session from 159.249.105.19 to the router 159.249.105.253. Five ICMP pings were then sent to 159.249.105.19 from the router. Bear in mind that these steps were performed purely to demonstrate the use of a Sniffer rather than being part of a troubleshooting strategy; the latter subject will be dealt with in detail in the upcoming chapters. The decode

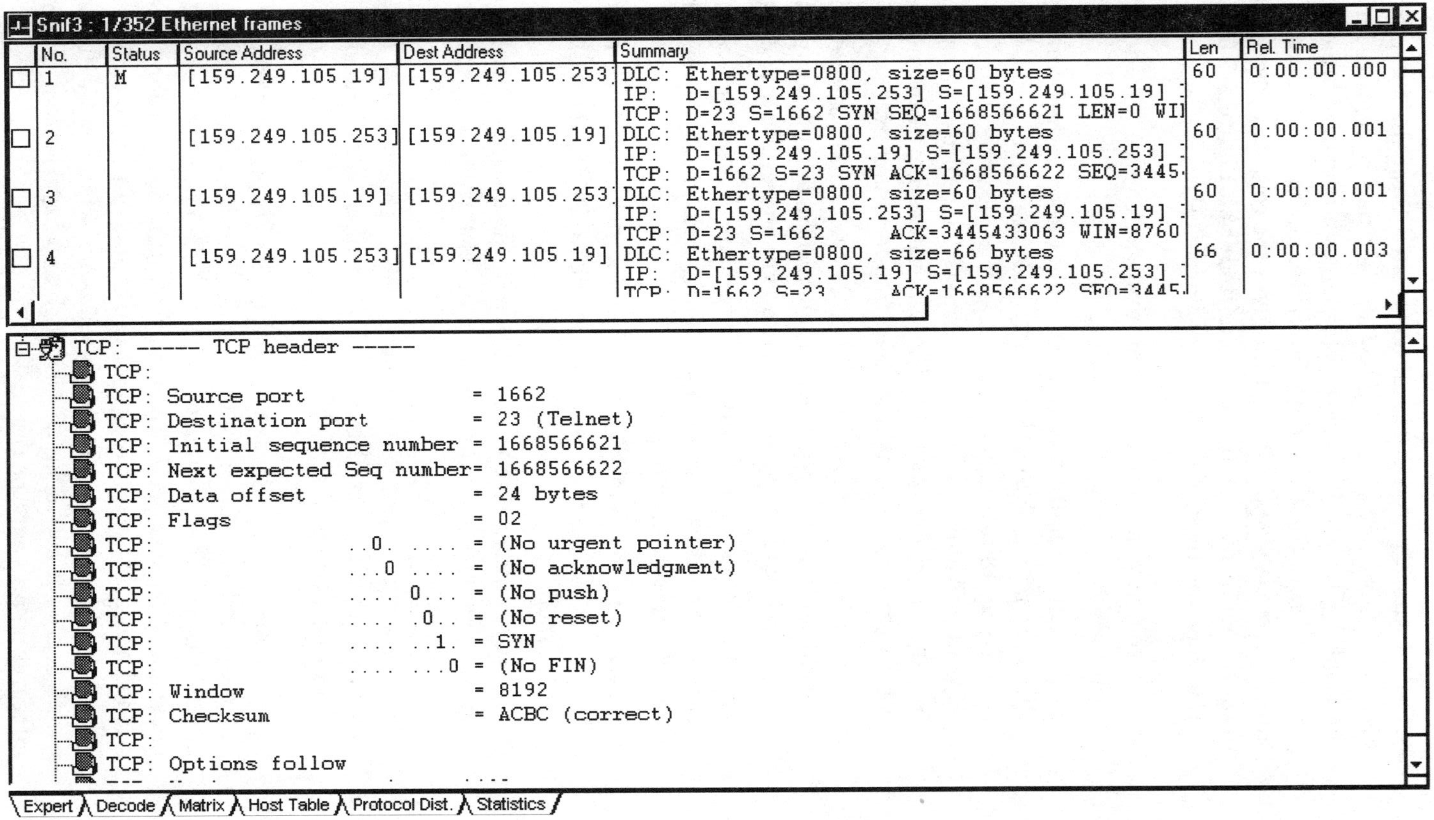

```
Snif3 : 1/352 Ethernet frames

No. Status Source Address     Dest Address        Summary                                                Len  Rel. Time
1   M      [159.249.105.19]   [159.249.105.253]   DLC:  Ethertype=0800, size=60 bytes                    60   0:00:00.000
                                                  IP:   D=[159.249.105.253] S=[159.249.105.19]
                                                  TCP:  D=23 S=1662 SYN SEQ=1668566621 LEN=0 WI
2          [159.249.105.253]  [159.249.105.19]    DLC:  Ethertype=0800, size=60 bytes                    60   0:00:00.001
                                                  IP:   D=[159.249.105.19] S=[159.249.105.253]
                                                  TCP:  D=1662 S=23 SYN ACK=1668566622 SEQ=3445
3          [159.249.105.19]   [159.249.105.253]   DLC:  Ethertype=0800, size=60 bytes                    60   0:00:00.001
                                                  IP:   D=[159.249.105.253] S=[159.249.105.19]
                                                  TCP:  D=23 S=1662      ACK=3445433063 WIN=8760
4          [159.249.105.253]  [159.249.105.19]    DLC:  Ethertype=0800, size=66 bytes                    66   0:00:00.003
                                                  IP:   D=[159.249.105.19] S=[159.249.105.253]

TCP: ----- TCP header -----
  TCP:
  TCP: Source port               = 1662
  TCP: Destination port          = 23 (Telnet)
  TCP: Initial sequence number   = 1668566621
  TCP: Next expected Seq number= 1668566622
  TCP: Data offset               = 24 bytes
  TCP: Flags                     = 02
  TCP:              ..0. ....    = (No urgent pointer)
  TCP:              ...0 ....    = (No acknowledgment)
  TCP:              .... 0...    = (No push)
  TCP:              .... .0..    = (No reset)
  TCP:              .... ..1.    = SYN
  TCP:              .... ...0    = (No FIN)
  TCP: Window                    = 8192
  TCP: Checksum                  = ACBC (correct)
  TCP:
  TCP: Options follow

Expert | Decode | Matrix | Host Table | Protocol Dist. | Statistics
```

Figure 2-7 Trace display showing a telnet session.

output of the captured data can be scrolled through. The part shown in Figure 2-7 has a summary window for each packet captured at the top of the display. The detail window below gives a complete breakdown of the packet contents from the data link layer up to the application layer. A third window is also available that gives the complete packet contents in hexadecimal form. This has been omitted from Figure 2-7 for clarity.

Consider the highlighted packet (marked *M*):

- It is the first packet captured, and the source and destination IP addresses are shown.
- The summary information shows that at layer 2 the frame is a 60-byte Ethernet frame. Ethertype=0800 indicates that it is IP over ARPA rather than 802.3 because 800=2,048 in decimal, which exceeds the maximum frame length for Ethernet. Therefore, this is a *Type* field rather than a *Length* field. The differences between the various flavors of Ethernet will be discussed in later chapters.
- Along with the IP addresses, the TCP source and destination ports are listed as well as the sequence numbers. The destination port is 23, the telnet port, and the source is a random, nonreserved TCP port.
- The summary and detail windows can be used to track the TCP sequencing, which may be particularly relevant if there is a high number of TCP retransmissions.
- Notice from the detail window that the Acknowledgment bit is set to zero. This means that you are viewing a TCP session that is not yet established.
- The TCP window size is also shown in the detailed output of the TCP header. This indicates how much data TCP will send without receiving an acknowledgment.
- Note that the detail window here merely shows the TCP header, but you will notice a scroll bar on the left-hand side that enables you to view the entire packet.

Depending on your level of knowledge and experience, the Sniffer data just described may have confused you. If it did, then I have good news and bad news. The good news is that much of the theory and practical knowledge required for competently interpreting Sniffer traces will be studied and discussed throughout the course of this book. The bad news is that this is an extremely simple example, which really illustrates that a high degree of networking knowledge and experience is essential when interpreting an analyzer trace.

Figure 2-8 shows an expanded detail window. The layer 2 Ethernet addresses are shown. The contents of the layer 3 IP packet are also displayed. It is an IP version 4 packet. Type-of-service parameters are not supported in IP v.4; hence all these fields are set to zero. The total length of the IP-encapsulated part of the packet is 40 bytes (including a 20-byte IP header). Notice that the "don't fragment (DF)" bit is set to 1. This is very significant if the MTU for a medium is exceeded and the frame cannot be fragmented. The IP packet also identifies TCP as the transport layer protocol. How can it be verified that this is a different frame from the one observed in Figure 2-7? The TCP sequence and acknowledgment numbers are one way of deducing this.

Figure 2-9 displays a small portion of each of the three "decode" windows: summary, detail, and hexadecimal. The hex decode is used for very detailed troubleshooting analysis. It can be particularly useful if the Sniffer cannot fully decode the protocol. This may happen in the case of a new version of a protocol or a new proprietary protocol that is not yet supported on the Sniffer. The hex code can be used by the vendor to decode the relevant portion of the frame.

In this figure, an ICMP Echo and Echo-Reply is observed between the two IP addresses in question. The summary window shows that the ping or ICMP Echo, of length 114 bytes, was sent from 159.249.105.253 to 159.249.105.19, with the latter station successfully sending an Echo-Reply. The detail window shows the ICMP header for the Echo. A portion of the IP header is also shown, which displays the IP address and the protocol identifier indicating that ICMP is encapsulated.

In Figure 2-10, summary statistics are displayed for the trace. The duration of the trace was just over 1 minute, which of course is a lot shorter than the average trace duration. A total for the number of packets and bytes captured is summarized along with the average utilization on the Ethernet segment, which is seen not to have been busy during the capture. MAC layer and network layer broadcasts and multicasts are totaled. This particular Sniffer only supports analysis of packets that are encapsulated in either IP or IPX, which explains why there are not rows for other desktop protocols. For IP, there is also a breakdown of the higher-layer components TCP, UDP, and ICMP. No UDP application was observed during this brief capture. The 10 ICMP packets relates to the 5 Echoes sent from the router to 159.249.105.19 and the corresponding 5 Echo-Replies, and it can be seen that these ping packets each had a total length of 118 bytes.

In this section I gave a brief introduction to network analyzers and, in particular, use of the Network Associates Sniffer tool. However, as you

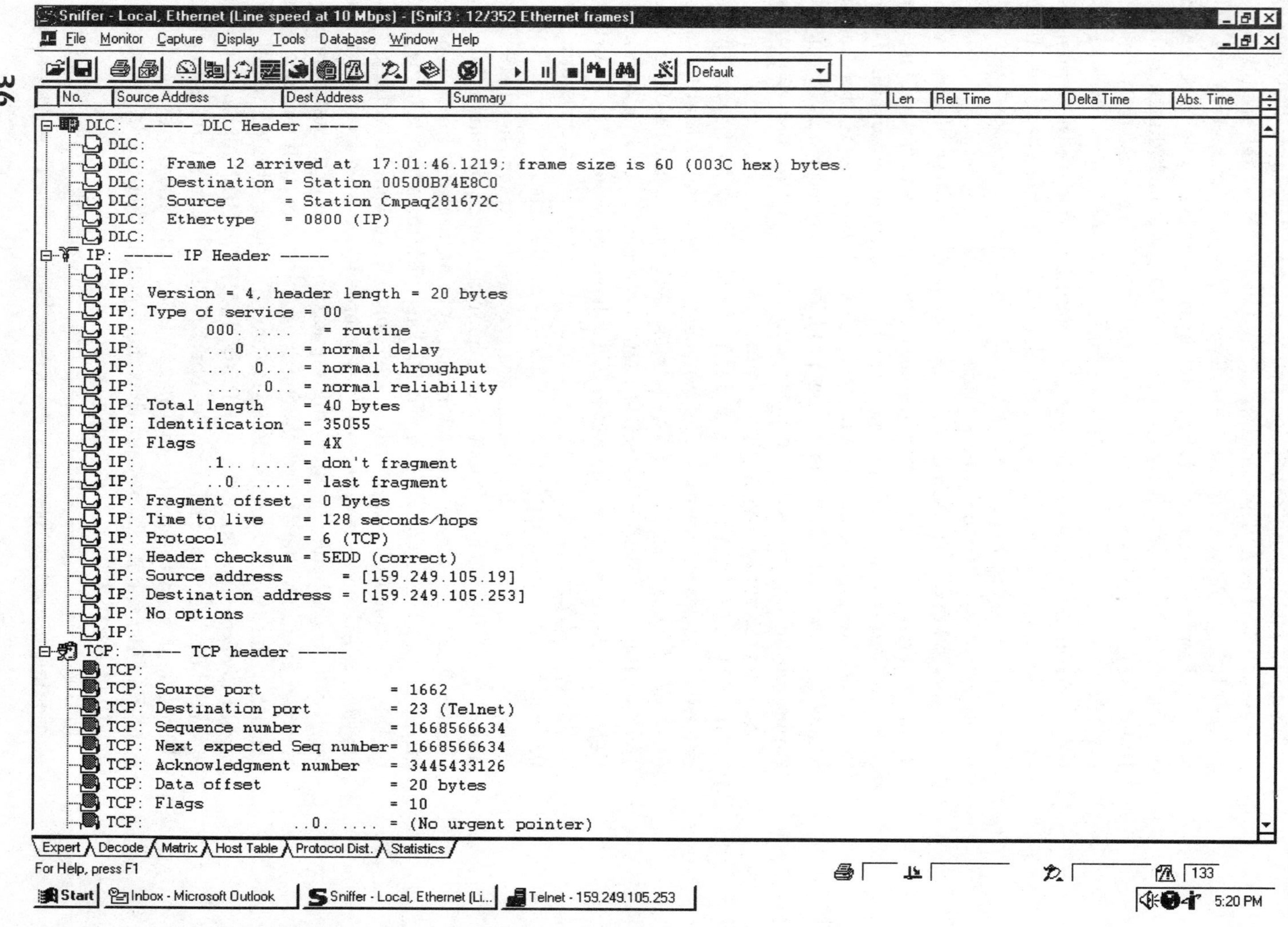

Figure 2-8 Display with the "detail" window extended.

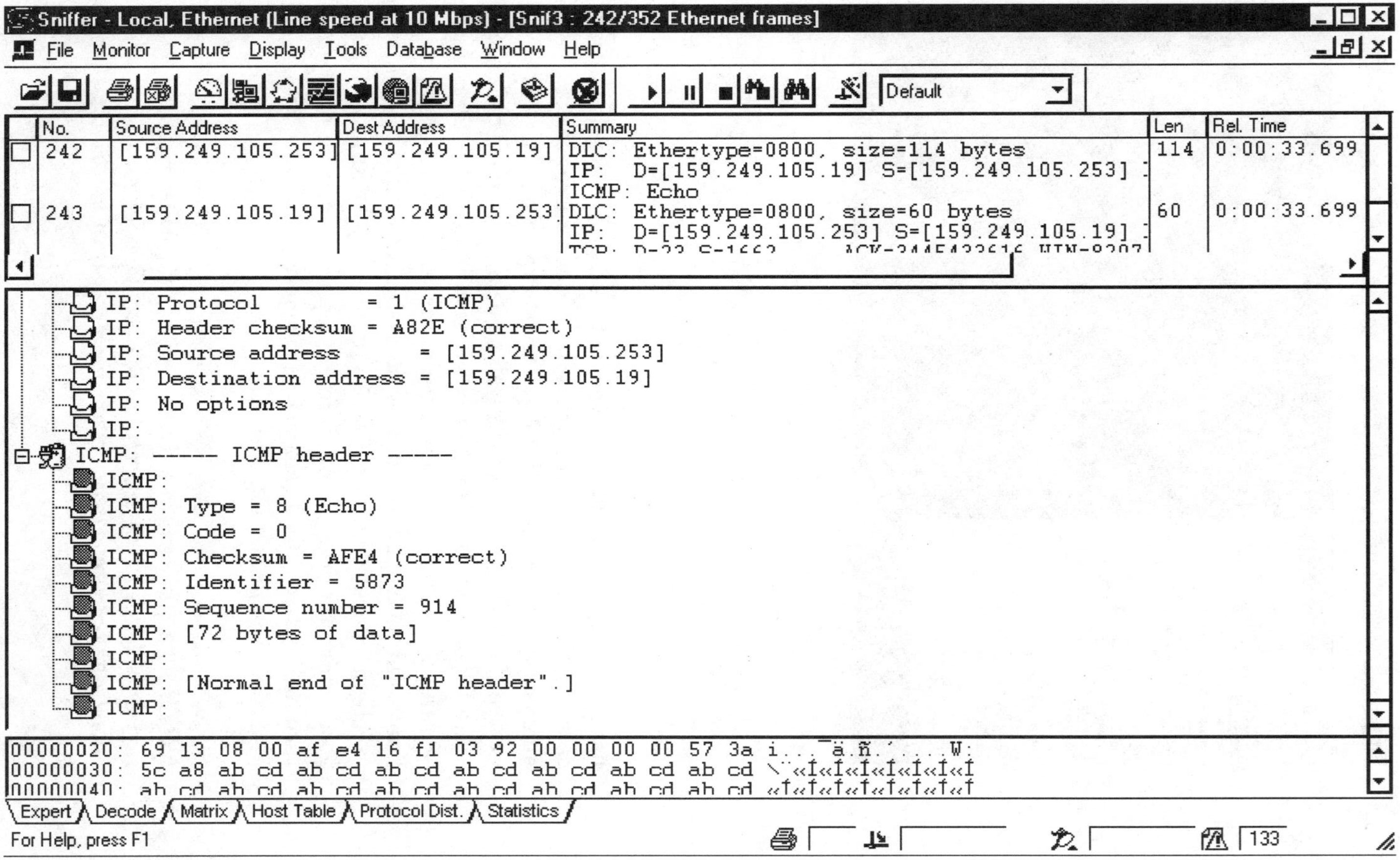

```
Sniffer - Local, Ethernet (Line speed at 10 Mbps) - [Snif3 : 242/352 Ethernet frames]
File  Monitor  Capture  Display  Tools  Database  Window  Help

No.  Source Address      Dest Address        Summary                                           Len  Rel. Time
242  [159.249.105.253]   [159.249.105.19]    DLC:  Ethertype=0800, size=114 bytes              114  0:00:33.699
                                             IP:   D=[159.249.105.19] S=[159.249.105.253]
                                             ICMP: Echo
243  [159.249.105.19]    [159.249.105.253]   DLC:  Ethertype=0800, size=60 bytes               60   0:00:33.699
                                             IP:   D=[159.249.105.253] S=[159.249.105.19]

IP: Protocol           = 1 (ICMP)
IP: Header checksum = A82E (correct)
IP: Source address       = [159.249.105.253]
IP: Destination address = [159.249.105.19]
IP: No options
IP:
ICMP: ----- ICMP header -----
ICMP:
ICMP: Type = 8 (Echo)
ICMP: Code = 0
ICMP: Checksum = AFE4 (correct)
ICMP: Identifier = 5873
ICMP: Sequence number = 914
ICMP: [72 bytes of data]
ICMP:
ICMP: [Normal end of "ICMP header".]
ICMP:

00000020: 69 13 08 00 af e4 16 f1 03 92 00 00 00 00 57 3a
00000030: 5c a8 ab cd ab cd ab cd ab cd ab cd ab cd ab cd

Expert  Decode  Matrix  Host Table  Protocol Dist.  Statistics
For Help, press F1                                                    133
```

Figure 2-9 Trace display showing ICMP Echo packets.

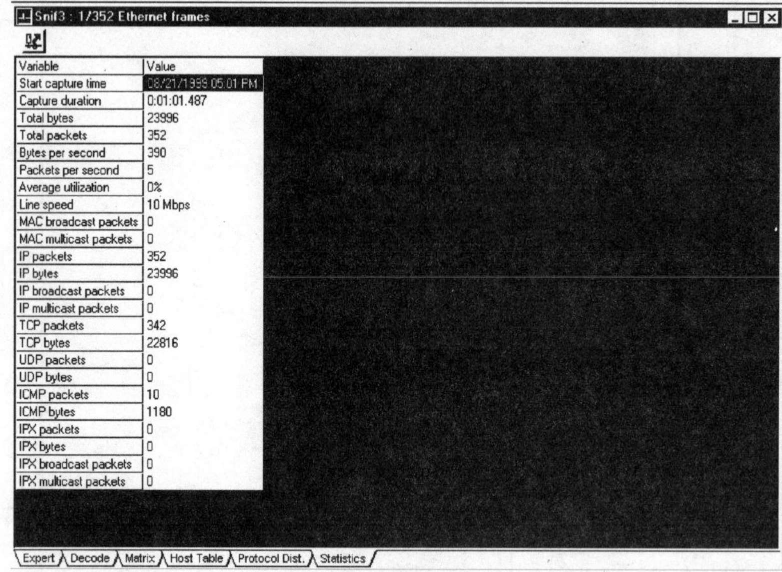

Variable	Value
Start capture time	08/21/1999 05:01 PM
Capture duration	0:01:01.487
Total bytes	23996
Total packets	352
Bytes per second	390
Packets per second	5
Average utilization	0%
Line speed	10 Mbps
MAC broadcast packets	0
MAC multicast packets	0
IP packets	352
IP bytes	23996
IP broadcast packets	0
IP multicast packets	0
TCP packets	342
TCP bytes	22816
UDP packets	0
UDP bytes	0
ICMP packets	10
ICMP bytes	1180
IPX packets	0
IPX bytes	0
IPX broadcast packets	0
IPX multicast packets	0

Figure 2-10
Summary statistics for a Sniffer trace.

have probably gathered, this was just a scratching of the surface. In the case of the Sniffer product, there is a broad range of data capture and analysis options that really have to be explored in practice to do them justice. Tools such as these, as well as being very powerful, are generally quite friendly to use. However, as I have indicated before, the real skill lies in possessing the knowledge necessary to interpret the results. A final point to note before moving on is that a tool like the Sniffer also has excellent educational benefits. By repeatedly looking at traces, a very good understanding of the different protocols can be built up. This, in turn, will put you in a position to use a network analyzer more effectively in a real troubleshooting scenario.

***NOTE:** The real skill in using a tool like the Sniffer is having the necessary knowledge for interpreting the data. One way to help build this knowledge is by repeatedly examining traces in nontroubleshooting situations.*

Network Management Packages and Platforms

CiscoWorks Network Management Software

CiscoWorks is a proprietary management package that was designed initially to provide SNMP-based management services for Cisco routers. CiscoWorks can be implemented using product versions for Windows as well as UNIX platforms, but it is really at its best running on the latter. It is a product that, like most management applications, really begins to come into its own on medium-sized to large networks. A full description of its many features can be found in the Cisco product catalog in hardcopy or online at *www.cisco.com*. From my own experience, two of the most useful features of CiscoWorks are

- *Backing up configurations*. This is an essential management function on any network, whatever its size. CiscoWorks allows the archiving of multiple configuration copies, which also can be compared against each other for any undocumented changes that may have taken place.
- A superbly useful feature known as *Snap-In Manager* allows the same configuration task to be carried out on a group of routers on the network. As an example of the use of Snap-In Manager, consider the case where your boss asks you to change the console password on every router on the network for security reasons. What if you have 250 routers? You get the idea.

CiscoWorks also has an ancillary graphics package called *CiscoView*. This gives a very detailed graphic representation of each device on the network. The capability for a certain amount of GUI-based (as opposed to command line) configuration is also supported. Again, since this is moving beyond the scope of this book, Cisco's Web page can be consulted for further information.

CiscoWorks for Switched Internetworks

CiscoWorks for Switched Internetworks (CWSI) is an SNMP-based management application for Cisco's LAN switches. It is available in different versions that run on Windows NT, Solaris, HP-UX, and AIX. It includes separate software modules that provide configuration and traffic management, VLAN management, and ATM and LANE management and configuration facilities.

These management packages, as with all Cisco products, are in a constant state of development and refinement as networking technologies evolve.

The next generation of NMS solutions from Cisco is CiscoWorks2000, which is intended to integrate the management of routers and switches, providing the potential for an enterprisewide network management solution. The CiscoWorks2000 family is also migrating to an increased use of a Web-based GUI and browser.

REVIEW QUESTIONS

For the exercises that are multiple-choice questions, there is only one correct answer unless the question is marked with an asterisk (*). Choose the most suitable answer.

1. List three parameters, apart from connectivity, that can be tested using a cable tester.
2. Estimate an acceptable signal-to-noise ratio.
3. Estimate an acceptable bit error rate.
4. Fiber cables usually are tested immediately after installation. True or false?
5. Time domain reflectometry is used solely to test the characteristics of a fiberoptic cable. True or false?
6. What are the five elements into which network management traditionally is broken?
7. List and explain four fundamental components of SNMP.
8. List and explain four types of SNMP messages or operations.
9. What are the nine MIBs or groups in RMON?
10. Explain the difference between network monitoring and network management.
11. Explain the difference between protocol analysis and packet analysis.
12. How can a specific amount of data be captured on a Sniffer?

13. A Sniffer can examine packet contents up to and including layer 3. True or false?

14. Explain the different means by which a LAN and a WAN Sniffer can tap into a network.

15. List five reasons why CiscoWorks might be a useful network management application.

CHAPTER 3

Cisco's Diagnostic Tools

Introduction

The objectives of this chapter are to

- Understand router hardware architecture and trace packet flow for the different switching technologies.
- Learn the appropriate use and interpretation of Cisco router diagnostic and troubleshooting commands, in particular: show commands, debug commands, ping and trace.
- Understand the logging and interpretation of Cisco error and informational messages.

Router Functionality and Architecture

Before examining the various troubleshooting and diagnostic tools available on Cisco routers, it is important to at least have a basic understanding of router architecture. The engineer should understand what is happening when these diagnostic commands are executed and how they may affect router performance. Therefore, the early part of this chapter will concentrate on the functions of a router and the different methods by which it implements these functions.

The Routing Function

All routing protocols rely fundamentally on the procedure of building a routing table based on updates received from attached routers, which are running the same protocol. This can be the relatively simple process used by distance-vector protocols such as RIP, or it can entail the more complicated workings of link-state protocols such as OSPF.

Routing could be taking place simultaneously for a number of different desktop protocols on the same router. For example, OSPF could be routing IP, and IPX RIP may be routing Novell packets. In this case, a separate and completely independent routing table would exist for IP and IPX. The independence of these types of routing processes is sometimes termed *ships in the night*, or *SIN*, *routing*.

The Switching Function

Routing and *switching* are two terms that are getting much use and abuse in the current internetworking marketplace. I am going to make some distinctions here. The switching process that I am going to discuss here relates to the internal workings of the router. This is not to be confused with frame-level local-area network (LAN) switching, which will be discussed in a later chapter.

The switching process, in this context, relates to how the router moves packets between its different interfaces. Consider the case of a router receiving a packet on its Ethernet 0 interface. The router strips away the Ethernet MAC header. It then examines the network layer packet header. It will look in its routing table for an entry that matches the destination address on the packet. Say the routing table has an entry with a next hop address of another router, which is reachable via the Token Ring 0 interface. The router then needs to check that it has a layer 2 address for this next hop. If it doesn't have one, then, in the case of IP or AppleTalk, for example, it will send an ARP broadcast out interface Token Ring 0. If there is no reply to the ARP request, the router drops the packet. If there is a reply, the router then constructs a Token Ring frame destined for the next hop router. In this example, the procedure that the router undergoes between receiving the Ethernet frame and constructing and sending the outgoing Token Ring frame is termed the *switching process*. It should be noted that ARP resolution is not normally considered part of the switching process.

In the preceding example, the fact that a routing table lookup was performed to find the next hop address means that process switching was being used. This is the simplest of the different switching methods, but it also causes the highest latency and overhead. We will now look at process switching along with the other faster switching methods that can be employed on the different Cisco hardware platforms.

Cisco 7000 Series Router Architecture

The type of switching used on the Cisco 7000 series routers depends on the router configuration and the version of Cisco IOS being used. Different desktop protocols can use different types of switching. In fact, the same protocol can use different switching methods on the different router interfaces. The type of switching being used for different protocols on various router interfaces is controlled by the router configuration on the *destination* interface.

The different types of switching that can be used on the Cisco 7000 are

- Process switching
- Fast switching
- Autonomous switching
- Silicon switching

The next section of this chapter describes process switching and the different fast-switching technologies. For the moment, it is sufficient to note that process switching makes decisions by consulting the routing table, whereas each of the faster-switching technologies employs caches that can be accessed at higher speeds.

Figure 3-1 shows a schematic diagram of the 7000 series hardware architecture. The basic components are as follows:

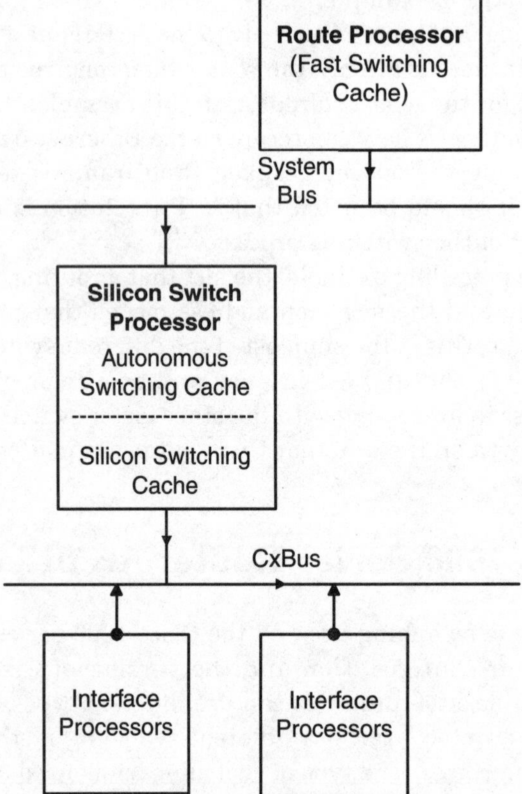

Figure 3-1 Cisco 7000 series hardware architecture.

- *Interface processor*. The network interfaces reside on these modular interface processors. They provide a direct connection between the CxBus and the external network.
- *Ciscobus or CxBus*. This provides a communication medium between the interface processors and the switch processor.
- *Switch processor*. This module manages the multilayer switching between different interface processors and between interface processors and the route processor. It also provides the capability for autonomous and silicon switching. For enhanced functionality, the Cisco 7000 can have a silicon switch processor (SSP) instead or an ordinary SP. With this module, silicon switching is possible, since it can contain the cache for both autonomous switching and silicon switching. On the other hand, an SP can only support the autonomous switching cache.
- *Multibus or system bus*. This bus enables communication between the route processor and the switch processor.
- *Route processor*. The route processor is responsible for generating routing updates and building the routing table, which is always used for routing decisions when only process switching is being employed on the router. The fast-switching cache also resides on the route processor.

Cisco 7500 Series Router Architecture

The Cisco 7500 router series has a number of architectural enhancements to the 7000 series (see Figure 3-2).

- The functions of the route processor and switch processor are incorporated into a single route-switch processor (RSP). This new structure eliminates the need for the system bus when doing fast switching. The integrated functionality of the route and switch processor also has been optimized for performance, stability, scalability, and security. This is particularly pertinent given the core role of the 7500 in the network.
- The communication between the interface processors and the RSP occur over a high-speed CyBus (this is the upgraded equivalent of the CxBus in the 7000 series). On the 7507 and 7513, this bus can be dual-mode communicating with master and slave RSPs. This redundancy feature is known as *high systems availability* and requires IOS version

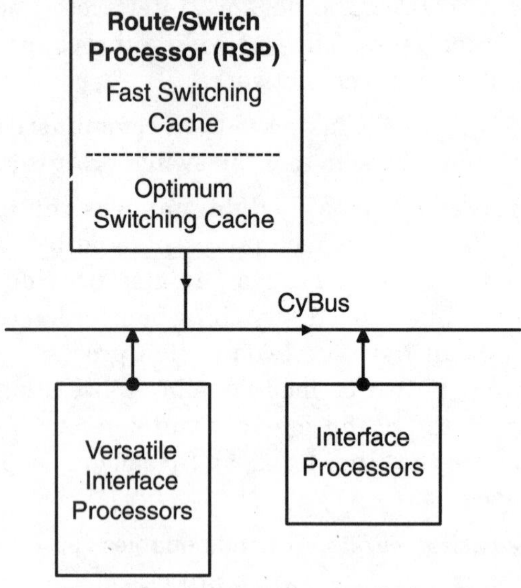

Figure 3-2 Cisco 7500 series hardware architecture.

11.1(4) or later. For clarity, only a single-bus implementation is shown in Figure 3-2.

- Neither autonomous switching nor silicon switching is performed on the 7500 series. Instead, *optimum switching* can be configured. This is similar to fast switching but provides more optimized performance using new data structures and caching methods that were developed for the 7500.

Cisco 4000/2500 Series Architecture

The Cisco 4000 and 2500 series routers have a significantly less complex hardware structure than their 7000/7500 series counterparts (see Figure 3-3). These devices only use shared memory during the switching process. All packet buffers and caches reside in this shared memory. Packets are copied for the network processor modules directly into shared memory. Here they are either fast switched or process switched depending on the configuration of the destination interface. A lookup of the fast-switching cache, which also resides in shared memory, is performed. If no matching entry is found, then the packet is process switched in the normal manner. The 4000 and 2500 series routers do not support autonomous or silicon switching.

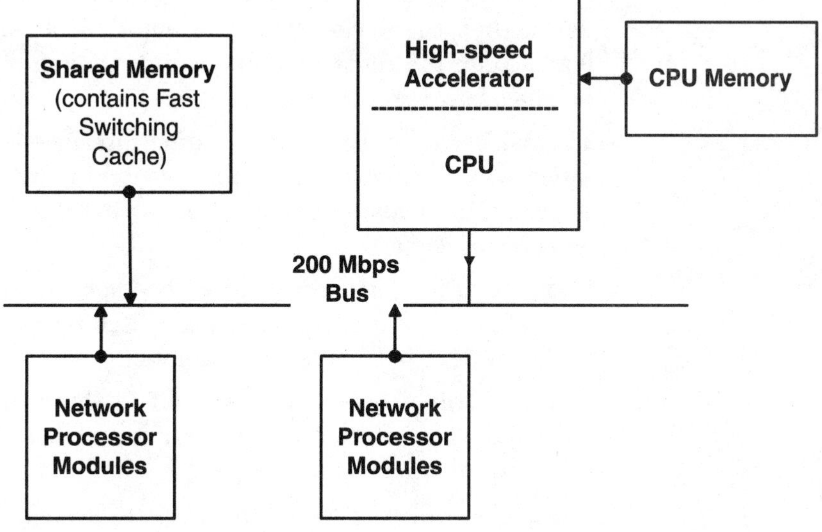

Figure 3-3 Cisco 4000 and 2500 series hardware architecture.

Process-Switched Packet Flow on a 7000 Series Router

Let's now examine and trace the flow of IP packets through a 7000 series router in the case where process switching is being used. Assume that IP fast switching has been turned off on all interfaces using the `no ip route-cache` interface command. This example is for IP but is equally applicable for other protocols.

- A packet arrives on interface processor hardware buffer.
- It is then copied across the CxBus to a packet buffer on the switch processor.
- The silicon-switching and autonomous-switching caches are checked, but no corresponding entry will be found in either of these caches.
- The packet header will be copied across the system bus to the route processor.
- The route processor will check the fast-switching cache for an entry that, of course, it will not find.
- The complete packet is then copied into the route processor memory, enabling the route processor to check the appropriate routing table for an entry corresponding to the destination network.

- If no entry exists, or if the table indicates that the route is in hold-down, then the packet will be dropped. If a corresponding entry is found, then the route processor builds the appropriate encapsulation for the destination interface.
- The configuration on the destination interface is then checked. If the interface is configured for silicon switching, then the encapsulation information is copied to the silicon-switching cache, where the copy will be stored.
- Likewise, if it is configured for autonomous switching, the encapsulation is copied to the autonomous-switching cache. Neither of these configurations is true in this example.
- Fast switching has been turned off in this example; therefore, the encapsulation information will not be copied to the fast-switching cache either.
- The packet will then be copied across the system bus to a packet buffer on the switch processor.
- The switch processor will then place the packet in an output queue for an interface processor.
- The packet will then be copied across the CxBus to a hardware buffer on the appropriate interface processor. From here the packet is sent to the destination interface.

Now that I have outlined the steps involved in process switching a packet, it can be seen why the procedure is considered slow. The main latency is incurred when the entire packet has to be copied from the switch processor to the route processor. In addition, the route processor has to be interrupted during this time interval. Through the appropriate use of caching, the entire procedure can be improved by eliminating unnecessary steps.

Fast Switching and Caching Technology

As mentioned previously, of the different switching technologies, process switching entails the most overhead and latency. Newer technologies have enabled router throughput to improve substantially. These switching technologies are mainly based on the concept of caching routing information so that the route processor does not have to be consulted to make routing decisions. This eliminates one or more steps in the switching process, depending on the location of the cache. In fact, each of the fast-switching technologies is mainly differentiated by the location of this cache. Silicon switching, for example, is faster than autonomous switching because the cache is located closer to the interface processors.

Fast Switching

The packet flow in fast switching can be summarized as follows:

- A packet arrives on interface processor hardware buffer.
- It is then copied across the CxBus to a packet buffer on the switch processor.
- The silicon-switching cache is checked, but no corresponding entry will be found for the destination address.
- The autonomous-switching cache is checked, but no corresponding entry will be found for the destination address.
- The packet header will be copied across the system bus to the route processor.
- The route processor will check the fast-switching cache for a corresponding entry and will discover one. It builds the appropriate encapsulation for the destination interface, which it receives from the fast cache in interrupt mode.
- The new encapsulation will then be copied across the system bus to the switch processor.
- The switch processor will then place the packet in an output queue for an interface processor.
- The packet will then be copied across the CxBus to a hardware buffer on the appropriate interface processor. From here the packet is sent to the destination interface.

Autonomous Switching

The packet flow in autonomous switching can be summarized as follows:

- A packet arrives on interface processor hardware buffer.
- It is then copied across the CxBus to a packet buffer on the switch processor.
- The silicon-switching cache is checked, but no corresponding entry will be found for the destination address.

- The switch processor then checks the autonomous-switching cache. An entry corresponding to the destination address should be found. The switch processor builds the new encapsulation that it receives from the cache.
- The switch processor will then place the packet in an output queue for an interface processor.
- The packet will then be copied across the CxBus to a hardware buffer on the appropriate interface processor. From here the packet is sent to the destination interface.

Silicon Switching

The packet flow in silicon switching can be summarized as follows:

- A packet arrives on interface processor hardware buffer.
- It is then copied across the CxBus to a packet buffer on the switch processor.
- The silicon switch processor checks the silicon-switching cache. An entry corresponding to the destination address should be found. The switch processor builds the new encapsulation that it receives from the cache.
- The switch processor will then place the packet in an output queue for an interface processor.
- The packet will then be copied across the CxBus to a hardware buffer on the appropriate interface processor. From here the packet is sent to the destination interface.

New Switching Technologies

The 7500 series supports newer switching technologies, namely, optimum switching and distributed switching. Optimum switching is, in simple terms, like a more optimized version of fast switching. It replaces autonomous switching and silicon switching for the 7500 series routers.

On 7500 series routers that contain versatile interface processors (VIPs), distributed switching is possible. This is a means of offloading the switching process to the VIP card when routing is performed between interfaces on the same VIP. It can be turned on using the `ip route-cache distributed` interface command. Remember that it can only be done on VIP cards, and currently, distributed switching is only available for IP.

Special Route Processor Functions

The route processor specifically handles certain tasks, even if fast switching is enabled on the destination interfaces. An example of this is when packets have to traverse an interface that is configured with an extended access list. The router may need to verify layer 4 protocol information; hence simple layer 3 caching will not suffice in making a routing decision.

The methods by which the router switches higher-layer protocols are improving continuously, with the advent of features such as Netflow. Newer IOS releases tend to remove more functionality from the route processor. Thus while it should be kept in mind that switching technology is improving rapidly, some functions are still handled by the route processor, namely

- *Broadcast handling*. MAC layer broadcast and routing updates that are broadcasts.
- *Protocol Translation*. Examples include DEC address translation, LAT to telnet, SDLLC, SR/TLB.
- *Tunneling*. For example, GRE tunneling.
- *Debugging*. It is important to remember that debugging activity avails of process switching.
- *SNMP and Syslog*.
- *Custom and priority queuing*.
- *Keepalives*. The sending and receiving of keepalive packets is process switched. For example, if IPX watchdog spoofing is enabled on a WAN interface, the router automatically inserts the `no ipx route-cache` command.
- *Link compression*.

Now I will present an example where we examine what proportion of the traffic on a certain interface is fast switched as opposed to process switched. We will do this using the `show interface statistic` command, which is an undocumented Cisco command. Generally, only very experienced support personnel should use or even have access to undocumented commands. However, I do not think that this particular one can cause too much damage.

On the following router, Token Ring 0/3 is fast switching a majority of its inbound packets, unlike the Token Ring 0/2, for example. Fast switching has not been disabled on any of these interfaces. The reason for the variation is that Token Ring 0/3 is processing significantly fewer broadcasts than the other interface. What is special about broadcasts again? Correct! They are process-switched. Also observe the comparison of the `show interface` commands for Token Rings 0/2 and 0/3 in Listings 3-1 through 3-3.

Queuing and Buffering on the Cisco 7000

The system buffers on the route processor are part of the main system memory on 7000 series router. The buffers' parameters have default values but can be further tuned in rare cases and with extreme caution. Tuning the buffers on the route processor obviously will not have any

Listing 3-1

```
Madrid#sh interface stat
TokenRing0/0
       Switching path   Pkts In  Chars In   Pkts Out  Chars Out
            Processor  35262851 2820191559   5640328 1766465582
          Route cache 183839625 3098184103 188037640  463973676
    Distributed cache         0          0         0          0
                Total 219102476 1623408366  193677968 2230439258
TokenRing0/1
       Switching path   Pkts In  Chars In    Pkts Out  Chars Out
            Processor  72180279  133005317   22290836 1355244997
          Route cache 170157712 3719332749  185863990 1160911073
    Distributed cache         0          0          0          0
                Total 242337991  557370770  208154827 2516156644
TokenRing0/2
       Switching path   Pkts In   Chars In   Pkts Out  Chars Out
            Processor  45870234  363383182   22718924 2304328533
          Route cache  26248636 3051151333   22695796 1229326719
    Distributed cache         0          0          0          0
                Total  72118870 3414534515   45414720 3533655252
TokenRing0/3
       Switching path     Pkts In    Chars In   Pkts Out  Chars Out
            Processor     371144    10615379   22728192 2305642742
          Route cache     859815   354413401     681794  151437085
    Distributed cache          0           0          0          0
                Total    1230959   365028780   23409986 2457079827
```

```
Madrid#sh interface to 0/2
TokenRing0/2 is up, line protocol is up
  Hardware is cxBus Token Ring, address is 0007.ef51.b640 (bia 0007.ef51.b640)
  Description: Open LAN seg=D9E
  Internet address is 165.48.50.1/25
  MTU 4464 bytes, BW 16000 Kbit, DLY 630 usec, rely 255/255, load 1/255
  Encapsulation SNAP, loopback not set, keepalive set (10 sec)
  ARP type: SNAP, ARP Timeout 04:00:00
  Ring speed: 16 Mbps, early token release
  Single ring node, Source Route Transparent Bridge capable
  Source bridging enabled, srn 3486 bn 1 trn 3485 (ring group)
    proxy explorers disabled, spanning explorer disabled, NetBIOS cache disabled
  Group Address: 0x00000000, Functional Address: 0x0880011A
  Ethernet Transit OUI: 0x00 0000
  Last Ring Status 8w4d <Soft Error> (0x2000)
  Last input 00:00:00, output 00:00:00, output hang never
  Last clearing of "show interface" counters 6w0d
  Queueing strategy: fifo
  Output queue 0/40, 0 drops; input queue 0/75, 194 drops
  5 minute input rate 62000 bits/sec, 21 packets/sec
  5 minute output rate 24000 bits/sec, 11 packets/sec
     72151907 packets input, 3425347331 bytes, 0 no buffer
     Received 45512304 broadcasts, 0 runts, 0 giants
     0 input errors, 0 CRC, 0 frame, 0 overrun, 0 ignored, 0 abort
     45436201 packets output, 3538699818 bytes, 0 underruns
     0 output errors, 0 collisions, 0 interface resets
     0 output buffer failures, 0 output buffers swapped out
     0 transitions
```

Listing 3-2

effect on traffic that is fast-switched. If performance problems are observed on process-switched traffic due to inadequate route processor buffer space, then it may be a better idea to use a type of fast switching for this traffic.

When a packet is awaiting an input or output interface processor queue, the system allocates the packet to one of the different buffer pools. The buffer pools are grouped according to the packet sizes they support:

Small buffers—104 bytes

Middle buffers—600 bytes

Big buffers—1524 bytes

Very big buffers—4520 bytes

Large buffers—5024 bytes

Huge buffers—18024 bytes

```
Madrid#sh interface to 0/3
TokenRing0/3 is up, line protocol is up
  Hardware is cxBus Token Ring, address is 0007.ef51.b6c0 (bia 0007.ef51.b6c0)
  Description: Open LAN seg=EFE
  Internet address is 165.48.50.129/25
  MTU 4464 bytes, BW 16000 Kbit, DLY 630 usec, rely 255/255, load 1/255
  Encapsulation SNAP, loopback not set, keepalive set (10 sec)
  ARP type: SNAP, ARP Timeout 04:00:00
  Ring speed: 16 Mbps, early token release
  Single ring node, Source Route Transparent Bridge capable
  Source bridging enabled, srn 3838 bn 1 trn 3485 (ring group)
    proxy explorers disabled, spanning explorer disabled, NetBIOS cache disabled
  Group Address: 0x00000000, Functional Address: 0x0880011A
  Ethernet Transit OUI: 0x000000
  Last Ring Status 1d16h < Error> (0x2000)
  Last input 00:00:08, output 00:00:08, output hang never
  Last clearing of "show interface" counters 6w0d
  Queueing strategy: fifo
  Output queue 0/40, 0 drops; input queue 0/75, 0 drops
  5 minute input rate 0 bits/sec, 0 packets/sec
  5 minute output rate 19000 bits/sec, 0 packets/sec
     1239768 packets input, 369506006 bytes, 0 no buffer
     Received 986 broadcasts, 0 runts, 0 giants
     0 input errors, 0 CRC, 0 frame, 0 overrun, 0 ignored, 0 abort
     23420696 packets output, 2461193000 bytes, 0 underruns
     35 output errors, 0 collisions, 0 interface resets
     0 output buffer failures, 0 output buffers swapped out
     0 transitions
```

Listing 3-3

Buffer Parameters

On bootup, the system allocates memory space to the buffer pools based on router configuration. If the buffer allocation has not been altered in the configuration, then the system will allocate memory based on default values for the buffer parameters. The most fundamental parameters are

Permanent. The number of permanent buffers allocated to a pool. Permanent buffers should never be reduced in number by the system.

Min-free. The minimum number of free or unallocated buffers that should exist in a pool. This parameter helps prevent packets from being dropped because of buffers filling up at an unusually fast rate. The system (i.e., route processor) *creates* more buffers when this threshold is reached in a given pool.

Max-free. The maximum number of free buffers that should exist in a pool. This parameter places an upper limit on the amount of memory that a pool can be allocated without necessity. If this threshold is exceeded, then the system *trims* the particular pool.

Initial. This parameter is particular to router initialization. Its function is to ensure that the router has adequate additional buffer space when booting up in a high-traffic environment.

If there are no free buffers into which an incoming packet can be placed, a *miss* is registered. A high number of misses indicates that the minimum number of free buffers or permanent buffers needs to be increased. On detecting a miss, the system will attempt to allocate more buffers to the appropriate pool. It may fail to allocate more buffers because the *max allowed* value (`show buffers` command) has been exceeded. In this case, a *failure* will be registered.

Interface Hold Queues

Each individual router interface has an input queue and an output queue. These queues may consist of buffers that are seized from different buffer pools depending on the size of the packets being queued. The default size for input queues is 75 packets, and the default output queue size is 40 packets. These queue sizes can be altered, although this will have no effect on fast-switched traffic. The fast-switching technologies do not use interface hold queues. Note that as of IOS 11.0, weighted fair queuing is on by default on WAN links that are T1 or less. In this case, weighted fair queuing must be turned off before default queue sizes can be manipulated.

If the input queue overflows before the router can empty it, packets will be dropped. This indicates that the router's CPU is overloaded and the router cannot process incoming packets quickly enough. This situation is often associated with heavy-loaded traffic conditions. However, it is certainly a cause for concern if it happens persistently. Output queue drops indicate that the router has switched the packet, but the output interface processor queue has overflowed. This is less serious than input drops because it indicates that the router is processing the packets. It also may be associated with unusually high traffic conditions.

Interface Buffers

The switch processor (SP) interface buffers store packets that are copied in from the interface processors via the CxBus (or CyBus in the case of the 7500 series). The SP or silicon switch processor (SSP) interface buffers have 512 kB of memory allocated to them. The autonomous switching cache is also contained within this memory.

If the SP interface buffers overflow, the system registers an *ignore* message. Ignores can occur when a high-speed interface such as HSSI is receiving data at a rate higher than the switch processor or CxBus can handle.

The hardware buffer on the interface processor is responsible for the initial receipt of packets. If this buffer cannot handle the rate at which it is receiving packets, then an *overrun* will be registered.

The `show buffers` Command

We are now finally ready to look at the `show buffers` command (see Listing 3-4). This command can be used if performance problems are reported on a router that is handling a lot of process-switched traffic. The only terms listed in this output that have not been addressed already (or are not self-explanatory) are *buffer elements* and *hits*. Buffer elements are used as placeholders for buffers in operating system queues. A hit is registered when a buffer is allocated successfully to a queue when required. Figure 3-4 shows a schematic diagram outlining the procedure for buffer allocation.

Before leaving the topic of buffers, I would like to emphasize that it is an area that should be treated with extreme caution. While it is important to have an understanding of how buffers are allocated, buffer tuning itself traditionally has been discouraged, except in last-resort cases. If a router that is predominantly doing process switching has performance problems, then it is usually a better alternative to turn on fast switching. Without a very detailed understanding of router memory architecture, buffer tuning may create problems that are additional to the one you are trying to solve. In the versions of Cisco's IOS from 11.0 onward, the operating system itself is more intelligent and adaptable with respect to memory allocation. Although it is still an area of some debate, for these versions of IOS, Cisco tends to advise that buffer tuning generally should no longer be necessary.

NOTE: *Buffer tuning should be performed infrequently and with caution. In more recent Cisco IOS versions it should not be necessary at all.*

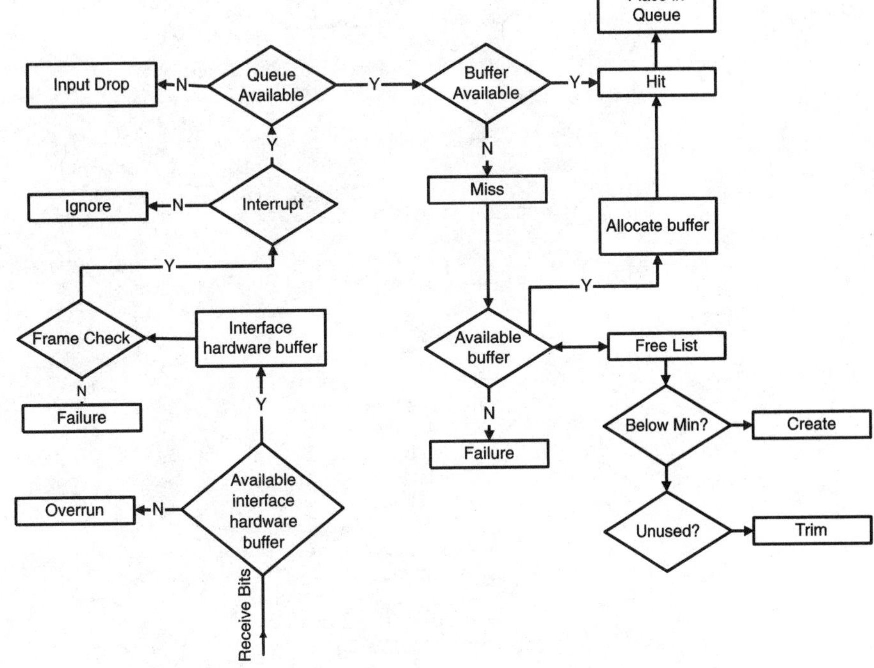

Figure 3-4 Flowchart for the allocation of buffer pools.

Queuing and Buffering on the Cisco 4000/2500

The buffering and queuing mechanisms in the Cisco 2500 and 4000 series routers are significantly less complex than in the 7000 series. All buffers and queues in the Cisco 2500 and 4000 series routers are contained in shared memory. Packets that are read from interface buffers are retained in shared memory until an output interface is selected. At this point, the packet is sent to an output queue for the appropriate network processor module before being transmitted to the destination interface.

Troubleshooting Commands

The Cisco IOS operating system software provides a tremendous selection of commands that greatly aid in troubleshooting, problem diagnosis, and performance monitoring. The commands can be divided most basically into show commands and debug commands. There is also a set of

Listing 3-4

```
Router8-prem#sh buffer
Buffer elements:
     499 in free list (500 max allowed)
     62464295 hits, 0 misses, 0 created

Public buffer pools:
Small buffers, 104 bytes (total 120, permanent 120):
     106 in free list (20 min, 250 max allowed)
     80193590 hits, 3 misses, 9 trims, 9 created
     0 failures (0 no memory)
Middle buffers, 600 bytes (total 90, permanent 90):
     88 in free list (10 min, 200 max allowed)
     45788908 hits, 7 misses, 4 trims, 4 created
     0 failures (0 no memory)
Big buffers, 1524 bytes (total 90, permanent 90):
     90 in free list (5 min, 300 max allowed)
     371233 hits, 0 misses, 0 trims, 0 created
     0 failures (0 no memory)
Very Big buffers, 4520 bytes (total 10, permanent 10):
     10 in free list (0 min, 300 max allowed)
     2499799 hits, 0 misses, 0 trims, 0 created
     0 failures (0 no memory)
Large buffers, 5024 bytes (total 10, permanent 10):
     10 in free list (0 min, 30 max allowed)
     0 hits, 0 misses, 0 trims, 0 created
     0 failures (0 no memory)
Huge buffers, 18024 bytes (total 3, permanent 0):
     2 in free list (0 min, 13 max allowed)
     250240 hits, 24 misses, 45 trims, 48 created
     0 failures (0 no memory)
Header pools:
```

clear commands, which usually are used in conjunction with the show and debug commands. For this reason, I am not treating the clear commands as a separate section but instead refer to them as they arise.

For the purpose of clarity, I have subdivided the show and debug commands that are referred to in this chapter. Dividing the commands into categories such as global, interface-related, system-related, and so on is mainly for illustration and is by no means written in stone. The engineer should develop an intuition as to what commands should be used in various situations through knowledge and experience.

Apart from simply learning different commands, one of my objectives is that you develop the skill to quickly navigate the Cisco IOS software to avail of an appropriate command that perhaps you never used before. When you get to this level, you are really using the full troubleshooting strength of the Cisco IOS. This concept applies equally to show commands, debug commands, and clear commands.

Show Commands

We will now examine some of the most useful show commands by exploring the output they provide and their significance in troubleshooting different types of problems. For clarity purposes, they have been loosely subdivided into global system commands, interface commands, and protocol commands. Only the more commonly used commands will be discussed in this particular section. However, many of the commands will be covered or revisited in greater detail in the appropriate chapters on the different LAN and WAN protocols.

Global System Commands This section presents the output of commands that relate to router software and hardware, including memory and power. The `show version` command is a fundamental command that is extremely useful in providing summary information about the router itself and the hardware and software that are employed. The `show hardware` command provides the same output (see Listing 3-5).

In this example, the information that is provided includes

- The IOS version is 11.1(17).
- The router has been up for almost 23 weeks and was last restarted by a reload as opposed to a power-on.
- We can see what the filename for the IOS image is and that the router was booted from Flash memory at slot 0.
- It is a 7000 series router, which is using an RSP.
- The router has 32 MB of main memory and 2 MB of shared memory.
- The router has 8 MB of both slot 0 Flash memory and internal SIMM.
- The configuration register value is 0x2102. This tells us that the router will be booted from Flash at the next reload. If the configuration register were set at 0x2101, then the next reboot would be from ROM.
- The different interface processors on the router are listed.

As you can see, the `show version` command provides a lot of very useful generic information on the router. It is often a good starting point when gathering facts on a particular problem.

If environmental factors need to be checked on the 7000 series router, then the `show environment all` command is very useful. The status of both power supplies (if the dual power supply is being used) can be checked at a glance. Temperature profile information is also available. This command could be used if there was an air conditioning failure in

```
R3#show version
Cisco Internetwork Operating System Software
IOS (tm) GS Software (RSP-JV-M), Version 11.1(17) CA, EARLY DEPLOYMENT RELEASE SO
FTWARE (fc1)
Synced to mainline version: 11.1(17)
Copyright (c) 1986-1998 by cisco Systems, Inc.
Compiled Tue 03-Feb-98 02:58 by richardd
Image text-base: 0x60010900, data-base: 0x60A52000

ROM: System Bootstrap, Version 5.3(9) [mkamson 9], RELEASE SOFTWARE (fc2)
ROM: GS Software (RSP-BOOT-M), Version 11.1(17)CA, EARLY DEPLOYMENT RELEASE SOFT
WARE (fc1)

R3 uptime is 22 weeks, 6 days, 13 hours, 44 minutes
System restarted by reload at 00:09:13 PDT Fri Jun 19 1998
System image file is "slot0:rsp-jv-mz.111-17.CA.bin", booted via slot0
Network configuration file is "pcmdi4f4Mqi406", booted via tftp from 165.48.67.1
47

cisco RSP7000 (R4600) processor with 32768K/2072K bytes of memory.
R4600 processor, Implementation 32, Revision 2.0
Last reset from power-on
G.703/E1 software, Version 1.0.
G.703/JT2 software, Version 1.0.
SuperLAT software copyright 1990 by Meridian Technology Corp).
Bridging software.
X.25 software, Version 2.0, NET2, BFE and GOSIP compliant.
TN3270 Emulation software (copyright 1994 by TGV Inc).
Chassis Interface.
3 EIP controllers (18 Ethernet).
2 TRIP controllers (8 Token Ring).
18 Ethernet/IEEE 802.3 interfaces.
8 Token Ring/IEEE 802.5 interfaces.
125K bytes of non-volatile configuration memory.

8192K bytes of Flash PCMCIA card at slot 0 (Sector size 128K).
8192K bytes of Flash internal SIMM (Sector size 256K).
Configuration register is 0x2102
```

Listing 3-5

an equipment room to detect the early stages of device overheating or thermal runaway. The `show environment table` command gives a listing of the temperature ranges for inlet, exhaust, and hot point that the router can tolerate. The commands are only available on the 7000 series (see Listing 3-6).

If a router is dropping packets on a number of different interfaces, then there is a possibility that the router may not have enough memory or that its CPU may be too busy. Memory availability is checked using

```
R3#sh environ all
Arbiter type 1, backplane type 70x0 (id 5)
Power supply #1 is 700W (id 2), power supply #2 is 700W (id 2)
Active fault conditions: none
Active trip points: none

            0123456
Dbus slots: XXXXXX

 card     inlet       hotpoint     exhaust
 CI(6)   21C/69F      32C/89F      23C/73F
Shutdown temperature source is 'hotpoint' on CI(6), requested CI(6)
+12V measured at 11.98
 +5V measured at 5.19
-12V measured at -11.98
+24V measured at 24.06
+2.5 reference is 2.49
```

Listing 3-6

the `show memory` command. CPU utilization is examined using the `show process` command.

The first two lines in Listing 3-7 give a generic memory summary indicating that there is sufficient available memory. They also indicate that memory fragmentation is not occurring, since the largest available block is approximately 11.25 MB in a 13.03-MB pool of free memory. Memory fragmentation is characterized by the memory splitting into a large number of smaller contiguous blocks. This is at best an extremely inefficient use of memory and at worst can produce memory errors that may adversely affect router performance. There then follows a detailed breakdown of processor memory blocks (see Listing 3-8). This is usually only analyzed by Cisco Technical Assistance Center (TAC) personnel.

Let us now examine a router that is exhibiting memory fragmentation (see Listing 3-9). Here we have an adequate amount of free memory (8.4 MB), but the largest block is just over 0.5 MB. Not having larger available blocks of contiguous memory can cause potentially serious memory allocation problems. The problem is sometimes characterized by one or more interfaces losing line protocol on intermittent basis. A memory fragmentation error message is also generated by the router.

Using the command `show memory free`, it can be seen that the available memory is split into many small fragments (a truncated output is shown in Listing 3-10 for illustration purposes). It should be noted that a certain amount of memory fragmentation is normal in a router.

```
Bilbao#sh memory
                Head     Total(b)     Used(b)     Free(b)   Lowest(b)  Largest(b)
Processor   60DB19C0     19195456     6162924    13032532    11615164    11250780
     Fast   60D919C0       131072      128344        2728        2728        2684
```

Listing 3-7

```
                   Processor memory
  Address   Bytes Prev.      Next     Ref  PrevF   NextF    Alloc PC  What
 60DB19C0    1056 0          60DB1E0C   1                   60133B44  List Elements
 60DB1E0C    2656 60DB19C0 60DB2898   1                   60133B44  List Headers
 60DB2898    9000 60DB1E0C 60DB4BEC   1                   60134D38  Interrupt Stack
 60DB4BEC    9000 60DB2898 60DB6F40   1                   60134D38  Interrupt Stack
 60DB6F40     160 60DB4BEC 60DB700C   1                   601745D0  *Init*
 60DB700C    2536 60DB6F40 60DB7A20   1                   60143724  TTY data
 60DB7A20    2000 60DB700C 60DB821C   1                   601466F4  TTY Input Buf
 60DB821C     512 60DB7A20 60DB8448   1                   60146728  TTY Output Buf
 60DB8448    9000 60DB821C 60DBA79C   1                   60134D38  Interrupt Stack
 60DBA79C    1056 60DB8448 60DBABE8   1                   60133B44  messages
 60DBABE8    1032 60DBA79C 60DBB01C   1                   60175668  Process Array
 60DBB01C     120 60DBABE8 60DBB0C0   1                   604A0C54  IPX NDB
 60DBB0C0      88 60DBB01C 60DBB144   1                   604A4EB8  IPX RIP RDB
 60DBB144      32 60DBB0C0 60DBB190   1                   602478D0  Router Init
 60DBB190      32 60DBB144 60DBB1DC   1                   603D40F8  EIGRP IIDB link
 60DBB1DC     120 60DBB190 60DBB280   1                   604A0C54  IPX NDB

Bilbao>
```

Listing 3-8

The example here, however, shows excessive fragmentation. There are no strict guidelines as to what is acceptable, but the largest available block certainly should not be less than half the free memory. The problem may be fixed by reloading the router. On boot up, the system reallocates memory and buffer space. The memory allocation should then be carefully monitored. If the condition begins to occur again, the Cisco TAC should be consulted.

To check if the router's CPU is being overloaded, use the `show process` command. This gives a snapshot of the overall CPU utilization, followed by a breakdown of the different processes and, more important, how much they are contributing to the CPU load. In the following example, the router does not appear to be overloaded. Very generally, a 5-minute average of less than 60 percent is acceptable. If a CPU utiliza-

```
Barcelona>sh mem
                Head    Total(b)     Used(b)     Free(b)   Lowest(b) Largest(b)
Processor   60DB19C0    19195456    10713712     8481744      192680     586748
     Fast   60D919C0      131072       90936       40136       40136      40092
```

Listing 3-9

tion problem is suspected, then this parameter should be monitored repeatedly at frequent intervals because it can vary rapidly over time. To demonstrate this, you should use the command on a live router and keep reentering it approximately every 10 seconds. In this way you will build up a good understanding of what range of values the utilization is fluctuating between.

If the CPU utilization is seen to be regularly exceeding 80 percent, then the router is likely overloaded. The next step is to check if one or more processes are making a major contribution to the load. In Listing 3-11, you can see that the processing of IPX SAP updates is the biggest single contributor to the CPU load, but it happens to be at an acceptable level. If, for example, the SRB *background* parameter were at a persist-

```
Barcelona>sh mem free
                Head    Total(b)     Used(b)     Free(b)   Lowest(b) Largest(b)
Processor   60DB19C0    19195456    10778764     8416692      192680     586748
     Fast   60D919C0      131072       90936       40136       40136      40092

            ---------   ------------  ---------------

            613F8504       24 613F844C 613F8548    0   6142D11 612F33C 6012FCB4
(fragment)
612F33C8        40 612F3310 612F341C   0   613F850 60F27B0 6012FCB4   (fragment)
60F27B00        32 60F27A48 60F27B4C   0   612F33C 614E7EA 6012FCB4   (fragment)
614E7EA8        24 614E7DF0 614E7EEC   0   60F27B0 610D3B0 6012FCB4   (fragment)
610D3B00        52 610D3A48 610D3B60   0   614E7EA 6152390 6012FCB4   (fragment)
61523900        36 61523848 61523950   0   610D3B0 6151A04 6012FCB4   (fragment)
6151A048        24 61519F90 6151A08C   0   6152390 6163C89 6012FCB4   (fragment)
6163C894        28 6163C7DC 6163C8DC   0   6151A04 61111D8 6012FCB4   (fragment)
61111D84        36 61111CE8 61111DD4   0   6163C89 6154721 6012FCB4   (fragment)
6154721C        44 61547180 61547274   0   61111D8 6142619 6012FCB4   (fragment)
6142619C        24 614260E4 614261E0   0   6154721 6198004 6012FCB4   (fragment)
```

Listing 3-10

```
Fulton_924>sh process cpu
CPU utilization for five seconds: 15%/4%; one minute: 17%; five minutes: 19%
 PID  Runtime(ms)   Invoked  uSecs     5Sec    1Min    5Min TTY Process
   1       460184   5380085     85    0.00%   0.00%   0.00%   0 NTP
   2    252749536   2384205 106010    0.00%   2.35%   2.65%   0 Check heaps
   3        28676     12855   2230    0.00%   0.00%   0.00%   0 Pool Manager
   4      3826920  18027652    212    0.00%   0.00%   0.00%   0 Timers
   5       971768    683376   1422    0.00%   0.00%   0.00%   0 ARP Input
   6            0         1      0    0.00%   0.00%   0.00%   0 SERIAL A'detect
   7         1600      3086    518    0.00%   0.00%   0.00%   0 RARP Input
   8     12020508   9837783   1221    0.24%   0.10%   0.08%   0 IP Input
   9       120392   1804348     66    0.00%   0.01%   0.00%   0 TCP Timer
  10          136        61   2229    0.00%   0.00%   0.00%   0 TCP Protocols
  11      2822048   1691386   1668    0.00%   0.01%   0.00%   0 CDP Protocol
  12        79364     23343   3399    0.00%   0.00%   0.00%   0 BOOTP Server
  13     26155236   9135958   2862    0.32%   0.25%   0.22%   0 IP Background
  14       317720    150150   2116    0.00%   0.00%   0.00%   0 IP Cache Ager
  15           52         2  26000    0.00%   0.00%   0.00%   0 Critical Bkgnd
  16         5856      4571   1281    0.00%   0.00%   0.00%   0 Net Background
  17          132        59   2237    0.00%   0.00%   0.00%   0 Logger
  18      2029800   8986220    225    0.00%   0.00%   0.00%   0 TTY Background
  19      1301540   8986278    144    0.00%   0.00%   0.00%   0 Per-Second Jobs
  20      4608976   8986301    512    0.00%   0.02%   0.01%   0 Net Periodic
  21      6566788  16585339    395    0.00%   0.00%   0.00%   0 Net Input
 PID  Runtime(ms)   Invoked  uSecs     5Sec    1Min    5Min TTY Process
  22      4582304    150150  30518    0.00%   0.02%   0.00%   0 Per-minute Jobs
  23     51598380 135094851    381    0.32%   0.24%   0.28%   0 IPX Input
  24     86792124  23662071   3667    0.98%   0.87%   0.89%   0 IPX RIP
  25    438480948 123384161   3553    7.94%   3.31%   3.91%   0 IPX SAP
  26       394636    738631    534    0.00%   0.00%   0.00%   0 IPX RSUpdate
  27       472276    114440   4126    0.00%   0.00%   0.00%   0 IPX GNS
  28            0         2      0    0.00%   0.00%   0.00%   0 IPX Forwarder
  29      8692052   7630006   1139    0.16%   0.07%   0.06%   0 IPX OutputFork
  30            0         2      0    0.00%   0.00%   0.00%   0 IPXWAN Input
  31            0         2      0    0.00%   0.00%   0.00%   0 IPXWAN Timer
  32     97862192 220402583    444    0.32%   0.61%   0.60%   0 LanNetMgr Supt
  33            0         9      0    0.00%   0.00%   0.00%   0 CLS Background
  34        16700    901181     18    0.00%   0.00%   0.00%   0 LLC2 Timer
  35            0         2      0    0.00%   0.00%   0.00%   0 VDLC Background
  36     15704404  24690843    636    0.00%   0.02%   0.05%   0 SRB Background
  37      6690020  11356484    589    0.00%   0.01%   0.00%   0 IP-EIGRP Hello
  38          564        82   6878    0.32%   0.50%   0.12%   2 Virtual Exec
  39      4761744    218153  21827    0.00%   0.00%   0.00%   0 IP SNMP
  40            0         2      0    0.00%   0.00%   0.00%   0 IPX SNMP
  41          660        23  28695    0.00%   0.00%   0.00%   0 SNMP Traps
  42       215532    150234   1434    0.00%   0.00%   0.00%   0 IP-RT Background
  43     13545760   9536446   1420    0.00%   0.00%   0.00%   0 IP-EIGRP Router
 PID  Runtime(ms)   Invoked  uSecs     5Sec    1Min    5Min TTY Process
  44           72        38   1894    0.00%   0.00%   0.00%   0 IPX SUO AB890780
  46           76        69   1101    0.32%   0.02%   0.00%   0 IPX SUO AB890780
Fulton_924>
```

Listing 3-11

ently high percentage, then this could indicate a source route bridging explorer storm.

The `show process memory` command first gives generic information on the available router memory. It then examines each of the processes, giving details on how much memory space they have been allocated (see Listing 3-12).

If a router completely crashed by doing an impromptu reload, a related error message may be included in the output of the `show version` command. The `show stack` command also can be used to see if the router did a stack trace, which provides information on why the reload occurred. The following output is for a router in a normal condition (Listing 3-13). If there had been an error-induced reload, the stack trace would appear at the end of the output. This stack trace needs to be decoded in order to extract the relevant information about the problem. A stack trace decode can be performed by a Cisco TAC engineer. Alternatively, a user with a privileged CCO logon ID can do the stack decode himself or herself by pasting the output of the `show stack` command at the appropriate section of CCO. The results of a stack trace decode can sometimes relate the problem to a known Cisco bug.

When reporting a case to the Cisco TAC, the support engineer assigned to the case frequently asks to be sent the output of the `show tech_support` command. This command causes each of the following commands to be executed sequentially:

- `Show version`
- `Show controllers`
- `Show buffers`
- `Show interface`
- `Show stack`
- `Show process cpu`
- `Show process memory`
- `Show running-config`

This combination of commands clearly gives a comprehensive overview of the router's configuration along with detailed information on most of the key performance parameters. The `show controllers` commands have not yet been discussed and will be covered in the next section. The output of `show tech_support` can be of great assistance to the Cisco TAC personnel when working on a complex problem.

```
R1>sh process memory
Total: 16367112, Used: 4669456, Free: 11697656
 PID  TTY  Allocated      Freed    Holding    Getbufs    Retbufs Process
   0    0      21720        300    1353708          0          0 *Init*
   0    0        336 3305106952        336          0          0 *Sched*
   0    0 2169734200 2292011292       6592     588792      30960 *Dead*
   1    2        860        492       5084          0          0 Virtual Exec
   2    0          0        672       2716          0          0 Check heaps
   3    0    8213912      10392      15856    6377280     419060 Pool Manager
   4    0        256        256       2716          0          0 Timers
   5    0       2108      27276       3096          0          0 ARP Input
   6    0         92          0       2808          0          0 SERIAL A'detect
   7    0        232          0       2948          0          0 Probe Input
   8    0        140          0       2856          0          0 RARP Input
   9    0   15890524       1496       6388     193200          0 IP Input
  10    0          0      10472       2716          0          0 TCP Timer
  11    0     101448       1496       6596          0          0 TCP Protocols
  12    0   14370192   14343288       3640      20160          0 CDP Protocol
  13    0     163032     128772       3752          0          0 BOOTP Server
  14    0       1536     128376       4888          0          0 IP Background
  15    0          0   14068056       2716          0          0 IP Cache Ager
  16    0        128          0       2844          0          0 Critical Bkgnd
  17    0       9624          0       2808       2268          0 Net Background
  18    0        348        256       4808          0          0 Logger
 PID  TTY  Allocated      Freed    Holding    Getbufs    Retbufs Process
  19    0        256        256       2716          0          0 TTY Background
  20    0          0        664       2716          0          0 Per-Second Jobs
  21    0      46876      43392       2716       2268          0 Net Periodic
  22    0        184          0       2900          0          0 Net Input
  23    0          0    2205804       2716          0   18670100 Per-minute Jobs
  24    0     137128          0       2716          0          0 IPX Input
  25    0   18695288   14712108       2716          0          0 IPX RIP
  26    0   15343144   73074256      65124          0          0 IPX SAP
  27    0  115847352      34184       2716       6804          0 IPX RSUpdate
  28    0       2056       2056       2716          0          0 IPX GNS
  29    0          0          0       2716          0          0 IPX Forwarder
  30    0 3305021104          0       2716          0          0 IPX OutputFork
  31    0          0          0       2716          0          0 IPXWAN Input
  32    0          0          0       2716          0          0 IPXWAN Timer
  33    0      16984        256      18892          0          0 ISDN
  34    0        504        256       2964          0          0 CCP manager
  35    0          0          0       2716          0          0 PPP manager
  36    0  496780020  496779124       2900          0          0 IP-EIGRP Hello
  38    0  165588980  165588980       2896          0          0 IPX-EIGRP Hello
  39    0 1059852064 1061033224     283980          0          0 IP-EIGRP Router
  40    0  175368788  162786932       7360   12253320          0 IP SNMP
  41    0          0          0       4716          0          0 IPX SNMP
 PID  TTY  Allocated      Freed    Holding    Getbufs    Retbufs Process
  42    0     118492      96140       2808      13608          0 SNMP Traps
  43    0          0          0       2716          0          0 IP-RT Background
 44    0   744991584  680352476    2778984          0          0 IPX EIGRP
                                   4651420 Total
```

Listing 3-12

Listing 3-13

```
CBS1>sh stacks
Minimum process stacks:
 Free/Size   Name
 9700/12000  Init
 5080/6000   Router Init
 9048/12000  Virtual Exec
 4692/6000   Config Probe

Interrupt level stacks:
Level    Called Unused/Size  Name
  1 1677545139   7264/9000  Network interfaces
  2  235675731   8624/9000  DMA/Timer Interrupt
  3          0   9000/9000  PA Management Int Handler
  4   13886855   8648/9000  Console Uart
  5          0   9000/9000  OIR/Error Interrupt
  7-  717235867  8608/9000  NMI Interrupt Handler
CBS1>
```

Interface-Related Commands This section examines some of the commands that directly relate to the router's active interfaces. I will start with the `show ip interface brief` command, which gives a useful summary of the IP address as well as the layer 2 status of each of the router interfaces (see Listing 3-14). A summary of other desktop protocols apart from IP also can be obtained using the appropriate options, e.g., `show ipx interface brief` and so on.

Many of the parameters that are observed in the output of a `show interface` command appear in all `show interface` commands. From an Ethernet example I will discuss all the general interface parameters as well as those which are specific to an Ethernet interface (see Listing 3-15).

Ethernet 2/0 is up, indicating that layer 1, in relation to the OSI model, is up.

Line protocol up indicates that layer 2 is up.

Description. This description is configurable by the user. It is important to use this facility by including a descriptive and concise comment. In a large organization, a field technician may have difficulty locating a faulty router.

MTU. This is the maximum transmission unit and is configurable.

BW, Dly, rely, load. Bandwidth, delay, reliability, and load: These parameters are relevant to the IGRP/EIGRP metric. Bandwidth and delay can be configured in order to influence routing decisions. Reliability

```
R3#sh ip in brief
Interface              IP-Address      OK? Method Status                Protocol
TokenRing0/0           165.48.48.3     YES NVRAM  up                    up
TokenRing0/1           165.48.49.3     YES NVRAM  up                    up
TokenRing0/2           165.48.50.1     YES NVRAM  up                    up
TokenRing0/3           165.48.50.129   YES NVRAM  up                    up
TokenRing1/0           165.48.59.1     YES NVRAM  up                    up
TokenRing1/1           unassigned      YES unset  administratively down down
TokenRing1/2           unassigned      YES unset  administratively down down
TokenRing1/3           unassigned      YES unset  administratively down down
Ethernet2/0            165.48.51.1     YES NVRAM  up                    up
Ethernet2/1            165.48.51.129   YES NVRAM  up                    up
Ethernet2/2            165.48.52.1     YES NVRAM  up                    up
Ethernet2/3            165.48.52.129   YES NVRAM  up                    up
Ethernet2/4            165.48.53.1     YES NVRAM  up                    up
Ethernet2/5            165.48.53.129   YES NVRAM  up                    up
R3#
```

Listing 3-14

```
R3#sh int e2/0
Ethernet2/0 is up, line protocol is up
  Hardware is cxBus Ethernet, address is 00e0.f78a.6d40 (bia 00e0.f78a.6d40)
  Description: seg=E2 LAB2 SRV1
  Internet address is 165.48.51.1/25
  MTU 1500 bytes, BW 10000 Kbit, DLY 1000 usec, rely 255/255, load 1/255
  Encapsulation ARPA, loopback not set, keepalive set (10 sec)
  ARP type: ARPA, ARP Timeout 04:00:00
  Last input 00:00:00, output 00:00:00, output hang never
  Last clearing of "show interface" counters 5w0d
  Queueing strategy: fifo
  Output queue 0/40, 44 drops; input queue 0/75, 66114 drops
  5 minute input rate 181000 bits/sec, 23 packets/sec
  5 minute output rate 43000 bits/sec, 26 packets/sec
     525599659 packets input, 2042735431 bytes, 0 no buffer
     Received 4004547 broadcasts, 10 runts, 0 giants
     139 input errors, 0 CRC, 129 frame, 0 overrun, 0 ignored, 0 abort
     0 input packets with dribble condition detected
     481020335 packets output, 1069273018 bytes, 47 underruns
     20 output errors, 95880485 collisions, 0 interface resets
     0 babbles, 0 late collision, 0 deferred
     0 lost carrier, 0 no carrier
     0 output buffer failures, 0 output buffers swapped out
R3#
```

Listing 3-15

should be 255 on a healthy interface. Except in very high traffic conditions, the load generally should not exceed 150/255.

Encapsulation. This is the layer 2 encapsulation on the interface. In the case of Ethernet, the Cisco default is ARPA for IP and Novell-Ether for IPX. I will discuss this in more detail in appropriate later chapters.

So what other information can we extract from the preceding output? We can see that the *ARP cache timeout* is 4 hours (which happens to be the default). Less than 1 second has elapsed since the last input and last output to and from the router interface. The output has never hung. The *interface counters* were last cleared just over 5 weeks ago. This is highly relevant when evaluating the interface statistics. In many cases, you should note the statistics and then clear the counters for further monitoring.

We see that the FIFO *queuing strategy* is employed on the interface. The *output* and *input queues* are at their default sizes of 40 and 75 packets, respectively. Neither queue currently contains any packets. The *input queue* has dropped a significant number of packets since the counters were last cleared. However, as noted previously, the counters have not been cleared for 5 weeks; therefore, this may or may not be significant. In this situation, the counters should be cleared and the number of input drops monitored carefully.

Information is also provided on the average bit rate and number of packets crossing the router interface per second. Totals are also available for these parameters. The total number of *broadcasts* that the router interface observed on the wire since the interface counters were last cleared is also shown. If this figure is seen to be incrementing rapidly, and in particular, if the number of broadcasts remains high relative to the total number of input packets, this could indicate a broadcast storm on the LAN segment. It is difficult to place a figure on what is acceptable because certain applications rely heavily on broadcasts. However, if broadcasts account for over 30 percent of the total input packets, then it may be a good idea to investigate further with a LAN protocol analyzer.

Information on errors detected by the interface is also available:

Runts are packets that are smaller than the minimum packet size for the medium. This value is 64 bytes in the case of Ethernet. A minimum packet size is specified in Ethernet because a station can only detect collisions when in transmit mode. This minimum packet size ensures that the station remains in transmit mode long enough to detect any collisions on the wire, assuming the segment is within proper Ethernet repeater and distance specifications.

Giants are packets that are larger than the maximum packet size for the medium. The MTU for Ethernet is usually just over 1500 bytes, or such that the maximum amount of encapsulated data is 1500 bytes.

Input errors are errors detected on incoming packets and may indicate a problem on the segment itself.

Output errors are errors on outgoing packets, which may indicate a problem with the router interface itself.

CRCs are cyclical redundancy check errors detected due to an invalid Ethernet checksum. They may be caused by noise on the segment, a bad NIC card, or deformed frames due to collisions. The rate of CRCs should only be of the order of 1 in every 100,000 input frames.

Frame errors are frame types received that were incompatible with the router's Ethernet frame type, which is ARPA for IP.

Aborts are issued when excessive retransmission attempts are made on detecting collisions. An Ethernet station can only retransmit up to a maximum of 15 times.

Dribble condition refers to frames received that were slightly greater than the MTU but are not classified as giants.

Babble is the receipt of persistent, spurious frames.

Deferred. Packets that are about to be transmitted are deferred or delayed in a queue if the line appears busy.

Interface resets. The router resets the interface after detecting excessive errors. These errors may be on the LAN segment or, alternatively, may be indicative of a problem with the interface itself. A definite conclusion cannot be made, but if the resets are coupled with a large number of output errors, then the problem may be with the router interface.

Collisions. In relation to Ethernet, collisions are classified as being early or late. An *early collision* is a collision detected by the sending station before the first 64 bytes of the frame have gone out onto the wire. Early collisions are a normal part of the CSMA/CD access method used for Ethernet. An early collision usually results in a small interrupted frame, or runt. *Late collisions* occur after 64 bytes have been passed out onto the wire. Ethernet is specified such that this condition should never occur in theory. It can and does happen in practice for the following reasons:

- 10Base5, 10Base2, or 10BaseT cabling that violates its distance specification rules
- A faulty NIC card that is not properly listening to the wire

Lost carrier. This quantifies the number of times the carrier or line protocol went down since the counters were last cleared. It usually indicates a problem that is external to the router. For example, carrier is lost if the cable connecting the router to the hub becomes disconnected.

Buffer parameters. The `show interface` command also provides information on problems relating to buffer allocation. These include *no buffer*, *overruns*, *ignored*, *underruns*, *buffer failures*, and *swapped out* buffers.

Now, having discussed Ethernet in a reasonable amount of detail, let's examine the other widely used `show interface` commands, along with their specific parameters.

The `show interface token ring` command provides the output in Listing 3-16. The output in this example includes the following information:

- The encapsulation is SNAP.
- The ring speed is 16 Mbps. Each station on the ring must agree on the ring speed. This is not to be confused with bandwidth, which is an IGRP metric.
- Early token release has been configured on this interface.
- The interface is configured for source route bridging. The ring number is 3876. The bridge number equivalent to this interface is 1, and the virtual ring is 3845.
- The caching of proxy explorers or NetBios names is not being used. Also, spanning tree explorers will not be forwarded from this interface.

Now examine the output for a token-ring interface that is not in a normal condition (Listing 3-17). In this example, a hardware fault and beacon have been detected. The router port has been removed from the ring. In this case, the cable between the router and the hub should be checked. Also, because the interface is down as well as the line protocol, a problem with the router interface cannot be discounted.

The FDDI protocol contains many sophisticated management features. Thus the `show interface` command provides information on a number of parameters that are useful for troubleshooting. I will now outline what these parameters mean and the different status levels they can be in (see Listing 3-18).

```
R3#sh int to 1/0
TokenRing1/0 is up, line protocol is up
  Hardware is cxBus Token Ring, address is 0007.ef51.b604 (bia 0007.ef51.b604)
  Description: User ring SEG=F4
  Internet address is 165.48.59.1/25
  MTU 4464 bytes, BW 16000 Kbit, DLY 630 usec, rely 255/255, load 1/255
  Encapsulation SNAP, loopback not set, keepalive set (10 sec)
  ARP type: SNAP, ARP Timeout 04:00:00
  Ring speed: 16 Mbps, early token release
  Single ring node, Source Route Transparent Bridge capable
  Source bridging enabled, srn 3876 bn 1 trn 3485 (ring group)
    proxy explorers disabled, spanning explorer disabled, NetBIOS cache disabled
  Group Address: 0x00000000, Functional Address: 0x0880011A
  Ethernet Transit OUI: 0x000000
  Last Ring Status 4w4d < Error> (0x2000)
  Last input 00:00:00, output 00:00:00, output hang never
  Last clearing of "show interface" counters 5w0d
  Queueing strategy: fifo
  Output queue 0/40, 74 drops; input queue 0/75, 75537 drops
  5 minute input rate 247000 bits/sec, 96 packets/sec
  5 minute output rate 61000 bits/sec, 96 packets/sec
     384463007 packets input, 2607685349 bytes, 0 no buffer
     Received 18330973 broadcasts, 0 runts, 0 giants
     3828 input errors, 0 CRC, 0 frame, 0 overrun, 0 ignored, 0 abort
     337677277 packets output, 1005177062 bytes, 0 underruns
     35 output errors, 0 collisions, 0 interface resets
     0 output buffer failures, 0 output buffers swapped out
     0 transitions
R3#
```

Listing 3-16

Phy-A/Phy-B The state that the physical A or physical B connection is in. This refers to the connection types that a dual FDDI ring has. This parameter can be in the following states:

Off Indicates that CMT (connection management) is off. If the interface is physically up, this could mean that the `cmt disconnect` command was issued for Phy-A or Phy-B.

Tra Trace state indicates a beacon condition.

Brk Break state is the first state in the setting up of a PCM (physical connection management) connection.

Con Connect state provides initial synchronization for each end of the physical connections.

Nxt The connection is in next state while the MAC local loop is performed.

```
Router1>sh in t0/0
TokenRing0/0 is down, line protocol is down
  Hardware is IBM2692, address is 0008.ded7.b741 (bia 0008.ded7.b741)
  Description: DEST=user ring SEG=9f8 FLR=43
  Internet address is 171.140.102.130/25
  MTU 4464 bytes, BW 16000 Kbit, DLY 630 usec, rely 255/255, load 1/255
  Encapsulation SNAP, loopback not set, keepalive set (10 sec)
  ARP type: SNAP, ARP Timeout 04:00:00
  Ring speed: 16 Mbps, early token release
  Single ring node, Source Route Transparent Bridge capable
  Group Address: 0x00000000, Functional Address: 0x08800000
  Ethernet Transit OUI: 0x000000
  Last Ring Status 01:14:41 <Hard Error,Ring Beacon,HW Removal,Ring Recovery> (0x5420)
  Last input 01:15:14, output 01:15:02, output hang never
  Last clearing of "show interface" counters never
  Queueing strategy: fifo
  Output queue 0/40, 253 drops; input queue 0/75, 0 drops
  5 minute input rate 0 bits/sec, 0 packets/sec
  5 minute output rate 0 bits/sec, 0 packets/sec
     3218453 packets input, 1271564342 bytes, 0 no buffer
     Received 0 broadcasts, 0 runts, 0 giants
     0 input errors, 0 CRC, 0 frame, 0 overrun, 0 ignored, 0 abort
     3170682 packets output, 1296373646 bytes, 0 underruns
     0 output errors, 0 collisions, 57 interface resets
     0 output buffer failures, 0 output buffers swapped out
     2 transitions
```

Listing 3-17

Sig Signal is the next state and is entered when a bit is ready to be transmitted.

Join Join is the first of the final three states in setting up communication with the physical neighbor.

Vfy Verify state verifies synchronization before the neighbor becomes active.

Act Active state indicates that communication has been established with the physical neighbor.

Neighbor This parameter can be in one of the following states:

A Indicates that the neighbor is a Phy-A-type dual attached station (DAS) or concentrator that attaches to primary ring IN and secondary ring OUT.

B Indicates that the neighbor is a Phy-B-type DAS or concentrator that attaches to primary ring OUT and secondary ring IN.

S Neighbor is a single attached station (SAS).

```
R2>sh in fddi2/0
Fddi2/0 is up, line protocol is up
  Hardware is cxBus FDDI, address is 0060.4776.b940 (bia 0060.4776.b940)
  Description: Utility Server Ring Seg=6B
  Internet address is 171.133.179.3/25
  MTU 4470 bytes, BW 100000 Kbit, DLY 100 usec, rely 255/255, load 1/255
  Encapsulation SNAP, loopback not set, keepalive not set
  ARP type: SNAP, ARP Timeout 04:00:00
  Phy-A state is connect, neighbor is unk, cmt signal bits 008/000, status QLS
  Phy-B state is  active, neighbor is   M, cmt signal bits 20C/00E, status ILS
  ECM is in, CFM is c_wrap_b, RMT is ring_op
  Requested token rotation 5000 usec, negotiated 5000 usec
  Configured tvx is 2500 usec ring operational 1w2d
  Upstream neighbor 0000.1d23.21da, downstream neighbor 0004.c107.9240
  Last input 00:00:21, output 00:00:07, output hang never
  Last clearing of "show interface" counters never
  Queueing strategy: fifo
  Output queue 0/40, 0 drops; input queue 0/75, 276 drops
  5 minute input rate 0 bits/sec, 0 packets/sec
  5 minute output rate 0 bits/sec, 0 packets/sec
     20009141 packets input, 1718529243 bytes, 3 no buffer
     Received 8551523 broadcasts, 0 runts, 0 giants, 4 throttles
     1 input errors, 0 CRC, 1 frame, 0 overrun, 0 ignored, 0 abort
     15369918 packets output, 2841708929 bytes, 0 underruns
     0 output errors, 0 collisions, 1 interface resets
     0 output buffer failures, 0 output buffers swapped out
     333 transitions, 0 traces,  799 claims, 0 beacon
```

Listing 3-18

M Neighbor is Phy-M-type concentrator that serves as master to a connected station.

Unk Router has not completed the CMT process; hence the neighbor is unknown.

CMT Signal Bits This indicates the total transmitted and received CMT bits since the counters were last cleared. If the connection is not active, then no bits will have been received.

Status This displays the actual status of the fiber cable:

NLS Noise line state

MLS Master line state

ILS Idle line state

HLS Halt line state

QLS Quiet line state (Can indicate that the carrier is down.)

ALS Active line state

LSU Link state unknown (Indicates that none of the other line state criteria have been met.)

ECM (entity coordination management) controls an optical bypass switch, which allows a station to stop repeating and bypass itself from the ring. When the router port is removed from the ring, for whatever reason, ECM allows the ring to remain operational. ECM starts and stops the PCM process. The ECM can be in one of the following states:

In The router is inserted into the ring.

Out The router is isolated from the ring.

Trace A beacon condition has been detected.

Leave The router is allowing a timer to expire before gracefully leaving the ring.

Path_test The router is testing its internal paths.

Insert The optical bypass is inserting.

Check The router is checking that the optical bypass is inserted correctly.

Deinsert The optical bypass is leaving the ring.

CFM (configuration management) gives information about the MAC connection. This field can have one of the following states:

Thru This is the normal mode for a DAS. It means that the router receives data on Phy-A and transmits on Phy-B.

Wrap a Data are received and transmitted on Phy-A.

C wrap b Data are received and transmitted on Phy-B.

Wrap s Data are received and transmitted on Phy-S. This is a normal for a SAS.

Isolated The MAC is not connected to any physical type.

RMT (ring management) is responsible for MAC circuitry. This parameter can have the following states:

Isolated This is the initial state, where the MAC is not attempting to participate in the ring.

Non_op The MAC is participating in ring recovery. Ring is therefore nonoperational.

Ring_op	The MAC is participating in an operational ring. This is a normal working state.
Detect	Ring has been nonoperational for an extended period. Duplicate address conditions are being detected.
Non_op_dup	Ring is nonoperational due to an indication of this station having a duplicate MAC address with another station on the ring.
Ring_op_dup	Ring is operational despite an indication of this station having a duplicate MAC address with another station on the ring.
Directed	The MAC is sending beacon frames.
Trace	This MAC has initiated trace; a path test will be done on the completion of trace.

The other parameters that can be seen from `show interface fddi` include

Token rotation. This value can be configured, or in the case of a nonoperational ring, it has a default value of 5 ms. In an operational ring, this parameter will be autonegotiated between all stations on the ring.

Ring operational. This parameter gives the ring uptime.

Upstream/downstream neighbor. This gives the MAC addresses of adjacent neighbors on the ring.

Listing 3-19 is the output of a `show interface serial` command for a serial line that is operating normally. It can be seen that ISDN dial backup is configured. Notice also that the queuing mechanism is weighted fair as opposed to FIFO. Weighted fair queuing is employed by default on serial interfaces up to and including T1 speed. This type of queuing is similar to custom queuing, but it gives preference to smaller packets. Interface hold queues cannot be manipulated when weighted fair queuing is enabled; however, it can be switched off using the `no fair-queue` interface command.

Now imagine that you get a call to your help desk reporting that users in Atlanta cannot connect to servers in New York, but all their other communication is fine. You check the appropriate serial interface and find the output in Listing 3-20.

The interface itself is up, as are the output leads RTS, DSR, and DTR. In fact, the input leads DCD and CTS are also up. More detail on these parameters will be provided in Chapter 4 on serial lines. For the moment, you should note that the fact that these input leads are up indi-

```
R1>sh in se0
Serial0 is up, line protocol is up
  Hardware is HD64570
  Description: DEST=Dublin2 SE 3/0 CCT ID= xxx_.yyy.001
  Internet address is 171.136.10.130/25
  Backup interface BRI0, kickin load not set, kickout load not set
      failure delay 0 sec, secondary disable delay 0 sec
  MTU 1500 bytes, BW 56 Kbit, DLY 20000 usec, rely 255/255, load 1/255
  Encapsulation HDLC, loopback not set, keepalive set (10 sec)
  Last input 00:00:00, output 00:00:00, output hang never
  Last clearing of "show interface" counters never
  Input queue: 0/75/24 (size/max/drops); Total output drops: 1271
  Queueing strategy: weighted fair
  Output queue: 0/64/1271 (size/threshold/drops)
     Conversations  0/72 (active/max active)
     Reserved Conversations 0/0 (allocated/max allocated)
  5 minute input rate 0 bits/sec, 0 packets/sec
  5 minute output rate 0 bits/sec, 0 packets/sec
     18187056 packets input, 418049142 bytes, 0 no buffer
     Received 931137 broadcasts, 0 runts, 0 giants
     1896 input errors, 1896 CRC, 22 frame, 0 overrun, 0 ignored, 1539 abort
     12150936 packets output, 1495129265 bytes, 0 underruns
     0 output errors, 0 collisions, 3 interface resets
     0 output buffer failures, 0 output buffers swapped out
     8 carrier transitions
     DCD=up  DSR=up  DTR=up  RTS=up  CTS=up
```

Listing 3-19

cates that the DSU is at least visible to the router. Line protocol is down, so HDLC keepalives are not being received from the far end of the link. A good strategy would be to check the newyork2 router interface and begin working out from there. The assistance of the telecommunications carrier, namely, by providing loopback tests, may be required to isolate the source of the problem.

We have now studied the more commonly used `show interface` commands. The output of these commands provides valuable information on a range of parameters that relate to the router interface and the medium to which it connects.

The `show controllers` commands often provide extremely detailed information on the physical cabling and medium that connects to the router interface. Its current status can be examined along with historical information. Some of the more detailed information is rarely examined in practice or is only used by TAC personnel in order to reasonably abstract problems. In this section you will see the typical output of `show controllers` for the most widely used media types. Only the parame-

```
Atlanta1>sh in s1/3
Serial1/3 is up, line protocol is down
  Hardware is M8T-V.35
  Description: DEST = newyork2 se0/0 OC12 #25 CKT ID 40xxxA001600-001PT
  Internet address is 171.144.252.45/30
  MTU 1500 bytes, BW 1536 Kbit, DLY 20000 usec, rely 255/255, load 1/255
  Encapsulation HDLC, loopback not set, keepalive set (10 sec)
  Last input never, output 00:00:03, output hang never
  Last clearing of "show interface" counters never
  Input queue: 0/75/0 (size/max/drops); Total output drops: 0
  Queueing strategy: weighted fair
  Output queue: 0/64/0 (size/threshold/drops)
     Conversations  0/1 (active/max active)
     Reserved Conversations 0/0 (allocated/max allocated)
  5 minute input rate 0 bits/sec, 0 packets/sec
  5 minute output rate 0 bits/sec, 0 packets/sec
     0 packets input, 0 bytes, 0 no buffer
     Received 0 broadcasts, 0 runts, 0 giants
     0 input errors, 0 CRC, 0 frame, 0 overrun, 0 ignored, 0 abort
     8398 packets output, 234280 bytes, 0 underruns
     0 output errors, 0 collisions, 2487 interface resets
     0 output buffer failures, 0 output buffers swapped out
     2498 carrier transitions     DCD=up  DSR=up  DTR=up  RTS=up  CTS=up
```

Listing 3-20

ters that are likely to be used in practical situations will be explicitly discussed.

In the sample output of `show controllers token` shown in Listing 3-21, notice that the interface is up and that the configured MAC address is the same as the burned-in address. This is pertinent in Token Ring because earlier versions of Texas Instruments NIC cards had problems interacting with MAC addresses that have the first 2 bytes set to zero, which is often the case on a Cisco router port. Hence the occasional need to reconfigure the router interface's MAC address. This information is also available from the `show interface token-ring` command, but the more detailed information that follows is not.

Each counter has two numbers separated by a slash. The number before or on the left of the slash is the current value of this counter. The number after the slash indicates the value of this counter since the system was last rebooted. Thus current and historical information can be combined to establish a pattern when troubleshooting. If the Token Ring interface counters are cleared, then the number before the slash will be set to zero and will be added to the number after the slash.

One of the most useful conditions that can be checked for using this command is whether or not the router port is the only station on the ring.

```
R2>sh control to 1/0
TokenRing1/0: state up
  current address: 0006.e26e.9d04, burned in address: 0006.e26e.9d04

  Last Ring Status: 1w1d < Error> (0x2000)
    Stats: soft: 0/110, hard: 0/11, sig loss: 0/0
           tx beacon: 0/0, wire fault 0/0, recovery: 0/40
           only station: 0/0, remote removal: 0/0
  Interface failures: 0

  Monitor state: (active), chip f/w: '000003.C24938A', [bridge capable]
    ring mode: 8, internal enables:
    internal functional: 08000000 (08000000), group: 00000000 (00000000)
    internal addrs: SRB: 0288, ARB: 02F6, EXB 0880, MFB: 07F4
                    Rev: 0170, Adapter: 02C4, Parms 01F6
    Microcode counters:
      MAC giants 0/1, MAC ignored 0/861
      Input runts 0/0, giants 0/0, overrun 0/0
      Input ignored 0/0, parity 0/0, RFED 0/0
      Input REDI 0/0, null rcp 0/0, recovered rcp 0/0
      Input implicit abort 0/1, explicit abort 0/190252
      Output underrun 0/0, tx parity 0/0, null tcp 0/0
      Output SFED 0/0, SEDI 0/0, abort 0/4
      Output False Token 0/2, PTT Expired 0/8
    Internal controller counts:
      line errors: 0/56,  internal errors: 0/0
      burst errors: 0/9,  ari/fci errors: 0/0
      abort errors: 0/0, lost frame: 0/11
      copy errors: 0/228, rcvr congestion: 0/0
      token errors: 0/0, frequency errors: 0/0
    Internal controller smt state:
      Adapter MAC:      0006.e26e.9d04, Physical drop:     00000000
      NAUN Address:     0007.7802.dc0a, NAUN drop:         00000000
      Last source:      0006.e29f.e200, Last poll:         0006.e29f.e200
      Last MVID:        0006,           Last attn code:    0006
      Txmit priority:   0003,           Auth Class:        7BFF
      Monitor Error:    0000,           Interface Errors:  0004
      Correlator:       0000,           Soft Error Timer:  00DC
      Local Ring:       0000,           Ring Status:       0000
      Beacon rcv type:  0003,           Beacon txmit type: 0004
      Beacon type:      0003,           Beacon NAUN:       0000.b818.2483
      Beacon drop:      00000000,       Reserved:          0000
      Reserved2:        0000
R2>
```

Listing 3-21

This can happen if the hub isolates the router from the ring; thus the router perceives itself as the only station on the ring. Sometimes this condition will result in an error message in the output of the `show interface token`, but this is not always the case. The most definite way to check is from the output of `show controllers token`. In the preceding example, notice that the NAUN address is different from the adapter MAC address for the interface. This confirms that the router port is not in only station mode.

The information extracted from `show controllers ethernet` that is most commonly analyzed is already provided from `show interface ethernet`. This is essentially in relation to addressing, buffering, and error conditions.

The most frequent use of `show controller serial` is to establish what type of cable is attached to the interface. In the example in Listing 3-22, notice that V.35 DTE cable is attached. Hence, clocking does not have to be configured on the interface, unlike in the case of having a DCE cable attached. Notice that this command also tells you which slot the serial card is in. It also defines the NIM (network interface module) version of the network processor module on a 4000 series router. This can be extremely relevant information because some known interface problems have been isolated to a particular NIM version, sometimes in combination with a particular version of IOS. Also bear in mind that newer NIM versions often are only supported by later versions of IOS. Cisco documentation or the TAC should be consulted if you think a NIM version upgrade may be required.

On the 7000 series routers, the `show controller cbus` command gives summary information on each of the interface processors that connect to the CiscoBus. The interface processor hardware and software or microcode versions are given. This command also can be used to check for the type of cable that is plugged into the interface processor (see Listing 3-23).

Interface processor hardware and microcode versions can be obtained for an FDDI interface using the `show controllers fddi` command. Most of the other information that this command makes available is only analyzed by TAC personnel in very specific circumstances. Microcode versions for each media type on a 7000 series router also can be checked using the `show microcode` command. (See Listing 3-24.)

Protocol-Related Commands This section summarizes how to use the various show commands that relate to the different protocols. The intention here is simply to demonstrate what types of commands are available. The detailed use of these commands will be examined in each of the appropriate chapters on IP, IPX, and AppleTalk.

The `show protocol` command gives very generic information on what protocols are running on the router and the addressing information for each interface that is routing that protocol (see Listing 3-25).

Here I will demonstrate use of the help facility when using and exploring the different Cisco IOS commands. If you type "help" or "?" after a

```
R2#sh control ser 0
MK5 unit 0, NIM slot 0, NIM type code 7, NIM version 1
idb = 0x60833C00, driver structure at 0x60837FE8, regaddr = 0x3C000300
IB at 0x40006DAC: mode=0x0108, local_addr=0, remote_addr=0
N1=1524, N2=1, scaler=100, T1=1000, T3=2000, TP=1
buffer size 1524
DTE V.35 serial cable attached
RX ring with 32 entries at 0x06E10 : RLEN=5, Rxhead 19
00 pak=0x6083BF44  ds=0xA8015780 status=80 max_size=1524 pak_size=44
01 pak=0x6083C2C4  ds=0xA80164F0 status=80 max_size=1524 pak_size=45
02 pak=0x6083D444  ds=0xA801A820 status=80 max_size=1524 pak_size=80
03 pak=0x60841884  ds=0xA802AE28 status=80 max_size=1524 pak_size=44
04 pak=0x6083D0C4  ds=0xA8019AB0 status=80 max_size=1524 pak_size=251
05 pak=0x608408C4  ds=0xA80271B0 status=80 max_size=1524 pak_size=44
06 pak=0x608401C4  ds=0xA80256D0 status=80 max_size=1524 pak_size=44
07 pak=0x6083F044  ds=0xA80213A0 status=80 max_size=1524 pak_size=44
08 pak=0x60840004  ds=0xA8025018 status=80 max_size=1524 pak_size=44
09 pak=0x6083C9C4  ds=0xA8017FD0 status=80 max_size=1524 pak_size=44
10 pak=0x6083BBC4  ds=0xA8014A10 status=80 max_size=1524 pak_size=44
11 pak=0x60841F84  ds=0xA802C908 status=80 max_size=1524 pak_size=257
12 pak=0x6083E244  ds=0xA801DDE0 status=80 max_size=1524 pak_size=45
13 pak=0x6083C644  ds=0xA8017260 status=80 max_size=1524 pak_size=265
14 pak=0x6083E784  ds=0xA801F208 status=80 max_size=1524 pak_size=44
15 pak=0x6083F904  ds=0xA8023538 status=80 max_size=1524 pak_size=45
16 pak=0x60840E04  ds=0xA80285D8 status=80 max_size=1524 pak_size=235
17 pak=0x60840A84  ds=0xA8027868 status=80 max_size=1524 pak_size=44
18 pak=0x6083F744  ds=0xA8022E80 status=80 max_size=1524 pak_size=46
19 pak=0x60842144  ds=0xA802CFC0 status=80 max_size=1524 pak_size=32
20 pak=0x6083ECC4  ds=0xA8020630 status=80 max_size=1524 pak_size=32
21 pak=0x60842304  ds=0xA802D678 status=80 max_size=1524 pak_size=44
22 pak=0x6083C804  ds=0xA8017918 status=80 max_size=1524 pak_size=44
23 pak=0x6083EE84  ds=0xA8020CE8 status=80 max_size=1524 pak_size=44
24 pak=0x6083D7C4  ds=0xA801B590 status=80 max_size=1524 pak_size=44
25 pak=0x6083E5C4  ds=0xA801EB50 status=80 max_size=1524 pak_size=119
26 pak=0x6083F3C4  ds=0xA8022110 status=80 max_size=1524 pak_size=44
27 pak=0x6083CF04  ds=0xA80193F8 status=80 max_size=1524 pak_size=44
28 pak=0x6083D984  ds=0xA801BC48 status=80 max_size=1524 pak_size=878
29 pak=0x6083E944  ds=0xA801F8C0 status=80 max_size=1524 pak_size=45
30 pak=0x60841A44  ds=0xA802B4E0 status=80 max_size=1524 pak_size=44
31 pak=0x60840544  ds=0xA8026440 status=80 max_size=1524 pak_size=45
TX ring with 2 entries at 0x07048 : TLEN=1, TWD=7
tx_count = 0, tx_head = 0, tx_tail = 0
00 pak=0x000000 ds=0xA812088E status=0x38 max_size=1524 pak_size=45
01 pak=0x000000 ds=0xA8091B06 status=0x38 max_size=1524 pak_size=46
XID/Test TX desc at 0xFFFFFF, status=0x30, max_buffer_size=0, packet_size=0
 XID/Test RX desc at 0xFFFFFF, status=0x0, max_buffer_size=0, packet_size=0
Status Buffer at 0x40007280: rcv=0, tcv=0, local_state=0, remote_state=0
phase=0, tac=0, currd=0x00000, curxd=0x00000
bad_frames=0, frmrs=0, T1_timeouts=0, rej_rxs=0, runts=0
0 missed datagrams, 0 overruns
0 bad datagram encapsulations, 0 memory errors
0 transmitter underruns
0 user primitive errors, 0 spurious primitive interrupts
0 provider primitives lost, 0 unexpected provider primitives
mk5025 registers: csr0 = 0x0E00, csr1 = 0x0302, csr2 = 0x4500
                  csr3 = 0x6DAC, csr4 = 0x0214, csr5 = 0x0008
```

Listing 3-22

```
sushi-wan#sh control cbus
MEMD at 40000000, 2097152 bytes (unused 320, recarves 1, lost 0)
  RawQ 48000100, ReturnQ 48000108, EventQ 48000110
  BufhdrQ 48000120 (2972 items)
  IpcbufQ_classic 48000138 (8 items, 4096 bytes)
  3570 buffer headers (48002000 - 4800FF10)
  pool0: 9 buffers, 256 bytes, queue 48000128
  pool1: 235 buffers, 1536 bytes, queue 48000130
  pool2: 342 buffers, 4512 bytes, queue 48000140
  pool3: 4 buffers, 4544 bytes, queue 48000148
  slot0: TRIP, hw 1.1, sw 20.01, ccb 5800FF20, cmdq 48000080, vps 4096
    software loaded from system
    TokenRing0/0, addr 0006.3a2d.2f00 (bia 0006.3a2d.2f00)
      gfreeq 48000140, lfreeq 48000150 (4512 bytes), throttled 0
      rxlo 4, rxhi 204, rxcurr 0, maxrxcurr 0
      txq 48000158, txacc 48000082 (value 0), txlimit 114
    TokenRing0/1, addr 0006.3a2d.2f80 (bia 0006.3a2d.2f80)
      gfreeq 48000140, lfreeq 48000160 (4512 bytes), throttled 0
      rxlo 4, rxhi 204, rxcurr 0, maxrxcurr 0
      txq 48000168, txacc 4800008A (value 0), txlimit 114
    TokenRing0/2, addr 0006.3a2d.2f40 (bia 0006.3a2d.2f40)
      gfreeq 48000140, lfreeq 48000170 (4512 bytes), throttled 0
      rxlo 4, rxhi 204, rxcurr 0, maxrxcurr 0
      txq 48000178, txacc 48000092 (value 0), txlimit 114
    TokenRing0/3, addr 0006.3a2d.2fc0 (bia 0006.3a2d.2fc0)
      gfreeq 48000140, lfreeq 48000180 (4512 bytes), throttled 0
      rxlo 4, rxhi 204, rxcurr 0, maxrxcurr 0
      txq 48000188, txacc 4800009A (value 0), txlimit 114
  slot1: FSIP, hw 1.1, sw 20.08, ccb 5800FF30, cmdq 48000088, vps 8192
    software loaded from system
    Serial1/0, applique is V.35 DTE
      gfreeq 48000130, lfreeq 48000190 (1536 bytes), throttled 75
      rxlo 4, rxhi 27, rxcurr 2, maxrxcurr 4
      txq 48000198, txacc 480000A2 (value 1), txlimit 6
    Serial1/1, applique is X.21 DCE
      gfreeq 48000130, lfreeq 480001A0 (1536 bytes), throttled 0
      rxlo 4, rxhi 27, rxcurr 0, maxrxcurr 0
      txq 480001A8, txacc 480000AA (value 6), txlimit 6
    Serial1/2, applique is Universal (cable unattached)
      gfreeq 48000130, lfreeq 480001B0 (1536 bytes), throttled 0
      rxlo 4, rxhi 27, rxcurr 0, maxrxcurr 0
      txq 480001B8, txacc 480000B2 (value 6), txlimit 6
    Serial1/3, applique is V.35 DTE
      gfreeq 48000130, lfreeq 480001C0 (1536 bytes), throttled 0
      rxlo 4, rxhi 27, rxcurr 3, maxrxcurr 4
      txq 480001C8, txacc 480000BA (value 6), txlimit 6
    Serial1/4, applique is V.35 DTE
```

Listing 3-23

```
R1>sh control fddi 1/0
Fddi1/0 - hardware version 2.9, microcode version 20.2
  Phy-A registers:
    cr0 3, cr1 3, cr2 0, status 3, cr3 0
  Phy-B registers:
    cr0 4, cr1 4, cr2 0, status 3, cr3 0
  FORMAC registers:
    irdtlb  7184, irdtneg F85E, irdthtt F982, irdmir  FFFF0BDC
    irdtrth F863, irdtmax FBC5, irdtvxt 8585, irdstmc 0810
    irdmode 6A21, irdimsk E000, irdstat 8060, irdtpri 0000
FIP registers
 ccbptr:         7F98  event_ptr:     0088  cmdreg:         0006  argreg:   0003
 memdptr:        0000  memdpage:      0000  memaptr:        0000  afaddr:   060B
 frptr:          000F  apptr:         0004  tx_channel:     0002  tx_claim: F002
 tx_claim_bc:    8011  tx_beacon:     F016  tx_beacon_bc:   8011  tx_clbn:  0000
 tx_pend:        0000  local_freeptr:00CC  hold_ctl:       0003  unused:   A000
 tx_active_cnt: 0000  txq_ptr:       00D0  tx_accptr:      0051  raw_ptr:  0080
 tx_state:       0003  rx_channel:    0000  rx_eof_channel:0000  rx_error: 0090
 rx_pool:        00A4  rx_buf0:       7C48  rx_buf1:        6BC0  rx_next0: 7940
 rx_next1:       7A78  rx_limit_lo:   0004  rx_limit_hi:    0081  rx_offset:0028
 enabled:        0001  return:        0000  phya_ls_flag:   0000  unused:   0005
 phya_tmin:      00CE  phya_tmax:     0000  unused:         0000  txq_fill: 0070
 lovenote:       0000  not_rcv_pkt:   0001  phyb_tmin:      0000  phyb_tmax:1388
 t0:             0030  t1:            000E  t2:             0003  t3:       0007
 txq_fill_txEof:0070  unused:        A793  cur:            7A78  cnt:      0000
 fop:            8004  phyb_ls_flag:  0001  lst_fint:       8004  rx_count: 0004
 unused:         0000  bogus_claim:   0000  robin:          0009  park:     0000
 Total LEM: phy-a 0, phy-b 671891
```

Listing 3-24

command, the router will automatically return with all the subcommand options. If you type "?" by itself, the router will prompt you with all the available commands at their highest level. Note that if you do this while in user mode rather than privileged mode, the router will only display user-mode commands. Listing 3-26 shows all the subcommand options for `show ipx` and `show ip`. Note that we are in privileged mode in both cases and therefore will get the full array of commands.

Now let's do the same for AppleTalk.

```
Fulton_924#sh apple ?
% Unrecognized command
```

Ooops! What happened here? The reason that the router does not recognize the `show apple` command is that it only has an IP/IPX software suite. Let us now repeat the same command on a router with enterprise-level software (see Listing 3-27).

Listing 3-25

```
Fulton_924#sh protocol
Global values:
  Internet Protocol routing is enabled
  Novell routing is enabled
Serial0 is up, line protocol is up
  Internet address is 171.137.8.130/25
  Novell address is AB890880.0000.30e8.b7c8
Serial1 is administratively down, line protocol is down
TokenRing0 is up, line protocol is up
  Internet address is 171.137.6.1/25
  Novell address is AB890600.0000.30e8.b7c8
TokenRing1 is up, line protocol is up
  Internet address is 171.137.6.129/25
  Novell address is AB890680.0000.30e8.b768
TokenRing2 is up, line protocol is up
  Internet address is 171.137.7.129/25
  Novell address is AB890780.0000.30e8.b728
TokenRing3 is up, line protocol is up
  Internet address is 171.137.8.1/25
  Novell address is AB890800.0000.30e8.b7e8
Fulton_924#
```

Debug Commands

A vast array of debugging commands is available through Cisco IOS software. These commands can enable you to get detailed information on the packets and frames being exchanged during normal protocol operation as well as during the course of a network problem. The debug commands provide an extremely powerful set of troubleshooting tools, which often eliminate the need for a protocol analyzer. There are a number of points that should be emphasized in relation to the use of debugging commands.

- Never use a debug command if you do not have at least a reasonable understanding of what it does and what information it provides.
- As mentioned previously, debugging packets are process-switched. Debug commands vary greatly in the load they place on the processor. While some commands result in minimal additional load, some can be extremely processor-intensive. It is strongly advised that you always do a `show process cpu` to estimate CPU load before enabling any debug command. Even if the CPU load is low, you should have some understanding of how processor-intensive the command you are considering using is. If you are in any doubt, the Cisco Debug Command Reference should be consulted. Very CPU-intensive commands usually carry a corresponding warning. Generally, the amount of data output that a debug command generates is indicative of resulting processor load.

```
Fulton_924#sh ipx ?
  accounting    The active IPX accounting database
  cache         IPX fast-switching cache
  compression   IPX compression information
  eigrp         IPX EIGRP show commands
  interface     IPX interface status and configuration
  nhrp          NHRP information
  nlsp          Show NLSP information
  route         IPX routing table
  servers       SAP servers
  spx-spoof     SPX Spoofing table
  traffic       IPX protocol statistics

Fulton_924#sh ip ?
  access-lists          List IP access lists
  accounting            The active IP accounting database
  aliases               IP alias table
  arp                   IP ARP table
  as-path-access-list   List AS path access lists
  bgp                   BGP information
  cache                 IP fast-switching route cache
  community-list        List community-list
  dvmrp                 DVMRP information
  egp                   EGP connections and statistics
  eigrp                 IP-EIGRP show commands
  igmp                  IGMP information
  interface             IP interface status and configuration
  irdp                  ICMP Router Discovery Protocol
  local                 IP local options
  masks                 Masks associated with a network
  mcache                IP multicast fast-switching cache
  mpacket               Display possible duplicate multicast packets
  mroute                IP multicast routing table
  nhrp                  NHRP information
  ospf                  OSPF information
  pim                   PIM information
  policy                Policy routing
  protocols             IP routing protocol process parameters and statistics
  redirects             IP redirects
  route                 IP routing table
  rpf                   Display RPF information for multicast source
  sd                    Session Directory cache
  sdr                   Session Directory (SDPv2) cache
  sockets               Open IP sockets
  tcp                   TCP/IP header-compression statistics
  traffic               IP protocol statistics
```

Listing 3-26

```
R3>sh appl ?
  access-lists     AppleTalk access lists
  adjacent-routes  AppleTalk adjacent routes
  arp              AppleTalk arp table
  aurp             AURP information
  cache            AppleTalk fast-switching cache
  domain           AppleTalk Domain(s) information
  eigrp            AppleTalk/EIGRP show commands
  globals          AppleTalk global parameters
  interface        AppleTalk interface status and configuration
  macip-clients    Mac IP clients
  macip-servers    Mac IP servers
  macip-traffic    Mac IP traffic
  name-cache       AppleTalk name cache
  nbp              AppleTalk NBP name table
  neighbors        AppleTalk Neighboring router status
  remap            AppleTalk remap table
  route            AppleTalk routing table
  sockets          AppleTalk protocol processing information
  static           AppleTalk static table
  traffic          AppleTalk protocol statistics
  zone             AppleTalk Zone table information
```

Listing 3-27

- Remember that debug commands are specific troubleshooting tools, and they should not be used for monitoring purposes. Any debugging that is turned on during troubleshooting should be switched off immediately when adequate information has been obtained.

I will now present an overview of the various debug commands available in Cisco IOS. For the purposes of clarity more than anything else, I have loosely categorized the commands into global, interface, and protocol debug commands. As I stated in relation to the show commands, there is no strict division of the commands into these categories. I will present sample outputs from a number of debug commands. In later chapters I will explain in detail how debugging commands can be used to troubleshoot problems relating to TCP/IP, IPX, AppleTalk, and different WAN media, in particular frame relay and ISDN. In this section, I will just introduce you to the different debug commands and some steps to be followed when these commands are used.

To first get an idea of the number of debug commands that are available, let's look at the help facility in relation to debugging (see Listing 3-28). Here you see an extensive list of commands. As you will later see, most of these commands have further subcommand options, thus providing a broad array of troubleshooting tools.

```
R1-wan#debug ?
  aaa                  AAA Authentication, Authorization and Accounting
  access-expression    Boolean access expression
  all                  Enable all debugging
  arp                  IP ARP and HP Probe transactions
  async                Async interface information
  bri-interface        bri network interface events
  broadcast            MAC broadcast packets
  bsc                  BSC information
  bstun                BSTUN information
  callback             Callback activity
  cdp                  CDP information
  chat                 Chat scripts activity
  cls                  CLS Information
  compress             COMPRESS traffic
  confmodem            Modem configuration database
  custom-queue         Custom output queueing
  dhcp                 DHCP client activity
  dialer               Dial on Demand
  dlsw                 Data Link Switching (DLSw) events
  dnsix                Dnsix information
  domain               Domain Name System
  eigrp                EIGRP Protocol information
  entry                Incoming queue entries
  ethernet-interface   Ethernet network interface events
  frame-relay          Frame Relay
  fras                 FRAS Debug
  ip                   IP information
  ipx                  Novell/IPX information
  isdn                 ISDN information
  lapb                 LAPB protocol transactions
  lex                  LAN Extender protocol
  list                 Set interface or/and access list for the next debug
                       command
  llc2                 LLC2 type II Information
  lnm                  Lan Network Manager information
  lnx                  generic qllc/llc2 conversion activity
  local-ack            Local ACKnowledgement information
  modem                Modem control/process activation
  netbios-name-cache   NetBIOS name cache tracing
  nhrp                 NHRP protocol
  ntp                  NTP information
  packet               Log unknown packets
  pad                  X25 PAD protocol
  pcbus                PCbus interface information
  ppp                  PPP (Point to Point Protocol) information
  printer              LPD printer protocol
  priority             Priority output queueing
  probe                HP Probe Proxy Requests
  dxi                  atm-dxi information
  qllc                 qllc debug information
  radius               RADIUS protocol
  rif                  RIF cache transactions
```

Listing 3-28

```
sdlc                    SDLC information
sdllc                   SDLLC media translation
serial                  Serial interface information
smf                     Software MAC filter
sna                     SNA Information
snapshot                Snapshot activity
snmp                    SNMP information
source                  Source bridging information
spanning                Spanning-tree information
standby                 Hot standby protocol
stun                    STUN information
tacacs                  TACACS authentication and authorization
tbridge                 Transparent Bridging
telnet                  Incoming telnet connections
tftp                    TFTP packets
token                   Token Ring information
tunnel                  Generic Tunnel Interface
v120                    V120 information
x25                     X.25 information
```

Listing 3-28 *(Cont.)*

Global Debugging When configuring Cisco routers, the distinction between global and interface commands is very precise. In this case I am simply using the term *global* to distinguish commands that do not refer directly to the debugging of an interface or a particular medium-type or protocol. In the example in Listing 3-29, the debugging of Cisco Discovery Protocol (CDP) packets has been enabled on a 2500 series router. I have connected to the Router1 through a telnet session. By default, the debug output is sent to the console, which is why the `terminal monitor` command is required to view the output via the telnet session. It can be seen that Router1 has just one CDP neighbor that it learns about through Serial0. In order to observe some activity, I then cleared the CDP table on Router1. We see CDP packets being sent out each of the routers' active interfaces, namely, Ethernet0 and Serial0. There is no Cisco device on the Ethernet segment; therefore, CDP packets are only received on Serial0 from Router9 at the other end of the serial link. Since the CDP table has been cleared, Router1 notes that this entry is not in its cache, and so it adds it in.

I will return to talk in greater detail about the Cisco Discovery Protocol in the chapter on LAN switching. This is an area where CDP is particularly useful.

EXERCISE What type of device is Router9, and which of its interfaces attaches to Router1?

Interface Debugging As an example of a debug command that relates directly to a router interface or medium type, let us examine `debug serial interface`. The example here is of a serial interface with HDLC encapsulation. End-to-end HDLC keepalives are seen being exchanged every 10 seconds. This indicates that the link is operating normally up to and including layer 2, and a `show interface serial0` would indicate that line protocol is up. Note carefully that debugging was turned off using `undebug all`. (See Listing 3-30.)

Protocol Debugging I have set out two examples of protocol debugging. Both are in relation to IP, but of course, all desktop and routing protocols have associated debugging commands.

The first example (Listing 3-31) shows the debugging of ARP. ARP debugging is turned on, and then the ARP cache is cleared to generate ARP requests and replies. This command clears the entire ARP cache on

```
Router1#debug cdp packet
Router1#terminal monitor
Router1#sh cdp nei
Capability Codes: R - Router, T - Trans Bridge, B - Source Route Bridge
                  S - Switch, H - Host, I - IGMP, r - Repeater

Device ID        Local Intrfce     Holdtme    Capability  Platform  Port ID
Router9             Ser 0          164           R        RSP7000   Ser 3/0
Router1#clear cdp table
Router1#
Dec 16 11:43:01 PST: CDP-AD: Deleted table entry for buckeye9-wan.gdn.bofa.com,
interface Serial0
Dec 16 11:43:15 PST: CDP-PA: Packet sent out on Ethernet0
Dec 16 11:43:15 PST: CDP-PA: Packet sent out on Serial0
Dec 16 11:43:39 PST: CDP-PA: Packet received from Router9 on interface Serial0
Dec 16 11:43:39 PST: **Entry NOT found in cache**
Router1#sh cdp nei
Capability Codes: R - Router, T - Trans Bridge, B - Source Route Bridge
                  S - Switch, H - Host, I - IGMP, r - Repeater

Device ID        Local Intrfce     Holdtme    Capability  Platform  Port ID
Router9             Ser 0          167           R        RSP7000   Ser 3/0
Router1#
```

Listing 3-29

```
R1#debug serial interface
Serial network interface debugging is on
R1#
*Jun  1 21:54:55 PDT: Serial0: HDLC myseq 171093, mineseen 171093*, yourseen 125
6540, line up
*Jun  1 21:55:05 PDT: Serial0: HDLC myseq 171094, mineseen 171094*, yourseen 125
6541, line up
*Jun  1 21:55:15 PDT: Serial0: HDLC myseq 171095, mineseen 171095*, yourseen 125
6542, line up
*Jun  1 21:55:25 PDT: Serial0: HDLC myseq 171096, mineseen 171096*, yourseen 125
6543, line up
*Jun  1 21:55:35 PDT: Serial0: HDLC myseq 171097, mineseen 171097*, yourseen 125
6544, line up
R1#undebug all
All possible debugging has been turned off
```

Listing 3-30

the router, therefore generating ARP traffic on each LAN segment that the router attaches to. Because I did not want to generate an excessive amount of traffic, I chose a router with just one Ethernet segment for this demonstration.

The second example (Listing 3-32) is the debugging of IP RIP. The routing table was not cleared after turning on the debugging, so this output reflects a periodic 30-second RIP update rather than a forced update. As in the first example, all debugging was turned off after sufficient information was displayed.

These two examples will not be explained in detail at this point. However, these identical examples will be returned to in the chapter on TCP/IP troubleshooting. Before you read that chapter, it would be a very useful exercise to examine both these debug outputs and list your observations.

Ping Commands

The term *ping* originates from an acronym for packet internetwork groper, which is an amusing and even slightly ridiculous name for one of the most useful troubleshooting tools you could ever use. A ping most basically consists of an ICMP echo request, and if it is successful, there is an echo reply. The ICMP messages are transported within IP datagrams; hence a successful ICMP echo reply verifies connectivity up to and including layer 3.

```
citygate1#debug arp
ARP packet debugging is on
citygate1#clear arp
citygate1#
*Jun  1 21:57:36 PDT: IP ARP: sent req src 171.136.10.1 00e0.1eb9.bbcd,
                 dst 171.136.10.34 00a0.24d1.5823 Ethernet0
*Jun  1 21:57:36 PDT: IP ARP: sent req src 171.136.10.1 00e0.1eb9.bbcd,
                 dst 171.136.10.10 0080.5f06.ca3d Ethernet0
*Jun  1 21:57:36 PDT: IP ARP: sent req src 171.136.10.1 00e0.1eb9.bbcd,
                 dst 171.136.10.13 00a0.2483.949d Ethernet0
*Jun  1 21:57:36 PDT: IP ARP: sent req src 171.136.10.1 00e0.1eb9.bbcd,
                 dst 171.136.10.14 0060.b002.9a08 Ethernet0
*Jun  1 21:57:36 PDT: IP ARP: sent req src 171.136.10.1 00e0.1eb9.bbcd,
                 dst 171.136.10.1 00e0.1eb9.bbcd Ethernet0
*Jun  1 21:57:36 PDT: IP ARP: sent req src 171.136.10.1 00e0.1eb9.bbcd,
                 dst 171.136.10.126 0000.1d22.d979 Ethernet0
*Jun  1 21:57:36 PDT: IP ARP: sent rep src 171.136.10.1 00e0.1eb9.bbcd,
                 dst 171.136.10.1 ffff.ffff.ffff Ethernet0
*Jun  1 21:57:36 PDT: IP ARP: sent rep src 171.136.10.1 00e0.1eb9.bbcd,
                 dst 171.136.10.1 ffff.ffff.ffff Ethernet0
*Jun  1 21:57:36 PDT: IP ARP: sent rep src 171.136.10.1 00e0.1eb9.bbcd,
                 dst 171.136.10.1 ffff.ffff.ffff Ethernet0
*Jun  1 21:57:36 PDT: IP ARP: sent rep src 171.136.10.1 00e0.1eb9.bbcd,
                 dst 171.136.10.1 ffff.ffff.ffff Ethernet0
*Jun  1 21:57:36 PDT: IP ARP: sent rep src 171.136.10.1 00e0.1eb9.bbcd,
                 dst 171.136.10.1 ffff.ffff.ffff Ethernet0
*Jun  1 21:57:36 PDT: IP ARP: sent rep src 171.136.10.1 00e0.1eb9.bbcd,
                 dst 171.136.10.1 ffff.ffff.ffff Ethernet0
*Jun  1 21:57:36 PDT: IP ARP: rcvd rep src 171.136.10.10 0080.5f06.ca3d, dst 171
.136.10.1 Ethernet0
*Jun  1 21:57:36 PDT: IP ARP: creating entry for IP address: 171.136.10.10, hw:
0080.5f06.ca3d
*Jun  1 21:57:36 PDT: IP ARP: rcvd rep src 171.136.10.13 00a0.2483.949d, dst 171
.136.10.1 Ethernet0
*Jun  1 21:57:36 PDT: IP ARP: creating entry for IP address: 171.136.10.13, hw:
00a0.2483.949d
*Jun  1 21:57:36 PDT: IP ARP: rcvd rep src 171.136.10.14 0060.b002.9a08, dst 171
.136.10.1 Ethernet0
*Jun  1 21:57:36 PDT: IP ARP: creating entry for IP address: 171.136.10.14, hw:
0060.b002.9a08
*Jun  1 21:57:36 PDT: IP ARP: rcvd rep src 171.136.10.126 0000.1d22.d979, dst 17
1.136.10.1 Ethernet0
*Jun  1 21:57:36 PDT: IP ARP: creating entry for IP address: 171.136.10.126, hw:
 0000.1d22.d979
```

Listing 3-31

Cisco supports ping implementations not only for IP but also for most desktop protocols. This section also discusses ping for IPX and AppleTalk. Let us first look at the simple ping facility for IP, IPX, and AppleTalk that can be implemented in user EXEC mode. The privileged-mode extended ping facility that includes a number of additional and powerful troubleshooting options will then be studied.

```
R2#debug ip rip events
RIP event debugging is on
R2#
Nov 27 13:55:45 PST: RIP: sending v1 update to 255.255.255.255 via TokenRing1/0
(165.48.65.136)
Nov 27 13:55:45 PST: RIP: Update contains 25 routes
Nov 27 13:55:45 PST: RIP: Update queued
Nov 27 13:55:45 PST: RIP: Update contains 6 routes
Nov 27 13:55:45 PST: RIP: Update queued
Nov 27 13:55:45 PST: RIP: Update sent via TokenRing1/0
Nov 27 13:55:45 PST: RIP: Update sent via TokenRing1/0
Nov 27 13:55:45 PST: RIP: sending v1 update to 255.255.255.255 via TokenRing1/0
(132.20.19.2)
Nov 27 13:55:45 PST: RIP: Update contains 18 routes
Nov 27 13:55:45 PST: RIP: Update queued
Nov 27 13:55:45 PST: RIP: Update sent via TokenRing1/0
Nov 27 13:55:45 PST: RIP: sending v1 update to 255.255.255.255 via TokenRing1/2
(132.20.44.1)
Nov 27 13:55:45 PST: RIP: Update contains 25 routes
Nov 27 13:55:45 PST: RIP: Update queued
Nov 27 13:55:45 PST: RIP: Update contains 25 routes
Nov 27 13:55:45 PST: RIP: Update queued
Nov 27 13:55:45 PST: RIP: Update contains 25 routes
Nov 27 13:55:45 PST: RIP: Update queued
Nov 27 13:55:45 PST: RIP: Update contains 25 routes
Nov 27 13:55:45 PST: RIP: Update queued
Nov 27 13:55:45 PST: RIP: Update contains 25 routes
Nov 27 13:55:45 PST: RIP: Update queued
Nov 27 13:55:45 PST: RIP: Update contains 25 routes
Nov 27 13:55:45 PST: RIP: Update queued
Nov 27 13:55:45 PST: RIP: Update contains 25 routes
Nov 27 13:55:45 PST: RIP: Update queued
Nov 27 13:55:45 PST: RIP: Update contains 25 routes
Nov 27 13:55:45 PST: RIP: Update queued
Nov 27 13:55:45 PST: RIP: Update contains 25 routes
Nov 27 13:55:45 PST: RIP: Update queued
Nov 27 13:55:45 PST: RIP: Update contains 1 routes
Nov 27 13:55:45 PST: RIP: Update queued
Nov 27 13:55:45 PST: RIP: Update sent via TokenRing1/2
Nov 27 13:55:45 PST: RIP: Update sent via TokenRing1/2
R2#undeb all
All possible debugging has been turned off
R2#
```

Listing 3-32

User EXEC Mode

IP PING Listing 3-33 is an example of a simple IP ping. Note that this can be done from user mode even though in this example we are in privileged mode. Five echo requests are sent, and the five exclamation marks

```
Galway1_14#ping 165.48.183.12

Type escape sequence to abort.
Sending 5, 100-byte ICMP Echoes to 165.48.183.12, timeout is 2 seconds:
!!!!!
Success rate is 100 percent (5/5), round-trip min/avg/max = 12/14/16 ms
Galway1_14#
```

Listing 3-33

indicate that all five requests have received a successful reply. Information on maximum, minimum, and average round-trip time is also included.

While an exclamation mark indicates that an echo reply was received successfully, the following symbols indicate the different reasons for an echo reply not being received:

!	Reply received
.	Request timed out
U	Destination unreachable
P	Protocol unreachable
N	Network unreachable
Q	Source quench
M	Could not fragment
?	Unknown packet type

IPX PING The IPX ping facility works on routers running IOS version 8.2 or later. The user EXEC IPX ping usually can only be used to test to Cisco router interfaces. In privileged mode, you can ping certain Novell stations. (See Listing 3-34.)

APPLETALK PING This ping uses the Apple Echo Protocol (AEP) to verify connectivity between AppleTalk nodes. Note that Cisco routers only currently support this echo protocol on Ethernet interfaces. (See Listing 3-35.)

```
R8#ping ipx a5304380.0007.7f12.0385

Type escape sequence to abort.
Sending 5, 100-byte IPX cisco Echoes to A5304380.0007.7f12.0385, timeout is 2 se
conds:
!!!!!
Success rate is 100 percent (5/5), round-trip min/avg/max = 1/1/4 ms
R8#
```

Listing 3-34

As in the case of IPX ping, the Apple keyword is normally used to indicate that you are attempting to ping an AppleTalk address. In newer versions of IOS, this may not be necessary because the router checks each of its routing tables for a matching destination address, and providing there is no conflict between protocols, the correct type of ping will be initiated.

The AEP provides the following error messages that distinguish it from IP ping:

B A malformed echo was received from the destination.

C Echo reply failed the Datagram Delivery Program (DDP) checksum. DDP is at layer 3 in the AppleTalk stack.

E Echo failed to the destination address.

R No route to the destination network.

Privileged EXEC Mode In privileged EXEC mode, an extended ping facility is available and can be implemented for each of the desktop protocols. This provides some powerful options that can be used to obtain more detailed information as to why pings may be failing on a consistent

```
Kildare1_10#ping apple 1000.48

Type escape sequence to abort.
Sending 5, 100-byte AppleTalk Echoes to 1000.48, timeout is 2 seconds:
!!!!!
Success rate is 100 percent (5/5), round-trip min/avg/max = 1/2/4 ms
Kildare1_10#
```

Listing 3-35

or intermittent basis. We will see that information also can be extracted about degraded performance rather than simple loss of service. An extended ping is always done by simply typing `ping`, and by then allowing the router to prompt you for the various options.

EXTENDED IP PING See Listing 3-36.

Let us now examine each of the options available in privileged-mode ping; the default value for each option is shown in brackets.

Protocol	The protocol under test.
Target address	Destination address under test.
Repeat count	A large number of pings may be used if intermittent failure or poor response is suspected.
Datagram size	The datagram size can be increased if it is suspected that packets are being dropped due to increased latency or fragmentation failure, for example. In this case, I used 1600 bytes in order to force fragmentation.
Timeout	The timeout should only be increased if you suspect that the timeout failures are due to extremely slow responses rather than dropped packets.

```
Galway1_14#ping
Protocol [ip]:
Target IP address: 165.48.183.12
Repeat count [5]: 10
Datagram size [100]: 1600
Timeout in seconds [2]:
Extended commands [n]: y
Source address or interface: 165.48.48.3
Type of service [0]:
Set DF bit in IP header? [no]:
Data pattern [0xABCD]:
Loose, Strict, Record, Timestamp, Verbose[none]:
Sweep range of sizes [n]:
Type escape sequence to abort.
Sending 10, 1600-byte ICMP Echoes to 165.48.183.12, timeout is 2 seconds:
!!!!!!!!!!
Success rate is 100 percent (10/10), round-trip min/avg/max = 36/39/48 ms
Galway1_14#
```

Listing 3-36

Extended commands	Answer yes to avail of the extended options.
Source address	This must be the address of one of the router's interfaces.
Type of service	This relates to RFC 791 TOS options. It is typically left at the default of 0.
Set DF bit in IP header?	Setting the DF bit prohibits fragmentation from occurring along the route even if the MTU of a medium is exceeded.
Data pattern [0xABCD]:	Choosing to vary the data pattern can have applications in testing a noisy serial link, for example.
Loose, Strict, Record, Timestamp, Verbose [none]:	These are IP header options. This chapter includes demonstrations of Record and Verbose. The other options are rarely used.
Sweep range of sizes [n]:	This option is useful to test if large packets are being dropped or processed too slowly or if fragmentation failure is occurring.

The example in Listing 3-37 shows the route record option being used. This option provides information on each hop not only along the route to the destination address but also along the return path. The fact that the route record option gives information on both the outbound route and the return path distinguishes it from the trace command that we will discuss in the next section. However, note also that trace does not have a nine-hop limitation.

You will notice that output commences with a number of zero strings. This indicates that the fields in the outgoing packets that will record the various nodal IP addresses along the route have been cleared.

As an exercise, you should write down each hop along the route from the source address, which is 171.133.1.1, to the destination address, which is 171.144.1.38.

Now let's look at an example of the *Verbose* option being availed of (see Listing 3-38). This gives you a breakdown of the response time for each echo reply. It may be useful if very specific information is required on delay variations. The *Timestamp* option gives a similar output, but time-stamps each response. The *Loose* and *Strict* options are rarely used. *Loose* allows you to specify certain nodes that must be traversed along the route to the destination, while *Strict* specifies nodes that must *only* be traversed along the route.

```
R1#ping
Protocol [ip]:
Target IP address: 171.144.1.38
Repeat count [5]:
Datagram size [100]:
Timeout in seconds [2]:
Extended commands [n]: y
Source address or interface: 171.133.1.1
Type of service [0]:
Set DF bit in IP header? [no]:
Validate reply data? [no]:
Data pattern [0xABCD]:
Loose, Strict, Record, Timestamp, Verbose[none]: r
Number of hops [ 9 ]:
Loose, Strict, Record, Timestamp, Verbose[RV]:
Sweep range of sizes [n]:
Type escape sequence to abort.
Sending 5, 100-byte ICMP Echoes to 171.144.1.38, timeout is 2 seconds:
Packet has IP options:  Total option bytes= 39, padded length=40
 Record route: <*> 0.0.0.0 0.0.0.0 0.0.0.0 0.0.0.0
         0.0.0.0 0.0.0.0 0.0.0.0 0.0.0.0 0.0.0.0

Reply to request 0 (8 ms).  Received packet has options
 Total option bytes= 40, padded length=40
 Record route: 171.133.1.1 165.48.7.130 171.144.1.3 171.144.1.38
         171.144.1.38 165.48.7.129 171.133.1.2 171.133.1.1 <*> 0.0.0.0
 End of list

Reply to request 1 (8 ms).  Received packet has options
 Total option bytes= 40, padded length=40
 Record route: 171.133.1.1 165.48.7.130 171.144.1.3 171.144.1.38
         171.144.1.38 165.48.7.129 171.133.1.2 171.133.1.1 <*> 0.0.0.0
 End of list

Reply to request 2 (8 ms).  Received packet has options
 Total option bytes= 40, padded length=40
 Record route: 171.133.1.1 165.48.7.130 171.144.1.3 171.144.1.38
         171.144.1.38 165.48.7.129 171.133.1.2 171.133.1.1 <*> 0.0.0.0
 End of list

Reply to request 3 (4 ms).  Received packet has options
 Total option bytes= 40, padded length=40
 Record route: 171.133.1.1 165.48.7.130 171.144.1.3 171.144.1.38
         171.144.1.38 165.48.7.129 171.133.1.2 171.133.1.1 <*> 0.0.0.0
 End of list

Reply to request 4 (8 ms).  Received packet has options
 Total option bytes= 40, padded length=40
 Record route: 171.133.1.1 165.48.7.130 171.144.1.3 171.144.1.38
         171.144.1.38 165.48.7.129 171.133.1.2 171.133.1.1 <*> 0.0.0.0
 End of list
Success rate is 100 percent (5/5), round-trip min/avg/max = 4/7/8 ms
R1#
```

Listing 3-37

```
R1#ping
Protocol [ip]:
Target IP address: 171.144.1.38
Repeat count [5]:
Datagram size [100]:
Timeout in seconds [2]:
Extended commands [n]: y
Source address or interface: 171.133.1.1
Type of service [0]:
Set DF bit in IP header? [no]:
Validate reply data? [no]:
Data pattern [0xABCD]:
Loose, Strict, Record, Timestamp, Verbose[none]: v
Loose, Strict, Record, Timestamp, Verbose[V]:
Sweep range of sizes [n]:
Type escape sequence to abort.
Sending 5, 100-byte ICMP Echoes to 171.144.1.38, timeout is 2 seconds:
Reply to request 0 (4 ms)
Reply to request 1 (4 ms)
Reply to request 2 (1 ms)
Reply to request 3 (4 ms)
Reply to request 4 (8 ms)
Success rate is 100 percent (5/5), round-trip min/avg/max = 1/4/8 ms
R1#
```

Listing 3-38

EXTENDED IPX PING The extended IPX ping also allows you to vary parameters such as packet size and repeat count, which can be extremely powerful. Another key enhancement from user-mode ping is the `Novell Standard Echo` option. By answering yes to this option, you can ping Novell workstations that have this IPX feature loaded. If you answer no, then Novell IPX devices will not respond, since they do not support the Cisco proprietary IPX ping protocol. Care should be exercised when drawing conclusions from ping failures to Novell IPX devices. You must verify that the device in question supports the feature. (See Listing 3-39.)

EXTENDED APPLETALK PING Listing 3-40 is a sample output of an extended AppleTalk ping. The same more basic enhancements apply here as in the case of an extended IPX ping. Notice that like IP and IPX extended ping, the *Verbose* option also can be chosen. This results in the same type of detailed output that we have already seen and discussed in the case of IP.

```
1R8#ping
Protocol [ip]: ipx
Target IPX address: a5304380.0007.7f12.0385
Repeat count [5]: 20
Datagram size [100]: 900
Timeout in seconds [2]:
Verbose [n]:
Novell Standard Echo [n]:
Type escape sequence to abort.
Sending 20, 900-byte IPX cisco Echoes to A5304380.0007.7f12.0385, timeout is 2
seconds:
!!!!!!!!!!!!!!!!!!!!
Success rate is 100 percent (20/20), round-trip min/avg/max = 1/2/4 ms
R8#
```

Listing 3-39

The `trace` Command

The `trace` command provides information about each hop along the route to a particular destination. It operates by manipulating the time-to-live (TTL) field in IP datagrams. An ICMP echo request with a TTL equal to 1 is sent out as the first probe. The first router along the path will discard the packet but will respond with an identifying error message. The error message is usually either an ICMP time-exceeded message, which indicates a successful hop on the path to the destination, or

```
R3#ping
Protocol [ip]: appl
Target AppleTalk address: 1000.48
Repeat count [5]: 20
Datagram size [100]: 500
Timeout in seconds [2]:
Verbose [n]:
Sweep range of sizes [n]:
Type escape sequence to abort.
Sending 20, 500-byte AppleTalk Echoes to 1000.48, timeout is 2 seconds:
!!!!!!!!!!!!!!!!!!!!
Success rate is 100 percent (20/20), round-trip min/avg/max = 1/2/4 ms
R3#
```

Listing 3-40

a port-unreachable message, indicating that the packet was received by the ultimate destination but could not be transferred up the IP stack.

In order to get information on round-trip delay times, the `trace` command sends two more probes and displays the resulting delay times. After three probes have been sent, `trace` then increments the TTL field by one and sends three more probes. These probes then reach the second hop along the route before either a time-exceeded or port-unreachable message is sent back. Using this principle, the `trace` command keeps incrementing the TTL field by one until a response is received from the ultimate target address.

Use of the `trace` command can be problematic at times. There are some known IOS bugs that relate to the use of `trace`. Information relating to the bugs is available on CCO. One problem can be that some destinations do not respond appropriately with an ICMP port-unreachable message. When the output of a trace displays a series of asterisks (`*`) until the maximum TTL is exceeded, then there is a possibility that this problem is occurring. To escape from this, use Ctrl-Shift-6.

User EXEC Mode Listing 3-41 is an example of a simple user EXEC-mode `trace` command. There are three hops to the destination. The first three probes with a TTL of one caused ICMP time-exceeded messages with two different source addresses. This happens here because Router1 and Router2 are dually attached to the same segment and they are both one hop away from Router3, so either of these routers may answer the probe.

```
Router3#trace 171.144.1.39

Type escape sequence to abort.
Tracing the route to Router9 (171.144.1.39)

  1 Router2 (165.48.48.2) 0 msec
    Router2 (165.48.48.2) 0 msec
    Router1 (165.48.48.1) 4 msec
  2 165.48.48.129 12 msec
    Router6 (165.48.49.129) 12 msec 12 msec
  3 Router4 (171.133.1.2) 12 msec 12 msec
    Router9 (171.144.1.39) 12 msec
Router3#
```

Listing 3-41

The following list shows the different characters that can appear in the output of the IP `trace` command:

`XY msec`	The round-trip delay in milliseconds before receiving a reply to the probe
`*`	Probe timed out
`?`	Unknown packet type
`U`	Port unreachable
`P`	Protocol unreachable
`N`	Network unreachable
`H`	Host unreachable
`Q`	ICMP source quench

Privileged-Mode Extended Trace Many of the options available to extended ping are also common to extended trace. The more particular options include

Numeric display. By default, DNS names along with IP addresses will be displayed in trace outputs. If you wish to suppress naming information, answer yes to this option.

Probe count. This can be varied from the default of 3.

TTL. The maximum and minimum TTL can be varied from their default values.

Port number. This is a useful option because it enables the engineer to trace to a particular transport layer port. This can be used to verify if a certain higher-layer service can be accessed between the source and destination, given that IP connectivity is okay. (See Listing 3-42.)

In the example in Listing 3-43, you can see a trace that verifies that the telnet port (port 23) can be accessed at the destination address 171.144.1.39 using the source address of 165.48.48.3. If telnet is available using one source address but not when using another, this may indicate an extended access list along the route.

A final issue in relation to the `trace` command is that care must be taken if there are multiple paths to the destination. In this case it is possible that packets are taking a different return path to the source. You should carefully compare the variation in delay time between the different probes to build up a picture of how the packets are returning. If you are still in doubt, it may be useful to telnet to one or more of the routers

```
R3#trace
Protocol [ip]:
Target IP address: 171.144.1.39
Source address: 165.48.48.3
Numeric display [n]:
Timeout in seconds [3]:
Probe count [3]:
Minimum Time to Live [1]:
Maximum Time to Live [30]:
Port Number [33434]:
Loose, Strict, Record, Timestamp, Verbose[none]:
Type escape sequence to abort.
Tracing the route to Router9 (171.144.1.39)

  1 Router1 (165.48.49.1) 0 msec
     Router2 (165.48.48.2) 4 msec
     Router3 (165.48.49.2) 0 msec
  2 165.48.48.129 12 msec 12 msec
      Router6 (165.48.49.129) 12 msec
  3 Router9 (171.144.1.39) 12 msec
    Router4 (171.133.1.2) 12 msec 12 msec
R3#
```

Listing 3-42

```
R3#trace
Protocol [ip]:
Target IP address: 171.144.1.39
Source address: 165.48.48.3
Numeric display [n]:
Timeout in seconds [3]:
Probe count [3]:
Minimum Time to Live [1]:
Maximum Time to Live [30]:
Port Number [33434]: 23
Loose, Strict, Record, Timestamp, Verbose[none]:
Type escape sequence to abort.
Tracing the route to 171.144.1.39

  1 Router2 (165.48.48.2) 4 msec
     Router2 (165.48.49.2) 0 msec
     Router1 (165.48.48.1) 0 msec
  2 165.48.48.129 12 msec
     Router6 (165.48.49.129) 12 msec 12 msec
  3 Router4 (171.133.1.2) 16 msec 12 msec
     Router9 (171.144.1.39) 16 msec
R3#
```

Listing 3-43

along the path and to repeat the tracing exercise to both the original source and original destination.

Understanding Cisco Error Messages

Error Message Format

The system error messages obey the following format:

```
%Facility - Subfacility - Severity - Mnemonic: Message Text
```

Facility This is the facility that the error message refers to. This can be for a protocol, hardware device, or module of the system software.

Subfacility This is only relevant in the case of the channel interface processor (CIP) card. More information can be obtained if required in the appropriate sections of Cisco documentation.

Severity This is a single-decimal digit ranging in value from 0 to 7. The lower the number, the greater is the severity.

Mnemonic A single-word code that uniquely identifies the error message. This code often gives a hint as to what the problem relates to.

Message Text This is a brief description of the error message and what aspects of the router hardware or software to which it refers.

The following are some sample error messages. As an exercise, you should research what they mean using the System Error Messages section of the CCO IOS documentation.

```
%DUAL-3-SIA: Route 171.155.148.192/26 stuck-in-active state
 in IP-EIGRP 211. Cleaning up
%LANCE-3-OWNERR: Unit 0, buffer ownership error
```

Note that not all error messages refer to faults or problem conditions. Some error messages are simply informational messages. For example, the following message simply means that the ISDN BRI0 interface is now connected to a particular remote number.

```
%ISDN-6-CONNECT:Interface BRI0 is now connected to 95551212
```

Traceback Reports

Some error messages that relate to internal problems on the router include what is known as *traceback information*. This is important information that should be included along with the error message when relaying a problem description to the Cisco TAC personnel.

Logging of Error Messages and Event Information

Cisco error messages of varying importance and significance can be logged to one or more of the following destinations:

- Console
- Virtual terminal
- Syslog server
- Internal buffer

The command `logging on` enables the output of logging messages to all these supported destinations. In the case of a Syslog server, the following global configuration command must be used to point to the IP address of the server:

```
logging ip-address
```

By issuing this command more than once, it is possible to build a list of Syslog servers that are written to in the same order. This typically might be done when managing a large network, and the use of redundant servers is a requirement.

The `logging buffered` command is used to send logging information to an internal buffer. The size of the buffer can be varied from 4096 bytes upward. The default value varies depending on the system platform. Choose the buffer size to suit the circumstances. If the buffer is too small, then it is likely that new messages will displace old ones, which may or may not be a problem. Obviously, making the buffer too large can place demands on system RAM. The `no logging buffered` command prevents messages from being written to the internal buffer.

```
R4(config)#logging buffered ?
  <4096-2147483647>  buffer size
  <cr>
R4(config)#no logging buffered
```

The `show logging` command displays the contents of the internal buffer. If you want the information timestamped, then you should first set the clock correctly either using NTP or manually as follows:

```
R4#clock set 11:37:00 11 December 1998
R4#sh clock
11:37:03.596 PST Fri Dec 11 1998
R4#
```

Timestamping of logging messages and debugging messages is achieved using the following global configuration commands:

```
R4(config)#service timestamps log datetime
R4(config)#service timestamps debug datetime
```

Now let's examine an excerpt of an internal buffer log that includes timestamped messages (Listing 3-44). The beginning of the output always provides summary information on all messages logged since the log was last cleared or since the system was last rebooted. Notice that the logging level is debugging; you are now about to learn exactly what that means.

```
CityGate1>sh logging
Syslog logging: enabled (0 messages dropped, 0 flushes, 0 overruns)
    Console logging: level debugging, 2421 messages logged
    Monitor logging: level debugging, 42 messages logged
    Trap logging: level informational, 2383 message lines logged
        Logging to 165.48.67.147, 2383 message lines logged
        Logging to 171.133.33.140, 2383 message lines logged
    Buffer logging: level debugging, 2421 messages logged

Log Buffer (4096 bytes):
Interface BRI0: B-Channel 1, changed state to down
Dec  4 14:30:57 PST: %ISDN-6-DISCONNECT: Interface BRI0: B-Channel 1  disconnect
ed from unknown , call lasted 1167 seconds
Dec  4 14:31:46 PST: %SYS-5-CONFIG_I: Configured from console on vty0
 (16.8.207.139)
Dec 10 13:27:21 PST: %LANCE-5-COLL: Unit 0, excessive collisions. TDR=0
```

Listing 3-44

The command `terminal monitor` will display logging information on the current terminal just as we have seen it work for debugging information. This command is not a configuration command; instead, it is applied at the privileged command line while connected to the router via telnet, and it is only relevant for that particular telnet session.

In most cases it is desirable to limit the logging messages to those of a certain priority or above. For this purpose, logging information is divided into the following eight levels, which are listed in *decreasing* order of importance:

- Emergencies
- Alerts
- Critical
- Errors
- Warnings
- Notifications
- Informational
- Debugging

For example, to limit the types of messages that go to the console to messages that are of a severity level equal to or more serious than a warning, use the following global configuration command:

```
logging console warning
```

Likewise, to limit the types of messages that are sent to the current terminal line, use

```
Logging monitor level
```

or

```
Logging trap level
```

in the case of a Syslog server.

The `logging monitor` command is entered as part of the router configuration, unlike `terminal monitor`. The latter command also does not allow for different severity levels to be detailed.

It is important to note that the different logging destinations entail a varying amount of system overhead. Logging to the console results in the most overhead, whereas logging to a virtual terminal line causes less overhead. Using a Syslog server results in even less overhead. The most efficient form of logging in terms of system overhead is the internal buffer.

Core Dumps

A number of commands are used to extract information after a router crash in order to help ascertain the cause of the failure. We have already examined the `show stacks` command.

A *core dump* is a full copy of the system memory image that can be written to a TFTP server. The resulting binary file can provide information relating to the router crash or serious malfunction that may be helpful for troubleshooting the underlying problem.

The following command, which is an undocumented configuration command, enables a core dump to be written to the IP address of a TFTP server:

```
exception dump ip-address
```

The `write core` command is normally used if the router is seriously malfunctioning but has not yet actually crashed.

Core dumps can only be obtained if the router is running IOS version 9.0 or later. However, it must be again noted that the commands relating to core dumps should only be used in conjunction with very experienced support personnel or the Cisco TAC.

SUMMARY

It is important to at least have a basic understanding of router architecture before examining the various troubleshooting and diagnostic tools available on Cisco routers. All routing protocols rely fundamentally on the procedure of building a routing table based on updates received from attached routers that are running the same protocol. This is termed the *routing process* and is facilitated by the route processor.

The *switching process* relates to how the router moves packets between its different interfaces. If the router must always check its routing table before deciding on the appropriate destination interface, then it is using process switching. The switch processor manages the multilayer switching between different interface processors and between interface processors and the route processor.

Faster switching technologies rely on the use of caching. The Cisco 7000 series supports three such switching technologies: fast switching, autonomous switching, and silicon switching. The main difference is the location of the cache. The fast-switching cache resides on the route processor, whereas the switch processor provides the capability for autonomous and silicon switching. Silicon switching is the fastest switching technology available on the 7000 series because its cache is closest to the interface processors.

The Cisco 7500 series routers integrate the route processor and switch processor functionality into a single (or dual) route-switch processor (RSP). The 7500 series also provides an enhanced CiscoBus and supports optimum switching, which is basically an optimized version of fast switching.

The 7000 series routers have a relatively complex system and interface buffer allocation mechanism. Different buffer pools are available for different ranges of packet size. A number of parameters can be manipulated to influence the buffer allocation process. This reconfiguration is generally only useful for process-switched traffic. Configuring fast switching is often a better alternative to buffer tuning. Also, newer versions of Cisco IOS contain automatic features that significantly reduce the requirement for buffer tuning.

The hardware and memory structure of the Cisco 2500/4000 series routers is significantly less complex than that of the 7000 series. All buffers and queues reside in shared memory. Only process switching and fast switching are supported on the 4000 series. The fast-switching cache also resides in shared memory.

The route processor handles some specific functions even if the router is configured for fast switching. These functions include the following: broadcast handling, debugging, SNMP, protocol translation, and tunneling.

The show commands on a Cisco device allow you to extract detailed information on the system itself, its configuration, the different active interfaces, and the different protocols running on the router. Some of the most useful show commands that provide fundamental router diagnostic information include `show version`, `show process`, `show memory`, and `show interface`.

Debugging commands are used to obtain detailed real-time packet- and frame-level information when troubleshooting a specific problem. Care must be taken not to overload the router while using the debug commands. Debugging commands can be used to troubleshoot generic system problems as well as interface- and protocol-specific problems.

`Ping` commands are used to verify connectivity up to and including layer 3 of the OSI model. Cisco supports ping for most desktop protocols, including IP, IPX, and AppleTalk. The extended ping facility is available in privileged mode, and it provides some powerful options that can be used to obtain more detailed information about degraded performance as well as simple loss of service.

The `trace` command provides the IP address of each hop along the route to a particular destination. Like ping, an extended version of trace is available in privileged mode.

Cisco system error messages obey the following format:

```
%Facility - Subfacility - Severity - Mnemonic: Message Text
```

The severity takes the form of a decimal digit from 0 to 7, with the lower numbers indicating increased severity. The other fields provide descriptive information on the nature of the error message.

Cisco error messages of varying importance and significance can be logged to one or more of the following destinations: console, virtual terminal, Syslog server, and internal buffer. The types of messages logged to any of these destinations can be filtered based on their level of significance.

Core dumps can be used to write a full copy of the system memory image to a TFTP server in the event of an overall system failure. This facility can provide valuable diagnostic information but should be used only in conjunction with experienced support personnel. The `show stacks` command also can be used to ascertain the cause of a router crash.

REVIEW QUESTIONS

For the exercises that are multiple-choice questions, there is only one correct answer unless the question is marked with an asterisk (*). Choose the most suitable answer.

1. The main latency incurred during process switching is due to
   a. The route processor looking up the routing table.
   b. Copying the packet from the SP to the RP, which is interrupt mode.

c. Copying the header across the system bus.

d. Reading the packet into the interface processor in interrupt mode.

e. Looking up the silicon-switching cache.

2. The 2500/4000 series routers use what type of memory for the switching process?

a. Main memory

b. Flash memory

c. NVRAM

d. Shared memory

e. Volatile memory

3. Debugging commands are used primarily for

a. monitoring a problem over time.

b. resetting all router defaults.

c. forcing a router reload to clear IOS software bugs.

d. long-term router performance monitoring.

e. troubleshooting a specific problem over an immediate time interval.

4. The command that copies debug output to the current terminal line is

a. `copy debug vty`

b. `terminal vty`

c. `terminal telnet`

d. `terminal monitor`

e. `no terminal console`

5. To verify that a DTE cable in connected to serial0, use

a. `show interface serial0`

b. `show running`

c. `show serial controllers`

d. `show interface summary`

e. `show controllers serial0`

6. Input drops on a router interface can indicate that the

a. router cannot access the routing table.

b. protocol has higher-layer retransmissions.

c. sytem bus is busy.

d. switch process cannot keep up with the input queue.

e. CPU cannot keep up with inbound packets.

7. To find the percentage CPU load on a router, use

a. `show process cpu`

b. `show memory`

c. `show process memory`

d. `show version`

e. `show snmp cpu`

8. The command that provides information on IOS version, memory, system uptime, and configuration register is

a. `show version`

b. `show system`

c. `show memory`

d. `show ios`

e. `show configuration`

9. A buffer failure is generated after

a. the router's attempt to allocate more buffers was unsuccessful.

b. there is a system hardware problem in interface memory.

c. there are no free buffers in the free list.

d. there are no permanent buffers in the buffer pool.

e. the output interface queues are full.

10. An Ethernet late collision occurs after

a. the entire packet has gone onto the wire.

b. more than 512 bits have gone onto the wire.

c. less than 512 bits have gone onto the wire.

d. the JAM signal was received by the sender.

e. a 9.6-ms interframe gap.

11. A packet that is smaller than the medium's minimum packet size is

a. an underrun.

b. an abort.

c. a runt.

d. a retransmission.

e. a discard.

12. The normal CFM state for a DAS on an FDDI ring is
    a. isolated.
    b. wrap a.
    c. wrap b.
    d. wrap s.
    e. thru.
13. The severity of a Cisco error message takes the form of a
    a. hex number that increases with higher severity level.
    b. decimal number from 1 to 10 that increases with higher severity level.
    c. decimal number from 0 to 7 that decreases with higher severity level.
    d. decimal number from 0 to 7 that increases with higher severity level.
    e. hex number that decreases with higher severity level.
14. Arrange the following logging levels in order of increasing significance.
    a. Critical
    b. Alerts
    c. Debugging
    d. Emergencies
    e. Errors

*15. Match up the following symbols in relation to IP ping: N, !, P, ., U.
    a. Network unreachable
    b. Protocol unreachable
    c. Timed out waiting for reply
    d. Destination unreachable
    e. Reply received

16. To get information on each hop in a route to a destination and along the return path, use
    a. extended ping with *Strict* option.
    b. extended ping with *Verbose* option.
    c. extended ping with *Record* option.
    d. trace.

17. The `show stack` command is used to troubleshoot a problem characterized by
    a. degraded router performance.
    b. a failure to load the TCP/IP stack.
    c. a router system crash.
    d. packets being dropped at each router interface.
    e. a high CPU load.
18. Match the following in relation to the trace command: P, N, *, U, H.
    a. Network unreachable
    b. Probe timed out
    c. Protocol unreachable
    d. Port unreachable
    e. Host unreachable
19. What state does an FDDI Phy-A or Phy-B enter after the Nxt (next) state?
    a. Active
    b. Verify
    c. Connect
    d. Signal
    e. Join
20. Write down the command used to check if a router's Token Ring 0 port has been isolated from the rest of the ring.

CHAPTER 4

WAN Media I

Troubleshooting Serial Lines and X.25

Introduction

This chapter examines the troubleshooting of problems with the more traditional serial line technologies. The Cisco HDLC encapsulation is the default serial line encapsulation on Cisco routers. There are still a large number of networks deploying X.25, but it is steadily being replaced by newer technologies such as frame relay and, where the need exists, ATM. Since the technology dealt with in this chapter generally belongs to legacy systems that are gradually being phased out, the subject matter will be covered in slightly less detail than frame relay, for example.

The objectives of this chapter are to

- Employ router diagnostic tools and loopback tests to troubleshoot HDLC-encapsulated serial links.
- Troubleshoot X.25 connectivity using router diagnostic commands.

Troubleshooting HDLC Serial Links

HDLC is a proprietary derivative of SDLC with slightly different implementations among the various major vendors. Since this discussion is limited to Cisco devices, interoperability issues do not apply.

The `show interface` Command

The `show interface` command is the single most powerful tool available for troubleshooting serial lines with HDLC encapsulation. It will indicate if the interface is physically okay at layer 1 and if layer 2 connectivity has been established with the remote end of the link. If such connectivity has not taken place, this command can help isolate where the problem might be. Listing 4-1 is for a correctly established serial link. The information that is provided includes

- The interface is up, indicating that the router interface itself is good and detects carrier at the physical layer.
- Line protocol is up, which means that HDLC keepalives are being seen coming back from the remote router. This verifies that the line is up all the way to and including the remote router.

```
r3#sh in s3/0
Serial3/0 is up, line protocol is up
  Hardware is 4T/MC68360
  Internet address is 172.16.1.3/24
  MTU 1500 bytes, BW 1544 Kbit, DLY 20000 usec, rely 254/255, load 1/255
  Encapsulation HDLC, loopback not set, keepalive set (10 sec)
  Last input 00:00:00, output 00:00:00, output hang never
  Last clearing of "show interface" counters never
  Input queue: 0/75/0 (size/max/drops); Total output drops: 0
  Queueing strategy: weighted fair
  Output queue: 0/64/0 (size/threshold/drops)
     Conversations  0/1 (active/max active)
     Reserved Conversations 0/0 (allocated/max allocated)
  5 minute input rate 1000 bits/sec, 1 packets/sec
  5 minute output rate 1000 bits/sec, 1 packets/sec
     53035 packets input, 3324067 bytes, 0 no buffer
     Received 35360 broadcasts, 0 runts, 0 giants
     3 input errors, 0 CRC, 3 frame, 0 overrun, 0 ignored, 0 abort
     46146 packets output, 2880991 bytes, 0 underruns
     0 output errors, 0 collisions, 4 interface resets
     0 output buffer failures, 0 output buffers swapped out
     39 carrier transitions     DCD=up  DSR=up  DTR=up  RTS=up  CTS=up
r3#
```

Listing 4-1

- All the leads are up at the interface:

  DCD (Data Carrier Detect) = up confirms again that carrier is detected. This can be thought of as an input lead with respect to the router.

  DSR (Data Send Ready) = up indicates that the DCE is available. This is an input lead on the router.

  DTR (Data Terminal Ready) = up means that the DTE (i.e., the router interface) is ready to receive a call. This is an output lead on the router.

  RTS (Request to Send) = up indicates that the DTE has free buffer space and therefore can receive a call from the DCE. This is an output lead.

  CTS (Clear to Send) = up confirms that the DCE has free buffer space enabling it to receive a call from the DTE. This is an input lead.

It is important to distinguish between input and output leads. Generally, if an input lead is down, then it suggests that the problem is external to the router. If an output lead is down, there is a possibility of a problem with the router interface.

- Weighted fair queuing is being employed. This is the default queuing mechanism for a serial link of T1 speed and lower. No input or output drops have been observed since the counters were last cleared. The dropping of packets would not be expected because the bandwidth utilization on the link appears low, as evidenced by the input and output rates. If the symptom of a problem was slow response across a serial link, then this command might indicate heavy utilization along with a high percentage of dropped packets. If there is no way to alleviate such a problem other than attempting to tune the interface queues, then fair queuing would have to first be disabled using the `no fair-queue` interface command. However, the latest versions of Cisco IOS contain automatic features that virtually eliminate the need for manual buffer and queue tuning.
- There have been a relatively large number of carrier transitions but far fewer interface resets. In a situation such as this, the interface statistics should be noted, and then the counters should be cleared. The interface statistics then should be monitored periodically to see if further carrier transitions occur.

It is important to differentiate between carrier transitions and interface resets. A carrier transition occurs if the router interface loses carrier detect, as indicated by the DCD lead changing to a down state. While this could conceivably be due to a router hardware problem, it is more likely that this input signal to the router was lost due to an external problem. It can be symptomatic of anything from a faulty cable on the router to a problem in the public telephone network.

The router performs an interface reset if it detects an excessive number of errors on the interface. The purpose of the reset is to attempt to clear the problem. Interface resets can be indicative not only of a problem that is external to the router but also of an interface hardware problem.

Refer to the appropriate section of Chapter 3 for a detailed explanation of the other parameter fields displayed in the output from a `show interface` command.

In the example in Listing 4-2, the interface is down, and the line protocol is down. All the interface leads are also in a down status. The fact that the interface itself is in a down state indicates that it is not detecting carrier. The following actions should be pursued:

- Verify that a cable is attached to the interface and that this is the correct cable. This can be checked easily using the `show controller serial 3/0` command, which will be demonstrated later.

```
r3#sh in s3/0
Serial3/0 is down, line protocol is down
  Hardware is 4T/MC68360
  Internet address is 172.16.1.3/24
  MTU 1500 bytes, BW 1544 Kbit, DLY 20000 usec, rely 255/255, load 1/255
  Encapsulation HDLC, loopback not set, keepalive set (10 sec)
  Last input 00:01:12, output 00:01:18, output hang never
  Last clearing of "show interface" counters never
  Input queue: 0/75/0 (size/max/drops); Total output drops: 0
  Queueing strategy: weighted fair
  Output queue: 0/64/0 (size/threshold/drops)
     Conversations  0/1 (active/max active)
     Reserved Conversations 0/0 (allocated/max allocated)
  5 minute input rate 0 bits/sec, 0 packets/sec
  5 minute output rate 0 bits/sec, 0 packets/sec
     53487 packets input, 3352960 bytes, 0 no buffer
     Received 35508 broadcasts, 0 runts, 0 giants
     5 input errors, 0 CRC, 4 frame, 0 overrun, 0 ignored, 1 abort
     46491 packets output, 2901430 bytes, 0 underruns
     0 output errors, 0 collisions, 4 interface resets
     0 output buffer failures, 0 output buffers swapped out
     42 carrier transitions     DCD=down  DSR=down  DTR=down  RTS=down  CTS=down
r3#
```

Listing 4-2

- If the cable is correct, perform a visual inspection of the LEDs on the CSU/DSU to verify that it sees carrier. If there is a manageable CSU/DSU in place, then a visual inspection may not be necessary.
- Use a breakout box or another type of cable tester to check the integrity of the connection between the DTE and the DCE.
- If carrier is being detected at the CSU/DSU but not at the router interface, change the cabling to the router and then, if necessary and possible, change the router port. Only perform one step at a time; otherwise, the fault cannot be isolated.
- If it is established that no incoming carrier is being detected from the public network, then the telecommunications company should be contacted.

Now let's look at an example where the serial interface is up but the line protocol is down. Interface serial 4/1 was brought administratively up (using `no shut`) at the local router, and you will notice, from the output that follows (Listing 4-3), that initially it appears that line protocol is up. Approximately 10 s after bringing up the interface, the line protocol changes state to down. The reason for this is that the line protocol

```
Router#sh in s4/1
Serial4/1 is up, line protocol is up
  Hardware is cyBus Serial
  Internet address is 130.10.11.1/30
  MTU 1500 bytes, BW 1544 Kbit, DLY 20000 usec,
     reliability 255/255, txload 1/255, rxload 1/255
  Encapsulation HDLC, loopback not set, keepalive set (10 sec)
  Last input never, output 00:00:04, output hang never
  Last clearing of "show interface" counters never
  Queueing strategy: fifo
  Output queue 0/40, 0 drops; input queue 0/75, 0 drops
  5 minute input rate 0 bits/sec, 0 packets/sec
  5 minute output rate 0 bits/sec, 0 packets/sec
     0 packets input, 0 bytes, 0 no buffer
     Received 0 broadcasts, 0 runts, 0 giants, 0 throttles
     0 input errors, 0 CRC, 0 frame, 0 overrun, 0 ignored, 0 abort
     119 packets output, 2300 bytes, 0 underruns
     0 output errors, 0 collisions, 48 interface resets
     0 output buffer failures, 0 output buffers swapped out
     38 carrier transitions
     RTS down, CTS up, DTR down, DCD up, DSR up
Router#
1d00h: %LINEPROTO-5-UPDOWN: Line protocol on Interface Serial4/1, changed state to
       down

Router#sh in s4/1
Serial4/1 is up, line protocol is down
  Hardware is cyBus Serial
  Internet address is 130.10.11.1/30
  MTU 1500 bytes, BW 1544 Kbit, DLY 20000 usec,
     reliability 255/255, txload 1/255, rxload 1/255
  Encapsulation HDLC, loopback not set, keepalive set (10 sec)
  Last input never, output 00:00:08, output hang never
  Last clearing of "show interface" counters never
  Queueing strategy: fifo
  Output queue 0/40, 0 drops; input queue 0/75, 0 drops
  5 minute input rate 0 bits/sec, 0 packets/sec
  5 minute output rate 0 bits/sec, 0 packets/sec
     0 packets input, 0 bytes, 0 no buffer
     Received 0 broadcasts, 0 runts, 0 giants, 0 throttles
     0 input errors, 0 CRC, 0 frame, 0 overrun, 0 ignored, 0 abort
     121 packets output, 2342 bytes, 0 underruns
     0 output errors, 0 collisions, 49 interface resets
     0 output buffer failures, 0 output buffers swapped out
     38 carrier transitions
     RTS down, CTS up, DTR down, DCD up, DSR up
Router#
```

Listing 4-3

was in an up state while waiting for the first HDLC keepalive, which never arrived, forcing the line protocol down. It is important to wait and verify that the line protocol remains stable and that packets are observed crossing the interface in both directions.

Carrier detect is present because the interface is up. The fact that HDLC keepalives are not being received from the remote end could be due to one or more of the following reasons:

- *A configuration error on the local or remote router interface*. This could be a mismatch of encapsulation types at the two ends of the link, e.g., HDLC at one end and PPP at the other.
- *A timing problem on the link*. This type of problem occurs frequently. The configuration of each CSU/DSU should be checked to verify that their timing parameters are set correctly. For example, both CSU/DSUs could be set to provide timing at different speeds. It also should be verified that all cabling at each end of the link is comfortably within its length specification.
- *A faulty CSU/DSU at the local or remote end*. In this case, DCD and CTS are up, which would indicate that there is not a fault at the local CSU/DSU. However, there could be a parameter mismatch between the two CSU/DSUs. Therefore, each device should have its LEDs checked for an indication of a possible fault, and the configuration should be checked to verify that all the parameters match at both ends.
- *Router hardware problem at the local or remote end*. Again, from this router's output, it is very unlikely that there is a problem at the local end. A `show interface serial` should be performed at the remote router to gather more complete information. Sometimes this is not possible if there is no out-of-band access (i.e., access that does not use the network itself, such as a modem). If there is no alternate path to the remote router, then this information obviously cannot be obtained. This leaves a number of choices. The line can be tested through the public network in conjunction with the telecommunications carrier to isolate the fault, or a technician can be dispatched to the remote site.
- *A fault in the public telecommunications network*. All you can tell from the interface parameters is that carrier is being received by the router; however, without checking the remote router, there is no way to verify if carrier is present end to end in the public network. This can be tested using the principle of the loopback test, which will be discussed now.

There are situations where very slow response is being reported across a serial link. In this case, the line protocol will be up. The line should be tested using extended pings. The packet size should be increased steadily, and the resulting variation in ping delay time can be observed. This can be indicative of a congested or noisy line. Sometimes pings will start to fail if the packet size is increased beyond a certain value. This may indicate that the MTU is set too low at the far end of the link.

CSU/DSU Loopback Tests

The loopback test is a very simple principle that provides an extremely useful tool for troubleshooting point-to-point serial links that have HDLC or PPP encapsulation. At certain designated points in the network the line can be looped back to one particular end of the link. A typical point to perform a loopback test is the CSU/DSU. The loop can be local or remote. In local loopback mode, the CSU/DSU uses its own timing instead of the timing from the public telephone network. This has the effect of "looping" the line back to the local router. A remote loopback employs the same principle, but the loop is sent in the direction of the public network. After the CSU/DSU is put in loopback mode, observing whether or not the line protocol is up may isolate the fault. The principle is illustrated in Figure 4-1.

Consider the case where RouterA in Figure 4-1 has its serial interface up but its line protocol is down. A typical test may involve first putting its CSU/DSU in local loopback. A software reconfiguration on the CSU/DSU itself can do this. If line protocol comes up, then the part of the link between the RouterA and the local CSU/DSU is clean. At this point the loopback should be removed from the local end, and the CSU/DSU at

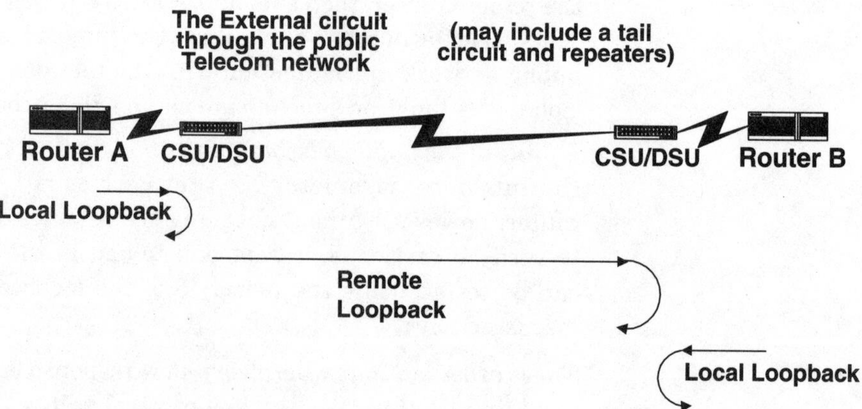

Figure 4-1 Schematic diagram of a loopback test.

the other end of the link should be put in a remote loopback state, i.e., pointing into the public telecommunications network. If line protocol is then seen as up (looped) at RouterA, the problem has been isolated to being between the remote CSU/DSU and the remote router. Conversely, if line protocol does not come up after the loopback has been put in place, then the fault has been isolated to being in the public network. The telecommunications carrier can then perform its own loopback tests to isolate the problem within its network. Loops can be provided at the router, at the CSU/DSU, or at various points within the public telecommunications network.

When a router "sees" a loop, the line protocol shows as being up (looped), as seen in the following example (Listing 4-4). It should then be possible to ping the interface IP address of the local router, as opposed to the remote end. Judging by the ping delay times, it can be observed whether it is a local or remote loopback. Of course, you should be perfectly aware of what type of loopback is being done if you are following a proper troubleshooting methodology.

```
Router#sh in s4/1
Serial4/1 is up, line protocol is up (looped)
  Hardware is cyBus Serial
  Internet address is 130.10.11.1/30
  MTU 1500 bytes, BW 1544 Kbit, DLY 20000 usec,
     reliability 255/255, txload 1/255, rxload 1/255
  Encapsulation HDLC, loopback set, keepalive set (10 sec)
  Last input 00:00:00, output 00:00:00, output hang never
  Last clearing of "show interface" counters never
  Queueing strategy: fifo
  Output queue 0/40, 0 drops; input queue 0/75, 0 drops
  5 minute input rate 0 bits/sec, 0 packets/sec
  5 minute output rate 0 bits/sec, 0 packets/sec
     2413 packets input, 1591711 bytes, 0 no buffer
     Received 0 broadcasts, 0 runts, 0 giants, 0 throttles
     0 input errors, 0 CRC, 0 frame, 0 overrun, 0 ignored, 0 abort
     2460 packets output, 1606683 bytes, 0 underruns
     0 output errors, 0 collisions, 65 interface resets
     0 output buffer failures, 0 output buffers swapped out
     80 carrier transitions
     RTS up, CTS up, DTR up, DCD up, DSR up
Router#ping 130.10.11.1

Type escape sequence to abort.
Sending 5, 100-byte ICMP Echos to 130.10.11.1, timeout is 2 seconds:
!!!!!
Success rate is 100 percent (5/5), round-trip min/avg/max = 32/33/36 ms
Router#
```

Listing 4-4

Not only is this type of test useful when the line protocol is down, it also can be used for troubleshooting a noisy line. The same procedure can be followed. Doing extended pings that stress the line does the fault isolation. Using a high repeat count and increasing the packet size can check the quality of the line.

Loopback tests in practice usually involve the coordination of different staff teams. For example, the person checking what the router is displaying is usually not the same person who is putting the loop on the CSU/DSU. It is very important that clear communication is maintained between these parties. Simple misunderstandings often needlessly increase the time that it takes to isolate and resolve the problem. If, for example, the CSU/DSU is put in loopback mode, it is obviously essential that all parties involved understand whether the loop is back to the router or out to the network.

CAUTION: *The loopback test is a simple and effective tool. Keep it that way by ensuring that all parties involved in the test are communicating clearly at all times.*

The `show controllers` Command

This command was already mentioned in passing when I discussed how to verify that the correct cable was plugged into the router's serial interface. The output of `show controller serial` provides an abundance of information about the interface relating to hardware type and version, along with detailed error statistics. A lot of this information is generally for the exclusive use of specialized technical support personnel, and the main use of this command is that it is the only way to verify what type of serial cable is plugged into the router's serial port.

The following truncated sample output (Listing 4-5) verifies that all the basic leads are up on the serial 3/0 interface. A V35 DCE cable is attached to this interface, and the clock rate is a mere 1200 bps. This is the minimum clock rate that can be configured on a DCE interface, and obviously, it is unacceptably slow. It should be reconfigured to a higher value such as 56,000 bps. It also should be verified that it is correct to have a DCE cable on this interface. DCE cables typically are used for applications such as back-to-back serial cables between routers in the same wiring closet or for connections to SDLC controllers. For most point-to-point serial links that connect over a wide-area network (WAN)

Listing 4-5

```
3#sh control se 3/0
Interface Serial3/0
PAS f/w rev 242, PAS h/w rev 122, CPU is 25Mhz
idb = 0x60A67ECC, ds = 0x60A6BB70, PCI cfg_regaddr = 0x60BB914C
IDB type = 0x22, status = 0x4218080, maxdgram = 1524
      DCD=up  DSR=up  DTR=up  RTS=up  CTS=up
4T(0) s4t_linestate: Up , cable type : DCE V.35 cable,
clockrate 1200 (index=1)
s4t_ds=0x60A6BB70, pa_info=0x60A67E70, ib=0x4B032080
PCI reg=0x3C300000, bus=6, D/L time=576
```

the cable type is DTE, with the clocking being provided via the CSU/DSU.

The `show buffers` Command

The `show buffers` command was discussed in detail in Chapter 3. It can be used along with the `show interface` command to investigate if packets are being dropped at the interface due to a lack of memory. The `hits`, `misses`, and `created` parameters should be tracked. For the interface buffer pools, the `hits`, `fallbacks`, and number of buffers in the free list can be monitored to ascertain if there are interface memory problems. However, with versions of Cisco IOS later than 11.0, buffer tuning is generally unnecessary and really should be treated as a last resort. (See Listing 4-6.)

Refer to Chapter 3 for a detailed explanation of the output displayed by the `show buffers` command.

The `debug serial interface` Command

The `debug serial interface` command will display HDLC keepalives that are being sent and received by the router. The following example (Listing 4-7) shows a serial interface that is sending and receiving keepalives in the correct sequence.

The `myseq` counter increments each time the router sends a keepalive packet.

The `mineseen` parameter reflects the last sent keepalive that was acknowledged by the remote router.

Listing 4-6

```
London-1D>sh buffer
Buffer elements:
     499 in free list (500 max allowed)
     271706743 hits, 0 misses, 0 created

Public buffer pools:
Small buffers, 104 bytes (total 50, permanent 50):
     46 in free list (20 min, 150 max allowed)
     49954041 hits, 120 misses, 241 trims, 241 created
     0 failures (0 no memory)
Middle buffers, 600 bytes (total 25, permanent 25):
     21 in free list (10 min, 150 max allowed)
     82811973 hits, 92998 misses, 185985 trims, 185985 created
     0 failures (0 no memory)
Big buffers, 1524 bytes (total 50, permanent 50):
     50 in free list (5 min, 150 max allowed)
     12759034 hits, 2435 misses, 4871 trims, 4871 created
     0 failures (0 no memory)
VeryBig buffers, 4520 bytes (total 10, permanent 10):
     10 in free list (0 min, 100 max allowed)
     17699009 hits, 0 misses, 0 trims, 0 created
     0 failures (0 no memory)
Large buffers, 5024 bytes (total 0, permanent 0):
     0 in free list (0 min, 10 max allowed)
     0 hits, 0 misses, 0 trims, 0 created
     0 failures (0 no memory)
Huge buffers, 18024 bytes (total 0, permanent 0):
     0 in free list (0 min, 4 max allowed)
     132756 hits, 19 misses, 19 trims, 19 created
     0 failures (0 no memory)

Interface buffer pools:
Serial0 buffers, 1524 bytes (total 96, permanent 96):
     32 in free list (0 min, 96 max allowed)
     64 hits, 0 fallbacks
     32 max cache size, 32 in cache
Serial1 buffers, 1524 bytes (total 96, permanent 96):
     32 in free list (0 min, 96 max allowed)
     64 hits, 0 fallbacks
     32 max cache size, 32 in cache
Fddi buffers, 4520 bytes (total 256, permanent 256):
     0 in free list (0 min, 256 max allowed)
     256 hits, 12 fallbacks
     256 max cache size, 130 in cache
     14 buffer threshold, 14 threshold transitions
TokenRing0 buffers, 4516 bytes (total 48, permanent 48):
8 in free list (0 min, 48 max allowed)
     160 hits, 8 fallbacks
     16 max cache size, 8 in cache
TokenRing1 buffers, 4516 bytes (total 48, permanent 48):
     0 in free list (0 min, 48 max allowed)
     112 hits, 0 fallbacks
     16 max cache size, 16 in cache
```

Listing 4-7

```
r3#debug serial interface
Serial network interface debugging is onr
3#term mon
% Console already monitors
r3#
Serial3/0: HDLC myseq 6, mineseen 6*, yourseen 7, line up
Serial3/0: HDLC myseq 7, mineseen 7*, yourseen 8, line up
Serial3/0: HDLC myseq 8, mineseen 8*, yourseen 9, line up
Serial3/0: HDLC myseq 9, mineseen 9*, yourseen 10, line up
Serial3/0: HDLC myseq 10, mineseen 10*, yourseen 11, line up
Serial3/0: HDLC myseq 11, mineseen 11*, yourseen 12, line up
```

The `yourseen` counter shows the sequence number of the last correctly sequenced keepalive received from the remote router.

In Listing 4-8, the router is attempting to reset the interface either because it is down or because of the detection of excessive errors. The interface is up after the restart. This would cause the `interface resets` parameter to increment.

Modem Connectivity

Now I will talk briefly about modem connectivity in the specific cases of a modem connecting to a router's auxiliary port or to an access server. While asynchronous modems are becoming increasingly less fashionable in today's high-technology environments, they can still provide an important application in the form of out-of-band access. The configuration and troubleshooting of the router only will be discussed, since the modems can be proprietary in nature.

The router configuration is quite straightforward for most applications. The type of input transport that is to be allowed across the inter-

Listing 4-8

```
r3#debug serial interface
Serial network interface debugging is on
r3#
Serial3/0: attempting to restart
Serial3/0: Interface is alive
 port_stat 0x30, cable_type 0x3
Serial3/0: attempting to restart
Serial3/0: Interface is alive
 port_stat 0x30, cable_type 0x3
```

Listing 4-9

```
Router-3#

!
line aux 0
 exec-timeout 5 30
 password 7 095F5A0800150206
 login
 transport input all
!
```

face should be specified. If "all" is specified, then telnet, pad, and mop are allowed. In the example given as Listing 4-9, an EXEC idle timeout of 5½ minutes has been specified along with a password. This is the password required of users who attempt to dial into the router's auxiliary port over the PSTN. Other parameters that may need to be configured include the type of flow control (usually hardware), baud rate, and the number of stop bits and data bits. In many cases the default value for these parameters will coincide with the modem. These settings on the router can be checked using the `show line` command.

The `show line` Command

The `show line` command by itself will list the current status of the console port, auxiliary port, and each of the vty lines. Historical session statistics since the last reload are also provided. An asterisk (*) at the left of the output indicates that the line is either in use or the last session has not been cleared down properly. The `clear line` command can be used to terminate unwanted sessions. The user cannot terminate its own session. For example, in the following output (Listing 4-10), the only active session is on the auxiliary port or line 1. If the user is connecting to the router over this line, then that user cannot clear line 1.

The `show line` command also can be used to get more detailed information about any specific line. The `status` parameter refers to the AUX port itself. The first of the following outputs (Listing 4-11) shows the line while a call is up; the second (Listing 4-12) displays the line status when idle. The only difference is that when a call is up, the status is shown as Ready, Active as opposed to Ready. In both cases, the modem state is Ready. This command displays a lot of information on parameters such as baud rate, parity, the number of stop bits and data bits. These param-

```
Router-3#sh line
 Tty Typ     Tx/Rx       A Modem  Roty AccO AccI  Uses    Noise   Overruns
   0 CTY                 -    -      -    -    -     0        0        0/0
*  1 AUX   9600/9600     -    -      -    -    -    10        0        0/0
   2 VTY                 -    -      -    -    -   272        0        0/0
   3 VTY                 -    -      -    -    -    27        0        0/0
   4 VTY                 -    -      -    -    -     0        0        0/0
   5 VTY                 -    -      -    -   10     0        0        0/0
   6 VTY                 -    -      -    -   10     0        0        0/0

Router-3#
```

Listing 4-10

eters are useful for troubleshooting the failure of an incoming call. If a call does succeed but a session cannot be activated with the router, then it is possible that the required transport (most usually telnet) is not allowed. Information on the terminal length and width and session and EXEC timeout values is also provided.

```
Router-3#sh line 1
 Tty Typ     Tx/Rx       A Modem  Roty AccO AccI  Uses    Noise   Overruns
*  1 AUX   9600/9600     -    -      -    -    -    10        0        0/0

Line 1, Location: "", Type: ""
Length: 24 lines, Width: 80 columns
Baud rate (TX/RX) is 9600/9600, no parity, 2 stopbits, 8 databits
Status: Ready, Active
Capabilities: none
Modem state: Ready
Special Chars: Escape  Hold  Stop  Start  Disconnect  Activation
                ^^x    none   -     -       none
Timeouts:       Idle EXEC    Idle Session   Modem Answer  Session    Dispatch
                0:05:30        never                        none     not set
Session limit is not set.
Time since activation: 0:01:06
Editing is enabled.
History is enabled, history size is 10.
Full user help is disabled
Allowed transports are pad telnet mop.  Preferred is telnet.
No output characters are padded
No special data dispatching characters
Router-3#
```

Listing 4-11

```
Router-3>sh lin 1
 Tty Typ     Tx/Rx     A Modem  Roty AccO AccI  Uses    Noise   Overruns
   1 AUX   9600/9600   -    -      -    -    -    10        0        0/0

Line 1, Location: "", Type: ""
Length: 24 lines, Width: 80 columns
Baud rate (TX/RX) is 9600/9600, no parity, 2 stopbits, 8 databits
Status: Ready
Capabilities: none
Modem state: Ready
Special Chars: Escape  Hold  Stop  Start  Disconnect  Activation
                ^^x    none   -      -      none
Timeouts:      Idle EXEC    Idle Session   Modem Answer  Session   Dispatch
               0:05:30       never                        none      not set
Session limit is not set.
Time since activation: never
Editing is enabled.
History is enabled, history size is 10.
Full user help is disabled
Allowed transports are pad telnet mop.  Preferred is telnet.
No output characters are padded
No special data dispatching characters
Router-3>
```

Listing 4-12

Troubleshooting X.25 Connectivity

X.25 is steadily being replaced by newer technology, in particular, frame relay. This packet-switching technology was designed in an era when WAN links were still relatively unreliable. For this reason, X.25 employs many error-checking features that in most of today's networks only serve to produce unnecessary overhead due to the inherent high reliability of modern WAN circuits. X.25 still warrants some attention because the robust nature of the protocol has served many clients well and there is a resulting inertia to change. However, because it is a technology whose days are ultimately numbered, it will be treated in less detail than frame relay in Chapter 5.

Listing 4-13 shows a simple and typical example of IP over X.25. This was set up in a laboratory as a simple point-to-point X.25 using back-to-back serial cables. Hence one end requires a DCE cable. You will notice that the DCE keyword also was included in the `encapsulation x25` command. This is essential for the link to work, since X.25 encapsulation defaults to being DTE.

```
interface Serial1
 ip address 172.16.1.6 255.255.255.0
 no ip mroute-cache encapsulation
 x25 x25 address 2222
 x25 map ip 172.16.1.3 3333 broadcast
!

r6#

!
interface Serial3/0
 ip address 172.16.1.3 255.255.255.0
 no ip mroute-cache
 encapsulation x25 dce
 x25 address 3333
 x25 map ip 172.16.1.6 2222 broadcast
 clockrate 56000
!

r3#
r3#pad 2222
Trying 2222...Open

User Access Verification

Password:
r6>

r3#ping 172.16.1.6Type escape sequence to abort.

Sending 5, 100-byte ICMP Echos to 172.16.1.6, timeout is 2 seconds:
!!!!!
Success rate is 100 percent (5/5), round-trip min/avg/max = 32/33/36 ms
r3#
```

Listing 4-13

Another point to note is that X.25 is a nonbroadcast medium; therefore, the broadcast keyword is required to enable the forwarding of broadcasts such as routing updates.

The X.25 connectivity can be verified by initiating an X.25 PAD session between the two routers. Here, a PAD is performed on R3 to the 2222 X.25 number, which causes a connection to be initiated to the R6 router. IP connectivity is verified using ping tests.

Show Commands

When used in the case of an X.25 encapsulated interface, the `show interface serial` command provides information about a range of X.25 circuit parameters along with the more familiar interface statistics. The following example (Listing 4-14) shows the interfaces at each end of a successfully negotiated point-to-point X.25 circuit, with one end DTE and the other DCE. X.25 connectivity is verified by opening a PAD session from R3 to 2222, which is R6's X.25 address.

If the DCE option is removed from R3's configuration, the X.25 line protocol is broken, and R3 is left in a state of having sent a SABM (Set Asynchronous Balanced Mode) message without receiving a reply. The `show controllers` command can be used to verify that there is in fact a DCE cable plugged into serial 3/0 (see Listing 4-15).

The X.25 parameters shown here are at the Cisco default values but are also configurable. Many of these parameters need to match either the other end of the circuit or the settings on the public network to which they attach. Other problems also can be caused if these parameters are configured incorrectly on the routers.

The range of channels available for incoming-only, outgoing-only, and two-way circuits must match at each end of an X.25 link. For connections to a public network, they must match the settings provided by the telecommunications carrier. The parameters are set on the router using `htc`, `ltc`, `hic`, `lic`, `hoc`, `loc`.

```
r6#sh in se 1
Serial1 is up, line protocol is up
  Hardware is MK5025
  Internet address is 172.16.1.6 255.255.255.0
  MTU 1500 bytes, BW 1544 Kbit, DLY 20000 usec, rely 255/255, load 1/255
  Encapsulation X25, loopback not set
  LAPB DTE, modulo 8, k 7, N1 12056, N2 20
      T1 3000, interface outage (partial T3) 0, T4 0
      State CONNECT, VS 5, VR 1, Remote VR 5, Retransmissions 0
      Queues: U/S frames 0, I frames 0, unack. 0, reTx 0
      IFRAMEs 85/81 RNRs 0/0 REJs 0/0 SABM/Es 1/0 FRMRs 0/0 DISCs 0/0
  X25 DTE, address 2222, state R1, modulo 8, timer 0
      Defaults: cisco encapsulation, idle 0, nvc 1
        input/output window sizes 2/2, packet sizes 128/128
      Timers: T20 180, T21 200, T22 180, T23 180, TH 0
      Channels: Incoming-only none, Two-way 1-1024, Outgoing-only none
```

Listing 4-14

```
        RESTARTs 1/1 CALLs 2+0/1+0/0+0 DIAGs 0/0
    Last input 0:02:25, output 0:00:06, output hang never
    Last clearing of "show interface" counters never
    Output queue 0/40, 0 drops; input queue 0/75, 0 drops
    5 minute input rate 0 bits/sec, 0 packets/sec
    5 minute output rate 0 bits/sec, 0 packets/sec
       3415 packets input, 215802 bytes, 0 no buffer
       Received 499 broadcasts, 0 runts, 0 giants
       10 input errors, 10 CRC, 0 frame, 0 overrun, 0 ignored, 0 abort
       3899 packets output, 246660 bytes, 0 underruns
       0 output errors, 0 collisions, 7 interface resets, 0 restarts
       0 output buffer failures, 0 output buffers swapped out
       42 carrier transitions
r6#
r3#sh in s3/0
Serial3/0 is up, line protocol is up
  Hardware is 4T/MC68360
  Internet address is 172.16.1.3/24
  MTU 1500 bytes, BW 1544 Kbit, DLY 20000 usec, rely 255/255, load 1/255
  Encapsulation X25, loopback not set
  LAPB DCE, modulo 8, k 7, N1 12056, N2 20
      T1 3000, interface outage (partial T3) 0, T4 0
      State CONNECT, VS 1, VR 5, Remote VR 1, Retransmissions 0
      Queues: U/S frames 0, I frames 0, unack. 0, reTx 0
      IFRAMEs 81/85 RNRs 0/0 REJs 0/0 SABM/Es 28/1 FRMRs 0/0 DISCs 0/0
  X25 DCE, address 3333, state R1, modulo 8, timer 0
      Defaults: cisco encapsulation, idle 0, nvc 1
        input/output window sizes 2/2, packet sizes 128/128
      Timers: T10 60, T11 180, T12 60, T13 60, TH 0
      Channels: Incoming-only none, Two-way 1-1024, Outgoing-only none
      RESTARTs 1/1 CALLs 1+0/2+0/0+0 DIAGs 0/0
  Last input 00:00:47, output 00:00:47, output hang never
  Last clearing of "show interface" counters 00:10:29
  Queueing strategy: fifo
  Output queue 0/40, 0 drops; input queue 0/75, 0 drops
  5 minute input rate 0 bits/sec, 0 packets/sec
  5 minute output rate 0 bits/sec, 0 packets/sec
     306 packets input, 13244 bytes, 0 no buffer
     Received 60 broadcasts, 0 runts, 0 giants
     3 input errors, 0 CRC, 3 frame, 0 overrun, 0 ignored, 0 abort
     248 packets output, 7903 bytes, 0 underruns
     0 output errors, 0 collisions, 0 interface resets
     0 output buffer failures, 0 output buffers swapped out
     7 carrier transitions     DCD=up  DSR=up  DTR=up  RTS=up  CTS=up
r3#
r3#pad 2222
Trying 2222...Open

User Access Verification

Password:
r6>
```

Listing 4-14 *(Cont.)*

```
r3#sh in s3/0
Serial3/0 is up, line protocol is down
  Hardware is 4T/MC68360
  Internet address is 172.16.1.3/24
  MTU 1500 bytes, BW 1544 Kbit, DLY 20000 usec, rely 255/255, load 1/255
  Encapsulation X25, loopback not set
  LAPB DTE, modulo 8, k 7, N1 12056, N2 20
      T1 3000, interface outage (partial T3) 0, T4 0
      State SABMSENT, VS 0, VR 0, Remote VR 0, Retransmissions 1
      Queues: U/S frames 0, I frames 0, unack. 0, reTx 0
      IFRAMEs 0/0 RNRs 0/0 REJs 0/0 SABM/Es 21/0 FRMRs 0/0 DISCs 0/0
  X25 DTE, address 3333, state R1, modulo 8, timer 0
      Defaults: cisco encapsulation, idle 0, nvc 1
        input/output window sizes 2/2, packet sizes 128/128
      Timers: T20 180, T21 200, T22 180, T23 180, TH 0
      Channels: Incoming-only none, Two-way 1-1024, Outgoing-only none
      RESTARTs 0/0 CALLs 0+0/0+0/0+0 DIAGs 0/0
  Last input 00:01:57, output 00:00:02, output hang never
  Last clearing of "show interface" counters 00:15:16
  Queueing strategy: fifo
  Output queue 0/40, 0 drops; input queue 0/75, 0 drops
  5 minute input rate 0 bits/sec, 0 packets/sec
  5 minute output rate 0 bits/sec, 0 packets/sec
     342 packets input, 14143 bytes, 0 no buffer
     Received 60 broadcasts, 0 runts, 0 giants
     4 input errors, 0 CRC, 4 frame, 0 overrun, 0 ignored, 0 abort
     290 packets output, 9062 bytes, 0 underruns
     0 output errors, 0 collisions, 1 interface resets
     0 output buffer failures, 0 output buffers swapped out
     13 carrier transitions     DCD=up  DSR=up  DTR=up  RTS=up  CTS=up
r3#
```

Listing 4-15

`htc` Highest value for a two-way circuit

`hic` Highest value for an incoming-only circuit

`lic` Lowest value for an incoming-only circuit

`hoc` Highest value for an outgoing-only circuit

`loc` Lowest value for an outgoing-only circuit

For example, the following configuration would mean that no two-way channels are allowed, since the highest-two-way-channel parameter has been configured to be zero.

```
interface serial 0
encapsulation x25
x25 htc 0
```

By default, the `htc` parameter is 1024, and no unidirectional channels are available unless the configuration is changed.

The flow-control parameters, namely, the input and output packet sizes and window sizes, should match across the X.25 network. The values seen in this example are the Cisco defaults and generally are accepted as being standard. Since X.25 heavily employs flow control, a mismatch in these parameters can produce errors across the link in the form of Clear and Reset events. Another consequence of the requirement to have identical flow-control parameters between the DTE and DCE is that any change in these parameters will not be reflected until X.25 restarts the packet service. This is also true of the `X.25 modulo` parameter, which numbers the X.25 packets in relation to their relative position within the X.25 window. The main X.25 flow-control parameters that are configurable on the interface are

`X25 win`	Receive window size
`X25 wout`	Transmit window size
`X25 ips`	Input maximum packet size
`X25 ops`	Outgoing maximum packet size
`X25 modulo`	Packet numbering modulo

Now let's look at examples of some of the other X.25 show commands, beginning with `show x25 map`. This displays the static mapping between destination virtual circuit X.25 addresses and corresponding desktop protocol addresses. This command also will display whether or not the broadcast keyword has been included in the mapping statement. The examples that follow are based on the network shown in Figure 4-2.

```
r6#sh x25 map
Serial1: X.121 1111 <-> ip 130.10.11.1
  PERMANENT, BROADCAST
```

To obtain detailed information on the current virtual circuit parameters and statistics, use the `show x25 vc` command. The current state of each X.25 VC will be displayed. Information is available on what the VC is connecting to and the settings for the X.25 interface parameters, along

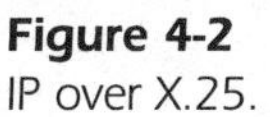

Figure 4-2
IP over X.25.

with activity and error information. For router R6 it can be observed that no traffic has passed on any of the VCs in over 2 minutes. In fact, none of the virtual circuits has passed data more than 20 seconds after they were created. This potentially could indicate a problem, but in this case it is simply due to very low traffic levels, as evidenced by the various byte counts. This conclusion is also fueled by the fact that none of the error counters has incremented. There are no Resets, RNRs, or REJs. Circuit Resets can be performed after the detection of errors on the circuit. Receiver Not Ready (RNR) messages can indicate congestion or a problem encountered during circuit setup at one end of the X.25 link. Frame Rejects (REJs) can indicate a compatibility problem or calls to or from an invalid remote end such as a closed user group.

Earlier I said that a mismatch of flow-control parameters such as window size and packet size would cause local procedure errors in the form of Clear and Reset events. The `show x25 vc` command is one means to check for Resets (see Listing 4-16).

Listing 4-16

```
r6#sh x25 vc
SVC 1,  State: D1,  Interface: Serial1
 Started 0:07:17, last input 0:07:11, output 0:07:11
 Connects 1111 <-> PAD
 Window size input: 2, output: 2
 Packet size input: 128, output: 128
 PS: 1  PR: 4  ACK: 4  Remote PR: 1  RCNT: 0  RNR: FALSE
 Retransmits: 0  Timer (secs): 0  Reassembly (bytes): 0
 Held Fragments/Packets: 0/0
 Bytes 61/61 Packets 9/4 Resets 0/0 RNRs 0/0 REJs 0/0 INTs 0/0

SVC 2,  State: D1,  Interface: Serial1
 Started 0:09:05, last input 0:08:50, output 0:08:59
 Connects 1111 <-> PAD
 Window size input: 2, output: 2
 Packet size input: 128, output: 128
 PS: 4  PR: 2  ACK: 1  Remote PR: 4  RCNT: 1  RNR: FALSE
 Retransmits: 0  Timer (secs): 0  Reassembly (bytes): 0
 Held Fragments/Packets: 0/0
 Bytes 64/196 Packets 12/10 Resets 0/0 RNRs 0/0 REJs 0/0 INTs 0/0

SVC 3,  State: D1,  Interface: Serial1
 Started 0:02:40, last input 0:02:37, output 0:02:37
 Connects 1111 <-> PAD
 Window size input: 2, output: 2
 Packet size input: 128, output: 128
 PS: 1  PR: 4  ACK: 4  Remote PR: 1  RCNT: 0  RNR: FALSE
 Retransmits: 0  Timer (secs): 0  Reassembly (bytes): 0
 Held Fragments/Packets: 0/0
 Bytes 61/61 Packets 9/4 Resets 0/0 RNRs 0/0 REJs 0/0 INTs 0/0
r6#
```

To obtain status information on current PAD connections, use the `show x25 pad` command. This command displays information that describes the connection itself, the parameter settings, and also activity and error information. As you can see, it also replicates much of the information provided by the `show x25 vc` command (see Listing 4-17).

Another X.25 command that displays similar information to some of the tools already discussed is the `show x25 interface` command. This is useful when multiple interfaces are configured with X.25. The sample output in Listing 4-18 is for the R7 router in Figure 4-2. Switched Virtual Circuit 2 (SVC 2) is supporting an X.25 PAD session to 2222. The session started 6 minutes and 54 seconds ago, but as you can see, no data have been transferred! SVC 1024 supports a telnet session to 130.10.11.2, which uses an X.25 mapping. This session commenced less than 5 minutes ago but is showing some packet transfer.

The `show x25 service` displays information on the X.25 software version and XOT (X.25 over TCP/IP) version. Summary information is also provided on the current status of the virtual circuits. This command is only available as of Cisco IOS 11.3. (See Listing 4-19).

The `debug x25 events` Command

The `debug x25 events` command displays all X.25 encapsulated packets except data and acknowledgments. The default X.25 debugging command is `debug x25`, which includes all X.25 traffic. In this example, you can see the traffic that is generated by doing an IP ping across an X.25 link (see Listing 4-20).

Referring again to Figure 4-2, a support engineer receives a complaint that IP applications are not working between R6 and R7, but a mainframe application that uses PAD is available. Removing the IP mapping statement on R6 has created this problem. It is then verified that pings fail, yet it is still possible to PAD between the two routers. It may seem confusing that IP is failing, yet a basic PAD session is working. The reason is that PAD simply relies on the existence of a virtual circuit, which has not been affected by the removal of the IP mapping statement. IP fails because without the static mapping there is no way for the router to relate the destination IP address to the virtual circuit (see Listing 4-21).

The `debug x25` output on R6 shows that data continue to be passed even after the IP mapping statement was removed. This simply means that these data are not IP traffic destined for the address that was

Listing 4-17

```
r6#sh x25 pad

tty0, connection 1 to host 1111

Total input: 10, control 2, bytes 115. Queued: 1 of 7 (81 bytes).
Total output: 12, control 2, bytes 64.
Flags: 1,   State: 3,   Last error: 1
 ParamsIn:  1:0, 2:0, 3:0, 4:0, 5:0, 6:0, 7:0,
    8:0, 9:0, 10:0, 11:0, 12:0, 13:0, 14:0, 15:0,
    16:0, 17:0, 18:0, 19:0, 20:0, 21:0, 22:0,
 ParamsOut:  1:1, 2:0, 3:2, 4:1, 5:0, 6:0, 7:21,
    8:0, 9:0, 10:0, 11:14, 12:0, 13:0, 14:0, 15:0,
    16:127, 17:21, 18:18, 19:0, 20:0, 21:0, 22:0,

SVC 2,  State: D1,  Interface: Serial1
 Started 0:07:55, last input 0:07:41, output 0:07:50
 Connects 1111 <-> PAD
 Window size input: 2, output: 2
 Packet size input: 128, output: 128
 PS: 4  PR: 2  ACK: 1  Remote PR: 4  RCNT: 1  RNR: FALSE
 Retransmits: 0  Timer (secs): 0  Reassembly (bytes): 0
 Held Fragments/Packets: 0/0
 Bytes 64/196 Packets 12/10 Resets 0/0 RNRs 0/0 REJs 0/0 INTs 0/0

tty0, connection 2 to host 1111

Total input: 4, control 2, bytes 61. Queued: 0 of 7 (0 bytes).
Total output: 9, control 2, bytes 61.
Flags: 1,   State: 3,   Last error: 1
 ParamsIn:  1:0, 2:0, 3:0, 4:0, 5:0, 6:0, 7:0,
    8:0, 9:0, 10:0, 11:0, 12:0, 13:0, 14:0, 15:0,
    16:0, 17:0, 18:0, 19:0, 20:0, 21:0, 22:0,
 ParamsOut:  1:1, 2:0, 3:2, 4:1, 5:0, 6:0, 7:21,
    8:0, 9:0, 10:0, 11:14, 12:0, 13:0, 14:0, 15:0,
    16:127, 17:21, 18:18, 19:0, 20:0, 21:0, 22:0,

SVC 1,  State: D1,  Interface: Serial1
 Started 0:06:14, last input 0:06:08, output 0:06:08
 Connects 1111 <-> PAD
 Window size input: 2, output: 2
 Packet size input: 128, output: 128
 PS: 1  PR: 4  ACK: 4  Remote PR: 1  RCNT: 0  RNR: FALSE
 Retransmits: 0  Timer (secs): 0  Reassembly (bytes): 0
 Held Fragments/Packets: 0/0
 Bytes 61/61 Packets 9/4 Resets 0/0 RNRs 0/0 REJs 0/0 INTs 0/0

tty0, connection 3 to host 1111

Total input: 4, control 2, bytes 61. Queued: 0 of 7 (0 bytes).
Total output: 9, control 2, bytes 61.
Flags: 1,   State: 3,   Last error: 1
 ParamsIn:  1:0, 2:0, 3:0, 4:0, 5:0, 6:0, 7:0,
    8:0, 9:0, 10:0, 11:0, 12:0, 13:0, 14:0, 15:0,
    16:0, 17:0, 18:0, 19:0, 20:0, 21:0, 22:0,
 ParamsOut:  1:1, 2:0, 3:2, 4:1, 5:0, 6:0, 7:21,
    8:0, 9:0, 10:0, 11:14, 12:0, 13:0, 14:0, 15:0,
    16:127, 17:21, 18:18, 19:0, 20:0, 21:0, 22:0,

r6#
```

```
r7#sh x25 inter s4/1
SVC 2,  State: D1,  Interface: Serial4/1/0
  Started 00:06:54, last input 00:00:00, output 00:00:00
  Line: 2   vty 0    Location:  Host: 2222
  2222 connected to 1111 PAD <-> X25
  Window size input: 2, output: 2
  Packet size input: 128, output: 128
  PS: 7  PR: 5  ACK: 5  Remote PR: 5  RCNT: 0  RNR: no
  Window is closed
  P/D state timeouts: 0  timer (secs): 0
  data bytes 6834/389 packets 367/325 Resets 0/0 RNRs 0/0 REJs 0/0 INTs 0/0
SVC 1024,  State: D1,  Interface: Serial4/1
  Started 00:04:49, last input 00:00:17, output 00:00:33
  Connects 2222 <-> ip 130.10.11.2
  Call PID cisco, Data PID none
  Window size input: 2, output: 2
  Packet size input: 128, output: 128
  PS: 2  PR: 0  ACK: 7  Remote PR: 2  RCNT: 1  RNR: no
  P/D state timeouts: 0  timer (secs): 0
  data bytes 2267/2141 packets 34/32 Resets 0/0 RNRs 0/0 REJs 0/0 INTs 0/0
r7#
```

Listing 4-18

removed. The PAD call connection sequence is then observed (see Listing 4-22).

Now let's clear the log on R6 by doing a `no logging buffered` followed by a `logging buffered` configuration command. When the ping to R7 again fails, as it will because the mapping statement is still missing, it is noticed that no output is generated by the `debug x25` command. This makes sense because there is currently no link between the IP pings and the X.25 virtual circuits on R6. This issue illustrates a simple yet very important principle when applying debugging tools for troubleshooting. You should think carefully about what information you might expect the debug command to provide you with, rather than blankly applying debug tools in the solution of problems. If you do not first attempt to char-

Listing 4-19

```
r7#sh x25 service
X.25 software, Version 3.0.0.
  1 configurations supporting 1 active contexts
  VCs allocated, freed and in use: 7 - 4 = 3
  VCs active and idle: 2, 1
XOT software, Version 2.0.0.
  not configured

r7#
```

```
r3#debug x25
X25 packet debugging is on
r3#ping 172.16.1.6
Type escape sequence to abort.
Sending 5, 100-byte ICMP Echos to 172.16.1.6, timeout is 2 seconds:
!!!!!
Success rate is 100 percent (5/5), round-trip min/avg/max = 32/33/36 ms
r3#
Serial3/0: X25 O D1 DATA (103) 8 lci 1024 PS 5 PR 5
Serial3/0: X25 I D1 DATA (103) 8 lci 1024 PS 5 PR 6
Serial3/0: X25 O D1 DATA (103) 8 lci 1024 PS 6 PR 6
Serial3/0: X25 I D1 DATA (103) 8 lci 1024 PS 6 PR 7
Serial3/0: X25 O D1 DATA (103) 8 lci 1024 PS 7 PR 7
Serial3/0: X25 I D1 DATA (103) 8 lci 1024 PS 7 PR 0
Serial3/0: X25 O D1 DATA (103) 8 lci 1024 PS 0 PR 0
Serial3/0: X25 I D1 DATA (103) 8 lci 1024 PS 0 PR 1
Serial3/0: X25 O D1 DATA (103) 8 lci 1024 PS 1 PR 1
Serial3/0: X25 I D1 DATA (103) 8 lci 1024 PS 1 PR 2
Serial3/0: X25 I D1 DATA (63) 8 lci 1024 PS 2 PR 2
Serial3/0: X25 O D1 RR (3) 8 lci 1024 PR 3
Serial3/0: X25 I D1 DATA (63) 8 lci 1024 PS 3 PR 2
```

Listing 4-20

acterize the nature of the problem, then the output from the debug tools may not be helpful in solving the problem. (See Listing 4-23.)

The output in Listing 4-23 confirms that the failed ping produced no output from `debug x25`, but this debugging command is still writing to log, as shown by the output produced by the PAD call.

```
r6#conf t
Enter configuration commands, one per line.  End with CNTL/Z.
r6(config)#in s1
r6(config-if)#no x25 map ip 130.10.11.1
r6(config-if)#^Z
r6#ping 130.10.11.1
Type escape sequence to abort.
Sending 5, 100-byte ICMP Echos to 130.10.11.1, timeout is 2 seconds:
.....
Success rate is 0 percent (0/5)
r6#pad 1111
Trying 1111...Open

User Access Verification

Password:
r7>
```

Listing 4-21

```
r6#debug x25
X25 packet debugging is onr6#sh log
Syslog logging: enabled (0 messages dropped, 0 flushes, 0 overruns)
    Console logging: level debugging, 706 messages logged
    Monitor logging: level debugging, 0 messages logged
    Trap logging: level informational, 70 message lines logged

*Mar  5 01:31:35: %SYS-5-CONFIG_I: Configured from console by console
*Mar  5 01:31:41: Serial1: X25 O D1 DATA (103) 8 lci 1 PS 0 PR 0
*Mar  5 01:31:41: Serial1: X25 I D1 DATA (103) 8 lci 1 PS 0 PR 1
*Mar  5 01:31:41: Serial1: X25 O D1 DATA (103) 8 lci 1 PS 1 PR 1
*Mar  5 01:31:41: Serial1: X25 I D1 DATA (103) 8 lci 1 PS 1 PR 2
*Mar  5 01:31:41: Serial1: X25 O D1 DATA (103) 8 lci 1 PS 2 PR 2
*Mar  5 01:31:41: Serial1: X25 I D1 DATA (103) 8 lci 1 PS 2 PR 3
*Mar  5 01:31:41: Serial1: X25 O D1 DATA (103) 8 lci 1 PS 3 PR 3
*Mar  5 01:31:41: Serial1: X25 I D1 DATA (103) 8 lci 1 PS 3 PR 4
*Mar  5 01:31:41: Serial1: X25 O D1 DATA (103) 8 lci 1 PS 4 PR 4
*Mar  5 01:31:41: Serial1: X25 I D1 DATA (103) 8 lci 1 PS 4 PR 5
*Mar  5 01:31:42: Serial1: X25 O D1 DATA (103) 8 lci 1 PS 5 PR 5
*Mar  5 01:31:42: Serial1: X25 I D1 DATA (103) 8 lci 1 PS 5 PR 6
*Mar  5 01:31:42: Serial1: X25 O D1 DATA (103) 8 lci 1 PS 6 PR 6
*Mar  5 01:31:42: Serial1: X25 I D1 DATA (103) 8 lci 1 PS 6 PR 7
*Mar  5 01:31:42: Serial1: X25 O D1 DATA (103) 8 lci 1 PS 7 PR 7
*Mar  5 01:31:42: Serial1: X25 I D1 DATA (103) 8 lci 1 PS 7 PR 0
*Mar  5 01:31:42: Serial1: X25 O D1 DATA (103) 8 lci 1 PS 0 PR 0
*Mar  5 01:31:43: Serial1: X25 I D1 DATA (103) 8 lci 1 PS 0 PR 1
*Mar  5 01:31:43: Serial1: X25 O D1 DATA (103) 8 lci 1 PS 1 PR 1
*Mar  5 01:31:43: Serial1: X25 I D1 DATA (103) 8 lci 1 PS 1 PR 2
*Mar  5 01:32:15: Serial1: X25 O P7 CLEAR REQUEST (5) 8 lci 1 cause 1 diag 122
*Mar  5 01:32:15: Serial1: X25 I P7 CLEAR CONFIRMATION (3) 8 lci 1
*Mar  5 01:32:16: %SYS-5-CONFIG_I: Configured from console by console
*Mar  5 01:32:32: Serial1: X25 O P3 CALL REQUEST (13) 8 lci 1
*Mar  5 01:32:32: From(4): 2222 To(4): 1111
*Mar  5 01:32:32:   Facilities: (0)
*Mar  5 01:32:32:   Call User Data (4): 0x01000000 (pad)
*Mar  5 01:32:32: Serial1: X25 I P3 CALL CONNECTED (5) 8 lci 1
*Mar  5 01:32:32: From(0):  To(0):
*Mar  5 01:32:32:   Facilities: (0)
*Mar  5 01:32:32: Serial1: X25 I P4 DATA (4) Q 8 lci 1 PS 0 PR 0
*Mar  5 01:32:32: Serial1: X25 O D1 DATA (48) Q 8 lci 1 PS 0 PR 1
*Mar  5 01:32:32: Serial1: X25 O D1 RR (3) 8 lci 1 PR 1
*Mar  5 01:32:32: Serial1: X25 I D1 DATA (45) 8 lci 1 PS 1 PR 0
*Mar  5 01:32:32: Serial1: X25 O D1 RR (3) 8 lci 1 PR 2
*Mar  5 01:32:32: Serial1: X25 I D1 DATA (12) Q 8 lci 1 PS 2 PR 1
*Mar  5 01:32:32: Serial1: X25 I D1 RR (3) 8 lci 1 PR 1
*Mar  5 01:32:32: Serial1: X25 O D1 DATA (12) Q 8 lci 1 PS 1 PR 3
*Mar  5 01:32:32: Serial1: X25 O D1 RR (3) 8 lci 1 PR 3
*Mar  5 01:32:32: Serial1: X25 I D1 RR (3) 8 lci 1 PR 2
*Mar  5 01:32:36: Serial1: X25 O D1 DATA (4) 8 lci 1 PS 2 PR 3
*Mar  5 01:32:36: Serial1: X25 I D1 RR (3) 8 lci 1 PR 3
r6#
```

Listing 4-22

```
r6#ping 130.10.11.1
Type escape sequence to abort.
Sending 5, 100-byte ICMP Echos to 130.10.11.1, timeout is 2 seconds:
.....
Success rate is 0 percent (0/5)
r6#sh log
Syslog logging: enabled (0 messages dropped, 0 flushes, 0 overruns)
    Console logging: level debugging, 707 messages logged
    Monitor logging: level debugging, 0 messages logged
    Trap logging: level informational, 71 message lines logged

r6#

r6#pad 1111
Trying 1111...Open

User Access Verification

Password:
r7>

r6#sh log
Syslog logging: enabled (0 messages dropped, 0 flushes, 0 overruns)
    Console logging: level debugging, 719 messages logged
    Monitor logging: level debugging, 0 messages logged
    Trap logging: level informational, 71 message lines logged

*Mar  5 01:35:58: %SYS-5-CONFIG_I: Configured from console by console
*Mar  5 01:37:12: Serial1: X25 O P3 CALL REQUEST (13) 8 lci 3
*Mar  5 01:37:12: From(4): 2222 To(4): 1111
*Mar  5 01:37:12:   Facilities: (0)
*Mar  5 01:37:12:   Call User Data (4): 0x01000000 (pad)
*Mar  5 01:37:12: Serial1: X25 I P3 CALL CONNECTED (5) 8 lci 3
*Mar  5 01:37:12: From(0):  To(0):
*Mar  5 01:37:12:   Facilities: (0)
r6#
```

Listing 4-23

Troubleshooting Dynamic Routing over X.25

Most dynamic routing protocols rely on broadcasting or multicasting to propagate routing information. As we have seen, X.25 is a nonbroadcast medium; therefore, it is essential to include the broadcast keyword in the mapping statement to facilitate the forwarding of routing updates (see Listing 4-24).

In the example in Listing 4-24, IPX RIP is also running on the X.25 network. A similar mapping statement is used, and the broadcast key-

Listing 4-24

```
interface Serial1
 ip address 172.16.1.6 255.255.255.0
 no ip mroute-cache
 encapsulation x25
 ipx network 22
 x25 address 2222
 x25 map ip 172.16.1.3 3333 broadcast
 x25 map ipx 22.0010.0d56.88a0 3333 broadcast
!

r6#
```

word must be included to enable the forwarding of IPX RIP and SAP updates.

NOTE: *If a mapping statement is being defined for a protocol that relies on the forwarding of broadcasts or multicasts, then the broadcast keyword must be included in that statement.*

Additional steps are sometimes required when using routing protocols that rely on the formation of neighbor relationships. Examples of these are EIGRP and OSPF. In the case of EIGRP, neighbors will be formed and the protocol can function correctly if the broadcast keyword is included in the IP mapping statement.

In the case of OSPF, the situation can be more complex, not just in the case of X.25 but for any nonbroadcast medium. OSPF will not form neighbors over a nonbroadcast medium unless the neighbor is statically defined. This scenario cannot be altered by the broadcast keyword. The following output (Listing 4-25) shows an X.25 interface that forms part of

```
r3>sh ip ospf int se 3/0Serial3/0 is up, line protocol is up
  Internet Address 172.16.1.3/24, Area 0
  Process ID 1, Router ID 172.16.229.3, Network Type NON_BROADCAST, Cost: 64
  Transmit Delay is 1 sec, State DR, Priority 1
  Designated Router (ID) 172.16.229.3, Interface address 172.16.1.3
  No backup designated router on this network
  Timer intervals configured, Hello 30, Dead 120, Wait 120, Retransmit 5
    Hello due in 00:00:00
  Neighbor Count is 0, Adjacent neighbor count is 0
  Suppress hello for 0 neighbor(s)
r3>
```

Listing 4-25

an OSPF backbone. You will notice that OSPF sees the network as being nonbroadcast and no neighbors have been formed.

Rather than statically defining neighbors, this problem is usually resolved by reconfiguring the OSPF network type. In the following example (Listing 4-26), the X.25 network in Figure 4-2 is defined as a broadcast network for OSPF, and a neighbor relationship is then formed between R6 and R7. The entire issue of running scalable routing protocols over nonbroadcast media will be discussed in great detail in Chapter 8. For the moment, it is sufficient to note that the configuration of both EIGRP and OSPF over X.25 is treated similarly to that of frame relay, which also will be discussed in detail.

```
r6#

!
interface Serial1
 ip address 130.10.11.2 255.255.255.252
 no ip mroute-cache
 encapsulation x25 dce
 ip ospf network broadcast
 x25 address 2222
 x25 map ip 130.10.11.1 1111 broadcast
 clockrate 56000
!
interface TokenRing0
 ip address 172.16.65.6 255.255.255.0
 ring-speed 16
!
router ospf 1
 network 0.0.0.0 255.255.255.255 area 0
!
logging buffered
!
r6#sh ip ospf int se 1
Serial1 is up, line protocol is up
  Internet Address 130.10.11.2 255.255.255.252, Area 0
  Process ID 1, Router ID 172.16.66.6, Network Type BROADCAST, Cost: 64
  Transmit Delay is 1 sec, State BDR, Priority 1
  Designated Router (ID) 172.16.254.1, Interface address 130.10.11.1
  Backup Designated router (ID) 172.16.66.6, Interface address 130.10.11.2
  Timer intervals configured, Hello 10, Dead 40, Wait 40, Retransmit 5
    Hello due in 0:00:08
  Neighbor Count is 1, Adjacent neighbor count is 1
    Adjacent with neighbor 172.16.254.1  (Designated Router)
r6#
```

Listing 4-26

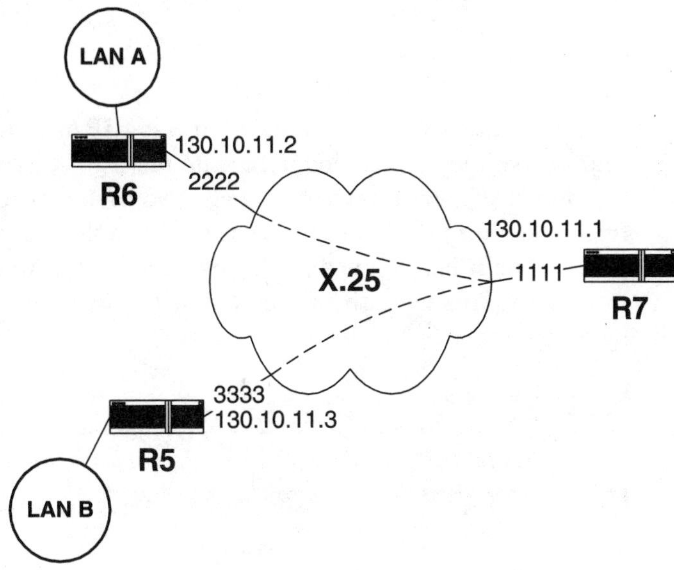

Figure 4-3 An illustration of EIGRP over X.25.

NOTE: *Neighbor formation for EIGRP and OSPF is facilitated in much the same way in X.25 as for frame relay.*

In the network in Figure 4-3, EIGRP is the WAN routing protocol. No subinterfaces are being used, and there is no VC between R5 and R6. A problem is reported that users on LAN A cannot communicate with users on LAN B. The reason for this is that split horizon is preventing R7 from forwarding routing updates back out the X.25 interface over which it learned the routes. Therefore, it will not propagate the route for LAN A to R5, and similarly, the route for LAN B will not be advertised to R6.

This situation would not apply if subinterfaces were being used at R7. In the case where subinterfaces are not used, the problem can be resolved by turning off split horizon for EIGRP. The configuration is

```
r7#
!

interface serial 0
ip address 130.10.11.1 255.255.255.0
encapsulation x25
x25 address 1111
x25 map ip 130.10.11.2 2222 broadcast
x25 map ip 130.10.11.3 3333 broadcast
no ip split-horizon eigrp 1
```

```
!
router eigrp 1
network 130.10.0.0
```

If the routing protocol in question was RIP or IGRP, then split horizon could be similarly disabled using the `no ip split-horizon` interface command. It is with regard to these two protocols that X.25 differs from frame relay in relation to its treatment of split horizon. When using RIP or IGRP, split horizon is disabled by default on frame-relay-encapsulated interfaces. This is distinct from EIGRP, which has split horizon enabled by default over frame relay.

NOTE: *Split horizon is enabled by default on X.25-encapsulated interfaces. This is different from frame relay, which, for RIP and IGRP, has split horizon disabled by default.*

REVIEW QUESTIONS

For the exercises that are multiple-choice questions, there is only one correct answer unless the question is marked with an asterisk (*). Choose the most suitable answer.

1. The command that verifies the cable type plugged into a serial interface is

a. `show controllers.`

b. `show interface.`

c. `debug serial interface.`

d. `show cable.`

e. `show cisco bus.`

2. What serial interface lead, when up, indicates that the router is detecting carrier?

a. RTS

b. DTR

c. DCD

d. DSR

e. CTS

3. Which of the following technologies can employ loopback tests?
   a. HDLC
   b. X.25
   c. PPP
   d. All of above
   e. a and c
4. Which of the following leads indicates that the DCE is available?
   a. RTS
   b. DSR
   c. DCD
   d. CTS
   e. DTR
5. If the serial interface is shut down, RTS will remain up. True or false?
6. Line protocol down on an HDLC interface means that
   a. Carrier is not being detected.
   b. Keepalives are not being seen from remote end.
   c. IP mapping statement is incorrect.
   d. Broadcast statement is missing.
   e. None of the above.
7. X.25 employs less error checking than newer technologies such as frame relay. True or false?
8. What keyword is required in an X.25 mapping statement to ensure the forwarding of routing updates?
9. Type the command that is used to troubleshoot modem connectivity into a router.
10. Split horizon is enabled by default on X.25 interfaces when using which of the following IP routing protocols?
    a. RIP
    b. IGRP
    c. EIGRP
    d. RIP version 2
    e. All of the above

11. What is the default X.25 encapsulation on Cisco router's serial interface?
    a. X25-DCE
    b. X25-DTE
    c. BFE
    d. HDLC
    e. PPP
12. What is the default encapsulation on a Cisco router's serial interface?
    a. X.25
    b. HDLC
    c. PPP
    d. ISDN
    e. There is no default.
13. IP is failing over X.25. How do you check if the X.25 itself is operational?
    a. Telnet
    b. Ping
    c. Show controllers
    d. PAD
    e. MOP
14. Which of the following commands does not give any information on current virtual circuit status?
    a. `show x25 interface`
    b. `show x25 vc`
    c. `show x25 pad`
    d. `show x25 map`
    e. `show x25 service`
15. A mismatch of the X.25 flow-control parameters between the DTE and DCE can result in which of the following error events?
    a. Clears
    b. Carrier transitions
    c. RNRs
    d. Virtual circuit resets
    e. a and b

CHAPTER 5

WAN Media II

Troubleshooting Frame Relay

Introduction

Frame relay is a packet-switched WAN technology that is still growing in its deployment. There is a trend whereby it is replacing older legacy technologies such as X.25 and point-to-point serial links. The design of the frame-relay protocol exploits the improved reliability of modern WAN circuits. The protocol itself employs no error checking, unlike X.25; it delegates error detection and correction procedures to the higher layers of the communications stack. Frame relay does include congestion control in the form of congestion notification messages.

One of the other motivating factors for moving to frame relay includes the ability to tailor the purchased bandwidth to the utilization profiles of the applications running on the network. Thus frame relay provides the potential for a more efficient and cost-effective use of the often expensive WAN bandwidth. Full or partial meshing of the permanent virtual circuits (PVCs) can be employed for network redundancy.

The objectives of this chapter are to

- Understand the frame relay configuration issues on Cisco routers that can be potentially troublesome.
- Learn how to configure and troubleshoot dynamic routing protocols that run on frame relay networks.
- Apply Cisco router `show` and `debug` commands to resolve problems on frame relay networks.

Understanding the Basics

I will now place a practical focus on the frame relay configuration parameters. Many of the problems that occur with the initial rollout of a frame-relay network or the extension of an existing network center around a misunderstanding of these parameters and how they are configured on Cisco routers.

Different Encapsulation Types

Two different types of frame-relay encapsulations can be configured on Cisco routers:

- *Cisco*. This is the default and does not require configuration of the Cisco keyword. This type encapsulation can be used when connecting to a Cisco frame-relay switch.
- *IETF*. This sets the encapsulation type to comply with the frame-relay IETF standard described in RFCs 1294 and 1490. This type of encapsulation is used when connecting to another vendor's frame-relay network. The IETF keyword must be included in the configuration statement

```
interface serial0
encapsulation frame-relay ietf
```

The encapsulation type also can be specific in the DLCI mapping statement, for example:

```
interface serial0
encapsulation frame-relay
frame-relay map ip 150.11.10.2 16 broadcast ietf
frame-relay map ip 150.11.10.3 17 broadcast ietf
```

Different LMI Types

Frame relay local management interface (LMI) messages are exchanged between the DTE (router) and the DCE (frame-relay switch) as a form of protocol keepalive. The DTE sends LMI status inquiry messages to the DCE every 10 seconds by default, and the DCE responds with status replies. It is required by the LMI protocol that the keepalive interval be less on the router than on the switch to which it connects. The purpose of the status inquiry and status reply messages is to verify configuration consistency as well as link integrity between the router and the switch, along with the status of configured PVCs. The reporting of PVC status is an extension to the LMI protocol along with other optional extensions such as multicasting, global addressing, and flow control.

A number of LMI parameters such as polling interval and error thresholds are configurable, but it is usually unnecessary to alter these defaults.

Cisco routers support three different LMI types:

- ANSI T1.617 Annex D
- Cisco
- ITU-T Q.933 Annex A

The default LMI type is Cisco, which uses DLCI 1023; the other two LMI types use DLCI 0. It is essential that the LMI type match between the router and the switch. Up to Cisco IOS version 11.2, the LMI type was configured in interface mode, whereas in recent IOS versions the option of LMI autosensing is available.

LMI Autosensing As of Cisco IOS version 11.2, the router can automatically sense the LMI type that is being implemented on the switch. It does so by sending out status inquiries using each of the different LMI types. The fact that this operating system level enables the router to simultaneously listen on both DLCI 0 and DLCI 1023 allows the router to process whatever reply is received. These messages are sent in rapid succession, and when a reply is received from the switch, the router then places this LMI type in the configuration. A practical example of LMI autosensing is demonstrated in the troubleshooting scenarios later in this chapter.

DLCI Mapping

The purpose of the DLCI mapping statement is to map a destination next-hop address for a desktop protocol to a local DLCI. It is important to be clear about what this means, since I have seen the issue of DLCI mapping cause confusion. Remember that the DLCI in the nonextended form is purely of local significance between the DTE and DCE. It distinguishes each of the logical channels on the physical link to the frame-relay switch. The frame-relay switch then switches each of these channels based on its own configuration for each DLCI. The DLCI mapping statement in effect tells the router in order to get to this destination address, use this DLCI. Multiple protocols can have addresses mapped over the same DLCI. Listing 5-1 gives some examples.

In the first example, the router will attempt to access 192.168.250.1 using DLCI 201 and 192.168.250.3 using DLCI 203. Decnet is also running on the PVC that is defined by DLCI 201, and the other end of this PVC is Decnet node 25.1.

The second example states that to get to the Novell destination network layer address 100.0000.0c3f.1234, use DLCI 200.

You will have noticed that the broadcast keyword is included at the end of each of the sample mapping statements. Frame relay is a nonbroadcast medium; hence this keyword is necessary to enable broadcasts to be forwarded across the frame-relay network. Without this statement,

Listing 5-1

```
interface Serial0
 ip address 192.168.250.2 255.255.255.0
 decnet cost 10
 encapsulation frame-relay IETF
 frame-relay lmi-type ansi
 frame-relay map ip 192.168.250.1 201 broadcast
 frame-relay map ip 192.168.250.3 203 broadcast
 frame-relay map decnet 25.1 201 broadcast

interface serial0
 encapsulation frame-relay
 ipx network 100
 frame-relay map ipx 100.0000.0c3f.1234 200 broadcast
```

routing updates, IPX SAPs, and any other broadcast-based traffic will not propagate across frame relay.

NOTE: *Since frame relay is a nonbroadcast medium, the broadcast keyword must be included in the mapping statement to ensure the propagation of broadcast-based traffic.*

Apart from static mapping, the router can discover the destination protocol address that is related to a particular DLCI using Inverse ARP. This is enabled by default on Cisco router frame-relay interfaces.

The contents of the frame-relay map table can be inspected using the `show frame-relay map` commands. In the following example (Listing 5-2), there are two entries in the table. One is the result of a static mapping statement, whereas the other was learned dynamically using Inverse ARP. Notice that the entry that was learned dynamically includes the broadcast statement; hence broadcasts can be forwarded over this DLCI without any additional configuration.

In the output shown in Listing 5-3, which is based on the network shown in Figure 5-1, the two IP destination addresses have static DLCI

Listing 5-2

```
r2#sh frame map
Serial0 (up): ip 192.168.250.1 dlci 201(0xC9,0x3090), static,
              broadcast,
              IETF, status defined, active
Serial0 (up): ip 192.168.250.3 dlci 203(0xCB,0x30B0), dynamic,
              broadcast,
              IETF, status defined, active
r2#
```

```
r1#sh frame map
Serial1 (up): ip 172.16.33.2 dlci 102(0x66,0x1860), static,
              broadcast,
              CISCO, status defined, active
Serial1 (up): ip 172.16.33.3 dlci 103(0x6A,0x18A0), static,
              broadcast,
              CISCO, status defined, active
Serial1 (up): ipx 33.0000.3020.f8ed dlci 102(0x66,0x1860), dynamic,
              broadcast,, status defined, active
r1#

r1#

!
interface serial1
ip address 172.16.33.1 255.255.255.0
encapsulation frame-relay
ipx network 33
frame-relay lmi-type ansi
frame-relay map ip 172.16.33.2 102 broadcast
frame-relay map ip 172.16.33.3 103 broadcast
!
```

Listing 5-3

mapping statements. The IPX network layer address 33.0000.3020.f8ed is reachable via DLCI 102; the router learned this dynamically. It is convenient that cumbersome mapping statements are not required for a protocol such as Novell. In this case, the only Novell interface configuration necessary is to give the frame-relay cloud an IPX network number.

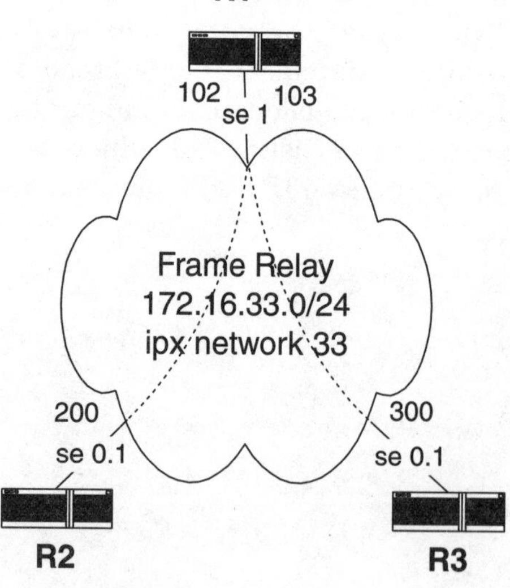

Figure 5-1 Frame-relay subinterfaces.

Subinterfaces in Frame Relay

Cisco routers have the ability to support subinterfaces in frame relay. A single physical interface that has a frame-relay encapsulation and LMI type configured can then be divided into multiple subinterfaces. Each subinterface must relate to a different network or subnet for routing purposes, just like physical router interfaces. A single or multiple PVCs can be run over a subinterface.

The same frame-relay network can support routers that use a mix of both subinterfaces along with main physical interfaces. This is demonstrated in Figure 5-2.

Point-to-Point versus Multipoint

Multiple PVCs can be defined for a main physical interface that is using frame relay. Such an interface is said to be a *point-to-multipoint interface*. With subinterfaces, there is an option to define the interface as point to point if only one PVC is being defined. If multiple PVCs are implemented on a subinterface, then that subinterface must be configured as point to multipoint. Listing 5-4 is a sample configuration for the Barcelona router relating to the network in Figure 5-2.

There are some points to note here:

- The frame-relay encapsulation and LMI type are configured on the main interface. Thus, in a fault scenario, the main interface can be checked to verify that LMI is being exchanged with the switch. This can be done independently of the PVCs that are defined on the subinterfaces.
- It is possible to mix point-to-point and multipoint subinterfaces on the same router and within the same frame-relay cloud.
- The two subinterfaces are on different IP subnets, as they must be. The point-to-point subinterface has a single PVC defined, whereas the point-to-multipoint subinterface happens to have two PVCs.
- The `frame-relay interface-dlci 501` command associates DLCI 501 with subinterface serial 0.1. This command automatically incorporates the `broadcast` keyword.
- On recent versions of Cisco IOS, an interface type (i.e., point to point or multipoint) must be specified when the subinterface is being

Figure 5-2
Frame relay with mixed topology of point-to-point and multipoint.

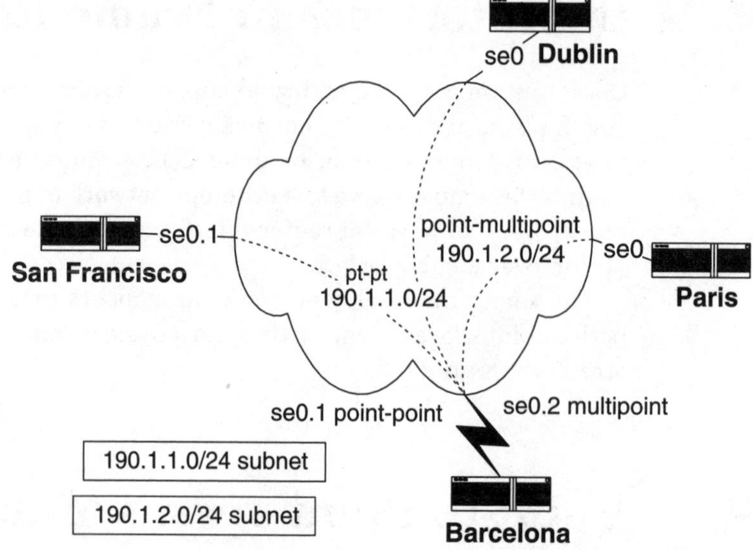

Listing 5-4

```
interface serial 0
encapsulation frame-relay
frame-relay lmi-type ansi

interface serial 0.1 point-to-point
ip address 190.1.1.1 255.255.255.0
frame-relay interface-dlci 501

interface serial 0.2 multipoint
ip address 190.1.2.1 255.255.255.0
frame-relay map ip 190.1.2.2 502 broadcast
frame-relay map ip 190.1.2.3 503 broadcast
```

defined. On earlier versions, pre-11.0, the subinterface defaulted to multipoint. This may create problems if it goes unnoticed, since multipoint interfaces rely on either static mapping or the use of Inverse ARP to resolve protocol addresses. A further issue was created by the fact that subinterfaces could not be deleted easily with these earlier versions of IOS. A router reload usually was required to fully delete subinterfaces that were configured incorrectly.

NOTE: *On older Cisco IOS versions, subinterfaces will default to multipoint unless otherwise specified. Also, a router reload may be required to fully delete subinterfaces.*

Routing over Frame Relay

I am now going to discuss some of the particular issues that are encountered when routing IP and other desktop protocols over frame relay. Frame relay offers configuration options such as the use of subinterfaces and the point-to-point versus the multipoint topology. These options enhance the flexibility of frame relay but also pose some configuration challenges for routing desktop protocols, particularly in light of the fact that frame relay is a nonbroadcast and multiaccess medium. Let us now look at these potential pitfalls.

Split Horizon

The principle of split horizon states that a router will not advertise routes that it learned over a particular interface back out that same interface. This is intended to help prevent routing loops in distance-vector routing protocols. Split horizon sometimes can cause problems in frame-relay networks that do not use subinterfaces. This is best demonstrated by an example. Refer again to the network shown in Figure 5-1, which has a main office router R1 that is not only responsible for providing access to the main office but also has to forward routing information between the various remote offices that need to communicate with each other. Router R1 uses one single main interface to access the frame-relay cloud; hence it will not forward routes that it learns from R2 to R3, and likewise, it will not forward routes learned from R3 on to R2. This is because split horizon prevents R1 from advertising routes out the same interface over which they were learned. If dynamic routing between the remote offices really is necessary, then there are a couple of options for solving the problem:

- Ensure that split horizon is disabled either by manually turning it off on the router interface or by using a routing protocol that has split horizon disabled by default on frame-relay interfaces.
- Use subinterfaces at the R1 router. This way the PVCs to R2 and R3 are seen as different logical interfaces; hence, split horizon does not apply.

Table 5-1 summarizes the default split horizon states when using each of the following routing protocols over frame relay.

TABLE 5-1
Default Split Horizon States

Routing Protocol	Default for Split Horizon on Frame Relay
RIP	Disabled
IGRP	Disabled
EIGRP for IP/IPX/Appletalk	Enabled
OSPF	Disabled
IPX RIP	Enabled and cannot be disabled
Appletalk RTMP	Enabled
Decnet	Enabled

Issues Created by the Nonbroadcast Medium

As already stated, frame relay is a nonbroadcast multiaccess medium. This means that by default broadcasts will not be forwarded across the frame-relay network. Thus routing updates that are broadcast-based or other services such as IPX SAPs will not be forwarded across frame relay by default.

This can be rectified using the broadcast keyword in the frame-relay mapping statement. Multicasts are treated the same as broadcasts in frame relay; hence this keyword is required to ensure that multicasts can propagate across the medium. Some protocols such as OSPF and EIGRP rely on multicasting to enable the formation of neighbors. We will study an example in the troubleshooting scenarios where the absence of the broadcast keyword disables an EIGRP relationship and hence breaks the routing.

The configuration of OSPF over frame relay is more complex. The specific issue of OSPF over frame relay, along with the overall challenges encountered when routing IP and other desktop protocols over frame relay, is examined in detail in the corresponding chapters of this book.

Frame Relay Show Commands

The `show interface` Command

The `show interface` command is useful for verifying that the frame-relay line protocol is up, LMI, queuing, and activity statistics and physical layer error statistics. The following output (Listing 5-5) tells us that

```
r3#sh in se3/3
Serial3/3 is up, line protocol is up
  Hardware is 4T/MC68360
  Internet address is 192.168.250.3/24
  MTU 1500 bytes, BW 1544 Kbit, DLY 20000 usec, rely 255/255, load 1/255
  Encapsulation FRAME-RELAY, loopback not set, keepalive set (10 sec)
  LMI enq sent  2, LMI stat recvd 2, LMI upd recvd 0, DTE LMI up
  LMI enq recvd 0, LMI stat sent  0, LMI upd sent  0
  LMI DLCI 0  LMI type is ANSI Annex D  frame relay DTE
  FR SVC disabled, LAPF state down
  Broadcast queue 0/64, broadcasts sent/dropped 0/0, interface broadcasts 0
  Last input 00:00:02, output 00:00:02, output hang never
  Last clearing of "show interface" counters 00:01:50
  Input queue: 0/75/0 (size/max/drops); Total output drops: 0
  Queueing strategy: weighted fair
  Output queue: 0/64/0 (size/threshold/drops)
     Conversations  0/1 (active/max active)
     Reserved Conversations 0/0 (allocated/max allocated)
  5 minute input rate 0 bits/sec, 0 packets/sec
  5 minute output rate 0 bits/sec, 0 packets/sec
     2 packets input, 28 bytes, 0 no buffer
     Received 0 broadcasts, 0 runts, 0 giants
     0 input errors, 0 CRC, 0 frame, 0 overrun, 0 ignored, 0 abort
     2 packets output, 28 bytes, 0 underruns
     0 output errors, 0 collisions, 0 interface resets
     0 output buffer failures, 0 output buffers swapped out
     8 carrier transitions     DCD=up  DSR=up  DTR=up  RTS=up  CTS=up
r3#
```

Listing 5-5

- The physical interface itself is up, indicating that it is detecting carrier.
- The frame-relay line protocol is up between the DTE and DCE. This does not confirm anything about the end-to-end state of any PVCs that are running over this interface.
- LMI is up between the router and the switch. The router is a frame-relay DTE that is exchanging LMI messages with the switch. Just two messages have been exchanged so far, indicating that the interface has just been brought up or reconfigured. The LMI type is ANSI, which uses DLCI 0 as shown.
- All queues are at their default values, and not surprisingly, no packets have as yet been queued or dropped. This includes broadcast queues and the interface input and output hold queues, which are employing weighted fair queuing.

- The familiar information provided by this command on the interface input and output rate along with physical layer error statistics is also included.

The following example (Listing 5-6) shows this command in the context of a subinterface. As you can see, the information is limited. By using `show interface serial 0`, more complete information could be obtained on the main interface and how it is talking to the switch.

The `show frame-relay lmi` command

To get more detailed information on the status and behavior of the LMI message exchange between the router and the switch, use the `show frame-relay lmi` command. The LMI type is displayed along with the configured frame-relay interface type. The most significant fields are highlighted. As you can see, the number of status inquiries sent tends to approximately equal the number of status messages received added to the number of timeouts. This is to be expected. The important issue is that in this example less than 1 status enquiry in 6000 timed out; all others were replied to (see Listing 5-7).

The `show frame-relay pvc` Command

The commands that have been discussed thus far give information on status of the DTE to DCE connection, along with more general information such as interface error statistics. The `show frame-relay pvc` command is used to obtain information that is specific to the PVCs that are configured on the router. The following sample output (Listing 5-8) relates to the network shown in Figure 5-1.

```
r2#sh in se 0.1
Serial0.1 is up, line protocol is up
  Hardware is MK5025
  Internet address is 192.168.250.2 255.255.255.0
  MTU 1500 bytes, BW 1544 Kbit, DLY 20000 usec, rely 255/255, load 1/255
  Encapsulation FRAME-RELAY
r2#
```

Listing 5-6

```
Router-1>sh fr lmi

LMI Statistics for interface Serial0 (Frame Relay DTE) LMI TYPE = ANSI
  Invalid Unnumbered info 0              Invalid Prot Disc 0
  Invalid dummy Call Ref 0               Invalid Msg Type 0
  Invalid Status Message 0               Invalid Lock Shift 0
  Invalid Information ID 0               Invalid Report IE Len 0
  Invalid Report Request 0               Invalid Keep IE Len 0
  Num Status Enq. Sent 60526             Num Status msgs Rcvd 60517
  Num Update Status Rcvd 0               Num Status Timeouts 10
Router-1>
```

Listing 5-7

The LOCAL use of the DLCI indicates that the interface is a frame-relay DTE rather than a switch. If the PVC is up and operational end to end, then an ACTIVE status will be displayed. An INACTIVE status for the PVC indicates that the DLCI is programmed at the switch; however, the PVC is not operational end to end. This could be due to a problem at the other end of the PVC. The status also can show as DELETED. In this case, either the DLCI has been deleted at the frame-relay switch or the

```
r1#sh fr pvc

PVC Statistics for interface Serial1 (Frame Relay DTE)

DLCI = 102, DLCI USAGE = LOCAL, PVC STATUS = ACTIVE, INTERFACE = Serial1

  input pkts 202632        output pkts 26264        in bytes 8490868
  out bytes 1863293        dropped pkts 0           in FECN pkts 0
  in BECN pkts 0           out FECN pkts 0          out BECN pkts 0
  in DE pkts 0             out DE pkts 0
  pvc create time 2d22  last time pvc status changed 2d22

DLCI = 103, DLCI USAGE = LOCAL, PVC STATUS = ACTIVE, INTERFACE = Serial1

  input pkts 59220         output pkts 30747        in bytes 4911382
  out bytes 2000793        dropped pkts 2           in FECN pkts 0
  in BECN pkts 0           out FECN pkts 0          out BECN pkts 0
  in DE pkts 0             out DE pkts 0
  pvc create time 2d22  last time pvc status changed 1d00
r1#
```

Listing 5-8

DLCI has been configured on the router before it was programmed on the switch.

PVC utilization information is also provided along with a counter for dropped packets. Congestion problems can be observed from the BECN, FECN, and discard eligible (DE) counters.

The time since the PVC was configured on the router, along with the last time it changed state, is also displayed.

There is a need for caution when using this command. Sometimes there is a time lag before the router detects the PVC as being down at the far end. In this case, the status will remain ACTIVE. If in doubt, you should ping across the PVC to verify network layer connectivity. Another problem is that PVCs sometimes can stay in the router's memory even after being deleted from the configuration. This can happen with older versions of Cisco IOS. It sometimes occurs if the PVCs have yet to be deleted at the switch and are being included in LMI status messages. My main point here is that while `show frame-relay pvc` is an extremely useful tool, its output should be treated with caution, particularly in instances where a lot of reconfiguration has taken place. This is similar to the issue that can be encountered when deleting subinterfaces and may require a router reload.

The `show frame-relay map` Command

The frame-relay map table is interrogated using the `show frame-relay map` command. The example shown here (Listing 5-9) again refers to the network in Figure 5-1.

```
r1#sh frame map
Serial1 (up): ip 172.16.33.2 dlci 102(0x66,0x1860), static,
              broadcast,
              CISCO, status defined, active
Serial1 (up): ip 172.16.33.3 dlci 103(0x6A,0x18A0), static,
              broadcast,
              CISCO, status defined, active
Serial1 (up): ipx 33.0000.3020.f8ed dlci 102(0x66,0x1860), dynamic,
              broadcast,, status defined, active
r1#
```

Listing 5-9

This table will show entries for any desktop protocol that is using frame-relay mapping. Entries that have been defined statically are shown along with entries that were learned using Inverse ARP. This command can be useful for verifying that PVC map statements have been configured correctly on the router and also if there are any problems with Inverse ARP. If no mapping statements were configured on the router, the frame-relay next-hop address should still show up in the output of `show frame-relay map` as a `dynamic` entry courtesy of Inverse ARP.

The most relevant fields have been highlighted in this sample, which include IP and IPX entries. This command confirms the frame-relay encapsulation type and also states whether broadcasts can be forwarded in the current configuration. Note that it is also stated whether the entry was statically configured or dynamically learned via Inverse ARP.

Frame-Relay Debug Commands

The `debug frame-relay lmi` Command

The show commands that have already been discussed often can be sufficient to indicate whether or not there is a problem with LMI. However, if further information is required to determine why LMI is down, the `debug frame-relay lmi` command can be used. This command does not produce a large amount of output and so can be used without adding significantly to the router's processor load. The output in Listing 5-10 is for a correctly operating LMI exchange between the router and the switch.

The following debug output (Listing 5-11) is from a router whose LMI type does not match that of the switch. Note that it shows DTE down, and although status inquiry messages are being sent (as evidenced by the incrementing `myseq` numbers), the switch does not reply (`yourseen =0`).

In the next example, the router was mistakenly configured as a DCE interface type. Since the router is a DCE, it is not sending LMI status inquiry messages, and the keepalive timer just keeps on expiring (see Listing 5-12).

The `debug frame-relay events` Command

The `debug frame-relay events` command provides an output of Inverse ARP traffic on the frame-relay network. PVC status changes are

Listing 5-10

```
r1#deb frame lmi
Frame Relay LMI debugging is on
r1#term mon
r1#
Serial1(out): StEnq, myseq 67, yourseen 66, DTE up
 datagramstart = 0x60008CC, datagramsize = 14
 FR encap = 0x00010308
00 75 95 01 01 01 03 02 43 42

Serial1(in): Status, myseq 67
RT IE 1, length 1, type 1
KA IE 3, length 2, yourseq 67, myseq 67
Serial1(out): StEnq, myseq 68, yourseen 67, DTE up
 datagramstart = 0x600079C, datagramsize = 14
 FR encap = 0x00010308
00 75 95 01 01 01 03 02 44 43

Serial1(in): Status, myseq 68
RT IE 1, length 1, type 1
KA IE 3, length 2, yourseq 68, myseq 68
Serial1(out): StEnq, myseq 69, yourseen 68, DTE up
 datagramstart = 0x60008CC, datagramsize = 14
 FR encap = 0x00010308
00 75 95 01 01 01 03 02 45 44

r1#undeb all
All possible debugging has been turned off
r1#
```

Listing 5-11

```
r1#debug frame lmi
Frame Relay LMI debugging is on
r1#term m
Serial0(out): StEnq, myseq 4, yourseen 0, DTE down
 datagramstart = 0x60001AC, datagramsize = 13
 FR encap = 0xFCF10309
00 75 01 01 00 03 02 04 00

Serial0(out): StEnq, myseq 5, yourseen 0, DTE down
 datagramstart = 0x600040C, datagramsize = 13
 FR encap = 0xFCF10309
00 75 01 01 00 03 02 05 00

Serial0(out): StEnq, myseq 6, yourseen 0, DTE down
 datagramstart = 0x600040C, datagramsize = 13
 FR encap = 0xFCF10309
00 75 01 01 00 03 02 06 00
```

Listing 5-12

```
r1#debug frame lmi

Serial3(down): DCE LMI timeout
Serial3(down): DCE LMI timeout
Serial3(down): DCE LMI timeout
Serial3(down): DCE LMI timeout
```

also reported in this output. This command can be useful in troubleshooting end-to-end problems on a PVC. The output from this command is not extensive and can be used without the possibility of overloading the router's processor.

In the following output (Listing 5-13), the DLCI is changing state because Inverse ARP was disabled on a multipoint interface. The DLCI became active again when it was enabled on a point-to-point interface. No additional output is generated because point-to-point interfaces do not require Inverse ARP, since there is only one possible end point to be resolved.

```
r1>sh log
Syslog logging: enabled (0 messages dropped, 0 flushes, 0 overruns)
    Console logging: level debugging, 176 messages logged
    Monitor logging: level debugging, 5 messages logged
    Trap logging: level informational, 115 message lines logged

%SYS-5-CONFIG_I: Configured from console by vty0 (192.168.250.2)
%FR-5-DLCICHANGE: Interface Serial0 - DLCI 102 state changed to INACTIVE
%FR-5-DLCICHANGE: Interface Serial0 - DLCI 102 state changed to ACTIVE
%FR-5-DLCICHANGE: Interface Serial0 - DLCI 102 state changed to INACTIVE
%FR-5-DLCICHANGE: Interface Serial0 - DLCI 102 state changed to ACTIVE
%FR-5-DLCICHANGE: Interface Serial0 - DLCI 102 state changed to INACTIVE
%FR-5-DLCICHANGE: Interface Serial0 - DLCI 102 state changed to ACTIVE
%FR-5-DLCICHANGE: Interface Serial0 - DLCI 102 state changed to INACTIVE
%FR-5-DLCICHANGE: Interface Serial0 - DLCI 102 state changed to ACTIVE
r1> sh debug
Frame Relay:
  Frame Relay events debugging is on
r1>
```

Listing 5-13

The output showing Inverse ARP replies for DLCI 102 and DLCI 103 is as follows:

```
Serial0(i): reply rcvd 192.168.250.2 102 Serial0(i): reply rcvd
192.168.250.3 103
```

The `debug frame-relay packet` Command

This command provides output for all frame-relay-encapsulated packets that are sent or received by the router. A facility exists to only apply this command to a particular interface or DLCI. This is usually a good idea, since this tool does generate a lot of output. In fact, according to Cisco recommendations, the `debug frame-relay` and `debug frame-relay packet` commands should not be applied unless the frame-relay traffic is below 25 packets per second. The following sample (Listing 5-14) is for a router that runs IP and DEC's LAT protocol over the frame-relay network.

Congestion Control and Traffic Shaping

This section discusses frame-relay bandwidth management and congestion control. This is important because there are a number of configurable features that can be implemented at the router to alleviate problems created by network congestion.

One of the key benefits of frame relay is that it affords the customer additional control over the type of bandwidth profile that it purchases from the telecommunications carrier. A *committed information rate* (CIR) is purchased that can be significantly less than the physical bandwidth of the public circuit. The carrier is guaranteeing transport at speeds up to this CIR value. A second bandwidth parameter known as the *enhanced information rate* (EIR) designates the maximum bandwidth that potentially could be available for a PVC. The frame-relay service provider does not guarantee the transport of traffic at speeds up to the EIR. When the bandwidth utilization exceeds the CIR, traffic is then marked Discard Eligible by the frame-relay switch. Setting the DE bit in the frame does this. If congestion is experienced in the frame-relay network, frames that are marked DE may be dropped. There is also a facility to set the DE bit at the Cisco router for types of traffic that are predefined in a Discard Eligible list.

```
r2#deb frame packet
Frame Relay packet debugging is on
r2#term mon
r2#
Serial1.1(o): dlci 200(0x3081), pkt type 0x800(IP), datagramsize 45
Serial1.1: broadcast search
Serial1.1(o): dlci 200(0x3081), pkt type 0x8038(DEC_SPANNING), datagramsize 31
Serial1(i): dlci 200(0x3081), pkt type 0x800, datagramsize 46
Serial1.1(o): dlci 200(0x3081), pkt type 0x800(IP), datagramsize 46
Serial1.1(o): dlci 200(0x3081), pkt type 0x800(IP), datagramsize 47
Serial1(i): dlci 200(0x3081), pkt type 0x800, datagramsize 44
Serial1.1: broadcast search
Serial1.1(o): dlci 200(0x3081), pkt type 0x8038(DEC_SPANNING), datagramsize 31
Serial1.1(o): dlci 200(0x3081), pkt type 0x800(IP), datagramsize 486
Serial1(i): dlci 200(0x3081), pkt type 0x800, datagramsize 44
Serial1.1: broadcast search
Serial1.1(o): dlci 200(0x3081), pkt type 0x8038(DEC_SPANNING), datagramsize 31
Serial1.1(o): dlci 200(0x3081), pkt type 0x800(IP), datagramsize 395
Serial1(i): dlci 200(0x3081), pkt type 0x800, datagramsize 44
```

Listing 5-14

The EIR is also sometimes termed the *maximum burst rate*. Obviously, the burst rate can have a maximum value of the physical line speed. A customer may decide that this bandwidth will not be required and therefore purchase a burst rate value that is lower than the actual line speed. This then sets the maximum available bandwidth on this PVC.

Different PVCs may have different CIR and burst rate values as required to fit the bandwidth utilization profile on a given network. For example, one PVC may be used to provide backup for a primary PVC.

The congestion messages in frame relay take the form of Backward Explicit Congestion Notifications (BECNs) or Forward Explicit Congestion Notifications (FECNs). These messages, along with a counter for packets marked Discard Eligible, can be displayed using the `show frame-relay pvc` command. BECN messages that are sent by the frame-relay network back to the source on detection of congestion are useful when the source controls the information rate, as is usual. FECN messages can be used if the destination controls the rate at which information is exchanged across the PVC. Until recently, the usefulness of FECN and BECN messages has been limited because not all higher-layer protocols are capable of processing this type of congestion notification. With Cisco IOS version 11.2, the frame-relay traffic-shaping feature automatically incorporates BECN feedback.

Frame-relay traffic shaping can provide the following facilities on a per-virtual-circuit basis:

- Rate enforcement at the router interface. The average and peak information rates can be configured.
- Automatic throttling back on the receipt of a BECN from the frame-relay network. This feature is enabled by default once traffic shaping is turned on at the router.
- The ability to apply configurable custom and priority queues that will help determine the traffic profile and prioritization between the different protocols in the events of congestion.

The following sample configuration (Listing 5-15) shows the traffic-shaping feature enabled on the main interface, with BECN feedback enabled by default. Two different frame-relay map classes are applied to the subinterfaces.

The first map class is labeled "primary" and sets a CIR of 112 kB and an EIR of 224 kB to the PVC defined by DLCI 301. This map class also contains a priority list that gives high priority to a particular application that uses UDP port 7900. The map class "secondary" sets a CIR of 16 kB and an EIR of 112 kB on subinterface serial 3/3.2. This class also gives priority to DLSW traffic by using custom queuing.

It is evident that traffic shaping provides a potentially powerful tool where the subscriber can have increased control over the type of traffic profile that occurs across the frame-relay network. For this feature to be effective, careful analysis must be done on the traffic that is accessing the frame-relay network. This should include auditing the type of traffic, its source and destination, its volume, and what percentage of packets is being dropped. The tools that we have used so far are helpful in performing this assessment because they also provide information on BECNs and packets that are marked Discard Eligible. In some instances it may be desirable or necessary to probe deeper using a network analyzer that supports frame relay.

Discard Eligible Lists

Prior to the advent of traffic shaping, Cisco routers provided a number of other configurable features that could help resolve frame-relay congestion problems. The first of these features is the ability to configure Discard Eligible lists. During heavy traffic periods when the CIR has been exceeded, switches in the frame-relay network will mark packets

Listing 5-15

```
interface Serial3/3
 no ip address
 encapsulation frame-relay
 frame-relay traffic-shaping
 frame-relay lmi-type ansi
!
interface Serial3/3.1 point-to-point
 ip address 192.168.250.3 255.255.255.0
 frame-relay class primary
 frame-relay interface-dlci 301
!
interface Serial3/3.2 point-to-point
 ip address 192.168.240.3 255.255.255.0
 frame-relay class secondary
 frame-relay interface-dlci 302
!
router eigrp 1
 network 192.168.250.0
 network 192.168.33.0
!
no ip classless
!
map-class frame-relay primary
 frame-relay traffic-rate 112000 224000
 frame-relay priority-group 1
!
map-class frame-relay secondary
 frame-relay traffic-rate 16000 112000
 frame-relay custom-queue-list 2
queue-list 2 protocol dlsw 1
queue-list 2 default 2
queue-list 2 queue 1 byte-count 4500
queue-list 2 queue 2 byte-count 4500
priority-list 1 protocol ip high udp 7900
priority-list 1 default medium
!
!
!
line con 0
line aux 0
line vty 0 4
 password cisco
 login
!
end

r3#
```

Discard Eligible by setting the DE bit. Traffic marked DE will be the first to be dropped if the frame-relay network cannot transport all traffic up to the burst rate. The ability to configure DE lists gives the subscriber more control over what type of packets should be dropped during heavy traffic conditions.

In the following example (Listing 5-16), DE-group 1, which in turn relates to DE-list 1, has been applied to DLCI 201. This DE list states that all IPX packets along with IP packets that are greater than 1000 bytes going over DLCI 201 will be marked DE by the router. No DE list has been applied to DLCI 203. This may be desirable in a scenario where interactive IP traffic takes precedence over batch IP and Novell traffic.

Listing 5-16

```
r2#wr t
Building configuration...

Current configuration:
!
version 11.0
service udp-small-servers
service tcp-small-servers
!
hostname r2
!
enable password cisco
!
ipx routing 0000.3020.f8ed
frame-relay de-list 1 protocol ip gt 1000
frame-relay de-list 1 protocol ipx
!
interface Loopback0
 ip address 192.168.222.2 255.255.255.0
 ipx network 2
!
interface Serial0
 no ip address
 encapsulation frame-relay
 no fair-queue
 frame-relay lmi-type ansi
!
interface Serial0.1 multipoint
 no ip address
 no frame-relay inverse-arp
!
interface Serial0.2 point-to-point
 ip address 192.168.250.2 255.255.255.0
 ipx network 911
 frame-relay de-group 1 201
 frame-relay interface-dlci 201
!
interface Serial0.3 point-to-point
 ip address 192.168.240.2 255.255.255.0
 ipx network 991
 frame-relay interface-dlci 203
!
```

The operation of the DE list can be verified as follows. Using the `show frame-relay pvc` command, it is noted that DLCI 201 has just one outbound DE on its counters. An extended ping with a datagram size of 2000 bytes is then sent over this DLCI. It can then be observed that the DE counter has incremented to six, as expected. Notice also that only the outbound DE counter incremented. (See Listing 5-17.)

Broadcast Queuing

If excessive broadcasts in the form of, say, routing updates, Novell SAPs, or Appletalk traffic are using a large portion of frame-relay bandwidth, then the broadcast queuing feature could be used to help curb the problem. A separate configurable queue for broadcasts is implemented by default on frame-relay interfaces. This can be particularly useful at a hub site where broadcasts need to be replicated on several different DLCIs to the remote sites. The broadcast queue, along with information on the level of broadcasts being sent, can be studied using the `show interface serial` command. The idea behind a broadcast queue is to limit the amount of frame-relay bandwidth that broadcasting consumes. The broadcast queue has priority at transmission rates below the configured maximum for the queue, thus guaranteeing an allocation of bandwidth for broadcast traffic.

The following broadcast queue parameters are configurable:

- Queue size for broadcasts. The default is 64 packets.
- Byte rate per second for the transmission of broadcasts.
- Maximum broadcast packet rate per second.

In the following example (Listing 5-18), the frame-relay broadcast queue has been tuned to a size of 32 packets. The maximum allowed rate for broadcast transmission is 13 kBps, or 20 packets per second. Up to this rate, broadcast packets have priority on this interface. The statistics for the broadcast queue and broadcast transmission can be checked using the `show interface` command. The broadcast queue is usually tuned using a combination of traffic and packet analysis along with a little bit of trial and error. One starting point is to set the broadcast byte rate to be less than a certain percentage of both the local access speed and the total of the remote access speeds. The queue ideally should be capable of containing a least one full routing update from each protocol configured to avoid the loss of routing information.

```
r2#sh frame pvc

PVC Statistics for interface Serial0 (Frame Relay DTE)

DLCI = 201, DLCI USAGE = LOCAL, PVC STATUS = ACTIVE, INTERFACE = Serial0.2

  input pkts 28347          output pkts 103250        in bytes 1522054
  out bytes 7012523         dropped pkts 0            in FECN pkts 0
  in BECN pkts 0            out FECN pkts 0           out BECN pkts 0
  in DE pkts 0              out DE pkts 1
  pvc create time 2d02  last time pvc status changed 2d02

DLCI = 203, DLCI USAGE = LOCAL, PVC STATUS = ACTIVE, INTERFACE = Serial0.3

  input pkts 344            output pkts 408           in bytes 35569
  out bytes 31804           dropped pkts 0            in FECN pkts 0
  in BECN pkts 0            out FECN pkts 0           out BECN pkts 0
  in DE pkts 0              out DE pkts 0
  pvc create time 2d02  last time pvc status changed 2d02
r2#ping
Protocol [ip]:
Target IP address: 192.168.250.1
Repeat count [5]:
Datagram size [100]: 2000
Timeout in seconds [2]:
Extended commands [n]:
Sweep range of sizes [n]:
Type escape sequence to abort.
Sending 5, 2000-byte ICMP Echos to 192.168.250.1, timeout is 2 seconds:
!!!!!
Success rate is 100 percent (5/5), round-trip min/avg/max = 1024/1028/1048 ms
r2#sh frame pvc

PVC Statistics for interface Serial0 (Frame Relay DTE)

DLCI = 201, DLCI USAGE = LOCAL, PVC STATUS = ACTIVE, INTERFACE = Serial0.2

  input pkts 28427          output pkts 103325        in bytes 1535352
  out bytes 7027285         dropped pkts 0            in FECN pkts 0
  in BECN pkts 0            out FECN pkts 0           out BECN pkts 0
  in DE pkts 0              out DE pkts 6
  pvc create time 2d02  last time pvc status changed 2d02

DLCI = 203, DLCI USAGE = LOCAL, PVC STATUS = ACTIVE, INTERFACE = Serial0.3

  input pkts 345            output pkts 410           in bytes 35873
  out bytes 32152           dropped pkts 0            in FECN pkts 0
  in BECN pkts 0            out FECN pkts 0           out BECN pkts 0
  in DE pkts 0              out DE pkts 0
  pvc create time 2d02  last time pvc status changed 2d02
r2#
```

Listing 5-17

```
interface Serial0
 ip address 192.168.250.1 255.255.255.0
 encapsulation frame-relay
 no ip split-horizon eigrp 1
 no fair-queue
 frame-relay broadcast-queue 32 13000 20
 frame-relay lmi-type ansi
 frame-relay map ip 192.168.250.2 102 broadcast
 frame-relay map ip 192.168.250.3 103 broadcast
!

r1#sh in se0
Serial0 is up, line protocol is up
  Hardware is MK5025
  Internet address is 192.168.250.1 255.255.255.0
  MTU 1500 bytes, BW 1544 Kbit, DLY 20000 usec, rely 255/255, load 1/255
  Encapsulation FRAME-RELAY, loopback not set, keepalive set (10 sec)
  LMI enq sent  60117, LMI stat recvd 59770, LMI upd recvd 0, DTE LMI up
  LMI enq recvd 0, LMI stat sent  0, LMI upd sent  0
  LMI DLCI 0  LMI type is ANSI Annex D  frame relay DTE
  Broadcast queue 0/32, broadcasts sent/dropped 31849/0, interface broadcasts 31883
  Last input 0:00:00, output 0:00:00, output hang never
  Last clearing of "show interface" counters 6d23
  Output queue 0/40, 0 drops; input queue 0/75, 0 drops
  5 minute input rate 3000 bits/sec, 3 packets/sec
  5 minute output rate 3000 bits/sec, 3 packets/sec
     457307 packets input, 30404175 bytes, 0 no buffer
     Received 0 broadcasts, 0 runts, 0 giants
     79 input errors, 79 CRC, 0 frame, 0 overrun, 0 ignored, 0 abort
     134126 packets output, 4891616 bytes, 0 underruns
     0 output errors, 0 collisions, 119 interface resets, 0 restarts
     0 output buffer failures, 0 output buffers swapped out
     358 carrier transitions
r1#
```

Listing 5-18

DLCI Prioritization

DLCI prioritization can be used to help accommodate the mixing of different traffic types on the same DLCI, biasing a particular DLCI toward a certain traffic type or helping facilitate certain remote sites that have lower access speeds than others. In the following example (Listing 5-19), DLCI 103 uses the high-priority queue (which is the first queue); this is reserved for batch IP traffic with packet sizes greater than 700 bytes. DLCI 102 uses the low-priority queue, the last queue, for interactive IP traffic of less than 200 bytes. All other traffic uses the normal or third queue.

```
!
interface Serial0
 ip address 192.168.250.1 255.255.255.0
 encapsulation frame-relay
 no ip split-horizon eigrp 1
 no fair-queue
 frame-relay broadcast-queue 32 3000 20
 frame-relay priority-dlci-group 1 103 102 102 102
 frame-relay lmi-type ansi
 frame-relay map ip 192.168.250.2 102 broadcast
 frame-relay map ip 192.168.250.3 103 broadcast
!
priority-list 1 protocol ip high gt 700
priority-list 1 protocol ip low lt 200
priority-list 1 default normal

r1#sh frame map
Serial0 (up): ip 192.168.250.2 dlci 102(0x66,0x1860), static,
              broadcast,
              CISCO, status defined, active
Serial0 (up): ip 192.168.250.3 dlci 103(0x67,0x1870), static,
              broadcast,
              CISCO, status defined, active
  Priority DLCI Group 1, DLCI 103 (HIGH), DLCI 102 (MEDIUM)
  DLCI 102 (NORMAL), DLCI 102 (LOW)
```

Listing 5-19

The configuration of the DLCI priority group also can be verified using the `show frame-relay map` command. It is important to have a good understanding of the type and nature of the desktop protocol traffic running over frame relay before attempting to resolve problems using DLCI prioritization.

Frame-Relay Troubleshooting Scenarios

Scenario 1: Parameter Mismatches

Consider the network shown in Figure 5-3. Full configurations for R1, R2, and the frame-relay switch are displayed, along with the relevant portions of R3's configuration. A Cisco 4000 router has been configured as a frame-relay switch. IP connectivity is not available across the three PVCs shown, so let's do some troubleshooting. (See Listing 5-20.)

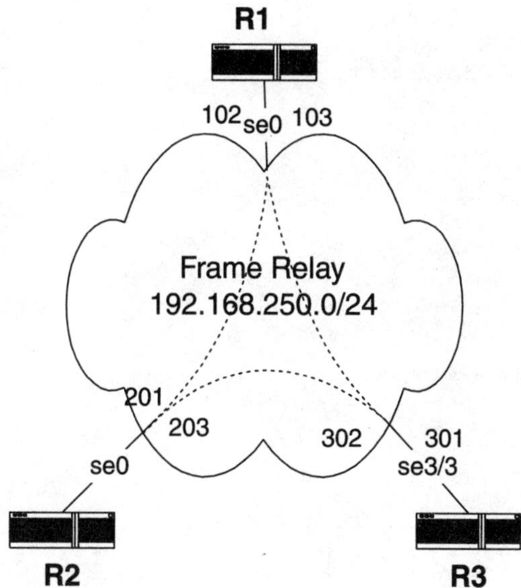

Figure 5-3
Frame-relay troubleshooting scenario 1.

We will begin our troubleshooting at R3, where pings are failing to both R1 and R2. The PVCs are shown as ACTIVE and have not changed state for over 20 minutes, as evidenced by the `show frame pvc` command. (See Listing 5-21.)

The fact that IP is failing on both PVCs could suggest a local problem, such as the DLCI mapping statements for IP. Before checking the configuration, it is always a good idea to check the interface and the LMI (see Listing 5-22).

It can be observed clearly that LMI packets are not being exchanged between the DTE and DCE. The LMI status inquiry packets that the router sends are timing out. The interface counters are cleared and then observed in order to confirm that LMI is not being exchanged across the interface. I am really doing this for emphasis and would not consider this to be a necessary step in practice.

So why is the LMI down? The answer is that the interface is configured as a frame-relay DCE; it should be a DTE in order to communicate with the switch port, which is DCE. (See Listing 5-23.)

The default frame-relay interface type is DTE, so this could be resolved by simply removing the DCE definition rather than having to explicitly configure a DTE interface type (see Listing 5-24).

The line protocol comes up after the interface is changed to DTE. LMI is now up, and the router is sending status inquiries and receiving status

Listing 5-20

```
FR-Switch#sh run
Building configuration...

Current configuration:
!
version 11.0
service udp-small-servers
service tcp-small-servers
!
hostname FR-Switch
!
enable password cisco
!
frame-relay switching
!
interface Serial0
 no ip address
 encapsulation frame-relay
 clockrate 56000
 frame-relay lmi-type ansi
 frame-relay intf-type dce
 frame-relay route 201 interface Serial1 102
 frame-relay route 203 interface Serial3 302
!
interface Serial1
 no ip address
 encapsulation frame-relay
 clockrate 56000
 frame-relay lmi-type ansi
 frame-relay intf-type dce
 frame-relay route 102 interface Serial0 201
 frame-relay route 103 interface Serial3 301
!
interface Serial2
 no ip address
 shutdown
!
interface Serial3
 no ip address
 encapsulation frame-relay
 clockrate 56000
 frame-relay lmi-type ansi
 frame-relay intf-type dce
 frame-relay route 301 interface Serial1 103
 frame-relay route 302 interface Serial0 203
!
interface TokenRing0
 no ip address
 shutdown
!
interface TokenRing1
 no ip address
 shutdown
!
logging buffered
!
```

Listing 5-20 (*Cont.*)

```
!
line con 0
line aux 0
 transport input all
line vty 0 4
 password cisco
 login
!
end

FR-Switch#

r2#sh run
Building configuration...

Current configuration:
!
version 11.0
service udp-small-servers
service tcp-small-servers
!
hostname r2
!
enable password cisco
!
!
interface Serial0
 ip address 192.168.250.2 255.255.255.0
 encapsulation frame-relay IETF
 no fair-queue
 frame-relay lmi-type ansi
 frame-relay map ip 192.168.250.1 201 broadcast
 frame-relay map ip 192.168.250.3 203 broadcast
!
interface Serial1
 no ip address
 shutdown
!
interface TokenRing0
 ip address 130.11.65.2 255.255.255.0
 ring-speed 16
!
interface TokenRing1
 no ip address
 shutdown
!
!
!
line con 0
line aux 0
 transport input all
line vty 0 4
 password cisco
 login
!
end
```

Listing 5-20 (*Cont.*)

```
r2#

r1#sh run
Building configuration...

Current configuration:
!
version 11.0
service udp-small-servers
service tcp-small-servers
!
hostname r1
!
enable password cisco
!
!
interface Serial0
 ip address 192.168.250.1 255.255.255.0
 encapsulation frame-relay
 no fair-queue
 frame-relay map ip 192.168.250.2 103 broadcast
 frame-relay map ip 192.168.250.3 102 broadcast
!
interface Serial1
 no ip address
 shutdown
!
interface TokenRing0
 ip address 130.11.65.1 255.255.255.0
 ring-speed 16
!
interface TokenRing1
 no ip address
 shutdown
!
!
!
line con 0
line aux 0
 transport input all
line vty 0 4
 password cisco
 login
!
end

r1#

r3#sh run
Building configuration...

Current configuration:
!
version 11.2
!
```

Listing 5-20 (*Cont.*)

```
hostname r3
!
enable password cisco
!
frame-relay switching
!
interface TokenRing1/0
 ip address 205.223.51.3 255.255.255.0
 bandwidth 100000
 appletalk cable-range 51-51 51.3
 appletalk zone token3
 ring-speed 16
!

interface Serial3/3
 ip address 192.168.250.3 255.255.255.0
 encapsulation frame-relay
 frame-relay map ip 192.168.250.1 301 broadcast
 frame-relay map ip 192.168.250.2 302 broadcast
 frame-relay lmi-type ansi
 frame-relay intf-type dce
!
no ip classless
!
!
line con 0
line aux 0
line vty 0 4
 password cisco
 login
!
end

r3#
```

messages from the switch. This is verified by both the `show interface` and `show frame-relay lmi` commands (see Listing 5-25).

One side issue to note before moving on is that the interface type on R3 could not have been configured to be DCE if the frame-relay switching command was not also configured. NNI (network-to-network interface) capability is not enabled by default. Perhaps someone once used this router as a frame-relay switch and did not fully remove the configuration?

While this problem was on, I had `debug frame-relay lmi` and `debug frame-relay packet` writing to log. At the start of the output, the LMI status inquiries are seen timing out; then, after the configuration change, DTE comes up followed by line protocol. Normal LMI messages then continue to be exchanged between the router and the switch. (See Listing 5-26.)

```
r3#ping 192.168.250.1

Type escape sequence to abort.
Sending 5, 100-byte ICMP Echos to 192.168.250.1, timeout is 2 seconds:
.....
Success rate is 0 percent (0/5)
r3#
r3#ping 192.168.250.2

Type escape sequence to abort.
Sending 5, 100-byte ICMP Echos to 192.168.250.2, timeout is 2 seconds:
.....
Success rate is 0 percent (0/5)
r3#sh fram pvc

PVC Statistics for interface Serial3/3 (Frame Relay DCE)

DLCI = 301, DLCI USAGE = LOCAL, PVC STATUS = ACTIVE, INTERFACE = Serial3/3

  input pkts 0            output pkts 0             in bytes 0
  out bytes 0             dropped pkts 0            in FECN pkts 0
  in BECN pkts 0          out FECN pkts 0           out BECN pkts 0
  in DE pkts 0            out DE pkts 0
  pvc create time 01:00:39, last time pvc status changed 00:23:48

DLCI = 302, DLCI USAGE = LOCAL, PVC STATUS = ACTIVE, INTERFACE = Serial3/3

  input pkts 404          output pkts 308           in bytes 18467
  out bytes 27478         dropped pkts 0            in FECN pkts 0
  in BECN pkts 0          out FECN pkts 0           out BECN pkts 0
  in DE pkts 0            out DE pkts 0
  pvc create time 01:00:26, last time pvc status changed 00:27:50
```

Listing 5-21

I have also highlighted something interesting and educational in the debug output. Cisco Discovery Protocol (CDP) broadcasts (or, more accurately, multicasts) are attempting to propagate across the interface after line protocol comes up. The “encaps failed” message indicates that CDP will not work because of a problem at a lower layer, in other words, what CDP is encapsulated in. This message could be occurring simply because CDP is disabled by default on frame-relay interfaces, or it could indicate a problem with the PVCs. As an important side note, the “encaps failed” message is often very useful in troubleshooting because it always indicates a problem at a lower layer.

```
r3#sh fram lmi

LMI Statistics for interface Serial3/3 (Frame Relay DCE) LMI TYPE = ANSI
  Invalid Unnumbered info 0              Invalid Prot Disc 0
  Invalid dummy Call Ref 0               Invalid Msg Type 0
  Invalid Status Message 0               Invalid Lock Shift 0
  Invalid Information ID 0               Invalid Report IE Len 0
  Invalid Report Request 0               Invalid Keep IE Len 0
  Num Status Enq. Rcvd 0                 Num Status msgs Sent 0
  Num Update Status Sent 0               Num St Enq. Timeouts 97

r3#sh in se3/3
Serial3/3 is up, line protocol is down
  Hardware is 4T/MC68360
  Internet address is 192.168.250.3/24
  MTU 1500 bytes, BW 1544 Kbit, DLY 20000 usec, rely 254/255, load 1/255
  Encapsulation FRAME-RELAY, loopback not set, keepalive set (10 sec)
  LMI enq sent  109, LMI stat recvd 109, LMI upd recvd 0
  LMI enq recvd 0, LMI stat sent  0, LMI upd sent  0, DCE LMI down
  LMI DLCI 0  LMI type is ANSI Annex D  frame relay DCE
  FR SVC disabled, LAPF state down
  Broadcast queue 0/64, broadcasts sent/dropped 0/0, interface broadcasts 0
  Last input 00:23:51, output 00:24:04, output hang never
  Last clearing of "show interface" counters 00:42:34
  Input queue: 0/75/0 (size/max/drops); Total output drops: 0
  Queueing strategy: weighted fair
  Output queue: 0/64/0 (size/threshold/drops)
     Conversations  0/1 (active/max active)
     Reserved Conversations 0/0 (allocated/max allocated)
  5 minute input rate 0 bits/sec, 0 packets/sec
  5 minute output rate 0 bits/sec, 0 packets/sec

r3#
```

Listing 5-22

NOTE: *An "encaps failed" message in a debug output indicates that the protocol in question detects a problem at a lower layer.*

It is now observed that DLCI 301 has changed state to INACTIVE (see Listing 5-21). Thus there was a problem with this particular PVC that was being masked by the fact that the line protocol was down. The DLCI was "frozen" in an ACTIVE state, and if you look back at the original `show frame-relay pvc`, it can be seen that the counters showed no traffic on this DLCI.

The mapping statements are correct for the two PVCs, and pings are successful to R2. This is worth verifying, although an incorrect mapping

```
r3#cle count se3/3
Clear "show interface" counters on this interface [confirm]
r3#
%CLEAR-5-COUNTERS: Clear counter on interface Serial3/3 by console

r3#sh in se3/3
Serial3/3 is up, line protocol is down
  Hardware is 4T/MC68360
  Internet address is 192.168.250.3/24
  MTU 1500 bytes, BW 1544 Kbit, DLY 20000 usec, rely 254/255, load 1/255
  Encapsulation FRAME-RELAY, loopback not set, keepalive set (10 sec)
  LMI enq sent  0, LMI stat recvd 0, LMI upd recvd 0
  LMI enq recvd 0, LMI stat sent  0, LMI upd sent  0, DCE LMI down
  LMI DLCI 0  LMI type is ANSI Annex D  frame relay DCE
  FR SVC disabled, LAPF state down
  Broadcast queue 0/64, broadcasts sent/dropped 0/0, interface broadcasts 0
  Last input 00:25:01, output 00:25:14, output hang never
  Last clearing of "show interface" counters 00:01:00
  Input queue: 0/75/0 (size/max/drops); Total output drops: 0
  Queueing strategy: weighted fair
  Output queue: 0/64/0 (size/threshold/drops)
     Conversations  0/1 (active/max active)
     Reserved Conversations 0/0 (allocated/max allocated)
  5 minute input rate 0 bits/sec, 0 packets/sec
  5 minute output rate 0 bits/sec, 0 packets/sec
     0 packets input, 0 bytes, 0 no buffer
     Received 0 broadcasts, 0 runts, 0 giants
     0 input errors, 0 CRC, 0 frame, 0 overrun, 0 ignored, 0 abort
     0 packets output, 0 bytes, 0 underruns
     0 output errors, 0 collisions, 0 interface resets
     0 output buffer failures, 0 output buffers swapped out
     4 carrier transitions     DCD=up  DSR=up  DTR=up  RTS=up  CTS=up
```

Listing 5-23

Listing 5-24

```
r3#conf t
Enter configuration commands, one per line.  End with CNTL/Z.
r3(config)#int se3/3
r3(config-if)#frame intf-type dte
r3(config-if)#^Z
r3#
%SYS-5-CONFIG_I: Configured from console by console
r3#
```

```
%LINEPROTO-5-UPDOWN: Line protocol on Interface Serial3/3, changed state to up
r3#sh in se3/3
Serial3/3 is up, line protocol is up
  Hardware is 4T/MC68360
  Internet address is 192.168.250.3/24
  MTU 1500 bytes, BW 1544 Kbit, DLY 20000 usec, rely 255/255, load 1/255
  Encapsulation FRAME-RELAY, loopback not set, keepalive set (10 sec)
  LMI enq sent  2, LMI stat recvd 2, LMI upd recvd 0, DTE LMI up
  LMI enq recvd 0, LMI stat sent  0, LMI upd sent  0
  LMI DLCI 0  LMI type is ANSI Annex D  frame relay DTE
  FR SVC disabled, LAPF state down
  Broadcast queue 0/64, broadcasts sent/dropped 0/0, interface broadcasts 0
  Last input 00:00:02, output 00:00:02, output hang never
  Last clearing of "show interface" counters 00:01:50
  Input queue: 0/75/0 (size/max/drops); Total output drops: 0
  Queueing strategy: weighted fair
  Output queue: 0/64/0 (size/threshold/drops)
     Conversations  0/1 (active/max active)
     Reserved Conversations 0/0 (allocated/max allocated)
  5 minute input rate 0 bits/sec, 0 packets/sec
  5 minute output rate 0 bits/sec, 0 packets/sec
     2 packets input, 28 bytes, 0 no buffer
     Received 0 broadcasts, 0 runts, 0 giants
     0 input errors, 0 CRC, 0 frame, 0 overrun, 0 ignored, 0 abort
     2 packets output, 28 bytes, 0 underruns
     0 output errors, 0 collisions, 0 interface resets
     0 output buffer failures, 0 output buffers swapped out
     8 carrier transitions     DCD=up  DSR=up  DTR=up  RTS=up  CTS=up
r3#sh frame lmi

LMI Statistics for interface Serial3/3 (Frame Relay DTE) LMI TYPE = ANSI
  Invalid Unnumbered info 0              Invalid Prot Disc 0
  Invalid dummy Call Ref 0               Invalid Msg Type 0
  Invalid Status Message 0               Invalid Lock Shift 0
  Invalid Information ID 0               Invalid Report IE Len 0
  Invalid Report Request 0               Invalid Keep IE Len 0
  Num Status Enq. Sent 2                 Num Status msgs Rcvd 2
  Num Update Status Rcvd 0               Num Status Timeouts 0
```

Listing 5-25

statement would not cause the PVC to move to the INACTIVE state. Locally, everything seems fine at R3; let's check the R1 end of this PVC to ascertain why it is not active end to end.

At R1 it can be seen that each of its PVCs are down (see Listing 5-28).

We will investigate further using `show interface` and `show frame-relay lmi`. Here, it can be seen that the line protocol is down, and the reason for this is that LMI is down, with no status inquiry replies being received from the switch. Any clues as to why LMI is not working? Well,

```
r3#sh log
Syslog logging: enabled (0 messages dropped, 0 flushes, 0 overruns)
    Console logging: level debugging, 253 messages logged
    Monitor logging: level debugging, 25 messages logged
    Trap logging: level informational, 114 message lines logged
    Buffer logging: level debugging, 253 messages logged

Log Buffer (8192 bytes):
Serial3/3(down): DCE LMI timeout
Serial3/3(down): DCE LMI timeout
Serial3/3(down): DCE LMI timeout
Serial3/3(down): DCE LMI timeout
Serial3/3(down): DCE LMI timeout
%SYS-5-CONFIG_I: Configured from console by console
Serial3/3(out): StEnq, myseq 74, yourseen 74, DTE up
datagramstart = 0x3967F74, datagramsize = 14
FR encap = 0x00010308
00 75 95 01 01 01 03 02 4A 4A

Serial3/3(in): Status, myseq 74
RT IE 1, length 1, type 1
KA IE 3, length 2, yourseq 1 , myseq 74
%LINEPROTO-5-UPDOWN: Line protocol on Interface Serial3/3, changed state to up
Serial3/3: broadcast search
Serial3/3:encaps failed on broadcast for link 65(CDP)
Serial3/3(out): StEnq, myseq 75, yourseen 1, DTE up
datagramstart = 0x39681F4, datagramsize = 14
FR encap = 0x00010308
00 75 95 01 01 01 03 02 4B 01

Serial3/3(in): Status, myseq 75
RT IE 1, length 1, type 1
KA IE 3, length 2, yourseq 2 , myseq 75
Serial3/3: broadcast search
Serial3/3:encaps failed on broadcast for link 65(CDP)
Serial3/3(out): StEnq, myseq 76, yourseen 2, DTE up
datagramstart = 0x3967F74, datagramsize = 14
FR encap = 0x00010308
00 75 95 01 01 00 03 02 4C 02

Serial3/3(in): Status, myseq 76
RT IE 1, length 1, type 0
KA IE 3, length 2, yourseq 3 , myseq 76
PVC IE 0x7 , length 0x3 , dlci 301, status 0x2
PVC IE 0x7 , length 0x3 , dlci 302, status 0x2
Serial3/3(out): StEnq, myseq 77, yourseen 3, DTE up
datagramstart = 0x39681F4, datagramsize = 14
FR encap = 0x00010308
00 75 95 01 01 01 03 02 4D 03

r3#undeb all
All possible debugging has been turned off
r3#
```

Listing 5-26

```
r3#
%FR-5-DLCICHANGE: Interface Serial3/3 - DLCI 301 state changed to INACTIVE

r3#sh fram pvc

PVC Statistics for interface Serial3/3 (Frame Relay DTE)

DLCI = 301, DLCI USAGE = LOCAL, PVC STATUS = INACTIVE, INTERFACE = Serial3/3

  input pkts 0           output pkts 0          in bytes 0
  out bytes 0            dropped pkts 0         in FECN pkts 0
  in BECN pkts 0         out FECN pkts 0        out BECN pkts 0
  in DE pkts 0           out DE pkts 0
  pvc create time 01:04:56, last time pvc status changed 00:01:33

DLCI = 302, DLCI USAGE = LOCAL, PVC STATUS = ACTIVE, INTERFACE = Serial3/3

  input pkts 0           output pkts 0          in bytes 0
  out bytes 0            dropped pkts 0         in FECN pkts 0
  in BECN pkts 0         out FECN pkts 0        out BECN pkts 0
  in DE pkts 0           out DE pkts 0
  pvc create time 01:04:45, last time pvc status changed 00:32:10

r3#sh fram map
Serial3/3 (up): ip 192.168.250.1 dlci 301(0x12D,0x48D0), static,
              broadcast,
              CISCO, status defined, inactive
Serial3/3 (up): ip 192.168.250.2 dlci 302(0x12E,0x48E0), static,
              broadcast,
              CISCO, status defined, active
r3#ping 192.168.250.2

Type escape sequence to abort.
Sending 5, 100-byte ICMP Echos to 192.168.250.2, timeout is 2 seconds:
!!!!!
Success rate is 100 percent (5/5), round-trip min/avg/max = 64/65/68 ms
r3#
```

Listing 5-27

both these commands confirm that the LMI type is Cisco, which is the default on a Cisco router. The problem is that the LMI type on the switch, as confirmed by the switch configuration, is ANSI. The LMI type must match between the router and the switch. An output of `debug frame-relay lmi` shows the LMI status inquiries from the router not receiving any inbound reply and the DTE is down (see Listing 5-29).

The LMI type does not show up as being Cisco in the configuration because this is the default. Since R1 is running 11.1 and not 11.2, there is no autodetect for the LMI type. The router is configured for Annex D ANSI, and the LMI and line protocol then comes up (see Listing 5-30).

```
r1#sh fram pvc

PVC Statistics for interface Serial0 (Frame Relay DTE)

DLCI = 102, DLCI USAGE = LOCAL, PVC STATUS = INACTIVE, INTERFACE = Serial0

  input pkts 0            output pkts 0             in bytes 0
  out bytes 0             dropped pkts 0            in FECN pkts 0
  in BECN pkts 0          out FECN pkts 0           out BECN pkts 0
  in DE pkts 0            out DE pkts 0
  pvc create time 0:47:28 last time pvc status changed 0:47:28

DLCI = 103, DLCI USAGE = LOCAL, PVC STATUS = INACTIVE, INTERFACE = Serial0

  input pkts 0            output pkts 0             in bytes 0
  out bytes 0             dropped pkts 0            in FECN pkts 0
  in BECN pkts 0          out FECN pkts 0           out BECN pkts 0
  in DE pkts 0            out DE pkts 0
  pvc create time 1:03:09 last time pvc status changed 0:50:57
```

Listing 5-28

The PVCs are also both active on R1, but there is a noticeable lack of traffic being passed. If the frame-relay mapping table is checked, two static maps are observed. Both R2 and R3 can be pinged, but one thing is noticeable: The average ping delay is 100 ms in each case. This is quite slow considering that the PVCs are not passing much traffic. If a traceroute is performed to R2, it can be observed that it goes via R3! Thus the mapping statements for R2 and R3 are mixed up. This can be verified by checking the switch configuration for these DLCIs. The reason that the pings succeed is because the network is fully meshed (see Listing 5-31).

The R1 router is now reconfigured. Note that the old mapping statements must first be removed before they can be altered (see Listing 5-32).

After verifying that the mapping table is now correct, notice that the average ping delay has been reduced to 65 ms, and the acid test of doing a traceroute reveals that there is just one hop.

I now want to point out some issues in relation to the configuration of R2 and R3 that deserve comment. You will notice from R2's configuration that the frame-relay encapsulation type is IETF. The frame-relay switch and the other router all have the default Cisco frame-relay encapsulation. This proves that while it is good practice to match up frame-relay encapsulations, it is not essential (see Listing 5-33).

```
r1#sh int se 0
Serial0 is up, line protocol is down
  Hardware is MK5025
  Internet address is 192.168.250.1 255.255.255.0
  MTU 1500 bytes, BW 1544 Kbit, DLY 20000 usec, rely 255/255, load 1/255
  Encapsulation FRAME-RELAY, loopback not set, keepalive set (10 sec)
  LMI enq sent  306, LMI stat recvd 0, LMI upd recvd 0, DTE LMI down
  LMI enq recvd 0, LMI stat sent  0, LMI upd sent  0
  LMI DLCI 1023  LMI type is CISCO  frame relay DTE
  Broadcast queue 0/64, broadcasts sent/dropped 0/0, interface broadcasts 0
  Last input 0:51:42, output 0:00:05, output hang never
  Last clearing of "show interface" counters 0:51:08
  Output queue 0/40, 0 drops; input queue 0/75, 0 drops
  5 minute input rate 0 bits/sec, 0 packets/sec
  5 minute output rate 0 bits/sec, 0 packets/sec
     0 packets input, 0 bytes, 0 no buffer
     Received 0 broadcasts, 0 runts, 0 giants
     67 input errors, 67 CRC, 0 frame, 0 overrun, 0 ignored, 0 abort
     306 packets output, 3978 bytes, 0 underruns
     0 output errors, 0 collisions, 102 interface resets, 0 restarts
     0 output buffer failures, 0 output buffers swapped out
     306 carrier transitions
r1#sh fr lmi

LMI Statistics for interface Serial0 (Frame Relay DTE) LMI TYPE = CISCO
  Invalid Unnumbered info 0             Invalid Prot Disc 0
  Invalid dummy Call Ref 0              Invalid Msg Type 0
  Invalid Status Message 0              Invalid Lock Shift 0
  Invalid Information ID 0              Invalid Report IE Len 0
  Invalid Report Request 0              Invalid Keep IE Len 0
  Num Status Enq. Sent 307              Num Status msgs Rcvd 0
  Num Update Status Rcvd 0              Num Status Timeouts 307

r1#
r1#debug frame lmi
Frame Relay LMI debugging is on
r1#term m
Serial0(out): StEnq, myseq 4, yourseen 0, DTE down
 datagramstart = 0x60001AC, datagramsize = 13
 FR encap = 0xFCF10309
00 75 01 01 00 03 02 04 00

Serial0(out): StEnq, myseq 5, yourseen 0, DTE down
 datagramstart = 0x600040C, datagramsize = 13
 FR encap = 0xFCF10309
00 75 01 01 00 03 02 05 00

Serial0(out): StEnq, myseq 6, yourseen 0, DTE down
 datagramstart = 0x600040C, datagramsize = 13
 FR encap = 0xFCF10309
00 75 01 01 00 03 02 06 00
```

Listing 5-29

```
r1#wr t
Building configuration...

Current configuration:
!
version 11.0
service udp-small-servers
service tcp-small-servers
!
hostname r1
!
enable password cisco
!
!
interface Serial0
 ip address 192.168.250.1 255.255.255.0
 encapsulation frame-relay
 no fair-queue
 frame-relay map ip 192.168.250.2 103 broadcast
 frame-relay map ip 192.168.250.3 102 broadcast
!
interface Serial1
 no ip address
 shutdown
!

r1#conf t
Enter configuration commands, one per line.  End with CNTL/Z.
r1(config)#int se 0
r1(config-if)#frame lmi-type ansi
r1(config-if)#^Z
r1#

r1#sh int se 0
Serial0 is up, line protocol is up
  Hardware is MK5025
  Internet address is 192.168.250.1 255.255.255.0
  MTU 1500 bytes, BW 1544 Kbit, DLY 20000 usec, rely 255/255, load 1/255
  Encapsulation FRAME-RELAY, loopback not set, keepalive set (10 sec)
  LMI enq sent  322, LMI stat recvd 11, LMI upd recvd 0, DTE LMI up
  LMI enq recvd 0, LMI stat sent  0, LMI upd sent  0
  LMI DLCI 0  LMI type is ANSI Annex D  frame relay DTE
  Broadcast queue 0/64, broadcasts sent/dropped 0/0, interface broadcasts 0
  Last input 0:00:00, output 0:00:00, output hang never
  Last clearing of "show interface" counters 0:53:53
  Output queue 0/40, 0 drops; input queue 0/75, 0 drops
  5 minute input rate 0 bits/sec, 0 packets/sec
  5 minute output rate 0 bits/sec, 0 packets/sec
     13 packets input, 228 bytes, 0 no buffer
     Received 0 broadcasts, 0 runts, 0 giants
     Received 0 broadcasts, 0 runts, 0 giants
     325 packets output, 4271 bytes, 0 underruns
     0 output errors, 0 collisions, 105 interface resets, 0 restarts
```

Listing 5-30

```
     0 output buffer failures, 0 output buffers swapped out
     315 carrier transitions
r1#sh fram pvc

PVC Statistics for interface Serial0 (Frame Relay DTE)

DLCI = 102, DLCI USAGE = LOCAL, PVC STATUS = ACTIVE, INTERFACE = Serial0

  input pkts 0            output pkts 0            in bytes 0
  out bytes 0             dropped pkts 0           in FECN pkts 0
  in BECN pkts 0          out FECN pkts 0          out BECN pkts 0
  in DE pkts 0            out DE pkts 0
  pvc create time 0:50:24 last time pvc status changed 0:01:34

DLCI = 103, DLCI USAGE = LOCAL, PVC STATUS = ACTIVE, INTERFACE = Serial0

  input pkts 1            output pkts 2            in bytes 30
  out bytes 60            dropped pkts 0           in FECN pkts 0
  in BECN pkts 0          out FECN pkts 0          out BECN pkts 0
  in DE pkts 0            out DE pkts 0
  pvc create time 1:06:07 last time pvc status changed 0:01:37
r1#
```

Listing 5-30 *(Cont.)*

In R2's frame-relay mapping table, you will notice that there are four entries instead of two. Apart from the two IETF static mappings, there are also two entries for Cisco encapsulation. There are no IP addresses against these DLCI entries. What this means is that the router was once configured with Cisco encapsulation but was then changed to IETF. Some frame-relay information requires a router reload in order to be cleared. It is not essential to clear these entries, since they will have no effect. (See Listing 5-34.)

Et voilà! The two spurious entries disappeared after the reload. While this is all very well in my laboratory, I would not suggest bringing down a live production router just to clear these entries.

Now let's turn our attention to R3 for an example of frame-relay autosensing. Router R3's configuration shows an LMI type of ANSI. This was not configured; it was autodetected, and just to prove it, I will remove it to see what happens. Remember the case of the R1 router running IOS version 11.1, which did not work when the incorrect LMI type was configured. Router R3 is running IOS version 11.2, so let's see if the autosensing feature really works (see Listing 5-35).

Initially, the LMI type changes to the Cisco default, and the DLCIs become inactive, but now look what happens (see Listing 5-36).

```
r1#sh frame map
Serial0 (up): ip 192.168.250.2 dlci 103(0x67,0x1870), static,
              broadcast,
              CISCO, status defined, active
Serial0 (up): ip 192.168.250.3 dlci 102(0x66,0x1860), static,
              broadcast,
              CISCO, status defined, active
r1#ping 192.168.250.2
Type escape sequence to abort.
Sending 5, 100-byte ICMP Echos to 192.168.250.2, timeout is 2 seconds:
!!!!!
Success rate is 100 percent (5/5), round-trip min/avg/max = 96/100/108 ms
r1#ping 192.168.250.3
Type escape sequence to abort.
Sending 5, 100-byte ICMP Echos to 192.168.250.3, timeout is 2 seconds:
!!!!!
Success rate is 100 percent (5/5), round-trip min/avg/max = 96/100/108 ms
r1#trace 192.168.250.2

Type escape sequence to abort.
Tracing the route to 192.168.250.2

  1 192.168.250.3 32 msec 32 msec 32 msec
  2 192.168.250.2 44 msec 44 msec *
r1#
```

Listing 5-31

Yes, autosensing really does work! As soon as the router receives a reply to the ANSI status request (remember it sends out LMI requests for each of the three types), it realizes that the switch is using ANSI and automatically puts this in the configuration, and all is well.

Scenario 2: Multipoint and Inverse ARP

For the network shown in Figure 5-4, users who locally attach to R2 have no WAN connectivity. The configuration for R2 is as shown in Listing 5-37.

The line protocol on the subinterface serial 0.1 is up; however, you cannot ping to R1 across the frame-relay cloud. It is then a good idea to check the frame-relay map table, which turns out to be empty. This is a point-to-multipoint subinterface that does not have any static mapping. Hence it must rely on Inverse ARP to resolve the destination IP address to the

```
r1#conf t
Enter configuration commands, one per line.  End with CNTL/Z.
r1(config)#in se 0
r1(config-if)#no fram map ip 192.168.250.2 103 broad
r1(config-if)#no fram map ip 192.168.250.3 102 broad
r1(config-if)#fram map ip 192.168.250.2 102 broad
r1(config-if)#fram map ip 192.168.250.2 102 broad
%FR-5-DLCICHANGE: Interface Serial0 no fram map ip 192.168.250.3 102 broad
%FR-5-DLCICHANGE: Interface Serial0 - DLCI 103 state changed to ACTIVE
r1(config-if)#fram map ip 192.168.250.3 103 broad
r1(config-if)#
%FR-5-DLCICHANGE: Interface Serial0 - DLCI 103 state changed to ACTIVE^Z
r1#
%SYS-5-CONFIG_I: Configured from console by console
r1#sh fram map
Serial0 (up): ip 192.168.250.2 dlci 102(0x66,0x1860), static,
              broadcast,
              CISCO, status defined, active
Serial0 (up): ip 192.168.250.3 dlci 103(0x67,0x1870), static,
              broadcast,
              CISCO, status defined, active

r1#ping 192.168.250.3
Type escape sequence to abort.
Sending 5, 100-byte ICMP Echos to 192.168.250.3, timeout is 2 seconds:
!!!!!
Success rate is 100 percent (5/5), round-trip min/avg/max = 64/65/68 ms

r1#trace 192.168.250.2

Type escape sequence to abort.
Tracing the route to 192.168.250.2

  1 192.168.250.2 36 msec 36 msec *
r1#
```

Listing 5-32

DLCI. From the configuration, it can be seen that Inverse ARP has been disabled. This explains why the map table is empty. (See Listing 5-38.)

There are two ways to solve this problem. Obviously, Inverse ARP can simply be enabled on the subinterface. Another solution that is viable for the current network topology is to configure a point-to-point subinterface on serial 0. This is currently sufficient, since R2 has just one PVC at the moment. A point-to-point subinterface does not require Inverse ARP because there is only one possible destination. I will solve the problem here by redefining the subinterface because it will also illustrate another issue (see Listing 5-39).

```
r2#sh in se0
Serial0 is up, line protocol is up
  Hardware is MK5025
  Internet address is 192.168.250.2 255.255.255.0
  MTU 1500 bytes, BW 1544 Kbit, DLY 20000 usec, rely 255/255, load 1/255
  Encapsulation FRAME-RELAY IETF, loopback not set, keepalive set (10 sec)
  LMI enq sent  388, LMI stat recvd 383, LMI upd recvd 0, DTE LMI up
  LMI enq recvd 0, LMI stat sent  0, LMI upd sent  0
  LMI DLCI 0  LMI type is ANSI Annex D  frame relay DTE
  Broadcast queue 0/64, broadcasts sent/dropped 0/0, interface broadcasts 0
  Last input 0:00:00, output 0:00:00, output hang never
  Last clearing of "show interface" counters never
  Output queue 0/40, 0 drops; input queue 0/75, 0 drops
  5 minute input rate 0 bits/sec, 2 packets/sec
  5 minute output rate 0 bits/sec, 1 packets/sec
     49821 packets input, 3070400 bytes, 0 no buffer
     Received 21546 broadcasts, 0 runts, 0 giants
     15 input errors, 15 CRC, 0 frame, 0 overrun, 0 ignored, 0 abort
     48137 packets output, 3005232 bytes, 0 underruns
     0 output errors, 0 collisions, 51 interface resets, 0 restarts
     0 output buffer failures, 0 output buffers swapped out
     177 carrier transitions
r2#sh fr pvc

PVC Statistics for interface Serial0 (Frame Relay DTE)

DLCI = 201, DLCI USAGE = LOCAL, PVC STATUS = ACTIVE, INTERFACE = Serial0

  input pkts 126          output pkts 94          in bytes 6403
  out bytes 8413          dropped pkts 0          in FECN pkts 0
  in BECN pkts 0          out FECN pkts 0         out BECN pkts 0
  in DE pkts 0            out DE pkts 0
  pvc create time 1:03:59  last time pvc status changed 0:20:11

DLCI = 203, DLCI USAGE = LOCAL, PVC STATUS = ACTIVE, INTERFACE = Serial0

  input pkts 247          output pkts 324         in bytes 20864
  out bytes 15473         dropped pkts 0          in FECN pkts 0
  in BECN pkts 0          out FECN pkts 0         out BECN pkts 0
  in DE pkts 0            out DE pkts 0
  pvc create time 1:04:00  last time pvc status changed 0:27:14

r2#sh frame map
Serial0 (up): ip 0.0.0.0 dlci 203(0xCB,0x30B0)
              broadcast,
              CISCO, status defined, active
Serial0 (up): ip 0.0.0.0 dlci 201(0xC9,0x3090)
              broadcast,
              CISCO, status defined, active
Serial0 (up): ip 192.168.250.1 dlci 201(0xC9,0x3090), static,
              broadcast,
              IETF, status defined, active
```

Listing 5-33

```
Serial0 (up): ip 192.168.250.3 dlci 203(0xCB,0x30B0), static,
              broadcast,
              IETF, status defined, active
r2#
```

Listing 5-33 *(Cont.)*

```
r2#sh version
Cisco Internetwork Operating System Software
IOS (tm) 4000 Software (XX-J-M), Version 11.0(17), RELEASE SOFTWARE (fc1)
Copyright (c) 1986-1997 by cisco Systems, Inc.
Compiled Thu 04-Sep-97 14:44 by richv
Image text-base: 0x00012000, data-base: 0x005E190C

ROM: System Bootstrap, Version 4.14(9), SOFTWARE

r2 uptime is 5 minutes
System restarted by reload
System image file is "xx-j-mz_110-17.bin", booted via flash

cisco 4000 (68030) processor (revision 0xA0) with 16384K/4096K bytes of memory.
Processor board ID 5008217
G.703/E1 software, Version 1.0.
Bridging software.
SuperLAT software copyright 1990 by Meridian Technology Corp).
X.25 software, Version 2.0, NET2, BFE and GOSIP compliant.
TN3270 Emulation software (copyright 1994 by TGV Inc).
2 Token Ring/IEEE 802.5 interfaces.
2 Serial network interfaces.
128K bytes of non-volatile configuration memory.
4096K bytes of processor board System flash (Read/Write)

Configuration register is 0x2102

r2#sh fr map
Serial0 (up): ip 192.168.250.1 dlci 201(0xC9,0x3090), static,
              broadcast,
              IETF, status defined, active
Serial0 (up): ip 192.168.250.3 dlci 203(0xCB,0x30B0), static,
              broadcast,
              IETF, status defined, active
r2#
```

Listing 5-34

```
r3#conf t
Enter configuration commands, one per line.  End with CNTL/Z.
r3(config)#in se 3/3
r3(config-if)#no frame lmi-type ansi
r3(config-if)#^Z
r3#
%SYS-5-CONFIG_I: Configured from console by console
%FR-5-DLCICHANGE: Interface Serial3/3 - DLCI 302 state changed to INACTIVE
%FR-5-DLCICHANGE: Interface Serial3/3 - DLCI 301 state changed to DELETED
%FR-5-DLCICHANGE: Interface Serial3/3 - DLCI 302 state changed to DELETED
%LINEPROTO-5-UPDOWN: Line protocol on Interface Serial3/3, changed state to down
r3#sh frame lmi

LMI Statistics for interface Serial3/3 (Frame Relay DTE) LMI TYPE = CISCO
  Invalid Unnumbered info 0              Invalid Prot Disc 0
  Invalid dummy Call Ref 0               Invalid Msg Type 0
  Invalid Status Message 0               Invalid Lock Shift 0
  Invalid Information ID 0               Invalid Report IE Len 0
  Invalid Report Request 0               Invalid Keep IE Len 0
  Num Status Enq. Sent 34                Num Status msgs Rcvd 29
  Num Update Status Rcvd 0               Num Status Timeouts 4
r3#
%FR-5-DLCICHANGE: Interface Serial3/3 - DLCI 301 state changed to INACTIVE
r3#
```

Listing 5-35

In configuration mode, the interface serial 0.1 was deleted. However, when the configuration is checked, the interface is still there, the only difference being that it has lost its DLCI and IP address. This is the issue that was discussed earlier in relation to removing subinterfaces on Cisco routers. For recent IOS versions, such as version 11.2, the preceding configuration step is usually sufficient to delete the subinterface. However, in earlier versions (R2 is running version 11.0), a reload is usually required to fully remove the interface. In this case I decided not to reload the router but to redefine a new point-to-point interface serial 0.2.

A point-to-point subinterface does not require a static mapping. The DLCI itself is simply displayed in the frame-relay map table. WAN connectivity is then verified by pinging R1 (see Listing 5-40).

Note that in some situations it may be desirable to turn off Inverse ARP. An example of this would be if a multipoint interface is attaching to a switch that still has a number of PVCs defined from that physical interface. If it is intended to not use all of the PVCs defined, then static maps could be defined for the PVCs that are to be currently used, and Inverse ARP must be disabled. If Inverse ARP is not disabled, then the

```
r3#wr t
Building configuration...

Current configuration:
!
version 11.2
!
hostname r3
!
enable password cisco
!
frame-relay switching
!
interface TokenRing1/0
 ip address 205.223.51.3 255.255.255.0
 bandwidth 100000
 appletalk cable-range 51-51 51.3
 appletalk zone token3
 ring-speed 16
!
interface Serial3/3
 ip address 192.168.250.3 255.255.255.0
 encapsulation frame-relay
 frame-relay map ip 192.168.250.1 301 broadcast
 frame-relay map ip 192.168.250.2 302 broadcast
 frame-relay lmi-type ansi
!

r3#sh frame lmi

LMI Statistics for interface Serial3/3 (Frame Relay DTE) LMI TYPE = ANSI
  Invalid Unnumbered info 0               Invalid Prot Disc 0
  Invalid dummy Call Ref 0                Invalid Msg Type 0
  Invalid Status Message 0                Invalid Lock Shift 0
  Invalid Information ID 0                Invalid Report IE Len 0
  Invalid Report Request 0                Invalid Keep IE Len 0
  Num Status Enq. Sent 37                 Num Status msgs Rcvd 32
  Num Update Status Rcvd 0                Num Status Timeouts 6
r3#sh in s3/3
%LINEPROTO-5-UPDOWN: Line protocol on Interface Serial3/3, changed state to up
Serial3/3 is up, line protocol is up
  Hardware is 4T/MC68360
  Internet address is 192.168.250.3/24
  MTU 1500 bytes, BW 1544 Kbit, DLY 20000 usec, rely 255/255, load 1/255
  Encapsulation FRAME-RELAY, loopback not set, keepalive set (10 sec)
  LMI enq sent  38, LMI stat recvd 33, LMI upd recvd 0, DTE LMI up
  LMI enq recvd 0, LMI stat sent  0, LMI upd sent  0
  LMI DLCI 0  LMI type is ANSI Annex D  frame relay DTE
  FR SVC disabled, LAPF state down
  Broadcast queue 0/64, broadcasts sent/dropped 0/0, interface broadcasts 0
  Last input 00:00:02, output 00:00:02, output hang never
  Last clearing of "show interface" counters 00:07:50
```

Listing 5-36

```
   Input queue: 0/75/0 (size/max/drops); Total output drops: 0
   Queueing strategy: weighted fair
   Output queue: 0/64/0 (size/threshold/drops)
      Conversations  0/1 (active/max active)
      Reserved Conversations 0/0 (allocated/max allocated)
   5 minute input rate 0 bits/sec, 0 packets/sec
   5 minute output rate 0 bits/sec, 0 packets/sec
      38 packets input, 1052 bytes, 0 no buffer
      Received 0 broadcasts, 0 runts, 0 giants
      0 input errors, 0 CRC, 0 frame, 0 overrun, 0 ignored, 0 abort
      46 packets output, 1086 bytes, 0 underruns
      0 output errors, 0 collisions, 0 interface resets
      0 output buffer failures, 0 output buffers swapped out
      12 carrier transitions     DCD=up  DSR=up  DTR=up  RTS=up  CTS=up
r3#
%FR-5-DLCICHANGE: Interface Serial3/3 - DLCI 302 state changed to ACTIVE
```

Listing 5-36 (Cont.)

latent PVCs that were not to be used could still potentially resolve protocol addresses. This could cause serious routing problems if it went unnoticed.

CAUTION: *It is sometimes necessary to disable Inverse ARP in order to avoid any undesirable effects due to "latent" PVCs.*

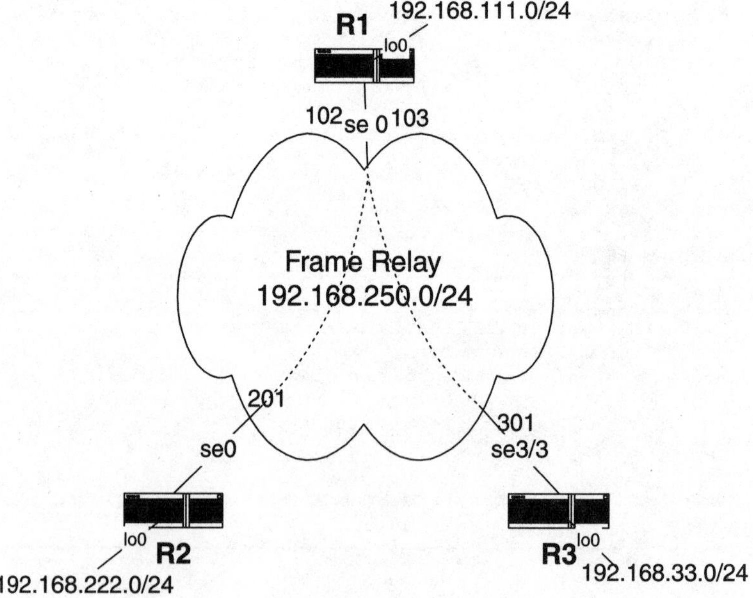

Figure 5-4 Routing problems over frame relay—troubleshooting scenarios 2 and 3.

Listing 5-37

```
r2#sh run
Building configuration...

Current configuration:
!
version 11.0
service udp-small-servers
service tcp-small-servers
!
hostname r2
!
enable password cisco
!
!
interface Loopback0
 ip address 192.168.222.2 255.255.255.0
!
interface Serial0
 no ip address
 encapsulation frame-relay
 no fair-queue
 frame-relay lmi-type ansi
!
interface Serial0.1 multipoint
 ip address 192.168.250.2 255.255.255.0
 frame-relay interface-dlci 201
 no frame-relay inverse-arp
!
interface Serial1
 no ip address
 shutdown
!
interface TokenRing0
 ip address 130.11.65.2 255.255.255.0
 ring-speed 16
!
interface TokenRing1
 no ip address
 shutdown
!
router eigrp 1
 network 192.168.222.0
 network 192.168.250.0
!
!
!
line con 0
line aux 0
 transport input all
line vty 0 4
 password cisco
 login
!
end

r2#
```

```
r2#sh in se0.1
Serial0.1 is up, line protocol is up
  Hardware is MK5025
  Internet address is 192.168.250.2 255.255.255.0
  MTU 1500 bytes, BW 1544 Kbit, DLY 20000 usec, rely 255/255, load 1/255
  Encapsulation FRAME-RELAY
r2#ping 192.168.250.1
Type escape sequence to abort.
Sending 5, 100-byte ICMP Echos to 192.168.250.1, timeout is 2 seconds:
.....
Success rate is 0 percent (0/5)
r2#sh frame map
r2#
```

Listing 5-38

Scenario 3: Routing over Frame Relay

The network shown in Figure 5-4 also will be used to display some of the problems that must be overcome when running dynamic routing protocols over frame relay. The network is using EIGRP to route IP; each of the routers has the indicated loopback address configured, which is also participating in EIGRP 1. There is no direct PVC between R2 and R3. Router R1 is not using subinterfaces, unlike the two spoke routers.

It is required that each router has a route to the loopback interface of each of the other two routers. It is reported that IP routing is not working between the three sites.

On first inspection, it can be seen that R2 is not seeing a route to 192.168.33.0/24, which is R3's loopback network. Likewise, R1 also does not have a route to this network (see Listing 5-41).

```
r2#conf t
Enter configuration commands, one per line.  End with CNTL/Z.
r2(config)#no interface se 0.1

!
interface Serial0.1 multipoint
 no ip address
 no frame-relay inverse-arp
!
```

Listing 5-39

```
!
interface Serial0.2 point-to-point
 ip address 192.168.250.2 255.255.255.0
 frame-relay interface-dlci 201
!
interface Serial1
 no ip address

r2#sh fram map
Serial0.2 (up): point-to-point dlci, dlci 201(0xC9,0x3090)
          status defined, active
r2#ping 192.168.250.1
Type escape sequence to abort.
Sending 5, 100-byte ICMP Echos to 192.168.250.1, timeout is 2 seconds:
!!!!!
Success rate is 100 percent (5/5), round-trip min/avg/max = 64/66/68 ms
r2#
```

Listing 5-40

```
r2#sh ip ro
Codes: C - connected, S - static, I - IGRP, R - RIP, M - mobile, B - BGP
       D - EIGRP, EX - EIGRP external, O - OSPF, IA - OSPF inter area
       E1 - OSPF external type 1, E2 - OSPF external type 2, E - EGP
       i - IS-IS, L1 - IS-IS level-1, L2 - IS-IS level-2, * - candidate default
Gateway of last resort is not set

D    192.168.111.0 [90/2297856] via 192.168.250.1, 00:00:18, Serial0.1
     130.11.0.0 255.255.255.0 is subnetted, 1 subnets
C       130.11.65.0 is directly connected, TokenRing0
C    192.168.250.0 is directly connected, Serial0.1
C    192.168.222.0 is directly connected, Loopback0
r2#

r1>sh ip ro
Codes: C - connected, S - static, I - IGRP, R - RIP, M - mobile, B - BGP
       D - EIGRP, EX - EIGRP external, O - OSPF, IA - OSPF inter area
       E1 - OSPF external type 1, E2 - OSPF external type 2, E - EGP
       i - IS-IS, L1 - IS-IS level-1, L2 - IS-IS level-2, * - candidate default

Gateway of last resort is not set

C    192.168.111.0 is directly connected, Loopback0
     130.11.0.0 255.255.255.0 is subnetted, 1 subnets
C       130.11.65.0 is directly connected, TokenRing0
C    192.168.250.0 is directly connected, Serial0
D    192.168.222.0 [90/2297856] via 192.168.250.2, 00:00:45, Serial0
r1>
```

Listing 5-41

When R3's routing table is inspected, it can be seen that it is not learning any routes from R1. Also, an EIGRP neighbor relationship has not been formed with R1, and there is no IP address for R3 in the mapping table (see Listing 5-42).

Let's revisit R1 to see if there are any clues as to why it is not at least forming an EIGRP neighbor with R3. What at first appears strange is that R1 sees both R2 and R3 as EIGRP neighbors. I then checked the frame-relay map table, and the answer to this problem is there. Notice that the broadcast keyword is included for DLCI 102 but is absent for DLCI 103, which points at R3. The effect of this is that R1 can receive broadcasts from R3 (because the configuration is correct on R3) but cannot send broadcasts to R3. EIGRP neighbor formation relies on the ability to exchange multicast hello messages. Even though these messages are multicasts rather than broadcasts, they will not propagate across frame relay by default. Thus R1 sees R3 as an EIGRP neighbor, but R3 does not see R1 as a neighbor. The possibility of forming one-way neighbor relationships is a peculiar property of EIGRP that we will learn more about in Chapter 8. (See Listing 5-43.)

```
r3>sh ip ro
Codes: C - connected, S - static, I - IGRP, R - RIP, M - mobile, B - BGP
       D - EIGRP, EX - EIGRP external, O - OSPF, IA - OSPF inter area
       N1 - OSPF NSSA external type 1, N2 - OSPF NSSA external type 2
       E1 - OSPF external type 1, E2 - OSPF external type 2, E - EGP
       i - IS-IS, L1 - IS-IS level-1, L2 - IS-IS level-2, * - candidate default
       U - per-user static route, o - ODR

Gateway of last resort is not set

C    205.223.51.0/24 is directly connected, TokenRing1/0
C    192.168.33.0/24 is directly connected, Loopback0
     159.249.0.0/23 is subnetted, 1 subnets
C       159.249.104.0 is directly connected, Ethernet2/0
C    192.168.250.0/24 is directly connected, Serial3/3.1
r3>

r3>sh ip eigrp nei
IP-EIGRP neighbors for process 1
r3>sh frame map
Serial3/3.1 (up): point-to-point dlci, dlci 301(0x12D,0x48D0), broadcast
          status defined, active
r3>
```

Listing 5-42

```
r1>sh ip eigrp nei
IP-EIGRP neighbors for process 1
H   Address                 Interface    Hold Uptime    SRTT   RTO  Q  Seq
                                         (sec)          (ms)       Cnt Num
0   192.168.250.3           Se0            13 0:00:14     0   5000  1  0
1   192.168.250.2           Se0            14 0:04:53    44    264  0  20
r1>sh fr map
Serial0 (up): ip 192.168.250.2 dlci 102(0x66,0x1860), static,
              broadcast,
              CISCO, status defined, active
Serial0 (up): ip 192.168.250.3 dlci 103(0x67,0x1870), static,
              CISCO, status defined, active
r1>en
Password:
r1#sh ip ro
Codes: C - connected, S - static, I - IGRP, R - RIP, M - mobile, B - BGP
       D - EIGRP, EX - EIGRP external, O - OSPF, IA - OSPF inter area
       E1 - OSPF external type 1, E2 - OSPF external type 2, E - EGP
       i - IS-IS, L1 - IS-IS level-1, L2 - IS-IS level-2, * - candidate default

Gateway of last resort is not set

C    192.168.111.0 is directly connected, Loopback0
     130.11.0.0 255.255.255.0 is subnetted, 1 subnets
C       130.11.65.0 is directly connected, TokenRing0
C    192.168.250.0 is directly connected, Serial0
D    192.168.222.0 [90/2297856] via 192.168.250.2, 00:04:30, Serial0
r1#
```

Listing 5-43

To solve the problem, the frame-relay mapping statement must be corrected on R1 to include the broadcast keyword. Note that the old mapping statement first has to be removed (see Listing 5-44).

The neighbor relationship is now up at each end, and R3 has R1's loopback network in its routing table (see Listing 5-45).

However, there is also a noticeable absentee from R3's routing table, and that is R2's loopback network. Similarly, when R2's routing table is checked, the R3 loopback network is not present (see Listing 5-46).

The next stop-off is to check if these routes are in R1's routing table. We confirm that it "sees" both remote loopback networks, so it appears that R1 is not forwarding these routes to R2 and R3, respectively (see Listing 5-47). Any ideas why this may be happening or not happening as the case may be?

```
r1#conf t
Enter configuration commands, one per line.  End with CNTL/Z.
r1(config)#in se 0
r1(config-if)#no frame map ip 192.168.250.3 103
r1(config-if)#frame map ip 192.168.250.3 103 broadcast
r1(config-if)#^Z
r1#
```

Listing 5-44

The answer is split horizon, which is on by default on frame-relay interfaces when routing with EIGRP. This is distinct from RIP or IGRP, which have split horizon disabled by default on frame-relay interfaces.

Split horizon for EIGRP 1 is disabled on the interface using the highlighted configuration commands. It is then verified that all routers see each other's loopback networks as required (see Listing 5-48).

Split horizon is an issue that we will be meeting numerous times during the course of this book, not only in relation to the IP routing protocols but also in the case of other desktop protocols such as IPX and AppleTalk.

```
r3>sh ip eigrp neigh
IP-EIGRP neighbors for process 1
H   Address                 Interface     Hold Uptime    SRTT   RTO  Q  Seq
                                          (sec)          (ms)       Cnt Num
0   192.168.250.1           Se3/3.1        151 00:02:14 1492   5000  0  24
r3>sh ip ro
Codes: C - connected, S - static, I - IGRP, R - RIP, M - mobile, B - BGP
       D - EIGRP, EX - EIGRP external, O - OSPF, IA - OSPF inter area
       N1 - OSPF NSSA external type 1, N2 - OSPF NSSA external type 2
       E1 - OSPF external type 1, E2 - OSPF external type 2, E - EGP
       i - IS-IS, L1 - IS-IS level-1, L2 - IS-IS level-2, * - candidate default
       U - per-user static route, o - ODR

Gateway of last resort is not set

D    192.168.111.0/24 [90/2297856] via 192.168.250.1, 00:02:20, Serial3/3.1
C    205.223.51.0/24 is directly connected, TokenRing1/0
C    192.168.33.0/24 is directly connected, Loopback0
     159.249.0.0/23 is subnetted, 1 subnets
C       159.249.104.0 is directly connected, Ethernet2/0
C    192.168.250.0/24 is directly connected, Serial3/3.1
r3>
```

Listing 5-45

```
r2>sh ip ro
Codes: C - connected, S - static, I - IGRP, R - RIP, M - mobile, B - BGP
       D - EIGRP, EX - EIGRP external, O - OSPF, IA - OSPF inter area
       E1 - OSPF external type 1, E2 - OSPF external type 2, E - EGP
       i - IS-IS, L1 - IS-IS level-1, L2 - IS-IS level-2, * - candidate default

Gateway of last resort is not set

D    192.168.111.0 [90/2297856] via 192.168.250.1, 00:08:57, Serial0.1
     130.11.0.0 255.255.255.0 is subnetted, 1 subnets
C       130.11.65.0 is directly connected, TokenRing0
C    192.168.250.0 is directly connected, Serial0.1
C    192.168.222.0 is directly connected, Loopback0
r2>
```

Listing 5-46

```
r1>sh ip ro
Codes: C - connected, S - static, I - IGRP, R - RIP, M - mobile, B - BGP
       D - EIGRP, EX - EIGRP external, O - OSPF, IA - OSPF inter area
       E1 - OSPF external type 1, E2 - OSPF external type 2, E - EGP
       i - IS-IS, L1 - IS-IS level-1, L2 - IS-IS level-2, * - candidate default

Gateway of last resort is not set

C    192.168.111.0 is directly connected, Loopback0
D    192.168.33.0 [90/2297856] via 192.168.250.3, 00:03:41, Serial0
     130.11.0.0 255.255.255.0 is subnetted, 1 subnets
C       130.11.65.0 is directly connected, TokenRing0
C    192.168.250.0 is directly connected, Serial0
D    192.168.222.0 [90/2297856] via 192.168.250.2, 00:09:10, Serial0
r1>
```

Listing 5-47

```
!
interface Serial0
 ip address 192.168.250.1 255.255.255.0
 encapsulation frame-relay
 no ip split-horizon eigrp 1
 no fair-queue
 frame-relay lmi-type ansi
 frame-relay map ip 192.168.250.2 102 broadcast
 frame-relay map ip 192.168.250.3 103 broadcast
!
interface Serial1

r1#

r2#sh ip ro
Codes: C - connected, S - static, I - IGRP, R - RIP, M - mobile, B - BGP
       D - EIGRP, EX - EIGRP external, O - OSPF, IA - OSPF inter area
       E1 - OSPF external type 1, E2 - OSPF external type 2, E - EGP
       i - IS-IS, L1 - IS-IS level-1, L2 - IS-IS level-2, * - candidate default

Gateway of last resort is not set

D    192.168.111.0 [90/2297856] via 192.168.250.1, 00:00:23, Serial0.1
D    192.168.33.0 [90/2809856] via 192.168.250.1, 00:00:23, Serial0.1
     130.11.0.0 255.255.255.0 is subnetted, 1 subnets
C       130.11.65.0 is directly connected, TokenRing0
C    192.168.250.0 is directly connected, Serial0.1
C    192.168.222.0 is directly connected, Loopback0
r2#

r3>sh ip ro
Codes: C - connected, S - static, I - IGRP, R - RIP, M - mobile, B - BGP
       D - EIGRP, EX - EIGRP external, O - OSPF, IA - OSPF inter area
       N1 - OSPF NSSA external type 1, N2 - OSPF NSSA external type 2
       E1 - OSPF external type 1, E2 - OSPF external type 2, E - EGP
       i - IS-IS, L1 - IS-IS level-1, L2 - IS-IS level-2, * - candidate default
       U - per-user static route, o - ODR

Gateway of last resort is not set

D    192.168.111.0/24 [90/2297856] via 192.168.250.1, 00:00:33, Serial3/3.1
C    205.223.51.0/24 is directly connected, TokenRing1/0
C    192.168.33.0/24 is directly connected, Loopback0
     159.249.0.0/23 is subnetted, 1 subnets
C       159.249.104.0 is directly connected, Ethernet2/0
C    192.168.250.0/24 is directly connected, Serial3/3.1
D    192.168.222.0/24 [90/2809856] via 192.168.250.1, 00:00:33, Serial3/3.1
r3>
```

Listing 5-48

REVIEW QUESTIONS

For the exercises that are multiple-choice questions, there is only one correct answer unless the question is marked with an asterisk (*). Choose the most suitable answer.

* **1.** The primary function of LMI is to verify link integrity

a. end to end across the PVC.

b. between the DTE and DCE.

c. between the DTE and local CO.

d. between the router and destination CO.

e. None of the above.

2. Which of the following is *not* an LMI type?

a. Annex A

b. IETF

c. Cisco

d. Annex D

e. All of the above

3. What is the Cisco default LMI type?

a. Annex A

b. IETF

c. Cisco

d. Annex D

e. There is no default.

4. What is the default frame-relay encapsulation on a Cisco router?

a. Annex A

b. IETF

c. Cisco

d. Annex D

e. There is no default.

5. The LMI protocol requires that the keepalive interval on the router be

a. greater than the switch.

b. less than the switch.

c. equal to the switch.

d. Does not matter.

6. Which of the following routing protocols has split horizon disabled by default on frame-relay interfaces?

a. IGRP

b. IP EIGRP

c. IPX EIGRP

d. Decnet

e. All of above

7. Multicasts will still be forwarded by a multipoint frame-relay interface that does not include the broadcast keyword in its mapping statement. True or False?

8. How many IP subnets are required for a four-node hub and spoke network using multipoint frame relay?

a. 1

b. 2

c. 3

d. 4

9. How many IP subnets are required for a four-node hub and spoke network using point-to-point frame relay without any meshing?

a. 1

b. 2

c. 3

d. 4

10. Which of the following frame-relay debug commands result in the most overhead on the router?

a. `debug frame-relay lmi`

b. `debug frame-relay events`

c. `debug frame-relay packet`

d. `debug frame-relay multipoint`

***11.** Which of the following commands will *not* tell you if LMI is being exchanged with the switch?

a. `show interface serial`

b. `show frame-relay lmi`

c. `show frame-relay map`

d. `show frame-relay pvc`

e. All of them will.

12. Automatic BECN feedback is enabled with which of the following features?

a. DE lists

b. Broadcast queuing

c. DLCI prioritization

d. Traffic shaping

e. All of the above

***13.** If frame-relay line protocol is down, which of the following tools is *not* a helpful option?

a. `show interface serial`

b. Loopback test

c. `show frame-relay lmi`

d. `show frame-relay map`

e. `debug frame-relay lmi`

14. Which Cisco IOS feature allows limits to be set on the amount of bandwidth that broadcasts use on a frame-relay interface?

15. What type of frame-relay congestion message is more useful if the information transfer rate is being controlled by the source?

a. DE

b. BECN

c. FECN

d. Dropped packet

e. Source quench

CHAPTER 6

Troubleshooting ISDN Connectivity

Introduction

The objectives of this chapter are to

- Address the configuration issues encountered with ISDN BRI connectivity using Cisco routers.
- Use Cisco router `show` and `debug` diagnostic commands for problem isolation and performance evaluation on ISDN BRI networks.
- Understand how these diagnostic tools relate to ISDN signaling and call setup.
- Learn the design issues relevant to ISDN that can potentially cause problems in network implementations.

ISDN Configuration Issues

ISDN Switch Type

The Cisco router must be globally configured with an ISDN switch type. This is the first ISDN parameter that must be defined on the router—there is no default. This must match the actual switch type at the central office. The most common types of ISDN switches encountered in the United States are AT+T 5ess, DMS-100, and the NI1. The appropriate Cisco global command is `isdn switch-type`. It should be noted that in some instances the router needs to be reloaded after the configured switch type is changed in order for the change to take effect. This depends on the actual switch type and the version of Cisco IOS. In some cases, the user will be prompted with a warning noting that a reload is required. If the incorrect switch type is configured on the router, ISDN q931 errors will be observed in the output of `debug isdn q931`. This will be discussed in more detail later in the chapter.

CAUTION: *In some cases, the router must be reloaded for a change in ISDN switch type to take effect.*

In a real-life situation, changing the configured switch type really should not be an option. After all, being less than 100 percent certain about the switch type that the router is connecting to hardly represents a satisfactory baseline for troubleshooting.

Service Profile Identifiers (SPIDs)

The *service profile identifier* (SPID) is a number assigned by the ISDN carrier to identify the line configuration of the BRI service. Each SPID points to line setup and configuration information contained in the central office ISDN switch.

The number of SPIDs to be configured can vary depending on the type of central office to which the router is connecting. AT+T 5ess switches can support up to eight SPIDs. The fact that multiple SPIDs can be applied to a single B-channel means that multiple services can be supported. In practice however, it is still uncommon to mix services on a given BRI line, and I generally will be confining the discussion to ISDN data calls. In such cases, even for a 5ess switch, only two SPIDs are configured. The DMS-100 and NI1 switches support only two SPIDs, one per B-channel.

The multiservice capability of ISDN also can cause problems if the service is not configured properly at the central office switch. A typical problem that can occur is when the router attempts to make a data call, but the SPIDs are set up only for voice at the switch. The call will be rejected by the switch, which will generate one of the following messages:

```
Bearer capability not authorized
Requested facility not subscribed
```

These signaling messages are picked up using ISDN debug commands, which will be discussed later in this chapter.

SPIDs can be crudely thought of as being equivalent to the analog telephone number. Unfortunately, the numbering rules and conventions are not nearly as simple or consistent. From my own experience, I have seen cases where the SPID numbering had to be modified because of different combinations of switch type, ISDN carrier, or even the geographic region where the switch is located. The user should work closely with the telecommunications carrier to be very clear about the exact SPID numbers to be configured on the router.

***CAUTION**: Clarify with your telecommunications carrier exactly what the SPIDs should be before configuring the router.*

Listing 6-1 is a sample configuration. The number of digits that you see in the SPID definition statements actually can occur in practice—hence the need to work closely with the telecommunications company to check their validity.

Listing 6-1

```
!
interface BRI0
 ip address 171.13.23.12 255.255.255.0
 encapsulation ppp
 isdn spid1 60221684731111
 isdn spid2 60221684741111
 dialer map ip 171.13.23.1 name Router2 broadcast 101033317026
 dialer-group 1
 ppp authentication chap
!
```

Dialer Map Statements

The purpose of the dialer map statement is to map a particular protocol address to an ISDN number. It tells the router "to get to this protocol address, dial this ISDN number." Put another way, this statement maps the destination address of a layer 3 or layer 2 protocol to an ISDN number. Most desktop protocols, including bridging, can be mapped to an ISDN number to be called. The following are some examples:

```
R1#
!
interface bri0
ip address 172.16.100.3 255.255.255.0
dialer map ip 172.16.100.3 name R3 broadcast 4313
!
R1#
```

This tells the router R1 that to get to IP address 172.16.100.3, it must dial 4313. The 172.16.100.3 address is the IP address of the BRI interface on the destination router, which has host name R3 (see Figure 6-1). The significance of the `broadcast` keyword is that it allows broadcasts to be forwarded across the BRI interface. Since ISDN, like X.25 and frame relay, is a nonbroadcast medium, this keyword is necessary to

Figure 6-1
Simple ISDN dialer map illustration.

allow routing updates and IPX SAPS, for example, to propagate across the ISDN network.

If IPX were being used across the wide-area network (WAN), then a similar map statement could be

```
dialer map ipx 10.0000.0c3f.1234 name R3 broadcast 4313
```

You need to be extremely careful with the ISDN number in the dialer map statement. As with the SPID configuration, what actually works does not always comply with what you might expect to be the correct dial-up number. This is another parameter that needs to be discussed carefully with your telecommunications carrier. If you are using Centrex, for example, then just four-digit dialing may be required. However, there are few hard and fast rules. I have seen instances of having to place a "1" before the dial-up number for a local call. Part of the reason for these apparent anomalies is that the level of standardization for ISDN in the United States is not sufficiently stringent. As a result of this, theory and practice do not always meet head-on with respect to parameters such as SPIDs and dial-up number.

An important option that can be set as part of the dialer map definition is the call speed that is requested at call setup. By default, calls are attempted at 64 kbps. There are situations where a particular telecommunications carrier may not support 64-kbps ISDN in that locality. This problem also can arise if the call is being switched across the networks of more than one carrier, and there may be cases where full 64-kbps ISDN is not supported end to end. Reducing the call speed to 56 kbps, as in the following configuration, usually averts the problem:

```
dialer map ip 2.2.2.2 name slowcoach broadcast speed 56 5552345
```

The speed keyword in the dialer map statement alters the speed of outgoing calls to avoid a speed mismatch across the network. However, what if it is required to alter the speed of an incoming call? By default, as for an outgoing call, the router expects to receive a 64-kbps call. There are situations where a call is originated at one speed during call setup but delivered by the network at another speed. This type of speed mismatch will prevent data from being transferred. The `isdn not-end-to-end` interface command can be used to override the speed at which the network delivers a call. Similarly to the speed keyword, this command is sometimes required to resolve compatibility issues due to a mix of different ISDN carriers. In the following example, calls were being set up at 56 kbps but were being delivered at 64 kbps; this configuration would resolve such a problem:

```
interface bri0
isdn not-end-to-end 56
```

Dialer Lists

Dialing cannot occur if the ISDN BRI interface is not assigned a dialer group. The dialer group is in turn related to a dialer list. The function of the dialer list is to define what type of traffic should cause dialing to be initiated. This list can be general in nature, or alternatively, it can be very specific.

You may wish to define a simple and general dialer list in order to ensure that the ISDN line will come up when the appropriate traffic needs to traverse the BRI interface. For example, the following dialer list simply allows any IP traffic to initiate dialing.

```
interface bri0
dialer-group 1

!
dialer-list 1 protocol ip permit
```

Note that the `dialer-list` command is global and that the interface command `dialer-group 1` is used to associate this list with the interface dialer group.

A typical concern with ISDN is that the line will be brought up needlessly due to periodic routing updates or, for example, IPX SAP updates. In the following example, IP EIGRP is being used across an ISDN backbone. If this is implemented without any filtering, then the EIGRP hellos will keep the line up indefinitely. The following global configuration would prevent EIGRP messages from initiating dialing.

```
dialer-list 1 protocol ip list 101

access-list 101 deny eigrp any any
access-list 101 permit ip any any
```

However, it would *not* prevent EIGRP updates once the line is up. This is a key difference between a dialer list and an access list. A dialer list simply controls what traffic can initiate dialing. Once the line is up, traffic that does not meet the criteria of the dialer list can still cross the interface. Traffic that meets the dialer-list criteria is termed *interesting* traffic, and it causes the idle timer to be reset. This means that if there is no interesting outbound traffic from the ISDN interface for a period greater than the idle timeout value, the line will then drop. It will not come up again until interesting traffic causes dialing to again be initiated.

NOTE: *It is important to understand the difference between an access list and a dialer list. The dialer list controls what traffic should initiate dialing; unlike an access list, it does not block that traffic when the line is up.*

Problems caused by unintended ISDN dialing are common on real networks, so I would like to emphasize some more points using an example. In the following ISDN configuration (Listing 6-2), the points that should be noted include

- Any IP traffic will cause a call to be initiated to R5.
- The idle timeout has been increased from its default value of 120 seconds to 5 minutes.
- The idle timer gets reset to zero when interesting outbound traffic (in this case, any IP traffic) crosses the interface. Note that only outgoing traffic can cause the idle timer to be reset.

There are some situations where it may be desirable to increase the idle timeout value. I once came across an interesting problem where both TFTP and BOOTP were intermittently failing across ISDN. Both these

Listing 6-2

```
R1#

!
interface BRI0
 ip address 171.13.23.12 255.255.255.0
 encapsulation ppp
 isdn spid1 60221684731111
 isdn spid2 60221684741111
 dialer idle-timeout 300
 dialer map ip 171.13.23.1 name R5 broadcast 1010333170265
 dialer-group 1
 ppp authentication chap
!
dialer-list 1 protocol ip permit

R1#
```

protocols were using UDP, which is unreliable. Hence there was no additional outbound traffic between initiating the session and ending it. The reason that the sessions were sometimes failing was due to the fact that there was no interesting outbound traffic resetting the idle timer during the session, which caused the idle timer to expire. Increasing the idle-timeout value solved the problem. This type of problem would not have occurred with, for example, a TCP-based service such as FTP because, due to the reliable nature of TCP, each windowed segment would require an acknowledgment that would reset the idle timer.

NOTE: *The idle timer only gets reset by interesting outgoing traffic.*

PPP and Multilink PPP

The Point-to-Point Protocol (PPP) is a layer 2 protocol derived from HDLC that can run over any DTE/DCE interface. It supports multiple layer 3 protocols and can support both synchronous and asynchronous transmission. The basic properties of PPP have made it ideally suited for ISDN networks.

PPP has a layer 2 Link Control Protocol (LCP) component that negotiates link layer establishment, management, and link termination. PPP also supports a family of Network Control Protocols (NCPs) that negotiate the support of most of the more common layer 3 desktop protocols, including IP, IPX, DECNET, and AppleTalk.

The most popular type of authentication used across PPP links is the Challenged Handshake Authentication Protocol (CHAP), although other security protocols such as the more sophisticated TACACS or the simpler Password Authentication Protocol (PAP) are also supported. CHAP is easy to configure, but I will give an example because it is something that causes problems in practice (see Listing 6-3).

The configuration in Listing 6-3 would fail CHAP authentication because the user name on one must exactly match the equivalent hostname on the other. The hostname for the Paris router is "paris-bri," but its defined user name on the London router is simply "paris." Also, the London WAN router has its user name beginning with a lowercase letter on the Paris router. Remember, everything must match exactly!

STAC compression can be configured for PPP. The throughput improvement can vary depending on the desktop protocol being transported. For example, IP usually would show a slightly higher compres-

Listing 6-3

```
hostname paris-bri
username london-wan password cisco
!
interface bri0
encapsulation ppp
dialer map ip 1.1.1.1 name london-wan broadcast 5554414
ppp authentication chap

hostname London-wan
username paris password cisco
!
interface bri0
encapsulation ppp
dialer map ip 1.1.1.2 name paris-bri broadcast 5554415
ppp authentication chap
```

sion ratio than IPX. When configuring compression, as with authentication, make sure that the configuration is consistent at both ends of the link. This may sound trite, but these are the simple things that cause far too many problems in practice.

A recent enhancement to PPP is Multilink PPP (MPPP). In the case of traditional PPP over ISDN, there have been problems obtaining an efficient utilization of the two B-channels simultaneously. Cisco routers can be configured to bring up the second B-channel either when an ISDN call is made or when a certain load threshold has been exceeded. This is based on the interface load, which ranges from 1 to 255. The following configuration would ensure that the channel always comes up after a 50 percent load has been exceeded:

```
interface bri0
dialer load-threshold 128
```

Traffic normally will just propagate across the first channel until the second channel is actually needed to support the throughput. This is often demonstrated by the fact that the second channel sometimes drops on an ISDN call as its idle timer expires, while the first channel remains up.

When the bandwidth requirements increase, the second channel gets used. Packets can get sent out randomly on either channel. There is, however, no guarantee that traffic across both channels will take an identical path through the public ISDN network; thus there is no guarantee that both channels will experience equal delay while getting to the destination. Hence there is a high probability of packets arriving out of sequence at the destination router. This can cause problems with unreliable protocols or extremely time-sensitive protocols. Even with reliable protocols, a very high number of retransmissions can nullify the effect of using both channels. For example, I have seen instances with IPX where a high percentage of SPX retransmissions meant that the throughput was not significantly greater with two channels than with one.

The solution to this problem is Multilink PPP. With this enhancement, a sequencing feature has been added that ensures that data are reassembled in the correct order at layer 2, thus eliminating the need for higher-layer retransmissions. MPPP is negotiated during the LCP setup stage, and both ends of the link must be configured to support it. The sequencing capability of MPPP allows it to view the two B-channels as a logically aggregated link.

An important configuration note is that with most versions of Cisco IOS, the dialer load threshold should be set to its minimum value of one to ensure that MPPP works correctly over the two channels:

```
interface bri0
encapsulation ppp
dialer load-threshold 1
ppp authentication chap
ppp multilink
```

Using ISDN for Backup

ISDN is frequently used as a means to provide backup to serial or frame-relay links in the event of link failure. It is also commonly employed as a cost-effective option to provide additional bandwidth when required. This is a simple principle, but it can be at the root of a number of network problems usually due to poor configuration or a badly thought out design. For this reason, I am going to briefly discuss these problems and how they are solved.

Dial Backup This is the simplest solution. A primary interface has an ISDN interface designated as its backup. The ISDN will only come up after the primary interface has been down for a configurable delay time. The router also can be configured to bring up the backup interface if a certain load is exceeded on the primary interface. Otherwise, the backup interface will only dial if the layer 2 protocol goes down on the primary. This is a serious limitation of dial backup. For example, if the LAN interface on the remote router goes down, dial backup will not take any action. Another example is if an Ethernet backbone was the primary interface, and the Ethernet interface has the "no keepalive" option configured. In this situation, the backbone hub or switch could crash, and no action would be taken because the Ethernet layer 2 would remain up.

The following example shows the bri0 interface backing up serial0. If the layer 2 protocol on serial0 is down for more than 10 seconds, bri0 will dial. The call will drop after serial0 has been up again for 5 minutes.

```
interface serial0
backup interface bri0
backup delay 10 300
```

In a dial backup configuration like this, the bri0 interface will be displayed as being in standby mode when the `show interface` command is used. Note also that the `show isdn status` command would indicate that ISDN layer 1 is DEACTIVATED, which is perfectly normal while the interface is in standby mode. This also means that the bri0 interface would not be in any of the routing tables.

One advantage of dial backup, apart from its simplicity, is the fact that complex dialer lists generally do not need to be configured to ensure that the ISDN line will not needlessly dial. I have one word of caution in relation to the initial testing of dial backup. It must be ensured that the backup timer that drops the calls (300 seconds in the example given) overrides the idle timer. This always should be the case, but I did see it fail in an early version of IOS version 11.2. In such a scenario, interesting packets could keep resetting the idle timer, and the ISDN call may not drop for a very long time after the primary interface has been restored.

Dial-on-Demand Dial-on-demand is usually implemented using floating static routes over the ISDN network. Routes to the rest of the network are learned dynamically over the primary interface, but if this interface fails, there is a static route pointing at the ISDN interface. The static route is configured with a higher administrative distance; hence it will not normally be preferred. This effect also can be achieved by running the same dynamic routing protocol over the ISDN but with a higher cost metric.

When configuring and testing ISDN dial-on-demand, caution again must be exercised to ensure that unwanted spurious dialing does not take place. You have already seen how an extended IP access list can be used as part of the dialer list to prevent EIGRP traffic from bringing up the line. This is just one example, and the same issue is equally relevant to such protocols as IPX and AppleTalk.

The following examples are indicative of the type of dialer-list filtering that needs to be performed to secure against spurious ISDN dialing:

```
access-list 101 deny any 255.255.255.255 0.0.0.0
access-list 101 permit any any

dialer-list 1 protocol ip list 101
```

The preceding configuration prevents any IP broadcasts from bringing up the line.

```
access-list 901 deny -1 FFFFFFFF 0 FFFFFFFF 452
access-list 901 deny -1 FFFFFFFF 0 FFFFFFFF 453
access-list 901 deny -1 FFFFFFFF 0 FFFFFFFF 457
access-list 901 permit -1

dialer-list 1 protocol ipx list 901
```

This configuration would prevent IPX RIP, SAP, or Netware serialization packets from causing an ISDN call to be initiated. These IPX packets, however, can flow across the ISDN network while the line is up. Since they are not defined to be interesting packets, they do not cause the idle timer to be reset and hence will not needlessly keep the call up. When using IPX over ISDN, it is imperative to have a good understanding of what Novell traffic needs to flow across the WAN. The network and router configurations must then be engineered to avoid keeping the ISDN link up for an excessive amount of time.

OSPF Demand Circuit OSPF, like EIGRP, uses the hello protocol to form neighbor relationships; this, along with its link-state nature, traditionally has made full OSPF operation difficult over ISDN. The OSPF demand circuit is a more sophisticated solution to the problem of running OSPF over ISDN. It is based on RFC 1793 and is supported in Cisco IOS versions 11.2 and later. The difficulties of using OSPF over ISDN and the demand-circuit feature are discussed in the section relating to OSPF in Chapter 8.

ISDN-Related Routing Problems

The network shown in Figure 6-2 is an example of ISDN dial backup. Each remote serial link is backed up by ISDN, which will dial router C at

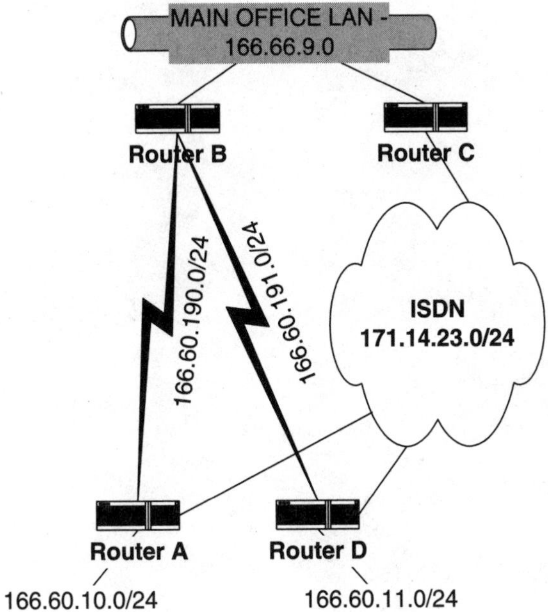

Figure 6-2 Discontiguous network with ISDN dial backup.

the main office. The network administrator noticed that when router A's serial link went down, the backup ISDN interface did dial up, but local users still cannot access an IP-based server at the main office.

The problem here is that the IP addressing and hence routing change when the ISDN is brought up. The ISDN belongs to a different class B network; hence EIGRP will summarize the 166.60.0.0/16 route, which will then become a discontiguous network. The solution here is either to disable autosummarization on the remote routers or to make the ISDN network part of the same class B network as the serial links. We will examine this type of problem again in each of the IP chapters. The point I am making here is that the situation can change dramatically when ISDN kicks in, and you must have thought out and tested the different networking scenarios after a link fails or gets overloaded. In the case of dial backup, it is easy to forget about an issue such as this because the ISDN could be inactive for a very long time before being called into use.

ISDN Sample Configuration

Listing 6-4 is a sample ISDN configuration that includes many of the features discussed so far. Go through the configuration as an exercise,

```
Galway1#wr t
Building configuration...

Current configuration:
!
version 11.1
service timestamps debug datetime localtime show-timezone
service timestamps log datetime localtime show-timezone
service password-encryption
service udp-small-servers
service tcp-small-servers
!
hostname Galway1
!
enable password 7 011D07145A525E
!
username Galway5-pri password 7 0213175A05130270
!
ipx routing 00e0.1ab9.b0cd
isdn switch-type basic-ni1
!
interface Ethernet0
 ip address 171.11.10.1 255.255.255.0
 ipx network 880A00
!
interface Serial0
 backup delay 10 300
 backup interface BRI0
 ip address 171.11.10.130 255.255.255.0
 bandwidth 56
 ipx network 880A80
!
interface Serial1
 no ip address
 shutdown
!
interface BRI0
 ip address 171.14.230.12 255.255.255.0
 no ip mroute-cache
 encapsulation ppp
 bandwidth 48
 ipx network 86E600
 isdn spid1 60224731111
 isdn spid2 60224741111
 dialer idle-timeout 100
 dialer map ip 171.14.230.1 name Galway5-pri broadcast 101036540134
 dialer hold-queue 100
 dialer load-threshold 150
 dialer-group 1
 no fair-queue
 compress stac
 ppp multilink
```

Listing 6-4

```
 ppp authentication chap
!
router eigrp 1
 network 171.11.0.0
 network 171.14.0.0
 no auto-summary
!
no ip classless
access-list 1090 permit 880A80
access-list 1090 permit 86E600
access-list 1090 permit 880A00
!
ipx router eigrp 1
 distribute-sap-list 1090 out BRI0
 distribute-sap-list 1090 out Serial0
 network 880A80
 network 86E600
!
!
dialer-list 1 protocol ip permit
!
line con 0
line aux 0
 exec-timeout 5 0
 transport input all
line vty 0 4
!
end

Galway1#
```

Listing 6-4 *(Cont.)*

ensuring that you understand what each of the configuration parameters means, and list possible reasons why the parameters are configured as they are. Use Cisco's Command Reference and Configuration Guide on CCO as an aid.

ISDN Show Commands

Show Interface—D-Channel

Between the router and the ISDN switch, the two B-channels get encapsulated in the D-channel signaling frame. Therefore a basic `show interface bri0` gives status information on the D-channel. For information on either or both B-channels, use `show interface bri0 1 2`, as you will see very soon. Now let's examine some points about the following sample D-channel output (Listing 6-5):

- bri0 up indicates that the router interface is up.
- Line protocol up (spoofing) means that D-channel information is being exchanged with the switch, but there happens to be no call up at the moment. This is a normal state for a healthy ISDN interface that is not at that moment supporting a call. If a layer 3 were currently connected, then the line protocol would simply read "up."
- Most of the other parameters from the output of `show interface bri0` are similar to other show interface commands. The D-channel output can indicate problems in the local loop between the router and the central office switch, since much of the D-channel information is stripped at the local switch.

Show Interface—B-Channels

In order to examine one or both of the B-channels, use `show interface bri0 1 2`. This most fundamentally will display whether or not there is a call active on each B-channel. In the following example (Listing 6-6), an

```
Router1#sh in bri0
BRI0 is up, line protocol is up (spoofing)
  Hardware is BRI
  Internet address is 171.14.23.14/24
  MTU 1500 bytes, BW 48 Kbit, DLY 20000 usec, rely 255/255, load 1/255
  Encapsulation PPP, loopback not set
  Last input 00:00:04, output 00:00:04, output hang never
  Last clearing of "show interface" counters never
  Queueing strategy: fifo
  Output queue 0/40, 0 drops; input queue 0/75, 0 drops
  5 minute input rate 0 bits/sec, 0 packets/sec
  5 minute output rate 0 bits/sec, 0 packets/sec
     2651 packets input, 15524 bytes, 0 no buffer
     Received 382 broadcasts, 0 runts, 0 giants
     0 input errors, 0 CRC, 0 frame, 0 overrun, 0 ignored, 0 abort
     2987 packets output, 18070 bytes, 0 underruns
     0 output errors, 0 collisions, 27 interface resets
     0 output buffer failures, 0 output buffers swapped out
     23 carrier transitions
Router1#
```

Listing 6-5

```
Router1#sh int bri0 1 2
BRI0: B-Channel 1 is up, line protocol is up
  Hardware is BRI
  MTU 1500 bytes, BW 64 Kbit, DLY 20000 usec, rely 255/255, load 1/255
  Encapsulation PPP, loopback not set, keepalive set (10 sec)
  LCP Open, multilink Open
  Open: ccp, ipcp
  Last input 00:00:00, output 00:00:02, output hang never
  Last clearing of "show interface" counters never
  Queueing strategy: fifo
  Output queue 0/40, 0 drops; input queue 0/75, 0 drops
  5 minute input rate 0 bits/sec, 2 packets/sec
  5 minute output rate 0 bits/sec, 0 packets/sec
     7141 packets input, 303391 bytes, 0 no buffer
     Received 6962 broadcasts, 0 runts, 0 giants
     0 input errors, 0 CRC, 0 frame, 0 overrun, 0 ignored, 0 abort
     7797 packets output, 228570 bytes, 0 underruns
     0 output errors, 0 collisions, 27 interface resets
     0 output buffer failures, 0 output buffers swapped out
     12 carrier transitions
BRI0: B-Channel 2 is up, line protocol is up
  Hardware is BRI
  MTU 1500 bytes, BW 64 Kbit, DLY 20000 usec, rely 255/255, load 1/255
  Encapsulation PPP, loopback not set, keepalive set (10 sec)
  LCP Open, multilink Open
  Closed: ipcp
  Listen: ccp
  Last input 00:00:05, output 00:00:05, output hang never
  Last clearing of "show interface" counters never
  Queueing strategy: fifo
  Output queue 0/40, 0 drops; input queue 0/75, 0 drops
  5 minute input rate 0 bits/sec, 0 packets/sec
  5 minute output rate 0 bits/sec, 0 packets/sec
     2627 packets input, 84303 bytes, 0 no buffer
     Received 2627 broadcasts, 0 runts, 0 giants
     0 input errors, 0 CRC, 0 frame, 0 overrun, 0 ignored, 0 abort
     2738 packets output, 73060 bytes, 0 underruns
     0 output errors, 0 collisions, 27 interface resets
     0 output buffer failures, 0 output buffers swapped out
     116 carrier transitions
Router1#
```

Listing 6-6

ISDN call is active on each B-channel. This is verified by the "channel up, line protocol up" status of both B-channels. If a call were not present, the B-channel would read "interface down, line protocol down."

Also, it can be seen that Multilink PPP has been negotiated successfully on both channels with the LCP state of OPEN. If PPP negotiation were still under way, then it would be in the LISTEN state. If PPP negotiation failed, or if no call was up, then its state would read CLOSED.

This command also can indicate what desktop protocols are being transported using PPP. IPCP is the PPP Network Control Protocol (NCP) that supports IP. Here you can see that IPCP is open on channel 1 but closed on channel 2, indicating that IP traffic is currently present on the first B-channel only. The reason that this is occurring is that the volume of traffic is particularly low, as evidenced by the low input and output packet rate. The Multilink PPP facility brings up both channels, but because of the low traffic volume, IP traffic only travels over the first physical channel. In this example it can be deduced that the `dialer load-threshold` must be set to 1 because there simply is not enough load to bring up the second channel otherwise. There is another parameter in the output that further illustrates this point, namely, the number of carrier transitions. Note that there are far more transitions on the second B-channel. This is so because the second B-channel is brought up for every ISDN call. However, there is minimal interesting traffic flowing over it, so the idle timer eventually expires, causing this channel to be dropped.

A large number of carrier transitions can indicate a line problem in the local loop between the router and the central office. It also can indicate a number of other problems that are characterized by a larger number of persistent short-duration calls. Examples of this will be presented later in this chapter.

By comparing the errors seen in the output of the respective `show interface` commands for the D-channel and B-channels, useful information can be obtained about the state of the local loop. For example, if a large number of physical errors (input errors, CRCs, etc.) is evident in the output of `show interface bri0` but not so for the B-channels, this could indicate a physical problem in the local loop, since most D-channel information is stripped off at the switch.

The show ISDN status Command

This command is extremely useful because it gives an immediate summary of the most pertinent information for the status of layers 1, 2, and 3. In the following example (Listing 6-7), the physical layer is okay, as indicated by the ACTIVE state. If there was a physical problem, or if the ISDN interface was configured in backup mode, then this state would indicate DEACTIVATED. If the interface has just been brought up, this state will read ACTIVATING for a short period before steadying to ACTIVE or DEACTIVATED depending on the physical condition of the line to the switch.

Listing 6-7

```
Router1#sh isdn status
The current ISDN Switchtype = basic-dms100
ISDN BRI0 interface
    Layer 1 Status:
        ACTIVE
    Layer 2 Status:
        TEI = 84, State = MULTIPLE_FRAME_ESTABLISHED
        TEI = 85, State = MULTIPLE_FRAME_ESTABLISHED
    Layer 3 Status:
        2 Active Layer 3 Call(s)
    Activated dsl 0 CCBs = 2
        CCB:callid=804B, sapi=0, ces=1, B-chan=1
        CCB:callid=804D, sapi=0, ces=2, B-chan=2
    Total Allocated ISDN CCBs = 2
Router1#
```

Two terminal end point identifiers (TEIs) have been obtained from the switch. In crude and practical terms, TEIs can be thought of as the ISDN equivalent of dial tone. Thus the ISDN router is conversing successfully with its local switch. While TEI is being established, a broadcast TEI of 255 can be observed. This should progress quickly to the establishment of proper TEI values; otherwise, there is a layer 2 problem between the router and the ISDN switch. If the switch type is NI1, then only one TEI value is established in the normal condition.

It also can be observed that both ISDN B-channels are engaged in a layer 3 call. There is no information as to which end initiated the call, its current duration, or whether or not both B-channels are connected to the same destination.

The `show dialer` Command

The `show dialer` command gives more detailed information on the status of any current layer 3 calls, along with providing some potentially useful historical data. The information that can be extracted from the following example (Listing 6-8) includes

- Just one number has been called since the dialer counter was last cleared. It has been called 78 times, with all calls connecting successfully to the remote end. A *success* is defined as the receipt of a connect message from the far end. This simply means that the remote end answered the call. PPP authentication still has to take place at this point. Hence a call could be deemed successful but then get hung up within 25 seconds due to an authentication failure.

```
Router1#sh dialer

BRI0 - dialer type = ISDN

Dial String       Successes   Failures    Last called   Last status
19256775085           78          0         00:00:21      successful
0 incoming call(s) have been screened.

BRI0: B-Channel 1
Idle timer (100 secs), Fast idle timer (20 secs)
Wait for carrier (30 secs), Re-enable (15 secs)
Time until disconnect 96 secs
Current call connected 00:00:21
Connected to 192567750 (Router2)

BRI0: B-Channel 2
Idle timer (100 secs), Fast idle timer (20 secs)
Wait for carrier (30 secs), Re-enable (15 secs)
Time until disconnect 80 secs
Current call connected 00:00:21
Connected to 192567750 (Router2)

Dialer0 - dialer type = NONE
Router1#
```

Listing 6-8

- The number was last called 21 seconds ago, which is the current call that is up. The fact that the current call on each B-channel is an outgoing call also can be verified by the fact that connection time information is given on each B-channel. If this were an incoming call, information on the duration that the call is up usually would not be available.
- The time until disconnect on an outgoing call is the current value of the idle timer. In the case of B-channel 1, it is 96 seconds. It can be seen that the idle timer decrements from a configured value of 100 seconds; hence it has been 4 seconds since interesting outbound traffic passed on B-channel 1. The time until disconnect on B-channel 2 is 80 seconds, implying that no interesting traffic has been passed on this channel since the call was set up.
- The purpose of the fast idle timer is to clear the B-channel of an existing call more quickly if no traffic is being passed and there is another new call attempt queued.

The counters for the output of `show dialer` can be reset using the `clear dialer` command.

The show isdn memory Command

The output of `show isdn memory` is usually only analyzed by a specialized technical support staff. However, there are instances where memory issues need to be checked in relation to ISDN. If one or more of the memory block types have their maximum allowed value in use, then there may be a fundamental ISDN problem on the router. This problem may only be characterized by intermittent call failures.

By doing your own research or consulting with appropriate technical support personnel, it should be verified that the router has sufficient memory for the ISDN modules it supports. For example, if an 8-port BRI card is installed in a Cisco 4500 series router, it is generally recommended that the router have a minimum of 8 MB of shared memory. (See Listing 6-9.)

ISDN Debug Commands

Cisco routers provide some powerful ISDN debugging tools, the output of which usually can be displayed without putting too much of a strain on the processor. Much of the output is intuitively understandable or even self-explanatory. Other error and debug messages need to be researched. Many of the error messages will be discussed here or encountered in practical examples. For ISDN debug messages that are not referenced here, the following URL is a good resource for explaining these codes: *www.cisco.com/univercd/cc/td/doc/product/software/ios11/dbook/disdn.htm*.

Listing 6-9

```
Router1#sh isdn memory
        MEMORY POOL STATISTICS (BlockType: in-use max-allowed)
        mail descriptors: 7 60
        exec timer blocks: 5 30
        LIF timer blocks: 31 120
        SBC_BTYPE: 0 8
        PRIM_BTYPE: 37 85
        PKT_BTYPE: 4 85
        HEADER_BTYPE: 1 85
        SML_INFO_BTYPE: 7 85
        LRG_INFO_BTYPE: 3 20
        PKG_BTYPE: 5 50
        CCBs: 2 6
        DLCBs: 2 2
        NLCBs: 3 10
Router1#
```

The debug isdn q921 Command

The debug isdn q921 command provides a trace of the layer 2 q921 signaling messages that are exchanged across the D-channel between the router and the switch. This D-channel signaling is in accordance with the user interface specification defined by ITU-T Recommendation Q.921. The output from this command is limited to commands and responses exchanged on the user side rather than on the network side of the ISDN switch. These messages will confirm whether or not TEI has been obtained from the switch.

The following output for router 1 shows TEI values of 84 and 85, which agrees with what was observed using the show isdn status command (see Listing 6-10).

These messages, which are periodic TEI management packets, continue to be exchanged like keepalives between the router and the ISDN switch, after TEI has been established initially.

The D-channel signals during call setup and teardown also can be monitored using debug isdn q921. However, once the D-channel signaling has been verified between the router and the switch, it is usually more useful to troubleshoot call failure using debug isdn events or debug isdn q931.

```
Router1#deb isdn q921
ISDN Q921 packets debugging is on
Router1#term mon
Router1#
.Nov 24 08:49:48 PST: ISDN BR0: TX ->  RRp sapi = 0  tei = 84 nr = 3
.Nov 24 08:49:48 PST: ISDN BR0: RX <-  RRf sapi = 0  tei = 84  nr = 3
.Nov 24 08:49:49 PST: ISDN BR0: TX ->  RRp sapi = 0  tei = 85 nr = 15
.Nov 24 08:49:49 PST: ISDN BR0: RX <-  RRf sapi = 0  tei = 85  nr = 19
.Nov 24 08:49:58 PST: ISDN BR0: TX ->  RRp sapi = 0  tei = 84 nr = 3
.Nov 24 08:49:58 PST: ISDN BR0: RX <-  RRf sapi = 0  tei = 84  nr = 3
.Nov 24 08:49:59 PST: ISDN BR0: TX ->  RRp sapi = 0  tei = 85 nr = 15
.Nov 24 08:49:59 PST: ISDN BR0: RX <-  RRf sapi = 0  tei = 85  nr = 19
```

Listing 6-10

While troubleshooting ISDN problems, it is sometimes prudent to use two or more of the debug commands simultaneously. The output will be intermingled and displayed as it gets generated.

The `debug isdn q931` Command

The ISDN network layer interface provided by the router conforms to the user interface specification defined by ITU-T Recommendation Q.931. The `debug isdn q931` command provides an extremely powerful way to track the progress of a layer 3 call through the ISDN network during the stages of call setup, call connect, and call teardown.

The sending and receipt of all layer 3 call-establishment and call-termination messages are monitored. In the following example (Listing 6-11), I turned on this debugging and then cleared down the existing ISDN calls by clearing the interface. The router is configured to allow any IP traffic to initiate a call; therefore, a new call setup follows promptly.

All the basic layer 3 signaling messages for the call setup on B-channel 1 have been highlighted in bold. The same messages are also seen when the second B-channel sets up its call. The example is indicative of a normal successful call setup. In the case of a call failing during setup, this type of debug output can be very helpful in isolating the problem.

The receipt of a call proceeding message, or CALL_PROC, indicates that the calling DCE (i.e., the local central office switch) has been reached successfully. The receipt of such a message usually, but not always, as you will see, indicates that there is no ISDN configuration problem between the router and the local switch.

The receipt of a connect message is the next critical stage. This indicates that the remote router answered the call and the resulting connect message has been sent back to the calling router. Getting this far verifies the following:

- The SPIDs have been configured correctly on the router; otherwise, a call-proceeding message would not have been received.
- The connect message indicates that the dialer map statement has been correctly configured. It also suggests that the fundamental ISDN configuration of the remote router is correct.
- In theory, this should confirm that the configured switch type is correct, and this is almost always true. However, I have seen an instance in practice where calls got dropped approximately a minute after being connected because of an incorrect switch type.

```
Router1#debug isdn q931
ISDN Q931 packets debugging is on
Router1#cle in br0
Clear this interface [confirm]
Router1#
Nov 24 08:53:42 PST: %ISDN-6-DISCONNECT: Interface BRI0: B-Channel 1  disconnected
  from 1925555085 Router2, call lasted 82 seconds
Nov 24 08:53:42 PST: %ISDN-6-DISCONNECT: Interface BRI0: B-Channel 2  disconnected
  from 1925555085 Router2, call lasted 78 seconds
Nov 24 08:53:42 PST: %LINK-3-UPDOWN: Interface BRI0: B-Channel 1, changed state to
  down
Nov 24 08:53:42 PST: %LINK-3-UPDOWN: Interface BRI0: B-Channel 2, changed state to
  down
Nov 24 08:53:42 PST: %LINK-3-UPDOWN: Interface BRI0, changed state to down
Nov 24 08:53:42 PST: %LINEPROTO-5-UPDOWN: Line protocol on Interface BRI0: B-Channel
  1, changed state to down
Nov 24 08:53:42 PST: %LINEPROTO-5-UPDOWN: Line protocol on Interface BRI0: B-Channel
  2, changed state to down
Nov 24 08:53:42 PST: ISDN BR0: Event: incoming ces value = 1
Nov 24 08:53:42 PST: ISDN BR0: Event: incoming ces value = 2
Nov 24 08:53:42 PST: ISDN BR0: Event: incoming ces value = 1
Nov 24 08:53:43 PST: ISDN BR0: Event: incoming ces value = 1
Nov 24 08:53:45 PST: ISDN BR0: TX ->  INFORMATION pd = 8  callref = (null)
        SPID Information i = 0x3635303638353136353030313031
Nov 24 08:53:45 PST: ISDN BR0: TX ->  SETUP pd = 8  callref = 0x56
Nov 24 08:53:45 PST:           Bearer Capability i = 0x8890
Nov 24 08:53:45 PST:           Channel ID i = 0x83
Nov 24 08:53:45 PST:           Called Party Number i = 0x80, '1925555085'
Nov 24 08:53:45 PST: ISDN BR0: RX <-  INFORMATION pd = 8  callref = (null)
        ENDPOINT IDent i = 0xF081
Nov 24 08:53:45 PST: ISDN BR0: Event: incoming ces value = 1
Nov 24 08:53:45 PST: ISDN BR0: RX <-  CALL_PROC pd = 8  callref = 0xD6
Nov 24 08:53:45 PST:           Channel ID i = 0x89
Nov 24 08:53:45 PST:           Locking Shift to Codeset 5
Nov 24 08:53:45 PST:           Codeset 5 IE 0x2A  i = 0x80880B, '1925555085',
  0x800109800114800114800114
Nov 24 08:53:45 PST: ISDN BR0: Event: incoming ces value = 1
Nov 24 08:53:46 PST: ISDN BR0: RX <-  CONNECT pd = 8  callref = 0xD6
Nov 24 08:53:46 PST: ISDN BR0: Event: incoming ces value = 1
Nov 24 08:53:46 PST: %LINK-3-UPDOWN: Interface BRI0: B-Channel 1, changed state to up
Nov 24 08:53:47 PST: ISDN BR0: TX ->  CONNECT_ACK pd = 8  callref = 0x56
Nov 24 08:53:47 PST: %LINEPROTO-5-UPDOWN: Line protocol on Interface BRI0: B-Channel
  1, changed state to up
Nov 24 08:53:49 PST: ISDN BR0: TX ->  INFORMATION pd = 8  callref = (null)
        SPID Information i = 0x3635303638353137343730313031
Nov 24 08:53:49 PST: ISDN BR0: TX ->  SETUP pd = 8  callref = 0x57
Nov 24 08:53:49 PST:           Bearer Capability i = 0x8890
Nov 24 08:53:49 PST:           Channel ID i = 0x83
Nov 24 08:53:49 PST:           Called Party Number i = 0x80, '1925555085'
Nov 24 08:53:49 PST: ISDN BR0: RX <-  INFORMATION pd = 8  callref = (null)
        ENDPOINT IDent i = 0xF181
Nov 24 08:53:49 PST: ISDN BR0: Event: incoming ces value = 2
```

Listing 6-11

```
Nov 24 08:53:49 PST: ISDN BR0: RX <-  CALL_PROC pd = 8  callref = 0xD7
Nov 24 08:53:49 PST:          Channel ID i = 0x8A
Nov 24 08:53:49 PST:          Locking Shift to Codeset 5
Nov 24 08:53:49 PST:          Codeset 5 IE 0x2A  i = 0x80880B, '1925555085',
  0x800109800114800114800114
Nov 24 08:53:49 PST: ISDN BR0: Event: incoming ces value = 2
Nov 24 08:53:50 PST: ISDN BR0: RX <-  CONNECT pd = 8  callref = 0xD7
Nov 24 08:53:50 PST: ISDN BR0: Event: incoming ces value = 2
Nov 24 08:53:50 PST: %LINK-3-UPDOWN: Interface BRI0: B-Channel 2, changed state to up
Nov 24 08:53:51 PST: ISDN BR0: TX ->  CONNECT_ACK pd = 8  callref = 0x57
Nov 24 08:53:51 PST: %LINEPROTO-5-UPDOWN: Line protocol on Interface BRI0: B-Channel
  2, changed state to up
Nov 24 08:53:57 PST: %ISDN-6-CONNECT:
```

Listing 6-11 *(Cont.)*

The `debug isdn events` Command

A similar information set to what we have just seen is available using the `debug isdn events` command. There is a slight difference in the output format. This command will indicate what the speed of the call is, an important and often troublesome parameter. It also includes a display of the CHAP user name of the remote router. Some non-layer 3 messages also can be included in the output of `debug isdn events`. It is not a problem to run both these debug commands concurrently. The output will be interleaved, and there should not be a processor load problem unless the router has several active ISDN interfaces.

In the following example (Listing 6-12), the interface was again cleared in order to generate a call teardown and new call setup. The output also includes the TEI messages, which are not layer 3. The most fundamental call setup messages also have been highlighted.

The `debug dialer` Command

The `debug dialer` tool provides information on traffic that can cause dialing to be initiated or interesting traffic as defined by the dialer list. It can be seen if dialing actually does occur, and if it does occur, the status of the interesting packets that caused the dialing to be initiated is reported on.

An explanation is given if dialing does not occur after interesting packets pass the dialer list. Obviously, this is extremely useful.

```
Router1#debug isdn ev
ISDN events debugging is on
Router1#cle in br0
Clear this interface [confirm]
Router1#
Nov 24 08:57:26 PST: %ISDN-6-DISCONNECT: Interface BRI0: B-Channel 1  disconnected
  from 1925555085 Router2, call lasted 28 seconds
Nov 24 08:57:26 PST: %ISDN-6-DISCONNECT: Interface BRI0: B-Channel 2  disconnected
  from 1925555085 Router2, call lasted 24 seconds
Nov 24 08:57:26 PST: %LINK-3-UPDOWN: Interface BRI0: B-Channel 1, changed state to
  down
Nov 24 08:57:26 PST: %LINK-3-UPDOWN: Interface BRI0: B-Channel 2, changed state to
  down
Nov 24 08:57:26 PST: %LINK-3-UPDOWN: Interface BRI0, changed state to down
Nov 24 08:57:26 PST: ISDN BR0: Physical layer is IF_DOWN
Nov 24 08:57:26 PST: ISDN BR0: L1 is IF_ACTIVE
Nov 24 08:57:26 PST: ISDN BR0: L1 ERR IF_ACTIVE
Nov 24 08:57:26 PST: ISDN BR0: Event: Hangup call to call id 0x805F  ces = 1
Nov 24 08:57:26 PST: ISDN BR0: Event: Hangup call to call id 0x8060  ces = 2
Nov 24 08:57:26 PST: ISDN BR0: Shutting down ME
Nov 24 08:57:26 PST: ISDN BR0: Shutting down ISDN Layer 3
Nov 24 08:57:26 PST: ISDN BR0: Event: incoming ces value = 1
Nov 24 08:57:26 PST: ISDN BR0: received HOST_QUERY_RESPONSE
        Call State i = 0x00
Nov 24 08:57:26 PST:     ----------
Nov 24 08:57:26 PST: ISDN BR0: Event: incoming ces value = 2
Nov 24 08:57:26 PST: ISDN BR0: received HOST_QUERY_RESPONSE
        Call State i = 0x00
Nov 24 08:57:26 PST:     ----------
Nov 24 08:57:26 PST: ISDN BR0: Event: Call to 1925555085 at 64 Kb/s
Nov 24 08:57:26 PST: ISDN BR0: Event: incoming ces value = 1
Nov 24 08:57:26 PST: ISDN BR0: received HOST_DISCONNECT_ACK
Nov 24 08:57:26 PST: ISDN BR0: Got a disconnect on a non-existent call (call id =
  0x8061).
Nov 24 08:57:26 PST: This probably is a call that we placed that never got answered.
Nov 24 08:57:26 PST: %LINEPROTO-5-UPDOWN: Line protocol on Interface BRI0: B-Channel
  1, changed state to down
Nov 24 08:57:26 PST: %LINEPROTO-5-UPDOWN: Line protocol on Interface BRI0: B-Channel
  2, changed state to down
Nov 24 08:57:29 PST: ISDN BR0: Event: Call to 1925555085 at 64 Kb/s
Nov 24 08:57:29 PST: ISDN BR0: Event: incoming ces value = 1
Nov 24 08:57:29 PST: ISDN BR0: received HOST_TERM_REGISTER_ACK - received eid
        ENDPOINT IDent i = 0xF081
Nov 24 08:57:30 PST: ISDN BR0: Event: incoming ces value = 1
Nov 24 08:57:30 PST: ISDN BR0: received HOST_PROCEEDING
        Channel ID i = 0x0101
Nov 24 08:57:30 PST:     ----------
        Channel ID i = 0x89
Nov 24 08:57:30 PST:          Locking Shift to Codeset 5
Nov 24 08:57:30 PST:          Codeset 5 IE 0x2A  i = 0x80880B, '1925555085',
  0x800109800114800114800114
Nov 24 08:57:31 PST: ISDN BR0: Event: incoming ces value = 1
```

Listing 6-12

```
Nov 24 08:57:31 PST: ISDN BR0: received HOST_CONNECT
        Channel ID i = 0x0101
Nov 24 08:57:31 PST:     ----------
Nov 24 08:57:31 PST: %LINK-3-UPDOWN: Interface BRI0: B-Channel 1, changed state to up
Nov 24 08:57:31 PST: ISDN BR0: Event: Connected to 1925555085 on B1 at 64 Kb/s
Nov 24 08:57:32 PST: %LINEPROTO-5-UPDOWN: Line protocol on Interface BRI0: B-Channel
  1, changed state to up
Nov 24 08:57:33 PST: ISDN BR0: Event: incoming ces value = 2
Nov 24 08:57:33 PST: ISDN BR0: received HOST_TERM_REGISTER_ACK - received eid
        ENDPOINT IDent i = 0xF181
Nov 24 08:57:34 PST: ISDN BR0: Event: Call to 1925555085 at 64 Kb/s
Nov 24 08:57:34 PST: ISDN BR0: Event: incoming ces value = 2
Nov 24 08:57:34 PST: ISDN BR0: received HOST_PROCEEDING
        Channel ID i = 0x0102
Nov 24 08:57:34 PST:     ----------
        Channel ID i = 0x8A
Nov 24 08:57:34 PST:           Locking Shift to Codeset 5
Nov 24 08:57:34 PST:           Codeset 5 IE 0x2A  i = 0x80880B, '1925555085', 0x8
00109800114800114800114
Nov 24 08:57:35 PST: ISDN BR0: Event: incoming ces value = 2
Nov 24 08:57:35 PST: ISDN BR0: received HOST_CONNECT
        Channel ID i = 0x0102
Nov 24 08:57:35 PST:     ----------
Nov 24 08:57:35 PST: %LINK-3-UPDOWN: Interface BRI0: B-Channel 2, changed state to up
Nov 24 08:57:35 PST: ISDN BR0: Event: Connected to 1925555085 on B2 at 64 Kb/s
Nov 24 08:57:36 PST: %LINEPROTO-5-UPDOWN: Line protocol on Interface BRI0: B-Channel
  2, changed state to up
Nov 24 08:57:42 PST: %ISDN-6-CONNECT: Interface BRI0: B-Channel 2 is now connected to
  1925555085 Router2
Router1#undeb all
All possible debugging has been turned off
```

Listing 6-12 ***(Cont.)***

First, let's look at an example of a successful call. Again, I cleared the interface in order to generate some action. This dialer list on this router is a simple one:

```
dialer-list 1 protocol ip permit
```

This means that any IP traffic can initiate a call. In the output (Listing 6-13), directed broadcast brings up the line. The "IP permit" dialer-list definition is quoted as the cause for dialing. This touches another topic, namely, the question of strictly defined dialer lists in order to prevent unnecessary and spurious ISDN calls and hence unnecessarily high phone bills. The `debug dialer` command is the ideal tool for troubleshooting unwanted dialing. In many cases it may be undesirable to

```
Router1#debug dialer
Dial on Demand debugging is on
Router1#cle in br0
Clear this interface [confirm]
Router1#
Nov 24 09:52:55 PST: BRI0: sending broadcast to ip 171.144.230.1
Nov 24 09:52:56 PST: %ISDN-6-DISCONNECT: Interface BRI0: B-Channel 1  disconnected
  from 1925555085 Router2, call lasted 27 seconds
Nov 24 09:52:56 PST: %ISDN-6-DISCONNECT: Interface BRI0: B-Channel 2  disconnected
  from 1925555085 Router2, call lasted 23 seconds
Nov 24 09:52:56 PST: %LINK-3-UPDOWN: Interface BRI0: B-Channel 1, changed state to
  down
Nov 24 09:52:56 PST: MLP: Change init idb: old = BRI0: B-Channel 1, new = BRI0:
B-Channel 2
Nov 24 09:52:56 PST: BRI0: B-Channel 1: disconnecting call
Nov 24 09:52:56 PST: %LINK-3-UPDOWN: Interface BRI0: B-Channel 2, changed state to
  down
Nov 24 09:52:57 PST: %LINK-3-UPDOWN: Interface BRI0, changed state to down
Nov 24 09:52:57 PST: BRI0: B-Channel 2: disconnecting call
Nov 24 09:52:57 PST: BRI0: sending broadcast to ip 171.14.23.1
Nov 24 09:52:57 PST: BRI0: Dialing cause: BRI0: ip PERMIT
Nov 24 09:52:57 PST: BRI0:Creating holdq 15F680
Nov 24 09:52:57 PST: BRI0: Attempting to dial 1925555085
Nov 24 09:52:57 PST: : Dialing remote, packet queued — failed, not connected
Nov 24 09:52:57 PST: BRI0: wait for carrier timeout, call id=0x8069
Nov 24 09:52:57 PST: freeing dialer holdq 15F680
Nov 24 09:52:57 PST: : Dialing failed, 1 packets unqueued and discarded
Nov 24 09:52:57 PST: %LINEPROTO-5-UPDOWN: Line protocol on Interface BRI0: B-Channel
  1, changed state to down
Nov 24 09:52:57 PST: %LINEPROTO-5-UPDOWN: Line protocol on Interface BRI0: B-Channel
  2, changed state to down
Nov 24 09:53:00 PST: BRI0: Dialing cause: BRI0: ip PERMIT
Nov 24 09:53:00 PST: BRI0:Creating holdq 15F680
Nov 24 09:53:00 PST: BRI0: Attempting to dial 19255555085
Nov 24 09:53:00 PST: : Dialing remote, packet queued
Nov 24 09:53:00 PST: BRI0: sending broadcast to ip 171.14.23.1
Nov 24 09:53:00 PST: : Still dialing, packet queued — failed, not connected
Nov 24 09:53:01 PST: %LINK-3-UPDOWN: Interface BRI0: B-Channel 1, changed state to up
Nov 24 09:53:01 PST: BRI0: B-Channel 1: 1925555085, multilink up, first link
Nov 24 09:53:01 PST: freeing dialer holdq 15F680
Nov 24 09:53:01 PST: BRI0: B-Channel 1: Call connected, 2 packets unqueued, 2 trans-
  mitted, 0 discarded
Nov 24 09:53:01 PST: BRI0: sending broadcast to ip 171.14.23.1
Nov 24 09:53:02 PST: BRI0: sending broadcast to ip 171.14.23.1
Nov 24 09:53:02 PST: BRI0: sending broadcast to ip 171.14.23.1
Nov 24 09:53:02 PST: %LINEPROTO-5-UPDOWN: Line protocol on Interface BRI0: B-Channel
  1, changed state to up
Nov 24 09:53:04 PST: BRI0: rotary group to 1925555085 overloaded (1)
Nov 24 09:53:04 PST: BRI0:Creating holdq 15A640
Nov 24 09:53:04 PST: BRI0: Attempting to dial 1925555085
Nov 24 09:53:04 PST: BRI0: sending broadcast to ip 171.14.23.1
Nov 24 09:53:05 PST: %LINK-3-UPDOWN: Interface BRI0: B-Channel 2, changed state to up
```

Listing 6-13

```
Nov 24 09:53:05 PST: BRI0: B-Channel 2: 1925555085, multilink up
Nov 24 09:53:05 PST: freeing dialer holdq 15A640
Nov 24 09:53:05 PST: : Multilink bundle member, 0 packets unqueued and discarded
Nov 24 09:53:06 PST: %LINEPROTO-5-UPDOWN: Line protocol on Interface BRI0: B-Channel
  2, changed state to up
Nov 24 09:53:09 PST: BRI0: sending broadcast to ip 171.14.23.1
Nov 24 09:53:12 PST: %ISDN-6-CONNECT: Interface BRI0: B-Channel 2 is now connected to
  19256775085 Router2
Nov 24 09:53:13 PST: BRI0: sending broadcast to ip 171.14.23.1

Router1#undeb all
All possible debugging has been turned off
Router1#term no mon
Router1#
```

Listing 6-13 (*Cont.*)

send any broadcasts across the ISDN network unless the line is already up. This entire issue is dealt with elsewhere in this chapter.

Further on in the `debug dialer` output, the packets get placed in the dialer hold queue. Packets clearly cannot be transmitted until the call is fully established, as is seen by the "failed, not connected" message. This command will continue to provide information on packets that match the dialer list even after both B-channel calls have been established.

The following is a sample `debug dialer` for a router that did not have a dialer group defined on the bri0 interface. The `debug dialer` output is quite self-explanatory (see Listing 6-14).

The `debug ppp authentication` Command

This command appears as `debug ppp chap` in the Cisco IOS versions earlier than 11.1 but the command has since been generalized to `debug ppp authentication`. If CHAP authentication is being used, then there is no difference in the displayed output.

This command should be used if an authentication problem is suspected. A CHAP authentication mismatch is often characterized by a large number of short-duration calls. After the ISDN call attempts to connect to the remote end, the PPP negotiation begins. Authentication is the last PPP parameter to be dealt with, since the call must have connected already to the remote end before CHAP handshaking can be veri-

```
Router1#
Nov 24 09:56:48 PST: BRI0: sending broadcast to ip 171.14.23.1
Nov 24 09:56:48 PST: BRI0: No dialer-group defined - dialing can not occur
Nov 24 09:56:48 PST: BRI0: Passive interfaces not supported on rotary group — failed,
  not connected
Nov 24 09:56:48 PST: BRI0: sending broadcast to default destination
Nov 24 09:56:48 PST: BRI0: No dialer-group defined - dialing can not occur
Nov 24 09:56:48 PST: BRI0: Passive interfaces not supported on rotary group — failed,
  not connected
Nov 24 09:56:48 PST: BRI0: No dialer-group defined - dialing can not occur
Nov 24 09:56:48 PST: BRI0: Passive interfaces not supported on rotary group
Nov 24 09:56:53 PST: BRI0: sending broadcast to ip 171.14.23.1
Nov 24 09:56:53 PST: BRI0: No dialer-group defined - dialing can not occur
Nov 24 09:56:53 PST: BRI0: Passive interfaces not supported on rotary group — failed,
  not connected
Router1#
```

Listing 6-14

fied. Both the calling end and the called router will exchange a CHAP challenge, where each checks the CHAP user name and password combination received from the other router against what is in its configuration. There must be an exact match of user name against the remote hostname, along with the correct password; otherwise, CHAP will fail, and the call will drop.

This example (Listing 6-15) has the user name missing from the configuration. Router 1 attempts to call Router 2, as defined in the dialer map statement, but there is no user name defined for Router 2 in Router 1's configuration. Hence the call is dropped within seconds of connecting.

Listing 6-16 is an example of the correct user name (Router 2) being configured on the router but with the wrong CHAP password. The call is dropped when it is detected that the two passwords do not match. Although it is not evident in these two examples, the call often drops about 10 seconds sooner if no user name has been defined. If a user name with an incorrect password is defined, then the call may take over 20 seconds to clear because of the additional steps in checking the password.

Listing 6-17 is the `debug ppp chap` output when the CHAP has been configured correctly.

```
Router1#

NO USERNAME Router2 DEFINED!!

!
int bri0
encapsulation ppp
dialer map ip 171.14.23.1 name Router2 broadcast 19255555085
ppp authentication chap
!

Router1#debug ppp authen
PPP authentication debugging is on

Nov 24 10:07:35 PST: %ISDN-6-DISCONNECT: Interface BRI0: B-Channel 2  disconnected
  from 1925555085 Router2, call lasted 100 seconds
Nov 24 10:07:36 PST: %LINK-3-UPDOWN: Interface BRI0: B-Channel 2, changed state to
  down
Nov 24 10:07:36 PST: %LINEPROTO-5-UPDOWN: Line protocol on Interface BRI0: B-Channel
  2, changed state to down
Nov 24 10:07:39 PST: %LINK-3-UPDOWN: Interface BRI0: B-Channel 2, changed state to up
Nov 24 10:07:39 PST: PPP BRI0: B-Channel 2: treating connection as a callout
Nov 24 10:07:39 PST: PPP BRI0: B-Channel 2: Send CHAP Challenge id=84
Nov 24 10:07:39 PST: PPP BRI0: B-Channel 2: CHAP Challenge id=8 received from Router2
Nov 24 10:07:39 PST: PPP BRI0: B-Channel 2: USERNAME Router2 not found.
Nov 24 10:07:39 PST: PPP BRI0: B-Channel 2: Unable to authenticate for peer.
Nov 24 10:07:39 PST: %LINK-3-UPDOWN: Interface BRI0: B-Channel 2, changed state to
  down
```

Listing 6-15

The `debug ppp negotiation` Command

The `debug ppp negotiation` command gives broader information on each of the steps involved in PPP startup negotiation. Authentication problems can be detected using this command, although the information is presented more clearly with `debug ppp authentication`, so that command should be used if an authentication problem is suspected. The `debug ppp negotiation` tool displays the PPP messages that are exchanged during LCP and then NCP negotiation. It will provide information as to why the LCP state will not open. This, again, is the PPP layer 2 Link Control Protocol. This tool also will display if a requested NCP (Network Control Protocol) is not supported at the other end of the link.

In the following output (Listing 6-18), the sending of CONFREQ messages and the receipt of equivalent CONFIG replies indicate the steps in

```
Nov 24 10:14:54 PST: %LINK-3-UPDOWN: Interface BRI0: B-Channel 1, changed state
to up
Nov 24 10:14:54 PST: PPP BRI0: B-Channel 1: treating connection as a callout
Nov 24 10:14:54 PST: PPP BRI0: B-Channel 1: Send CHAP Challenge id=27
Nov 24 10:14:54 PST: PPP BRI0: B-Channel 1: CHAP Challenge id=180 received from
  Router2
Nov 24 10:14:54 PST: PPP BRI0: B-Channel 1: Send CHAP Response id=180
Nov 24 10:14:54 PST: PPP BRI0: B-Channel 1: Failed CHAP authentication with remote.
Nov 24 10:14:54 PST: Remote message is: MD compare failed
Nov 24 10:14:55 PST: %LINK-3-UPDOWN: Interface BRI0: B-Channel 1, changed state to
  down
```

Listing 6-16

```
Router1#
Nov 24 10:09:09 PST: PPP BRI0: B-Channel 2: treating connection as a callout
Nov 24 10:09:09 PST: PPP BRI0: B-Channel 2: Send CHAP Challenge id=87
Nov 24 10:09:09 PST: PPP BRI0: B-Channel 2: CHAP Challenge id=11 received from
  Router2
Nov 24 10:09:09 PST: PPP BRI0: B-Channel 2: Send CHAP Response id=11
Nov 24 10:09:09 PST: PPP BRI0: B-Channel 2: Passed CHAP authentication with remote.
Nov 24 10:09:09 PST: PPP BRI0: B-Channel 2: CHAP Response id=87 received from Router2
Nov 24 10:09:09 PST: PPP BRI0: B-Channel 2: Send CHAP Success id=87
Nov 24 10:09:09 PST: PPP BRI0: B-Channel 2: remote passed CHAP authentication.
Nov 24 10:09:10 PST: %LINEPROTO-5-UPDOWN: Line protocol on Interface BRI0: B-Channel
  2, changed state to up
Nov 24 10:09:16 PST: %ISDN-6-CONNECT: Interface BRI0: B-Channel 2 is now connected to
  1925555085 Router2
Router1#
```

Listing 6-17

basic LCP negotiation. NCP negotiation only had to take place for IP or IPCP because IP is the only desktop protocol being transported across the link. The LCP and NCP negotiation was successful, and in the final step, the line protocol comes up.

Now let's look at the debug output for an unsuccessful PPP negotiation (Listing 6-19). Here, you see LCP negotiation failing because there is no reply being received to the CONFREQ messages. The requests then time out, and LCP moves to a LISTEN state. If a `show interface serial4/1/0` is now done, the LCP state will be LISTEN, and the IPCP

```
r6#debug ppp negotiat
PPP protocol negotiation debugging is on
r6#Mar  1 00:33:45: %SYS-5-CONFIG_I: Configured from console by console
*Mar  1 00:33:55: PPP Serial1: Unsupported or un-negotiated protocol. Link = cdp
*Mar  1 00:33:56: %SYS-5-CONFIG_I: Configured from console by console
*Mar  1 00:33:57: %LINK-3-UPDOWN: Interface Serial1, changed state to up
*Mar  1 00:33:57: PPP Serial1: treating connection as a dedicated line
*Mar  1 00:33:57: ppp: sending CONFREQ, type = 5 (CI_MAGICNUMBER), value = 0x4FB8EE
*Mar  1 00:33:57: PPP Serial1: received config for type = 5 (MAGICNUMBER) value =
  0x554F6F7B acked
*Mar  1 00:33:57: PPP Serial1: state = ACKsent fsm_rconfack(0xC021): rcvd id 2
*Mar  1 00:33:57: ppp: config ACK received, type = 5 (CI_MAGICNUMBER), value =
  0x4FB8EE
*Mar  1 00:33:57: ipcp: sending CONFREQ, type = 3 (CI_ADDRESS), Address = 130.10.11.2
*Mar  1 00:33:57: ppp Serial1: Negotiate IP address: her address 130.10.11.1 (ACK)
*Mar  1 00:33:57: ppp: ipcp_reqci: returning CONFACK.
*Mar  1 00:33:57: ppp: cdp_reqci: returning CONFACK
*Mar  1 00:33:57: PPP Serial1: state = ACKsent fsm_rconfack(0x8021): rcvd id 2
*Mar  1 00:33:57: ipcp: config ACK received, type = 3 (CI_ADDRESS), Address =
  130.10.11.2
*Mar  1 00:33:57: Serial1: install route to 130.10.11.1
*Mar  1 00:33:57: PPP Serial1: state = ACKsent fsm_rconfack(0x8207): rcvd id 2
*Mar  1 00:33:57: ppp: cdp_reqci: received CONFACK
*Mar  1 00:33:58: %LINEPROTO-5-UPDOWN: Line protocol on Interface Serial1, changed
  state to up
r6#
```

Listing 6-18

state will be CLOSED. The reason for the failure in this case is that the other end of the link does not have PPP encapsulation enabled.

Two other PPP debugging commands are frequently used:

- `debug ppp error` This displays PPP protocol error information and statistics. Some of its output can be obtained from the other PPP debug commands. It can be useful to leave the output of this command writing to a log if the problem under investigation is intermittent and cannot be diagnosed otherwise.
- `debug ppp packet` This will give an output of all PPP-encapsulated packets. This can cause processor load issues, especially if the router has multiple ISDN interfaces, and therefore should be used with caution. The output of `debug ppp packet` command also can result in excessive information, making it difficult to isolate the most relevant parts. Only use this command if you have still failed to diagnose the problem using the other PPP debugging commands.

```
Router#debug ppp negot
PPP protocol negotiation debugging is on
Router#
1d00h: Se4/1/0 LCP: TIMEout: Time 0x527F0F0 State REQsent
1d00h: Se4/1/0 LCP: O CONFREQ [REQsent] id 9 len 10
1d00h: Se4/1/0 LCP:    MagicNumber 0x553323CD (0x0506553323CD)
1d00h: Se4/1/0 LCP: TIMEout: Time 0x527F8C0 State REQsent
1d00h: Se4/1/0 LCP: O CONFREQ [REQsent] id 10 len 10
1d00h: Se4/1/0 LCP:    MagicNumber 0x553323CD (0x0506553323CD)
1d00h: Se4/1/0 LCP: TIMEout: Time 0x5280090 State REQsent
1d00h: Se4/1/0 LCP: O CONFREQ [REQsent] id 11 len 10
1d00h: Se4/1/0 LCP:    MagicNumber 0x553323CD (0x0506553323CD)
1d00h: Se4/1/0 LCP: TIMEout: Time 0x5280860 State REQsent
1d00h: Se4/1/0 LCP: State is Listen
1d00h: Se4/1/0 LCP: TIMEout: Time 0x5287D94 State Listen
1d00h: Se4/1/0 LCP: O CONFREQ [Listen] id 12 len 10
1d00h: Se4/1/0 LCP:    MagicNumber 0x5533F282 (0x05065533F282)
1d00h: Se4/1/0 LCP: TIMEout: Time 0x5288564 State REQsent
1d00h: Se4/1/0 LCP: O CONFREQ [REQsent] id 13 len 10
1d00h: Se4/1/0 LCP:    MagicNumber 0x5533F282 (0x05065533F282)
1d00h: Se4/1/0 LCP: TIMEout: Time 0x5288D34 State REQsent
1d00h: Se4/1/0 LCP: O CONFREQ [REQsent] id 14 len 10
1d00h: Se4/1/0 LCP:    MagicNumber 0x5533F282 (0x05065533F282)
1d00h: Se4/1/0 LCP: TIMEout: Time 0x5289504 State REQsent
1d00h: Se4/1/0 LCP: O CONFREQ [REQsent] id 15 len 10
1d00h: Se4/1/0 LCP:    MagicNumber 0x5533F282 (0x05065533F282)
1d00h: Se4/1/0 LCP: TIMEout: Time 0x5289CD4 State REQsent
1d00h: Se4/1/0 LCP: O CONFREQ [REQsent] id 16 len 10
1d00h: Se4/1/0 LCP:    MagicNumber 0x5533F282 (0x05065533F282)
1d00h: Se4/1/0 LCP: TIMEout: Time 0x528A4A4 State REQsent
1d00h: Se4/1/0 LCP: O CONFREQ [REQsent] id 17 len 10
1d00h: Se4/1/0 LCP:    MagicNumber 0x5533F282 (0x05065533F282)
1d00h: Se4/1/0 LCP: TIMEout: Time 0x528AC74 State REQsent
1d00h: Se4/1/0 LCP: O CONFREQ [REQsent] id 18 len 10
1d00h: Se4/1/0 LCP:    MagicNumber 0x5533F282 (0x05065533F282)
1d00h: Se4/1/0 LCP: TIMEout: Time 0x528B444 State REQsent
1d00h: Se4/1/0 LCP: O CONFREQ [REQsent] id 19 len 10
1d00h: Se4/1/0 LCP:    MagicNumber 0x5533F282 (0x05065533F282)
1d00h: Se4/1/0 LCP: TIMEout: Time 0x528BC14 State REQsent
1d00h: Se4/1/0 LCP: O CONFREQ [REQsent] id 20 len 10
1d00h: Se4/1/0 LCP:    MagicNumber 0x5533F282 (0x05065533F282)
1d00h: Se4/1/0 LCP: TIMEout: Time 0x528C3E4 State REQsent
1d00h: Se4/1/0 LCP: O CONFREQ [REQsent] id 21 len 10
1d00h: Se4/1/0 LCP:    MagicNumber 0x5533F282 (0x05065533F282)
1d00h: Se4/1/0 LCP: TIMEout: Time 0x528CBB4 State REQsent
1d00h: Se4/1/0 LCP: O CONFREQ [REQsent] id 22 len 10
1d00h: Se4/1/0 LCP:    MagicNumber 0x5533F282 (0x05065533F282)
1d00h: Se4/1/0 LCP: TIMEout: Time 0x528D384 State REQsent
1d00h: Se4/1/0 LCP: State is Listen
```

Listing 6-19

ISDN Troubleshooting Summary

ISDN Problem or Symptom	Troubleshooting Tool
Router not properly connected to the appropriate NT (Network Termination at the Customer Premises)	`show interface bri0` (D-channel) `show isdn status`
Physical problem in local loop	`show interface bri0` (D-channel) `show isdn status`
Incorrect SPIDs configured	`debug isdn q931` `debug isdn events`
Incorrect switch type configured	`debug isdn q931`
Incorrect dialer map number	`debug isdn q931` `debug isdn events`
One or both ends not commissioned by the telco to support data (e.g., voice only)	`debug isdn q931, debug isdn events` Message: `Bearer capability not authorized` or `Requested facility not subscribed`
No dialer group or dialer list defined	`debug dialer`
Packets being dropped because dialer hold queue is not big enough	`debug dialer`
Spurious dialing	`debug dialer`
CHAP authentication problem	`debug ppp chap` `debug ppp negotiation`
Speed mismatch across the network	`debug isdn events`
Incompatible remote end (non-ISDN)	`debug isdn q931, debug isdn events` Message: `Incompatible destination`

REVIEW QUESTIONS

1. Which command displays summary information on ISDN layers 1, 2, and 3?
   a. `show isdn q931`
   b. `show isdn status`
   c. `show dialer`

d. `show interface bri0`

e. None of the above

2. To find out how many successful and unsuccessful ISDN calls have been placed by the router, use

a. `show dialer.`

b. `show isdn memory.`

c. `show isdn status.`

d. `show interface bri0.`

e. `show isdn q931.`

3. The debug command that verifies whether or not the router is getting TEI from the switch is

a. `debug isdn q921.`

b. `debug isdn q931.`

c. `debug isdn events.`

d. `debug dialer.`

e. `debug isdn TEI.`

4. Type the command that gives information on why, or why not, dialing was initiated.

5. Which of the following commands gives setup information on layer 3 calls?

a. `debug isdn q921`

b. `debug isdn q931`

c. `debug isdn events`

d. `debug dialer`

e. `debug ppp negotiation`

6. Type the debug command that could indicate if the incorrect ISDN switch type has been configured on the router.

7. The data link layer of the ISDN signaling protocol is

a. D-channel.

b. B-channel.

c. LAPD.

d. LAPB.

e. HDLC.

8. Type the interface command that tells the router to drop the ISDN line if there is no interesting outgoing traffic for 5 min.
9. Calls being dropped after less than 30 s most likely indicate
   a. CHAP problem.
   b. Incorrect SPIDs.
   c. Incorrect switch type.
   d. Dialer map not configured.
   e. A routing loop.
10. Type the command that displays how long current calls have been connected.
11. Which of the following commands can be used to analyze suspected CHAP problems?
    a. `debug ppp chap`.
    b. `debug ppp negotiation`.
    c. `debug ppp authentication`.
    d. b and c
    e. a, b, and c
12. If the second ISDN B-channel will not come up, which of the following is *not* a possible cause?
    a. Problem with load threshold
    b. Router incorrectly configured for second B-channel
    c. ISDN switch incorrectly configured for second B-channel
    d. Second B-channel cannot authenticate with TACACS server
    e. Dialer list only configured for one channel
13. Type the command that enables multilink PPP.
14. What command can be used to suppress the sending of OSPF hellos over an ISDN interface?
15. Which of the following IPX sockets should *not* be filtered by the dialer list?
    a. 451
    b. 452
    c. 453
    d. 456
    e. 457

CHAPTER 7

IP I

Static, RIP, IGRP, EIGRP

Introduction

The objectives of this chapter are to

- Learn how to apply a structured troubleshooting methodology to IP networks.
- Become familiar with the Cisco router IP diagnostic commands.
- Understand the configuration and troubleshooting issues relating to IP desktop connectivity.
- Be capable of configuring and troubleshooting RIP, IGRP, and EIGRP.
- Understand the power and pitfalls of IP access lists.
- Use ICMP as a network diagnostic tool.

TCP/IP Diagnostic Commands

Ping and Trace Commands

Ping and trace commands have been discussed already to a reasonable level of detail in Chapter 3. This chapter focuses more on how they are to be applied when troubleshooting problems relating to IP connectivity.

Ping Commands

Here we will see how the simple `ping` command can be used to verify basic IP connectivity between two hosts on a network. Then we will explore how the extended ping facility provides better capabilities for troubleshooting more complex IP connectivity problems.

User EXEC Mode

IP PING For the purposes of refreshment, let me remind you of what a successful IP ping looks like, where all five echoes receive a reply. Since echo requests and replies are Internet Control Message Protocol (ICMP) messages that are transported in IP datagrams, this result verifies IP connectivity up to and including layer 3. ICMP will be described in more detail later in this chapter. More specifically, the following result (Listing 7-1) verifies that:

```
Router1#ping 15.48.18.12

Type escape sequence to abort.
Sending 5, 100-byte ICMP Echoes to 15.48.18.12, timeout is 2 seconds:
!!!!!
Success rate is 100 percent (5/5), round-trip min/avg/max = 12/14/16 ms
Router1#
```

Listing 7-1

- Router 1 can connect to 15.48.18.12 up to and including layer 3.
- 15.48.18.12 can connect to router 1 up to and including layer 3.

Now for some examples of when things are not going so perfectly. In Listing 7-2 we try to ping 15.125.10.1 from router 1, and all the echo requests fail. A good starting point when troubleshooting such a problem is to check that router 1 has a route to the destination using the `show ip route` command. We see that it does not.

The next question to resolve is why there is no route in the routing table for 15.125.10.1. Here are some possibilities:

- The destination router interface is down.
- The destination router is down.
- A network or router along the route is down, without any redundancy.
- The routing update for 15.125.10.1 is not being redistributed to router 1. This may be due to badly configured distribute lists, route maps, or a route redistribution problem.

```
Router1>ping 15.125.10.1

Type escape sequence to abort.
Sending 5, 100-byte ICMP Echoes to 15.125.10.1, timeout is 2 seconds:
.....
Success rate is 0 percent (0/5)
Router1>sh ip route 15.125.10.1
% Network not in table
Router1>
```

Listing 7-2

In this situation, since there is no route to 15.125.10.1, it would be a good idea to telnet to a router that you know to be closer to 15.125.10.1 and check if that has a route to the destination. You can then repeat this process in an iterative manner until you have isolated the point at which the route is being lost.

In the following example (Listing 7-3), we try to ping 161.41.18.12, which is known to be the address of a port on another router. We find that we cannot ping 161.41.18.12 from router 1, but we do have a route to that network. We see that we learn a summary route for 161.41.0.0 via EIGRP over our serial 0 interface.

Thus, if we have a route to the destination network, why are our pings failing? Remember that having a route to the destination is only part of the battle. Some of the other potential problems that could be causing the pings to fail are

- The destination router may not have a route back to router 1.
- A router along the return path may not have a route back to router 1.

There are a number of options in troubleshooting this further. You could use `trace 161.41.18.12` to see where along the route the ICMP messages are failing. Or you could telnet to the destination router and check if it has a route back to router 1.

If the destination router does not have a route back to router 1, then you should move back along the path to router 1 by doing a telnet to each

```
Router1>ping 161.41.18.12
Type escape sequence to abort.
Sending 5, 100-byte ICMP Echoes to 15.125.10.1, timeout is 2 seconds:
.....
Success rate is 0 percent (0/5)

Router1>sh ip route 161.41.18.12
Routing entry for 161.41.0.0/16
  Known via "eigrp 211", distance 90, metric 46244096, type internal
  Redistributing via eigrp 1
  Last update from 171.136.10.129 on Serial0, 00:00:34 ago
  Routing Descriptor Blocks:
  * 171.136.10.129, from 171.136.10.129, 00:00:34 ago, via Serial0
      Route metric is 46244096, traffic share count is 1
      Total delay is 20700 microseconds, minimum bandwidth is 56 Kbit
      Reliability 255/255, minimum MTU 1500 bytes
      Loading 19/255, Hops 5
```

Listing 7-3

router until you find the router that has a route back to router 1. At this point, you are close to isolating the problem. The problem could relate to a distribute list that is blocking router 1's networks from propagating back to the 161.41.18.12 router. We know that it is not a redistribution issue because the EIGRP route for 161.41.18.12 is internal with a distance of 90. More about this later in this chapter.

Privileged EXEC Mode

EXTENDED IP PING Now we are ready to examine the usefulness of the additional troubleshooting features that extended ping gives us. We receive a report from a network administrator that one of his clients cannot connect to a remote IP-based server but can connect to a server on its local-area network (LAN). The client's IP address is 15.48.18.12. When we begin troubleshooting, we observe that we can ping 15.48.18.12 from its local router. This means that that client can connect to the router on its local LAN. (See Listing 7-4.)

The next step is to do an extended ping with a source address of one of the other router interfaces. Here we choose the address of serial 0 to be the source address inserted in the datagrams sent by the router to 15.48.18.12. (See Listing 7-5.)

The fact that this extended ping fails indicates that workstation 15.48.18.12 cannot communicate with hosts that are on a different subnet. We have already established that it can connect to its local router port. However, it could not send ICMP echo replies to 15.48.24.3. Assuming that the workstation is not meant to be running any dynamic routing protocol, the problem is likely to be with the default gateway configuration. We will discuss this topic in relation to Windows NT/95 workstations later in this chapter.

Let us look at another example of the power of extended ping before moving on. You receive a report that an Ethernet client with an IP

```
Router2#ping 15.48.18.12

Type escape sequence to abort.
Sending 5, 100-byte ICMP Echoes to 15.48.18.12, timeout is 2 seconds:
!!!!!
Success rate is 100 percent (5/5), round-trip min/avg/max = 1/2/4 ms
Router2#
```

Listing 7-4

```
Router2#ping
Protocol [ip]:
Target IP address: 15.48.18.12
Repeat count [5]: 10
Datagram size [100]:
Timeout in seconds [2]:
Extended commands [n]: y
Source address or interface: 15.48.24.3
Type of service [0]:
Set DF bit in IP header? [no]:
Validate reply data? [no]:
Data pattern [0xABCD]:
Loose, Strict, Record, Timestamp, Verbose[none]:
Sweep range of sizes [n]:
Type escape sequence to abort.
Sending 10, 1600-byte ICMP Echoes to 15.48.18.12, timeout is 2 seconds:
..........
Success rate is 0 percent (0/5)
Router2#
```

Listing 7-5

address of 10.10.100.99 is having very slow response connecting to the server on a token-ring segment at 172.16.11.11. We know in advance that there is basic IP connectivity between the client and server. Thus we test further by doing extended pings with various different datagram sizes. When the datagram size is increased from the default of 100 bytes to 900 bytes, the round-trip delays increase proportionally, which is normal. The datagram size is then increased to 1600 bytes, and the following occurs (see Listing 7-6).

All packets are dropped when the datagram size is increased to 1600 bytes. Given that the client is on an Ethernet segment and the server is on token ring, the problem is likely to relate to exceeding the MTU for Ethernet. The configuration of the workstation IP stack should be checked either directly on the workstation itself or by using a protocol analyzer on the Ethernet segment. It is likely that the DF (do not fragment) bit is being set at the workstation. With fragmentation not being allowed, any packets that exceed the MTU size will be dropped.

Trace Commands

User EXEC Mode As we saw in Chapter 3, the `trace` command is used to obtain a router IP address for each hop along the route to a des-

```
Router3#ping
Protocol [ip]:
Target IP address: 172.16.11.11
Repeat count [5]: 20
Datagram size [100]: 1600
Timeout in seconds [2]:
Extended commands [n]: y
Source address or interface: 10.10.100.1
Type of service [0]:
Set DF bit in IP header? [no]:
Validate reply data? [no]:
Data pattern [0xABCD]:
Loose, Strict, Record, Timestamp, Verbose[none]:
Sweep range of sizes [n]:
Type escape sequence to abort.
Sending 20, 1600-byte ICMP Echoes to 172.16.11.11, timeout is 2 seconds:
....................
Success rate is 0 percent (0/20)
Router3#
```

Listing 7-6

tination. To demonstrate a typical example of how `trace` might be used, let us return to a previous example where we could not ping 161.41.18.12 from router 1 even though it did have a route to that network (see Listing 7-7).

We will use `trace` to attempt to ascertain where the route back to router 1 is being lost or suppressed. From the following output (Listing 7-8), we see that the first three hops to the destination have a route back to router 1. The next troubleshooting step should be to telnet to router 15 at 161.168.11.1 and see how it gets to 161.41.18.12.

An alternative approach would be to telnet to the router that is locally attached to 161.41.18.12 and work back from there. This was the approach that was described earlier in the same example in relation to IP ping.

Privileged Mode Extended Trace To demonstrate the use of extended trace, let us look at the following problem: In Figure 7-1, router R3 has two local LANs—one is 165.48.48.0/24 and the other is 165.48.10.0/24. Users on 165.48.48.0/24 can connect to remote server 172.144.1.55. Users on the other LAN cannot access this server, but they can access other remote servers.

```
Router1>ping 161.41.18.12
Type escape sequence to abort.
Sending 5, 100-byte ICMP Echoes to 15.125.10.1, timeout is 2 seconds:
.....
Success rate is 0 percent (0/5)

Router1>sh ip ro 161.41.18.12
Routing entry for 161.41.0.0/16
  Known via "eigrp 211", distance 90, metric 46244096, type internal
  Redistributing via eigrp 211
  Last update from 171.136.10.129 on Serial0, 00:00:34 ago
  Routing Descriptor Blocks:
  * 171.136.10.129, from 171.136.10.129, 00:00:34 ago, via Serial0
      Route metric is 46244096, traffic share count is 1
      Total delay is 20700 microseconds, minimum bandwidth is 56 Kbit
      Reliability 255/255, minimum MTU 1500 bytes
      Loading 19/255, Hops 5
```

Listing 7-7

```
Router1#trace 161.41.18.12

Type escape sequence to abort.
Tracing the route to 161.41.18.12

  1 Router11 (171.136.10.129) 16 msec 12 msec 12 msec
  2 Router6 (171.137.1.1) 16 msec 12 msec 12 msec
  3 Router15 (161.168.11.1) 24 msec 24 msec 24 msec
  4  *  *  *
```

Listing 7-8

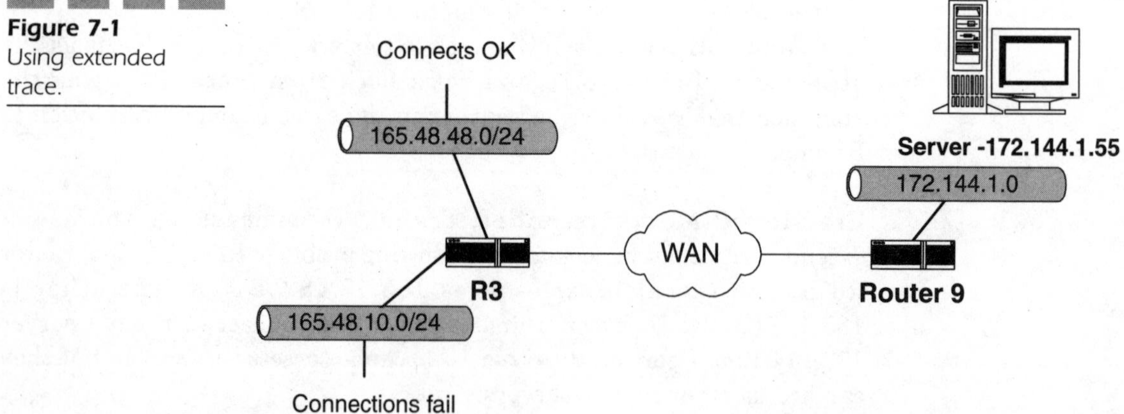

Figure 7-1 Using extended trace.

We will first demonstrate and verify that connectivity is okay from 165.48.48.0/24 to the router port of the destination server (172.144.1.39). We are only tracing as far as the destination router port because not all LAN devices respond to trace ICMP requests with an appropriate ICMP message (this depends on proprietary issues and their IP stack configuration). Also, we know that the server can communicate with remote devices, and it is unlikely that it is just missing a route to the specific 165.48.10.0 subnet, without having a default gateway. (See Listing 7-9.)

Now that we have verified connectivity from the 165.48.48.0 subnet, we will repeat the exercise from the 165.48.10.0 subnet. We find that the trace begins to fail after router 6. Therefore, it seems likely that the problem is at router 9, the next hop after router 6. Router 9's IP address is 172.144.1.39, which is the same segment as the server in question. It is likely that router 9 does not have a route back to 165.48.10.0 even though it does have a route to 165.48.48.0. The next step is to telnet to router 9 to see why this is the case. We have used `trace` to isolate the problem. To fully resolve the problem, the IP commands that we are about to discuss need to be used. (See Listing 7-10.)

```
R3#trace
Protocol [ip]:
Target IP address: 172.144.1.39
Source address: 165.48.48.3
Numeric display [n]:
Timeout in seconds [3]:
Probe count [3]:
Minimum Time to Live [1]:
Maximum Time to Live [30]:
Port Number [33434]:
Loose, Strict, Record, Timestamp, Verbose[none]:
Type escape sequence to abort.
Tracing the route to Router9 (172.144.1.39)

  1 Router1 (165.48.49.1) 0 msec
     Router2 (165.48.48.2) 4 msec
     Router3 (165.48.49.2) 0 msec
  2 165.48.48.129 12 msec 12 msec
      Router6 (165.48.49.129) 12 msec
  3 Router9 (172.144.1.39) 12 msec
    Router4 (172.133.1.2) 12 msec 12 msec
R3#
```

Listing 7-9

```
R3#trace
Protocol [ip]:
Target IP address: 172.144.1.39
Source address: 165.48.10.3
Numeric display [n]:
Timeout in seconds [3]:
Probe count [3]:
Minimum Time to Live [1]:
Maximum Time to Live [30]:
Port Number [33434]:
Loose, Strict, Record, Timestamp, Verbose[none]:
Type escape sequence to abort.
Tracing the route to Router9 (172.144.1.39)

  1 Router1 (165.48.49.1) 0 msec
     Router2 (165.48.48.2) 4 msec
     Router3 (165.48.49.2) 0 msec
  2 165.48.48.129 12 msec 12 msec
      Router6 (165.48.49.129) 12 msec
  3  *  *  *
R3#
```

Listing 7-10

Show Commands

The broad array of IP show commands can be seen in the Cisco Command Reference on Cisco Connection Online (CCO) or in hard copy. Alternatively, you can use the privileged mode help facility to get a complete summary of these commands. (See Listing 7-11.) If you do this exercise while in user EXEC mode, obviously, you will only see commands that can be executed without entering privileged mode.

The following sections of this chapter examine the more commonly used commands in detail, but as always, it is important to be able to navigate the Cisco IOS and explore new commands as appropriate.

Debug Commands

Cisco has a Debug Command Reference available in hard copy as part of the IOS documentation suite. It is also available in the documentation

```
Router1#sh ip ?
  access-lists          List IP access lists
  accounting            The active IP accounting database
  aliases               IP alias table
  arp                   IP ARP table
  as-path-access-list   List AS path access lists
  bgp                   BGP information
  cache                 IP fast-switching route cache
  community-list        List community-list
  dvmrp                 DVMRP information
  egp                   EGP connections and statistics
  eigrp                 IP-EIGRP show commands
  igmp                  IGMP information
  interface             IP interface status and configuration
  irdp                  ICMP Router Discovery Protocol
  local                 IP local options
  masks                 Masks associated with a network
  mcache                IP multicast fast-switching cache
  mpacket               Display possible duplicate multicast packets
  mroute                IP multicast routing table
  nhrp                  NHRP information
  ospf                  OSPF information
  pim                   PIM information
  policy                Policy routing
  protocols             IP routing protocol process parameters and statistics
  redirects             IP redirects
  route                 IP routing table
  rpf                   Display RPF information for multicast source
  sd                    Session Directory cache
  sdr                   Session Directory (SDPv2) cache
  sockets               Open IP sockets
  tcp                   TCP/IP header-compression statistics
  traffic               IP protocol statistics
```

Listing 7-11

section of CCO. The help facility also can be used as a quick means to get a command summary. Since debug commands can only be executed while in privileged mode, this exercise cannot be performed in user EXEC mode. Unlike in the case of the show commands, you should be careful to suppress any temptation to experiment with debug commands that you do not fully understand. (See Listing 7-12.)

The more commonly used IP debugging commands will be demonstrated in the appropriate sections of this chapter.

```
dunlap1-wan#debug ip ?
  bgp        BGP information
  cache      IP cache operations
  cgmp       CGMP protocol activity
  dvmrp      DVMRP protocol activity
  egp        EGP information
  eigrp      IP-EIGRP information
  error      IP error debugging
  http       HTTP connections
  icmp       ICMP transactions
  igmp       IGMP protocol activity
  igrp       IGRP information
  mcache     IP multicast cache operations
  mobile     Mobility protocols
  mpacket    IP multicast packet debugging
  mrouting   IP multicast routing table activity
  ospf       OSPF information
  packet     General IP debugging and IPSO security transactions
  peer       IP peer address activity
  pim        PIM protocol activity
  policy     Policy routing
  rip        RIP protocol transactions
  routing    Routing table events
  sd         Session Directory (SD)
  security   IP security options
  tcp        TCP information
  udp        UDP based transactions
```

Listing 7-12

Fault Resolution TCP/IP

We have already seen how tools such as `ping` and `trace` in user and privileged EXEC mode can be applied to isolate and diagnose IP connectivity problems. Now we will firm up on the standard methodology that should be applied when troubleshooting such problems. Figure 7-2 shows a flowchart that outlines a very fundamental methodology that can be applied for troubleshooting TCP/IP connectivity. The complexity of IP connectivity problems varies dramatically, but this model can be applied to the diagnosis of many problems. It is important to remember that particularly in the case of more complex problems, which may include multiple routing protocols, it is important not to lose sight of the fundamental troubleshooting model. I have decided to introduce the TCP/IP model

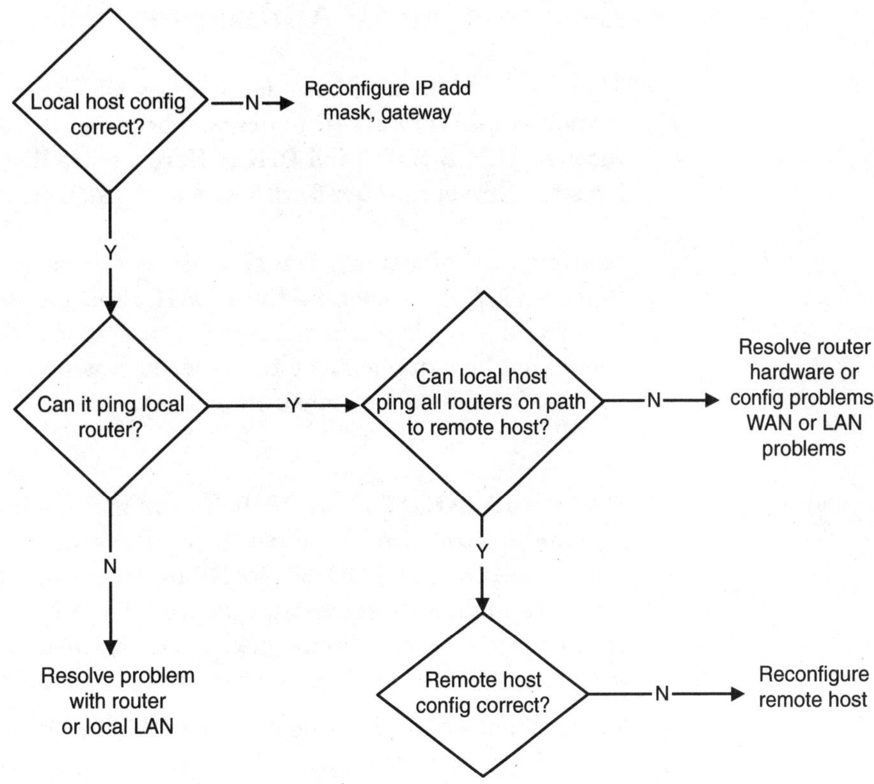

Figure 7-2
TCP/IP troubleshooting flowchart.

only after discussing the applications of `ping` and `trace` so that you would have a better sense of each of the steps.

LAN Connectivity Problems

As can be seen from the troubleshooting flowchart (Figure 7-2), it is usually a good idea to check that a particular host has IP connectivity on its local LAN before analyzing any possible problems in the wide-area network (WAN). In this section we will take a look at the typical problems encountered with local host configuration and LAN connectivity. In particular, we will discuss these problems as they relate to Windows NT/95 platforms.

Designating IP Addresses

There are a number of basic methods by which a Windows NT/95 workstation can obtain an IP address. These include static configuration, Reverse ARP, BOOTP, and DHCP. Here we will discuss the typical problems that are encountered with each of these mechanisms.

Static Configuration The IP address can be configured statically in Windows NT/95 by opening the TCP/IP Properties window. The address configured here should be the correct one intended for the workstation; it should not be a duplicate of any other host address on the segment, and it must have a subnet mask that is consistent with the LAN segment that it is on.

RARP and BOOTP Two of the traditional methods by which a workstation obtains its IP address are Reverse ARP (RARP) and the Bootstrap Protocol (BOOTP). RARP uses a server that maintains a listing of IP addresses against hardware addresses. The server is usually contacted through a client-initiated broadcast. The typical problems encountered with RARP resolution are

- The client's broadcasts do not reach the RARP server because there is a router along the path. This can be solved by configuring an IP helper address on the router. It should be noted that it is possible to configure the router to be an RARP server.
- The RARP server does not have an IP address that corresponds to the client's hardware address.

BOOTP is more sophisticated than RARP. It runs over UDP using a particular port for client requests and another port for server responses. The response from a BOOTP server also contains additional information such as the IP address of the local router gateway. Some typical problems encountered with BOOTP include

- The client's broadcasts do not reach the BOOTP server because there is a router along the path. As in the case of RARP, this can be solved by configuring a helper address on the router.
- There is an IP connectivity problem between the client's segment and the segment that the BOOTP server is on. Check this by doing an extended ping to the server using a source address of the local router's LAN interface in question.

- The UDP ports that BOOTP uses are not being forwarded along the entire path in both directions. This may be so because there is a `no ip forward-protocol udp` command configured on the router or there is an extended access list that is filtering out these UDP ports.
- The BOOTP server has a configuration problem or is out of available IP addresses.

DHCP Dynamic Host Configuration Protocol (DHCP) is the most advanced mechanism by which a workstation can obtain its IP address dynamically. DHCP also uses UDP as a transport mechanism. The two most fundamental enhancements that DHCP offers over BOOTP are (1) a DHCP response also includes the client's subnet mask, and (2) IP addresses are leased to the clients for a configurable period of time without any static mapping of IP addresses to hardware addresses. These features are particularly useful in modern networking environments that also may include mobile users. Some of the typical DHCP-related problems include

- DHCP has not been enabled on the client. In Windows NT/95, this is a straightforward task that is done under TCP/IP Properties.
- There is an IP connectivity problem between the client's segment and the segment that the DHCP server is on.
- The client's broadcasts do not reach the DHCP server because there is a router along the path. As in the previous cases, this can be solved by configuring an IP helper address on the router.
- The UDP port that DHCP uses (port 67) is not being forwarded along the entire path in both directions.
- The DHCP server has a configuration problem or is out of available IP addresses.

ARP

The `show arp` command displays the contents of the router's Address Resolution Protocol (ARP) cache. This includes ARP mappings of IP addresses versus hardware addresses for all LAN segments to which the router attaches. Information is provided on the age of the entry and the encapsulation type of the frames. Cisco routers age out ARP entries after 4 hours by default. (See Listing 7-13.)

```
citygate1#show arp
Protocol  Address          Age (min)  Hardware Addr   Type   Interface
Internet  165.4.3.150            80   0007.ef51.b004  SNAP   TokenRing1/3
Internet  165.4.3.151            83   0006.7c66.8ac4  SNAP   TokenRing1/3
Internet  165.4.3.148            85   0006.e2d6.ab84  SNAP   TokenRing1/3
Internet  165.4.3.146            85   0007.2ca8.1401  SNAP   TokenRing1/3
Internet  165.4.3.147            82   0006.e2d6.a384  SNAP   TokenRing1/3
Internet  165.4.3.145            84   0007.7802.dc9c  SNAP   TokenRing1/3
Internet  165.4.185.38            2   0000.f6b2.8b28  SNAP   TokenRing1/1
Internet  165.4.3.152            82   0006.7c66.92c4  SNAP   TokenRing1/3
```

Listing 7-13

ARP debugging can be used to monitor the ARP transactions on a router. Some examples of where this tool is particularly useful include

- When you cannot ping between two hosts on the same LAN segment and you need to check whether or not the source host is resolving the hardware address of the destination host.
- In order to investigate a duplicate IP address on a segment. In this case, the ARP cache should be cleared using `clear arp` after ARP debugging is turned on. Then ping the duplicate IP address. It should then be observed that two different hardware addresses are answering the ARP request for that IP address.

Listing 7-14 is a sample output of ARP debugging. The ARP cache is cleared in order to stimulate some activity. There are some peculiar features to be noticed here. First, after the ARP cache is cleared, we see the router sending ARP requests, the purpose of which is to verify that the same IP address to hardware address mappings exist as before clearing of the cache. You can then observe the router repeatedly broadcasting its own IP and hardware address pair. This is sometimes termed *gratuitous ARP* and is intended to reduce the overall amount of ARP broadcasts on the segment. Finally, in this output we see the router rebuilding its ARP cache as it receives replies to its own ARP broadcast requests.

IP Name Resolution

There are a number of different name-resolution mechanisms that can be implemented in TCP/IP environments. Here we discuss the main name-resolution methods with particular focus on the Windows NT/95 platform.

```
citygate1#debug arp
ARP packet debugging is on
citygate1#clear arp
citygate1#
*Jun  1 21:57:36 PDT: IP ARP: sent req src 171.136.10.1 00e0.1eb9.bbcd,
                  dst 171.136.10.34 00a0.24d1.5823 Ethernet0
*Jun  1 21:57:36 PDT: IP ARP: sent req src 171.136.10.1 00e0.1eb9.bbcd,
                  dst 171.136.10.10 0080.5f06.ca3d Ethernet0
*Jun  1 21:57:36 PDT: IP ARP: sent req src 171.136.10.1 00e0.1eb9.bbcd,
                  dst 171.136.10.13 00a0.2483.949d Ethernet0
*Jun  1 21:57:36 PDT: IP ARP: sent req src 171.136.10.1 00e0.1eb9.bbcd,
                  dst 171.136.10.14 0060.b002.9a08 Ethernet0
*Jun  1 21:57:36 PDT: IP ARP: sent req src 171.136.10.1 00e0.1eb9.bbcd,
                  dst 171.136.10.1 00e0.1eb9.bbcd Ethernet0
*Jun  1 21:57:36 PDT: IP ARP: sent req src 171.136.10.1 00e0.1eb9.bbcd,
                  dst 171.136.10.126 0000.1d22.d979 Ethernet0
*Jun  1 21:57:36 PDT: IP ARP: sent rep src 171.136.10.1 00e0.1eb9.bbcd,
                  dst 171.136.10.1 ffff.ffff.ffff Ethernet0
*Jun  1 21:57:36 PDT: IP ARP: sent rep src 171.136.10.1 00e0.1eb9.bbcd,
                  dst 171.136.10.1 ffff.ffff.ffff Ethernet0
*Jun  1 21:57:36 PDT: IP ARP: sent rep src 171.136.10.1 00e0.1eb9.bbcd,
                  dst 171.136.10.1 ffff.ffff.ffff Ethernet0
*Jun  1 21:57:36 PDT: IP ARP: sent rep src 171.136.10.1 00e0.1eb9.bbcd,
                  dst 171.136.10.1 ffff.ffff.ffff Ethernet0
*Jun  1 21:57:36 PDT: IP ARP: sent rep src 171.136.10.1 00e0.1eb9.bbcd,
                  dst 171.136.10.1 ffff.ffff.ffff Ethernet0
*Jun  1 21:57:36 PDT: IP ARP: sent rep src 171.136.10.1 00e0.1eb9.bbcd,
                  dst 171.136.10.1 ffff.ffff.ffff Ethernet0
*Jun  1 21:57:36 PDT: IP ARP: rcvd rep src 171.136.10.10 0080.5f06.ca3d, dst
  171.136.10.1 Ethernet0
*Jun  1 21:57:36 PDT: IP ARP: creating entry for IP address: 171.136.10.10,
  hw:0080.5f06.ca3d
*Jun  1 21:57:36 PDT: IP ARP: rcvd rep src 171.136.10.13 00a0.2483.949d, dst
  171.136.10.1 Ethernet0
*Jun  1 21:57:36 PDT: IP ARP: creating entry for IP address: 171.136.10.13,
  hw:00a0.2483.949d
*Jun  1 21:57:36 PDT: IP ARP: rcvd rep src 171.136.10.14 0060.b002.9a08, dst
  171.136.10.1 Ethernet0
*Jun  1 21:57:36 PDT: IP ARP: creating entry for IP address: 171.136.10.14,
  hw:0060.b002.9a08
*Jun  1 21:57:36 PDT: IP ARP: rcvd rep src 171.136.10.126 0000.1d22.d979, dst
  171.136.10.1 Ethernet0
*Jun  1 21:57:36 PDT: IP ARP: creating entry for IP address: 171.136.10.126,
  hw:0000.1d22.d979
citygate1#undeb all
All possible debugging has been turned off
citygate1#
```

Listing 7-14

With the exception of the static methods such as LMHOSTS, all the other methods require IP connectivity to a name server. In some cases this is a unicast to an address that must be configured on the client (e.g., p-node), and in other cases it is a broadcast (e.g., b-node). Problems connecting to a name server can be diagnosed easily by pinging a host's IP address and then pinging it by name. If a name-resolution problem is found, then you must first understand how name resolution is being performed in that environment and then follow the usual IP connectivity troubleshooting steps.

Broadcasting The use of broadcasts to resolve names is inefficient and on most platforms has been replaced by more sophisticated methods. The only thing to check when broadcasting is being used for name resolution is whether or not a router is blocking the broadcasts. An IP helper address configured on the local router's LAN interface can solve this problem. The helper address feature converts broadcasts to unicasts destined for the configured helper address. Since the broadcast packets become unicasts, the router will not block them.

NetBIOS over TCP/IP Name Resolution NetBIOS over TCP/IP has four different name-resolution methods defined. The goal of the following methods is to resolve NetBIOS names to IP addresses:

- *p-Node.* The client contacts the WINS or NBNS server using a directed unicast. The address of the WINS server must be configured on the client. Here the client simply needs IP connectivity to the server.
- *b-Node.* The client attempts to contact the NBNS server using a broadcast. If the server is on a different IP subnet, then there must be a mechanism for forwarding the broadcasts to the server such as the use of helper addresses.
- *h-Node.* With this configuration, the client first uses a p-node unicast to contact the server. If no reply is received before the timeout period expires, the client then uses a b-node broadcast.
- *m-Node.* In this case, the client uses b-node first and then p-node if no reply is received to the initial broadcast. m-Node may be appropriate if the local LAN segment is first checked for a server and the p-node unicast is sent to a remote server that will not see the b-node broadcast.

Windows Internet Name Service (WINS) The Windows Internet Name Service (WINS) is a Microsoft implementation of the NetBIOS

Name Service (NBNS) protocol. WINS is dynamic and distributed, and the name-to-address mappings are contained on a WINS server. WINS does not reply to b-node broadcasts, and it is interrogated using p-node unicasts. Hence the IP address of the WINS server must be configured explicitly on the clients. More than one WINS server can be specified in the TCP/IP Properties window. Obviously, full IP connectivity must exist between the client and the WINS server. The two basic types of transactions that the client initiates with the WINS server is name registration and name query. After registering with the WINS server, the client receives the IP address of the primary domain controller (PDC) and backup domain controller (BDC) for logging onto the domain.

LMHOSTS This is a static file that must be configured, distributed, and updated by the network administrator. In a NetBIOS over TCP/IP environment, if a station is configured as h-node, then the LMHOST file is usually only consulted after the p-node and b-node methods both fail to produce name resolution.

Domain Name Service Domain Name Service (DNS) is a distributed and hierarchical name-resolution service that resolves internet-based name formats to IP addresses. The address of one or more DNS servers can be configured on the router using the `ip name-server` command.

WAN Connectivity Issues

The Default Gateway

An end station on a LAN can communicate with stations on different IP networks or subnets using a number of different methods. Probably the most common method is to manually configure a default gateway on the station.

Many problems occur in practice due to not only incorrectly configured default gateways but also errors in the basic IP configuration on the workstation. Sometimes it could be as simple as an incorrect IP address on the station or, more commonly, an incorrect subnet mask. At this point it should be noted that some operating systems require you to reboot the workstation for a change of IP configuration to take effect.

NOTE: Some LAN operating systems require that the workstation be rebooted before changes in its IP configuration take effect. Check your operating system manuals!

An important question to ask a user who is reporting trouble with an IP application is whether he or she can ping other hosts on the same subnet. If the user can do this but cannot ping hosts on other subnets, then the default gateway should be checked.

Static and Dynamic Routing

A dynamic routing protocol can be run on the workstation, enabling it to communicate with the nearest router. This protocol can only be RIP or OSPF, since IGRP and EIGRP are proprietary Cisco routing protocols. The router, of course, also must be running RIP or OSPF on the same network.

A gateway discovery protocol such as Internet Gateway Discovery Protocol (IGDP) also could be implemented on the end station. Exactly how end stations should communicate with hosts on different IP subnets is a design and policy issue to be agreed on between the LAN, WAN, and applications support engineers within an organization.

Proxy ARP

Proxy ARP can be used if the workstation is not configured with a subnet mask. Say, for example, station A has an IP address of 150.10.10.47. If no mask is configured, the station will assume that no subnetting is taking place. Therefore, a default class B mask of 255.255.0.0 is assumed. Now consider the following scenario. The actual subnet mask being used is 255.255.255.0. Therefore, if the station needs to communicate with station B at 150.10.9.22, it must go through its local router. However, the station "thinks" that the destination is on its own network, since it belongs to the same class B network. Hence, station A will do an ARP broadcast for 150.10.9.22. If proxy ARP is not enabled on the router, then station A will receive no response because the router will drop the ARP broadcast. Proxy ARP, on the other hand, allows the router to respond to the ARP broadcast with its own MAC address. The router will only respond to ARP broadcasts for IP addresses that are on different subnets to the one on which the ARP originated. This prevents the router from interfering in the normal ARP process on a given LAN subnet. The router also will check its routing table for a route to 150.10.9.22 before responding. Thus station A is "fooled" into thinking that station B is on its own subnet with a MAC address of the local router's interface.

Proxy ARP is enabled by default on Cisco router LAN interfaces. It can be switched off using the `no ip proxy-arp` interface command. While it can be an extremely useful feature, especially when the stations have no configured mask, it also can potentially cause problems. For example, it can allow unintended communication between stations that are configured with the wrong subnet mask. Sometimes a network administrator may decide to turn off proxy ARP on the routers in order to clean up various LAN segments.

IP Access Lists

The most fundamental use for IP access lists is to control and restrict the availability of IP-based services across router interfaces. Two different types of IP access lists can be configured on Cisco routers. The simplest type of list is the *standard access list*, which performs filtering based on the source IP address. More sophisticated filtering can be achieved using the *extended access list*. This enables more powerful access control, which also can relate to destination address and protocol type.

Access lists also can be applied to many of the functional processes that the router performs. They can, for example, be used to limit the sending or accepting of routing updates or the sending of SNMP traps. These are just some of the many applications of access lists that will be discussed during the course of this book. However, not only are access lists extremely powerful, they are also complex and provide the potential for serious problems resulting from poorly configured lists.

Standard Access Lists

The standard IP access list performs filtering based on source IP addresses only. This type of list is given a numerical label between 1 and 99. As of Cisco IOS version 11.2, the keyword *standard* can be used, and the list can be labeled by name. The source addresses to which the list refers can be those of individual IP hosts or summarized ranges of IP addresses. The summarization of contiguous address blocks is achieved through the use of wildcards. The default wildcard is 0.0.0.0; for example, the following two lines mean the same thing:

```
access-list 1 permit 172.16.83.32
```

```
access-list 1 permit 172.16.83.32 0.0.0.0
```

In the preceding example, the host 172.16.83.12 is all that matches access list 1. If we wish to match access list 1 to the entire range of addresses from 172.16.83.0 to 172.16.83.255, then the following line could be used:

```
access-l 1 permit 172.16.83.0 0.0.0.255
```

An essential point to remember in relation to all access lists, regardless of their type, is that the order in which lines are written is always obeyed. Sometimes inexperienced engineers overlook this fact, often resulting in unintended effects. For example, if it is required to allow WAN access to 172.16.83.32 but to deny WAN access to all other hosts on 172.16.83.0/24, the following list could be used:

```
access-list 1 permit 172.16.83.32
access-list 1 deny 172.16.83.0 0.0.0.255

interface ethernet0
ip address 172.16.83.1 255.255.255.0

interface serial0
ip address 172.16.1.1 255.255.255.0
ip access-group 1 out
```

In fact, given that there is an implicit deny-all at the end of a list of permitted addresses, the second line is not actually necessary.

However, the following configuration for access list 1 would not have the desired effect:

```
access-list 1 deny 172.16.83.0 0.0.0.255
access-list 1 permit 172.16.83.32
```

The reason is that the first line denies all the 172.16.83.0/24 subnet. Therefore, given the significance of ordering, the second line referring to 172.16.83.32 is rendered meaningless.

CAUTION: *All access lists must be configured with the correct ordering. Also, don't forget that there is an implicit deny-all at the end of the list.*

Listing 7-15

```
R2>sh access-l 1

Standard IP access list 1
    permit 171.13.181.139
    permit 171.13.181.138
    permit 171.13.181.141
    permit 171.13.181.140
    permit 165.4.183.10
    permit 165.4.67.147
    permit 171.13.33.141
R2>
```

The access lists that are configured on a router can be viewed using the `show access-list` command. In the example in Listing 7-15, is access list 1 referring to a group of IP hosts or a group of IP subnets? What wildcard is being used?

Extended Access Lists

The extended IP access list is a powerful tool that also can be troublesome if careful thought is not given to its application. This particular type of access list is labeled numerically in the range 100 to 199. As for standard access lists, newer versions of Cisco IOS also support named access lists. It should be noted that Cisco IOS version 11.1 contained some significant changes to the way in which access lists are configured. The appropriate Cisco documentation should be consulted if a router containing access lists is being downgraded to an earlier image.

Filtering can be performed based on source or destination address or protocol type. As the following example (Listing 7-16) of an extended access list shows, the protocol filtering can be performed up to the socket level. A useful feature of the `show access-list` command is that the number of matches for each access list entry is displayed. The keyword `logging`, when added to the end of an access list entry, achieves the same result. This can be a very useful tool for troubleshooting.

The following is a typical example of a network problem resulting from a poorly configured extended access list. The local host (199.18.2.88) is to be allowed to FTP from a remote server (152.46.7.19), and this is the only FTP service to be allowed to any host. Telnet is to be available to all hosts. Before reading on, try to find three problems in this configuration (see Listing 7-17).

```
R2>sh access-l 101

Extended IP access list 101

    permit ip host 165.47.47.57 host 165.48.67.22 (330 matches)
    permit tcp host 165.47.110.45 host 133.50.16.20 eq telnet
    permit icmp any any (102281 matches)
    permit udp any any (50090 matches)
    permit tcp host 171.132.20.15 host 165.48.67.11 eq ftp-data
    permit tcp host 171.132.20.15 host 165.48.67.11 eq ftp
    permit tcp host 171.132.20.15 host 165.48.67.12 eq ftp-data
    permit tcp host 171.132.20.15 host 165.48.67.12 eq ftp
    permit ip 133.3.24.0 0.0.0.255 host 165.48.67.22
    permit ip 133.3.33.0 0.0.0.255 host 165.48.67.22
    permit ip 133.3.34.0 0.0.0.255 host 165.48.67.22
    permit ip 133.3.35.0 0.0.0.255 host 165.48.67.22
    permit ip 133.3.36.0 0.0.0.255 host 165.48.67.22
    permit ip 133.50.10.0 0.0.0.255 host 165.48.67.22 (5088 matches)
    permit ip 133.60.31.0 0.0.0.255 host 165.48.67.22
    permit ip 133.60.32.0 0.0.0.255 host 165.48.67.22
    permit ip 133.60.50.0 0.0.0.255 host 165.48.67.22
    permit ip 133.60.51.0 0.0.0.255 host 165.48.67.22
    permit ip 133.60.60.0 0.0.0.255 host 165.48.67.22
    permit ip 133.60.61.0 0.0.0.255 host 165.48.67.22
    permit ip 133.60.64.0 0.0.0.255 host 165.48.67.22
    permit ip 133.60.70.0 0.0.0.255 host 165.48.67.22

R2>
```

Listing 7-16

In this configuration, neither FTP nor telnet works, and here is why:

- Allowing the FTP socket without allowing FTP-DATA is not really much use, is it?
- Access list 103 is applied to packets coming from the router port out onto the Ethernet. If 199.18.2.88 attempts to start an FTP session

```
access-list 102 permit tcp host 199.18.2.88 host 152.46.7.19 eq ftp
access-list 103 permit tcp host 152.46.7.19 host 199.18.2.88 eq ftp

in ethernet0
ip address 199.18.2.1 255.255.255.0
ip access-group 102 in
ip access-group 103 out
```

Listing 7-17

with 152.46.7.19, then the return packets from this server will use a random port number above 1023 as the destination port. Access list 103 only allows the FTP port!

- Even if the preceding problems are solved, telnet still will not work because of the implicit deny-all to other TCP services.

The configuration for access lists 102 and 103 shown in Listing 7-18 would be one way to solve these problems.

There are usually a number of different ways to configure access lists that meet your security goals. It is most important to first be clear on the precise security and filtering policies that need to be implemented. The second task is to implement these policies using the simplest and most concise access list configuration. Even in the preceding example, it is questionable whether both an inbound and an outbound list is really necessary.

Two examples of the use of temporary extended access lists in troubleshooting will now be demonstrated. In the first example, it is suspected that some hosts on the 151.10.12.0/24 subnet are configured with the wrong mask. If, for example, the 151.10.12.33 host were configured with a 28-bit mask, then it would consider 151.10.12.130 to be on a different subnet and would send the packets to the router port, assuming the correct default gateway has been configured. This type of traffic can be monitored using the following configuration (Listing 7-19), which logs all traffic that is needlessly sent to the router port that should be staying on the same subnet.

The first line of access list 102 is used to separate out any traffic that is legitimately destined for the router port itself. The second line is used to log any traffic that has a source and destination address that is local to the Ethernet segment but is still being sent to the router port. The third line is essential to ensure that all other traffic is allowed (remember the implicit deny-all). If many matches are found against the second

```
access-list 102 permit tcp host 199.18.2.88 host 152.46.7.19 eq ftp
access-list 102 permit tcp host 199.18.2.88 host 152.46.7.19 eq ftp-data
access-list 102 permit tcp any any eq telnet
access-list 102 permit tcp any any gt 1023
access-list 103 permit tcp any any eq telnet
access-list 103 permit tcp any any gt 1023
```

Listing 7-18

```
access-list 102 permit ip 151.10.12.0 0.0.0.255 host 151.10.12.1
access-list 102 permit ip 151.10.12.0 0.0.0.255 151.10.12.0 0.0.0.255 logging
access-list 102 permit ip any any

int ethernet0
ip address 151.10.12.1 255.255.255.0
ip access-group 102 in
```

Listing 7-19

entry, then an incorrect host mask is a distinct possibility. To find out which hosts have an incorrect mask, there are a number of options:

- The IP configuration of each host can be verified manually.
- If there are many hosts on the subnet, the first option may not be practical. The `debug ip packet` command could be used. Great caution must be exercised here because of the potentially high processor overhead generated by this command. The command should be bounded by an access list that preferably refers to only a portion of the IP hosts at a single time. For example:

```
debug ip packet 11

access-list 11 permit ip 151.10.12.0 0.0.0.127
```

In this case, only the hosts up to and including .127 would match the debugging criterion. After this is complete, the higher end of the subnet could be analyzed.

- The ICMP mask-reply facility could be used. The analysis of ICMP messages will be discussed in the next section.
- Finally, be sure to turn off all debugging and remove any access lists that were configured for temporary troubleshooting. Of course, this sounds very obvious, but many of the problems with access list configuration and troubleshooting are caused by not enough attention being given to the simple things.

The second example of a temporary access list being used for troubleshooting purposes relates to verifying the UDP port number that a particular application is assumed to be using. Users are complaining that their UDP-based application is not working at all. The applications engineer previously had stated that the application only uses port numbers between 3170 and 3190 in both directions. After much troubleshooting has been performed, she is now beginning to express doubt about this. The remote server's IP address is 141.10.10.19. The following access list checks if there are matches to these port numbers:

```
access-list 102 permit udp any host 141.10.10.19 range 3170 3190
  logging
access-list 102 permit ip any any

in ethernet0
ip access-group 102 out
```

Internet Control Message Protocol

The Internet Control Message Protocol (ICMP) contains a set of different message types, many of which are extremely useful for IP network management and troubleshooting. We have already seen the integral uses for ping, which employs ICMP echo and echo reply. Traceroute also has been discussed in detail, and this uses ICMP traceroute and time-exceeded messages for monitoring the hop count time to live (TTL). Listing 7-20 is a list of the different ICMP messages; only the more commonly encountered ICMP messages will be discussed here.

Apart from the messages that are used by ping and trace, the following ICMP messages are encountered frequently when managing IP internetworks:

- *ICMP unreachables.* An IP host generates an ICMP unreachable message if that host does not have a valid path to a requested host, network, protocol, or port. The family of such ICMP messages is collectively termed *ICMP unreachables*. Routers can generate these messages if a local access list is denying access to the requested resource. These messages are helpful for troubleshooting purposes. However, there are instances where the sending of such messages may be undesirable for security reasons, since unreachable messages include the address that generated them. The different types of ICMP unreachable messages can be filtered using extended IP access lists. Alternatively, all types of unreachable messages can be blocked using the `no ip unreachables` interface command.
- *ICMP redirects.* A router generates an ICMP redirect if it receives a packet on a given interface and the route that it has to the destination address is also out on that interface. The routers that receive the redi-

```
administratively-prohibited  Administratively prohibited
alternate-address            Alternate address
conversion-error             Datagram conversion
dod-host-prohibited          Host prohibited
dod-net-prohibited           Net prohibited
echo                         Echo (ping)
echo-reply                   Echo reply
general-parameter-problem    Parameter problem
host-isolated                Host isolated
host-precedence-unreachable  Host unreachable for precedence
host-redirect                Host redirect
host-tos-redirect            Host redirect for TOS
host-tos-unreachable         Host unreachable for TOS
host-unknown                 Host unknown
host-unreachable             Host unreachable
information-reply            Information replies
information-request          Information requests
log                          Log matches against this entry
mask-reply                   Mask replies
mask-request                 Mask requests
mobile-redirect              Mobile host redirect
net-redirect                 Network redirect
net-tos-redirect             Net redirect for TOS
net-tos-unreachable          Network unreachable for TOS
net-unreachable              Net unreachable
network-unknown              Network unknown
no-room-for-option           Parameter required but no room
option-missing               Parameter required but not present
packet-too-big               Fragmentation needed and DF set
parameter-problem            All parameter problems
port-unreachable             Port unreachable
precedence                   Match packets with given precedence value
precedence-unreachable       Precedence cutoff
protocol-unreachable         Protocol unreachable
reassembly-timeout           Reassembly timeout
redirect                     All redirects
router-advertisement         Router discovery advertisements
router-solicitation          Router discovery solicitations
source-quench                Source quenches
source-route-failed          Source route failed
time-exceeded                All time exceededs
timestamp-reply              Timestamp replies
timestamp-request            Timestamp requests
tos                          Match packets with given TOS value
traceroute                   Traceroute
ttl-exceeded                 TTL exceeded
unreachable                  All unreachables
```

Listing 7-20

rect messages can then update their routing tables appropriately. ICMP redirects can be useful for detecting routing loops. If it is required to suppress the sending of ICMP redirects for security reasons, the `no ip redirects` interface command can be used. If Cisco's Hot Standby Routing Protocol (HSRP) is configured, then the sending of redirects is automatically suppressed. This is so because the router that happens to be in standby mode would persistently generate redirects to the active router.

- *ICMP mask request and reply.* For hosts that do not have statically defined subnet masks and have no other means of dynamically learning their subnet mask, an ICMP mask request can be used. In such a scenario, the host issues an ICMP mask request message, and the local router returns an ICMP mask reply.
- *ICMP source quench.* Source-quench messages provide a means of congestion control using ICMP. If a router detects congestion by having to drop packets that overflow its interface or system buffers, it will send an ICMP source-quench message back to the source of these packets. ICMP source-quench messages further illustrate two important points about ICMP that deserve emphasis. First, messages are always sent back to the source rather than to the last hop. Second, the messages are simply reporting congestion rather than attempting to alleviate it. ICMP should be thought of as a fault-reporting protocol; it is not a fault-correction protocol.
- *Fragmentation needed but DF bit set.* This type of ICMP message is generated when an IP packet is received that is larger than the MTU for the LAN or WAN medium, but the packet also has its DF (do not fragment) bit set to 1. In this situation, the packet cannot be forwarded, but this ICMP message offers an explanation to the source as to why the packet was dropped. The DF bit could be getting set as a result of the configuration of the IP stack on the sender's station. An example of this type of scenario could be a token-ring station that sets the DF bit and also generates large packets that are destined for an Ethernet segment or are required to cross a WAN medium that has a smaller MTU.

***NOTE:** ICMP messages are sent back to the source rather than to the last hop.*

NOTE: ICMP is a fault-reporting rather than a fault-correction protocol.

The following examples of ICMP messages (Listing 7-21) illustrate not only their usefulness in troubleshooting but also their relatively self-explanatory format. ICMP messages that are sent or received can be logged using `debug ip icmp`. The first two sample messages show how redirects that are sent or received can be logged. In the first message, the router has sent a redirect to 152.31.18.39 indicating that it should use 152.31.18.2 as a gateway or next hop in order to reach 172.16.1.3.

Troubleshooting RIP

RIP—the Old and the New

Routing Information Protocol (RIP) version 1 is the most traditional and simplest routing protocol that is still in popular use on many LANs and WANs. Its popularity stems from the fact that it was the first standardized IP routing protocol to be supported by all major vendors in the industry. Its simplicity further fueled its growth as a ubiquitous routing protocol. However, along with its simplicity comes a number of limitations that are problematic in today's era of increasingly complex internetworks. The limitations of RIP version 1 include

- A maximum network diameter of 15 hops is inadequate for large networks.

```
ICMP: redirect sent to 152.31.18.39 for dest 172.16.1.3 use gw 152.31.18.2

ICMP: redirect rcvd from 172.16.65.5 – for 172.16.97.3 use gw 172.16.33.2

ICMP: dst (172.16.33.33) host unreachable sent to 172.16.34.2

ICMP: dst (172.16.33.33) host unreachable rcv from 172.16.254.1

ICMP: time exceeded (time to live) sent to 150.10.34.2 (dest was 172.16.33.1)

ICMP: source quench sent to 172.16.33.2 (dest was 172.16.97.5)
```

Listing 7-21

- The hop-count metric is unsophisticated and can lead to suboptimal routing decisions.
- The periodic exchange of routing tables with neighboring routers every 30 seconds is a crude way to exchange routing information and leads to the unnecessary use of valuable WAN bandwidth.
- Variable length subnet masking (VLSM) is not supported because RIP updates do not include mask information. This results in the potentially inefficient use of IP address space.
- Address summarization cannot be configured manually. RIP networks are simply summarized based on class when a network boundary is crossed.

These issues render RIP unsuitable for use in large networks because of its poor scalability, slow speed of convergence, and inefficient bandwidth usage. The motivation for the development of an enhanced version of RIP is obvious, and it came in the form of RIP version 2, which addresses many of its predecessor's limitations.

RIP version 2 supports

- *Route summarization.* Like RIP version 1, summarization is performed automatically when crossing classful network boundaries. However, an extremely useful differentiating feature is that automatic summarization can be disabled using the `no auto-summary` router configuration command. As we will see later, this feature has an application in resolving problems caused by discontiguous networks.
- *VLSM.*
- *Classless interdomain routing (CIDR).* This most fundamentally means that routing can be performed while ignoring the constraints of network class type. Each network or subnet is routed on the basis of its network address and mask without any regard for it being class A, B, or C.

RIP version 1 is the default version on Cisco routers. If the Cisco IOS image supports version 2, then it can be easily configured:

```
router rip
 version 2
```

A router running RIP version 1 will by default only send RIP version 1 updates but has the capability to receive both version 1 and version 2 updates. The sending and receiving of different RIP versions is configurable on a per-interface basis. However, we will see that this can cause problems if it is not handled carefully.

Show Commands

The `show ip protocol` command displays what IP routing protocols have been configured on the router and for each protocol gives useful summary information. In this example (Listing 7-22), we see that RIP is routing for the 165.4.0.0 and 132.2.0.0 networks. The following information is also provided:

- The version of RIP that is sent and receivable on each interface is listed.
- We also see that EIGRP 211 is being redistributed into RIP with a default metric of 9 hops.
- Token ring 1/1 is a passive interface for RIP, meaning that RIP updates are received but not sent out this interface.

```
R2>sh ip protocol
Routing Protocol is "rip"
  Sending updates every 30 seconds, next due in 24 seconds
  Invalid after 180 seconds, hold down 180, flushed after 240
  Outgoing update filter list for all interfaces is not set
  Incoming update filter list for all interfaces is not set
  Default redistribution metric is 9
  Redistributing: eigrp 211, rip
  Default version control: send version 1, receive any version
    Interface        Send  Recv   Key-chain
    TokenRing1/0     1     1 2
    TokenRing1/3     1     1 2
    Ethernet2/0      1     1 2
Routing for Networks:
    165.4.0.0
    132.2.0.0
  Passive Interface(s):
    TokenRing1/1
Routing Information Sources:
    Gateway          Distance      Last Update
    165.4.65.131         120      00:00:02
    132.2.19.8           120      00:00:15
Distance: (default is 120)
```

Listing 7-22

- The routing timers are all at their default values.
  - The *update* timer controls the sending of routing updates and is the most fundamental timing parameter.
  - A route is marked invalid if no updates have been received about that route for the duration of the *invalid* timer. This is typically three times the update interval.
  - A route is marked in the *hold down* state when the router receives an update indicating that this route is inaccessible. During the hold down period, the route continues to be advertised as inaccessible, and the router will not process any further updates about that route. The purpose of the hold down state is to avoid routing convergence loops with distance vector routing protocols. A routing loop can occur if routers have inconsistent information about whether the route is up or down, as well as what the best path to that destination is. After the hold down timer expires, the router will accept new updates about that particular route.
  - The *flush* timer must expire before the old route can be removed from the routing table. Obviously, the flush timer must have a value greater than that of each of the other timers.

The default value for each of these timers can be altered using the `timers basic` router configuration command. Generally, this is not a good idea unless it is somehow determined to be absolutely necessary. The timer values should match across the RIP routing domain.

- 165.4.65.131 and 132.2.19.8 are neighbor routers that provide RIP updates for R2.
- Any filter or distribute lists that control inbound or outbound distribution of routing information also will be listed using the `show ip protocol` command. In this example there are none.
- The final parameter listed is a highly significant one, the *administrative distance*. This parameter can be thought of as the method that the router uses to assign credibility to information obtained from different IP routing protocols. It is only relevant if the router is receiving updates from more than one routing protocol. The router will choose the update with the lower administrative distance and place that route in its routing table.

Administrative distance should in no way be confused with routing metrics. A metric is used to enable the routing protocol to choose between different routes to a destination.

Administrative distance is used to choose between updates from different protocols. We see that RIP has its administrative distance at the default value of 120. Administrative distance is another fundamental routing parameter that should only be altered from its default value by an experienced network engineer who knows exactly what he or she is doing! Table 7-1 is a summary of the default values for the different IP routing protocols that we are about to study.

NOTE: *Administrative distance enables the router to choose between updates received via* different *routing protocols. It is not to be confused with routing metric, which enables choice of the best route from multiple routes received via the* same *routing protocol.*

The `show ip route` command can display the entire contents of the routing table, or it can be applied to a particular network or an individual subnet. In this example (Listing 7-23), the 11.0.0.0/24 subnet is seen with a 24-bit mask. RIP updates, as mentioned previously, do not include masking information. Here RIP receives the update from 11.11.11.1; this segment is directly connected and has a 24-bit mask. Hence, RIP makes the assumption that the 11.0.0.0 network is using a 24-bit subnet mask. If the router Dublin2 did not have any interface in the 11.0.0.0 class A network, it would simply show a summarized 11.0.0.0/8 route. It also can be noted that this RIP-derived route is one hop away (metric 1), is being

TABLE 7-1

Default Values for Various IP Routing Protocols

Routing Protocol or Network Type	Administrative Distance
Connected	0
Static routes	1
RIP	120
OSPF	110
IGRP	100
EIGRP (internal)	90
EIGRP (external)	170
External BGP	20
Internal BGP	200

```
Dublin2#sh ip ro 11.0.0.0
Routing entry for 11.0.0.0/24, 2 known subnets
  Attached (1 connections)
  Redistributing via rip, igrp 1
  Advertised by rip

C       11.11.11.0 is directly connected, TokenRing4/1
R       11.11.20.0 [90/1] via 11.11.11.1, 00:00:08, TokenRing4/1

Dublin2#sh ip ro 11.11.20.0
Routing entry for 11.11.20.0/24
  Known via "rip", distance 90, metric 1
  Redistributing via rip, igrp 1
  Last update from 11.11.11.1 on TokenRing4/1, 00:00:11 ago
  Routing Descriptor Blocks:
  * 11.11.11.1, from 11.11.11.1, 00:00:11 ago, via TokenRing4/1
      Route metric is 1, traffic share count is 1

Dublin2#
```

Listing 7-23

redistributed into IGRP1, and that its administrative distance has been altered to 90 instead of the default value of 120.

The `show ip route` command also can be used to check for routes that were derived from a particular routing protocol. In the following case (Listing 7-24), we are simply checking what static routes are configured on the router. What form would the command take to check only for RIP-derived routes?

Debug Commands

The most basic type of RIP debugging is the `debug ip rip events` command. This displays a summary of the number of routes being sent

```
R2>sh ip route static
     165.4.0.0/16 is variably subnetted, 33 subnets, 2 masks
S       165.4.220.0/25 [1/0] via 165.4.67.4
S       165.4.64.128/25 [1/0] via 165.4.65.1
R2>
```

Listing 7-24

and received on different interfaces. In the output shown here (Listing 7-25), the outgoing update contains a relatively large number of routes and in some cases has to be queued before being sent. An update sent out token ring 1/0 had 6 routes queued before the remainder of the RIP routing table was transmitted out this interface. The entire 25 routes are advertised out the token ring 1/2 interface. This output also demonstrates the broadcast nature of RIP updates. In some troubleshooting scenarios, a nonbroadcast medium such as X.25 or frame relay may need to be modified to ensure that these types of broadcasts are forwarded across it.

NOTE: *Configuration changes may be required to ensure that nonbroadcast media such as X.25 or frame relay forward broadcast-based routing updates.*

For a more detailed analysis of which networks are included in routing updates, the `debug ip rip` command is used. In the following output (Listing 7-26), the entire routing table was cleared using `clear ip route *`. Otherwise, it would be necessary to wait for the next set of updates. Which show command is used to tell when the next update is due?

```
R2#debug ip rip events
RIP event debugging is on
R2#
Nov 27 13:55:45 PST: RIP: Update contains 6 routes
Nov 27 13:55:45 PST: RIP: Update queued
Nov 27 13:55:45 PST: RIP: Update sent via TokenRing1/0
Nov 27 13:55:45 PST: RIP: Update sent via TokenRing1/0
Nov 27 13:55:45 PST: RIP: sending v1 update to 255.255.255.255 via TokenRing1/0
(132.2.19.2)
Nov 27 13:55:45 PST: RIP: Update contains 18 routes
Nov 27 13:55:45 PST: RIP: Update queued
Nov 27 13:55:45 PST: RIP: Update sent via TokenRing1/0
Nov 27 13:55:45 PST: RIP: sending v1 update to 255.255.255.255 via TokenRing1/2
(132.2.44.1)
Nov 27 13:55:45 PST: RIP: Update contains 25 routes
Nov 27 13:55:45 PST: RIP: Update queued
Nov 27 13:55:45 PST: RIP: Update contains 25 routes
Nov 27 13:55:45 PST: RIP: Update queued
Nov 27 13:55:45 PST: RIP: Update contains 25 routes
```

Listing 7-25

```
r3#debug ip rip
RIP protocol debugging is on
r3#term mon
r3#cle ip ro *
r3#
.Mar  6 19:33:44: RIP: sending general request on Ethernet2/0 to 255.255.255.255
.Mar  6 19:33:44: RIP: received v1 update from 150.10.97.5 on Ethernet2/0
.Mar  6 19:33:44:      150.10.55.0 in 1 hops
.Mar  6 19:33:44:      150.10.97.0 in 1 hops
.Mar  6 19:33:44: RIP: sending v1 update to 255.255.255.255 via Ethernet2/0
(150.10.97.3)
.Mar  6 19:33:44:      subnet  150.10.34.0, metric 3
.Mar  6 19:33:44:      network 172.16.0.0, metric 3
.Mar  6 19:33:47: RIP: sending v1 update to 255.255.255.255 via Ethernet2/0
(150.10.97.3)
.Mar  6 19:33:47:      subnet  150.10.34.0, metric 3
.Mar  6 19:33:47:      network 172.16.0.0, metric 3
.Mar  6 19:33:49: RIP: received v1 update from 150.10.97.5 on Ethernet2/0
.Mar  6 19:33:49:      150.10.55.0 in 1 hops
r3#undeb all
All possible debugging has been turned off
```

Listing 7-26

If the routing table is large, then it may be wiser just to clear the particular routes that you may be troubleshooting, e.g., `clear ip route 150.10.55.0`. Notice that the update entries are routes with the corresponding hop counts as seen by the advertising router. No masking information is included with any of the routes advertised.

Troubleshooting Scenarios for RIP—Part I

Now I will address some of the typical troubleshooting scenarios encountered with RIP. Use of the tools that we have studied will be demonstrated in practical examples. A summary of typical network problems that are encountered in RIP-based networks also will be presented. In many of the practical examples, basic router configuration skills are assumed, and I will only provide the very relevant portions of these configurations. In cases where the configuration is particularly straightforward, I may not provide any details. This is in line with my goal that you should focus on the troubleshooting tools rather than on the router configurations.

Mismatch of RIP Versions In Figure 7-3, both R3 and R5 are running RIP for the 150.10.0.0 network. R5 does not have version 2 enabled.

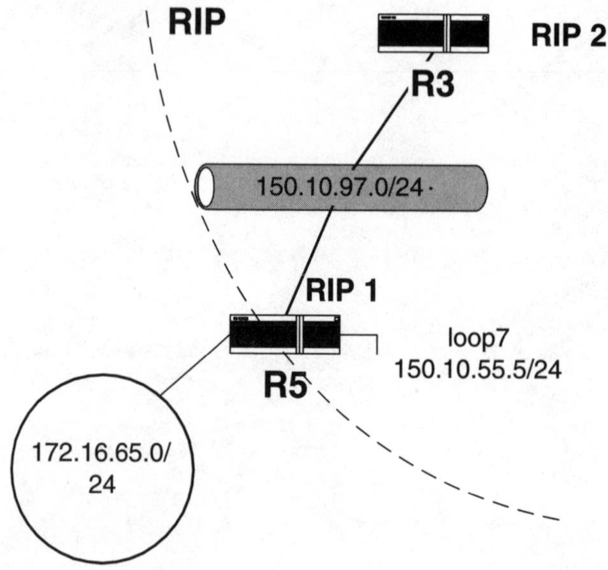

Figure 7-3 RIP version 1 and version 2 interactivity problems.

Since R3 has been configured explicitly for version 2, it would have to be reconfigured to receive version 1 updates. The output of the `show ip protocol` command verifies that R3 will not accept RIP version 1 updates. Hence R3 does not have a route to 150.10.55.0, which is a loopback network on R5. (See Listing 7-27.)

R3 can be made compatible with R5 either by configuring its Ethernet 2/0 interface to accept RIP version 1 or simply by disabling RIP version 2 as shown in Listing 7-28. As expected, R3 now sees the 150.10.55.0 network via RIP version 1. The routing table was cleared just to speed things up.

Now let's look closer at the RIP updates that R3 is sending and receiving on its Ethernet interface. The 150.10.55.0 network is being received from R5. We also can see that R3 is sending 150.10.34.0 and 172.16.0.0 both with a metric of 3. Since the default metric is set at 3 hops in the configuration, it is likely that these two routes were redistributed into RIP from EIGRP (see Listing 7-29).

It can be verified that these routes appear in the R5 routing table. The 150.10.34.0 network appears as an RIP route, but the 172.16.0.0 summary route is absent. This is so because R5 already has a connected interface in the 172.16.0.0 network, namely, token ring 0, which uses the 172.16.65.0 subnet. In such a situation, the router will drop the summary route that came in over a different interface. This makes sense because it is inconsistent to say that "to get to the entire 172.16.0.0 net-

```
R3#

!
router rip
 version 2
 redistribute eigrp 1
 network 150.10.0.0
 default-metric 3
!
no ip classless

r3#conf t
Enter configuration commands, one per line.  End with CNTL/Z.
r3(config)#^Z
r3#sh ip route 150.10.55.0
% Subnet not in table

r3#sh ip protocol
Routing Protocol is "rip"
  Sending updates every 30 seconds, next due in 3 seconds
  Invalid after 180 seconds, hold down 180, flushed after 240
  Outgoing update filter list for all interfaces is not set
  Incoming update filter list for all interfaces is not set
  Redistributing: rip
  Default version control: send version 2, receive version 2
  Routing for Networks:
    150.10.0.0.0
  Routing Information Sources:
    Gateway         Distance      Last Update
  Distance: (default is 120)
```

Listing 7-27

work, go out Ethernet 0" when the 172.16.65.0 subnet is already connected via token ring 0. (See Listing 7-30.)

Thus, what is the likely effect of configuring R3 to send RIP version 2 updates out its Ethernet 2/0 interface? We can do this easily, as shown in Listing 7-31.

Yes, you guessed it. The RIP route that R5 learns from R3 (i.e., 150.10.34.0) would disappear from its routing table, since R5 can still only receive RIP version 1 updates (see Listing 7-32).

Troubleshooting Scenarios for RIP—Part II

VLSM, Split Horizon, and Passive Interfaces These three topics—VLSM, Split Horizon, and Passive Interfaces—are not necessarily in any

```
r3#
r3#conf t
Enter configuration commands, one per line.  End with CNTL/Z.
r3(config)#router rip
r3(config-router)#no version 2
r3(config-router)#^Z
r3#cle ip ro *
r3#sh ip ro 150.10.55.0
Routing entry for 150.10.55.0/24
  Known via "rip", distance 120, metric 1
  Redistributing via rip
  Last update from 150.10.97.5 on Ethernet2/0, 00:00:05 ago
  Routing Descriptor Blocks:
  * 150.10.97.5, from 150.10.97.5, 00:00:05 ago, via Ethernet2/0
      Route metric is 1, traffic share count is 1

r3#
```

Listing 7-28

```
r3#deb ip rip
RIP protocol debugging is on
r3#term mon
r3#cle ip ro *
r3#
.Mar  6 19:33:44: RIP: sending general request on Ethernet2/0 to 255.255.255.255

.Mar  6 19:33:44: RIP: received v1 update from 150.10.97.5 on Ethernet2/0
.Mar  6 19:33:44:      150.10.55.0 in 1 hops
.Mar  6 19:33:44:      150.10.97.0 in 1 hops
.Mar  6 19:33:44: RIP: sending v1 update to 255.255.255.255 via Ethernet2/0 (150
.10.97.3)
.Mar  6 19:33:44:      subnet  150.10.34.0, metric 3
.Mar  6 19:33:44:      network 172.16.0.0, metric 3
.Mar  6 19:33:47: RIP: sending v1 update to 255.255.255.255 via Ethernet2/0 (150
.10.97.3)
.Mar  6 19:33:47:      subnet  150.10.34.0, metric 3
.Mar  6 19:33:47:      network 172.16.0.0, metric 3
.Mar  6 19:33:49: RIP: received v1 update from 150.10.97.5 on Ethernet2/0
.Mar  6 19:33:49:      150.10.55.0 in 1 hops
r3#undeb all
All possible debugging has been turned off
```

Listing 7-29

```
r5#sh ip ro
Codes: C - connected, S - static, I - IGRP, R - RIP, M - mobile, B - BGP
       D - EIGRP, EX - EIGRP external, O - OSPF, IA - OSPF inter area
       E1 - OSPF external type 1, E2 - OSPF external type 2, E - EGP
       i - IS-IS, L1 - IS-IS level-1, L2 - IS-IS level-2, * - candidate default

Gateway of last resort is not set

     150.10.0.0 255.255.255.0 is subnetted, 3 subnets
C       150.10.55.0 is directly connected, Loopback7
R       150.10.34.0 [120/3] via 150.10.97.3, 00:00:28, Ethernet0
C       150.10.97.0 is directly connected, Ethernet0
     172.16.0.0 255.255.255.0 is subnetted, 1 subnets
C       172.16.65.0 is directly connected, TokenRing0
r5#
```

Listing 7-30

way interrelated. However, they all have the potential to create serious network problems if they are not understood properly. The next example (Listing 7-33) is an RIP version 2 network that demonstrates each of these topics. There isn't any network problem in place in Figure 7-4, but I will use the troubleshooting tools to point out relevant routing issues in relation to the network itself.

The network shown has RIP version 2 running on all subnets that are labeled. The network addressing follows a typical convention that is very suitable for a laboratory environment:

- All interfaces have a last octet of .x on each router Rx.
- Each Rx router has a loopback address of the form 172.16.254.x /32.

```
r3#conf t
Enter configuration commands, one per line.  End with CNTL/Z.
r3(config)#in e2/0
r3(config-if)#ip rip send version 2
r3(config-if)#^Z
r3#cle ip ro
.Mar  6 19:36:25: %SYS-5-CONFIG_I: Configured from console by vty0 (150.10.97.5)
 *
r3#
r3#
```

Listing 7-31

```
r5#cle ip ro *
r5#sh ip ro
Codes: C - connected, S - static, I - IGRP, R - RIP, M - mobile, B - BGP
       D - EIGRP, EX - EIGRP external, O - OSPF, IA - OSPF inter area
       E1 - OSPF external type 1, E2 - OSPF external type 2, E - EGP
       i - IS-IS, L1 - IS-IS level-1, L2 - IS-IS level-2, * - candidate default

Gateway of last resort is not set

     150.10.0.0 255.255.255.0 is subnetted, 2 subnets
C       150.10.55.0 is directly connected, Loopback7
C       150.10.97.0 is directly connected, Ethernet0
     172.16.0.0 255.255.255.0 is subnetted, 1 subnets
C       172.16.65.0 is directly connected, TokenRing0
r5#
```

Listing 7-32

Let's now check some of the routing tables to verify that all routes are being distributed correctly. R2 can see all routes on the network. Note that the 172.16.0.0 network is subnetted using three different masks: 24 bit, 27 bit, and 32 bit. All are present in R2's routing table, indicating that variable length subnet masking (VLSM) is supported.

R2 is learning RIP routes over both its frame-relay interface and the token ring. Since this is a reasonably symmetrical network, the same is

```
r2#sh ip ro
Codes: C - connected, S - static, I - IGRP, R - RIP, M - mobile, B - BGP
       D - EIGRP, EX - EIGRP external, O - OSPF, IA - OSPF inter area
       E1 - OSPF external type 1, E2 - OSPF external type 2, E - EGP
       i - IS-IS, L1 - IS-IS level-1, L2 - IS-IS level-2, * - candidate default

Gateway of last resort is not set

     150.10.0.0 255.255.255.224 is subnetted, 1 subnets
C       150.10.34.0 is directly connected, TokenRing0
     172.16.0.0 is variably subnetted, 6 subnets, 3 masks
C       172.16.254.2 255.255.255.255 is directly connected, Loopback0
R       172.16.254.1 255.255.255.255
           [120/1] via 172.16.33.1, 00:00:02, Serial1.1
R       172.16.254.6 255.255.255.255
           [120/1] via 172.16.65.6, 00:00:02, TokenRing1
C       172.16.33.0 255.255.255.224 is directly connected, Serial1.1
R       172.16.1.0 255.255.255.0 [120/1] via 172.16.65.6, 00:00:02, TokenRing1
C       172.16.65.0 255.255.255.0 is directly connected, TokenRing1
```

Listing 7-33

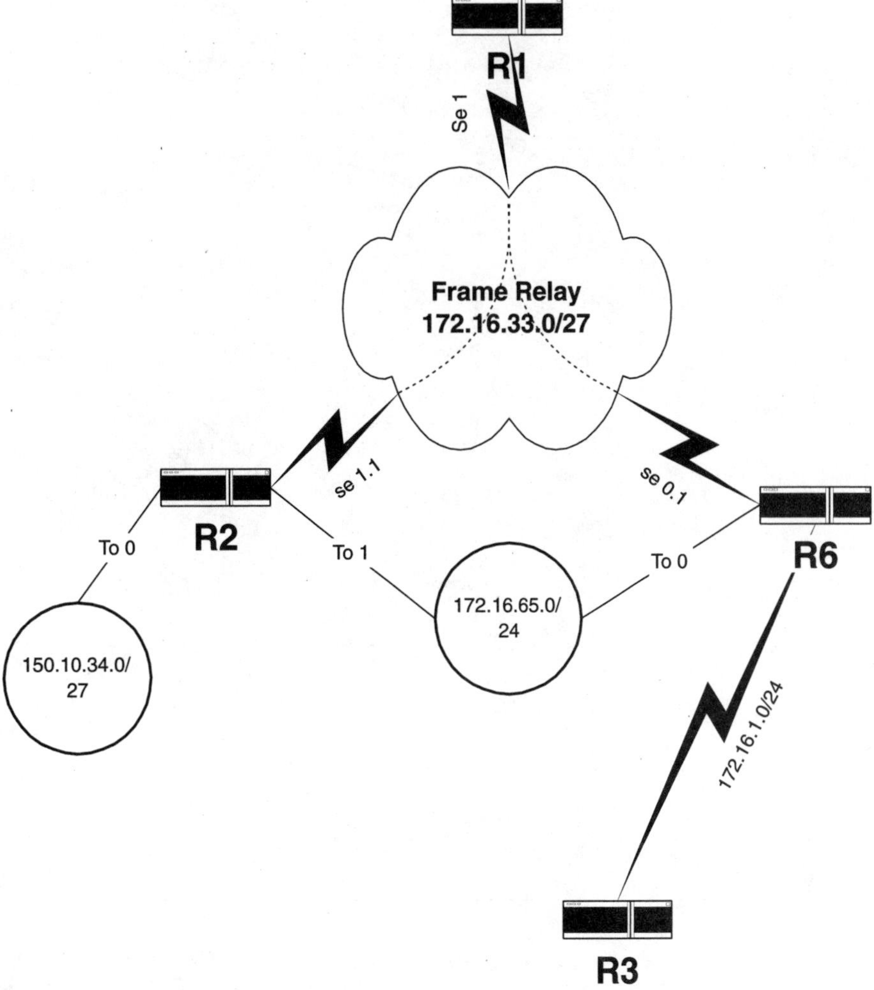

Figure 7-4 RIP version 2 network with VLSM.

true of R6. Let's now make things a little more interesting by making token ring 1 passive for RIP on R2 (see Listing 7-34).

There are a number of points to be made after examining R6's routing table:

- With the passive interface command on R2's token ring, R6 is no longer receiving RIP updates over the shared token ring. Hence R2's loopback network is learned via serial 0.1 and is therefore 2 hops away instead of just 1.
- R1 does not use subinterfaces for its frame-relay connectivity. Hence the fact that R6 can see R2's locally connected network means that

```
r2#conf t
Enter configuration commands, one per line.  End with CNTL/Z.
r2(config)#router rip
r2(config-router)#passive-interface tok1
r2(config-router)#^Z
r2#cle ip ro *
r2#

r6#cle ip ro *
r6#sh ip ro
Codes: C - connected, S - static, I - IGRP, R - RIP, M - mobile, B - BGP
       D - EIGRP, EX - EIGRP external, O - OSPF, IA - OSPF inter area
       E1 - OSPF external type 1, E2 - OSPF external type 2, E - EGP
       i - IS-IS, L1 - IS-IS level-1, L2 - IS-IS level-2, * - candidate default

Gateway of last resort is not set

R    150.10.0.0 [120/2] via 172.16.33.1, 00:00:02, Serial0.1
     172.16.0.0 is variably subnetted, 6 subnets, 3 masks
R       172.16.254.2 255.255.255.255
           [120/2] via 172.16.33.1, 00:00:02, Serial0.1
R       172.16.254.1 255.255.255.255
           [120/1] via 172.16.33.1, 00:00:02, Serial0.1
C       172.16.254.6 255.255.255.255 is directly connected, Loopback0
C       172.16.33.0 255.255.255.224 is directly connected, Serial0.1
C       172.16.1.0 255.255.255.0 is directly connected, Serial1
C       172.16.65.0 255.255.255.0 is directly connected, TokenRing0
r6#ping 172.16.254.2
Type escape sequence to abort.
Sending 5, 100-byte ICMP Echos to 172.16.254.2, timeout is 2 seconds:
!!!!!
Success rate is 100 percent (5/5), round-trip min/avg/max = 128/132/140 ms
```

Listing 7-34

split horizon is turned off on R1's serial 1 interface. This did not have to be configured. Split horizon is turned off by default on frame-relay and SMDS interfaces (but not X.25) when RIP is being used. As we will see later, this is not true of all routing protocols.

NOTE: *When using RIP, split horizon is turned off by default on frame-relay and SMDS encapsulated interfaces. This is not so for X.25!*

- Note that R6 has a summary route to the class B network 150.10.0.0 that it received from R1. No specific route to the 150.10.34.0 subnet will be found on any router other than R2, where, of course, it appears as a connected subnet. R1 receives a 150.10.0.0/16 summary from R2 because the network bit boundary is crossed at this point. To put it another way, R1 does not have any interfaces with IP addresses in the 150.10.0.0 network.

If we now check back with R2, there is one further point to note. R2 learns R6's loopback interface over the shared token ring and therefore sees it as being one hop away. But didn't we make R2's token ring 1 interface passive for RIP? Yes, we did. But that only blocks outgoing updates; unlike R6, R2 is still receiving RIP updates on its shared token ring 1 interface (see Listing 7-35).

Discontiguous Networks The automatic summarization of networks when a network boundary is crossed sometimes can create a condition known as a *discontiguous network*. The network shown in Figure 7-5 can be used to illustrate how a discontiguous network is created.

In the example shown, router A would receive a summary route 172.16.0.0/16 from both router B and router C. Hence it will not have a specific route to either 172.16.18.0 or 172.16.27.0. These networks will become inaccessible from router A because it will have two conflicting summary routes to 172.16.0.0. This is termed a *discontiguous network*.

If RIP version 1 is the routing protocol, there is only one way to solve the problem, and that is to remove the discontiguous network by putting subnets of 172.16.0.0 on the serial links between router A and the other two routers. The addressing on the serial links could be changed, or they

```
r6#172.16.33.2
Trying 172.16.33.2 ... Open

User Access Verification

Password:
r2>sh ip ro 172.16.254.6
Routing entry for 172.16.254.6 255.255.255.255
  Known via "rip", distance 120, metric 1
  Redistributing via rip
  Advertised by rip (self originated)
  Last update from 172.16.65.6 on TokenRing1, 00:00:15 ago
  Routing Descriptor Blocks:
  * 172.16.65.6, from 172.16.65.6, 00:00:15 ago, via TokenRing1
      Route metric is 1, traffic share count is 1

r2>q
```

Listing 7-35

could take the form of secondary addresses. The discontiguous network condition would no longer exist because the 172.16.0.0 network boundary would not be crossed by any of the routers, and therefore, summarization would not take place.

Using RIP version 2, there is another solution. RIP version 2 allows for automatic summarization to be turned off using the `no auto-summary` router configuration command. If automatic summarization is turned off on router B and router C, a discontiguous network is avoided, and router A will receive specific routes for the 172.16.18.0 and 172.16.27.0 subnets.

RIP Version 2 authentication RIP version 2 supports md5 authentication. It can be quite difficult to troubleshoot a suspected RIP authentication mismatch using the debug tools. If such a problem is suspected, the configuration on all the relevant routers should be checked for consistency. It should be clearly noted that it is the key-string not the key-chain label that must match on a given network. In the following example (Listing 7-36), the key string `cisco` for key 1 must match on the neighboring router that is authenticating with router A on the Ethernet segment. The key chain could have a name other than `watchdog` on the other router.

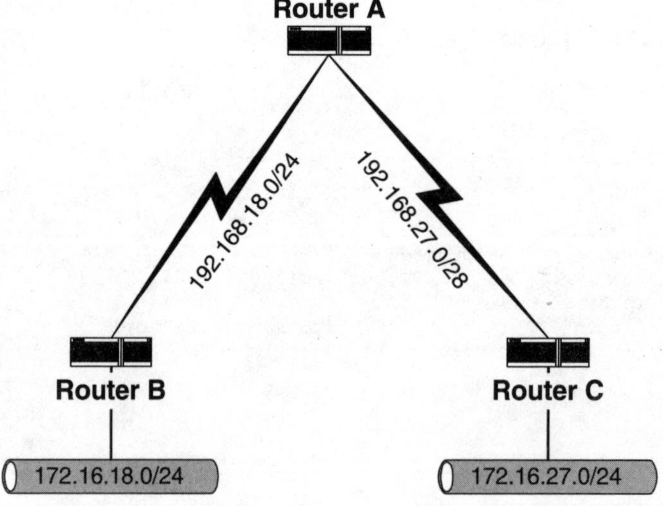

Figure 7-5
A discontiguous network.

Listing 7-36

```
Router A:

interface ethernet0
ip rip authentication key-chain watchdog
ip rip authentication mode md5

key-chain watchdog
key 1
key-string cisco
```

Problems Related to RIP Inefficiency

HOP COUNT LIMITATION The limitation to 15 hops frequently creates problems on relatively large networks that are running RIP in the WAN, and there are a lot of networks still out there that fit this description. Sometimes networks that are only moderately large have this type of problem because of poor design. In such cases, packets often incur unnecessary router hops to get to their destination. The only long-term solution to such a problem is a network redesign, possibly coupled with migration to a more scalable routing protocol.

If it is suspected that hop count is becoming an issue, ICMP debugging can be run, and the router at the final hop that detects the hop count violation will send an ICMP time-exceeded or TTL-exceeded message back to the source. For example:

```
ICMP: time exceeded (time to live) sent to 150.10.34.2 (dest was
172.16.33.1)
```

BANDWIDTH UTILIZATION The default update interval for RIP is 30 seconds. Because it is a distance-vector protocol, this means that a router running RIP will exchange its entire routing table with each adjacent neighbor every 30 seconds. Clearly, this can result in excessive bandwidth utilization. On WAN links that may already have high utilization, RIP updates can have a serious effect on network performance, particularly if the routing tables contain many routes.

We have already seen that split horizon is off by default on interfaces that use frame-relay encapsulation. In the case of a hub and spoke type of network where the remote offices only communicate with the central office and not with each other, it may be advantageous to turn on split horizon on the central site's serial interface. In this way, needless updates would not be sent to the remote offices, thus minimizing bandwidth utilization.

Troubleshooting IGRP

The Interior Gateway Routing Protocol (IGRP) is a Cisco-proprietary IP routing protocol that was developed as an early enhancement to RIP version 1. Because it is a purely distance-vector protocol, it still shares some of the limitations that are evident with RIP, namely

- Mask information is not exchanged; hence VLSM cannot be supported.
- Route summarization cannot be configured manually. Like RIP, IGRP summarizes on class when crossing a network boundary.

However, IGRP is without question a more sophisticated routing protocol than RIP, and it includes a number of significant enhancements:

- The default maximum network diameter for IGRP is 100 hops. Hop count is noted in order to set the maximum network diameter and to limit a "count to infinity" routing loop to a maximum of 100 hops. It must be noted, however, that hop count does not form any component of the IGRP metric.
- The IGRP metric is more sophisticated and more complex than that of RIP. The metric is by default influenced by bandwidth and delay. In order to troubleshoot routing problems with IGRP, it is important to understand exactly what influences the metric. The IGRP metric is calculated using a set of constants K1, K2, K3, K4, and K5. These constants act as multipliers for *Bandwidth, Reliability, Delay, Load*, and *MTU*. By default, K1 and K3 are set to 1, and the other three constants are zero. Hence, by default, only *Bandwidth* and *Delay* influence calculation of the metric value. These constants can be altered from their default values, but it is hard to imagine why anybody would want to make an already complex calculation even more difficult. I have never seen an IGRP routing problem where changing these metric weights was an appropriate solution.

Now we need to clarify what exactly is meant by the *Bandwidth* and *Delay* parameters. *Bandwidth* refers to the minimum bandwidth that the routers see along the route to the destination network. *Delay* is the total aggregate delay along that path. The value of the *Bandwidth* and *Delay* parameters on a given interface can be seen using the `show interface` command. These parameters can be configured to be different from their default values on a given interface. This is a potentially useful technique for influencing routing decisions, but it should only be done after careful analysis.

- Unlike RIP, IGRP will generate a flash or triggered update on detecting a new route or the loss of a route. This speeds up convergence.
- IGRP periodically sends updates every 90 s, which results in a slightly more efficient use of network bandwidth. With the triggered update feature, the convergence speed is less likely to be compromised by the less frequent periodic updates.

Show Commands

We have already met the `show ip protocol` command, which gives information about any IP routing protocol that is configured on the router. In the following example (Listing 7-37), IGRP is configured with an autonomous system number of 1. It can be seen that all the routing timers are at their default values, no route distribute lists are configured, and RIP is being redistributed into IGRP 1. Some parameters that we have not already encountered need to be discussed:

- Default routes can be redistributed into IGRP 1. This occurs by default in IGRP, unlike some of the other IP protocols, where the redistribution of default routes needs to be configured.

```
r6#show ip protocol
Routing Protocol is "igrp 1"
  Sending updates every 90 seconds, next due in 18 seconds
  Invalid after 270 seconds, hold down 280, flushed after 630
  Outgoing update filter list for all interfaces is not set
  Incoming update filter list for all interfaces is not set
  Default networks flagged in outgoing updates
  Default networks accepted from incoming updates
  IGRP metric weight K1=1, K2=0, K3=1, K4=0, K5=0
  IGRP maximum hopcount 100
  IGRP maximum metric variance 1
  Redistributing: rip, igrp 1
  Routing for Networks:
    172.16.0.0
  Passive Interface(s):
    Ethernet0
  Routing Information Sources:
    Gateway         Distance      Last Update
    172.16.12.2          100      00:01:14
  Distance: (default is 100)

r6#
```

Listing 7-37

- We see that of the five IGRP metric weights, K1 and K3 are set to one, with the other three being zero. K1 and K3 control the *Bandwidth* and *Delay* parameters. This is the default condition for calculating the IGRP metric, and it means that only *Delay* and *Bandwidth* are part of the calculation.
- The maximum hop count is at the default value of 100. Again, it should be emphasized that while IGRP tracks the hop count to avoid counting to infinity, hop count does not influence the IGRP route selection metric.
- The metric variance is a feature available with IGRP and EIGRP that can be used for symmetrical load balancing. The *Variance* parameter is set to one by default, which means that load balancing will be equal or symmetrical across multiple paths. I have rarely seen this feature used in practice. Great caution needs to be exercised when using *Variance* to bias more traffic toward one path over another. If the *Variance* were set to two, it would mean that twice as much traffic would traverse the first path compared with the second-choice path. If the packets are being process switched, then the load balancing takes place on a per-packet basis. However, if fast switching is being employed, caching twice as many destinations against the more favorable route performs load balancing. This could potentially cause congestion if many of the less busy destinations were cached against what is supposed to be the better path.

The contents of the routing table can be displayed using the `show ip route` command. In the output shown (Listing 7-38), the 172.16.200.0 and 172.16.13.0 networks are both learned via IGRP over the Ethernet 0 interface. Both routes have an administrative distance of 100, the default for IGRP. The 172.16.200.0 network has a metric of 1600, whereas the 172.16.13.0 network has a metric equal to 1163. It is noticeable that no mask information is included with the route entries. At the top of the routing table, 172.16.0.0 is stated to have 4 subnets, each being of a 24-bit prefix length. This assumption is made because the directly connected subnets on Ethernet 0 and Serial 0.100 have 24-bit masks.

More detailed information can be obtained by using the `show ip route` command for a particular network or subnet. Some points to be noted about the following sample output (Listing 7-39) are

- The term *self-originated* sometimes causes confusion. It refers to the routing protocol, not the router. It essentially means that this route was learned via IGRP and is being readvertised using the same IGRP

```
r6#clear ip ro *
r6#sh ip ro
Codes: C - connected, S - static, I - IGRP, R - RIP, M - mobile, B - BGP
       D - EIGRP, EX - EIGRP external, O - OSPF, IA - OSPF inter area
       N1 - OSPF NSSA external type 1, N2 - OSPF NSSA external type 2
       E1 - OSPF external type 1, E2 - OSPF external type 2, E - EGP
       i - IS-IS, L1 - IS-IS level-1, L2 - IS-IS level-2, * - candidate default
       U - per-user static route, o - ODR

Gateway of last resort is not set

     172.16.0.0/24 is subnetted, 4 subnets
I       172.16.200.0 [100/1600] via 172.16.12.2, 00:01:21, Ethernet0
C       172.16.12.0 is directly connected, Ethernet0
I       172.16.13.0 [100/1163] via 172.16.12.2, 00:01:21, Ethernet0
C       172.16.10.0 is directly connected, Serial0.100
r6#
```

Listing 7-38

routing process. It does *not* mean that the route originated from this particular router.

- The *Total delay* and *Minimum bandwidth* values that are shown are used to calculate the route metric. The other parameters, such as *Delay, Reliability*, and *Loading*, do not influence metric calculation unless the default metric weights are altered, which almost always is not a good idea.

```
Router-3#sh ip ro 192.168.11.0
Routing entry for 192.168.11.0 255.255.255.0
  Known via "igrp 1", distance 100, metric 781
  Redistributing via igrp 1
  Advertised by igrp 1 (self originated)
  Last update from 192.168.7.1 on TokenRing2/0, 00:00:13 ago
  Routing Descriptor Blocks:
  * 192.168.7.1, from 192.168.7.1, 00:00:13 ago, via TokenRing2/0
      Route metric is 781, traffic share count is 1
      Total delay is 1560 microseconds, minimum bandwidth is 16000 Kbit
      Reliability 255/255, minimum MTU 1500 bytes
      Loading 6/255, Hops 2
Router-3#
```

Listing 7-39

Debug Commands

The `debug ip igrp transactions` command is quite a powerful debugging tool. It lists the entries present in each routing update that is sent and received on each of the router's interfaces. In the following example (Listing 7-40), there are some points to note:

- The routing table was cleared using `clear ip ro *`. This is to avoid having to wait for the next set of updates, which could be up to 90 s away.
- The updates are sent in the form of a broadcast out each interface that is participating in the IGRP process. Care should be taken when dealing with nonbroadcast media such as X.25 or frame relay to ensure that the interfaces are configured to forward broadcasts.
- In this example, updates are also being broadcast out the loopback 0 interface. This is so because loopback 0 is logically participating in IGRP, but of course, the update has no physical significance.

Troubleshooting Scenarios for IGRP

Exploring VLSM and Split Horizon Issues Figure 7-6 shows a network that will be used to demonstrate some principles and properties of

```
*r5#debug ip igrp transactions
IGRP protocol debugging is on
r5#term mon
r5#cle ip ro *
r5#
IGRP: broadcasting request on Ethernet0
IGRP: broadcasting request on Loopback0
IGRP: broadcasting request on TokenRing0
IGRP: edition is now 3
IGRP: sending update to 255.255.255.255 via Ethernet0 (172.16.12.2)
subnet 172.16.200.0, metric=501
subnet 172.16.13.0, metric=688
IGRP: sending update to 255.255.255.255 via Loopback0 (172.16.200.1)
subnet 172.16.12.0, metric=1100
subnet 172.16.13.0, metric=688
IGRP: sending update to 255.255.255.255 via TokenRing0 (172.16.13.2)
subnet 172.16.200.0, metric=501
subnet 172.16.12.0, metric=1100
```

Listing 7-40

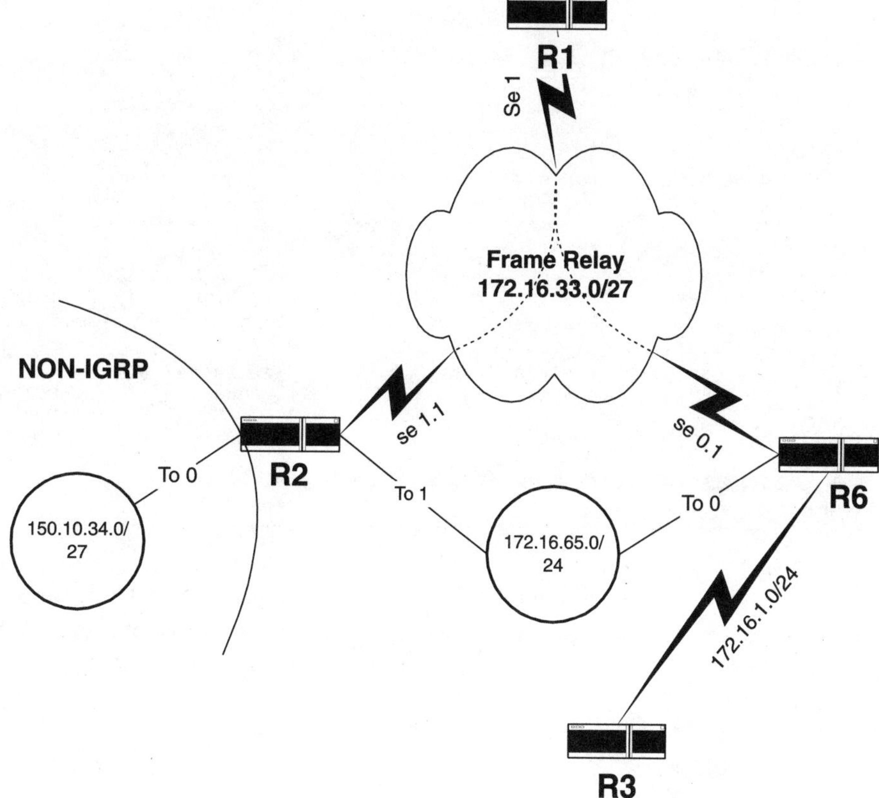

Figure 7-6
IGRP and VLSM.

the IGRP protocol. We will see some of the problems caused by the limitations of the protocol, along with some possible solutions.

As usual, all router interfaces for each router Rx have a last octet equal to x. Also, each router has a loopback address of the form 172.16.254.x /32. All the 172.16.0.0 subnets are participating in IGRP. The 150.10.0.0 network is not. This initial network configuration shows various subnets of 172.16.0.0 that include three different masks. The loopback networks are all 32-bit masks, the frame relay uses a 27-bit mask, and all other subnets are 24 bits in length.

To verify whether or not the different subnets are being distributed correctly around the network, we can first check R2's routing table (see Listing 7-41). Here it can be observed that R2 does not learn any of the remote loopback networks over IGRP. The only route it learns over IGRP is the 172.16.1.0/24 subnet; it learns this over the token ring 1 interface, which also has a 24-bit mask. Thus it retains this in its routing table. This routing table is a good illustration of how IGRP does not support

```
r2#sh ip ro
Codes: C - connected, S - static, I - IGRP, R - RIP, M - mobile, B - BGP
       D - EIGRP, EX - EIGRP external, O - OSPF, IA - OSPF inter area
       E1 - OSPF external type 1, E2 - OSPF external type 2, E - EGP
       i - IS-IS, L1 - IS-IS level-1, L2 - IS-IS level-2, * - candidate default

Gateway of last resort is not set

     150.10.0.0 255.255.255.224 is subnetted, 1 subnets
C       150.10.34.0 is directly connected, TokenRing0
     172.16.0.0 is variably subnetted, 4 subnets, 3 masks
C       172.16.254.2 255.255.255.255 is directly connected, Loopback0
C       172.16.33.0 255.255.255.224 is directly connected, Serial1.1
I       172.16.1.0 255.255.255.0
           [100/8539] via 172.16.65.6, 00:00:08, TokenRing1
C       172.16.65.0 255.255.255.0 is directly connected, TokenRing1
r2#
```

Listing 7-41

variable length subnet masking (VLSM). Chapter 8 will show a variety of techniques for allowing the redistribution of variable-length subnets into routing protocols that do not support VLSM.

NOTE: *IGRP, like RIP version 1, does not support VLSM.*

Okay, let's experiment a little further. We will make the shared token-ring interface on R6 passive for IGRP (see Listing 7-42). Is there anything surprising here? We made the R6 token ring 0 passive for IGRP, yet R2 appears to be still learning about 172.16.1.0 from 172.16.65.6 (the same interface we made passive). At first sight this does not make sense, but note that the last update was 46 seconds ago. Thus we need to wait for the next update, which will not come in this interface, or we can clear the routing table manually (see Listing 7-43).

NOTE: *With distance-vector protocols like RIP and IGRP, you often need to clear routing table entries to speed up the convergence of the network.*

Now, having cleared R2's routing table, we see that there are no routes being learned dynamically. Before we go on, can you think of the reason why R2 is not learning about 172.16.1.0/24 over the frame relay from R1? (See Listing 7-44.)

```
r6#conf t
Enter configuration commands, one per line.  End with CNTL/Z.
r6(config)#router igr 1
r6(config-router)#passive-inter tok 0
r6(config-router)#^Z
r6#

r2>sh ip route
Codes: C - connected, S - static, I - IGRP, R - RIP, M - mobile, B - BGP
       D - EIGRP, EX - EIGRP external, O - OSPF, IA - OSPF inter area
       E1 - OSPF external type 1, E2 - OSPF external type 2, E - EGP
       i - IS-IS, L1 - IS-IS level-1, L2 - IS-IS level-2, * - candidate default

Gateway of last resort is not set

     150.10.0.0 255.255.255.224 is subnetted, 1 subnets
C       150.10.34.0 is directly connected, TokenRing0
     172.16.0.0 is variably subnetted, 4 subnets, 3 masks
C       172.16.254.2 255.255.255.255 is directly connected, Loopback0
C       172.16.33.0 255.255.255.224 is directly connected, Serial1.1
I       172.16.1.0 255.255.255.0
           [100/8539] via 172.16.65.6, 00:00:46, TokenRing1
C       172.16.65.0 255.255.255.0 is directly connected, TokenRing1
r2>
```

Listing 7-42

```
r2>en
Password:
r2#clear ip route *
r2#sh ip ro
Codes: C - connected, S - static, I - IGRP, R - RIP, M - mobile, B - BGP
       D - EIGRP, EX - EIGRP external, O - OSPF, IA - OSPF inter area
       E1 - OSPF external type 1, E2 - OSPF external type 2, E - EGP
       i - IS-IS, L1 - IS-IS level-1, L2 - IS-IS level-2, * - candidate default

Gateway of last resort is not set

     150.10.0.0 255.255.255.224 is subnetted, 1 subnets
C       150.10.34.0 is directly connected, TokenRing0
     172.16.0.0 is variably subnetted, 3 subnets, 3 masks
C       172.16.254.2 255.255.255.255 is directly connected, Loopback0
C       172.16.33.0 255.255.255.224 is directly connected, Serial1.1
C       172.16.65.0 255.255.255.0 is directly connected, TokenRing1
r2#
```

Listing 7-43

```
r1#sh ip ro
Codes: C - connected, S - static, I - IGRP, R - RIP, M - mobile, B - BGP
       D - EIGRP, EX - EIGRP external, O - OSPF, IA - OSPF inter area
       E1 - OSPF external type 1, E2 - OSPF external type 2, E - EGP
       i - IS-IS, L1 - IS-IS level-1, L2 - IS-IS level-2, * - candidate default

Gateway of last resort is not set

     172.16.0.0 is variably subnetted, 2 subnets, 2 masks
C       172.16.254.1 255.255.255.255 is directly connected, Loopback0
C       172.16.33.0 255.255.255.224 is directly connected, Serial1
r1#
```

Listing 7-44

For those of you who might have guessed that it is because of split horizon, I'm sorry to say you were wrong! Split horizon is off by default on NMBA interfaces such as frame relay and SMDS (not so for X.25) when IGRP is the routing protocol.

NOTE: *When using IGRP, split horizon is off by default on frame relay (and on by default on X.25).*

It can be seen from R1's routing table that R1 is not learning about 172.16.1.0/24 from R6. Again, this demonstrates IGRP's lack of support for VLSM. The frame-relay cloud uses a 172.16.0.0 subnet with a 27-bit mask. R1 will not process any 172.16.0.0 routes it receives on this interface that are other than 27 bit.

Before we made R6's token ring 0 interface passive for IGRP, R2 was learning about this network from R6. The reason that this worked is that the shared token-ring segment on which the update was arriving was 172.16.65.0/24, so there was no conflict in the mask lengths.

Just to prove the point, let's give the 172.16.1.0 serial subnet a 27-bit mask. It can be seen in R6's table as the connected network on serial 1 (see Listing 7-45).

As expected, we now see the route in R1's routing table. We also see the route in R2's table as being learned over the frame-relay network. There is no conflict in masking because the entire frame-relay cloud is a 27-bit subnet.

Note also that the fact that R1 propagated the route to R2 further illustrates that split horizon is off by default on frame-relay-encapsu-

```
r6#sh ip route
Codes: C - connected, S - static, I - IGRP, R - RIP, M - mobile, B - BGP
       D - EIGRP, EX - EIGRP external, O - OSPF, IA - OSPF inter area
       E1 - OSPF external type 1, E2 - OSPF external type 2, E - EGP
       i - IS-IS, L1 - IS-IS level-1, L2 - IS-IS level-2, * - candidate default

Gateway of last resort is not set

     172.16.0.0 is variably subnetted, 4 subnets, 3 masks
C       172.16.254.6 255.255.255.255 is directly connected, Loopback0
C       172.16.33.0 255.255.255.224 is directly connected, Serial0.1
C       172.16.1.0 255.255.255.224 is directly connected, Serial1
C       172.16.65.0 255.255.255.0 is directly connected, TokenRing0
r6#
```

Listing 7-45

lated interfaces. We will see later that this is not true of all IP routing protocols. (See Listing 7-46.)

For further demonstration purposes, we will turn on IGRP debugging on R2. The output (Listing 7-47) can be studied in the context of the discussion so far.

Note again the broadcasting nature of IGRP. R2's debug output shows IGRP updates being broadcast on serial 1.1. However, in R2's configuration, there is no `broadcast` keyword where the DLCI is being defined. This is so because the `frame-relay interface dlci` command automatically enables broadcast forwarding. Conversely, the mapping commands on R1 do require the `broadcast` keyword to achieve this goal. (See Listing 7-48.)

The `debug ip igrp events` command is not as powerful in that it simply gives the total number of routes being sent and received on each interface. Unlike the case of `debug ip igrp transactions`, individual subnets are not listed. (See Listing 7-49.)

Discontiguous Networks in IGRP The network in Figure 7-7 is going to be used to illustrate a discontiguous network that is running IGRP. It is required that the 150.10.66.0 network is propagated to R2 for use as an IBM internetworking peer. R6 is using 150.10.22.2 as its remote peer definition for R2. Hence R6 must have a route to 150.10.22.0/24.

When IGRP transaction debugging is run on R6, it can be observed that only a summary route for 150.10.0.0/16 is being received from the

```
r1>sh ip route
Codes: C - connected, S - static, I - IGRP, R - RIP, M - mobile, B - BGP
       D - EIGRP, EX - EIGRP external, O - OSPF, IA - OSPF inter area
       E1 - OSPF external type 1, E2 - OSPF external type 2, E - EGP
       i - IS-IS, L1 - IS-IS level-1, L2 - IS-IS level-2, * - candidate default

Gateway of last resort is not set

     172.16.0.0 is variably subnetted, 3 subnets, 2 masks
C       172.16.254.1 255.255.255.255 is directly connected, Loopback0
C       172.16.33.0 255.255.255.224 is directly connected, Serial1
I       172.16.1.0 255.255.255.224
           [100/10476] via 172.16.33.6, 00:01:15, Serial1
r1>

r2>sh ip route
Codes: C - connected, S - static, I - IGRP, R - RIP, M - mobile, B - BGP
       D - EIGRP, EX - EIGRP external, O - OSPF, IA - OSPF inter area
       E1 - OSPF external type 1, E2 - OSPF external type 2, E - EGP
       i - IS-IS, L1 - IS-IS level-1, L2 - IS-IS level-2, * - candidate default

Gateway of last resort is not set

     150.10.0.0 255.255.255.224 is subnetted, 1 subnets
C       150.10.34.0 is directly connected, TokenRing0
     172.16.0.0 is variably subnetted, 4 subnets, 3 masks
C       172.16.254.2 255.255.255.255 is directly connected, Loopback0
C       172.16.33.0 255.255.255.224 is directly connected, Serial1.1
I       172.16.1.0 255.255.255.224
           [100/12476] via 172.16.33.1, 00:00:16, Serial1.1
C       172.16.65.0 255.255.255.0 is directly connected, TokenRing1
r2>
```

Listing 7-46

WAN. Since R6 already has 150.10.66.0 directly connected, it will ignore a summary route for a major network. Therefore, the discontiguous network has created a fundamental routing problem.

The `debug ip igrp transactions` command was used here instead of `debug ip igrp events` because it was required to see whether the routes being advertised were summary routes or specific routes. In other words, it was not good enough just to see the total number of routes in each update. The following output (Listing 7-50) shows that R6 is sending and receiving a 150.10.0.0 class B summary route.

By checking R1's routing table, it can be verified that it is not R1 that is doing the summarization for the 150.10.0.0 network. As expected, both R2 and R6 are summarizing this route, since the updates cross a major network boundary into 172.16.0.0, which is the frame-relay network. In

```
r2#debug ip igrp trans
IGRP protocol debugging is on
r2#term mon
r2#cle ip route *
r2#
Mar  6 20:33:43: IGRP: broadcasting request on Loopback0
Mar  6 20:33:43: IGRP: broadcasting request on Serial1.1
Mar  6 20:33:43: IGRP: broadcasting request on TokenRing1
Mar  6 20:33:43: IGRP: received update from 172.16.33.1 on Serial1.1
Mar  6 20:33:43:       subnet 172.16.33.0, metric 10476 (neighbor 8476)
Mar  6 20:33:43:       subnet 172.16.1.0, metric 12476 (neighbor 10476)
Mar  6 20:33:43: IGRP: edition is now 3
Mar  6 20:33:43: IGRP: sending update to 255.255.255.255 via Loopback0 (172.16.2
54.2) - suppressing null update
Mar  6 20:33:43: IGRP: sending update to 255.255.255.255 via Serial1.1 (172.16.3
3.2) - suppressing null update
Mar  6 20:33:43: IGRP: sending update to 255.255.255.255 via TokenRing1 (172.16.
65.2) - suppressing null update
Mar  6 20:33:50: IGRP: sending update to 255.255.255.255 via Loopback0 (172.16.2
54.2) - suppressing null update
Mar  6 20:33:50: IGRP: sending update to 255.255.255.255 via Serial1.1 (172.16.3
3.2) - suppressing null update
Mar  6 20:33:50: IGRP: sending update to 255.255.255.255 via TokenRing1 (172.16.
65.2) - suppressing null update
r2#undeb all
All possible debugging has been turned off
r2#
```

Listing 7-47

```
R1#

interface serial 1
encapsulation frame-relay
frame-relay lmi-type ansi
ip address 172.16.33.1 255.255.255.224
frame-relay map ip 172.16.33.2 102 broadcast
frame-relay map ip 172.16.33.6 106 broadcast

R2#

interface serial 1
encapsulation frame-relay
frame-relay lmi-type ansi
!
interface serial 1.1 point-to-point
ip address 172.16.33.1 255.255.255.224
frame-relay interface-dlci 200
```

Listing 7-48

```
r2#deb ip igrp event
IGRP event debugging is on
r2#term mon
r2#cle ip ro *
r2#
Mar  6 20:38:05: IGRP: broadcasting request on Loopback0
Mar  6 20:38:05: IGRP: broadcasting request on Serial1.1
Mar  6 20:38:05: IGRP: broadcasting request on TokenRing1
Mar  6 20:38:05: IGRP: received update from 172.16.33.1 on Serial1.1
Mar  6 20:38:05: IGRP: Update contains 2 interior, 0 system, and 0 exterior routes.
Mar  6 20:38:05: IGRP: Total routes in update: 2
Mar  6 20:38:05: IGRP: edition is now 4
Mar  6 20:38:05: IGRP: sending update to 255.255.255.255 via Loopback0 (172.16.254.2)
Mar  6 20:38:05: IGRP: Update contains 0 interior, 0 system, and 0 exterior routes.
Mar  6 20:38:05: IGRP: Total routes in update: 0 - suppressing null update
Mar  6 20:38:05: IGRP: sending update to 255.255.255.255 via Serial1.1 (172.16.33.2)
Mar  6 20:38:05: IGRP: Update contains 0 interior, 0 system, and 0 exterior routes.
Mar  6 20:38:05: IGRP: Total routes in update: 0 - suppressing null update
Mar  6 20:38:05: IGRP: sending update to 255.255.255.255 via TokenRing1 (172.16.65.2)
Mar  6 20:38:05: IGRP: Update contains 0 interior, 0 system, and 0 exterior routes.
Mar  6 20:38:05: IGRP: Total routes in update: 0 - suppressing null update
Mar  6 20:38:12: IGRP: received update from 172.16.33.1 on Serial1.1
Mar  6 20:38:12: IGRP: Update contains 2 interior, 0 system, and 0 exterior routes.
Mar  6 20:38:12: IGRP: Total routes in update: 2
r2#undeb all
All possible debugging has been turned off
r2#
```

Listing 7-49

this scenario, R1 is receiving the 150.10.0.0/16 summarized route from both R2 and R6 (see Listing 7-51).

It can then be easily verified that neither R6 nor R2 put this summary route in their respective routing tables (see Listing 7-52).

Automatic summarization cannot be turned off for IGRP; hence IGRP does not have any inherent means of supporting discontiguous networks. There are a couple of workaround solutions:

- Use a subnet of 150.10.0.0/24 for the frame relay. This could mean changing the addressing or applying secondary addressing. In this case, a network boundary would not be crossed, thus avoiding summarization.
- Use IP unnumbered for the frame-relay network. If you are unfamiliar with IP unnumbered, do a search for it on CCO, where you will find sample configurations along with guidelines.

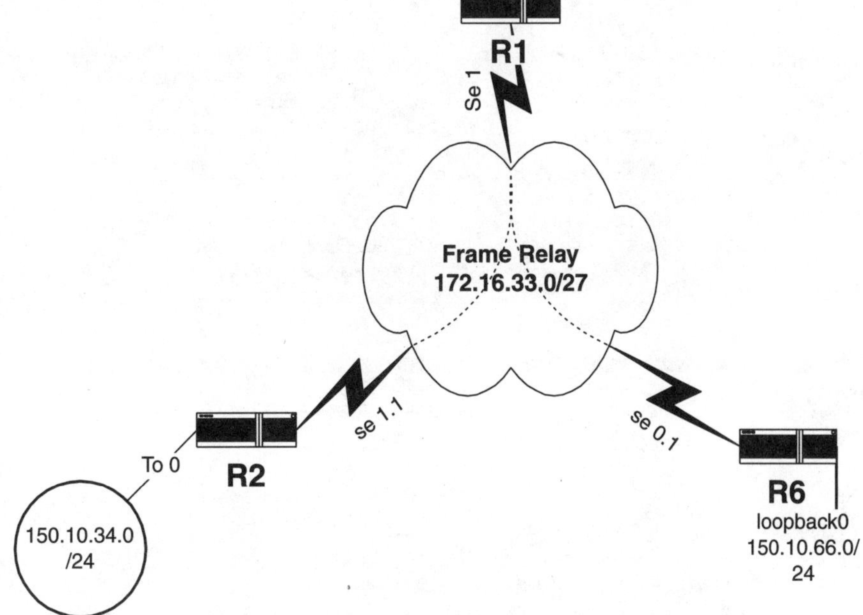

Figure 7-7
A discontiguous network in IGRP.

```
r6#deb ip igr trans
IGRP protocol debugging is on
r6#cle ip ro *
r6#term mon
r6#cle ip ro *
r6#
Mar  7 00:16:48: IGRP: broadcasting request on Loopback0
Mar  7 00:16:48: IGRP: broadcasting request on Serial0.1
Mar  7 00:16:48: IGRP: edition is now 5
Mar  7 00:16:48: IGRP: sending update to 255.255.255.255 via Loopback0 (150.10.66.6)
Mar  7 00:16:48:       network 172.16.0.0, metric=8476
Mar  7 00:16:48: IGRP: sending update to 255.255.255.255 via Serial0.1 (172.16.33.6)
Mar  7 00:16:48:       network 150.10.0.0, metric=501
Mar  7 00:16:48: IGRP: received update from 172.16.33.1 on Serial0.1
Mar  7 00:16:48:       subnet 172.16.33.0, metric 10476 (neighbor 8476)
Mar  7 00:16:48:       network 150.10.0.0, metric 10539 (neighbor 8539)
r6#undeb all
All possible debugging has been turned off
r6#
```

Listing 7-50

```
r1>sh ip ro
Codes: C - connected, S - static, I - IGRP, R - RIP, M - mobile, B - BGP
       D - EIGRP, EX - EIGRP external, O - OSPF, IA - OSPF inter area
       E1 - OSPF external type 1, E2 - OSPF external type 2, E - EGP
       i - IS-IS, L1 - IS-IS level-1, L2 - IS-IS level-2, * - candidate default

Gateway of last resort is not set

I    150.10.0.0 [100/8539] via 172.16.33.2, 00:00:55, Serial1
     172.16.0.0 255.255.255.224 is subnetted, 1 subnets
C       172.16.33.0 is directly connected, Serial1
r1>
```

Listing 7-51

```
r6>sh ip ro
Codes: C - connected, S - static, I - IGRP, R - RIP, M - mobile, B - BGP
       D - EIGRP, EX - EIGRP external, O - OSPF, IA - OSPF inter area
       E1 - OSPF external type 1, E2 - OSPF external type 2, E - EGP
       i - IS-IS, L1 - IS-IS level-1, L2 - IS-IS level-2, * - candidate default

Gateway of last resort is not set

     150.10.0.0 255.255.255.0 is subnetted, 1 subnets
C       150.10.66.0 is directly connected, Loopback0
     172.16.0.0 255.255.255.224 is subnetted, 1 subnets
C       172.16.33.0 is directly connected, Serial0.1
r6>

r2>sh ip ro
Codes: C - connected, S - static, I - IGRP, R - RIP, M - mobile, B - BGP
       D - EIGRP, EX - EIGRP external, O - OSPF, IA - OSPF inter area
       E1 - OSPF external type 1, E2 - OSPF external type 2, E - EGP
       i - IS-IS, L1 - IS-IS level-1, L2 - IS-IS level-2, * - candidate default

Gateway of last resort is not set

     150.10.0.0 255.255.255.0 is subnetted, 1 subnets
C       150.10.22.0 is directly connected, TokenRing0
     172.16.0.0 is variably subnetted, 2 subnets, 2 masks
C       172.16.254.2 255.255.255.255 is directly connected, Loopback0
C       172.16.33.0 255.255.255.224 is directly connected, Serial1.1
r2>
```

Listing 7-52

Troubleshooting IP EIGRP

The Enhanced Interior Gateway Routing Protocol (EIGRP) is a significant development by Cisco Systems in providing a scalable IP routing protocol suitable for large networks. It is a substantially more powerful protocol than IGRP. What I appreciate most about EIGRP is that while it provides an adequate routing solution for most large and complex networks, the protocol itself is no more complicated than it is required to be.

Before moving on, I would like to clarify a point in relation to the integrated routing feature of EIGRP. It is claimed that EIGRP is a protocol that provides integrated routing for IP, IPX, and AppleTalk. Technically speaking, this could be argued to be true; however, in practice, you are talking about three different sets of configurations, three different routing tables, and three different topology databases. While all three protocols are efficient and powerful, it is just worth reiterating for anyone who is inexperienced in this particular area that EIGRP is not some magic protocol that automatically routes IP, IPX, and AppleTalk. In this chapter I will confine the discussion to IP EIGRP. In the respective chapters on Novell and AppleTalk, you will meet its cousins.

EIGRP Characteristics

Here I will discuss the features and characteristics of EIGRP that need to be most clearly understood in order to troubleshoot the typical problems that can be encountered in EIGRP networks. As in most sections of this book, I am not going to give an exhaustive reiteration of the fundamental theory of the EIGRP protocol, since this information is readily available from a multitude of sources. Instead, I am going to explore how some of the characteristics of EIGRP relate to common network problems.

EIGRP Packet Types EIGRP has four basic packet types that need to be understood:

- *Hellos and Acks.* These packets are used for the discovery and recovery of neighbors. Hellos are multicast messages. Acks are unicast packets. Hellos and Acks are not transmitted reliably.
- *Updates.* These are routing updates, which are of unicast nature when neighbors are building up each other's topology databases. Updates use multicasting for incremental topology changes. Update

messages always use reliable transmission, which requires an acknowledgment.

- *Queries.* These are sent when a router does not have a feasible successor in its topology database for a route that is lost. The queries are sent to each neighbor, and they require an acknowledgment. Queries are multicast in nature unless they are in response to a received query.
- *Replies.* These are in response to queries. They are unicast packets that are sent to the originator of the query. Replies are also transmitted reliably. During the stage when a router is exchanging queries and replies for a particular route, the router is said to be in an *EIGRP active state* for that route.

Neighbor Formation EIGRP will form neighbors with every router on each of its interfaces that is participating in the EIGRP process for the overlapping network. Hence a router can potentially form an EIGRP neighbor relationship with the same router on several different interfaces or with several different routers on the same interface.

In Figure 7-8, router A will see router B as an EIGRP neighbor three times, with a neighbor relationship being formed over each token-ring

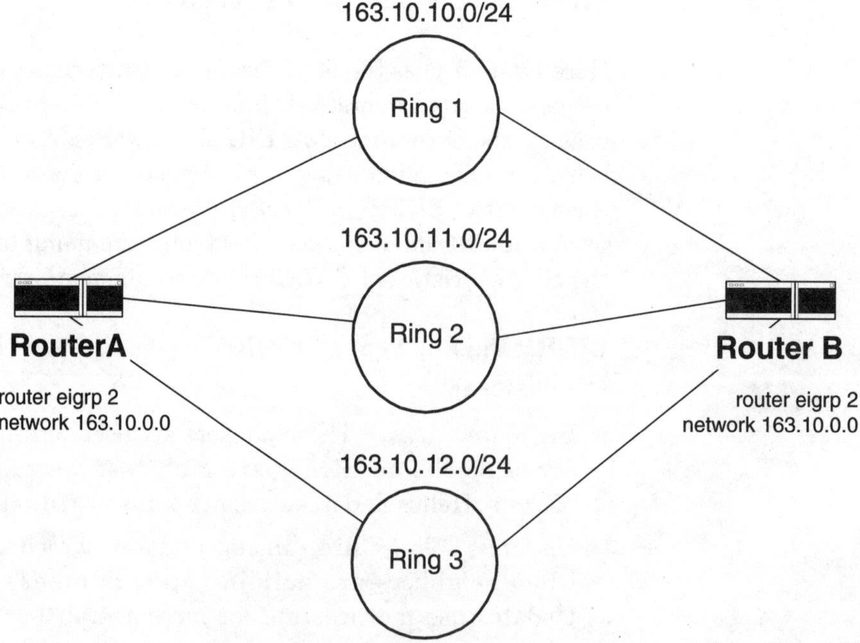

Figure 7-8
A repeated EIGRP neighbor on multiple interfaces.

segment. The same would be true of router B. In Figure 7-9, each router on the collapsed backbone ring will see the other routers as EIGRP neighbors.

Sometimes having a large number of EIGRP neighbors can cause problems with convergence speed after a link or subnet is lost. This can be especially true if the neighbors are formed over serial links, which already may be burdened with other traffic, causing a slow response to EIGRP queries.

The following issues relating to a potentially excessive number of EIGRP neighbors should be kept in mind when either designing or troubleshooting a very large EIGRP network.

- *Memory constraints.* A very large number of neighbor relationships results in a large topology database. The appropriate Cisco documentation of the Technical Assistance Center should be consulted if it is suspected that the routers do not have enough memory to support a large EIGRP network.
- *Convergence problems.* If a neighbor receives a query for a route that it does not have a feasible successor, it will in turn query each of its neighbors for a successor for that route. If the number of neighbors is large, then this could have a snowballing effect, which could produce a convergence problem. The likelihood of such a problem occurring increases if the queries are taking place over heavily utilized serial links, for example. Also, imagine what could happen in the case of a flapping link? Later we will discuss safeguards against this possibility.

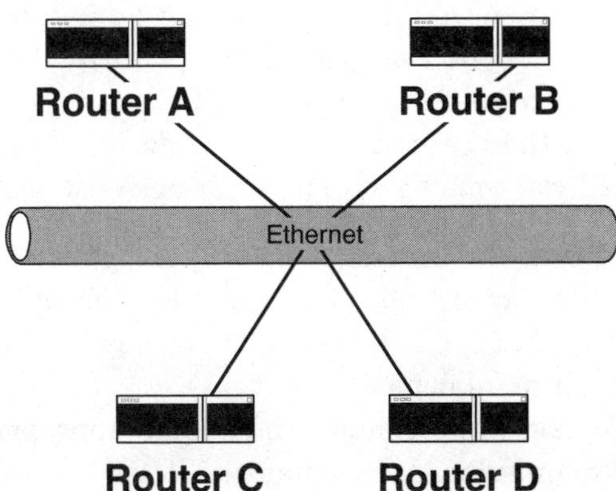

Figure 7-9 Multiple EIGRP neighbors on the same interface.

Convergence When a router running EIGRP detects a lost route, it will check its own topology database for a feasible successor to that route. If the topology database does not have a successor, then the router will query each of its neighbors for such a successor. During this process, in which the router is trying to find another route to succeed the one that was lost, the router is said to be in an *active state* for that route. If the router receives a reply from one of its neighbors with a feasible successor, then it will recompute its topology database in accordance with the DUAL algorithm and place the route in its routing table and then update each of its neighbors with the new route. Convergence will then have taken place, and the route will appear in the routing table as being in a *passive state*.

Sometimes the router will not receive a reply from any of its neighbors, and the request will timeout. The route is then said to be *stuck-in-active* (SIA), and an appropriate EIGRP error message will be generated. This can happen for one of the following reasons:

- If a router is querying neighbors over serial links that are heavily congested with other traffic. Thus EIGRP query request and query reply packets may be getting dropped.
- If the autonomous system is so large that routers keep on querying their respective neighbors, and the convergence timer expires. Queries can be bounded to a particular range of networks using distribute lists. In this situation, the solution is to either "boundary" the queries with access lists or, alternatively, to run more than one autonomous system. Bear in mind that running a second autonomous system is effectively running another routing protocol and therefore should be viewed as an extreme measure. Using distribute lists to bound the queries is a more realistic solution; however, it should only be necessary on networks that are extremely large or contain design flaws or both. I would not view this as a routine troubleshooting option, and so I will not develop the point further. If you suspect that this may be required on your EIGRP network, I would recommend that you further research the Cisco documentation and not do anything until you consult with a senior network engineer.

The first issue arises more frequently in practice. The best approach is to avoid regular occurrence of the problem through good design, as well as by ensuring that serial links are not so heavily loaded that these timeouts occur on a regular basis.

If the problem is persistent, then some appropriate EIGRP parameters can be manipulated. By default, EIGRP occupies a maximum of 50 percent of the bandwidth on a link. This can be altered from its default value using the following command:

```
interface serial 0
bandwidth 56
ip bandwidth-percent eigrp 1 75
```

With this configuration, EIGRP 1 could use up to $0.75 \times 56 = 42$ kbps for its traffic.

Keep in mind that this only sets the maximum amount of bandwidth that EIGRP can use, and in the stable passive state, EIGRP generally will occupy only a small amount of link bandwidth.

The *Bandwidth* parameter that EIGRP uses to calculate how much actual bandwidth it may use for EIGRP traffic is the bandwidth that is displayed using the `show interface` command. This, of course, can be altered from its default and often may be altered to a value above or below the actual physical bandwidth to influence routing decisions or satisfy policy requirements.

The EIGRP *Active timeout* also can be increased from its default value of 3 minutes using the `timers active-time` router configuration command, thus reducing the likelihood of getting router `stuck-in-active` messages.

A very important point to note from the preceding discussion is that these measures are really only addressing the symptom of a problem rather than the cause. In a well-designed environment, these EIGRP parameters should not have to be changed from their default values.

Of course, you also should note that the default values of EIGRP parameters should not be changed unless there is a clear understanding that by doing so a problem will be fixed without other side effects.

NOTE: *If it is not broken, don't fix it! Do not change EIGRP parameter defaults without understanding exactly what you are doing and why you are doing it!*

Addressing and VLSM EIGRP supports variable length subnet masking (VLSM), which allows for a more efficient use of IP address space in the WAN and on small LAN segments. If a company's network is migrating from a non-VLSM protocol such as IGRP to EIGRP, and if major networks in the EIGRP domain are employing VLSM, clearly there are issues that need resolution. IGRP can only accept subnets of a single mask length. Hence subnets using VLSM that are redistributed from EIGRP to IGRP will not be visible in the IGRP process.

If this situation arises, one solution is to use static routes for the VLSM subnets, which summarize all the subnets as being of the same mask length. These static routes can then be redistributed into IGRP. Alternatively, EIGRP's manual summarization feature (which I will be discussing very soon) can be used to summarize all the subnets using VLSM as having the same mask.

Route Summarization

AUTOMATIC SUMMARIZATION Both IGRP and EIGRP automatically summarize based on class on crossing a network bit boundary. For example, if network 172.16.0.0 is running in IGRP or EIGRP on a given router with a 24-bit subnet mask, and if this router broadcasts this network to an adjacent neighbor that does not have any of its interfaces in the 172.16.0.0 major network, then the adjacent router will receive a summary route of 172.16.0.0/16 for this network.

In EIGRP, this automatic summarization feature can be disabled using the `no auto-summary` command. This may be required in cases where there is a discontiguous network, which will be discussed later.

MANUAL SUMMARIZATION Another enhancement that EIGRP has with respect to route summarization is that it supports manual configuration of the route summarization. This can be done using the `ip summary-address eigrp <autonomous system> ip address mask` interface command. For example:

```
int se0
ip address 171.100.10.1 255.255.255.0
ip summary-address eigrp 1 130.0.0.0 254.0.0.0
```

This would cause a single routing update of 130.0.0.0/7 for any network whose first octet is 130 or 131.

Manual summarization may be configured in the following instances:

1. To support supernetting.
2. To enable the summarization of external routes within EIGRP. By *external*, I mean routes that were redistributed into EIGRP from another routing protocol. EIGRP does not summarize these routes even when crossing the network bit boundary into a new major network. This may cause problems because EIGRP will always

choose the longest prefix match regardless of metric or administrative distance when making routing decisions.

3. To allow VLSM networks to be redistributed into non-VLSM protocols.

Discontiguous Networks If the addressing shown in Figure 7-10 is used with either IGRP or EIGRP, a discontiguous network will be formed. This is so because both these routing protocols automatically summarize based on class when a network bit boundary is crossed. This means that in the example shown, router A would receive a summary route (172.16.0.0/16) from both router B and router C. Hence it will not have a specific route to either 172.16.18.0 or 172.16.27.0. These networks will become inaccessible from router A because it will have two conflicting summary routes to 172.16.0.0.

With EIGRP, there are a number of ways to solve this problem: Manual summarization for 172.16.18.0/24 could be configured on router B's serial link, and likewise for router C and 172.16.27.0/24. However, a simpler solution would be to switch off automatic summarization for the EIGRP process on router B and router C. If these routers connect to stub networks, switching off automatic summarization will not increase the routing table sizes because, due to split horizon, they will only advertise

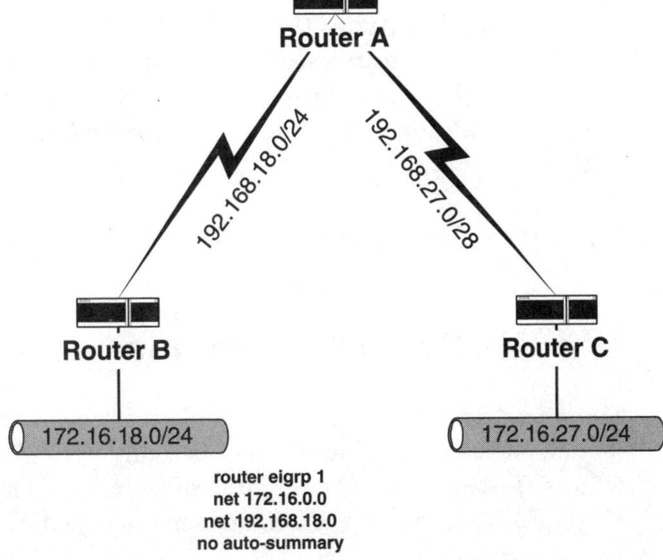

Figure 7-10 EIGRP's solution for discontiguous networks.

locally attached networks. For nonstub networks, distribute lists could be used to curtail any unnecessary advertised routes.

Automatic summarization is turned off as follows:

```
router eigrp 1
no auto-summary
```

If IGRP were the routing protocol, then there is only one way to solve the problem, since manual summarization cannot be configured and automatic summarization cannot be turned off. The formation of a discontiguous network can only be avoided by having 24-bit subnets of 172.16.0.0 on the serial links that attach router A to routers B and C.

Common EIGRP Error Messages

- Neighbor changes can be logged if it is suspected that the EIGRP network is not totally stable. This is done using the `eigrp log-neighbor` router configuration command. It is usually a good idea to use this command when the network is initially being rolled out. After the network has been seen to be stable, the logging of neighbor changes should only be required in specific problem conditions. Error messages that result from EIGRP neighbor changes take the following format:

```
%DUAL-5-NBRCHANGE: [chars] [dec]: Neighbor [chars] ([chars]) is
[chars]: [chars]
```

- *Routes Stuck-in-Active (SIA).* EIGRP stuck-in-active error messages will be written to the log if *Logging buffered* is on. Frequent occurrences of these messages are indicative of convergence problems in the EIGRP network. Stuck-in-active messages take the following format:

```
%DUAL-3-SIA: Route [chars] stuck-in-active state in [chars] [dec]
```

IP EIGRP Show Commands

The `show ip protocol` command gives the familiar summary information on the protocol and how it is configured. Most of the output that follows (Listing 7-53) should be familiar to you after the discussion on IGRP. However, as ever, there are some particular points to be made in relation to EIGRP:

```
R2>sh ip protocol
Routing Protocol is "eigrp 1"
  Outgoing update filter list for all interfaces is not set
  Incoming update filter list for all interfaces is not set
  Default networks flagged in outgoing updates
  Default networks accepted from incoming updates
  EIGRP metric weight K1=1, K2=0, K3=1, K4=0, K5=0
  EIGRP maximum hopcount 100
  EIGRP maximum metric variance 1
  Redistributing: static, eigrp 1, rip
  Automatic network summarization is in effect
  Automatic address summarization:
    132.20.0.0/16 for TokenRing0/1, TokenRing3/1, TokenRing4/2
      Loopback0
      Summarizing with metric 176128
    171.14.0.0/16 for TokenRing0/1, TokenRing3/1, TokenRing4/2
      Loopback0
      Summarizing with metric 176128
  Routing for Networks:
    165.14.0.0
    132.20.0.0
    171.14.0.0
  Passive Interface(s):
    TokenRing0/0
 Routing Information Sources:
    Gateway         Distance      Last Update
    165.14.65.194         90      00:05:51
    165.14.3.170          90      20w4d
 Distance: internal 90 external 170
```

Listing 7-53

- The 132.20.0.0 and 171.14.0.0 class B networks are being summarized based on class. This is so because these routes are being advertised into different major networks.
- The administrative distance for internal EIGRP routes is seen to be 90. The distance for external routes that are redistributed into EIGRP is 170. This is the default value for each of these parameters.
- Note the two sources from which R2 gets EIGRP updates. 165.14.65.194 last sent an update just under 6 minutes ago, while it has been over 20 weeks since an update was received from 165.14.3.170. This illustrates the incremental nature of EIGRP updates once the initial topology table has been built.
- EIGRP is also routing for the 132.20.0.0 and 171.14.0.0 major networks, yet R2 sees no EIGRP routing information sources on these networks. This implies that these are stub networks in relation to EIGRP at least.

```
r2#sh ip rou 172.16.131.0
Routing entry for 172.16.131.0 255.255.255.240
  Known via "eigrp 1", distance 90, metric 2185984, type internal
  Redistributing via eigrp 1
  Last update from 172.16.33.1 on Serial1.1, 00:10:18 ago
  Routing Descriptor Blocks:
  * 172.16.33.1, from 172.16.33.1, 00:10:18 ago, via Serial1.1
      Route metric is 2185984, traffic share count is 1
      Total delay is 20630 microseconds, minimum bandwidth is 1544 Kbit
      Reliability 255/255, minimum MTU 1500 bytes
      Loading 1/255, Hops 1

r2#
```

Listing 7-54

By executing a `show ip route` for a specific route, it can be seen how EIGRP displays the mask information (see Listing 7-54).

The `show ip eigrp neighbor` command is a useful means to obtain information on the status of the EIGRP neighbor relationships. I will explain the most pertinent parameters:

- *H* relates to the time since the last hello packet was received. The default hello interval is 5 seconds for broadcast media, point-to-point serial links, or high-bandwidth (greater than T1) multipoint WAN links. The hello interval is 60 seconds by default on multipoint WAN links that are of T1 speed or below. What type of serial link is shown in the example below?
- The *Hold time* is the length of time that a neighbor is declared up without receiving a hello packet from it. Typically, this is three times the hello interval. When a hello is received, the hold timer is reset to zero. The value in the hold column should never go above the hold time. With EIGRP, the hello and hold times are configurable. Another important point to note is that EIGRP can form neighbors across an interface where the hello and hold times do not match on each end of the link. We will see later that this is not true of OSPF.
- The neighbor *Uptime* will tell you how often the neighbor relationship is being lost. If this parameter were frequently getting reset, this would indicate that R1 is experiencing a stability problem that at the very least relates to its directly connected networks. Further troubleshooting would have to be done in such an instance. In the example below (Listing 7-55), the last three neighbors are all stable. The

```
R1>sh ip eigrp nei
IP-EIGRP neighbors for process 211
H   Address                   Interface    Hold Uptime     SRTT    RTO  Q   Seq
                                           (sec)           (ms)        Cnt  Num
13  171.14.205.130           Se3/2          14 02:02:30    76    456   0   525343
3   171.14.248.22            Se2/6          14 1d16h       32    200   1   3147277
10  171.14.252.34            Se2/0          14 2d07h       61   2604   0   831811
8   171.13.253.2             Se3/6          14 3d01h       32   2604   0   155200
R1>
```

Listing 7-55

171.14.205.130 neighbor has been up for just over 2 hours. This may or may not be a problem. If logging is turned on, then it could be checked whether or not this coincided with a link failure on either router.

- *SRTT* and *RTO* are round-trip timers and request timeout values that are automatically negotiated across the link. They can vary depending on the speed of the link and its utilization.
- The *Q* count parameter can be useful for troubleshooting. It displays a nonzero value if a query has been sent to a neighbor and a corresponding reply has yet to be received. In the sample output (Listing 7-55), we can see that R1 is awaiting a reply to a query sent to 171.14.248.22. If this value is incrementing or not decreasing over time, then it could indicate a routing loop, flapping route, convergence problem, or other type of network instability.

The contents of the topology table can be examined using the `show ip eigrp topology` command. In a stable network, all routes should appear in a passive state. The *Feasible distance* (FD) is actually the metric required for a successor route to be deemed "feasible." This is not to be confused with the *Administrative distance* parameter that is used to distinguish between different IP routing protocols. Notice in the following output (Listing 7-56) that the metric for each successor route is less than the feasible distance. For this example I also have printed the contents of the routing table for the same router so that you can relate the two tables.

The `show ip eigrp traffic` command provides global summary information for the EIGRP process on the router. It gives information on input queue drops; apart from this, I have found it to be of limited use in practice. (See Listing 7-57.)

```
r1#sh ip ro
Codes: C - connected, S - static, I - IGRP, R - RIP, M - mobile, B - BGP
       D - EIGRP, EX - EIGRP external, O - OSPF, IA - OSPF inter area
       E1 - OSPF external type 1, E2 - OSPF external type 2, E - EGP
       i - IS-IS, L1 - IS-IS level-1, L2 - IS-IS level-2, * - candidate default

Gateway of last resort is not set

     150.10.0.0 is variably subnetted, 3 subnets, 2 masks
D       150.10.22.0 255.255.255.0
           [90/2185984] via 172.16.33.2, 00:01:01, Serial1
D       150.10.0.0 255.255.0.0 [90/2707456] via 172.16.33.6, 00:01:02, Serial1
D       150.10.66.0 255.255.255.0
           [90/2297856] via 172.16.33.6, 00:01:02, Serial1
     172.16.0.0 is variably subnetted, 5 subnets, 2 masks
D       172.16.254.2 255.255.255.255
           [90/2297856] via 172.16.33.2, 00:01:02, Serial1
D       172.16.254.3 255.255.255.255
           [90/2809856] via 172.16.33.6, 00:01:02, Serial1
C       172.16.254.1 255.255.255.255 is directly connected, Loopback0
C       172.16.33.0 255.255.255.224 is directly connected, Serial1
D       172.16.1.0 255.255.255.224
           [90/2681856] via 172.16.33.6, 00:01:02, Serial1

r1#sh ip eig topology
IP-EIGRP Topology Table for process 1

Codes: P - Passive, A - Active, U - Update, Q - Query, R - Reply,
       r - Reply status

P 172.16.254.2 255.255.255.255, 1 successors, FD is 2297856
         via 172.16.33.2 (2297856/128256), Serial1
P 172.16.254.3 255.255.255.255, 1 successors, FD is 2809856
         via 172.16.33.6 (2809856/2297856), Serial1
P 172.16.254.1 255.255.255.255, 1 successors, FD is 128256
         via Connected, Loopback0
P 150.10.22.0 255.255.255.0, 1 successors, FD is 2185984
         via 172.16.33.2 (2185984/176128), Serial1
P 150.10.0.0 255.255.0.0, 1 successors, FD is 2707456
         via 172.16.33.6 (2707456/2195456), Serial1
P 172.16.33.0 255.255.255.224, 1 successors, FD is 2169856
         via Connected, Serial1
P 172.16.1.0 255.255.255.224, 1 successors, FD is 2681856
         via 172.16.33.6 (2681856/2169856), Serial1
P 150.10.66.0 255.255.255.0, 1 successors, FD is 2297856
         via 172.16.33.6 (2297856/128256), Serial1
r1#
```

Listing 7-56

```
R1>sh ip eigrp traffic
IP-EIGRP Traffic Statistics for process 1
  Hellos sent/received: 32330289/47943555
  Updates sent/received: 4681262/6760176
  Queries sent/received: 2413083/775395
  Replies sent/received: 694540/2777216
  Acks sent/received: 9408734/9752496
  Input queue high water mark 113, 0 drops
```

Listing 7-57

To check which interfaces are participating in EIGRP, use `show ip eigrp interface`. Peers can be taken to mean neighbors in this output. Unlike OSPF, the EIGRP process cannot be applied to some interfaces and not to others that are all part of the same major network. That is to say, a mask cannot be applied to the network command when EIGRP is being enabled. The entire major network must participate in the process.

```
router eigrp 1
network 172.16.0.0
```

A mask cannot be applied here to limit the scope of EIGRP on 172.16.0.0.

However, we will see that the `passive-interface` command achieves something similar. For a protocol that relies on the formation of neighbors such as EIGRP, the `passive-interface` command will completely kill the process on the interface because neighbors cannot be formed without the sending of hello packets. We will meet this concept again in a later section in this chapter. In the following example (Listing 7-58), if serial 2/4 had been made passive for EIGRP, then it would not appear in the displayed output.

Debugging IP EIGRP

The `debug eigrp packet` command can provide useful troubleshooting output, but like many debug commands, it must be used with caution. In the following output (Listing 7-59), we just see hello packets being sent and received on each interface that is partaking in EIGRP (the autonomous system is 211 in this example). This is the normal, stable situation for EIGRP.

```
R1>sh ip eigrp int s2/4
IP-EIGRP interfaces for process 1

                        Xmit Queue   Mean   Pacing Time   Multicast    Pending
Interface       Peers  Un/Reliable  SRTT   Un/Reliable   Flow Timer   Routes
Se2/4             1        0/0        24       0/15          115 .         0
R1>
```

Listing 7-58

If we wanted to simulate a route being lost, we could use the `clear ip route` command. In this example (Listing 7-60), we will take router R1, whose topology table is shown in Listing 7-61. In order to force a query, we are going to clear route 172.16.1.0 and watch what happens.

All that is to be observed is the hello messages that we saw in the last debug output. There appears to have been no effect as a result of clearing the 172.16.1.0 route. If you check the topology table, you will see that this actually makes sense. R1 has a feasible successor for 172.16.1.0; hence it does not need to send any queries to its neighbors.

```
Router1#debug  eigrp packet
EIGRP Packets debugging is on
    (UPDATE, REQUEST, QUERY, REPLY, HELLO, IPXSAP, PROBE, ACK)
Router1#
*Jun  1 22:14:49 PDT: EIGRP: Received HELLO on Serial0 nbr AB880A80.00e0.f786.6100
*Jun  1 22:14:49 PDT:   AS 211, Flags 0x0, Seq 0/0 idbQ 0/0 iidbQ un/rely 0/0 peerQ
  un/rely 0/0
*Jun  1 22:14:49 PDT: EIGRP: Sending HELLO on Ethernet0
*Jun  1 22:14:49 PDT:   AS 211, Flags 0x0, Seq 0/0 idbQ 0/0 iidbQ un/rely 0/0
*Jun  1 22:14:49 PDT: EIGRP: Sending HELLO on Serial0
*Jun  1 22:14:49 PDT:   AS 211, Flags 0x0, Seq 0/0 idbQ 0/0 iidbQ un/rely 0/0
*Jun  1 22:14:51 PDT: EIGRP: Sending HELLO on Loopback0
*Jun  1 22:14:51 PDT:   AS 211, Flags 0x0, Seq 0/0 idbQ 0/0 iidbQ un/rely 0/0
*Jun  1 22:14:51 PDT: EIGRP: Received HELLO on Loopback0 nbr 171.136.254.10
*Jun  1 22:14:51 PDT:   AS 211, Flags 0x0, Seq 0/0 idbQ 0/0
*Jun  1 22:14:51 PDT: EIGRP: Packet from ourselves ignored
*Jun  1 22:14:52 PDT: EIGRP: Sending HELLO on Serial0
*Jun  1 22:14:52 PDT:   AS 211, Flags 0x0, Seq 0/0 idbQ 0/0 iidbQ un/rely 0/0
```

Listing 7-59

```
r1#cle ip route 172.16.1.0
r1#sh log
Syslog logging: enabled (0 messages dropped, 0 flushes, 0 overruns)
    Console logging: level debugging, 2024 messages logged
    Monitor logging: level debugging, 0 messages logged
    Trap logging: level informational, 27 message lines logged

Apr  7 23:37:32: %SYS-5-CONFIG_I: Configured from console by console
Apr  7 23:37:49: EIGRP: Received HELLO on Serial1 nbr 172.16.33.6
Apr  7 23:37:49:   AS 1, Flags 0x0, Seq 0/0 idbQ 0/0 iidbQ un/rely 0/0 peerQ un/rely 0/0
Apr  7 23:37:50: EIGRP: Received HELLO on Serial1 nbr 172.16.33.2
Apr  7 23:37:50:   AS 1, Flags 0x0, Seq 0/0 idbQ 0/0 iidbQ un/rely 0/0 peerQ un/rely 0/0
Apr  7 23:37:54: EIGRP: Received HELLO on Serial1 nbr 172.16.33.6
Apr  7 23:37:54:   AS 1, Flags 0x0, Seq 0/0 idbQ 0/0 iidbQ un/rely 0/0 peerQ un/rely 0/0
Apr  7 23:37:55: EIGRP: Received HELLO on Serial1 nbr 172.16.33.2
Apr  7 23:37:55:   AS 1, Flags 0x0, Seq 0/0 idbQ 0/0 iidbQ un/rely 0/0 peerQ un/rely 0/0
r1#
```

Listing 7-60

```
r1#sh ip eig topol
IP-EIGRP Topology Table for process 1

Codes: P - Passive, A - Active, U - Update, Q - Query, R - Reply,
       r - Reply status

P 172.16.254.2 255.255.255.255, 1 successors, FD is 2297856
         via 172.16.33.2 (2297856/128256), Serial1
P 172.16.254.3 255.255.255.255, 1 successors, FD is 2809856
         via 172.16.33.6 (2809856/2297856), Serial1
P 172.16.254.1 255.255.255.255, 1 successors, FD is 128256
         via Connected, Loopback0
P 150.10.22.0 255.255.255.0, 1 successors, FD is 2185984
         via 172.16.33.2 (2185984/176128), Serial1
P 150.10.0.0 255.255.0.0, 1 successors, FD is 2707456
         via 172.16.33.6 (2707456/2195456), Serial1
P 172.16.33.0 255.255.255.224, 1 successors, FD is 2169856
         via Connected, Serial1
P 172.16.1.0 255.255.255.224, 1 successors, FD is 2681856
         via 172.16.33.6 (2681856/2169856), Serial1
P 150.10.66.0 255.255.255.0, 1 successors, FD is 2297856
         via 172.16.33.6 (2297856/128256), Serial1
r1#
```

Listing 7-61

NOTE: *EIGRP does not send a query to its neighbors if it has a feasible successor for the route in its topology table.*

Troubleshooting Scenarios for EIGRP

Now it is time to demonstrate the use of the EIGRP troubleshooting tools in some practical examples. Figure 7-11 shows a hub and spoke type of

Figure 7-11
A VLSM network running EIGRP.

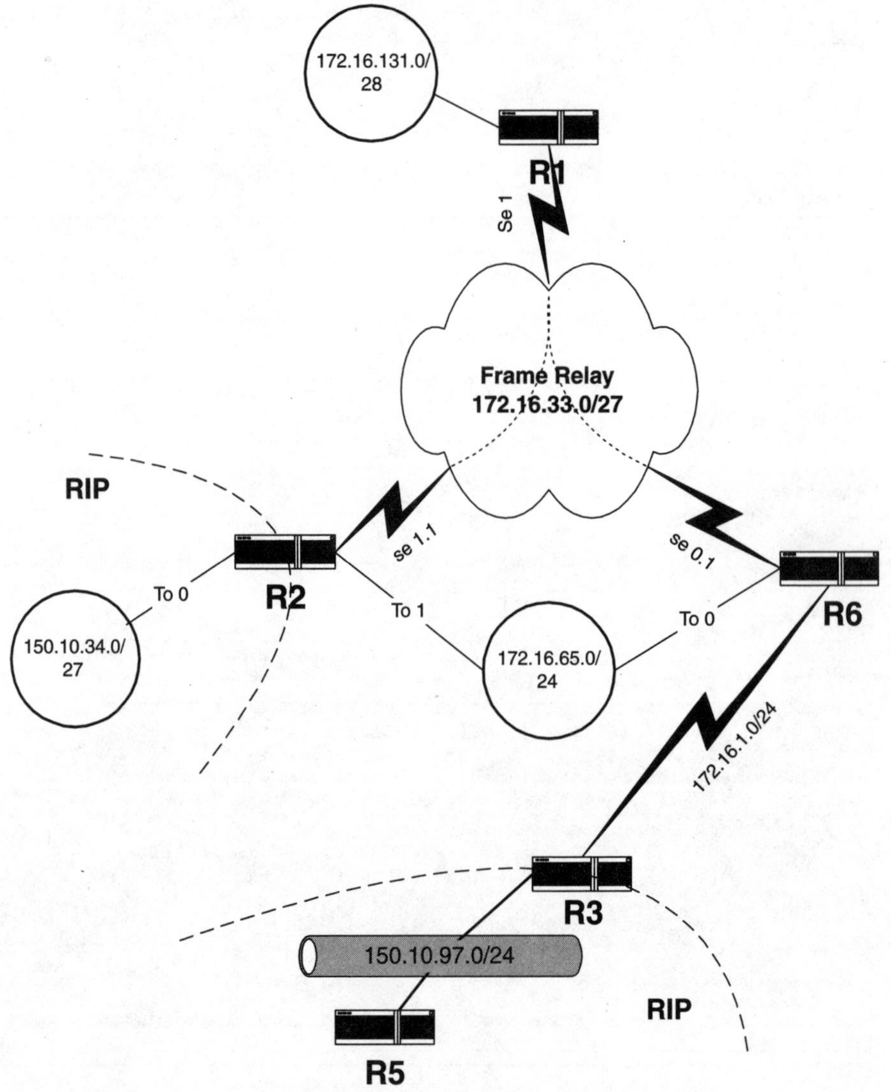

network running EIGRP 1 between routers R1, R2, and R6. R2 and R6 are also connected via token ring. Each router has a loopback address in the form 172.16.254.x for router Rx. EIGRP is being run for the 172.16.0.0 network on all routers. R2, R3, and R5 also have a 150.10.0.0 subnet running RIP. We will ignore this part of the network for the moment. If we examine R2's routing table, we see that it correctly learns all of R1's and R6's routes. It also has formed EIGRP neighbors with R1 over its serial 1.1 interface and with R6 over its token ring 1 interface. The fact that the routing table shows four different masks for 172.16.0.0 illustrates how EIGRP supports VLSM (see Listing 7-62).

Now, suppose that R2's token ring 1 must be made passive for EIGRP for security reasons. The basic effect is that it will not send EIGRP updates out that interface. This should not cause a problem, since R6 will learn all the routes from R1 in any case, right? (See Listing 7-63.)

It looks like something happened that we had not bargained for! All the routes previously learned from R6 (namely, 172.16.254.6/32 and

```
r2#sh ip ro
Codes: C - connected, S - static, I - IGRP, R - RIP, M - mobile, B - BGP
       D - EIGRP, EX - EIGRP external, O - OSPF, IA - OSPF inter area
       E1 - OSPF external type 1, E2 - OSPF external type 2, E - EGP
       i - IS-IS, L1 - IS-IS level-1, L2 - IS-IS level-2, * - candidate default

Gateway of last resort is not set

     172.16.0.0 is variably subnetted, 7 subnets, 4 masks
D       172.16.131.0 255.255.255.240
           [90/2185984] via 172.16.33.1, 00:00:02, Serial1.1
C       172.16.254.2 255.255.255.255 is directly connected, Loopback0
D       172.16.254.1 255.255.255.255
           [90/2297856] via 172.16.33.1, 00:00:02, Serial1.1
D       172.16.254.6 255.255.255.255
           [90/304128] via 172.16.65.6, 00:00:11, TokenRing1
C       172.16.33.0 255.255.255.224 is directly connected, Serial1.1
D       172.16.1.0 255.255.255.0
           [90/2185984] via 172.16.65.6, 00:00:11, TokenRing1
C       172.16.65.0 255.255.255.0 is directly connected, TokenRing1

r2#sh ip eigrp neig
IP-EIGRP neighbors for process 1
H   Address                 Interface   Hold Uptime   SRTT   RTO  Q  Seq
                                        (sec)         (ms)       Cnt Num
1   172.16.33.1             Se1.1        150 0:00:31  1213  5000  0  5
0   172.16.65.6             To1           12 0:01:07   145   870  0  4
r2#
```

Listing 7-62

```
r2(config)#router eigrp 1
r2(config-router)#passive-int tok 1
r2(config-router)#^Z
r2#sh ip ro
Codes: C - connected, S - static, I - IGRP, R - RIP, M - mobile, B - BGP
       D - EIGRP, EX - EIGRP external, O - OSPF, IA - OSPF inter area
       E1 - OSPF external type 1, E2 - OSPF external type 2, E - EGP
       i - IS-IS, L1 - IS-IS level-1, L2 - IS-IS level-2, * - candidate default

Gateway of last resort is not set

     172.16.0.0 is variably subnetted, 5 subnets, 4 masks
D       172.16.131.0 255.255.255.240
           [90/2185984] via 172.16.33.1, 00:11:41, Serial1.1
C       172.16.254.2 255.255.255.255 is directly connected, Loopback0
D       172.16.254.1 255.255.255.255
           [90/2297856] via 172.16.33.1, 00:11:41, Serial1.1
C       172.16.33.0 255.255.255.224 is directly connected, Serial1.1
C       172.16.65.0 255.255.255.0 is directly connected, TokenRing1
r2#sh ip eig nei
IP-EIGRP neighbors for process 1
H   Address                 Interface   Hold Uptime   SRTT   RTO  Q  Seq
                                        (sec)         (ms)       Cnt Num
1   172.16.33.1             Se1.1        172 0:11:58   827  4962  0  6
r2#
```

Listing 7-63

172.16.1.0/24) have disappeared from R2's routing table. It also can be seen that R2 lost its neighbor relationship with R6 over the token ring. This is so because the `passive-interface` command does not just block outgoing updates, it also blocks EIGRP hellos. If hellos cannot be sent, a neighbor relationship cannot be formed. Therefore, the `passive-interface` command effectively kills the EIGRP process on the interface to which it is applied. As we will also see in the case of OSPF, this is true of any routing protocol that relies on the formation of neighbors.

CAUTION: The `passive-interface` command completely kills the EIGRP process on the interface to which it is applied.

Now that we understand why the neighbor relationship is broken with R6, the next question is why does R2 not learn about R6's routes from R1? R2 is still a neighbor of R1 after all, and as we see from R1's routing table, it does contain all of R6's routes (see Listing 7-64).

```
r1#sh ip ro
Codes: C - connected, S - static, I - IGRP, R - RIP, M - mobile, B - BGP
       D - EIGRP, EX - EIGRP external, O - OSPF, IA - OSPF inter area
       E1 - OSPF external type 1, E2 - OSPF external type 2, E - EGP
       i - IS-IS, L1 - IS-IS level-1, L2 - IS-IS level-2, * - candidate default

Gateway of last resort is not set

     172.16.0.0 is variably subnetted, 7 subnets, 4 masks
C       172.16.131.0 255.255.255.240 is directly connected, TokenRing0
D       172.16.254.2 255.255.255.255
           [90/2297856] via 172.16.33.2, 00:04:14, Serial1
C       172.16.254.1 255.255.255.255 is directly connected, Loopback0
D       172.16.254.6 255.255.255.255
           [90/2297856] via 172.16.33.6, 00:04:25, Serial1
C       172.16.33.0 255.255.255.224 is directly connected, Serial1
D       172.16.1.0 255.255.255.0
           [90/2681856] via 172.16.33.6, 00:04:25, Serial1
D       172.16.65.0 255.255.255.0
           [90/2185984] via 172.16.33.6, 00:15:59, Serial1
           [90/2185984] via 172.16.33.2, 00:15:59, Serial1
```

Listing 7-64

We also can verify that R1 sees R2 and R6 as neighbors (see Listing 7-65).

Thus R1 is simply not forwarding R6's routes to R2, even though it sees both routers as EIGRP neighbors. A point to notice from the neighbor table is that both neighbors are formed over serial 1; in other words, subinterfaces are not being used. This should remind us immediately of split horizon, which means that R1 will not readvertise any routes that it learns over serial 1 back out that same interface. Hence R2 will not see R6's local routes, and likewise, R6 will not see R2's local routes.

EIGRP's use of the split-horizon principle is more complex than RIP or IGRP. For those protocols, we saw that split horizon is off by default on frame-relay interfaces. This is not true of EIGRP.

```
r1#sh ip eig nei
IP-EIGRP neighbors for process 1
H   Address                 Interface   Hold Uptime   SRTT   RTO  Q  Seq
                                        (sec)         (ms)       Cnt Num
1   172.16.33.2             Se1           14 0:16:50    52   312  0  7
0   172.16.33.6             Se1           13 0:17:06   547  3282  0  7
r1#
```

Listing 7-65

Listing 7-66

```
R1#

interface Serial1
 ip address 172.16.33.1 255.255.255.224
 encapsulation frame-relay
 no ip split-horizon eigrp 1
 frame-relay lmi-type ansi
 frame-relay map ip 172.16.33.2 102 broadcast
 frame-relay map ip 172.16.33.6 106 broadcast

R1#
```

NOTE: *EIGRP does not disable split horizon by default on frame-relay-encapsulated interfaces. It may have to be turned off manually.*

An important feature of EIGRP is that split horizon can be turned off on any given interface. The configuration in Listing 7-66 shows how it could be done on R1.

If R2's routing table is now checked, it can be seen that R6's local routes have been restored (see Listing 7-67). If R6's routing table were checked, it would now also display R2's connected routes.

```
r2#sh ip ro
Codes: C - connected, S - static, I - IGRP, R - RIP, M - mobile, B - BGP
       D - EIGRP, EX - EIGRP external, O - OSPF, IA - OSPF inter area
       E1 - OSPF external type 1, E2 - OSPF external type 2, E - EGP
       i - IS-IS, L1 - IS-IS level-1, L2 - IS-IS level-2, * - candidate default

Gateway of last resort is not set

     172.16.0.0 is variably subnetted, 7 subnets, 4 masks
D       172.16.131.0 255.255.255.240
           [90/2185984] via 172.16.33.1, 00:00:30, Serial1.1
C       172.16.254.2 255.255.255.255 is directly connected, Loopback0
D       172.16.254.1 255.255.255.255
           [90/2297856] via 172.16.33.1, 00:00:30, Serial1.1
D       172.16.254.6 255.255.255.255
           [90/2809856] via 172.16.33.1, 00:00:30, Serial1.1
C       172.16.33.0 255.255.255.224 is directly connected, Serial1.1
D       172.16.1.0 255.255.255.0
           [90/3193856] via 172.16.33.1, 00:00:30, Serial1.1
C       172.16.65.0 255.255.255.0 is directly connected, TokenRing1
r2#
```

Listing 7-67

Another issue that can sometimes lead to routing problems or at best unpredictable results if it has not been foreseen is the fact that EIGRP does not summarize external routes by default. The term *external* means routes that have been redistributed into EIGRP from another protocol. These routes show up in the routing table with an administrative distance of 170 instead of the internal EIGRP distance of 90. Referring again to Figure 7-11, R2 has a local ring segment 150.10.34.0/27 that uses RIP, and this network is redistributed in to EIGRP. (See Listing 7-68.)

When we check R1's routing table (Listing 7-69), the 150.10.34.0 network has the same 27-bit mask that was configured on the R2 token ring 0 segment. It appears as an external route in EIGRP with a distance of 170. It has not been summarized based on class, even though it has crossed a network boundary; i.e., R2's serial link to R1 does not use addressing on the 150.10.0.0 class B network.

If the 150.10.34.0 route were an internal EIGRP route, it would appear in R1's routing table as a summarized 150.10.0.0/16 route in accordance with the rules of EIGRP automatic summarization. This may not necessarily pose a problem for routing, and the most important point is to understand the manner in which EIGRP deals with external routes.

EIGRP will always choose the route with the longest prefix match regardless of metric. For example, when routing to the 152.34.10.0 network, EIGRP would choose 152.34.10.0 above 152.34.0.0 even if the summary route had a significantly better metric. Therefore, it is vital

Listing 7-68

```
!
interface TokenRing0
 ip address 150.10.34.2 255.255.255.224
 ring-speed 16
!
interface TokenRing1
 ip address 172.16.65.2 255.255.255.0
 ring-speed 16
!
router eigrp 1
 redistribute rip
 passive-interface TokenRing1
 network 172.16.0.0
 default-metric 15000 10000 255 1 1500
!
router rip
 network 150.10.0.0
!

r2#
```

that the network engineer understands which prefix length is being advertised with each route in the network. In the next example I am going to create a scenario where this EIGRP feature creates a fundamental network access problem.

Routers R3 and R5 share the Ethernet segment 150.10.97.0/24, which has RIP as its routing protocol. Hosts on R5's token-ring segment (not shown in Figure 7-11) are required to access a server on the remote R2 token ring 0 segment—150.10.34.0/27. Thus it is necessary that R5 have a route to this network. We have already seen that this route appears in R1's routing table as an external EIGRP route.

Therefore, it also will be an external route in R3's table. R3 redistributes EIGRP into RIP, and distribute-list 9 ensures that all 150.10.0.0

```
r1#sh ip ro
Codes: C - connected, S - static, I - IGRP, R - RIP, M - mobile, B - BGP
       D - EIGRP, EX - EIGRP external, O - OSPF, IA - OSPF inter area
       E1 - OSPF external type 1, E2 - OSPF external type 2, E - EGP
       i - IS-IS, L1 - IS-IS level-1, L2 - IS-IS level-2, * - candidate default

Gateway of last resort is not set

     150.10.0.0 255.255.255.224 is subnetted, 1 subnets
D EX    150.10.34.0 [170/4729856] via 172.16.33.2, 00:03:34, Serial1
     172.16.0.0 is variably subnetted, 6 subnets, 3 masks
D       172.16.254.2 255.255.255.255
           [90/2297856] via 172.16.33.2, 00:25:31, Serial1
C       172.16.254.1 255.255.255.255 is directly connected, Loopback0
D       172.16.254.6 255.255.255.255
           [90/2297856] via 172.16.33.6, 00:25:33, Serial1
C       172.16.33.0 255.255.255.224 is directly connected, Serial1
D       172.16.1.0 255.255.255.0
           [90/2681856] via 172.16.33.6, 00:25:33, Serial1
D       172.16.65.0 255.255.255.0
           [90/2185984] via 172.16.33.2, 00:25:35, Serial1
           [90/2185984] via 172.16.33.6, 00:25:35, Serial1

r1#sh ip ro 150.10.34.0
Routing entry for 150.10.34.0 255.255.255.224
  Known via "eigrp 1", distance 170, metric 4729856, type external
  Redistributing via eigrp 1
  Last update from 172.16.33.2 on Serial1, 00:03:51 ago
  Routing Descriptor Blocks:
  * 172.16.33.2, from 172.16.33.2, 00:03:51 ago, via Serial1
      Route metric is 4729856, traffic share count is 1
      Total delay is 120000 microseconds, minimum bandwidth is 1544 Kbit
      Reliability 255/255, minimum MTU 1500 bytes
      Loading 1/255, Hops 1

r1#
```

Listing 7-69

routes will be advertised in RIP updates, which will go out interface Ethernet 2/0 only because RIP only runs on 150.10.0.0 interfaces (see Listing 7-70).

```
R3#

in ethernet2/0
ip add 150.10.97.3 255.255.255.0
!
in serial3/0
ip add 172.16.1.3 255.255.255.0
!
router eigrp 1
 network 172.16.0.0
!
router rip
 redistribute eigrp 1
 network 150.10.0.0
 default-metric 3
 distribute-list 9 out eigrp 1
!
no ip classless

access-list 9 permit 150.10.0.0 0.0.255.255

r3#

R5#

interface Ethernet0
 ip address 150.10.97.5 255.255.255.0
 media-type 10BaseT
!
interface Ethernet1
 no ip address
 shutdown
!
router rip
 network 150.10.0.0
!

r5#sh ip route
Codes: C - connected, S - static, I - IGRP, R - RIP, M - mobile, B - BGP
       D - EIGRP, EX - EIGRP external, O - OSPF, IA - OSPF inter area
       E1 - OSPF external type 1, E2 - OSPF external type 2, E - EGP
       i - IS-IS, L1 - IS-IS level-1, L2 - IS-IS level-2, * - candidate default

Gateway of last resort is not set

     150.10.0.0 255.255.255.0 is subnetted, 1 subnets
C       150.10.97.0 is directly connected, Ethernet0
r5#
```

Listing 7-70

However, the 150.10.34.0/27 network is not present in R5's routing table. This is so because it has a 27-bit mask in EIGRP that conflicts with the 24-bit mask for 150.10.97.0 that exists on the Ethernet segment shared by R3 and R5 (remember RIP does not support VLSM).

This is where we use another important EIGRP feature: manual summarization. The 150.10.34.0/27 network can be summarized manually on R6's serial link to R3. The network can be summarized as 24 bit; hence there is no conflict with the 150.10.97.0 network on R3 and R5. The relevant configuration is shown in Listing 7-71.

We can verify that the network appears as a 24-bit summary in R3's routing table. Note also that not only does it have a 24-bit mask, it has a distance of 90, as distinct from the distance value of 170 that the 150.10.34.0/27 route has in R1's routing table. There is an additional side effect to manual summarization in that it makes the route appear to have originated in the EIGRP process. It is no longer an external EIGRP route. (See Listing 7-72.)

Listing 7-71

```
r6#
!
interface Serial1
 ip address 172.16.1.6 255.255.255.0
 ip summary-address eigrp 1 150.10.34.0 255.255.255.0
!

r6#
```

```
r3>sh ip ro 150.10.34.0
Routing entry for 150.10.34.0/24
  Known via "eigrp 1", distance 90, metric 5753856, type internal
  Redistributing via eigrp 1, rip
  Advertised by rip
  Last update from 172.16.1.6 on Serial3/0, 00:01:51 ago
  Routing Descriptor Blocks:
  * 172.16.1.6, from 172.16.1.6, 00:01:51 ago, via Serial3/0
      Route metric is 5753856, traffic share count is 1
      Total delay is 160000 microseconds, minimum bandwidth is 1544 Kbit
      Reliability 255/255, minimum MTU 1500 bytes
      Loading 1/255, Hops 3

r3>
```

Listing 7-72

```
r5>sh ip ro
Codes: C - connected, S - static, I - IGRP, R - RIP, M - mobile, B - BGP
       D - EIGRP, EX - EIGRP external, O - OSPF, IA - OSPF inter area
       E1 - OSPF external type 1, E2 - OSPF external type 2, E - EGP
       i - IS-IS, L1 - IS-IS level-1, L2 - IS-IS level-2, * - candidate default

Gateway of last resort is not set

     150.10.0.0 255.255.255.0 is subnetted, 2 subnets
R       150.10.34.0 [120/3] via 150.10.97.3, 00:00:01, Ethernet0
C       150.10.97.0 is directly connected, Ethernet0
r5>
```

Listing 7-73

And finally, we can verify the happy news that R5 has a route to the 150.10.34.0 network. Of course, there is still some unfinished business with the current set of configurations. R2 needs a route to the 150.10.97.0 network in order for communication to take place. To achieve this, RIP must be redistributed into EIGRP on the R3 router. This would be a good exercise if you have access to laboratory facilities. (See Listing 7-73.)

Now let's revisit the question of discontiguous networks and demonstrate how they are supported with EIGRP. You may feel that I am laboring this issue in relation to each of the IP routing protocols that we have studied so far. What motivates me to give this level of emphasis to the topic is the number of network problems I have seen in practice centered around the issue of discontiguous networks not being understood properly. Sometimes the issue is not addressed at the design phase; other times I have seen new subnets being commissioned that created an unforeseen discontiguous network.

Figure 7-12 shows the network that we will use to explore the topic in EIGRP. A discontiguous network is created as both R2 and R6 automatically summarize the 150.10.0.0 network (see Listing 7-74). R1 thus receives two equal cost summary routes for this network which prevents it from being able to route to any specific subnets on this network because the summary routes came with different source addresses.

It can be seen from R2 and R6's routing tables (Listing 7-75) that they include the summary route only as a route to Null0, i.e., the bit bucket. The net result is that R2 has no route to the 150.10.66.0, and likewise, R6 does not see the 150.10.22.0 network.

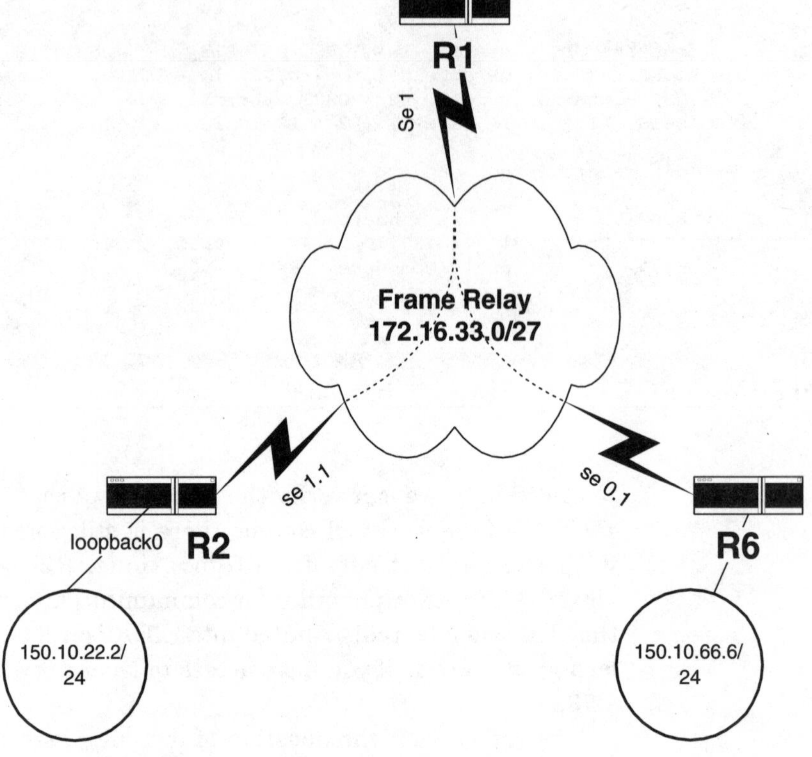

Figure 7-12 An EIGRP network using discontiguous subnets.

The simplest way to solve the discontiguous subnet problem with EIGRP is simply to turn off automatic summarization. This solution involves no readdressing on the network. Automatic summarization must be turned off on both R2 and R6. Listing 7-76 displays it in the case of R6.

After disabling automatic summarization on R2 and R6, we can now see that R1 receives specific route information about 172.16.22.0 and 172.16.66.0 (see Listing 7-77).

Of course, in order for these appropriate routes to be propagated back to R2 and R6, we need to turn off split horizon on R1 (see Listing 7-78).

After clearing the routing table on R2, we see the appearance of the 172.16.66.0 network. Similarly, R6 has a route to 172.16.22.0, and connectivity can be verified by pinging the remote loopback interface. (See Listing 7-79.)

```
r2>sh ip ro
Codes: C - connected, S - static, I - IGRP, R - RIP, M - mobile, B - BGP
       D - EIGRP, EX - EIGRP external, O - OSPF, IA - OSPF inter area
       E1 - OSPF external type 1, E2 - OSPF external type 2, E - EGP
       i - IS-IS, L1 - IS-IS level-1, L2 - IS-IS level-2, * - candidate default

Gateway of last resort is not set

     150.10.0.0 is variably subnetted, 2 subnets, 2 masks
C       150.10.22.0 255.255.255.0 is directly connected, TokenRing0
D       150.10.0.0 255.255.0.0 is a summary, 00:01:04, Null0
     172.16.0.0 is variably subnetted, 2 subnets, 2 masks
C       172.16.33.0 255.255.255.224 is directly connected, Serial1.1
D       172.16.0.0 255.255.0.0 is a summary, 00:01:04, Null0
r2>sh ip ro 150.10.0.0
Routing entry for 150.10.0.0 255.255.0.0, 2 known subnets
  Attached (1 connections)
  Variably subnetted with 2 masks
  Redistributing via eigrp 1

C       150.10.22.0 255.255.255.0 is directly connected, TokenRing0
D       150.10.0.0 255.255.0.0 is a summary, 00:01:28, Null0
r2>ping 150.10.66.6
Type escape sequence to abort.
Sending 5, 100-byte ICMP Echos to 150.10.66.6, timeout is 2 seconds:
.....
Success rate is 0 percent (0/5)
r2>
```

Listing 7-74

```
r6>sh ip ro
Codes: C - connected, S - static, I - IGRP, R - RIP, M - mobile, B - BGP
       D - EIGRP, EX - EIGRP external, O - OSPF, IA - OSPF inter area
       E1 - OSPF external type 1, E2 - OSPF external type 2, E - EGP
       i - IS-IS, L1 - IS-IS level-1, L2 - IS-IS level-2, * - candidate default

Gateway of last resort is not set

     150.10.0.0 is variably subnetted, 2 subnets, 2 masks
D       150.10.0.0 255.255.0.0 is a summary, 00:01:38, Null0
C       150.10.66.0 255.255.255.0 is directly connected, Loopback0
     172.16.0.0 is variably subnetted, 2 subnets, 2 masks
C       172.16.33.0 255.255.255.224 is directly connected, Serial0.1
D       172.16.0.0 255.255.0.0 is a summary, 00:01:38, Null0
r6>ping 150.10.22.2
Type escape sequence to abort.
Sending 5, 100-byte ICMP Echos to 150.10.22.2, timeout is 2 seconds:
.....
Success rate is 0 percent (0/5)
r6>

r1#sh ip ro
Codes: C - connected, S - static, I - IGRP, R - RIP, M - mobile, B - BGP
       D - EIGRP, EX - EIGRP external, O - OSPF, IA - OSPF inter area
       E1 - OSPF external type 1, E2 - OSPF external type 2, E - EGP
       i - IS-IS, L1 - IS-IS level-1, L2 - IS-IS level-2, * - candidate default

Gateway of last resort is not set

D    150.10.0.0 [90/2185984] via 172.16.33.2, 00:01:50, Serial1
     172.16.0.0 255.255.255.224 is subnetted, 1 subnets
C       172.16.33.0 is directly connected, Serial1
r1#
```

Listing 7-75

Listing 7-76

```
r6#conf t
Enter configuration commands, one per line.  End with CNTL/Z.
r6(config)#router eigrp 1
r6(config-router)#no auto-summary
r6(config-router)#^Z
r6#cle ip ro *
r6#
```

```
r1#sh ip ro
Codes: C - connected, S - static, I - IGRP, R - RIP, M - mobile, B - BGP
       D - EIGRP, EX - EIGRP external, O - OSPF, IA - OSPF inter area
       E1 - OSPF external type 1, E2 - OSPF external type 2, E - EGP
       i - IS-IS, L1 - IS-IS level-1, L2 - IS-IS level-2, * - candidate default

Gateway of last resort is not set

     150.10.0.0 255.255.255.0 is subnetted, 2 subnets
D       150.10.22.0 [90/2185984] via 172.16.33.2, 00:01:44, Serial1
D       150.10.66.0 [90/2297856] via 172.16.33.6, 00:02:01, Serial1
     172.16.0.0 255.255.255.224 is subnetted, 1 subnets
C       172.16.33.0 is directly connected, Serial1
r1#
```

Listing 7-77

```
r1(config)#in se 1
r1(config-if)#no ip split-horizon eigrp 1
r1(config-if)#^Z
r1#cle ip ro *
r1#

r2#sh ip ro
Codes: C - connected, S - static, I - IGRP, R - RIP, M - mobile, B - BGP
       D - EIGRP, EX - EIGRP external, O - OSPF, IA - OSPF inter area
       E1 - OSPF external type 1, E2 - OSPF external type 2, E - EGP
       i - IS-IS, L1 - IS-IS level-1, L2 - IS-IS level-2, * - candidate default

Gateway of last resort is not set

     150.10.0.0 255.255.255.0 is subnetted, 1 subnets
C       150.10.22.0 is directly connected, TokenRing0
     172.16.0.0 255.255.255.224 is subnetted, 1 subnets
C       172.16.33.0 is directly connected, Serial1.1
r2#cle ip ro *
r2#sh ip ro
Codes: C - connected, S - static, I - IGRP, R - RIP, M - mobile, B - BGP
       D - EIGRP, EX - EIGRP external, O - OSPF, IA - OSPF inter area
       E1 - OSPF external type 1, E2 - OSPF external type 2, E - EGP
       i - IS-IS, L1 - IS-IS level-1, L2 - IS-IS level-2, * - candidate default

Gateway of last resort is not set

     150.10.0.0 255.255.255.0 is subnetted, 2 subnets
C       150.10.22.0 is directly connected, TokenRing0
D       150.10.66.0 [90/2809856] via 172.16.33.1, 00:00:11, Serial1.1
     172.16.0.0 255.255.255.224 is subnetted, 1 subnets
C       172.16.33.0 is directly connected, Serial1.1
r2#
```

Listing 7-78

```
r6>sh ip ro
Codes: C - connected, S - static, I - IGRP, R - RIP, M - mobile, B - BGP
       D - EIGRP, EX - EIGRP external, O - OSPF, IA - OSPF inter area
       E1 - OSPF external type 1, E2 - OSPF external type 2, E - EGP
       i - IS-IS, L1 - IS-IS level-1, L2 - IS-IS level-2, * - candidate default

Gateway of last resort is not set

     150.10.0.0 255.255.255.0 is subnetted, 2 subnets
D       150.10.22.0 [90/2697984] via 172.16.33.1, 00:00:24, Serial0.1
C       150.10.66.0 is directly connected, Loopback0
     172.16.0.0 255.255.255.224 is subnetted, 1 subnets
C       172.16.33.0 is directly connected, Serial0.1
r6>ping 150.10.22.2
Type escape sequence to abort.
Sending 5, 100-byte ICMP Echos to 150.10.22.2, timeout is 2 seconds:
!!!!!
Success rate is 100 percent (5/5), round-trip min/avg/max = 136/148/192 ms
r6>
```

Listing 7-79

REVIEW QUESTIONS

Review Questions for Chapters 7 and 8 are grouped at the end of Chapter 8.

CHAPTER 8

IP II
Troubleshooting OSPF and BGP

Introduction

The objectives of this chapter are to

- Develop a better understanding of OSPF and its configuration on Cisco networks.
- Apply OSPF router diagnostic commands to spot issues and resolve problems.
- Understand the characteristics of internal and external BGP and how BGP attributes can be configured and manipulated.
- Apply Cisco troubleshooting tools to BGP networking scenarios.

Troubleshooting OSPF

Open Shortest Path First (OSPF) is a sophisticated link-state IP routing protocol. It is hierarchical in nature, employing the concept of multiple routing areas within the same routing process. Like EIGRP, it uses incremental updates to provide a more efficient means of exchanging routing information. It also supports features such as VLSM, configurable route summarization, and discontiguous networks.

OSPF is more complex in nature than any IP routing protocol that we have examined so far. For this reason, I will discuss the most pertinent OSPF principles and characteristics in a practical rather than a theoretical context. Because of its relative complexity and rich feature set, a significant proportion of OSPF network problems are due to configuration errors. For this reason, I will place more emphasis on the configuration of OSPF than I have done with some of the other protocols.

OSPF Characteristics

Neighbor and Adjacency Formation

NEIGHBOR FORMATION For a neighbor relationship to be formed between two OSPF routers, the routers must agree on the following parameters:

- *Area ID.* The segment that connects the two routers together must appear as being in the same area on each router.

- *Hello and dead intervals.* The *Dead interval* is the amount of time a router will wait without receiving a hello packet before declaring the neighbor to be down. It is usually four times the *Hello interval*. These two parameters must match on the respective router interfaces that connect to the common OSPF network segment. The parameters are configurable. The default hello and dead intervals on a broadcast or point-to-point segment are 10 and 40 seconds, respectively. On a non-broadcast network or a point-to-multipoint network, the corresponding default values are 30 and 120 seconds.
- *Authentication.* OSPF supports simple authentication along with MD5. The interface authentication parameters must match in order for neighbor formation to take place.
- *Stub area flag.* Both routers must agree whether or not the area through which they are attempting to form neighbors is a stub area. The area cannot be configured as stub on one router and not on the other.

ADJACENCY FORMATION After an OSPF neighbor relationship has been formed, the two routers may proceed to form a full adjacency. This entails exchanging link-state databases. OSPF routers on a particular segment may not necessarily all need to become adjacent with each other. On a broadcast network, for example, a designated router (DR) and backup designated router (BDR) are elected using the hello protocol. These act as centralized points for the exchange of routing information across the segment. Thus all routers do not need to exchange link-state databases with each other; they only do this with the DR and BDR.

On this type of broadcast network (e.g., an Ethernet segment), each router will only form an adjacency with the DR and BDR, while it will see all other OSPF routers as two-way neighbors.

The following is a sequential list of the different states that neighbor formation and eventually adjacency formation go through. Most of the states are quite self-explanatory.

- *Down.* No information has been detected on the segment.
- *Attempt.* The router has not received any hello but is attempting to send a hello packet.
- *Init.* A hello packet has been received; now bidirectional communication has to be established.
- *Two-way.* At this point, a two-way neighbor relationship has been formed.

- *Exstart.* This indicates that the routers have begun to negotiate the exchange of databases.
- *Exchange.* This is the initial stage of information exchange.
- *Loading.* This is the final stage, which enables database exchange.
- *Full.* This final state indicates that a full adjacency has been formed.

OSPF Network Types OSPF can be classified as having four basic network types:

- Broadcast
- Nonbroadcast
- Point to point
- Point to multipoint

OSPF will automatically detect a network type from the router configuration. All of these with the exception of a point-to-point network type are configurable. We will now look at each of these network types in more detail. They need to be understood in order to ensure that OSPF neighbors are formed in the correct manner across different local-area network (LAN) and wide-area network (WAN) media types.

BROADCAST NETWORKS This refers to broadcast media such as Ethernet or token-ring LANs. A designated router (DR) and backup designated router (BDR) are elected on OSPF broadcast networks. This provides a more efficient means for routers to exchange link-state advertisements on the network by providing centralized points to update the entire segment. Each ordinary (i.e., nondesignated) router sends its link-state advertisements (LSAs) to the designated router rather than to all other routers on the network. The DR is then responsible for ensuring that all routers on the broadcast segment have their topology database updated with the same information.

On a broadcast type of network, all routers will see each other as neighbors, but they will only be adjacent to the DR and BDR. If OSPF does not automatically see the network segment as being a broadcast medium, it can be configured to appear as a broadcast network for the purposes of OSPF. For example:

```
interface serial 1
encapsulation frame-relay
ip address 172.16.33.1 255.255.255.224
ip ospf network broadcast
```

In this case, all routers that have a multipoint frame-relay interface connecting to the 172.16.33.0/27 subnet also should have that interface configured to be an OSPF broadcast network.

To verify the OSPF network type on a given interface use the `show ip ospf interface` command (see Listing 8-1). Changing the OSPF network type on an interface may be desirable to facilitate neighbor formation, as we will see with the other network types.

If a point-to-multipoint network is configured as an OSPF broadcast network, there are some issues that need to be remembered:

- Configuring the medium to be a broadcast network for the purposes of OSPF does not make it a broadcast medium. If in the case of multipoint frame relay the appropriate PVCs are not in place between the routers, or if the necessary frame-relay mapping statements are not configured, then OSPF will not work as desired. This brings me to a more basic secondary point, and this is that altering the OSPF network types should be thought of as something that is done solely for the purposes of OSPF. It does not alter the physical or logical topology of the medium in question.
- If a multipoint network is configured as a broadcast network, then it is essential that the designated router have a PVC to all the other routers. For example, in the network shown in Figure 8-1, consider the frame-relay backbone that is OSPF area 0. R1 is the only suitable choice for the designated router on this segment because it is the only router with a PVC to each of the other two.

```
r1#sh ip osp in ser 1
Serial1 is up, line protocol is up
  Internet Address 172.16.33.1 255.255.255.224, Area 0
  Process ID 1, Router ID 172.16.254.1, Network Type BROADCAST, Cost: 64
  Transmit Delay is 1 sec, State DR, Priority 100
  Designated Router (ID) 172.16.254.1, Interface address 172.16.33.1
  Backup Designated router (ID) 172.16.254.6, Interface address 172.16.33.6
  Timer intervals configured, Hello 10, Dead 40, Wait 40, Retransmit 5
    Hello due in 0:00:05
  Neighbor Count is 2, Adjacent neighbor count is 2
    Adjacent with neighbor 172.16.254.2
    Adjacent with neighbor 172.16.254.6  (Backup Designated Router)
r1#
```

Listing 8-1

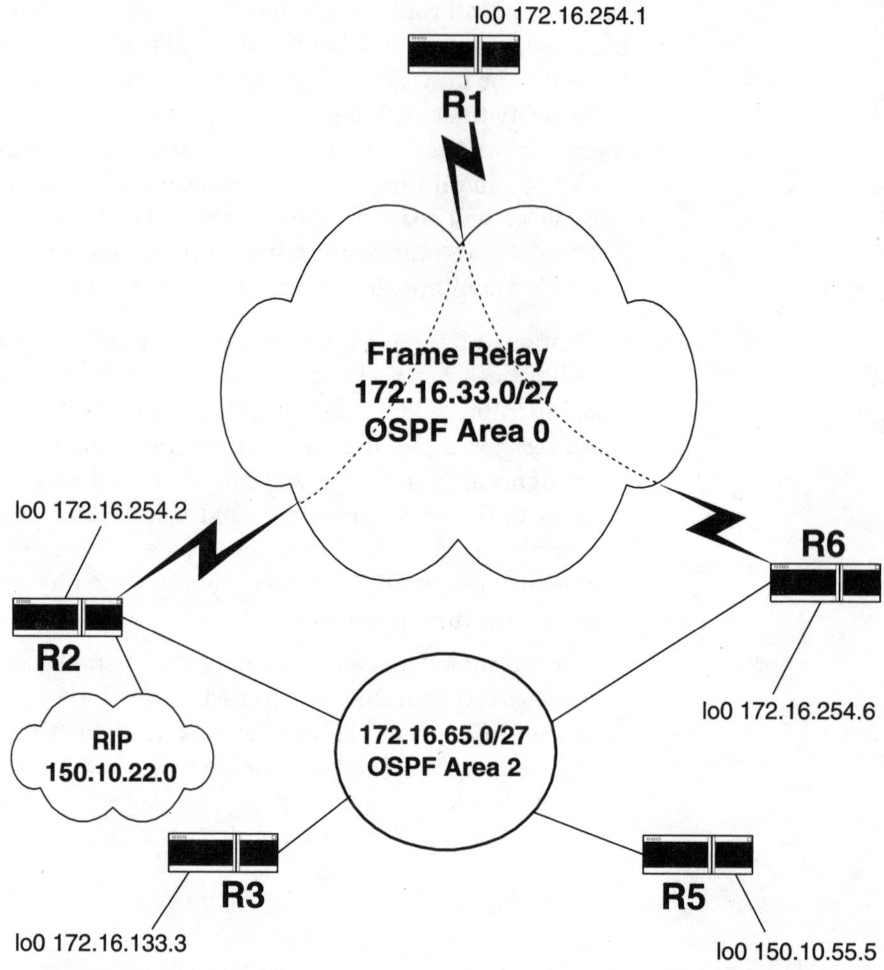

Figure 8-1
An OSPF network with multiple areas.

This leads me to a final and very important point in relation to OSPF broadcast networks, and this is how the designated routers are elected. Here are the criteria:

- *Priority*. This is the overriding parameter that determines which router becomes the DR. The default OSPF priority on a router interface, regardless of network type, is 1. It is a configurable parameter. In the case of the network in Figure 8-1, we could ensure that R1 becomes the DR with the following configuration:

```
R1#

interface serial 1
encapsulation frame-relay
```

```
ip address 172.16.33.1 255.255.255.224
ip ospf network broadcast
ip ospf priority 10
```

- *Router ID.* The router ID in OSPF is the highest IP address on the router. If a loopback address is configured, then it will override any other address. The router with the highest ID will become the DR on the segment. As we will see later, the router ID address does not even have to belong to a network that is participating in OSPF. The router ID only becomes relevant to designated router election if the OSPF priority is left at its default value.

NONBROADCAST NETWORKS A multipoint frame-relay main interface would be seen by OSPF as a nonbroadcast network. On a nonbroadcast network, neighbor formation usually cannot occur unless the neighbor is statically defined. There are cases where frame-relay Inverse ARP can facilitate neighbor formation. This happens when Inverse ARP is enabled on multipoint frame relay and the OSPF hello interval matches at each end of the PVC. In this section I want to discuss OSPF neighbor formation in a variety of scenarios, so I will assume that the network topology is not doing us any favors. A static neighbor is easily configured as follows:

```
interface serial 0
neighbor 144.22.27.2
```

The output in Listing 8-2 shows the default state of a multipoint frame-relay interface that does not use subinterfaces. It sees the designated router as itself but has not formed any neighbors.

```
r1#sh ip ospf int serial 1
Serial1 is up, line protocol is up
  Internet Address 172.16.33.1 255.255.255.224, Area 0
  Process ID 1, Router ID 172.16.254.1, Network Type NON_BROADCAST, Cost: 64
  Transmit Delay is 1 sec, State DR, Priority 1
  Designated Router (ID) 172.16.254.1, Interface address 172.16.33.1
  No backup designated router on this network
  Timer intervals configured, Hello 30, Dead 120, Wait 120, Retransmit 5
    Hello due in 0:00:28
  Neighbor Count is 0, Adjacent neighbor count is 0
r1#
```

Listing 8-2

A more popular alternative to the static configuration of neighbors is to configure the interface to be either a point-to-multipoint or a broadcast network in OSPF. The following command would achieve this:

```
interface serial 0
ip ospf network point-to-multipoint
```

NOTE: *OSPF cannot be assumed to form neighbors over a nonbroadcast network unless they are statically defined. Alternatively, the network type can be reconfigured to be broadcast or point to multipoint.*

POINT-TO-POINT NETWORKS In the case of point-to-point frame relay using subinterfaces, OSPF will automatically detect that this is a point-to-point network. A neighbor relationship can then be formed with the router at the other end of the link.

This network type cannot be configured manually to be point to point for the purposes of OSPF because this is not a configuration option on Cisco routers. Listing 8-3 is an example of a point-to-point OSPF subnet. Notice in this output that R6 has not formed a neighbor relationship over the point-to-point serial 0.100 interface. Later we will study examples showing why this might be the case.

POINT-TO-MULTIPOINT NETWORKS As mentioned previously, a multipoint frame-relay main interface would be seen by OSPF as a nonbroadcast network. Other than statically defining neighbors, one option is to configure the network manually to be point to multipoint for the purpose of OSPF. The following command only needs to be used on the routers that have multiple PVCs, provided there is no mismatching hello intervals on the other routers that connect to the cloud.

```
r6#sh ip ospf int s0.100
Serial0.100 is up, line protocol is up
  Internet Address 172.16.10.2/24, Area 0
  Process ID 1, Router ID 172.16.12.1, Network Type POINT_TO_POINT, Cost: 64
  Transmit Delay is 1 sec, State POINT_TO_POINT,
  Timer intervals configured, Hello 5, Dead 20, Wait 20, Retransmit 5
    Hello due in 00:00:01
  Neighbor Count is 0, Adjacent neighbor count is 0
  Suppress hello for 0 neighbor(s)
```

Listing 8-3

```
interface serial 1
ip ospf network point-to-multipoint
```

This enables the router with the multiple PVCs to form a neighbor relationship with each router to which it has a PVC. This is demonstrated in Listing 8-4 in relation to the network in Figure 8-1.

Rules for OSPF Areas OSPF is a complex protocol. Sometimes in practice the simple matter of a single link failing can produce additional effects. This may be so because the loss of a single route could mean that a basic OPSF principle is violated. Below I have summarized some of the principles in relation to OSPF area architecture that the design or support engineer should always be particularly mindful of.

- All OSPF areas must connect to area 0 in the form of an area border router. An exception to this rule is the use of an OSPF virtual link. Generally, virtual links are not considered good design practice and usually are only used as part of interim solutions.
- All interarea traffic must cross the backbone area 0. Hence all routers in a given area must have a route, default or otherwise, to area 0.
- Areas cannot be "broken up." In other words, a single area cannot have two area border routers that have no physical path between them. This would mean that traffic between these two routers would have to go from area *x* to area 0 and back to area *x*. The hierarchical principles of OSPF deem that traffic within the local area should not have to enter area 0. In such a scenario, connectivity between the two area border routers would have to be provided within area *x*. Otherwise, area *x* would have to be split into two distinct areas.

```
r1>sh ip ospf int ser 1
Serial1 is up, line protocol is up
  Internet Address 172.16.33.1 255.255.255.224, Area 0
  Process ID 1, Router ID 172.16.254.1, Network Type POINT_TO_MULTIPOINT, Cost:64
  Transmit Delay is 1 sec, State POINT_TO_MULTIPOINT,
  Timer intervals configured, Hello 30, Dead 120, Wait 120, Retransmit 5
    Hello due in 0:00:27
  Neighbor Count is 2, Adjacent neighbor count is 2
    Adjacent with neighbor 172.16.254.2
    Adjacent with neighbor 172.16.254.6
r1>
```

Listing 8-4

Route Summarization Route summarization does not take place automatically in OSPF, even if major network boundaries are crossed. This feature, combined with the fact that OSPF routing updates include full mask information, also enables OSPF to automatically support discontiguous networks without any additional configuration. Two types of route summarization can be configured in OSPF: interarea and external route summarization.

NOTE:

- *OSPF automatically supports discontiguous networks.*
- *Route summarization is never automatic in OSPF, even when crossing a major network boundary. It must be configured manually.*

INTERAREA SUMMARIZATION This type of summarization should be configured on an area border router (ABR), i.e., routers that have interfaces in area 0 and one other area. The purpose of this type of summarization can be threefold:

- To reduce the size of routing tables and link-state databases for the OSPF process. Area 0 routers would see summary routes to each of the other areas. Non-Area 0 routers also would see summary routes from the adjacent nonzero areas.
- By summarizing the routes that get injected into the backbone from each area, and hence propagated into all other areas, convergence can be improved and overhead reduced. For example, if a specific route is lost in a given area, the OSPF Dijkstra algorithm only needs to be recomputed for that area. This would not be the case if that specific route had been injected into each of the other areas.
- Interarea summarization also can be used to make different sets of routes of the same major network all appear as if they use the same mask. This can be a useful trick if OSPF is being redistributed into a protocol that does not support VLSM. We will see an example of this later.

If OSPF area 2 used subnets from 172.16.17.0 to 172.16.30.0, then the following configuration could be used to summarize all these subnets into a single update of 172.16.16.0 255.255.240.0:

```
router ospf 1
area 2 range 172.16.16.0 255.255.240.0
```

EXTERNAL ROUTE SUMMARIZATION External route summarization is used to aggregate the routing updates that are redistributed from another routing protocol into OSPF. This summarization is configured on the autonomous system's border router (ASBR). OSPF will view another routing protocol or another OSPF process as a separate autonomous system.

The example in Listing 8-5 would summarize all 151.10.11.0 routes that are being redistributed into OSPF into a single 151.10.11.0/24 summary route. Note that only part of the configuration is shown.

OSPF Demand Circuit A newer OSPF feature that complies with RFC 1793 and is available as of Cisco IOS version 11.2 is the OSPF demand circuit. The primary application for this feature is to facilitate a more effective implementation of OSPF over dial-up networks such as ISDN, as well as backup serial link applications.

OSPF traditionally has been problematic over ISDN for two main reasons:

- The hello packets would tend to keep the line up unless a complex dialer list was configured. This in any case would break the OSPF adjacency over the ISDN network. Another possible solution is to make the hello and hold times very long. This is also less than ideal.
- Every time the ISDN link changes state, the OSPF area would be flooded with LSAs.

The demand circuit feature addresses the first issue by suppressing the hellos and periodic LSA refreshes once the initial adjacency is formed. The adjacency is then maintained without requiring periodic hello packets. The demand circuit will only become active if there are topology changes within the area.

If combined with a higher cost metric, the ISDN link can then provide dial on demand or dial backup while still remaining part of the OSPF topology.

Listing 8-5

```
router eigrp 1
network 151.10.0.0

router ospf 1
redistribute eigrp 1 subnets metric 100
summary-address 151.10.11.0 255.255.255.0
```

```
interface bri0
ip ospf demand-circuit
ip ospf cost 100
```

Use of the demand circuit feature is not restricted to ISDN. The output in Listing 8-6 demonstrates a serial link that uses the demand circuit feature for backup purposes. Notice how the hellos are suppressed but the neighbor relationship is still active.

Before moving on, I would like to comment on the OSPF metric, i.e., cost, which has not been discussed until now. OSPF dynamically assigns a cost to each interface that is inversely proportional to the interface bandwidth:

Cost = 10^8/bandwidth

This makes the default cost for Ethernet 10 and the default for FDDI equal to 1. The cost metric is configurable and therefore can be manipulated to influence routing decisions. The overall cost associated with a route is the sum of the interface costs along the path to the destination.

OSPF Show Commands

The `show ip ospf interface` command can be used to verify that OSPF has been configured on a given interface. It also provides a lot of other useful information. From the following sample output (Listing 8-7) we can extract the following information:

```
r3#sh ip ospf in se 3/0
Serial3/0 is up, line protocol is up
  Internet Address 133.10.1.3/24, Area 5
  Process ID 1, Router ID 172.16.254.3, Network Type POINT_TO_POINT, Cost: 100
  Configured as demand circuit.
  Run as demand circuit.
  DoNotAge LSA not allowed (Number of DCbitless LSA is 9).
  Transmit Delay is 1 sec, State POINT_TO_POINT,
  Timer intervals configured, Hello 10, Dead 40, Wait 40, Retransmit 5
    Hello due in 00:00:00
  Neighbor Count is 1, Adjacent neighbor count is 1
    Adjacent with neighbor 172.16.254.6
  Suppress hello for 0 neighbor(s)
r3#
```

Listing 8-6

```
r6#sh ip ospf int s0.100
Serial0.100 is up, line protocol is up
  Internet Address 172.16.10.2/24, Area 0
  Process ID 1, Router ID 172.16.12.1, Network Type POINT_TO_POINT, Cost: 64
  Transmit Delay is 1 sec, State POINT_TO_POINT,
  Timer intervals configured, Hello 5, Dead 20, Wait 20, Retransmit 5
    Hello due in 00:00:01
  Neighbor Count is 0, Adjacent neighbor count is 0
  Suppress hello for 0 neighbor(s)
r6#
```

Listing 8-7

- The interface is in area 0 for OSPF 1.
- It is a point-to-point OSPF network type.
- We see the hello and dead timer values.
- We also can observe that it has not formed a neighbor relationship over this link.

When troubleshooting why an adjacency has not been formed here, the first step is to go to the other end of the PVC and verify that the hello and dead timers match. It is also quite possible that the other end of the PVC is configured as multipoint frame relay. In this case, OSPF would see it as a nonbroadcast network by default, which could be rectified by reconfiguring it as a point-to-multipoint or a broadcast network type.

In the preceding example, I solved the problem by making a configuration change at the remote end router. We can use the `show ip ospf neighbor` command to check that an adjacency was formed by R6. Also, let's try to deduce what configuration change was made at the far end (see Listing 8-8).

The FULL state indicates that an adjacency has been formed. The other end of the link is 172.16.10.1, but the neighbor's router ID (i.e., highest IP address or loopback address) is 172.145.16.1. So what was done to make the adjacency possible? The fact that the neighbor has a priority of 100 should be a clue. The remote multipoint frame-relay interface was configured to be an OSPF broadcast network and was given a priority of 100 to ensure that it became the designated router.

In the following example (Listing 8-9) we see a token-ring interface appearing as a broadcast network, as expected. However, no adjacencies have been formed. The reason here is that this happens to be a stub network segment that has no other routers on it. I include this to emphasize that you should never overlook the obvious.

```
r6#sh ip ospf neighbor

Neighbor ID     Pri   State           Dead Time   Address         Interface
172.45.16.1     100   FULL/  -        00:00:39    172.16.10.1     Serial0.100
r6#
```

Listing 8-8

Before a designated router election can take place, the wait timer must expire. This timer has the same value as the dead timer, and its purpose is to allow sufficient time for routers to join a new segment that has no designated router assigned, before having a DR election. (See Listing 8-10.)

On a broadcast network, each router will have a neighbor relationship with all other routers on the segment but will only form an adjacency with the DR and BDR. This will be demonstrated in Listing 8-11. In Figure 8-1, four routers, R2, R3, R5, and R6, all connect to a single token-ring segment, 172.16.65.0/27, which is part of OSPF area 2. R6 and R2 become the DR and BDR, respectively, because they have the highest router IDs. The output from R5 in Listing 8-11 verifies that it has three neighbors on the segment but is only adjacent to the DR and BDR. R5 has the lowest ID on the segment (150.10.55.5); if it were configured with a loopback address in the format 172.16.254.5, then it would have been the BDR. Note also that the neighbor state is FULL with respect to the DR and BDR, while the state is 2WAY with respect to R1. Check back to the section on adjacency formation if you do not know why this is so.

```
r1>sh ip osp in to0
TokenRing0 is up, line protocol is up
  Internet Address 172.16.131.1 255.255.255.240, Area 0
  Process ID 1, Router ID 172.16.254.1, Network Type BROADCAST, Cost: 6
  Transmit Delay is 1 sec, State DR, Priority 1
  Designated Router (ID) 172.16.254.1, Interface address 172.16.131.1
  No backup designated router on this network
  Timer intervals configured, Hello 10, Dead 40, Wait 40, Retransmit 5
    Hello due in 0:00:08
  Neighbor Count is 0, Adjacent neighbor count is 0
r1>
```

Listing 8-9

```
RouterA#sh ip ospf in to0/0
TokenRing0/0 is up, line protocol is up
  Internet Address 172.16.65.65/27, Area 2
  Process ID 1,Router ID 172.45.16.1,Network Type BROADCAST, Cost: 6
  Transmit Delay is 1 sec, State WAITING, Priority 1
  No designated router on this network
  No backup designated router on this network
  Timer intervals configured, Hello 10,Dead 40,Wait 40, Retransmit 5
    Hello due in 00:00:00
    Wait time before Designated router selection 00:00:30
  Neighbor Count is 0, Adjacent neighbor count is 0
          RouterA#
```

Listing 8-10

The `show ip protocol` command can be used to obtain summary information on the OSPF process configured on the router. Listing 8-12 shows that OSPF is enabled on all interfaces that fall within the 172.16.0.0 major network. The presence of a wildcard enables OSPF to specify only certain ranges within the same major network if so desired. Apart from this, it can be observed that this is in a stable network with no topology changes in 1 day and 15 hours.

```
r5#sh ip ospf in to0
TokenRing0 is up, line protocol is up
  Internet Address 172.16.65.5 255.255.255.224, Area 2
  Process ID 1, Router ID 150.10.55.5, Network Type BROADCAST, Cost: 6
  Transmit Delay is 1 sec, State DROTHER, Priority 1
  Designated Router (ID) 172.16.254.6, Interface address 172.16.65.6
  Backup Designated router (ID) 172.16.254.2, Interface address 172.16.65.2
  Timer intervals configured, Hello 10, Dead 40, Wait 40, Retransmit 5
    Hello due in 0:00:08
  Neighbor Count is 3, Adjacent neighbor count is 2
    Adjacent with neighbor 172.16.254.2  (Backup Designated Router)
    Adjacent with neighbor 172.16.254.6  (Designated Router)
r5#sh ip ospf nei

Neighbor ID     Pri   State           Dead Time   Address         Interface
172.16.254.2      1   FULL/BDR        0:00:37     172.16.65.2     TokenRing0
172.16.254.6      1   FULL/DR         0:00:35     172.16.65.6     TokenRing0
172.16.133.3      1   2WAY/DROTHER    0:00:32     172.16.65.1     TokenRing0
r5#
```

Listing 8-11

Listing 8-12

```
r1>sh ip protocol
Routing Protocol is "ospf 1"
  Sending updates every 0 seconds
  Invalid after 0 seconds, hold down 0, flushed after 0
  Outgoing update filter list for all interfaces is not set
  Incoming update filter list for all interfaces is not set
  Redistributing: ospf 1
  Routing for Networks:
    172.16.0.0 0.0.255.255
  Routing Information Sources:
    Gateway         Distance      Last Update
    172.16.254.2         110      1d15
    172.16.254.6         110      1d15
  Distance: (default is 110)

r1>
```

Now let's examine the contents of a typical routing table for a router running OSPF (see Listing 8-13). Here are some points to note from R1's routing table in Figure 8-1 (some routes have been omitted for clarity):

- A route marked as O indicates an OSPF-derived route from within the same area in which the router resides, termed an *intraarea route*. If

```
r1#sh ip route
Codes: C - connected, S - static, I - IGRP, R - RIP, M - mobile, B - BGP
       D - EIGRP, EX - EIGRP external, O - OSPF, IA - OSPF inter area
       E1 - OSPF external type 1, E2 - OSPF external type 2, E - EGP
       i - IS-IS, L1 - IS-IS level-1, L2 - IS-IS level-2, * - candidate default

Gateway of last resort is not set

     150.10.0.0 255.255.255.0 is subnetted, 1 subnets
O E2    150.10.22.0 [110/100] via 172.16.33.2, 00:00:11, Serial1
     172.16.0.0 is variably subnetted, 6 subnets, 3 masks
C       172.16.131.0 255.255.255.240 is directly connected, TokenRing0
O       172.16.254.2 255.255.255.255
           [110/65] via 172.16.33.2, 00:12:54, Serial1
C       172.16.254.1 255.255.255.255 is directly connected, Loopback0
O       172.16.254.6 255.255.255.255
           [110/65] via 172.16.33.6, 00:12:54, Serial1
C       172.16.33.0 255.255.255.224 is directly connected, Serial1
O IA    172.16.65.0 255.255.255.224
           [110/70] via 172.16.33.2, 00:05:42, Serial1
           [110/70] via 172.16.33.6, 00:05:42, Serial1
r1#
```

Listing 8-13

the router is an ABR, then any route that originated from either area 0 or the other area that it borders will be marked as O.

- Routes that originate in areas other than the area(s) in which the router is located, and hence are learned by transiting through area 0, show up as interarea or O IA routes in the routing table.
- Routes that originate from another routing protocol or a different OSPF process to the one running on the router are said to be *external routes*. There are two types of external routes in OSPF. The difference between the two types is how they calculate the cost metric. E2 routes are the default type of external route, and their metric consists only of the external metric when the route was redistributed into OSPF. The metric for an E1 route is the sum of the external and internal costs, as seen by that router. E1 routes generally are preferred over E2 because their metric has a greater accuracy. Note that external routes in OSPF have an administrative distance of 110, just like internal routes.

The output in Listing 8-14 gives more detailed information about the interarea route 172.16.65.0 and the external E2 route 150.10.22.0. Note that the external route is displayed as being known via OSPF 1. This is so because it was already redistributed into OSPF when the update reached R1. It did not, however, originate in OSPF.

Listing 8-14

```
r1#sh ip ro 172.16.65.0
Routing entry for 172.16.65.0 255.255.255.224
  Known via "ospf 1", distance 110, metric 70, type inter area
  Redistributing via ospf 1
  Last update from 172.16.33.2 on Serial1, 00:08:29 ago
  Routing Descriptor Blocks:
  * 172.16.33.6, from 172.16.254:6, 00:08:29 ago, via Serial1
      Route metric is 70, traffic share count is 1
    172.16.33.2, from 172.16.254.2, 00:08:29 ago, via Serial1
      Route metric is 70, traffic share count is 1

r1#sh ip ro 150.10.22.0
Routing entry for 150.10.22.0 255.255.255.0
Known via "ospf 1", distance 110, metric 100, type extern 2,
forward metric 64
Redistributing via ospf 1
  Last update from 172.16.33.2 on Serial1, 00:08:48 ago
  Routing Descriptor Blocks:
  * 172.16.33.2, from 172.16.254.2, 00:08:48 ago, via Serial1
      Route metric is 100, traffic share count is 1

r1#
```

The contents of the link-state database can be examined using the `show ip ospf database` command. This command also can be used to look for a particular route or a particular OSPF link type. In Listing 8-15 we look in R1's link-state database for all external link types. As expected, we find just one—150.10.22.0.

Debugging OSPF

Because OSPF is a link-state routing protocol, it does not provide an abundance of periodic information that facilitates the use of debugging tools. We have seen how useful the show commands are. The most helpful OSPF debugging command is `debug ip ospf adj`, which can be extremely useful when troubleshooting why neighbor formation has not occurred. In Listing 8-16, this command pinpoints a mismatch in the hello and dead intervals; hence 172.16.10.2 cannot become a neighbor. An incorrect subnet mask also would be highlighted in this output. Later, when we are working through some troubleshooting scenarios, we will see how this command can be used to display authentication failure.

The following output (Listing 8-17) is from `debug ip ospf adj` for normal successful adjacency formation. Here, R1 is attempting to form neighbors over its serial 1 and token ring 0 interfaces. It successfully

Listing 8-15

```
r1#sh ip ospf data external

       OSPF Router with ID (172.16.254.1) (Process ID 1)

                AS External Link States

  Routing Bit Set on this LSA
  LS age: 1791
  Options: (No TOS-capability)
  LS Type: AS External Link
  Link State ID: 150.10.22.0 (External Network Number )
  Advertising Router: 172.16.254.2
  LS Seq Number: 80000052
  Checksum: 0xA109
  Length: 36
  Network Mask: 255.255.255.0
        Metric Type: 2 (Larger than any link state path)
        TOS: 0
        Metric: 100
        Forward Address: 0.0.0.0
        External Route Tag: 0

r1#
```

```
r1#deb ip osp adj
OSPF adjacency events debugging is on
r1#term mon
r1#
OSPF: Mismatched hello parameters from 172.16.10.2
Dead R 20 C 120, Hello R 5 C 30  Mask R 255.255.255.0 C 255.255.255.0
r1#undeb all
All possible debugging has been turned off
r1#
```

Listing 8-16

forms a full adjacency with router ID 172.16.254.6; over the WAN. Note that the serial interface to which it sends the initial packets is 172.16.33.6; it then receives the router ID. R1 (ID of 172.16.254.1) becomes the designated router on the token ring in absence of any other router.

```
Apr 12 17:17:59: OSPF: 2 Way Communication to neighbor 172.16.254.6
Apr 12 17:17:59: OSPF: send DBD packet to 172.16.33.6 seq 0x323
Apr 12 17:17:59: OSPF: send DBD packet to 172.16.33.6 seq 0x323
Apr 12 17:17:59: OSPF: NBR Negotiation Done  We are the SLAVE
Apr 12 17:17:59: OSPF: send DBD packet to 172.16.33.6 seq 0x236E
Apr 12 17:17:59: OSPF: Receive dbd from 172.16.254.6 seq 0x236F
Apr 12 17:17:59: OSPF: send DBD packet to 172.16.33.6 seq 0x236F
Apr 12 17:17:59: OSPF: Database request to 172.16.254.6
Apr 12 17:17:59: OSPF: sent LS REQ packet to 172.16.33.6, length 60
Apr 12 17:17:59: OSPF: Receive dbd from 172.16.254.6 seq 0x2370
Apr 12 17:17:59: OSPF: Exchange Done with neighbor 172.16.254.6
Apr 12 17:17:59: OSPF: send DBD packet to 172.16.33.6 seq 0x2370
Apr 12 17:17:59: OSPF: Synchronized with neighbor 172.16.254.6, state:FULL
Apr 12 17:17:59: OSPF: Build router LSA, router ID 172.16.254.1
Apr 12 17:18:11: OSPF: end of Wait on interface TokenRing0
Apr 12 17:18:11: OSPF: DR/BDR election on TokenRing0
Apr 12 17:18:11: OSPF: Elect BDR 172.16.254.1
Apr 12 17:18:11: OSPF: Elect DR 172.16.254.1
Apr 12 17:18:11: OSPF: Elect BDR 0.0.0.0
Apr 12 17:18:11: OSPF: Elect DR 172.16.254.1
Apr 12 17:18:11:        DR: 172.16.254.1 (Id)   BDR: none
Apr 12 17:18:11: OSPF: Build network LSA, router ID 172.16.254.1
Apr 12 17:18:11: OSPF: No full nbrs to build Net Lsa
Apr 12 17:18:11: OSPF: Flush network LSA on TokenRing0 for area 172.16.254.1
Apr 12 17:18:11: OSPF: Build router LSA, router ID 172.16.254.1
r1#
```

Listing 8-17

There are no other routers on the token ring 0 segment, which explains why neighbors cannot be formed on this interface. R1 elects itself the BDR and then the DR for this segment.

In Cisco IOS version 11.2 there is a further debugging command, `debug ip ospf events`, that displays equivalent information on neighbor and adjacency formation.

Troubleshooting Scenarios for OSPF

In the network shown in Figure 8-2, R2, R5, and R6 each attach to the token-ring OSPF backbone area 0. The problem is that R2 is not learning any remote routes over the backbone.

If we first examine R2's configuration, it can be seen that MD5 authentication is configured across the area 0 backbone. This information also could have been obtained using the `sh ip ospf interface token 1` command. It is also observed that R2 has failed to form any OSPF neighbors. The hello interval or network type has not been changed from the defaults, but what about the authentication parameters? We can choose to check R6 to verify that the parameter values match. On R6 token ring 0, the hello interval and network type are at the default values. The 172.16.65.0/24 segment is also in area 0, so everything is in place for neighbor formation except the authentication parameters. From the configuration (Listing 8-18), we see the mismatch, the password for key 1 is `cisco-ospf` on R2, and it is `cisco` on R6.

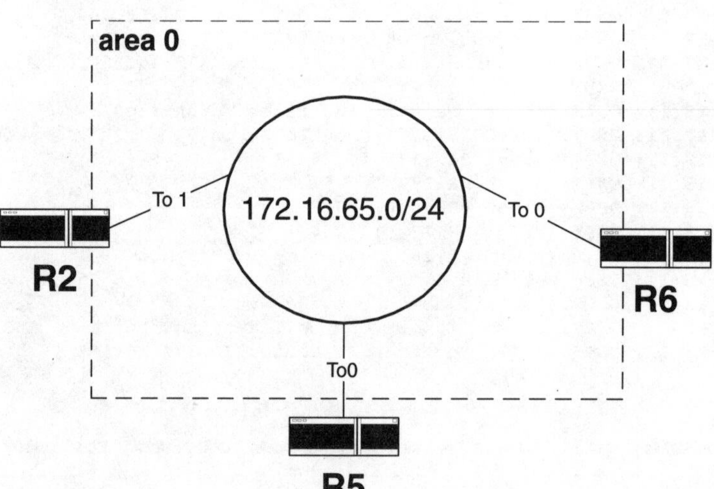

Figure 8-2
OSPF troubleshooting scenario.

Listing 8-18

```
r2#

!
interface TokenRing1
 ip address 172.16.65.2 255.255.255.0
 ip ospf message-digest-key 1 md5 cisco-ospf
 ring-speed 16
!
router ospf 1
 network 172.16.65.0 0.0.0.255 area 0
 area 0 authentication message-digest
!

r2#sh ip ospf neig
r2#

R6#

interface TokenRing0
 ip address 172.16.65.6 255.255.255.0
 ip ospf message-digest-key 1 md5 cisco
 ring-speed 16
!
router ospf 1
 network 172.16.0.0 0.0.255.255 area 0
 area 0 authentication message-digest
```

Another way to pick up this authentication problem would be to use the `debug ip ospf adj` tool. The output from R2 confirms an authentication mismatch with both R5 and R6 (see Listing 8-19).

It can be verified that R5 has formed an adjacency with R6 over the token ring; hence there is no authentication mismatch between these two routers. The MD5 password for key 1 is `cisco` for R5 and R6 (see Listing 8-20).

Now I am going to break the adjacency between R5 and R6 by changing the hello interval to 5 seconds on R5. I will then demonstrate the use of debugging to isolate the problem. (See Listing 8-21.)

As you can see, R5 no longer sees R6 as a neighbor. The reason can be provided from the output of `debug ip ospf adj`, as shown in Listing 8-22. The best way to restore the adjacency is simply to return the hello interval value on R5 to the default of 10 seconds for a broadcast network. If R6 had its hello interval also changed to 5 seconds, the adjacency with R5 would be restored, but there would then be a mismatch with R2.

The network in Figure 8-3 consists of two OSPF areas 0 and 2. A RIP stub network is to be redistributed into OSPF by R2. OSPF is to be redistributed into IGRP at R6 such that R3 has a route to the 172.16.65.0/27 token-ring network.

```
r2#sh log
Syslog logging: enabled (0 messages dropped, 0 flushes, 0 overruns)
    Console logging: level debugging, 407 messages logged
    Monitor logging: level debugging, 296 messages logged
    Trap logging: level informational, 103 message lines logged

 Mismatch Authentication Key - Message Digest Key 1
OSPF: Send with youngest Key 1
OSPF: Rcv pkt from 172.16.65.5, TokenRing1 : Mismatch Authentication Key - Message
  Digest Key 1
OSPF: Rcv pkt from 172.16.65.6, TokenRing1 : Mismatch Authentication Key - Message
  Digest Key 1
OSPF: Send with youngest Key 1
OSPF: Rcv pkt from 172.16.65.5, TokenRing1 : Mismatch Authentication Key - Message
  Digest Key 1
OSPF: Rcv pkt from 172.16.65.6, TokenRing1 : Mismatch Authentication Key - Message
  Digest Key 1
```

Listing 8-19

```
r5>sh ip osp nei

Neighbor ID     Pri   State           Dead Time   Address         Interface
172.16.254.6      1   FULL/DR         0:00:33     172.16.65.6     TokenRing0
r5>

interface TokenRing0
 ip address 172.16.65.5 255.255.255.0
 ip ospf message-digest-key 1 md5 cisco
 ring-speed 16
!
router ospf 1
 network 172.16.0.0 0.0.255.255 area 0
 area 5 authentication message-digest

r5#sh ip ospf int to0
TokenRing0 is up, line protocol is up
  Internet Address 172.16.65.5 255.255.255.0, Area 5
  Process ID 1, Router ID 172.16.65.5, Network Type BROADCAST, Cost: 6
  Transmit Delay is 1 sec, State BDR, Priority 1
  Designated Router (ID) 172.16.254.6, Interface address 172.16.65.6
  Backup Designated router (ID) 172.16.65.5, Interface address 172.16.65.5
  Timer intervals configured, Hello 10, Dead 40, Wait 40, Retransmit 5
    Hello due in 0:00:09
  Neighbor Count is 1, Adjacent neighbor count is 1
    Adjacent with neighbor 172.16.254.6  (Designated Router)
  Message digest authentication enabled
    Youngest key id is 1
```

Listing 8-20

```
r5#conf t
Enter configuration commands, one per line.  End with CNTL/Z.
r5(config)#in to0
r5(config-if)#ip ospf hello 5
r5(config-if)#^Z
r5#
r5#sh ip osp in to0
TokenRing0 is up, line protocol is up
  Internet Address 172.16.65.5 255.255.255.0, Area 5
  Process ID 1, Router ID 172.16.65.5, Network Type BROADCAST, Cost: 6
  Transmit Delay is 1 sec, State DR, Priority 1
  Designated Router (ID) 172.16.65.5, Interface address 172.16.65.5
  No backup designated router on this network
  Timer intervals configured, Hello 5, Dead 20, Wait 20, Retransmit 5
    Hello due in 0:00:01
  Neighbor Count is 0, Adjacent neighbor count is 0
  Message digest authentication enabled
    Youngest key id is 1
r5#sh ip osp nei
r5#
```

Listing 8-21

Multiple problems are being experienced. I have provided the configurations for each of the four routers (Listing 8-23). We will use these combined with the other troubleshooting tools to resolve all problems.

A good place to start checking out how well this network is working is to view the routing table at a hub site like R1 (see Listing 8-24).

Thus R1 has not learned any OSPF routes, and it has not even formed any adjacencies. We see that the frame-relay serial interface is a nonbroadcast OSPF network, which is the normal default but is not very

```
r5#
OSPF: Mismatched hello parameters from 172.16.65.6
Dead R 40 C 20, Hello R 10 C 5  Mask R 255.255.255.0 C 255.255.255.0
OSPF: Send with youngest Key 1
OSPF: Send with youngest Key 1
OSPF: Mismatched hello parameters from 172.16.65.6
Dead R 40 C 20, Hello R 10 C 5  Mask R 255.255.255.0 C 255.255.255.0
OSPF: Send with youngest Key 1
OSPF: Send with youngest Key 1
OSPF: Mismatched hello parameters from 172.16.65.6
Dead R 40 C 20, Hello R 10 C 5  Mask R 255.255.255.0 C 255.255.255.0
r5#
```

Listing 8-22

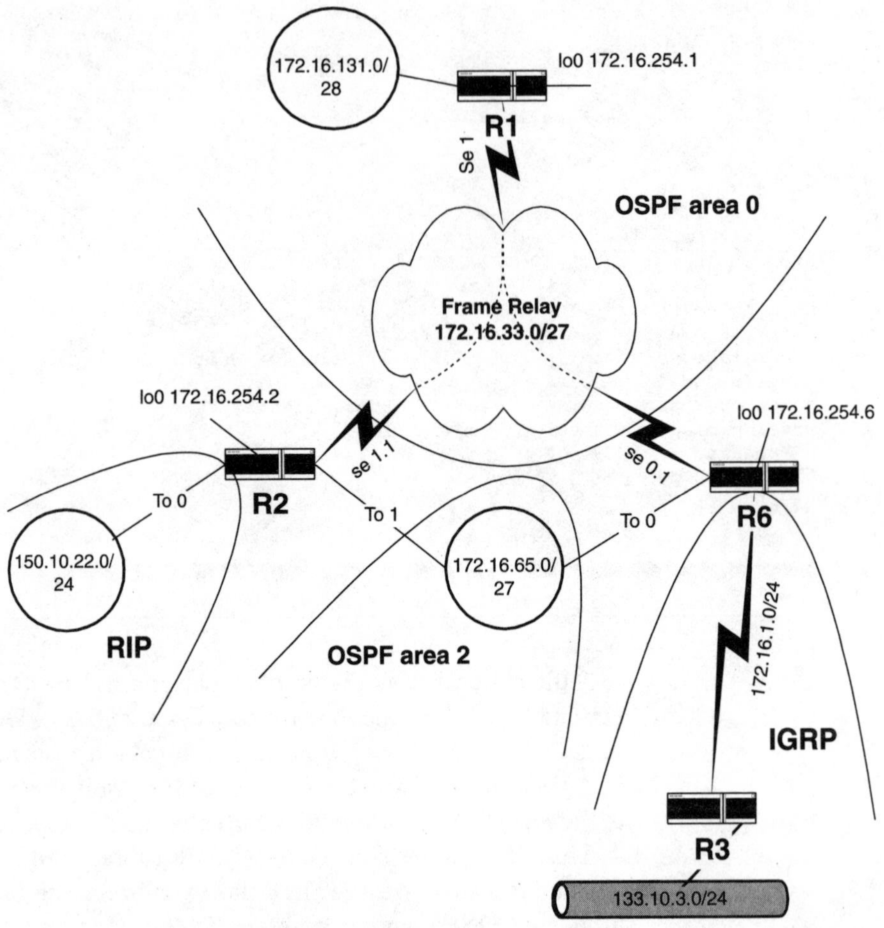

Figure 8-3 Complex multiprotocol troubleshooting scenario.

useful in this instance. We will reconfigure it as a broadcast network (see Listing 8-25).

Now we see that R1 has formed neighbor relationships with R2 and R6 and has already become adjacent to R6, which is the designated router. It is not desirable for R6 to be the DR because R6 does not have a PVC to R2. We must change the priority on R1 to make it the DR for the subnet (see Listing 8-26).

We also have to make the subinterfaces on R2 and R6 broadcast networks. The reason that they formed neighbors as point-to-point networks with R1, which was a broadcast network, is because the default hello and dead timer values for these two network types are the same (see Listing 8-27).

Listing 8-23

```
r1#sh run
Building configuration...

Current configuration:
!
! Last configuration change at 17:57:20 PDT Thu Apr 8 1999
!
version 11.0
service timestamps debug datetime
service timestamps log datetime
service udp-small-servers
service tcp-small-servers
!
hostname r1
!
enable password cisco
!
!
interface Loopback0
 ip address 172.16.254.1 255.255.255.255
!
interface Serial0
 no ip address
 shutdown
 no fair-queue
!
interface Serial1
 ip address 172.16.33.1 255.255.255.224
 encapsulation frame-relay
 frame-relay lmi-type ansi
 frame-relay map ip 172.16.33.2 102 broadcast
 frame-relay map ip 172.16.33.6 106 broadcast
!
interface TokenRing0
 ip address 172.16.131.1 255.255.255.240
 ring-speed 16
!
interface TokenRing1
 no ip address
 shutdown
!
router ospf 1
 network 172.16.33.0 0.0.0.255 area 0
!
logging buffered
!
!
!
line con 0
line aux 0
 transport input all
line vty 0 4
 password cisco
 login
!
end
```

Listing 8-23 (*Cont.*)

```
r1#

r2#sh run
Building configuration...

Current configuration:
!
! Last configuration change at 18:10:27 PDT Thu Apr 8 1999
!
version 11.0
service timestamps debug datetime
service timestamps log datetime
service udp-small-servers
service tcp-small-servers
!
hostname r2
!
enable password cisco
!
!
interface Loopback0
 ip address 172.16.254.2 255.255.255.255
!
interface Serial0
 no ip address
 shutdown
 no fair-queue
!
interface Serial1
 no ip address
 encapsulation frame-relay
 frame-relay lmi-type ansi
!
interface Serial1.1 point-to-point
 ip address 172.16.33.2 255.255.255.224
 frame-relay interface-dlci 200
!
interface TokenRing0
 ip address 150.10.22.2 255.255.255.0
 ring-speed 16
!
interface TokenRing1
 ip address 172.16.65.2 255.255.255.224
 ring-speed 16
!
router ospf 1
 redistribute rip
 passive-interface TokenRing1
 network 172.16.33.0 0.0.0.255 area 0
 network 172.16.65.0 0.0.0.255 area 2
 default-metric 100
!
router rip
 network 150.10.0.0
!
logging buffered
!
```

Listing 8-23 (*Cont.*)

```
!
!
line con 0
line aux 0
 transport input all
line vty 0 4
 password cisco
 login
!
end

r2#

r6#sh run
Building configuration...

Current configuration:
!
! Last configuration change at 18:12:11 PDT Thu Apr 8 1999
!
version 11.0
service timestamps debug datetime
service timestamps log datetime
service udp-small-servers
service tcp-small-servers
!
hostname r6
!
enable password cisco
!
!
interface Loopback0
 ip address 172.16.254.6 255.255.255.255
!
interface Serial0
 no ip address
 encapsulation frame-relay
 no fair-queue
 frame-relay lmi-type ansi
!
interface Serial0.1 point-to-point
 ip address 172.16.33.6 255.255.255.224
 frame-relay interface-dlci 600
!
interface Serial1
 ip address 172.16.1.6 255.255.255.0
!
interface TokenRing0
 ip address 172.16.65.6 255.255.255.224
 ip ospf network non-broadcast
 decnet cost 5
 ring-speed 16
!
router ospf 1
 network 172.16.33.0 0.0.0.255 area 0
 network 172.16.65.0 0.0.0.255 area 2
!
```

Listing 8-23 (*Cont.*)

```
router igrp 1
 redistribute ospf 1
 network 172.16.0.0
!
logging buffered
!
line con 0
line aux 0
 transport input all
line vty 0 4
 password cisco
 login
!
end

r6#

r3#sh run
Building configuration...

Current configuration:
!
! Last configuration change at 16:42:41 PDT Wed Apr 7 1999
!
version 11.2
service timestamps debug datetime
service timestamps log datetime
!
hostname r3
!
enable password cisco
!
!
interface Loopback0
 ip address 172.16.254.3 255.255.255.255
!
interface Loopback7
 ip address 150.10.71.3 255.255.240.0
 shutdown
!
interface Ethernet2/0
 ip address 133.10.3.3 255.255.255.0
!
interface Serial3/0
 ip address 172.16.1.3 255.255.255.0
 clockrate 56000
!
router igrp 1
 network 172.16.0.0
!
no ip classless
!
!
line con 0
line aux 0
line vty 0 4
 password cisco
```

Listing 8-23 (*Cont.*)

```
 login
!
end

r3#
```

If we again check R1, we see that it is now the designated router on the segment, with R6 being the BDR (see Listing 8-28).

The routing table also shows the interarea route from area 2 that is learned from both R2 and R6 (see Listing 8-29).

However, none of the remote loopback interfaces are participating in OSPF. Also, R1 token ring 0 has not been included in the OSPF process. This can be seen from the initial configurations and can be verified as shown in Listing 8-30.

We will now enable OSPF on each of these networks, putting them all in area 0 (see Listing 8-31).

```
r1#sh ip ro
Codes: C - connected, S - static, I - IGRP, R - RIP, M - mobile, B - BGP
       D - EIGRP, EX - EIGRP external, O - OSPF, IA - OSPF inter area
       E1 - OSPF external type 1, E2 - OSPF external type 2, E - EGP
       i - IS-IS, L1 - IS-IS level-1, L2 - IS-IS level-2, * - candidate default

Gateway of last resort is not set

     172.16.0.0 is variably subnetted, 3 subnets, 3 masks
C       172.16.131.0 255.255.255.240 is directly connected, TokenRing0
C       172.16.254.1 255.255.255.255 is directly connected, Loopback0
C       172.16.33.0 255.255.255.224 is directly connected, Serial1

r1#sh ip osp nei

r1#sh ip osp int ser 1
Serial1 is up, line protocol is up
  Internet Address 172.16.33.1 255.255.255.224, Area 0
  Process ID 1, Router ID 172.16.254.1, Network Type NON_BROADCAST, Cost: 64
  Transmit Delay is 1 sec, State DR, Priority 1
  Designated Router (ID) 172.16.254.1, Interface address 172.16.33.1
  No backup designated router on this network
  Timer intervals configured, Hello 30, Dead 120, Wait 120, Retransmit 5
    Hello due in 0:00:28
  Neighbor Count is 0, Adjacent neighbor count is 0
r1#
```

Listing 8-24

```
r1#conf t
Enter configuration commands, one per line.  End with CNTL/Z.
r1(config)#int serial 1
r1(config-if)#ip ospf network broadcast
r1(config-if)#^Z
r1#

r1#sh ip osp ne

Neighbor ID      Pri   State            Dead Time   Address         Interface
172.16.254.2       1   2WAY/DROTHER     0:00:37     172.16.33.2     Serial1
172.16.254.6       1   FULL/DR          0:00:37     172.16.33.6     Serial1
r1#sh ip osp int ser 1
Serial1 is up, line protocol is up
  Internet Address 172.16.33.1 255.255.255.224, Area 0
  Process ID 1, Router ID 172.16.254.1, Network Type BROADCAST, Cost: 64
  Transmit Delay is 1 sec, State DROTHER, Priority 1
  Designated Router (ID) 172.16.254.6, Interface address 172.16.33.6
  Backup Designated router (ID) 172.16.254.6, Interface address 172.16.33.6
  Timer intervals configured, Hello 10, Dead 40, Wait 40, Retransmit 5
    Hello due in 0:00:04
  Neighbor Count is 2, Adjacent neighbor count is 1
    Adjacent with neighbor 172.16.254.6  (Designated Router)
r1#
```

Listing 8-25

```
r1#conf t
Enter configuration commands, one per line.  End with CNTL/Z.
r1(config)#int serial 1
r1(config-if)#ip ospf priority 100
r1(config-if)#^Z
r1#
```

Listing 8-26

Now we will check the other routers to verify that their routing tables and neighbor relationships have been formed correctly. All OSPF routes appear in R2's routing table, but there is no neighbor relationship with R6 (see Listing 8-32).

By doing a `show ip ospf interface token ring 1`, we can see one problem (see Listing 8-33). Token ring 1 is a passive interface for OSPF. This suppresses hellos, making neighbor formation impossible. We have already seen this principle with EIGRP, where the `passive-interface` command not only blocks outgoing updates but also com-

```
r2#conf t
Enter configuration commands, one per line.  End with CNTL/Z.
r2(config)#in serial 1.1
r2(config-subif)#ip ospf network broadcast
r2(config-subif)#^Z
r2#q

r6#conf t
Enter configuration commands, one per line.  End with CNTL/Z.
r6(config)#in se 0.1
r6(config-subif)#ip ospf network broadcast
r6(config-subif)#^Z
r6#
```

Listing 8-27

```
r1#sh ip osp in ser 1
Serial1 is up, line protocol is up
  Internet Address 172.16.33.1 255.255.255.224, Area 0
  Process ID 1, Router ID 172.16.254.1, Network Type BROADCAST, Cost: 64
  Transmit Delay is 1 sec, State DR, Priority 100
  Designated Router (ID) 172.16.254.1, Interface address 172.16.33.1
  Backup Designated router (ID) 172.16.254.6, Interface address 172.16.33.6
  Timer intervals configured, Hello 10, Dead 40, Wait 40, Retransmit 5
    Hello due in 0:00:05
  Neighbor Count is 2, Adjacent neighbor count is 2
    Adjacent with neighbor 172.16.254.2
    Adjacent with neighbor 172.16.254.6  (Backup Designated Router)
r1#sh ip osp nei

Neighbor ID     Pri   State           Dead Time   Address         Interface
172.16.254.2      1   FULL/DROTHER    0:00:32     172.16.33.2     Serial1
172.16.254.6      1   FULL/BDR        0:00:34     172.16.33.6     Serial1
r1#
```

Listing 8-28

pletely kills the process on that interface by disabling neighbor formation.

NOTE: *The* `passive-interface` *command completely kills the OSPF process on the interface to which it is applied.*

However, even after removing the `passive-interface` command, R2 still has not become a neighbor with R6 (see Listing 8-34).

```
r1#sh ip ro
Codes: C - connected, S - static, I - IGRP, R - RIP, M - mobile, B - BGP
       D - EIGRP, EX - EIGRP external, O - OSPF, IA - OSPF inter area
       E1 - OSPF external type 1, E2 - OSPF external type 2, E - EGP
       i - IS-IS, L1 - IS-IS level-1, L2 - IS-IS level-2, * - candidate default

Gateway of last resort is not set

     172.16.0.0 is variably subnetted, 4 subnets, 3 masks
C       172.16.131.0 255.255.255.240 is directly connected, TokenRing0
C       172.16.254.1 255.255.255.255 is directly connected, Loopback0
C       172.16.33.0 255.255.255.224 is directly connected, Serial1
O IA    172.16.65.0 255.255.255.224
           [110/70] via 172.16.33.2, 00:01:04, Serial1
           [110/70] via 172.16.33.6, 00:01:04, Serial1
r1#
```

Listing 8-29

Listing 8-30

```
r1>sh ip ospf int loop0
Loopback0 is up, line protocol is up
   OSPF not enabled on this interface
r1>sh ip ospf int tok 0
TokenRing0 is up, line protocol is up
   OSPF not enabled on this interface
```

Now check the R6 router (see Listing 8-35). It can be seen that the token ring 0 interface is configured as nonbroadcast, which explains why it will not form neighbors over this interface in the absence of statically defined neighbors. When the interface is returned to its default broadcast network type, it readily forms a neighbor relationship with R2. The reason that R2 becomes the DR, despite having a lower router ID, is because it became a broadcast network before R6 did.

When R2's routing table is checked, there is one interesting point to note: R6's loopback network has been learned over the frame-relay network (see Listing 8-36). The lower-cost path is over token ring 1. However, all loopback networks are in area 0. Hence R2, being an area border router, will learn about this route over an interface that is also in area 0, namely, the frame-relay interface. This particular example may not make a lot of sense from a design standpoint, but it is an excellent illustration of the hierarchical nature and rules of OSPF. This underscores the need to have a very good understanding of how OSPF routes in order to troubleshoot this type of a network.

Listing 8-31

```
r6#conf t
Enter configuration commands, one per line.  End with CNTL/Z.
r6(config)#router osp 1
r6(config-router)#net 172.16.254.0 0.0.0.255 area 0
r6(config-router)#^Z
r6#
r1>en
Password:
r1#conf t
Enter configuration commands, one per line.  End with CNTL/Z.
r1(config)#router osp 1
r1(config-router)#net 172.16.0.0 0.0.255.255 area 0
r1(config-router)#^Z
r1#172.16.33.2
Trying 172.16.33.2 ... Open

User Access Verification

Password:
r2>en
Password:
r2#conf t
Enter configuration commands, one per line.  End with CNTL/Z.
r2(config)#router osp 1
r2(config-router)#net 172.16.254.0 0.0.0.255 area 0
r2(config-router)#^Z
r2#
```

Now let's examine some of the other problems on the network. When R1's routing table is checked, it can be seen that the 150.10.22.0 RIP network does not appear there (See Listing 8-37). It should have been redistributed into OSPF by R2, and therefore, R1, like the other routers, should see it as an external OSPF route.

We know from R1's configuration that there are no inbound filters blocking this route, so the next step is to check R2's configuration for clues as to why the redistribution is not taking place (see Listing 8-38).

We see that R2 specifies a default metric of 100. This needs to be specified when redistributing RIP, since the hop count metric has to be translated into an OSPF cost.

CAUTION: *Always specify a metric, default or otherwise, when redistributing between two routing protocols that have a dissimilar metric type.*

If the metric is being dealt with, then what is the problem? The issue results from a configuration peculiarity that frequently causes problems.

```
r2#sh ip ro
Codes: C - connected, S - static, I - IGRP, R - RIP, M - mobile, B - BGP
       D - EIGRP, EX - EIGRP external, O - OSPF, IA - OSPF inter area
       E1 - OSPF external type 1, E2 - OSPF external type 2, E - EGP
       i - IS-IS, L1 - IS-IS level-1, L2 - IS-IS level-2, * - candidate default

Gateway of last resort is not set

     150.10.0.0 255.255.255.0 is subnetted, 1 subnets
C       150.10.22.0 is directly connected, TokenRing0
     172.16.0.0 is variably subnetted, 6 subnets, 3 masks
O       172.16.131.0 255.255.255.240
          [110/70] via 172.16.33.1, 00:05:29, Serial1.1
C       172.16.254.2 255.255.255.255 is directly connected, Loopback0
O       172.16.254.1 255.255.255.255
          [110/65] via 172.16.33.1, 00:05:29, Serial1.1
O       172.16.254.6 255.255.255.255
          [110/65] via 172.16.33.6, 00:05:29, Serial1.1
C       172.16.33.0 255.255.255.224 is directly connected, Serial1.1
C       172.16.65.0 255.255.255.224 is directly connected, TokenRing1
r2#

r2>sh ip ospf nei

Neighbor ID     Pri   State           Dead Time   Address         Interface
172.16.254.1    100   FULL/DR         0:00:38     172.16.33.1     Serial1.1
r2>
```

Listing 8-32

```
r2>sh ip os in tok 1
TokenRing1 is up, line protocol is up
  Internet Address 172.16.65.2 255.255.255.224, Area 2
  Process ID 1, Router ID 172.16.254.2, Network Type BROADCAST, Cost: 6
  Transmit Delay is 1 sec, State DR, Priority 1
  Designated Router (ID) 172.16.254.2, Interface address 172.16.65.2
  No backup designated router on this network
  Timer intervals configured, Hello 10, Dead 40, Wait 40, Retransmit 5
    No Hellos (Passive interface)
  Neighbor Count is 0, Adjacent neighbor count is 0
r2>
```

Listing 8-33

```
r2#conf t
Enter configuration commands, one per line.  End with CNTL/Z.
r2(config)#router ospf 1
r2(config-router)#no passive-int token 1
r2(config-router)#^Z
r2#sh ip os in tok 1
TokenRing1 is up, line protocol is up
  Internet Address 172.16.65.2 255.255.255.224, Area 2
  Process ID 1, Router ID 172.16.254.2, Network Type BROADCAST, Cost: 6
  Transmit Delay is 1 sec, State DR, Priority 1
  Designated Router (ID) 172.16.254.2, Interface address 172.16.65.2
  No backup designated router on this network
  Timer intervals configured, Hello 10, Dead 40, Wait 40, Retransmit 5
    Hello due in 0:00:05
  Neighbor Count is 0, Adjacent neighbor count is 0
r2#
```

Listing 8-34

When redistributing into OSPF, the keyword `subnets` must be included after the `redistribute <protocol>` statement. This is required so that those major networks which are subnetted will be redistributed. Without this keyword, only major networks that employ no subnetting will be redistributed into OSPF. Given that most networks are subnetted, the actual rationale behind the `subnets` keyword has always escaped me. But let's put it in and make this thing work (see Listing 8-39).

NOTE: *When redistributing into OSPF, don't forget the* `subnets` *keyword!*

Now the 150.10.22.0 route is displayed in the OSPF domain as an external type E2 route, which is what we would expect by default. Note that it has a metric of 100, the same external metric that was applied to it by R2. If R2 was configured to make this route type E1, then it would appear in R1's routing table with a higher cost because its metric would then also include the internal OPSF cost.

There is one final issue that must be verified on this network, namely, is the 172.16.65.0 subnet visible to R3 in the IGRP domain? (See Listing 8-40.)

We see that no OSPF routes have been redistributed into IGRP. When R6's configuration is checked, we find that no metric was specified for

```
r6>sh ip os n

Neighbor ID     Pri   State           Dead Time   Address         Interface
172.16.254.1    100   FULL/DR         0:00:36     172.16.33.1     Serial0.1
r6>sh ip ospf int to 0
TokenRing0 is up, line protocol is up
  Internet Address 172.16.65.6 255.255.255.224, Area 2
  Process ID 1, Router ID 172.16.254.6, Network Type NON_BROADCAST, Cost: 6
  Transmit Delay is 1 sec, State DR, Priority 1
  Designated Router (ID) 172.16.254.6, Interface address 172.16.65.6
  No backup designated router on this network
  Timer intervals configured, Hello 30, Dead 120, Wait 120, Retransmit 5
    Hello due in 0:00:11
  Neighbor Count is 0, Adjacent neighbor count is 0
r6>en
Password:
r6#conf t
Enter configuration commands, one per line.  End with CNTL/Z.
r6(config)#in to0
r6(config-if)#no ip ospf network non-broadcast
r6(config-if)#^Z
r6#sh ip os int to 0
TokenRing0 is up, line protocol is up
  Internet Address 172.16.65.6 255.255.255.224, Area 2
  Process ID 1, Router ID 172.16.254.6, Network Type BROADCAST, Cost: 6
  Transmit Delay is 1 sec, State BDR, Priority 1
  Designated Router (ID) 172.16.254.2, Interface address 172.16.65.2
  Backup Designated router (ID) 172.16.254.6, Interface address 172.16.65.6
  Timer intervals configured, Hello 10, Dead 40, Wait 40, Retransmit 5
    Hello due in 0:00:08
  Neighbor Count is 1, Adjacent neighbor count is 1
     Adjacent with neighbor 172.16.254.2  (Designated Router)
r6#sh ip osp n

Neighbor ID     Pri   State           Dead Time   Address         Interface
172.16.254.1    100   FULL/DR         0:00:38     172.16.33.1     Serial0.1
172.16.254.2      1   FULL/DR         0:00:39     172.16.65.2     TokenRing0
r6#
```

Listing 8-35

OSPF routes redistributed into IGRP, so the default metric was added as shown. Also, the 172.16.65.0 network uses a 27-bit mask, which IGRP will not accept because this network is using a 24-bit mask on R3.

Interarea summarization can be used to make the 172.16.65.0 appear as a 24-bit mask. The configuration is shown for R6 and is also done on R2, which are the two border routers.

```
r2#sh ip ro

Codes: C - connected, S - static, I - IGRP, R - RIP, M - mobile, B - BGP
       D - EIGRP, EX - EIGRP external, O - OSPF, IA - OSPF inter area
       E1 - OSPF external type 1, E2 - OSPF external type 2, E - EGP
       i - IS-IS, L1 - IS-IS level-1, L2 - IS-IS level-2, * - candidate default

Gateway of last resort is not set

     150.10.0.0 255.255.255.0 is subnetted, 1 subnets
C       150.10.22.0 is directly connected, TokenRing0
     172.16.0.0 is variably subnetted, 6 subnets, 3 masks
O       172.16.131.0 255.255.255.240
           [110/70] via 172.16.33.1, 00:00:51, Serial1.1
C       172.16.254.2 255.255.255.255 is directly connected, Loopback0
O       172.16.254.1 255.255.255.255
           [110/65] via 172.16.33.1, 00:00:51, Serial1.1
O       172.16.254.6 255.255.255.255
           [110/65] via 172.16.33.6, 00:00:17, Serial1.1
C       172.16.33.0 255.255.255.224 is directly connected, Serial1.1
C       172.16.65.0 255.255.255.224 is directly connected, TokenRing1
r2#
```

Listing 8-36

```
r1#sh ip ro
Codes: C - connected, S - static, I - IGRP, R - RIP, M - mobile, B - BGP
       D - EIGRP, EX - EIGRP external, O - OSPF, IA - OSPF inter area
       E1 - OSPF external type 1, E2 - OSPF external type 2, E - EGP
       i - IS-IS, L1 - IS-IS level-1, L2 - IS-IS level-2, * - candidate default

Gateway of last resort is not set

     172.16.0.0 is variably subnetted, 6 subnets, 3 masks
C       172.16.131.0 255.255.255.240 is directly connected, TokenRing0
O       172.16.254.2 255.255.255.255
           [110/65] via 172.16.33.2, 00:10:19, Serial1
C       172.16.254.1 255.255.255.255 is directly connected, Loopback0
O       172.16.254.6 255.255.255.255
           [110/65] via 172.16.33.6, 00:10:20, Serial1
C       172.16.33.0 255.255.255.224 is directly connected, Serial1
O IA    172.16.65.0 255.255.255.224
           [110/70] via 172.16.33.2, 00:03:09, Serial1
           [110/70] via 172.16.33.6, 00:03:09, Serial1
r1#
```

Listing 8-37

Listing 8-38

```
R2
!
router ospf 1
 redistribute rip
 network 172.16.33.0 0.0.0.255 area 0
 network 172.16.65.0 0.0.0.255 area 2
 network 172.16.254.0 0.0.0.255 area 0
 default-metric 100
!
router rip
 network 150.10.0.0
```

```
r2#conf t
Enter configuration commands, one per line.  End with CNTL/Z.
r2(config)#router osp 1
r2(config-router)#redistrib rip subnets
r2(config-router)#^Z
r2#cle ip ro *
r2#
r1#sh ip ro
Codes: C - connected, S - static, I - IGRP, R - RIP, M - mobile, B - BGP
       D - EIGRP, EX - EIGRP external, O - OSPF, IA - OSPF inter area
       E1 - OSPF external type 1, E2 - OSPF external type 2, E - EGP
       i - IS-IS, L1 - IS-IS level-1, L2 - IS-IS level-2, * - candidate default

Gateway of last resort is not set

     150.10.0.0 255.255.255.0 is subnetted, 1 subnets
O E2    150.10.22.0 [110/100] via 172.16.33.2, 00:00:11, Serial1
     172.16.0.0 is variably subnetted, 6 subnets, 3 masks
C       172.16.131.0 255.255.255.240 is directly connected, TokenRing0
O       172.16.254.2 255.255.255.255
           [110/65] via 172.16.33.2, 00:12:54, Serial1
C       172.16.254.1 255.255.255.255 is directly connected, Loopback0
O       172.16.254.6 255.255.255.255
           [110/65] via 172.16.33.6, 00:12:54, Serial1
C       172.16.33.0 255.255.255.224 is directly connected, Serial1
O IA    172.16.65.0 255.255.255.224
           [110/70] via 172.16.33.2, 00:05:42, Serial1
           [110/70] via 172.16.33.6, 00:05:42, Serial1
r1#
```

Listing 8-39

```
r3#sh ip ro
Codes: C - connected, S - static, I - IGRP, R - RIP, M - mobile, B - BGP
       D - EIGRP, EX - EIGRP external, O - OSPF, IA - OSPF inter area
       N1 - OSPF NSSA external type 1, N2 - OSPF NSSA external type 2
       E1 - OSPF external type 1, E2 - OSPF external type 2, E - EGP
       i - IS-IS, L1 - IS-IS level-1, L2 - IS-IS level-2, * - candidate default
       U - per-user static route, o - ODR

Gateway of last resort is not set

     133.10.0.0/24 is subnetted, 1 subnets
C       133.10.3.0 is directly connected, Ethernet2/0
     172.16.0.0/16 is variably subnetted, 2 subnets, 2 masks
C       172.16.254.3/32 is directly connected, Loopback0
C       172.16.1.0/24 is directly connected, Serial3/0
r3#
```

Listing 8-40

NOTE: *Interarea summarization can be used to enable the redistribution of VLSM subnets into a protocol that does not support VLSM.*

Now we will configure the interarea summarization and observe the results (see Listing 8-41).

By specifying a metric for the OSPF routes, two routes have been redistributed into IGRP: the 172.16.131.0/24 route and the 150.10.0.0 route, which originated in RIP and has now been summarized across the network boundary by IGRP (note that OSPF does *not* do any such automatic summarization).

But what about the 172.16.65.0 network? This should now be 24 bit and thus be accepted by IGRP. We will check R6's routing table for a clue as to why it is not being seen by R3 (see Listing 8-42).

The 172.16.65.0 network still only appears in R6's table as a directly connected 27-bit subnet, which is exactly what it is. *The router will not accept summary information for a network to which it is directly connected*. This makes perfectly good sense when you think about it. In technical terms, it can be explained by realizing that a connected network has an administrative distance of zero, as opposed to the OSPF distance of 110.

One way to make this work and further illustrate this OSPF routing principle is to remove the connected network by shutting down token ring 0. (In practice, a more realistic solution could be to readdress this token-ring segment.) (See Listing 8-43.)

```
R6#

router ospf 1
 network 172.16.33.0 0.0.0.255 area 0
 network 172.16.65.0 0.0.0.255 area 2
 network 172.16.254.0 0.0.0.255 area 0
!
router igrp 1
 redistribute ospf 1
 network 172.16.0.0
 default-metric 1500 10000 255 1 1500

r6(config)#router ospf 1
r6(config-router)#area 2 range 172.16.65.0 255.255.255.0
r6(config-router)#^Z
r6#

r3#sh ip ro
Codes: C - connected, S - static, I - IGRP, R - RIP, M - mobile, B - BGP
       D - EIGRP, EX - EIGRP external, O - OSPF, IA - OSPF inter area
       N1 - OSPF NSSA external type 1, N2 - OSPF NSSA external type 2
       E1 - OSPF external type 1, E2 - OSPF external type 2, E - EGP
       i - IS-IS, L1 - IS-IS level-1, L2 - IS-IS level-2, * - candidate default
       U - per-user static route, o - ODR

Gateway of last resort is not set

     133.10.0.0/24 is subnetted, 1 subnets
C       133.10.3.0 is directly connected, Ethernet2/0
I    150.10.0.0/16 [100/18666] via 172.16.1.6, 00:00:01, Serial3/0
     172.16.0.0/24 is subnetted, 2 subnets
I       172.16.131.0 [100/18666] via 172.16.1.6, 00:00:01, Serial3/0
C       172.16.1.0 is directly connected, Serial3/0
r3#
```

Listing 8-41

Now it can be observed that the 172.16.65.0 network is displayed in R3's routing table. The summarization that made this possible was done on the ABR. The route is then redistributed successfully into IGRP, appearing in R3's routing table. This, of course, now means that R3 would have to route to R2 all the way across the frame relay to access the 172.16.65.0 network. This example does underline the point that solutions to network problems are not always ideal. Sometimes there are so many constraints at play, both technical and practical, that tradeoffs have to be made. Often the final solution is not necessarily the solution that you sought initially.

A final note that I think is worth emphasizing is that in a real-life scenario hosts on the 172.16.65.0 network also would need a route back to

```
r6#sh ip ro
Codes: C - connected, S - static, I - IGRP, R - RIP, M - mobile, B - BGP
       D - EIGRP, EX - EIGRP external, O - OSPF, IA - OSPF inter area
       E1 - OSPF external type 1, E2 - OSPF external type 2, E - EGP
       i - IS-IS, L1 - IS-IS level-1, L2 - IS-IS level-2, * - candidate default

Gateway of last resort is not set

     150.10.0.0 255.255.255.0 is subnetted, 1 subnets
O E2    150.10.22.0 [110/100] via 172.16.65.2, 00:01:36, TokenRing0
     172.16.0.0 is variably subnetted, 9 subnets, 3 masks
O       172.16.131.0 255.255.255.0
           [110/206] via 172.16.33.1, 00:01:36, Serial0.1
O       172.16.254.2 255.255.255.255
           [110/265] via 172.16.33.1, 00:01:36, Serial0.1
O       172.16.254.1 255.255.255.255
           [110/201] via 172.16.33.1, 00:01:36, Serial0.1
C       172.16.254.6 255.255.255.255 is directly connected, Loopback0
O       172.16.33.1 255.255.255.255
           [110/200] via 172.16.33.1, 00:01:36, Serial0.1
C       172.16.33.0 255.255.255.224 is directly connected, Serial0.1
O       172.16.33.2 255.255.255.255
           [110/264] via 172.16.33.1, 00:01:36, Serial0.1
C       172.16.1.0 255.255.255.0 is directly connected, Serial1
C       172.16.65.0 255.255.255.224 is directly connected, TokenRing0
r6#
```

Listing 8-42

the IGRP domain. This could be achieved by redistributing IGRP into OSPF on R6.

Troubleshooting BGP

The Border Gateway Protocol (BGP) is a complex IP routing protocol that has a specialized application. It is used primarily for routing between different autonomous systems or routing domains. Typical niches for BGP are to be found with Internet service providers (ISPs) and very large corporate networks. Companies also frequently use BGP over connections to the computer networks of their business partner companies. The corporate merger culture of the 1990s also has fueled a more extensive use of BGP because it provides a good solution for routing between the networks of two recently merged corporations.

```
r6#conf t
Enter configuration commands, one per line.  End with CNTL/Z.
r6(config)#in to0
r6(config-if)#shut
r6(config-if)#^Z
r6#sh ip ro 172.16.65.0
Routing entry for 172.16.65.0 255.255.255.0
  Known via "ospf 1", distance 110, metric 270, type inter area
  Redistributing via ospf 1, igrp 1
  Advertised by igrp 1
  Last update from 172.16.33.1 on Serial0.1, 00:03:45 ago
  Routing Descriptor Blocks:
  * 172.16.33.1, from 172.16.254.2, 00:03:45 ago, via Serial0.1
      Route metric is 270, traffic share count is 1

r6#

r3>sh ip ro
Codes: C - connected, S - static, I - IGRP, R - RIP, M - mobile, B - BGP
       D - EIGRP, EX - EIGRP external, O - OSPF, IA - OSPF inter area
       N1 - OSPF NSSA external type 1, N2 - OSPF NSSA external type 2
       E1 - OSPF external type 1, E2 - OSPF external type 2, E - EGP
       i - IS-IS, L1 - IS-IS level-1, L2 - IS-IS level-2, * - candidate default
       U - per-user static route, o - ODR

Gateway of last resort is not set

     133.10.0.0/24 is subnetted, 1 subnets
C       133.10.3.0 is directly connected, Ethernet2/0
I    150.10.0.0/16 [100/18666] via 172.16.1.6, 00:01:13, Serial3/0
     172.16.0.0/24 is subnetted, 3 subnets
I       172.16.131.0 [100/18666] via 172.16.1.6, 00:01:13, Serial3/0
C       172.16.1.0 is directly connected, Serial3/0
I       172.16.65.0 [100/18666] via 172.16.1.6, 00:01:13, Serial3/0
r3>
```

Listing 8-43

BGP Characteristics

I will now discuss some characteristics of BGP that must be understood in order to correctly configure the protocol, spot configuration errors, and troubleshoot routing problems with BGP.

Neighbor Formation Neighbors in BGP are almost always statically defined, and their formation relies on the setting up of a TCP connection. The `show ip bgp neighbor` command is used to verify the status of a router's BGP neighbors (see Listing 8-44).

```
router bgp 35
 neighbor 172.16.254.3 remote-as 35

r5#sh ip bgp neigh
BGP neighbor is 172.16.254.3,  remote AS 35, internal link
  BGP version 4, remote router ID 172.16.254.3
  BGP state = Established, table version = 2, up for 0:02:24
  Last read 0:00:24, hold time is 180, keepalive interval is 60 seconds
  Minimum time between advertisement runs is 5 seconds
  Received 5 messages, 0 notifications, 0 in queue
  Sent 6 messages, 0 notifications, 0 in queue
  Connections established 1; dropped 0
Connection state is ESTAB, I/O status: 1, unread input bytes: 0
Local host: 130.10.254.5, Local port: 179
Foreign host: 172.16.254.3, Foreign port: 11012

Enqueued packets for retransmit: 0, input: 0, saved: 0

Event Timers (current time is 9617704):
Timer:        Retrans   TimeWait    AckHold    SendWnd  KeepAlive
Starts:             7          0          5          0          0
Wakeups:            0          0          0          0          0
Next:               0          0          0          0          0

iss: 3643886838  snduna: 3643886998  sndnxt: 3643886998     sndwnd:  16225
irs: 3057539614  rcvnxt: 3057539720  rcvwnd:       16279  delrcvwnd:    105

SRTT: 583 ms, RTTO: 4036 ms, RTV: 1435 ms, KRTT: 0 ms
minRTT: 4 ms, maxRTT: 396 ms, ACK hold: 300 ms
Flags: passive open, nagle, gen tcbs

Datagrams (max data segment is 536 bytes):
Rcvd: 11 (out of order: 0), with data: 5, total data bytes: 105
Sent: 7 (retransmit: 0), with data: 6, total data bytes: 159
r5#
```

Listing 8-44

The most pertinent data are to be found in the first few lines of this output. The single most important parameter is the BGP state. This state goes from *Idle* to *Active* to *Open* to *Established* as neighbor formation takes place. If the state is anything other than *Established*, then neighbor formation has not taken place. BGP neighbors tend to take a little longer to form than in the case of other routing protocols, which should be kept in mind when using the preceding command.

NOTE: *If the BGP state shows anything other than* Established, *the neighbor relationship has not been formed.*

Other parameters to note are the BGP version. BGP 4 is the latest version and is supported by default on Cisco routers. If a neighbor relationship is attempted with a router running version 3, then BGP will autonegotiate down to the lower version. The table version increments when there is a change in the BGP routing information. A persistently increasing table version could indicate an unstable network or a flapping route. The neighbor uptime is also useful in indicating such a problem. Note that the defined neighbor's IP address may vary from the neighbor's router ID. The BGP router ID is the highest IP address or loopback address on the box. In the preceding example, a loopback address is being used, so they are the same.

External BGP External BGP, or EBGP, is run between two different autonomous systems. Usually, EBGP neighbors are defined on directly connected networks. For example, in Figure 8-4, R6, which is in AS 62, defines R3 as an EBGP neighbor in AS 35 by specifying the address of its directly attached serial link (see Listing 8-45).

If it were desired to use the loopback interfaces on R3 and R6 to define the preceding neighbor relationship, the configuration would have to be altered as shown in Listing 8-46.

The `ebgp-multihop` option is required because R3's loopback interface is not a directly connected network for R6. The `update-source` option is required if anything other than the interface address of the net-

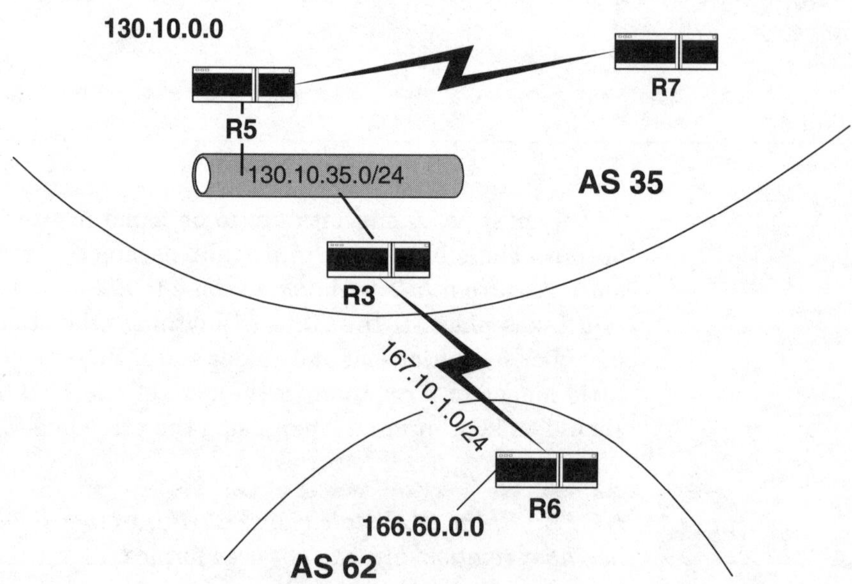

Figure 8-4
Network illustrating EBGP and IBGP.

Listing 8-45

```
router bgp 62
 neighbor 167.10.1.3 remote-as 35
!
!
line con 0
line aux 0
 transport input all

r6#
```

work that attaches to the remote router is being used for updates and neighbor definition. In this case, the network is the serial link; hence, when using loopback addresses, the `update-source` option is required. This option is also telling R6 that R3 is defining the neighbor relationship at the other end using R6's loopback address. A similar configuration using `ebgp-multihop` and `update-source` would have to be used with R3.

The BGP protocol ignores any BGP routes that have originated in its own AS. This is to ensure a loop-free topology. This principle becomes relevant when routing between multiple autonomous systems or if parallel paths exist between the same two autonomous systems. For example, consider a case where there is more than one path between two autonomous systems 10 and 20. BGP updates that originate in AS 10 are sent to AS 20 over the preferred path. These updates will then go back into AS 10 from AS 20 via the second path. BGP will discard these updates because they originated within AS 10.

Internal BGP Internal BGP, or IBGP, refers to a BGP process between neighbors that are in the same autonomous system. Referring again to Figure 8-4, R3 and R5 are running IBGP between them, with both routers being in AS 35. The configuration on R5 is shown in Listing 8-47.

Listing 8-46

```
router bgp 62
 neighbor 172.16.254.3 remote-as 35
 neighbor 172.16.254.3 update-source Loopback0
 neighbor 167.10.1.3 ebgp-multihop
!
!
line con 0
line aux 0
 transport input all

r6#
```

Listing 8-47

```
router bgp 35
 neighbor 172.16.254.3 remote-as 35
 neighbor 172.16.254.3 update-source Loopback0
!
!
!
line con 0
line aux 0
 transport input all
line vty 0 4
 password cisco
 login
!
end

r5#
```

Loopback addresses are also being used here, hence the need for the `update-source loopback0` option. The `multi-hop` option is not required because it is only relevant to EBGP.

I will now discuss some features and rules of IBGP that must be clearly understood to correctly configure and troubleshoot BGP networks.

- IBGP will not propagate routes that it learns from an IBGP neighbor onto any other IBGP neighbor. It will only send this routing information to EBGP neighbors. For this reason, if IBGP is being used extensively for routing within an autonomous system, it is important to maintain a full mesh of IBGP neighbors. For example, in Figure 8-4, if R5 were made an IBGP neighbor of R7, it would not propagate routing information that it learns from R7 onward to R3. Similarly, R5 would not propagate to R7 any BGP information that its learns from R3. Apart from full meshing, there is another way to resolve problems caused by this IBGP property. The concept of *route reflectors* causes this feature to be relaxed for the configured router-reflector clients. We will see a practical example of this type of scenario.
- If a router receives an update from an EBGP neighbor about a particular network, it will propagate that route to its IBGP neighbor with the same next hop. In other words, the next hop address is carried into IBGP and maintained. For example, in Figure 8-4, if R6 sends an update about 166.60.0.0 to R3, R3 will receive this route with a next hop address of 167.10.1.6. It will then advertise 166.60.0.0 to R5 with the same next hop of 167.10.1.6. This can create a problem if R5 does not have a route to 167.10.1.0/24.

- If there is no way of providing R5 with a route to 167.10.1.0, the other solution is to use the `next-hop-self` command. If the `next-hop-self` option is used as shown in Listing 8-48, R3 will now send all its BGP routes to R5 with a next hop of 172.16.254.3 (i.e., R3's own loopback address, because that neighbor definition between R3 and R5 happens to be using loopback addresses).

NOTE:

- *IBGP will not advertise routes learned from one IBGP neighbor onto a third IBGP neighbor.*
- *The next hop address associated with a route learned via EBGP is propagated though the IBGP domain without being altered.*

The `network` Command The `network` command in BGP is fundamentally different in its meaning and application to the `network` command in interior gateway IP routing protocols that we have studied so far. In those protocols, the `network` command is used to enable the routing protocol on interfaces that belong to that network.

In BGP, the `network` command is used to redistribute that network into the BGP process. In order for this to work correctly, the router must have learned about the network through an Interior Gateway Protocol (IGP), a static route, or as a directly connected network. For example:

```
route bgp 10
network 144.44.0.0
```

This configuration would, assuming the router already has an entry for 144.44.0.0 in its IP routing table, redistribute the 144.44.0.0 class B network into BGP 10. If it was only desired to redistribute a particular subnet such as 144.44.20.0, the mask option could be used as follows:

Listing 8-48

```
R3#

router bgp 35
 neighbor 130.10.254.5 remote-as 35
 neighbor 130.10.254.5 update-source Loopback0
 neighbor 130.10.254.5 next-hop-self
 neighbor 167.10.1.6 remote-as 62
```

```
router bgp 10
network 144.44.20.0 mask 255.255.255.0
```

In Figure 8-4, R5 has an Ethernet segment that belongs to the 130.10.0.0 network. R5 is configured to redistribute that 130.10.0.0 into BGP 35 using the `network` command. The BGP routing table for R5 will then indicate that the 130.10.0.0 network has originated locally by indicating a next hop of 0.0.0.0. This network is then propagated to the other routers participating in BGP. The BGP table is examined using the `show ip bgp` command (see Listing 8-49).

```
router bgp 35
 network 130.10.0.0
 neighbor 172.16.254.3 remote-as 35
 neighbor 172.16.254.3 update-source Loopback0
!
!
!
line con 0
line aux 0
 transport input all
line vty 0 4
 password cisco
 login
!
end

r5#

r5# sh ip bgp
BGP table version is 2, local router ID is 130.10.254.5
Status codes: s suppressed, d damped, h history, * valid, > best, i - internal
Origin codes: i - IGP, e - EGP, ? - incomplete

   Network          Next Hop            Metric LocPrf Weight Path
*> 130.10.0.0       0.0.0.0                  0         32768 i
r5#
r3#sh ip bgp
BGP table version is 2, local router ID is 172.16.254.3
Status codes: s suppressed, d damped, h history, * valid, > best, i - internal
Origin codes: i - IGP, e - EGP, ? - incomplete

   Network          Next Hop            Metric LocPrf Weight Path
*>i130.10.0.0       130.10.254.5             0    100      0 i
r3#
```

Listing 8-49

NOTE: The `network` *command has a different meaning in BGP than in any of the interior gateway protocols.*

BGP Attributes BGP attributes describe key features of the BGP and in particular how it performs path selection. Some attributes are termed *mandatory* because they provide essential descriptive information that is part of all BGP routing updates. Other attributes, such as the community attribute, are described as being *optional* because they provide a facility for influencing policy decisions.

AS-PATH As a BGP update passes through an autonomous system, that AS number gets appended to the update. If a router receives an update that originated from a distant AS and the update traversed through a number of autonomous systems before reaching the router in question, that router will have path information associated with the route, which tracks each of the intermediate autonomous systems. This is best illustrated by an example. In Figure 8-5, each of the routers distributes the network shown using the `network` command. The path information that router B would have to get to 130.1.0.0 would be (10 30); to get to 180.11.0.0, the path is (10). Similarly, for router C the path to 120.0.0.0 is (10 20), and to reach 180.11.0.0, the path is (10). What path information should router A have for the routes to 120.0.0.0 and the 130.1.0.0 network?

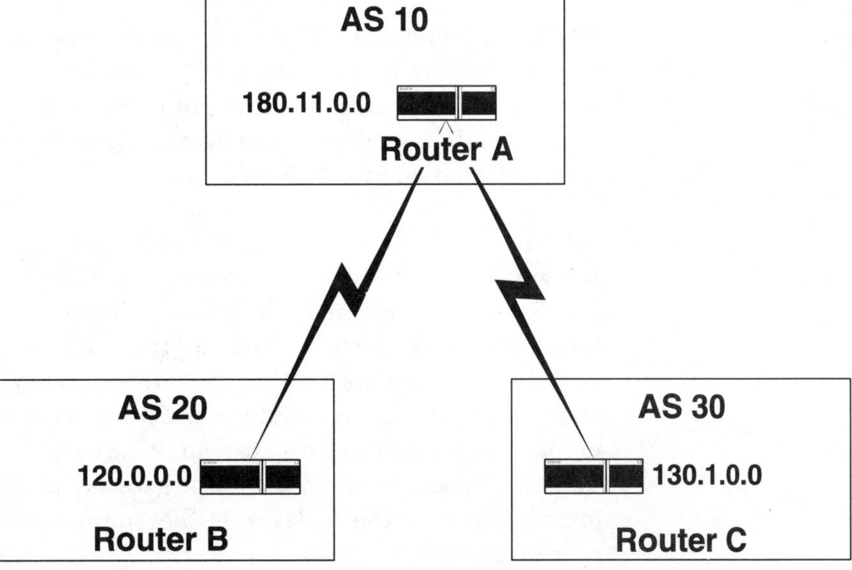

Figure 8-5
BGP *AS-path* example.

ORIGIN The *Origin* attribute is included in all BGP routing updates, and its purpose is to indicate the origin of the path information. It can have one of three values:

- *IGP / "i"*. This indicates that the network was redistributed from an interior gateway protocol into BGP using the `network` command or the `redistribute` command.
- *EGP / "e"*. The origin is EGP.
- *INCOMPLETE / "?"*. The origin is unknown. This can happen when a static route is redistributed into BGP using the `redistribute static` command.

NEXT-HOP We have already discussed this attribute. It is the IP address of the next hop associated with a BGP update. The fact that IBGP advertises the same next hop that it learns from EBGP potentially can cause problems with the downstream IBGP neighbor that has no route to that next hop. This issue will be illustrated by an example.

WEIGHT *Weight* is a Cisco-specified attribute. It influences path selection from a router when there is more than one route to the destination network. It is configurable on a per-neighbor basis but has no significance outside that router. Weights with higher numerical values are preferred. The default weight for a route that is originated by the local router is 32768, and it is zero for all other routes. The *Weight* attribute is never propagated between BGP neighbors.

LOCAL PREFERENCE The *Local preference* attribute is distributed between routers in the same AS. It is designed to influence the choice of a preferred exit point from the autonomous system. A higher value for this attribute is preferred—its default value is 100. The local preference is not distributed to EBGP neighbors.

METRIC The *Metric* attribute (also known as the Multi_ Exit_ Discriminator, or MED) is advertised to EBGP neighbors, and its purpose is to influence the path selection for entering the autonomous system from another AS. A lower metric value is preferred. The *Metric* attribute is distributed within an autonomous system in order to decide on the best path into the AS from which it was received. The metric is not propagated onto a third AS; instead, it is reset to its default value of zero. This is different from most interior gateway protocols, where the metric increments with the updates as they propagate throughout the entire routing domain.

In the network shown in Figure 8-6, R1 receives updates about the 152.16.0.0 network from two sources in AS 20 and from one source in AS 40. R1 will choose R2 as the next hop to 152.16.0.0 because R2 advertised the route with a lower metric than R3.

By default, neighboring EBGP routers will only compare metrics associated with a particular route if the updates come from the same AS. This is so because the *Metric* attribute is most fundamentally intended to set the best entry point into a particular AS. Sometimes, in order to execute certain routing policies, it may be desirable to have a router compare metrics for a route that it learns about from more than one AS. In this case, the `bgp always-compare-med` router configuration command is used.

In Figure 8-6, if R1 were configured with the `bgp always-compare-med` command it would choose R4 as the next hop to 152.16.0.0. Without enabling this command, R1 could not compare the R4 metric with that of R2. It could only choose R4 as the next hop to 152.16.0.0 if another attribute overrode the metric attribute. The hierarchy of the relative importance of BGP attributes is outlined in the section on BGP route selection.

COMMUNITY The *Community* attribute is a way to group a set of destinations so that a common policy can be applied to them. It is an optional attribute, which I am not going to discuss at length because of the intended broad scope of this book. The *Community* attribute is mainly used by ISPs to set routing policies. Here I will mention in passing three

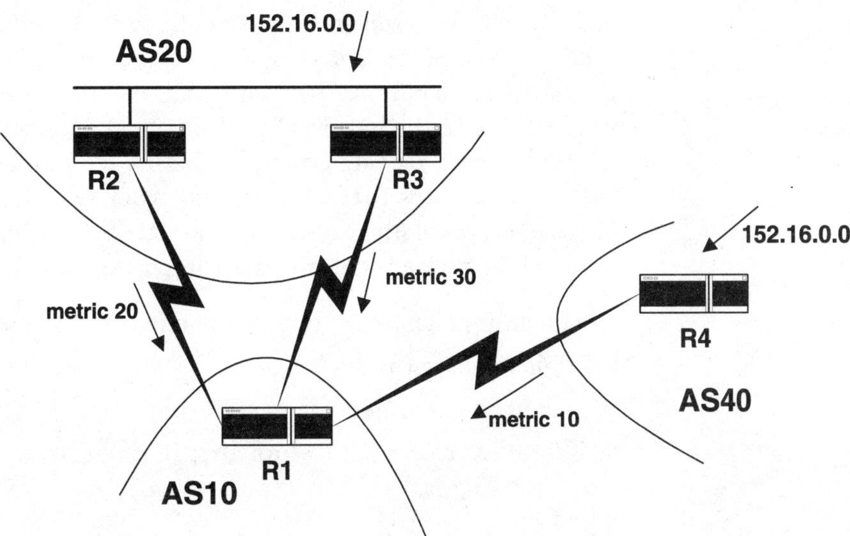

Figure 8-6 Demonstration of the BGP *Metric* attribute.

predefined communities that can be set in BGP routing updates to implement a particular policy.

- *No-export.* A route that is in this community should not be advertised to EBGP peers; i.e., it should not be exported beyond the AS.
- *No-advertise.* Marking a route as being in this community prevents it from being advertised further to any BGP peers (internal or external).
- *Internet.* Every router belongs to the Internet community. Therefore, this community places no restraints on an advertised route.

Synchronization The synchronization principle dictates that a BGP router will not advertise a route to its BGP neighbors until it learns about that route via IGP. Synchronization is enabled by default, and it is required in two scenarios:

- When BGP is transiting information from one autonomous system onto a third AS. If the intermediate AS advertises a BGP route to the third AS to which it does not yet have an IGP route, there is a possibility that packets will be dropped if a BGP router in the third AS attempts to access that route.
- When IBGP full meshing is not in place. Synchronization can be disabled if full meshing is in place because there is no need to wait for the route to be learned via IGP.

BGP Route Selection The BGP by default chooses one best path to a destination and propagates that path to its neighbors. It can be configured to forward packets over more than one path using the `maximum-paths` router configuration command, but this is not done commonly in practice due to the nature of BGP's typical applications.

Unlike other routing protocols, there are a number of different parameters or attributes that BGP can use when deciding route selection. The following is a sequenced list of the attributes that BGP uses for path selection beginning with the most important attributes:

- The path is ignored if the next hop is inaccessible.
- Highest weight is preferred.
- Highest local preference is preferred.
- Prefer a route that has originated from the router that is advertising it.

- Shortest AS path.
- Lowest origin code (IGP < EGP < INCOMPLETE).
- Lowest metric.
- External path is preferred to internal. The administrative distance for an EBGP route is 20; for an IBGP route, it is 200.
- If there are only internal paths and IGP synchronization is turned off, the path through the closest IGP neighbor is preferred.
- Choose the path through the router with the *lowest* BGP router ID.

BGP Show Commands

The following sample `show` commands relate to the network in Figure 8-7, which we will be studying later.

The `show ip protocol` command also can be applied to get basic summary information for the router's BGP configuration (see Listing 8-50). For R5, the following can be observed:

- No distribute lists, path filter lists, or route maps have been configured. The *Weight* attribute also has not been altered from its default behavior.
- The IGP synchronization default has been disabled.
- BGP uses automatic route summarization by default based on class. This default is in place.
- The only configured neighbor is 172.16.254.3—R3's loopback address.
- It is injecting 130.10.0.0 into BGP using the `network` command.
- How can it be deduced that the 172.16.254.3 neighbor is an IBGP neighbor in AS 35? The administrative distance for this source is 200, which is the default for IBGP.

We have already met the `show ip bgp neighbor` command, which is the way to check on the status of the router's neighbor relationship (see Listing 8-51).

The `show ip bgp` command examines the contents of the BGP table. You have also seen this before, but now you should be able to analyze the output in more detail. The following example (Listing 8-52) checks R3's BGP table. R3 is an IBGP peer of 130.10.254.5, which is R5's loopback address. R5 has originated 130.10.0.0 using the `network` command; hence the origin is IGP. The next hop is R5. The *Metric* and *Local prefer-*

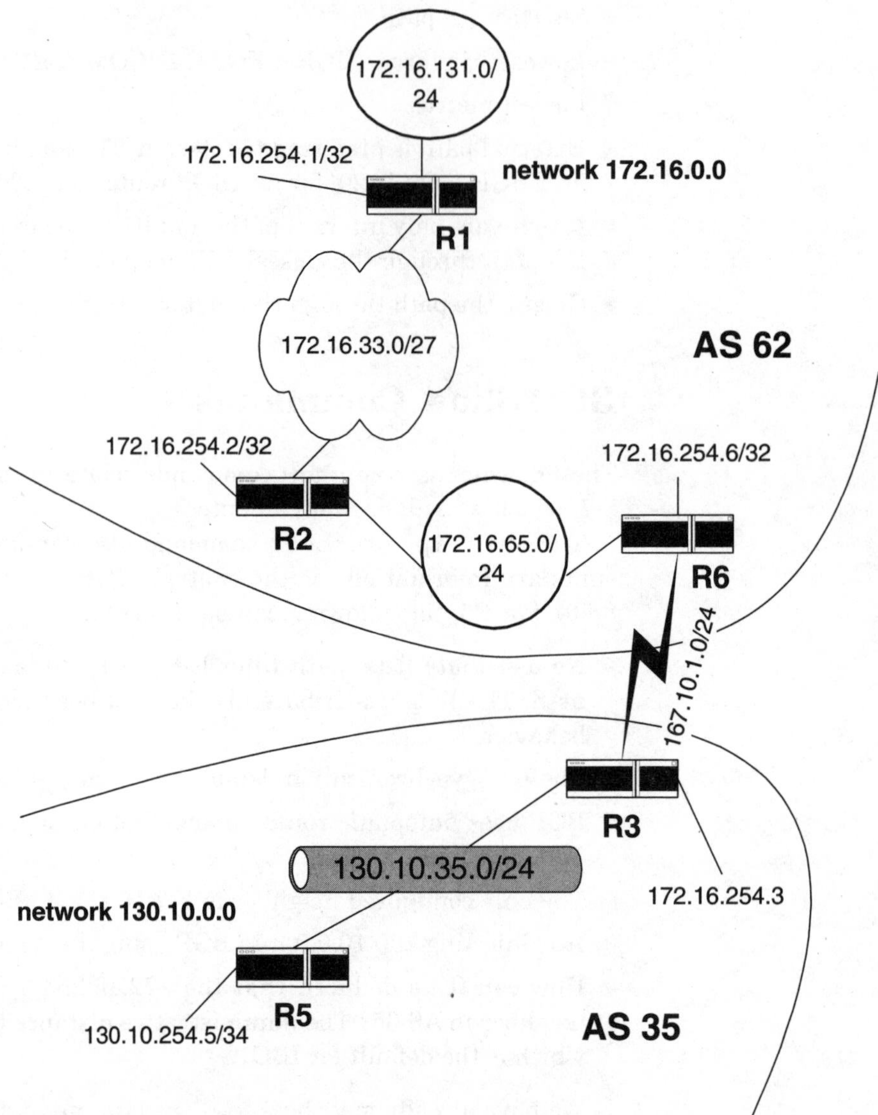

Figure 8-7 BGP troubleshooting scenario 1.

ence attributes are at their respective default values. Since the route did not originate from R3, the weight of zero is also a default value. The path shows up as "i," which means the route originated from IGP and was distributed into the same BGP AS that R3 is in; i.e., it is seen by R3 as an internal BGP route.

The `show ip route` command can be used to verify that the BGP-derived route has been placed in the IP routing table. Sometimes it is

```
r5#show ip protocol
Routing Protocol is "bgp 35"
  Sending updates every 60 seconds, next due in 0 seconds
  Outgoing update filter list for all interfaces is not set
  Incoming update filter list for all interfaces is not set
  IGP synchronization is disabled
  Automatic route summarization is enabled
  Neighbor(s):
    Address          FiltIn FiltOut DistIn DistOut Weight RouteMap
    172.16.254.3
  Routing for Networks:
    130.10.0.0
  Routing Information Sources:
    Gateway         Distance      Last Update
    172.16.254.3         200      0:01:26
  Distance: external 20 internal 200 local 200

r5#
```

Listing 8-50

necessary to disable synchronization to ensure that a BGP route appears in the IP routing table. By disabling synchronization, the router is forced to advertise the BGP route without waiting for an IGP update about that same route (see Listing 8-53).

After altering the BGP configuration on the router, the `clear ip bgp *` command can be used to reset the BGP neighbor connection. In recent Cisco IOS versions, BGP soft configuration is a feature that is intended to make it unnecessary to reset the BGP neighbors.

Debugging BGP

The `debug ip bgp` command can be used to investigate why neighbor formation is not taking place. In the output in Listing 8-54, the connection moves from the idle state to the active state; however, the neighbor does not become established. The connection could be getting refused because there is not an IGP route each way between the defined peers.

In the following output (Listing 8-55), the `debug ip bgp events` command is used to display the correct reestablishment of neighbors and resulting BGP updates after the BGP connections were reset on R3. The steps involved in establishing a neighbor relationship with 167.10.1.6 after resetting all the BGP neighbors are traced in bold print.

```
r5#sh ip bgp nei
BGP neighbor is 172.16.254.3,  remote AS 35, internal link
  BGP version 4, remote router ID 172.16.254.3
  BGP state = Established, table version = 2, up for 0:02:24
  Last read 0:00:24, hold time is 180, keepalive interval is 60 seconds
  Minimum time between advertisement runs is 5 seconds
  Received 5 messages, 0 notifications, 0 in queue
  Sent 6 messages, 0 notifications, 0 in queue
  Connections established 1; dropped 0
Connection state is ESTAB, I/O status: 1, unread input bytes: 0
Local host: 130.10.254.5, Local port: 179
Foreign host: 172.16.254.3, Foreign port: 11012

Enqueued packets for retransmit: 0, input: 0, saved: 0

Event Timers (current time is 9617704):
Timer:        Retrans   TimeWait   AckHold    SendWnd  KeepAlive
Starts:             7          0         5          0          0
Wakeups:            0          0         0          0          0
Next:               0          0         0          0          0

iss: 3643886838  snduna: 3643886998  sndnxt: 3643886998     sndwnd:  16225
irs: 3057539614  rcvnxt: 3057539720  rcvwnd:       16279  delrcvwnd:    105

SRTT: 583 ms, RTTO: 4036 ms, RTV: 1435 ms, KRTT: 0 ms
minRTT: 4 ms, maxRTT: 396 ms, ACK hold: 300 ms
Flags: passive open, nagle, gen tcbs

Datagrams (max data segment is 536 bytes):
Rcvd: 11 (out of order: 0), with data: 5, total data bytes: 105
Sent: 7 (retransmit: 0), with data: 6, total data bytes: 159
r5#
```

Listing 8-51

```
r3#sh ip bgp
BGP table version is 2, local router ID is 172.16.254.3
Status codes: s suppressed, d damped, h history, * valid, > best, i - internal
Origin codes: i - IGP, e - EGP, ? - incomplete

   Network          Next Hop            Metric LocPrf Weight Path
*>i130.10.0.0       130.10.254.5             0    100      0 i
r3#
```

Listing 8-52

```
r2#sh ip ro 130.10.0.0
Routing entry for 130.10.0.0 255.255.0.0
  Known via "bgp 62", distance 200, metric 0
  Tag 35, type internal
  Last update from 172.16.65.6 00:00:35 ago
  Routing Descriptor Blocks:
  * 172.16.65.6, from 172.16.65.6, 00:00:35 ago
      Route metric is 0, traffic share count is 1

r2#sh ip route
Codes: C - connected, S - static, I - IGRP, R - RIP, M - mobile, B - BGP
       D - EIGRP, EX - EIGRP external, O - OSPF, IA - OSPF inter area
       E1 - OSPF external type 1, E2 - OSPF external type 2, E - EGP
       i - IS-IS, L1 - IS-IS level-1, L2 - IS-IS level-2, * - candidate default

Gateway of last resort is not set

B    130.10.0.0 [200/0] via 172.16.65.6, 00:00:42
r2#
```

Listing 8-53

Listing 8-54

```
debug ip bgp

r5#
BGP: 172.16.254.3 open active, delay 8564ms
BGP: 172.16.254.3 open active, local address 130.10.35.5
BGP: 172.16.254.3 open failed: Connection refused by remote host
```

The other available BGP debug commands can be checked using the help facility (see Listing 8-56).

Troubleshooting Scenarios for BGP

The network shown in Figure 8-7 has a mixture of EBGP and IBGP. The goal is that BGP should distribute its routes across all routers, with R5 injecting 130.10.0.0 into BGP 35 and R1 injecting 172.16.0.0 into BGP 62 using the `network` command. At the moment, the routers have been configured, but no BGP neighbors have been formed. Only the relevant portions of the configurations will be shown (see Listing 8-57). Each router has a loopback address with a 32-bit mask, as indicated in Figure 8-7. The last octet of all addresses on the network again corresponds to the

```
r3#deb ip bgp events
BGP events debugging is on
r3#term mon
r3#cle ip bgp *
r3#
BGP: reset all neighbors
BGP: 130.10.254.5 went from Established to Idle
BGP: 167.10.1.6 went from Established to Idle
BGP: 130.10.254.5 went from Idle to Active
BGP: 167.10.1.6 went from Idle to Active
BGP: 130.10.254.5 went from Active to OpenSent
BGP: 130.10.254.5 went from OpenSent to OpenConfirm
BGP: 130.10.254.5 went from OpenConfirm to Established
BGP: 130.10.254.5 computing updates, neighbor version 0, table version 1, starting at
  0.0.0.0
BGP: 130.10.254.5 update run completed, ran for 0ms, neighbor version 0, start ver-
  sion 1, throttled to 1, check point net 0.0.0.0
BGP: 130.10.254.5 computing updates, neighbor version 1, table version 2, starting at
  0.0.0.0
BGP: 130.10.254.5 update run completed, ran for 0ms, neighbor version 1, start ver-
  sion 2, throttled to 2, check point net 0.0.0.0
BGP: 167.10.1.6 went from Active to OpenSent
BGP: 167.10.1.6 went from OpenSent to OpenConfirm
BGP: 167.10.1.6 went from OpenConfirm to Established
BGP: 167.10.1.6 computing updates, neighbor version 0, table version 2, starting at
  0.0.0.0
BGP: 167.10.1.6 update run completed, ran for 0ms, neighbor version 0, start version
  2, throttled to 2, check point net 0.0.0.0
BGP: 130.10.254.5 computing updates, neighbor version 2, table version 3, starting at
  0.0.0.0
BGP: 130.10.254.5 update run completed, ran for 0ms, neighbor version 2, start ver-
  sion 3, throttled to 3, check point net 0.0.0.0
BGP: 167.10.1.6 computing updates, neighbor version 2, table version 3, starting at
  0.0.0.0
BGP: 167.10.1.6 update run completed, ran for 0ms, neighbor version 2, start version
  3, throttled to 3, check point net 0.0.0.0
BGP: scanning routing tables
r3#
```

Listing 8-55

Listing 8-56

```
r3#deb ip bgp ?
  dampening   BGP dampening
  events      BGP events
  keepalives  BGP keepalives
  updates     BGP updates
  <cr>
```

```
r5#

router bgp 35
 neighbor 172.16.254.3 remote-as 35
!
!
!
line con 0
line aux 0
 transport input all
line vty 0 4
 password cisco
 login

r5#sh ip bgp nei
BGP neighbor is 172.16.254.3,  remote AS 35, internal link
  BGP version 4, remote router ID 0.0.0.0
  BGP state = Active, table version = 0
  Last read 0:00:04, hold time is 180, keepalive interval is 60 seconds
  Minimum time between advertisement runs is 5 seconds
  Received 0 messages, 0 notifications, 0 in queue
  Sent 0 messages, 0 notifications, 0 in queue
  Connections established 0; dropped 0
  No active TCP connection
r5#
```

Listing 8-57

router number. Note again that this is not an exercise in design; it is an exercise in configuration and troubleshooting for the purpose of illustrating the use of the troubleshooting tools.

IBGP is running between R3 and R5, and the routers use each other's loopback interfaces to define the neighbor relationships. Since R3 and R5 are in the same AS, there is no need for the `ebgp-multihop` option.

A neighbor relationship has not formed between R5 and R3. R3 does not have a route to R5's peer address (130.10.254.5). To correct this, we can bring the 130.10.0.0 network into OSPF area 0 on R5 and place both 130.10.0.0 and 172.16.0.0 into OSPF area 0 on R3; thus there is now IGP connectivity between the peers (see Listing 8-58).

After enabling OSPF, the IP connectivity can be verified by pinging the defined peers for the respective route. Even though this connectivity is now working, the neighbors still have not been established. This is so because we are using an address other than the closest address to define the peers; therefore, the `update-source` option must be used. Both R3 and R5 must be configured as shown in Listing 8-59.

```
r3#sh ip ro 130.10.254.5
% Subnet not in table
r3#

r5#debug ip bgp

r5#
BGP: 172.16.254.3 open active, delay 8564ms
BGP: 172.16.254.3 open active, local address 130.10.35.5
BGP: 172.16.254.3 open failed: Connection refused by remote host

r3#sh ip bgp n
BGP neighbor is 130.10.254.5,  remote AS 35, internal link
  BGP version 4, remote router ID 0.0.0.0
  BGP state = Active, table version = 0
  Last read 00:00:27, hold time is 180, keepalive interval is 60 seconds
  Minimum time between advertisement runs is 5 seconds
  Received 0 messages, 0 notifications, 0 in queue
  Sent 0 messages, 0 notifications, 0 in queue
  Connections established 0; dropped 0
  No active TCP connection
r3#
r3#ping 130.10.254.5

Type escape sequence to abort.
Sending 5, 100-byte ICMP Echos to 130.10.254.5, timeout is 2 seconds:
!!!!!
Success rate is 100 percent (5/5), round-trip min/avg/max = 1/3/4 ms
r3#
```

Listing 8-58

The neighbors have now been established. It can be observed that R5 is redistributing the 130.10.0.0 network into BGP. R3 sees the network with a next hop of 130.10.254.5 as expected (see Listing 8-60).

However, if R3's IP routing table is checked (see Listing 8-61), the 130.10.0.0 network does not show up as a BGP-derived route. This is so because synchronization is enabled by default. R3 has an IGP route for 130.10.254.5/32, but it does not have an IGP route for 130.10.0.0/16, the route that BGP is distributing. Therefore, R3 will not advertise the 130.10.0.0/16 network. Since AS 35 is not transiting between two other autonomous systems, synchronization can be turned off. When this is done, R3 now displays 130.10.0.0/16 as a BGP route.

R3 also has an EBGP neighbor relationship defined with R6. Each router to define the relationship uses the serial link subnet 167.10.1.0/24 that connects R6 to R3. Hence the configuration is straightforward. The output in Listing 8-62 verifies that R6 sees the neighbor as established.

```
r5#
!
router bgp 35
 network 130.10.0.0
 neighbor 172.16.254.3 remote-as 35
 neighbor 172.16.254.3 update-source Loopback0
!
!
!
line con 0
line aux 0
 transport input all
line vty 0 4
 password cisco
 login
!
end

r5#

r5#sh ip bgp nei
BGP neighbor is 172.16.254.3,  remote AS 35, internal link
  BGP version 4, remote router ID 172.16.254.3
  BGP state = Established, table version = 2, up for 0:02:24
  Last read 0:00:24, hold time is 180, keepalive interval is 60 seconds
  Minimum time between advertisement runs is 5 seconds
  Received 5 messages, 0 notifications, 0 in queue
  Sent 6 messages, 0 notifications, 0 in queue
  Connections established 1; dropped 0
Connection state is ESTAB, I/O status: 1, unread input bytes: 0
Local host: 130.10.254.5, Local port: 179
Foreign host: 172.16.254.3, Foreign port: 11012

Enqueued packets for retransmit: 0, input: 0, saved: 0

Event Timers (current time is 9617704):
Timer:        Retrans   TimeWait    AckHold    SendWnd  KeepAlive
Starts:             7          0          5          0          0
Wakeups:            0          0          0          0          0
Next:               0          0          0          0          0

iss: 3643886838  snduna: 3643886998  sndnxt: 3643886998     sndwnd:  16225
irs: 3057539614  rcvnxt: 3057539720  rcvwnd:      16279  delrcvwnd:    105

SRTT: 583 ms, RTTO: 4036 ms, RTV: 1435 ms, KRTT: 0 ms
minRTT: 4 ms, maxRTT: 396 ms, ACK hold: 300 ms
Flags: passive open, nagle, gen tcbs

Datagrams (max data segment is 536 bytes):
Rcvd: 11 (out of order: 0), with data: 5, total data bytes: 105
Sent: 7 (retransmit: 0), with data: 6, total data bytes: 159
r5#
```

Listing 8-59

```
r5# sh ip bgp
BGP table version is 2, local router ID is 130.10.254.5
Status codes: s suppressed, d damped, h history, * valid, > best, i - internal
Origin codes: i - IGP, e - EGP, ? - incomplete

   Network          Next Hop            Metric LocPrf Weight Path
*> 130.10.0.0       0.0.0.0                  0         32768 i
r5#

r3#sh ip bgp
BGP table version is 2, local router ID is 172.16.254.3
Status codes: s suppressed, d damped, h history, * valid, > best, i - internal
Origin codes: i - IGP, e - EGP, ? - incomplete

   Network          Next Hop            Metric LocPrf Weight Path
*>i130.10.0.0       130.10.254.5             0    100      0 i
r3#
```

Listing 8-60

It also learns about the 130.10.0.0 route with a next hop of R3, and it places the route in its routing table.

Note that the link type is external for this neighbor relationship. This verifies that R3 and R6 are EBGP neighbors with R6 in AS 62. In R6's BGP table, the path to the 130.10.0.0 network is shown correctly as going through AS 35. In the routing table shown in Listing 8-63, it is also worth noticing that the 130.10.0.0 route has an administrative distance of 20 because it was learned over EBGP. R3 shows the same route with a distance of 200, since it learned the route using IBGP.

R6 is also an IBGP neighbor of R2. However, when R2's routing table is checked, the 130.10.0.0 BGP route is not there. Why is that?

OSPF is not enabled across the 167.10.1.0 serial link; this is evident because R6 is not learning any OSPF routes across the serial 1 interface. The result of this is that R6 has no way of learning about 130.10.0.0 over IGP. Hence the synchronization principle dictates that R6 will not advertise this route to R2. We will disable synchronization on R6 and R2 to ensure that BGP routes propagate through AS 62 (see Listing 8-64).

The 130.10.0.0 route is propagated to R2, but it is not in the IP routing table. Also, R6 has advertised it with a next hop of 167.10.1.3 (remember that the EBGP next hop gets carried into IBGP). R6 has no route to 167.10.1.3; hence it will not put the 130.10.0.0 network in its routing table. Without enabling R2 to learn an IGP route to 167.10.1.3, the `next-hop-self` command can be used to manipulate the next hop that R6 advertises to R2. With the configuration shown in Listing 8-65,

```
r3#sh ip ro
Codes: C - connected, S - static, I - IGRP, R - RIP, M - mobile, B - BGP
       D - EIGRP, EX - EIGRP external, O - OSPF, IA - OSPF inter area
       N1 - OSPF NSSA external type 1, N2 - OSPF NSSA external type 2
       E1 - OSPF external type 1, E2 - OSPF external type 2, E - EGP
       i - IS-IS, L1 - IS-IS level-1, L2 - IS-IS level-2, * - candidate default
       U - per-user static route, o - ODR

Gateway of last resort is not set

     130.10.0.0/16 is variably subnetted, 3 subnets, 3 masks
O       130.10.254.5/32 [110/11] via 130.10.35.5, 00:26:03, Ethernet2/0
C       130.10.35.0/24 is directly connected, Ethernet2/0
     167.10.0.0/24 is subnetted, 1 subnets
C       167.10.1.0 is directly connected, Serial3/0
     172.16.0.0/32 is subnetted, 1 subnets
C       172.16.254.3 is directly connected, Loopback0
r3#

R3#

router bgp 35
 no synchronization
 neighbor 130.10.254.5 remote-as 35
 neighbor 130.10.254.5 update-source Loopback0
 neighbor 167.10.1.6 remote-as 62
!
no ip classless

r3#sh ip ro
Codes: C - connected, S - static, I - IGRP, R - RIP, M - mobile, B - BGP
       D - EIGRP, EX - EIGRP external, O - OSPF, IA - OSPF inter area
       N1 - OSPF NSSA external type 1, N2 - OSPF NSSA external type 2
       E1 - OSPF external type 1, E2 - OSPF external type 2, E - EGP
       i - IS-IS, L1 - IS-IS level-1, L2 - IS-IS level-2, * - candidate default
       U - per-user static route, o - ODR

Gateway of last resort is not set

     130.10.0.0/16 is variably subnetted, 3 subnets, 3 masks
O       130.10.254.5/32 [110/11] via 130.10.35.5, 00:26:03, Ethernet2/0
B       130.10.0.0/16 [200/0] via 130.10.254.5, 00:01:45
C       130.10.35.0/24 is directly connected, Ethernet2/0
     167.10.0.0/24 is subnetted, 1 subnets
C       167.10.1.0 is directly connected, Serial3/0
     172.16.0.0/32 is subnetted, 1 subnets
C       172.16.254.3 is directly connected, Loopback0
r3#
```

Listing 8-61

```
r6>sh ip bgp nei
BGP neighbor is 167.10.1.3,  remote AS 35, external link
  BGP version 4, remote router ID 172.16.254.3
  BGP state = Established, table version = 1, up for 0:02:18
  Last read 0:00:18, hold time is 180, keepalive interval is 60 seconds
  Minimum time between advertisement runs is 30 seconds
  Received 5 messages, 0 notifications, 0 in queue
  Sent 5 messages, 0 notifications, 0 in queue
  Connections established 1; dropped 0
Connection state is ESTAB, I/O status: 1, unread input bytes: 0
Local host: 167.10.1.6, Local port: 11005
Foreign host: 167.10.1.3, Foreign port: 179

r6>
```

Listing 8-62

```
r6>sh ip bgp
BGP table version is 5, local router ID is 172.16.254.6
Status codes: s suppressed, d damped, h history, * valid, > best, i - internal
Origin codes: i - IGP, e - EGP, ? - incomplete

   Network          Next Hop          Metric LocPrf Weight Path
*> 130.10.0.0       167.10.1.3                           0 35 i
r6>
r6>sh ip ro
Codes: C - connected, S - static, I - IGRP, R - RIP, M - mobile, B - BGP
       D - EIGRP, EX - EIGRP external, O - OSPF, IA - OSPF inter area
       E1 - OSPF external type 1, E2 - OSPF external type 2, E - EGP
       i - IS-IS, L1 - IS-IS level-1, L2 - IS-IS level-2, * - candidate default

Gateway of last resort is not set

B    130.10.0.0 [20/0] via 167.10.1.3, 00:04:21
     167.10.0.0 255.255.255.0 is subnetted, 1 subnets
C       167.10.1.0 is directly connected, Serial1
     172.16.0.0 is variably subnetted, 6 subnets, 3 masks
O       172.16.254.2 255.255.255.255
          [110/7] via 172.16.65.2, 00:27:43, TokenRing0
C       172.16.254.6 255.255.255.255 is directly connected, Loopback0
C       172.16.65.0 255.255.255.0 is directly connected, TokenRing0
r6>
```

Listing 8-63

Listing 8-64

```
r6#

router bgp 62
 no synchronization
 neighbor 167.10.1.3 remote-as 35
 neighbor 172.16.65.2 remote-as 62
!
!
!
line con 0
line aux 0
 transport input all

r6#

r2#

router bgp 62
 no synchronization
 neighbor 172.16.65.6 remote-as 62
!
!

r2#sh ip bgp
BGP table version is 1, local router ID is 172.16.254.2
Status codes: s suppressed, d damped, h history, * valid, > best,
  i - internal
Origin codes: i - IGP, e - EGP, ? - incomplete
   Network          Next Hop            Metric LocPrf Weight Path
* i130.10.0.0       167.10.1.3                    100      0 35 i
r2#sh ip ro 130.10.0.0
% Network not in table
r2#sh ip ro 167.10.1.3
% Network not in table
r2#
```

R6 will advertise all routes to R2 with a next hop of 172.16.65.6 (i.e., R6 itself).

***NOTE**: The behavior of the* Next-hop *attribute in IBGP can be manipulated using* `next-hop-self`.

Thus, by manipulating the *Next-hop* attribute on R6, R2's problem was solved. R2 in turn has an IBGP relationship with R1. The neighbor is established, but R1 has not learned any BGP routes from R2. This is evidenced by the blank response to the `show ip bgp` command.

The reason for this is another fundamental principle of IBGP. R2 will not propagate any routes that it learns over IBGP from R6 to another

```
r6#conf t
Enter configuration commands, one per line.  End with CNTL/Z.
r6(config)#router bgp 62
r6(config-router)#nei 172.16.65.2 next-hop-self
r6(config-router)#^Z
r6#cle ip bgp *

r2#cle ip bgp *
r2#sh ip bgp
BGP table version is 2, local router ID is 172.16.254.2
Status codes: s suppressed, d damped, h history, * valid, > best, i - internal
Origin codes: i - IGP, e - EGP, ? - incomplete

   Network          Next Hop            Metric LocPrf Weight Path
*>i130.10.0.0       172.16.65.6                   100      0 35 i
r2#sh ip ro 130.10.0.0
Routing entry for 130.10.0.0 255.255.0.0
  Known via "bgp 62", distance 200, metric 0
  Tag 35, type internal
  Last update from 172.16.65.6 00:00:35 ago
  Routing Descriptor Blocks:
  * 172.16.65.6, from 172.16.65.6, 00:00:35 ago
      Route metric is 0, traffic share count is 1

r2#sh ip ro
Codes: C - connected, S - static, I - IGRP, R - RIP, M - mobile, B - BGP
       D - EIGRP, EX - EIGRP external, O - OSPF, IA - OSPF inter area
       E1 - OSPF external type 1, E2 - OSPF external type 2, E - EGP
       i - IS-IS, L1 - IS-IS level-1, L2 - IS-IS level-2, * - candidate default

Gateway of last resort is not set

B    130.10.0.0 [200/0] via 172.16.65.6, 00:00:42
     172.16.0.0 is variably subnetted, 6 subnets, 3 masks
O       172.16.131.0 255.255.255.0
           [110/70] via 172.16.33.1, 00:53:54, Serial1.1
C       172.16.254.2 255.255.255.255 is directly connected, Loopback0
O       172.16.254.1 255.255.255.255
           [110/65] via 172.16.33.1, 00:53:54, Serial1.1
O       172.16.254.6 255.255.255.255
           [110/7] via 172.16.65.6, 00:53:54, TokenRing1
C       172.16.33.0 255.255.255.224 is directly connected, Serial1.1
C       172.16.65.0 255.255.255.0 is directly connected, TokenRing1
r2#
```

Listing 8-65

IBGP neighbor, namely, R1. If R1 were an EBGP neighbor, it *would* see the 130.10.0.0 route. The solution is to define R1 as a route-reflector client of R2. This enables an exception of this IBGP principle to be made for R1 (see Listing 8-66).

```
r1#sh ip bgp n
BGP neighbor is 172.16.33.2,  remote AS 62, internal link
  BGP version 4, remote router ID 172.16.254.2
  BGP state = Established, table version = 1, up for 0:00:28
  Last read 0:00:28, hold time is 180, keepalive interval is 60 seconds
  Minimum time between advertisement runs is 5 seconds
  Received 3 messages, 0 notifications, 0 in queue
  Sent 3 messages, 0 notifications, 0 in queue
  Connections established 1; dropped 0

r1#
r1#sh ip bgp
r1#

r2#

router bgp 62
 no synchronization
 neighbor 172.16.33.1 remote-as 62
 neighbor 172.16.33.1 route-reflector-client
 neighbor 172.16.65.6 remote-as 62
!
!

r2#

r1>sh ip bgp
BGP table version is 2, local router ID is 172.16.254.1
Status codes: s suppressed, d damped, h history, * valid, > best, i - internal
Origin codes: i - IGP, e - EGP, ? - incomplete

   Network          Next Hop            Metric LocPrf Weight Path
*>i130.10.0.0       172.16.65.6                   100      0 35 i
r1>ping 172.16.65.6
Type escape sequence to abort.
Sending 5, 100-byte ICMP Echos to 172.16.65.6, timeout is 2 seconds:
!!!!!
Success rate is 100 percent (5/5), round-trip min/avg/max = 72/78/104 ms
r1>sh ip ro 130.10.0.0
Routing entry for 130.10.0.0 255.255.0.0
  Known via "bgp 62", distance 200, metric 0
  Tag 35, type internal
  Last update from 172.16.65.6 00:00:43 ago
  Routing Descriptor Blocks:
  * 172.16.65.6, from 172.16.33.2, 00:00:43 ago
      Route metric is 0, traffic share count is 1

r1>
```

Listing 8-66

Note that the next hop is still preserved as being R6, as expected. This is not a problem because R2 and R1 are fully participating together in OSPF, as verified by R2's routing table, which shows R1's loopback address as an OSPF-derived route. Hence R1 has a route to the next hop 172.16.65.6 and will therefore put the 130.10.0.0 network in its IP routing table.

NOTE: *Route reflectors can be used to facilitate route propagation within IBGP.*

A second goal for this network is that R1 should inject 172.16.0.0 into BGP, and this route should propagate back to R5 as an EBGP route (see Listing 8-67).

The 172.16.0.0 network is displayed in R1's BGP table with a next hop of 0.0.0.0 and a weight of 32768. This is consistent with a route that has been distributed into BGP by that router.

It can be observed that the route is visible in R2's BGP table and also propagates onto R6 with the same next hop being preserved. Before moving on, this gives me an opportunity to further generalize a principle that I have already presented. We have seen that IBGP preserves the next hop for routes learned via EBGP. Now we see that it also preserves the

```
r1#

router bgp 62
 no synchronization
 network 172.16.0.0
 neighbor 172.16.33.2 remote-as 62
!
!
!

r1#sh ip bgp
BGP table version is 3, local router ID is 172.16.254.1
Status codes: s suppressed, d damped, h history, * valid, > best, i - internal
Origin codes: i - IGP, e - EGP, ? - incomplete

   Network          Next Hop            Metric LocPrf Weight Path
*>i130.10.0.0       172.16.65.6                   100      0 35 i
*> 172.16.0.0       0.0.0.0                  0         32768 i
r1#
```

Listing 8-67

next hop for any route being distributed among IBGP speakers. This is something that is only noticeable if route reflectors are being used; otherwise, the principle never gets tested, because IBGP does not propagate routes to a third IBGP router.

This leads us to the next question. Why did R2 propagate the 172.16.0.0 network to R6? Normally, you would expect to have to configure R6 as a route-reflector client of R2 to achieve this. This demonstrates another principle of operation for router reflectors that is not usually documented. The typical operation of router reflectors is that if the best path to a destination is a nonclient, then this route should be reflected to clients. The converse is also true—if the best path is through a client (such as R1), then the route reflector will reflect this path to nonclients such as R6. Hence R2 propagates the route to R6. I found this result surprising, so I decided to verify it in the laboratory. I removed the R2-R1 route-reflector relationship, and the 172.16.0.0 route then disappeared from R6's BGP table (see Listing 8-68).

All routers are advertising the 172.16.0.0 BGP route because synchronization already has been disabled on each router. Now we can verify that R3 sees the 172.16.0.0 network with a path of AS 62 and an EBGP next hop of 167.10.1.6. This is correct because the IBGP next hop does *not* get carried into EBGP routes (see Listing 8-69).

Now we run into trouble with R5. The 172.16.0.0 route is carried into IBGP with a next hop of 167.10.1.6. Since OSPF is not running on this segment, R5 has no route to this subnet and hence will not place the 172.16.0.0 BGP route in its IP routing table (see Listing 8-70).

Like all these next-hop problems, this can be solved two ways: using `next-hop-self` or providing an IGP route to the advertised next hop. First, we will look at our, by now, old friend, the `next-hop-self` command. This is configured on R3 as shown in Listing 8-71. It can then be seen that R5 receives the 172.16.0.0 route with a next hop of 172.16.254.3 from R3. R5 does have an OSPF route to this next hop, so it happily places the network in its IP routing table.

The other solution would be to remove the `next-hop-self` command on R3 and give R5 a route to 167.10.1.0 by including this network in the OSPF process on R3. Now R3 sees the 167.10.1.6 as an OSPF-derived route, and all is well (see Listing 8-72).

The final BGP troubleshooting scenario that we will examine concerns the network shown in Figure 8-8. The are two paths between AS 21 and AS 43. R1 will be injecting 130.11.0.0 into BGP 21, and R4 will be distributing 143.10.0.0 into BGP 43. There are two particular design requirements that need to be fulfilled, namely:

```
r2#sh ip bgp
BGP table version is 7, local router ID is 172.16.254.2
Status codes: s suppressed, d damped, h history, * valid, > best, i - internal
Origin codes: i - IGP, e - EGP, ? - incomplete

   Network          Next Hop            Metric LocPrf Weight Path
*>i130.10.0.0       172.16.65.6                   100      0 35 i
*>i172.16.0.0       172.16.33.1              0    100      0 i
r2#q

r6#sh ip bgp
BGP table version is 7, local router ID is 172.16.254.6
Status codes: s suppressed, d damped, h history, * valid, > best, i - internal
Origin codes: i - IGP, e - EGP, ? - incomplete

   Network          Next Hop            Metric LocPrf Weight Path
*> 130.10.0.0       167.10.1.3                             0 35 i
*>i172.16.0.0       172.16.33.1              0    100      0 i
r6#sh ip ro 172.16.0.0
Routing entry for 172.16.0.0 255.255.0.0, 7 known subnets
  Attached (3 connections)
  Variably subnetted with 4 masks
  Redistributing via ospf 1

O       172.16.131.0 255.255.255.0
           [110/25] via 172.16.33.1, 00:40:25, TokenRing0
O       172.16.254.2 255.255.255.255
           [110/7] via 172.16.65.2, 00:40:25, TokenRing0
O       172.16.254.1 255.255.255.255
           [110/25] via 172.16.33.1, 00:40:25, TokenRing0
C       172.16.254.6 255.255.255.255 is directly connected, Loopback0
B       172.16.0.0 255.255.0.0 [200/0] via 172.16.33.1, 00:00:45
C       172.16.65.0 255.255.255.0 is directly connected, TokenRing0
r6#
```

Listing 8-68

- R4 should choose R2 as its entry point into AS 21 for the 130.11.0.0 network. The *Metric* attribute is being used to manipulate the routing, so R4 sees a lower metric from R2 than R1. The problem is that R4 is still choosing R1 as its next hop for 130.11.0.0.
- R1 should be the exit point from AS 21, but traceroute analysis is showing that R2 is the preferred exit point from this autonomous system.

With the aid of the configurations, the routing tables, and the Cisco IOS troubleshooting tools, let us now resolve these two problems. (See Listing 8-73.)

```
r3>sh ip bgp
BGP table version is 8, local router ID is 172.16.254.3
Status codes: s suppressed, d damped, h history, * valid, > best, i - internal
Origin codes: i - IGP, e - EGP, ? - incomplete

   Network          Next Hop            Metric LocPrf Weight Path
*>i130.10.0.0       130.10.254.5             0    100      0 i
*> 172.16.0.0       167.10.1.6                             0 62 i
r3>
r3>sh ip ro
Codes: C - connected, S - static, I - IGRP, R - RIP, M - mobile, B - BGP
       D - EIGRP, EX - EIGRP external, O - OSPF, IA - OSPF inter area
       N1 - OSPF NSSA external type 1, N2 - OSPF NSSA external type 2
       E1 - OSPF external type 1, E2 - OSPF external type 2, E - EGP
       i - IS-IS, L1 - IS-IS level-1, L2 - IS-IS level-2, * - candidate default
       U - per-user static route, o - ODR

Gateway of last resort is not set

     130.10.0.0/16 is variably subnetted, 3 subnets, 3 masks
O       130.10.254.5/32 [110/11] via 130.10.35.5, 00:43:18, Ethernet2/0
B       130.10.0.0/16 [200/0] via 130.10.254.5, 00:40:44
C       130.10.35.0/24 is directly connected, Ethernet2/0
     167.10.0.0/24 is subnetted, 1 subnets
C       167.10.1.0 is directly connected, Serial3/0
     172.16.0.0/16 is variably subnetted, 2 subnets, 2 masks
C       172.16.254.3/32 is directly connected, Loopback0
B       172.16.0.0/16 [20/0] via 167.10.1.6, 00:02:33
r3>
```

Listing 8-69

```
r5>sh ip bgp
BGP table version is 5, local router ID is 130.10.254.5
Status codes: s suppressed, d damped, h history, * valid, > best, i - internal
Origin codes: i - IGP, e - EGP, ? - incomplete

   Network          Next Hop            Metric LocPrf Weight Path
*> 130.10.0.0       0.0.0.0                  0         32768 i
* i172.16.0.0       167.10.1.6                    100      0 62 i
r5>sh ip ro 167.10.1.6
% Network not in table
r5>
```

Listing 8-70

```
r3#

router bgp 35
 no synchronization
 neighbor 130.10.254.5 remote-as 35
 neighbor 130.10.254.5 update-source Loopback0
 neighbor 130.10.254.5 next-hop-self
 neighbor 167.10.1.6 remote-as 62
!

r3#q

r5#sh ip bgp
BGP table version is 7, local router ID is 130.10.254.5
Status codes: s suppressed, d damped, h history, * valid, > best, i - internal
Origin codes: i - IGP, e - EGP, ? - incomplete

   Network          Next Hop            Metric LocPrf Weight Path
*> 130.10.0.0       0.0.0.0                  0         32768 i
*>i172.16.0.0       172.16.254.3                   100      0 62 i

r5#sh ip ro 172.16.0.0
Routing entry for 172.16.0.0 255.255.0.0, 2 known subnets
  Variably subnetted with 2 masks
  Redistributing via ospf 1

O       172.16.254.3 255.255.255.255
            [110/11] via 130.10.35.3, 00:55:31, Ethernet0
B       172.16.0.0 255.255.0.0 [200/0] via 172.16.254.3, 00:00:18
r5#
```

Listing 8-71

The first problem is that R4 is choosing R1 as the next hop to the 130.11.0.0 network even though R2 has a metric of 20 for this route, which is less than that of R1. The explanation for this can be found by looking at R4's BGP table. The R1 next hop of 10.10.21.1 has a weight of 21, whereas the 10.10.22.2 next hop has a weight of zero, which is the default for routes not originated by the local router. In the BGP route selection process, *Weight* has a higher priority than *Metric*; hence R2's lower metric is overridden. We will solve the problem simply by giving R2 a higher weight (see Listing 8-74).

Now it can be observed that R4 sees 10.10.22.2 as the preferred next hop to the 130.10.0.0 network in AS 21.

We will now turn our attention to the second problem, which entailed R2 being the exit point out of AS 21 instead of R1. The first issue that can be seen from the configurations and the BGP tables of R1 and R2 is that R2 was given a local preference of 150 for routes received from R4. R1

```
r5>sh ip ro 167.10.1.0
Routing entry for 167.10.1.0 255.255.255.0
  Known via "ospf 1", distance 110, metric 74, type intra area
  Redistributing via ospf 1
  Last update from 130.10.35.3 on Ethernet0, 00:00:12 ago
  Routing Descriptor Blocks:
  * 130.10.35.3, from 172.16.254.3, 00:00:12 ago, via Ethernet0
      Route metric is 74, traffic share count is 1

r5>sh ip bgp
BGP table version is 9, local router ID is 130.10.254.5
Status codes: s suppressed, d damped, h history, * valid, > best, i - internal
Origin codes: i - IGP, e - EGP, ? - incomplete

   Network          Next Hop            Metric LocPrf Weight Path
*> 130.10.0.0       0.0.0.0                  0         32768 i
* i172.16.0.0       167.10.1.6                    100      0 62 i

r5>sh ip ro 172.16.0.0
Routing entry for 172.16.0.0 255.255.0.0, 2 known subnets
  Variably subnetted with 2 masks
  Redistributing via ospf 1

O       172.16.254.3 255.255.255.255
           [110/11] via 130.10.35.3, 00:00:31, Ethernet0
B       172.16.0.0 255.255.0.0 [200/0] via 167.10.1.6, 00:00:14
r5>sh ip ro
Codes: C - connected, S - static, I - IGRP, R - RIP, M - mobile, B - BGP
       D - EIGRP, EX - EIGRP external, O - OSPF, IA - OSPF inter area
       E1 - OSPF external type 1, E2 - OSPF external type 2, E - EGP
       i - IS-IS, L1 - IS-IS level-1, L2 - IS-IS level-2, * - candidate default

Gateway of last resort is not set

     130.10.0.0 is variably subnetted, 2 subnets, 2 masks
C       130.10.254.5 255.255.255.255 is directly connected, Loopback0
C       130.10.35.0 255.255.255.0 is directly connected, Ethernet0
     167.10.0.0 255.255.255.0 is subnetted, 1 subnets
O       167.10.1.0 [110/74] via 130.10.35.3, 00:00:36, Ethernet0
     172.16.0.0 is variably subnetted, 2 subnets, 2 masks
O       172.16.254.3 255.255.255.255
           [110/11] via 130.10.35.3, 00:00:36, Ethernet0
B       172.16.0.0 255.255.0.0 [200/0] via 167.10.1.6, 00:00:18
r5>
```

Listing 8-72

has a default local preference of 200; this should override R2 because the *Local preference* attribute is distributed within the AS. However, it does not, and the 143.10.0.0 network appears with a local preference of 150 and a next hop of 10.10.22.4 in both BGP tables. This implies that there is another problem preventing the propagation of this routing informa-

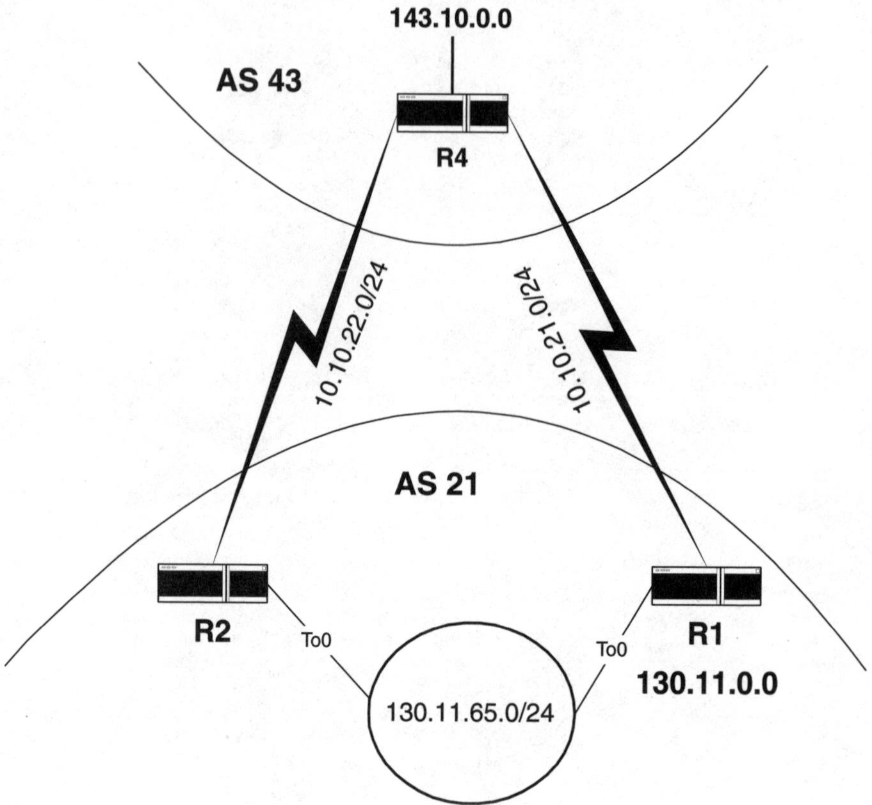

Figure 8-8 BGP troubleshooting scenario 2.

tion. Before addressing this further, I generally do not like to use defaults to influence routing decisions. Therefore, I will eliminate local preference as an issue by giving R1 a higher local preference of 300 for routes specifically received from R4 (see Listing 8-75).

Even after this change, R1's BGP table has not altered. The reason for this is the filter list 9 on R4, which is blocking any updates that originate in R4's local AS from being sent to R1. Let's remove the filter list and see what happens (see Listing 8-76).

Now R1 has a next hop to 143.10.0.0 as 10.10.21.4, which is the exit point that was required in the design. We also need to check that R2 agrees on this exit point from AS 21 to the 143.10.0.0 network (see Listing 8-77).

R2's IP routing table and BGP table still show 10.10.22.4 as the preferred next hop to 143.10.0.0, even though it has a lower local preference. The reason for this is an elementary oversight that can sometimes hap-

```
r1#sh run
Building configuration...

Current configuration:
!
version 11.0
service udp-small-servers
service tcp-small-servers
!
hostname r1
!
enable password cisco
!
!
interface Serial0
 ip address 10.10.21.1 255.255.255.0
 no fair-queue
!
interface Serial1
 no ip address
 shutdown
!
interface TokenRing0
 ip address 130.11.65.1 255.255.255.0
 ring-speed 16
!
interface TokenRing1
 no ip address
 shutdown
!
router bgp 21
 no synchronization
 bgp default local-preference 200
 network 130.11.0.0
 neighbor 10.10.21.4 remote-as 43
 neighbor 10.10.21.4 route-map metric out
 neighbor 130.11.65.2 remote-as 21
!
route-map metric permit 10
 set metric 30
!
!
!
line con 0
line aux 0
 transport input all
line vty 0 4
 password cisco
 login
!
end
```

Listing 8-73

```
r1#

r2#sh run
Building configuration...

Current configuration:
!
version 11.0
service udp-small-servers
service tcp-small-servers
!
hostname r2
!
enable password cisco
!
!
interface Serial0
 ip address 10.10.22.2 255.255.255.0
 no fair-queue
!
interface Serial1
 no ip address
 shutdown
!
interface TokenRing0
 ip address 130.11.65.2 255.255.255.0
 ring-speed 16
!
router bgp 21
 no synchronization
 neighbor 10.10.22.4 remote-as 43
 neighbor 10.10.22.4 route-map setloc in
 neighbor 10.10.22.4 route-map setmet out
 neighbor 130.11.65.1 remote-as 21
!
route-map setloc permit 10
 set local-preference 150
!
route-map setmet permit 10
 set metric 20
!
!
!
line con 0
line aux 0
 transport input all
line vty 0 4
 password cisco
 login
!
end
```

Listing 8-73 ***(Cont.)***

```
r2#

r4#sh run
Building configuration...

Current configuration:
!
version 11.0
service udp-small-servers
service tcp-small-servers
!
hostname r4
!
enable password cisco
!
!
interface Loopback0
 ip address 143.10.44.4 255.255.255.0
!
interface Serial0
 ip address 10.10.22.4 255.255.255.0
 no fair-queue
 clockrate 56000
!
interface Serial1
 ip address 10.10.21.4 255.255.255.0
 clockrate 56000
!
router bgp 43
 network 143.10.0.0
 neighbor 10.10.21.1 remote-as 21
 neighbor 10.10.21.1 filter-list 9 out
 neighbor 10.10.21.1 weight 21
 neighbor 10.10.22.2 remote-as 21
!
ip as-path access-list 9 deny ^$
ip as-path access-list 9 permit .*
!
!
line con 0
line aux 0
 transport input all
line vty 0 4
 password cisco
 login
!
end

r4#

r1#sh ip bgp
BGP table version is 5, local router ID is 130.11.65.1
```

Listing 8-73 (*Cont.*)

```
Status codes: s suppressed, d damped, h history, * valid, > best, i - internal
Origin codes: i - IGP, e - EGP, ? - incomplete

   Network          Next Hop          Metric LocPrf Weight Path
*> 130.11.0.0       0.0.0.0                0         32768 i
* i143.10.0.0       10.10.22.4             0    150      0 43 i
r1#sh ip ro
Codes: C - connected, S - static, I - IGRP, R - RIP, M - mobile, B - BGP
       D - EIGRP, EX - EIGRP external, O - OSPF, IA - OSPF inter area
       E1 - OSPF external type 1, E2 - OSPF external type 2, E - EGP
       i - IS-IS, L1 - IS-IS level-1, L2 - IS-IS level-2, * - candidate default

Gateway of last resort is not set

     10.0.0.0 255.255.255.0 is subnetted, 1 subnets
C       10.10.21.0 is directly connected, Serial0
     130.11.0.0 255.255.255.0 is subnetted, 1 subnets
C       130.11.65.0 is directly connected, TokenRing0
r1#

r2#sh ip bgp
BGP table version is 11, local router ID is 130.11.65.2
Status codes: s suppressed, d damped, h history, * valid, > best, i - internal
Origin codes: i - IGP, e - EGP, ? - incomplete

   Network          Next Hop          Metric LocPrf Weight Path
*>i130.11.0.0       130.11.65.1            0    200      0 i
*> 143.10.0.0       10.10.22.4             0    150      0 43 i
r2#sh ip ro
Codes: C - connected, S - static, I - IGRP, R - RIP, M - mobile, B - BGP
       D - EIGRP, EX - EIGRP external, O - OSPF, IA - OSPF inter area
       E1 - OSPF external type 1, E2 - OSPF external type 2, E - EGP
       i - IS-IS, L1 - IS-IS level-1, L2 - IS-IS level-2, * - candidate default

Gateway of last resort is not set

     10.0.0.0 255.255.255.0 is subnetted, 1 subnets
C       10.10.22.0 is directly connected, Serial0
B    143.10.0.0 [20/0] via 10.10.22.4, 00:06:58
     130.11.0.0 is variably subnetted, 2 subnets, 2 masks
B       130.11.0.0 255.255.0.0 [200/0] via 130.11.65.1, 00:20:36
C       130.11.65.0 255.255.255.0 is directly connected, TokenRing0
r2#

r4#sh ip bgp
BGP table version is 4, local router ID is 143.10.44.4
Status codes: s suppressed, d damped, h history, * valid, > best, i - internal
Origin codes: i - IGP, e - EGP, ? - incomplete

   Network          Next Hop          Metric LocPrf Weight Path
*  130.11.0.0       10.10.22.2            20             0 21 i
*>                  10.10.21.1            30            21 21 i
```

Listing 8-73 (*Cont.*)

```
*> 143.10.0.0        0.0.0.0                 0         32768 i
r4#sh ip ro
Codes: C - connected, S - static, I - IGRP, R - RIP, M - mobile, B - BGP
       D - EIGRP, EX - EIGRP external, O - OSPF, IA - OSPF inter area
       E1 - OSPF external type 1, E2 - OSPF external type 2, E - EGP
       i - IS-IS, L1 - IS-IS level-1, L2 - IS-IS level-2, * - candidate default

Gateway of last resort is not set

     10.0.0.0 255.255.255.0 is subnetted, 2 subnets
C       10.10.21.0 is directly connected, Serial1
C       10.10.22.0 is directly connected, Serial0
     143.10.0.0 255.255.255.0 is subnetted, 1 subnets
C       143.10.44.0 is directly connected, Loopback0
B    130.11.0.0 [20/30] via 10.10.21.1, 00:06:45
r4#
```

Listing 8-73 *(Cont.)*

pen in BGP networks. R2 has no route to 10.10.21.4, because network 10.0.0.0 is not participating in BGP or any IGP. There are, of course, many ways to resolve this; we will do so by enabling OSPF on the 10.0.0.0 network but will not allow for any redistribution between OSPF and BGP (see Listing 8-78).

R2 now has a route to 10.10.21.4, so let's examine the impact that this has on the BGP routing (see Listing 8-79).

Now R2 and R1 both agree that the preferred exit point from AS 21 to the 143.10.0.0 network is via R1 with a next hop of 10.10.21.4. Thus the problem has been resolved, and our final design goal has been satisfied.

Redistribution Revisited

There are a number of issues that frequently cause problems when redistributing between two or more IP routing protocols. We have come across many of them already, such as the issue of having to redistribute VLSM subnets into a protocol that does not support VLSM. We also have dealt with issues such as default metrics.

I think it is worthwhile to again summarize the typical problems encountered when redistributing between IP routing protocols, since this is a topic that is commonly at the root of very many IP routing problems.

```
r4#conf t
Enter configuration commands, one per line.  End with CNTL/Z.
r4(config)#router bgp 43
r4(config-router)#neighbor 10.10.22.2 weight 30
r4(config-router)#^Z
r4#cle ip bgp *
r4#sh ip bgp
BGP table version is 3, local router ID is 143.10.44.4
Status codes: s suppressed, d damped, h history, * valid, > best, i - internal
Origin codes: i - IGP, e - EGP, ? - incomplete

   Network          Next Hop          Metric LocPrf Weight Path
*> 130.11.0.0       10.10.22.2            20            30 21 i
*                   10.10.21.1            30            21 21 i
*> 143.10.0.0       0.0.0.0                0         32768 i
r4#sh ip ro
Codes: C - connected, S - static, I - IGRP, R - RIP, M - mobile, B - BGP
       D - EIGRP, EX - EIGRP external, O - OSPF, IA - OSPF inter area
       E1 - OSPF external type 1, E2 - OSPF external type 2, E - EGP
       i - IS-IS, L1 - IS-IS level-1, L2 - IS-IS level-2, * - candidate default

Gateway of last resort is not set

     10.0.0.0 255.255.255.0 is subnetted, 2 subnets
C       10.10.21.0 is directly connected, Serial1
C       10.10.22.0 is directly connected, Serial0
     143.10.0.0 255.255.255.0 is subnetted, 1 subnets
C       143.10.44.0 is directly connected, Loopback0
B    130.11.0.0 [20/20] via 10.10.22.2, 00:01:04
r4#
```

Listing 8-74

Manipulating Route Metrics

A routing metric must be defined to facilitate redistribution between two protocols that have a dissimilar metric type. For example, OSPF uses a cost metric that inversely relates to bandwidth, whereas EIGRP employs a composite metric that is influenced by two or more parameters such as *Bandwidth* and *Delay*.

This metric definition can take the form of a default metric that is applied to all routes that do not have a specified metric (e.g., routes that are being redistributed into the protocol). A metric also can be defined explicitly along with the redistribute statement. The following is an example of each method:

```
r1#

!
router bgp 21
 no synchronization
 bgp default local-preference 200
 network 130.11.0.0
 neighbor 10.10.21.4 remote-as 43
 neighbor 10.10.21.4 route-map setlocal in
 neighbor 10.10.21.4 route-map metric out
 neighbor 130.11.65.2 remote-as 21
!
route-map metric permit 10
 set metric 30
!
route-map setlocal permit 10
 set local-preference 300
!
!
!
line con 0
line aux 0
 transport input all

r1#sh ip bgp
BGP table version is 2, local router ID is 130.11.65.1
Status codes: s suppressed, d damped, h history, * valid, > best, i - internal
Origin codes: i - IGP, e - EGP, ? - incomplete

   Network          Next Hop           Metric LocPrf Weight Path
*> 130.11.0.0       0.0.0.0                 0         32768 i
* i143.10.0.0       10.10.22.4              0    150      0 43 i
r1#
```

Listing 8-75

```
router ospf 1
redistribute eigrp 1 subnets
default-metric 100

router eigrp 1
redistribute ospf 1 metric 1500 1000 255 1 1500
```

Applying Distribute Lists

Distribute lists are used to control the routes that are advertised or accepted in routing updates. They can be applied in a number of ways.

- To the entire routing protocol, inbound or outbound. For example:

```
r4#conf t
Enter configuration commands, one per line.  End with CNTL/Z.
r4(config)#router bgp 43
r4(config-router)#no neighbor 10.10.21.1 filter-lis 9 out
r4(config-router)#^Z
r4#cle ip bgp *
r4#

r1#sh ip bgp
BGP table version is 4, local router ID is 130.11.65.1
Status codes: s suppressed, d damped, h history, * valid, > best, i - internal
Origin codes: i - IGP, e - EGP, ? - incomplete

   Network          Next Hop            Metric LocPrf Weight Path
*> 130.11.0.0       0.0.0.0                  0         32768 i
* i143.10.0.0       10.10.22.4               0    150      0 43 i
*>                  10.10.21.4               0    300      0 43 i
r1#sh ip ro
Codes: C - connected, S - static, I - IGRP, R - RIP, M - mobile, B - BGP
       D - EIGRP, EX - EIGRP external, O - OSPF, IA - OSPF inter area
       E1 - OSPF external type 1, E2 - OSPF external type 2, E - EGP
       i - IS-IS, L1 - IS-IS level-1, L2 - IS-IS level-2, * - candidate default

Gateway of last resort is not set

     10.0.0.0 255.255.255.0 is subnetted, 1 subnets
C       10.10.21.0 is directly connected, Serial0
B    143.10.0.0 [20/0] via 10.10.21.4, 00:00:17
     130.11.0.0 255.255.255.0 is subnetted, 1 subnets
C       130.11.65.0 is directly connected, TokenRing0
r1#
```

Listing 8-76

```
router rip
distribute-list 1 in
distribute-list 2 out

access-list 1 permit 172.20.0.0 0.0.255.255
access-list 2 permit 172.20.0.0 0.0.63.255
```

This configuration would limit RIP to accepting routes from the 172.20.0.0 class B network only. This router can then only advertise subnets 0 through 63 from the same class B in its outgoing RIP updates.

- To a routing protocol running on a particular interface, inbound or outbound. For example:

```
router rip
distribute-list 1 in ethernet0
distribute-list 2 out serial0
```

```
r2#sh ip bgp
BGP table version is 3, local router ID is 130.11.65.2
Status codes: s suppressed, d damped, h history, * valid, > best, i - internal
Origin codes: i - IGP, e - EGP, ? - incomplete

   Network          Next Hop          Metric LocPrf Weight Path
*>i130.11.0.0       130.11.65.1            0    200      0 i
* i143.10.0.0       10.10.21.4             0    300      0 43 i
*>                  10.10.22.4             0    150      0 43 i
r2#sh ip ro 143.10.0.0
Routing entry for 143.10.0.0 255.255.0.0
  Known via "bgp 21", distance 20, metric 0
  Tag 43, type external
  Last update from 10.10.22.4 00:03:33 ago
  Routing Descriptor Blocks:
  * 10.10.22.4, from 10.10.22.4, 00:03:33 ago
      Route metric is 0, traffic share count is 1

r2#
```

Listing 8-77

```
access-list 1 permit 172.20.0.0 0.0.255.255
access-list 2 permit 172.20.0.0 0.0.63.255
```

In this case, access list 1 is only applied to RIP updates received on Ethernet 0. Access list 2 is only applied to outgoing updates on serial 0.

- To all routes that were learned from another particular routing protocol; this can be applied outbound only. For example:

```
router rip
redistribute igrp 100 metric 3
distribute-list 2 out igrp 100
```

This configuration applies access list 2 to a certain type of outbound RIP update, those routes which were learned via IGRP 100. Distribute list 2 will *not* be applied to RIP-derived routes.

Distribute lists also can have a useful troubleshooting application in killing routing loops or convergence loops, e.g., a link that was down comes back up and there is a transition period where some routers are advertising the route as valid and some are advertising it as inaccessible. For distance-vector protocols, the hold-down timer should take care of such a problem. Despite this, however, these problems can occur in real-life situations, particularly if there is a flapping route. Distribute lists can be used to temporarily prevent the relevant routers from advertising

```
r2#ping 10.10.21.4
Type escape sequence to abort.
Sending 5, 100-byte ICMP Echos to 10.10.21.4, timeout is 2 seconds:
.....
Success rate is 0 percent (0/5)
r2#

r2#conf t
Enter configuration commands, one per line.  End with CNTL/Z.
r2(config)#router ospf 1
r2(config-router)#net 10.0.0.0 0.255.255.255 area 0
r2(config-router)#^Z
r2#
r4#conf t
Enter configuration commands, one per line.  End with CNTL/Z.
r4(config)#router ospf 1
r4(config-router)#net 10.0.0.0 0.255.255.255 area 0
r4(config-router)#^Z
r4#sh ip ospf neigh

Neighbor ID     Pri   State           Dead Time   Address         Interface
130.11.65.2       1   FULL/  -        0:00:37     10.10.22.2      Serial0
r4#

r2#sh ip ro 10.10.21.0
Routing entry for 10.10.21.0 255.255.255.0
  Known via "ospf 1", distance 110, metric 128, type intra area
  Redistributing via ospf 1
  Last update from 10.10.22.4 on Serial0, 00:00:17 ago
  Routing Descriptor Blocks:
  * 10.10.22.4, from 143.10.44.4, 00:00:17 ago, via Serial0
      Route metric is 128, traffic share count is 1

r2#ping 10.10.21.4
Type escape sequence to abort.
Sending 5, 100-byte ICMP Echos to 10.10.21.4, timeout is 2 seconds:
!!!!!
Success rate is 100 percent (5/5), round-trip min/avg/max = 36/36/36 ms
```

Listing 8-78

or from accepting updates about a particular route. This can "kill" the routing loop. The distribute lists should then be removed when network stability is regained.

NOTE: *Temporary distribute lists can be a useful tool when troubleshooting routing loops.*

```
r2#cle ip bgp *
r2#sh ip ro
Codes: C - connected, S - static, I - IGRP, R - RIP, M - mobile, B - BGP
       D - EIGRP, EX - EIGRP external, O - OSPF, IA - OSPF inter area
       E1 - OSPF external type 1, E2 - OSPF external type 2, E - EGP
       i - IS-IS, L1 - IS-IS level-1, L2 - IS-IS level-2, * - candidate default

Gateway of last resort is not set

     10.0.0.0 255.255.255.0 is subnetted, 2 subnets
O       10.10.21.0 [110/128] via 10.10.22.4, 00:01:08, Serial0
C       10.10.22.0 is directly connected, Serial0
B    143.10.0.0 [200/0] via 10.10.21.4, 00:00:26
     130.11.0.0 is variably subnetted, 2 subnets, 2 masks
B       130.11.0.0 255.255.0.0 [200/0] via 130.11.65.1, 00:00:26
C       130.11.65.0 255.255.255.0 is directly connected, TokenRing0
r2#
```

Listing 8-79

The Power of Route Maps

Route maps provide a powerful means to control the redistribution between two IP routing protocols. They can be applied inbound or outbound, and they have the capability not only to control the routes present in routing updates but also to manipulate route characteristics such as metric, next hop, and route tagging, among others. Route maps usually must be used with OSPF because, being a link-state protocol, distribute lists cannot filter its routing updates. This is so because OSPF does not exchange its entire routing table with adjacent neighbors as a distance-vector protocol does. Distribute lists still work with EIGRP, which is technically a distance vector protocol that exhibits a number of "pseudo" link-state features.

Listing 8-80 is an example of a poorly configured route map. The 150.10.0.0 class B network employs 24-bit subnetting in the EIGRP 1 domain. It is required to block the redistribution from EIGRP to OSPF of 150.10.x.0 subnets where x<32 and to assign a metric of 50 to subnets where 31<x<64. All other redistributed subnets of 150.10.0.0 should pick up the default metric of 100.

The symptom of the problem is that only a small number of subnets of 150.10.x.0/24 are visible in the OSPF domain, all of which have a metric of 50. When troubleshooting the problem, the route map in Listing 8-80 was found in the configuration of the router responsible for redistributing from EIGRP to OSPF.

This is a common problem in route maps. The first two route-map entries correctly achieve their goals; namely, 150.10.0-31.0 subnets are "denied" into the OSPF domain, whereas 150.10.32-63.0 subnets are "permitted" and assigned a metric of 50. The numbers 10 and 20 at the end of the route-map statements are simply sequence numbers that dictate the order in which the `match` and `set` statements are to be executed. However, no match was defined for subnets 150.10.64.0 and above. If there is no match in the route map, the routes get dropped rather than passed by default.

Route maps can be relatively complex and should be mastered in a laboratory environment before you attempt to configure or troubleshoot issues that may relate to route maps on a live network. The preceding route map requires the following additional statements to achieve the desired routing policy:

```
route-map eig-ospf permit 30
match ip address 9

access-list 9 permit 150.10.0.0 0.0.255.255
```

CAUTION: *Packets that do not explicitly match the defined route-map criteria will be dropped by default.*

Listing 8-80

```
router ospf 1
redistribute eigrp 1 subnets route-map eig-ospf
default-metric 100

route-map eig-ospf deny 10
match ip address 7

route-map eig-ospf permit 20
match ip address 8
set metric 50

access-list 7 permit 150.10.0.0 0.0.31.255
access-list 8 permit 150.10.32.0 0.0.31.255
```

REVIEW QUESTIONS FOR CHAPTERS 7 AND 8

For the exercises that are multiple-choice questions, there is only one correct answer unless the question is marked with an asterisk (*). Choose the most suitable answer.

1. Which of the following could a Windows NT station *not* use to attach to a remote network?

a. IGRP

b. EIGRP

c. RIP

d. Default gateway

e. a and b

2. What type of route will a router use only if it has no other route to a destination?

a. Static route

b. Floating static route

c. Default gateway

d. OSPF-derived route

e. RIP-derived route

3. Which of the following routing protocols do *not* support VLSM?

a. RIP version 1

b. RIP version 2

c. IGRP

d. OSPF

e. a and c

4. Type the router configuration command that prevents routing updates from propagating from the Ethernet 0 interface.

5. The Cisco command that displays the contents of the IP routing table is

a. `show ip route`.

b. `show ip routing`.

c. `show ip network`.

d. `show routing`.

e. none of the above.

6. Type the command that displays which IP routing protocols are configured on a router.

7. For two routers to form an OSPF neighbor relationship, which of the following interface parameters must agree?

   a. Hello interval

   b. Dead interval

   c. Area ID

   d. Stub area flag

   e. All of the above

8. Distribute list 1 will allow the summary route 172.16.0.0 but will block all the more specific subnets. Type the two lines of access list 1.

9. The debug commands that allow analysis of IP RIP updates are

   a. `debug ip rip updates.`

   b. `debug ip rip transactions.`

   c. `debug ip rip.`

   d. `debug ip rip events.`

   e. c and d.

10. Which of the following debug commands can have its scope limited by an access list?

    a. `debug ip packet`

    b. `debug ip rip events`

    c. `debug ip igrp transactions`

    d. `debug ip ospf events`

    e. None of the above

11. Which of the following routing protocols have debug commands that can have their scope limited, specifying the IP address of a neighbor?

    a. RIP

    b. IGRP

    c. EIGRP

    d. OSPF

    e. b and c

12. Type the interface command that disables all types of IP fast switching on an interface.

13. Which of the following is *not* an IP name resolution mechanism?

a. DHCP

b. WINS

c. LMHOSTS

d. DNS

e. Broadcasting

14. The Windows NT DOS prompt that gives information on IP address, default gateway, node type, and adapter MAC address is

a. `ipconfig`.

b. `set logon`.

c. `ip config`.

d. `ipconfig /all`.

e. all of the above

15. For a Windows NT station using NetBIOS over TCP/IP configured as h-node, put the following name resolution steps in the correct order.

a. LMHOST

b. DNS

c. p-node unicast

d. b-node broadcast

16. To configure a static route on a Windows NT station, use

a. `set ip route`.

b. `netstat-add`.

c. `netstat-r`.

d. `route add`.

e. `ip route add`.

17. How many bytes are in the sequence field of a UDP packet?

a. Zero

b. One

c. Two

d. Four

e. Six

18. Which bit in the header of an IP packet when set prevents fragmentation from being an option?

19. Type the command that clears the entire IP routing table.

20. Which debug command allows an analysis of all ICMP transactions on a router?

    a. `debug icmp`

    b. `debug ip icmp`

    c. `debug ping`

    d. `debug ip echo`

    e. `debug ip ping`

21. Type the command that allows manual summarization for EIGRP 21.

22. Which of the following EIGRP packet types is transmitted unreliably?

    a. Hellos/Acks

    b. Updates

    c. Queries

    d. Replies

23. The difference between route summarization in IGRP and EIGRP is that

    a. IGRP autosummarizes on class.

    b. EIGRP autosummarizes on class.

    c. EIGRP supports manual summarization.

    d. autosummary is off by default on IGRP.

    e. autosummary can be turned off with EIGRP.

*24. Which of the following protocols can support discontiguous networks?

    a. RIP

    b. IGRP

    c. EIGRP

    d. OSPF

    e. RIP version 2

25. What does an incrementing "Q" count in the output of `show ip eigrp neighbors` indicate?

*26. On which of the following routing protocols would the `passive-interface` command block *incoming* updates?

    a. RIP

b. IGRP

c. EIGRP

d. OSPF

e. RIP version 2

27. Which of the following protocols has split horizon on by default on a frame-relay interface?

a. RIP

b. IGRP

c. EIGRP

28. What is the default OSPF interface priority?

a. 0

b. 1

c. 10

d. 100

e. 10^8

29. On what type of OSPF router should interarea route summarization be configured?

30. What standards-based Cisco router feature allows for optimized OSPF operation over ISDN?

***31.** If an OSPF route is marked "O E1," then it

a. is an external summarized route.

b. has been redistributed into OSPF without manipulation.

c. is favored over an E2 route of equal metric.

d. has a cost consisting of external and internal costs.

e. has a cost consisting of external cost only.

32. What OSPF debug command is useful for monitoring the formation of neighbors?

a. `debug ip ospf adj`

b. `debug ospf adj`

c. `debug ip ospf neighbor`

d. `debug ospf neighbor`

e. `debug ip ospf network`

33. Type the keyword required by OSPF to ensure that networks that are subnetted get redistributed into OSPF.

34. What BGP neighbor state indicates successful neighbor formation?

   a. Active
   b. Openconfirm
   c. Opensent
   d. Established
   e. Connect

*35. Which of the following BGP attributes can get advertised between autonomous systems?

   a. *Weight*
   b. *Local-preference*
   c. *Metric*
   d. *AS-path*

36. Type the router configuration command that modifies the RIP and IGRP routing timers.

37. Arrange the following protocols in order of increasing default administrative distance.

   a. RIP
   b. IGRP
   c. Static
   d. Connected
   e. OSPF

38. By default, IGRP considers which of the following in its metric calculation?

   a. *Bandwidth*
   b. *Bandwidth* and *Delay*
   c. *Bandwidth, Delay, Load, Reliability,* and *MTU*
   d. *Bandwidth* and *Hop-count*
   e. *Bandwidth, Delay*, and *Hop-count*

39. To enable a BGP router to forward updates it receives from one IBGP neighbor on to another IBGP neighbor, use

   a. `next-hop-self`.
   b. route reflectors.
   c. BGP peer groups.

d. BGP communities.

e. BGP confederation.

40. Arrange the following attributes in order of *decreasing* significance as they relate to the BGP route selection process.

a. *Metric*

b. *Weight*

c. *BGP router ID*

d. *Local-preference*

e. Length of the *AS-path*

CHAPTER 9

Troubleshooting Novell Connectivity

Introduction

This chapter begins by reviewing some Novell client-server theory that must be understood in order to troubleshoot IPX networks. The overall subject matter discussed in this chapter will range from the local-area network (LAN) environment to the issues faced when routing IPX across a large wide-area enterprise network. All the Cisco router diagnostic tools available for use in IPX RIP and IPX EIGRP networks will be demonstrated. Troubleshooting scenarios and tips on how to avoid problems in each of these environments also will be examined.

The objectives of this chapter are to

- Understand the Novell client-server connection sequence.
- Identify all the key technology issues in relation to IPX internetworking, in particular, SAP, GNS, and encapsulation type.
- Appreciate the challenges of using IPX in the WAN.
- Apply Cisco router diagnostic tools to solve problems in IPX RIP and IPX EIGRP networks.

Novell Client-Server Connection Sequence

In order to troubleshoot Novell connectivity problems, it is essential to have a good understanding of the connection sequence between the time an IPX client boots up and that same client successfully attaches to its server. The connection sequence that a Novell client engages in after boot-up is illustrated schematically in Figure 9-1. The following is a summary of the basic steps. While there can be slight variations depending on whether the client has a preferred server configured and what version of Novell is being used, the fundamental steps remain the same.

- The client sends a Get Nearest Server (GNS) request for the Service Advertising Protocol (SAP) that it requires. For example, this would be SAP type 4 to log onto a file server.
- A server or router can answer the GNS request with the name and network address of an appropriate server in its SAP table. Routers

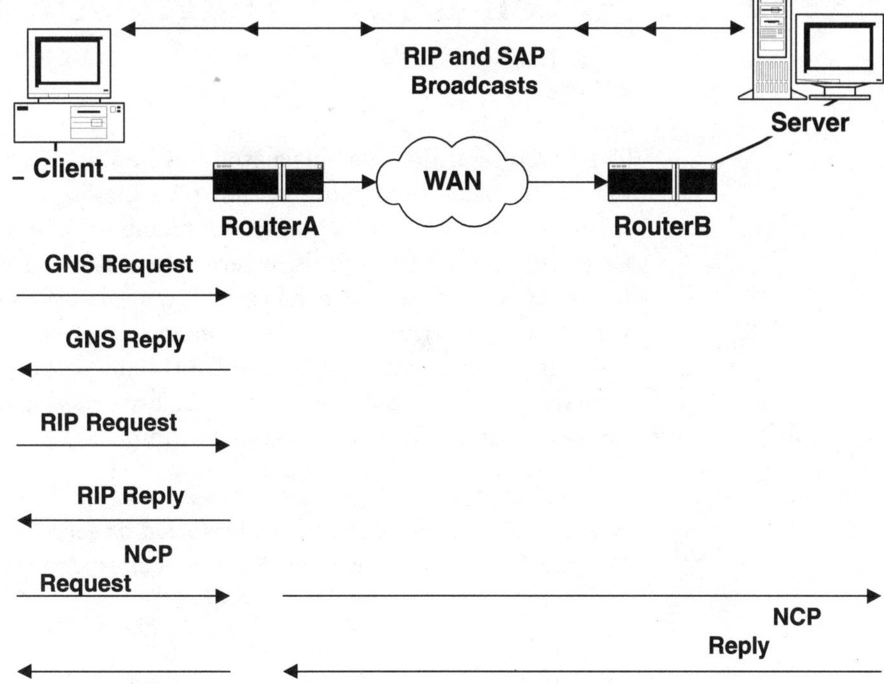

Figure 9-1 Novell client-server connection sequence.

build up their own SAP tables by listening to the SAPs that are advertised by servers.

- On receiving the GNS reply, the client sends an IPX Routing Information Protocol (RIP) request to obtain a route to the nearest server.
- A server that is running IPX RIP could answer the RIP request, but usually the router provides the route to the nearest server.
- The client then issues a Netware Core Protocol (NCP) request to attach to the nearest server.
- The server answers with an NCP reply to the client. This enables the client to log onto the server. In some cases, the client may have a preferred server configured and rather than logging onto the nearest server; the client simply uses it as a transport mechanism for attaching to the preferred server.

Novell Router Diagnostic Tools

Ping

The IPX ping utility was discussed in Chapter 3. A sample of both a simple and extended IPX ping is shown in Listing 9-1 just to refresh your memory. One important point to remember is that a simple ping uses Cisco IPX echoes by default, whereas an extended ping gives the option to use Novell standard echoes. The default IPX ping can be changed using the `ipx ping-default` command, but not all Novell devices have the Netware Loadable Module (NLM) loaded that supports the Novell echo feature. You need to check this before drawing any conclusions from pings failing to a Novell server, for example.

NOTE: *If pings to a Novell workstation or server are failing, verify that the station supports Novell echoes before drawing any conclusions.*

```
R8#ping ipx a5304380.0007.7f12.0385

Type escape sequence to abort.
Sending 5, 100-byte IPX cisco Echoes to A5304380.0007.7f12.0385, timeout is
  2 seconds:
!!!!!
Success rate is 100 percent (5/5), round-trip min/avg/max = 1/1/4 ms
R8#

R8#ping
Protocol [ip]: ipx
Target IPX address: a5304380.0007.7f12.0385
Repeat count [5]: 20
Datagram size [100]: 900
Timeout in seconds [2]:
Verbose [n]:
Novell Standard Echo [n]:
Type escape sequence to abort.
Sending 20, 900-byte IPX cisco Echoes to A5304380.0007.7f12.0385, timeout is
  2 seconds:
!!!!!!!!!!!!!!!!!!!!
Success rate is 100 percent (20/20), round-trip min/avg/max = 1/2/4 ms
R8#
```

Listing 9-1

Show Commands

The `show ipx interface` Command The `show ipx interface` command can be applied to any interface to display specific IPX information.

- It will indicate whether the interface is up and running IPX. If it is, then the IPX network and node number is displayed.
- The IPX delay in ticks (55 ms) is shown in Listing 9-2. The displayed value could be the default or a configured value and is used by both IPX RIP and EIGRP when making routing decisions. In older versions of IPX RIP, ticks were used as a tiebreak when the hop counts on two routes were equal. In newer versions, the tick count is the predominant parameter for route selection.
- The IPX encapsulation is shown. This is highly significant because Novell supports multiple encapsulation types for Ethernet, Token Ring, and FDDI. Sometimes different encapsulations must be configured on secondary or subinterface networks to support different flavors of Novell that reside on the same LAN segment. Encapsulation mismatches can cause IPX connectivity problems, and an example of this will be demonstrated.
- The SAP update interval is at the default value of 60 seconds in the example in Listing 9-2. The IPX RIP update and multiplier intervals are also at their defaults. The multiplier interval is the period of time without an update after which the route is put in holddown. This is three times the update interval by default. Information is also given on the interpacket delay and maximum packet size for SAPs and RIPs, as well as the total number of these packets that have been sent and received by this interface since the counters were last cleared. Later we will see reasons why these parameters may need to be tuned from their default settings.
- The IPX type 20 propagation command enables the forwarding of NetBIOS over IPX. This is disabled by default.
- IPX filtering will be discussed in some detail because access lists frequently cause connectivity problems in Novell networks. In this example, the only type of filter applied to the interface is SAP filter 1099, which is applied to outbound SAP packets.
- The fast switching of IPX packets is also enabled on the interface.

```
R1#sh ipx int e0
Ethernet0 is up, line protocol is up
  IPX address is 82F600.00e0.1e3e.5d8d, NOVELL-ETHER [up] line-up, RIPPQ: 0, SAPPQ: 0
  Delay of this IPX network, in ticks is 1 throughput 0 link delay 0
  IPXWAN processing not enabled on this interface.
  IPX SAP update interval is 1 minute(s)
  IPX type 20 propagation packet forwarding is disabled
  Incoming access list is not set
  Outgoing access list is not set
  IPX helper access list is not set
  SAP GNS processing enabled, delay 0 ms, output filter list is not set
  SAP Input filter list is not set
  SAP Output filter list is 1099
  SAP Router filter list is not set
  Input filter list is not set
  Output filter list is not set
  Router filter list is not set
  Netbios Input host access list is not set
  Netbios Input bytes access list is not set
  Netbios Output host access list is not set
  Netbios Output bytes access list is not set
  Updates each 60 seconds, aging multiples RIP: 3 SAP: 3
  SAP interpacket delay is 55 ms, maximum size is 480 bytes
  RIP interpacket delay is 55 ms, maximum size is 432 bytes
  IPX accounting is disabled
  IPX fast switching is configured (enabled)
  RIP packets received 794, RIP packets sent 2680900
  SAP packets received 161, SAP packets sent 298586
R1#
```

Listing 9-2

The `show ipx route` Command The `show ipx route` command displays the contents of the IPX routing table. Different routes may have been derived from different IPX routing protocols. In the example shown in Listing 9-3, only IPX RIP is running on R3.

- The routing table can hold up to three paths to the same network, as distinct from the default of just one path. This can be configured globally using `ipx maximum-paths 3`. In recent Cisco IOS versions, the load balancing over these parallel paths can be configured to be on a per-packet or per-host basis. Also notice that IPX RIP has the same hop-count limitation as for IP RIP.
- The R3 router has four interfaces running IPX; three are WAN interfaces, along with an interface to an FDDI ring. The corresponding IPX encapsulations are shown.
- Consider the route to IPX network 1. There are two routes learned from different stations on the FDDI ring. R3 sees the advertised

```
R3>sh ipx route
Codes: C - Connected primary network,    c - Connected secondary network
       S - Static, F - Floating static, L - Local (internal), W - IPXWAN
       R - RIP, E - EIGRP, N - NLSP, X - External, A - Aggregate
       s - seconds, u - uses

10 Total IPX routes. Up to 3 parallel paths and 16 hops allowed.

No default route known.

C   D1500 (FRAME-RELAY-IETF),  Se4/0.726
C   07680 (HDLC),           Se2/1
C   50100 (SNAP),           Fd1/0
C   10F80 (HDLC),           Se2/3
R          1 [05/04] via 50100.0060.7056.6020,   42s, Fd1/0
                     via 50100.0060.7056.6820,   31s, Fd1/0
R          2 [05/04] via 50100.0060.7056.6020,   47s, Fd1/0
                     via 50100.0060.7056.6820,   31s, Fd1/0
R          3 [14/08] via 50100.0060.4763.7500,   18s, Fd1/0
R          5 [08/07] via 50100.0060.4763.7500,   18s, Fd1/0
R          B [14/08] via 50100.0060.4763.7500,   19s, Fd1/0
R          C [06/05] via 50100.0060.7056.6020,   48s, Fd1/0
                     via 50100.0060.7056.6820,   32s, Fd1/0

R3>
```

Listing 9-3

route from each of these sources as being 4 hops and 5 ticks away. The two sources sent their last RIP updates 42 and 31 seconds ago, respectively.

The `show ipx servers` Command To display the contents of the router's SAP table, use `show ipx servers`. This will display all SAPs that the router receives originating from networks to which it has a route. If the router does not have a route to a server's network, it will not display any of that server's SAPs in its SAP table. Also, if the router learns the route to the server's network over a different interface than the one from which it received the SAP, it also will refrain from placing the SAP in its table. This can be demonstrated by attempting to configure a static SAP on a router that does not have a route to the network on which the server is located:

```
Router-1(config)#ipx sap 4 FSERV44 44.0000.2022.1212 451 4
%no route to 44, FSERV44 won't be announced until route is learned
Router-1(config)#
```

NOTE: A router will not place a SAP in its SAP table unless it has a route to that server's network over the same interface from which it received the SAP.

Listing 9-4 is a truncated version of a router's SAP table that contains 115 entries. In the left-most column, the "P" indicates a periodic update, since the network is running IPX RIP. The type of service, along with its name and network address, is then provided.

Notice that many of the SAPs have a MAC address of 0000.0000.0001. This is a typical notation for an IPX SAP that was advertised using the server's internal IPX address. In this case, the network part of the address is the internal IPX address of the server. When the internal IPX network number is used, the service will always appear to be one additional hop away, because obviously the internal network can never appear as directly connected even to its local router.

Two SAPs whose addresses are not of this format have been highlighted. One is a SAP type 47 Microsoft File and Print Services for Netware (FPNW) server, and the other is an HP LaserJet, as indicated by SAP type 30C. These non-Novell products generally use a physical network address and MAC address as opposed to an internal network to

```
Sarah1#sh ipx server
Codes: S - Static, P - Periodic, E - EIGRP, N - NLSP, H - Holddown, + = detail
115 Total IPX Servers

Table ordering is based on routing and server info

   Type Name                    Net     Address     Port       Route Hops Itf
P+     4 SRV-30401              201.0000.0000.0001:0451        3/02    2  Fd1/0
P+     4 SRV-40502              102.0000.0000.0001:0451        3/02    2  To0/0
P+     4 SRV-40801              401.0000.0000.0001:0451        3/02    2  To0/0
P+     4 SRV-41801              101.0000.0000.0001:0451        3/02    2  To0/0
P+     4 SRV-DCS01              501.0000.0000.0001:0451        3/02    2  To0/0
P+     4 SRV-NDS0               701.0000.0000.0001:0451        3/02    2  To0/0
P+     4 SRV-SAA01              901.0000.0000.0001:0451        3/02    2  To0/0
P+     4 SRV-LAF01              601.0000.0000.0001:0451        3/02    2  Fd1/0
P+    47 R_PSERVER              502.0800.5a94.3b0c:8060        2/01    2  To0/0
P    107 SRV-SRL03              302.0000.0000.0001:8104        8/02    2  Se2/0
P+   30C 00060D13CE82PS-HP      551.0006.0d13.ce82:400C        2/01    2  Fd1/0
P+   130 SRV-SAA01              221.0000.0000.0001:1F80        3/02    2  To0/0
Sarah1#
```

Listing 9-4

advertise their SAPs. As we will see later, this can sometimes cause problems when these servers appear to be fewer hops away as a result of not using an internal network.

The port or socket number used to log onto the service is also displayed. For example, all the Novell file servers in this case use 451, which is NCP. The route to the network that the server is on is shown in ticks and hops along with the interface over which the route and SAP were learned.

A "P+" in the left-hand column indicates that more information is available, which can be obtained using `show ipx servers detailed`. The additional information is usually multiple routes to the server's network, as demonstrated in Listing 9-5.

The router periodically sorts the SAP table information by service type, tick and hop count, and order in which it was received. It also can be requested to display the SAP table sorted by other parameters. These include service name, network or a matching regular expression. This facility can be useful when searching for a particular SAP on a large IPX network (see Listing 9-6).

The `show ipx traffic` Command The `show ipx traffic` command displays a summary about each of the different possible IPX traffic types. This ranges from summary totals of all IPX packets sent and received by the router along with error information to specific IPX traffic types such as SAPs and traffic generated by different IPX routing protocols.

The *Format errors* are a total for the number of packets received by the router that had different encapsulations to the router interface on

```
Sarah1#sh ipx server detail
Codes: S - Static, P - Periodic, E - EIGRP, N - NLSP, H - Holddown, + = detail
115 Total IPX Servers

Table ordering is based on routing and server info

   Type Name                    Net     Address     Port      Route Hops Itf
P+    4 SRV-30401             201.0000.0000.0001:0451      3/02   2  Fd1/0
        - via Fd1/0:10000.0060.2fde.2e00,  25s
        - via To0/0:100.0006.f47b.b486,  25s
P+    4 SRV-40502             102.0000.0000.0001:0451      3/02   2  To0/0
        - via To0/0:100.0006.f47b.b486,  25s
        - via Fd1/0:10000.0060.2fde.2e00,  25s
```

Listing 9-5

```
Sarah1#sh ipx server sorted ?
  name     Sort by name
  net      Sort by net
  regexp   Display server list elements whose name matches a regular expression
  type     Sort by type
  <cr>
```

Listing 9-6

which they were received. An excessive number of format errors indicates an encapsulation mismatch between the router interface and one or more locally attached Novell stations or servers (see Listing 9-7).

An incrementing bad hop count can be indicative of a routing loop or the presence of a "backdoor bridge" between two routed segments. A diagram for this type of scenario is shown in Figure 9-2. The fact that a bridge is connecting to two different IPX network numbers will cause a routing loop, with packets having their TTL incrementing up to 16 before disappearing from the routing table and then reappearing. This can cause client-server connectivity problems. When a router receives a packet with a TTL of 16, it will drop the packet and register a bad hop count on the `show ipx traffic` counters.

The problem can be resolved by putting a LAN analyzer on the segment that is suspected of having the backdoor bridge. When it is noticed that frames arriving from another network have a source node address of something other than that of the router, that is the MAC address of the backdoor bridge.

This type of technique also can be used to troubleshoot problems caused by a dual-attached server undesirably routing packets using IPX RIP or Novell's Multi-Protocol Router (MPR). This can lead to very slow response and other unpredictable results if the server is not intended to act as a router. Such a problem could be verified if it is seen on a LAN analyzer that packets arriving from another network have the server's MAC address rather than the router's address. Disabling IPX RIP or MPR on a Novell server is not always trivial, since a separate NLM may need to be loaded.

CAUTION: *Be aware of potential problems caused by backdoor bridges or dual-attached servers acting as routers on Novell networks.*

```
R3>sh ipx traffic
System Traffic for 0.0000.0000.0001 System-Name: sarahl-wan
Rcvd:    449578 total, 885 format errors, 0 checksum errors, 43 bad hop count,
         390 packets pitched, 1180797 local destination, 0 multicast
Bcast:   118307 received, 287124 sent
Sent:    295976 generated, 279055 forwarded
         24 encapsulation failed, 4609 no route
SAP:     84 SAP requests, 0 SAP replies, 257 servers
         73116 SAP advertisements received, 263121 sent
         0 SAP flash updates sent, 1 SAP format errors, last seen from
  AB90CF86.d8d8.302c.0f1c
RIP:     85 RIP requests, 0 RIP replies, 2167 routes
         40983797 RIP advertisements received, 71902663 sent
         2323896 RIP flash updates sent, 0 RIP format errors
Echo:    Rcvd 0 requests, 0 replies
         Sent 20 requests, 0 replies
         0 unknown: 0 no socket, 0 filtered, 0 no helper
         0 SAPs throttled, freed NDB len 0
Watchdog:
         0 packets received, 0 replies spoofed
Queue lengths:
         IPX input: 0, SAP 0, RIP 0, GNS 0
         SAP throttling length: 0/(no limit), 0 nets pending lost route reply
         Delayed process creation: 0
EIGRP:   Total received 4750085, sent 4757998
         Updates received 246274, sent 227780
         Queries received 107763, sent 93797
         Replies received 94259, sent 107043
         SAPs received 517327, sent 662522
NLSP:    Level-1 Hellos received 0, sent 0
         PTP Hello received 0, sent 0
         Level-1 LSPs received 0, sent 0
         LSP Retransmissions: 0
         LSP checksum errors received: 0
         LSP HT=0 checksum errors received: 0
         Level-1 CSNPs received 0, sent 0
         Level-1 PSNPs received 0, sent 0
         Level-1 DR Elections: 0
         Level-1 SPF Calculations: 0
         Level-1 Partial Route Calculations: 0
R3>
```

Listing 9-7

Debug Commands

The `debug ipx routing` Command There are two commands for debugging IPX RIP updates, namely, `debug ipx routing events` and `debug ipx routing activity`. Both commands give a similar type of information, with more detail about hop and tick counts being included in the output of `debug ipx routing activity`. Refer to the network

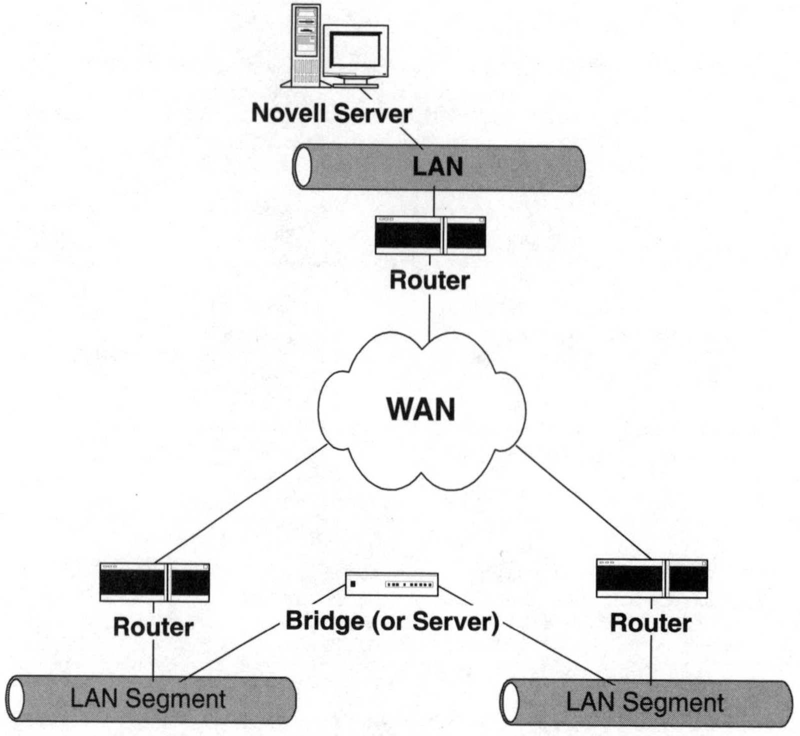

Figure 9-2
A backdoor bridge or routing server scenario.

shown in Figure 9-3. The IPX network numbers are shown, and routers R1, R2, R3, and R5 have IPX internal network numbers of 111, 222, 333, and 555, respectively. Router R5's routing is cleared using `clear ipx route *`, and the output of each of these debug commands is then demonstrated. Routes are first deleted after clearing the table, and then flash updates are sent. In the case of `debug ipx routing events`, some of the general routing events such as the sending and receipt of updates are highlighted along with events relating to specific route 913. It can be seen that `debug ipx routing activity` includes a breakdown of the actual routes in each update and hence is more processor-intensive. (See Listing 9-8.)

The `debug ipx packet` Command The `debug ipx packet` command is both an extremely useful tool and a very dangerous one. This should not be enabled on a router that has a large routing table or even more particularly a large SAP table. The cutoff point for too large is very difficult to assess because it relates to the router's processor load and how many interfaces are participating in IPX. I would say that a very

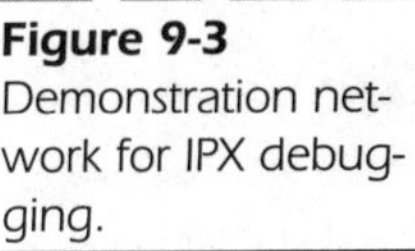

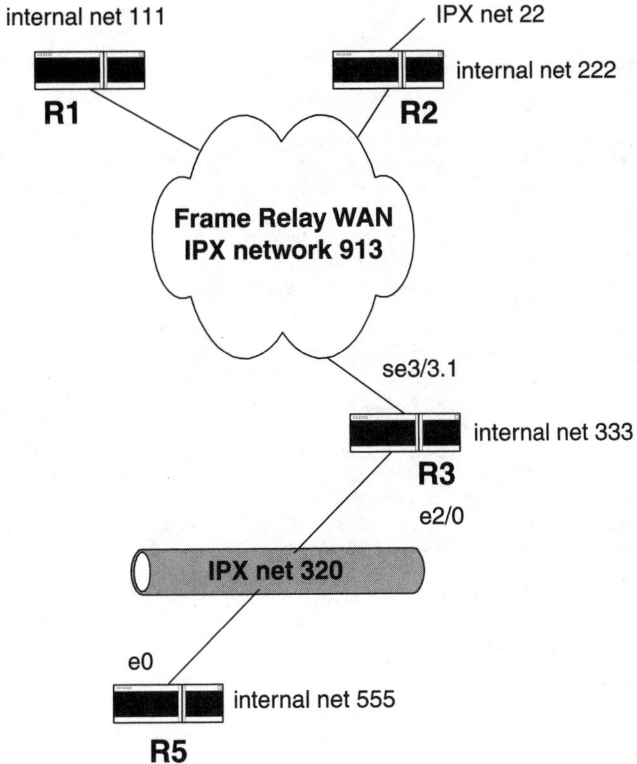

Figure 9-3 Demonstration network for IPX debugging.

conservative approach to the use of this command is advisable, since I have seen this debug command crash routers on live networks.

Referring again to the network in Figure 9-3, the routing table was cleared while IPX packet debugging was enabled. The MAC address of R5's Ethernet port is 0000.0c05.c067, and R3's Ethernet MAC address is 0010.1fc8.9c10. R5 is seen sending and receiving broadcast packets on the Ethernet segment. The source of the received broadcasts is R3. Unicast packets are also exchanged between R5 and R3. The packet length is given, and all these packets have a tick count of zero because each router is attached directly to the segment. The IPX cache is cleared after the clearing of the routing table and the receipt of new routing updates (see Listing 9-9).

The `debug ipx sap activity` Command This is another IPX debug command that is quite processor-intensive, so the same little cautionary speech that I gave in relation to `debug ipx packet` applies to almost the same degree here.

```
r5#debug ipx routing events
IPX routing events debugging is on
r5#cle ipx ro *
r5#
IPXRIP: Deleting network 913 in table-wide purge
IPXRIP: Marking network 913 for Flash Update
IPXRIP: Deleting network 111 in table-wide purge
IPXRIP: Marking network 111 for Flash Update
IPXRIP: Deleting network 222 in table-wide purge
IPXRIP: Marking network 222 for Flash Update
IPXRIP: Deleting network 333 in table-wide purge
IPXRIP: Marking network 333 for Flash Update
IPXRIP: General Query src=555.0000.0000.0001, dst=555.ffff.ffff.ffff, packet sent
IPXRIP: General Query src=320.0000.0c05.c067, dst=320.ffff.ffff.ffff, packet sent
IPXRIP: positing flash update to 320.ffff.ffff.ffff via Ethernet0 (broadcast)
IPXRIP: sending flash update to 320.ffff.ffff.ffff via Ethernet0
IPXRIP: Marking network 222 for Flash Update
IPXRIP: Marking network 111 for Flash Update
IPXRIP: Marking network 913 for Flash Update
IPXRIP: Marking network 333 for Flash Update
IPXRIP: positing flash update to 320.ffff.ffff.ffff via Ethernet0 (broadcast)
IPXRIP: sending flash update to 320.ffff.ffff.ffff via Ethernet0
r5#undeb all
All possible debugging has been turned off

r5#debug ipx routing activity
IPX routing activity debugging is on
r5#cle ipx ro *

r5#sh log
Syslog logging: enabled (0 messages dropped, 0 flushes, 0 overruns)
    Console logging: level debugging, 355 messages logged
    Monitor logging: level debugging, 285 messages logged
        Logging to: vty2(285)
    Trap logging: level informational, 23 message lines logged

%SYS-5-CONFIG_I: Configured from console by vty0 (172.16.50.3)
IPXRIP: Deleting network 913 in table-wide purge
IPXRIP: Marking network 913 for Flash Update
IPXRIP: Deleting network 111 in table-wide purge
IPXRIP: Marking network 111 for Flash Update
IPXRIP: Deleting network 222 in table-wide purge
IPXRIP: Marking network 222 for Flash Update
IPXRIP: Deleting network 333 in table-wide purge
IPXRIP: Marking network 333 for Flash Update
IPXRIP: General Query src=555.0000.0000.0001, dst=555.ffff.ffff.ffff, packet sent
IPXRIP: General Query src=320.0000.0c05.c067, dst=320.ffff.ffff.ffff, packet sent
IPXRIP: positing flash update to 320.ffff.ffff.ffff via Ethernet0 (broadcast)
IPXRIP: sending flash update to 320.ffff.ffff.ffff via Ethernet0
IPXRIP: update from 320.0010.1fc8.9c10
    222 in 1 hops, delay 3
    111 in 1 hops, delay 3
```

Listing 9-8

```
    913 in 1 hops, delay 2
    333 in 1 hops, delay 2
IPXRIP: positing full update to 320.ffff.ffff.ffff via Ethernet0 (broadcast)
IPXRIP: sending update to 320.ffff.ffff.ffff via Ethernet0
IPXRIP: src=320.0000.0c05.c067, dst=320.ffff.ffff.ffff, packet sent
    network 555, hops 1,  delay 2
IPXRIP: update from 320.0010.1fc8.9c10
IPXRIP: create route to 222 via 0010.1fc8.9c10, delay 3, hops 1
IPXRIP: Marking network 222 for Flash Update
    222 in 1 hops, delay 3
IPXRIP: create route to 111 via 0010.1fc8.9c10, delay 3, hops 1
IPXRIP: Marking network 111 for Flash Update
    111 in 1 hops, delay 3
IPXRIP: create route to 913 via 0010.1fc8.9c10, delay 2, hops 1
IPXRIP: Marking network 913 for Flash Update
    913 in 1 hops, delay 2
IPXRIP: create route to 333 via 0010.1fc8.9c10, delay 2, hops 1
IPXRIP: Marking network 333 for Flash Update
    333 in 1 hops, delay 2
IPXRIP: positing flash update to 320.ffff.ffff.ffff via Ethernet0 (broadcast)
IPXRIP: sending flash update to 320.ffff.ffff.ffff via Ethernet0
r5#
```

Listing 9-8 ***(Cont.)***

In Figure 9-3, the R3 router has two entries in its SAP table. IPX RIP is running on the LAN segment, and if you examine the output of `debug ipx sap activity`, you will see that IPX EIGRP is running on the serial 3/3.1 interface. Periodic SAP updates (IPX SAP) are also being sent but not received on this interface. This implies that IPX RIP has not been disabled for the 913 network on R3, but it is not running at the other end of this WAN link; hence R3 is not receiving RIP updates.

To avoid confusion, note that FERV320 is a static SAP configured on R3 and given a hop count of 2. PSERV22 is also a static SAP configured on R2; this was given a hop count of 1. This illustrates that static SAPs do not have their hop count incremented as they propagate through the network.

The other SAP queries seen in the output (Listing 9-10) are IPX EIGRP queries. You also will notice that the SAP relating to network 320 was rejected when received over the serial interface. FSERV320 is eventually designated as being unreachable (hop count of 16) from R3 over the serial interface. This is equivalent to a poison reverse update from R1 to R3 about FSERV320, since R1 learned this SAP from R3. It is a

```
r5#deb ipx packet
IPX packet debugging is on
r5#
r5#cle ipx ro *
r5#
IPX: cache flush
IPX: local:320.0000.0c05.c067->320.ffff.ffff.ffff ln= 40 tc=00,
  gw=Et0:320.ffff.ffff.ffff
IPX: local:320.0000.0c05.c067->320.ffff.ffff.ffff ln= 34 tc=00,
  gw=Et0:320.ffff.ffff.ffff
IPX: Et0:320.0010.1fc8.9c10->320.0000.0c05.c067 ln= 72 tc=00, rcvd
IPX: Et0:320.0010.1fc8.9c10->320.0000.0c05.c067 ln= 72 tc=00, local
IPX: Et0:320.0010.1fc8.9c10->320.0000.0c05.c067 ln= 96 tc=00, rcvd
IPX: Et0:320.0010.1fc8.9c10->320.0000.0c05.c067 ln= 96 tc=00, local
IPX: local:320.0000.0c05.c067->320.ffff.ffff.ffff ln= 96 tc=00,
  gw=Et0:320.ffff.ffff.ffff
IPX: Et0:320.0010.1fc8.9c10->320.ffff.ffff.ffff ln= 96 tc=00, rcvd
IPX: Et0:320.0010.1fc8.9c10->320.ffff.ffff.ffff ln= 96 tc=00, local
IPX: Et0:320.0010.1fc8.9c10->320.ffff.ffff.ffff ln= 72 tc=00, rcvd
IPX: Et0:320.0010.1fc8.9c10->320.ffff.ffff.ffff ln= 72 tc=00, local
IPX: cache flush
IPX: cache flush
IPX: cache flush
IPX: cache flush
IPX: cache flush
IPX: Et0:AA11.0000.8106.8af7->0.ffff.ffff.ffff ln= 96 tc=00, rcvd
IPX: Et0:AA11.0000.8106.8af7->0.ffff.ffff.ffff ln= 96 tc=00, bad pkt
IPX: Et0:AA11.0000.8106.8af7->0.ffff.ffff.ffff ln= 34 tc=00, rcvd
IPX: Et0:AA11.0000.8106.8af7->0.ffff.ffff.ffff ln= 34 tc=00, local
r5#undeb all
All possible debugging has been turned off
r5#
```

Listing 9-9

further illustration of the principle that for a SAP to be placed in the SAP table, it must be received on the same interface as the existing route to its network. This is, of course, not the case in relation to this particular SAP update for FSERV320.

The `debug ipx sap events` Commmand This tool gives a good level of SAP information while being less processor-intensive than `debug ipx sap activity`. The output in Listing 9-11 relates to the same set of SAP updates on R3. As you can see, this command gives less detail but sometimes can be a better option on a large and busy IPX network.

```
r3#sh ipx server
Codes: S - Static, P - Periodic, E - EIGRP, N - NLSP, H - Holddown, + = detail
2 Total IPX Servers

Table ordering is based on routing and server info

   Type Name                       Net      Address     Port       Route Hops Itf
S     4 FERV320                    320.0000.0323.34c1:0451         conn    2  Et2/0
E     7 PSERV22                     22.0000.0c3f.1123:0451 267520000/00    1  Se3/3.1
r3#

r3#sh log
Syslog logging: enabled (0 messages dropped, 0 flushes, 0 overruns)
    Console logging: level debugging, 69 messages logged
    Monitor logging: level debugging, 0 messages logged
    Trap logging: level informational, 41 message lines logged
    Buffer logging: level debugging, 69 messages logged

Log Buffer (8192 bytes):

%SYS-5-CONFIG_I: Configured from console by console
%SYS-5-CONFIG_I: Configured from console by console
IPXSAP: General Query src=333.0000.0000.0001, dst=333.ffff.ffff.ffff, packet sent
IPXSAP: General Query src=320.0010.1fc8.9c10, dst=320.ffff.ffff.ffff, packet sent
IPXSAP: General Query src=913.0010.1fc8.9c10, dst=913.ffff.ffff.ffff, packet sent
IGRP SAP sent
IPXEIGRP: Sending EIGRP SAP general query
IPXEIGRP: SAP from 913 rejected, route 320 in table via different interface
IPXEIGRP: Received EIGRP SAP from 913.0000.3060.1faa
IPXSAP: Response (in) type 0x2 len 160 src:913.0000.3060.1faa
  dest:913.0010.1fc8.9c10(85BE)
 type 0x4, "FERV320", 320.0000.0323.34c1(451), 2 hops
 type 0x7, "PSERV22", 22.0000.0c3f.1123(451), 1 hops
IPXEIGRP: SAP from 913 rejected, route 320 in table via different interface
IPXEIGRP: Received EIGRP SAP from 913.0000.3060.1faa
IPXSAP: Response (in) type 0x2 len 96 src:913.0000.3060.1faa
  dest:913.0010.1fc8.9c10(85BE)
  type 0x4, "FERV320", 320.0000.0323.34c1(451), 16 hops
IPXEIGRP: SAP from 913 rejected, route 320 in table via different interface
IPXSAP: positing update to 320.ffff.ffff.ffff via Ethernet2/0 (broadcast) (full)
IPXSAP: Update type 0x2 len 96 src:320.0010.1fc8.9c10 dest:320.ffff.ffff.ffff(452)
 type 0x7, "PSERV22", 22.0000.0c3f.1123(451), 1 hops
r3#
```

Listing 9-10

```
IPXSAP: General Query src=333.0000.0000.0001, dst=333.ffff.ffff.ffff, packet sent
IPXSAP: General Query src=320.0010.1fc8.9c10, dst=320.ffff.ffff.ffff, packet sent
IPXSAP: General Query src=913.0010.1fc8.9c10, dst=913.ffff.ffff.ffff, packet sent
IGRP SAP sent
IPXEIGRP: SAP from 913 rejected, route 320 in table via different interface
IPXEIGRP: Received EIGRP SAP from 913.0000.3060.1faa
IPXEIGRP: SAP from 913 rejected, route 320 in table via different interface
IPXEIGRP: Received EIGRP SAP from 913.0000.3060.1faa
IPXEIGRP: SAP from 913 rejected, route 320 in table via different interface
IPXSAP: positing update to 320.ffff.ffff.ffff via Ethernet2/0 (broadcast) (full)
IPX: I SAP query type 3 for server type 0x4 from AA11.0000.8106.8af7
IPXEIGRP: Received EIGRP SAP from 913.0000.3060.1faa
IPXEIGRP: SAP from 913 rejected, route 320 in table via different interface
IPXSAP: positing update to 320.ffff.ffff.ffff via Ethernet2/0 (broadcast) (full)
r3#
```

Listing 9-11

IPX Encapsulation Mismatches

Novell supports multiple encapsulation types for Ethernet, Token Ring, and FDDI. Sometimes different encapsulations must be configured on secondary or subinterface networks to support stations or servers residing on the same physical LAN segment that have different Novell encapsulations.

Encapsulation mismatches can cause client-server connectivity problems not only on the local LAN segment but also for remote server access if the router port and the Novell station have different encapsulation types. The different IPX encapsulation types can be viewed as follows:

```
Router-1(config-if)#ipx network 99 encapsulation ?
  arpa          IPX Ethernet_II
  hdlc          HDLC on serial links
  novell-ether  IPX Ethernet_802.3
  novell-fddi   IPX FDDI RAW
  sap           IEEE 802.2 on Ethernet, FDDI, Token Ring
  snap          IEEE 802.2 SNAP on Ethernet, Token Ring, and FDDI
```

Table 9-1 shows the different available encapsulation types for each LAN medium along with the Cisco default. Ethernet in particular can be a source of confusion because four encapsulation types are supported, and each is referred to by a different name depending on whether your documentation is from Novell, Cisco, or the industry in general.

TABLE 9-1

Different Encapsulation Types for Various LAN Media

Lan Medium	Cisco Default Encapsulation	Configurable Encapsulations
Ethernet	Novell-Ether	ARPA, SAP, SNAP
Token Ring	SAP	SNAP
FDDI	SNAP	SAP, Novell-FDDI

- *ETHERNET_II*. This is the Novell term for an ARPA frame that includes the *Type* field.
- *ETHERNET_802.2*. This is the Novell term for the standard IEEE 802.3 frame type, which includes the *Length* field and 802.2 SAPs. The Cisco term is SAP.
- *ETHERNET_802.3*. This is Novell's term for its own version of 802.3 that does not include 802.2 SAPs. Cisco calls this *Novell-Ether*, and it is the default IPX encapsulation on a Cisco router's Ethernet interface. A common industry term for this frame type is *Novell 802.3 raw*.
- *ETHERNET_SNAP*. This frame type is like ETHERNET_802.2 with a SNAP header included. Both Cisco and the industry refer to this encapsulation as *SNAP*.

Now that you are suitably confused about the different IPX Ethernet encapsulations, try using Figure 9-4 to clear your head.

Now let's examine a scenario in which an encapsulation mismatch causes an IPX connectivity problem. Routers R5 and R6 share a common Ethernet segment—IPX network 6. IPX pings are failing between the two routers. The relevant portions of the router configuration are as shown in Listing 9-12.

It can be seen from R6's configuration that the Ethernet 0 interface is configured with a SNAP encapsulation, whereas R5 has the default Novell-Ether encapsulation. This mismatch explains why pings are failing (see Listing 9-13).

Notice that R6's routing table shows IPX network 5, R5's loopback network, as being in holddown. It is to be expected that R6 should not see R5's loopback network because of the encapsulation mismatch. The fact that R6 has the route in holddown implies that the encapsulation has just been changed on one of the router's to produce the mismatch. IPX connectivity will be restored between the two routers by changing R6's Ethernet encapsulation to Novell-Ether (see Listing 9-14).

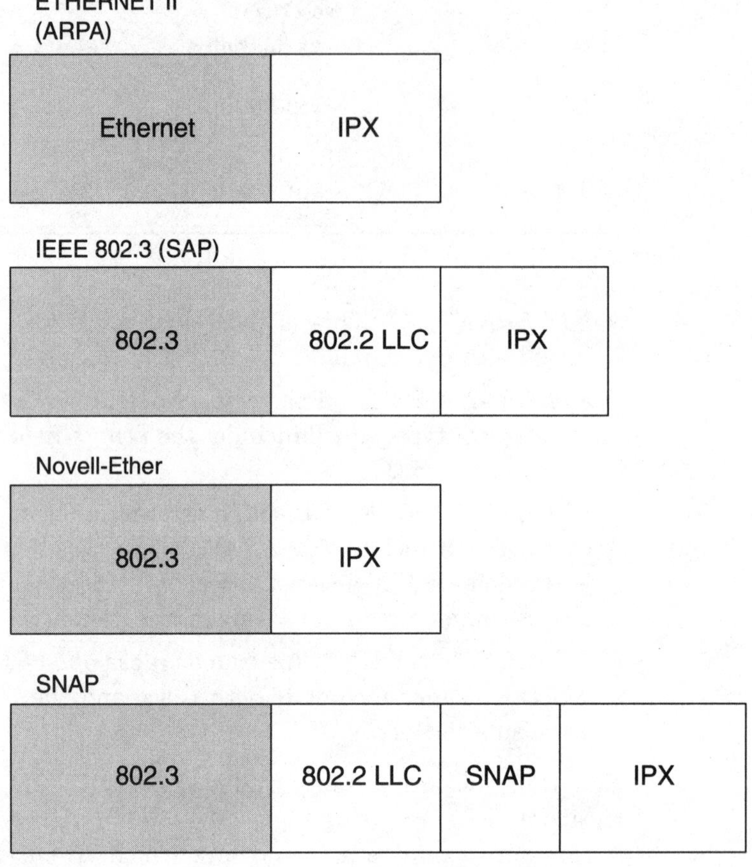

Figure 9-4 The different Ethernet/802.3 IPX encapsulations.

Now R6 has learned R5's loopback network and can ping R5's Ethernet interface.

This simple example of an encapsulation mismatch between two routers illustrates how such a mismatch can break client-server connectivity on a LAN or can prohibit WAN access for a client or server due to a mismatch between it and the local router port.

Adding a secondary network or a subinterface to the router port that uses a different encapsulation type can solve this type of problem. All stations using the second encapsulation must belong to that corresponding secondary network number.

```
interface Ethernet0
  ipx network 6
  ipx network 6b encapsulation SNAP secondary
```

Listing 9-12

```
r#6sh  run
Building configuration...

Current configuration:
!
version 11.2
no service udp-small-servers
no service tcp-small-servers
!
hostname r6
!
enable secret 5 $1$CHe/$QUDWaIX2zfd1/5cxz6QXy/
enable password cisco1
!
ipx routing 0000.0c34.9400
!
interface Ethernet0
 ip address 172.16.12.1 255.255.255.0
 ipx encapsulation SNAP
 ipx network 6
!
!
line con 0
line aux 0
line vty 0 4
 password cisco
 login
!
end

r6#

r5#sh run
Building configuration...

Current configuration:
!
version 11.2
no service udp-small-servers
no service tcp-small-servers
!
hostname r5
!
enable secret 5 $1$XiWp$4kOfaw/QqQx8wjxtLK98U.
enable password cisco1
!
ipx routing 0000.0c16.fa42
!
interface Loopback0
 ip address 172.16.200.1 255.255.255.0
 ipx network 5
!
interface Ethernet0
 mac-address 0007.0c16.fa42
 ip address 172.16.12.2 255.255.255.0
 media-type 10BaseT
```

Listing 9-12 (*Cont.*)

```
 ipx network 6
!
interface Ethernet1
 no ip address
 shutdown
!
line con 0
line aux 0
line vty 0 4
 password cisco
 login
!
end

r5#sh ipx route
Codes: C - Connected primary network,    c - Connected secondary
  network
       S - Static, F - Floating static, L - Local (internal), W -
  IPXWAN
       R - RIP, E - EIGRP, N - NLSP, X - External, A - Aggregate
       s - seconds, u - uses
2 Total IPX routes. Up to 1 parallel paths and 16 hops allowed.

No default route known.

C          5 (UNKNOWN),        Lo0
C          6 (NOVELL-ETHER),  Et0
r5#
```

```
r6#sh ipx ro
Codes: C - Connected primary network,    c - Connected secondary network
       S - Static, F - Floating static, L - Local (internal), W - IPXWAN
       R - RIP, E - EIGRP, N - NLSP, X - External, A - Aggregate
       s - seconds, u - uses

2 Total IPX routes. Up to 1 parallel paths and 16 hops allowed.

No default route known.

C          6 (SNAP),           Et0
RH         5 [**/**]
r6#
```

Listing 9-13

```
r6#conf t
Enter configuration commands, one per line.  End with CNTL/Z.
r6(config)#in e0
r6(config-if)#ipx encapsulation novell-ether
r6(config-if)#^Z
r6#

r6#cle ipx ro *
r6#sh ipx ro
Codes: C - Connected primary network,    c - Connected secondary network
       S - Static, F - Floating static, L - Local (internal), W - IPXWAN
       R - RIP, E - EIGRP, N - NLSP, X - External, A - Aggregate
       s - seconds, u - uses

2 Total IPX routes. Up to 1 parallel paths and 16 hops allowed.

No default route known.
C          6 (NOVELL-ETHER),  Et0
R          5 [02/01] via       6.0007.0c16.fa42,     1s, Et0
r6#ping ipx 6.0007.0c16.fa42
Type escape sequence to abort.
Sending 5, 100-byte IPX cisco Echoes to 6.0007.0c16.fa42, timeout is 2 seconds:
!!!!!
Success rate is 100 percent (5/5), round-trip min/avg/max = 4/4/4 ms
r6#
```

Listing 9-14

SAP, Route, and Access Filtering

SAP Filtering

SAP filtering is used to reduce the propagation of IPX SAPs to networks that do not require those particular SAP types. It is a powerful tool for reducing unnecessary bandwidth consumption by SAPs, especially in the WAN. SAP access lists are also used to minimize the size of SAP tables in the routers and in some cases to avoid several duplicate SAP updates from being advertised on the same network.

The following SAP filter blocks any HP DeskJet SAPs from being advertised out the serial 0 interface regardless of the network on which they originated. File services advertised by the server FileSRV2 on network aa23 are also filtered. All other SAPs in the router's SAP table will be advertised out serial 0. Note that there is no implicit permit-all, and the policy of allowing all other SAPs must be configured using `permit -1` at the end of the access list. This is displayed in the configuration as permit FFFFFFFF, which allows any SAP from any source network.

```
!
interface serial0
ipx output-sap-filter 1000
!
access-list 1000 deny FFFFFFFF 30C
access-list 1000 deny aa23 4 FileSRV2
access-list 1000 permit FFFFFFFF
```

NOTE: On IPX SAP filters there is an implicit deny-all but not an implicit permit-all. If it is desired to forward all unspecified SAPs, then permit -1 *must be configured at the end of the list.*

IPX SAP filters can be at the root of many connectivity problems in part due to poorly configured filters. There are also cases where a new server is brought on the network and filters that are in place along the path that clients will take to this new server have not been modified appropriately. The issue of filters also should be kept in mind if a server is being moved to a different segment, even if it maintains the same internal network number; there could be a filter along the client-server path to the new segment that blocks SAPs from this network number.

NOTE: If a new server is commissioned or an existing server moved between segments, carefully ensure that there are no legacy filters that could block the new path for client-server traffic flow.

Manipulating GNS Responses

A router responds to GNS requests if appropriate. For example, if a local server with a better metric exists, then the router does not respond to the GNS request on that segment. When the router does respond to a GNS request, the GNS reply that it sends contains the name and address of the server whose availability was learned most recently.

There are instances where inappropriate GNS responses from the router can cause problems:

- The router "thinks" it has a better metric than a local server due to the configuration of the server or because a static SAP on the router has a low configured hop count. This is undesirable because the response to GNS requests should only be a router function when there is no suitable local server. Configuring an `output-gns-filter` could alleviate the problem. Alternatively, a static SAP could be configured on the router giving the server a high hop count. Yet another possibility is to increase the GNS response delay on the router's interface in milliseconds using `ipx gns-response-delay`. This may allow a server to answer first. Care should be taken when using this command because the default delay, which can be checked using `show ipx interface`, varies depending on the Cisco IOS version. Also, some clients, such as OS/2 workstations, can have problems getting a connection if the delay is greater than 500 ms.

- The router persistently answers GNS requests with the details of the same server causing that server to become overloaded. This may happen if a given server remains higher in the router's SAP table because it was learned most recently. The solution here is to use the `ipx gns-round-robin` global command, which tells the router to alternate the servers detailed in its GNS responses.
- The router responds with the details of a server that should not be used for communications purposes. This is particularly relevant, but by no means exclusively relevant, to cases where a preferred server has not been configured on the client, and therefore, it may be required to first log onto the nearest server before accessing any other server. I will give three examples of related problem scenarios:
  - *FPNW.* If a Microsoft File and Print Services for Netware server replies as the nearest server, there are a number of issues. First of all, an FPNW is likely to be a nearest server because by default it does not use internal addresses and therefore appears as being one hop closer to the client. It also may advertise network 0, which is not a valid IPX network, as its IPX network number unless it is configured with an internal or physical network number. An additional problem with FPNW is that it does not support IPX RIP, preventing it from routing to the preferred server. FPNW servers are noticeable in the router's SAP table because they also use their physical MAC address to advertise SAPs. An FPNW server can be prevented from becoming the nearest server by not including it in an `output-gns-filter` on the router or by configuring a static SAP on the router for the FPNW server that features an unfavorable hop count.
  - The nearest server cannot see the preferred server due to a SAP filter on one or both of the servers. This can be checked for using the Novell `display servers` facility.

- *Insufficient user licenses on the nearest server.* If the server that most often answers GNS requests is a server with insufficient user licenses, then some clients will have their connection dropped when they attempt to attach to it. This problem also will occur if the router answers a GNS request with the details of such a server. Even if the server has the *Reply to GNS* parameter set to OFF, the router may still answer. One solution is to configure an `output-gns-filter` on the router, which blocks the advertisement of the server in question. Another possibility is to configure a static SAP with a high hop count, thus placing that SAP lower in the router's table. Note that SAA gateways can make good communications servers because they have a 255-user license.

Here are some examples of the tools mentioned to solve GNS-related problems. In the configuration in Listing 9-15, the router is told to rotate the servers that it uses in its GNS replies in a round-robin manner, thus preventing any one server from becoming the exclusive gateway for IPX initialization. The router also has a delay of 1 tick (55 ms) configured on Ethernet 0 in order to give servers on the this LAN segment the opportunity to answer the GNS requests first.

A GNS filter has been configured on the Ethernet 0 interface that only allows the router to respond to GNS requests on that segment with the details of two servers on the AA40 and AA54 networks. The filter also tells the router that any SAA gateway server (SAP type 130) is suitable for replying to GNS requests.

A static SAP has been configured for the fileserver BADBOY on network AA54; this has been given a fictitiously high hop count of 5 to move it lower in the router's SAP table.

Listing 9-15

```
ipx routing 0000.3021.0e0d
ipx gns-round-robin
!
interface ethernet0
ipx network 100
ipx output-gns-filter 1010
ipx gns-response-delay 55
!
access-list 1010 permit AA40
access-list 1010 permit AA54
access-list 1010 permit FFFFFFFF 130
!
ipx sap 4 BADBOY AA54.0000.2022.1212 451 5
!
```

There are a couple of points to note here before moving on. First, it is unlikely that all the tools discussed in the preceding example would be used to solve a problem relating to inappropriate GNS replies. In practice, one or two of the configuration features would be sufficient to solve the problem. How they are applied depends on each individual case, and all that is required of the network engineer is to precisely understand the rationale and effect of any configuration alterations.

There is also an issue in relation to the use of static SAPs to manipulate the perceived hop count to a given server. In newer Cisco IOS versions, the delay or tick count overrides the hop count in determining IPX routing decisions. The tick count can only be manipulated using the `ipx delay` interface command.

One other alternative that was not discussed is that the router can be prevented from answering any GNS requests on a given segment by using the `ipx gns-reply-disable` interface command.

Route Filters

As in the case of route filters for other desktop protocols, IPX route filters are configured for the following reasons:

- To reduce unnecessary bandwidth consumption by routing updates.
- To reduce the size of IPX routing tables where possible.
- To implement security policies.

IPX route filters can cause similar problems to SAP filters if they have been configured incorrectly or not updated appropriately as the network changes. Remember that a SAP will not appear in the router's SAP table unless it has a route to the server's network over the same interface on which it received the SAP update. A situation can occur where a SAP is not present in the router's table even though it is receiving the SAP update, because there is no route to the server's network. A route filter could be blocking the route, while the SAPs are propagating freely through the network.

Another scenario that is slightly more complex to troubleshoot is where the SAP is not present in the router's SAP table even though it has a route to the server's network. A possible reason for this is that there are multiple paths to the server's network and the router is receiving the SAP from a source other than what is displayed in its routing table as the next hop to that network.

Listing 9-16

```
interface TokenRing0
 no ip address
 ipx output-network-filter 801
 ipx network 22
 ring-speed 16
!
access-list 801 permit 30
access-list 801 permit 20
```

Listing 9-16 is a sample configuration that filters outbound IPX RIP updates on a token-ring interface allowing only IPX networks 20 and 30 to be forwarded onto the ring.

IPX Access Filters

IPX access control is achieved using standard and extended IPX access lists. Standard access lists can filter on the source network or node and optionally the destination also. This type of access list falls in the range 800-899, and the format is as follows:

```
Router-1(config)#access-list 800 per -1 ?
  -1              Any IPX net
  <0-FFFFFFFF>    Destination net
  N.H.H.H         Destination net.host address
  <cr>
```

An extended access list is designated by the 900-999 range and is significantly more sophisticated and powerful. Filtering is available on the basis of protocol type, source and destination address, and source and destination socket. As ever, along with increased sophistication come increased complexity and the possibility of configuration errors. It is very important to clearly understand the exact meaning and consequences of an extended access list before applying it to a configuration or before attempting to troubleshoot a possible access-list problem.

As an exercise, consider the network shown in Figure 9-5. Access list 800 is applied to outbound packets on router RA's serial 1 interface. The extended access list 901 is applied to inbound packets on the same router's Ethernet 0 interface. The two access lists are shown in Listing 9-17; using the Cisco Command Reference and Configuration Guide documentation, determine what is the effect of these access lists and any potential problems that you may see.

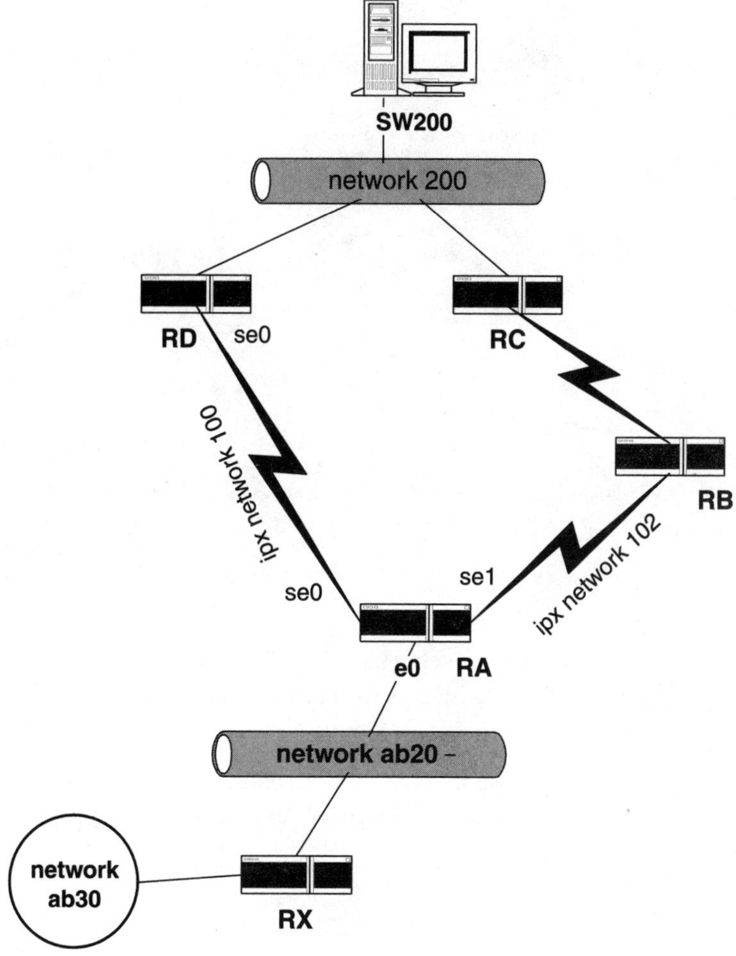

Figure 9-5 Filtering on an IPX RIP network.

Another issue to note is that access filters also can block routing updates and SAPs if the router sending the updates has its IPX network blocked by the access filter.

We will now consider one more scenario relating to filtering for the network in Figure 9-5. Clients on the ab20 network cannot attach to the SW200 file server that is on IPX network 200. On inspection, it is found that the appropriate SAP for this server is not present in RA's SAP table. RA does have a route to network 200 (see Listing 9-18).

Here it can be seen that the route is learned from over the serial 0 interface from the RD router. When the two directly connected routers

Listing 9-17

```
RA#
!
interface serial1
ipx network 102
ipx access-group 800 out
!
interface ethernet0
ipx network ab20
ipx access-group 901 in
!

RA#sh access-l 800
IPX access list 800
    permit AB20 200
    deny AB20

RA#sh access-list 901
IPX access list 901
    deny any AB30 all 200 ncp
    deny any AB20 all any eigrp
    permit any
RA#
```

RD and RB are checked, it is found that both have an entry for SW200 in their SAP tables. The configuration of each of these routers is then checked, and the following is found:

- RB does not have any outbound filter; hence it can be assumed pending further investigation that it is forwarding the SAP to RA.
- RD has the following filter configured:

```
RA#sh ipx rou 200
Codes: C - Connected primary network,    c - Connected secondary network
       S - Static, F - Floating static, L - Local (internal), W - IPXWAN
       R - RIP, E - EIGRP, N - NLSP, X - External, A - Aggregate
       s - seconds, u - uses

90 Total IPX routes. Up to 1 parallel paths and 16 hops allowed.

No default route known.

R       200 [02/01] via      100.0010.0d58.6860,   58s, Se0
RA#
```

Listing 9-18

```
interface serial0
ipx network 100
ipx output-sap-filter 1005
!
access-list 1005 permit FFFFFFFF 30C
access-list 1005 deny FFFFFFFF
```

This filter is likely to be a configuration error. It suggests that it was intended to filter SAP type 30C (HP DeskJet) and allow everything else. Instead, it is allowing SAP type 30C only. Therefore, the filer server SAP for SW200 is not being sent by RD to RA. This explains why the SAP is absent from RA's SAP table. However, what about the update that RA is receiving from RB? Check again the route that RA has to network 200, and it will be noticed that the route is learned from RD, and only one path is allowed. Hence, while RA is receiving SW200's SAP from RB, it does not have a route to network 200 over this interface, so it will not put the SAP in its table.

There are two ways to solve this problem. The most pressing issue is to reconfigure the SAP filter on RD as follows:

```
access-list 1005 deny FFFFFFFF 30C
access-list 1005 permit FFFFFFFF
```

Another solution, which may be a desirable thing to do in any case, is to allow RA to put multiple routes to the same destination in its routing table using the `ipx maximum-paths` command. This would enable RA to learn about network 200 from RB, and even though this route would have a higher hop and tick count, its presence in RA's routing table would mean that RA could place the SAP received from RB in its SAP table.

Client-Server Remote Connectivity

In order to apply any Novell problem-isolation techniques, a clear understanding is required of the client-server connection sequence that was outlined at the start of this chapter. Beyond this, practice and intuition in using the troubleshooting tools are the keys to success. When confronted with a problem such as the inability of a client to attach to a remote server, there are two basic approaches. You can choose to troubleshoot the network starting from the client's end or from the server. Choosing the most appropriate option here can save a lot of time in resolving the problem, especially on a large network. Two important pieces of information should be gathered:

- Can the client attach to a local server or any other remote server?
- Can any other clients attach to the server in question, and if so, are they local or remote to this server?

If it is found that clients on other networks can attach to this server, then it may be appropriate to begin troubleshooting at the client's end. A possible strategy could be

- Check that the client's local router has a SAP for the remote server and that it is the correct type of SAP. For example, the problem could be that the client cannot RCONSOLE to the server. In this case, SAP 107 must be in the local router's SAP table. If this SAP is not present, then check if the router has a route to the server's network. Repeat this process on each router along the path between the client and server. The problem may be due to multiple paths not being supported by a given router, or it may be due to a SAP, route, or access filter. Finding the router that does have the correct SAP and/or routing information usually can isolate this type of problem. It is possible that either this router has an outbound filter or the last router without the SAP has an inbound SAP or route filter.
- If the SAP is present in the local router's table. Then check that the server's router has a route back to the client's network. This is something that can get overlooked in the heat of battle. There could be a routing issue such as multiple paths or a filter blocking the propagation of this route.
- If the SAP is present in the client's router, another possibility is a GNS-related problem. For example, the router may be answering GNS requests with the details of a server that cannot route to the preferred server or a server that has a small number of licenses. This type of problem has been discussed already in some detail, and there are a number of configuration options available to resolve the problem. The difficult part here is establishing which server or servers are contained in GNS replies. If the Novell client cannot provide the information, then it may be necessary to run `debug ipx packet`, which is hazardous. A more ideal way to get the information is the use of a LAN analyzer.

SAP Bandwidth Consumption

With IPX RIP, periodic routing and SAP updates are sent every 60 seconds by default. This can cause congestion problems on slow-speed WAN links and on shared LAN or campus backbones. Sometimes the problem can manifest itself as slow response for attaching to Novell servers, but it also can have broader consequences, such as using up an excessive amount of bandwidth that is required by other protocols sharing the medium such as IP or SNA.

The case of a 56-kbps serial link is an obvious potential bottleneck when running IPX RIP. A less obvious problem could be a shared token-ring LAN backbone that has six routers attached to it. Each of these routers could be flooding the backbone with the same RIP and SAP updates every 60 seconds, resulting in a potentially serious traffic bottleneck.

SAP updates are particularly troublesome because they contain more information than a routing update. SAP packets are 480 bytes by default, which means that each packet can contain seven SAPs. This may cause critical bottlenecks on a large network that has several hundred entries in the router's SAP tables.

Here are some possible solutions:

- Increase the SAP interval on each end of a slow-speed WAN link. If this interval is set to 3 or 5 minutes, then the bandwidth consumption is reduced by an equivalent factor.
- The RIP and SAP interpacket delay can be increased by a small number of ticks on slow-speed WAN links and also on LAN server segments to ensure that the servers can keep pace with the SAP updates coming from the router. The default interval value for these parameters should first be checked using `show ipx interface` because it can vary depending on the Cisco IOS version. The configured delay should exceed the default by no more than a factor of 3. As in the case of adjusting update intervals, the delays should match on all interfaces connecting to the same WAN link or LAN segment.
- As already stated, the default maximum size of SAP updates sent out an interface is 480 bytes. This size allows for seven servers (64 bytes each), plus a 32-byte IPX SAP header. The maximum packet size can be increased up to a value of 4096 bytes using the following interface command: `ipx sap-max-packetsize`. This will reduce the percentage overhead in the transmission of SAPs and also will allow the

routers to process the SAP updates more efficiently. Again, this parameter should match on all interfaces connecting to the same network.

- On a LAN segment that only contains clients, periodic SAP updates are not actually required because the clients will not process them in any case. By setting the `sap-interval` to 0, the sending of periodic updates is disabled, resulting in a very significant bandwidth saving on that segment.

The other option that is available to use an IPX routing protocol that only sends incremental SAPs, such as IPX EIGRP or NLSP, particularly on the WAN links. This brings us to our next topic in a timely manner.

IPX EIGRP

IPX EIGRP is a scalable IPX routing protocol that is particularly suitable for large IPX networks that feature a large number of SAPs. Contrary to popular belief, while this protocol employs many similar principles to IP EIGRP, such as neighbor formation, the DUAL algorithm, feasible succession, and reliable update transmission, it is actually a totally separate protocol with its own routing table and topology database.

IPX routes that were derived using EIGRP will be displayed in the IPX routing table alongside other IPX routes if more than one IPX routing protocol is running on the router. Redistribution is automatic between IPX RIP and IPX EIGRP. Frequently, IPX EIGRP is only applied to WAN links, with RIP routing in the LAN environment. This is so because EIGRP is a more resource-intensive protocol that can increase the memory requirements on the router. Also, LAN Novell workstations or servers do not support IPX EIGRP.

After neighbor formation and the initial exchange of topology databases, all subsequent IPX EIGRP routing updates are incremental. Incremental SAP updates are sent by default on WAN links, whereas these updates are periodic on LAN interfaces. The sending of incremental SAPs can be configured on LAN interfaces, but this should *not* be done on any segments containing servers that still expect updates every 60 seconds.

Some of the tools used to monitor and troubleshoot IPX EIGRP will now be demonstrated.

Diagnostic Tools for IPX EIGRP

Show IPX EIGRP Neighbors The status and stability of the EIGRP neighbors can be checked using `show ipx eigrp neighbor` command. This will display the network and node address of all EIGRP neighbors and the interface over which they were learned. The current value of the hold timer is displayed, and the hello time can be inferred from this value, since it is one-third the hold time. For example, if the hold time usually varies between 10 and 15 seconds, it is probable that the hello interval is 5 seconds. The neighbor uptime is shown along with the round-trip timer to that neighbor and the negotiated retransmission timeout value. The Q counter displays the number of outstanding queries, and an incrementing value here could indicate a route convergence problem (see Listing 9-19).

Show IPX EIGRP Topology The contents of the topology database can be displayed using `show ipx eigrp topology`. The "P" in the left-hand column of Listing 9-20 indicates a passive state for that route; in other words, the protocol is not actively seeking a successor for this route. This is the normal stable state for all routes. The route to a feasible successor is shown for each route in the database along with its corresponding feasible distance.

Show IPX EIGRP Interface Information on all router interfaces that have IPX EIGRP enabled can be obtained from the output of `show ipx`

```
R1>sh ipx eigrp nei

IPX EIGRP Neighbors for process 211
H   Address                    Interface     Hold Uptime    SRTT    RTO  Q  Seq
                                             (sec)          (ms)        Cnt Num
0   AB82FD0C.0090.bf7e.8820 Se0                13 5w6d         8    216  0  588412
R1>
```

Listing 9-19

```
R1>sh ipx eigrp topol
IPX EIGRP Topology Table for process 211

Codes: P - Passive, A - Active, U - Update, Q - Query, R - Reply,
       r - Reply status

P 666666, 1 successors, FD is 276864000
         via A82FD0C.0090.bf7e.8820 (276864000/276352000), Serial0
P 390A, 1 successors, FD is 276864000
         via A82FD0C.0090.bf7e.8820 (276864000/276352000), Serial0
P A301580, 1 successors, FD is 282496000
         via A82FD0C.0090.bf7e.8820 (282496000/281984000), Serial0
P FFFF, 1 successors, FD is 282496000
         via A82FD0C.0090.bf7e.8820 (282496000/281984000), Serial0
P EEEE, 1 successors, FD is 283904000
         via A82FD0C.0090.bf7e.8820 (283904000/283392000), Serial0
P 2B2BAD, 1 successors, FD is 278272000
         via A82FD0C.0090.bf7e.8820 (278272000/277760000), Serial0
R1>
```

Listing 9-20

interface. The number of peers or neighbors formed over each interface is displayed along with information on interface timers and the contents of EIGRP transmission queues. In the example in Listing 9-21, notice that no peers have been formed over the BRI0 interface, implying that the interface may be in dial-backup mode.

Show IPX Route The `show ipx route` command will display the entire contents of the IPX routing table, including all routes, regardless

```
R1#sh ipx eigrp interface

IPX EIGRP Interfaces for process 211

                    Xmit Queue   Mean   Pacing Time   Multicast    Pending
Interface    Peers  Un/Reliable  SRTT   Un/Reliable   Flow Timer   Routes
BRI0           0        0/0         0      16/16           0           0
Se0            1        0/0        23       1/36         140           0
R1#
```

Listing 9-21

of the IPX routing protocol from which they were learned. An "E" in the left-hand column designates IPX EIGRP routes. In the example of the route to network 2 (Listing 9-22), the route has a metric of 276864000 and a tick count of 7. IPX EIGRP metric calculation relates to interface bandwidth and delay as in the case of IP EIGRP. The next-hop address that sent the update is shown, and there have been no incremental updates for this route in over 4 days and 20 hours.

Show IPX Servers If SAPs have been received in an incremental fashion through EIGRP, then they will be displayed in the SAP table with an "E" in the left-hand column. The other difference to note is that the route metric will have the EIGRP format as distinct from a simple hop count (see Listing 9-23).

Show IPX EIGRP Traffic Summary information on the different types of IPX EIGRP traffic sent and received by the router can be obtained using the show ipx eigrp traffic command (see Listing 9-24).

```
R1#sh ipx route
Codes: C - Connected primary network,    c - Connected secondary network
       S - Static, F - Floating static, L - Local (internal), W - IPXWAN
       R - RIP, E - EIGRP, N - NLSP, X - External, A - Aggregate
       s - seconds, u - uses

6 Total IPX routes. Up to 1 parallel paths and 16 hops allowed.

No default route known.

C   A82F600 (NOVELL-ETHER),  Et0
C   A82FD0C (HDLC),          Se0
E          2 [276864000/7] via A82FD0C.0090.bf7e.8820, age 4d20h,
                          1u, Se0
E          3 [288128000/10] via A82FD0C.0090.bf7e.8820, age 1w5d,
                          49723u, Se0
E          B [288128000/10] via A82FD0C.0090.bf7e.8820, age 1d03h,
                          3409u, Se0
E          C [282496000/11] via A82FD0C.0090.bf7e.8820, age 4d08h,
                          2154u, Se0

R1#
```

Listing 9-22

```
R1#sh ipx servers
Codes: S - Static, P - Periodic, E - EIGRP, N - NLSP, H - Holddown, + = detail
5 Total IPX Servers

Table ordering is based on routing and server info

   Type Name                   Net     Address    Port     Route Hops Itf
E     4 BAT90119            000037.0000.f609.fa22:0451 269824000/02   3  Se0
E     4 BAT2000             110001.0000.0000.0001:0451 271232000/03   3  Se0
E     4 BAT90101            101001.0000.0000.0001:0451 271232000/03   3  Se0
E     4 BAT90105            91053A.0000.0000.0001:0451 271232000/03   3  Se0
E     4 BAT90106             10601.0000.0000.0001:0451 271232000/03   3  Se0

R1#
```

Listing 9-23

EIGRP Distribute Lists

The ipx input, output-route, and sap-filter commands are used for filtering IPX RIP updates and the corresponding periodic SAPs. These commands do not apply to IPX EIGRP. To filter routing and SAP information in EIGRP, appropriate distribute lists must be configured within the IPX EIGRP process. These distribute lists will be featured in some of the troubleshooting scenarios that we will study later in this chapter. They can be configured as shown in Listing 9-25.

In this example, IPX EIGRP 1 is running on network 913. There is an outbound route distribute list that allows networks 220 and 320 to be broadcast. Similarly, the outbound SAP filter 1000 denies file services from network 320 but allows print services from that same network to be advertised.

Listing 9-24

```
R1#sh ipx eigrp traffic
IP-EIGRP Traffic Statistics for process 11
  Hellos sent/received: 771847/772580
  Updates sent/received: 53257/53618
  Queries sent/received: 29560/23128
  Replies sent/received: 23057/29487
  Acks sent/received: 213237/105283
  Input queue high water mark 4, 0 drops

R1#
```

Listing 9-25

```
access-list 801 permit 220
access-list 801 permit 320
access-list 1000 deny 320 4
access-list 1000 permit 320 7
!
!
!
ipx router eigrp 1
 distribute-sap-list 1000 out
 distribute-list 801 out
 network 913
!
```

NetBIOS over IPX

A router will drop IPX broadcasts by default unless an IPX helper address is configured on the appropriate interface. This technique can be used to propagate IPX broadcast packets such as type 20 packets, which is NetBIOS over IPX.

If it is reported that a NetBIOS application is not working in a Novell environment, the routers should be checked to ensure that one of the following configuration options is appropriately in place.

The following configuration uses a helper address to forward type 20 broadcast packets:

```
interface ethernet0/0
ipx type-20-helpered
ipx helper-address 100.0000.0c05.c067
```

However, the method that fully complies with Novell specifications is use of the `ipx type-20-propagation` interface command.

```
ipx type-20-input-checks
ipx type-20 output-checks
!
interface ethernet0/0
ipx type-20-propagation
```

The input and output checks are an enhanced form of the IPX loop detection performed after the forwarding of a broadcast.

Another issue to be considered when troubleshooting NetBIOS is the existence of a NetBIOS filter. In a Novell environment, NetBIOS can be filtered on host name or on byte pattern as relating to the IPX network address. NetBIOS host name filtering will be discussed in detail in

Chapter 11. Filtering by byte offset can have an adverse effect on the packet transmission rate because each packet must be examined. This type of NetBIOS access control should only be used when there are no other options.

IPX in the Wide-Area Network

IPX over Frame Relay

When routing IPX over frame relay, one of the main issues to be careful about is split horizon. This has already been discussed at length in relation to IP, and the same issues hold true for IPX. Both RIP and IPX EIGRP have split horizon enabled by default on frame-relay-encapsulated interfaces. This will create problems in a hub and spoke type of network where the hub site is using a multipoint main interface as opposed to subinterfaces.

Split horizon can be disabled manually for IPX EIGRP, but this is not true for IPX RIP. This important point is another reason why IPX RIP is not a suitable WAN routing protocol in the particular case of multipoint frame relay.

NOTE: *Split horizon cannot be disabled for IPX RIP on frame-relay interfaces.*

The network shown in Figure 9-6 demonstrates a troubleshooting scenario for IPX over frame relay where RIP is the WAN routing protocol. Clients on IPX network 3 cannot attach to a server on IPX network 2. When R3's routing table is checked, it is found not to contain a route to network 2 (see Listing 9-26). The hub router R1 has a route to both networks 2 and 3. It is not propagating these networks to R2 and R3 over interface serial 0 because it learned the routes over that same interface. Hence split horizon applies. Because the protocol is IPX RIP, split horizon cannot be disabled. The solution here is to either use frame-relay subinterfaces or use a protocol such as IPX EIGRP for the frame-relay cloud.

I will demonstrate the use of IPX EIGRP to resolve this problem. IPX EIGRP is enabled on all routers for the frame-relay network (911). IPX

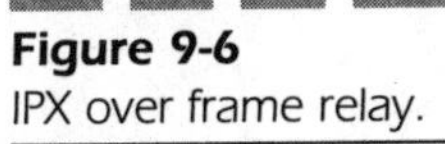

Figure 9-6
IPX over frame relay.

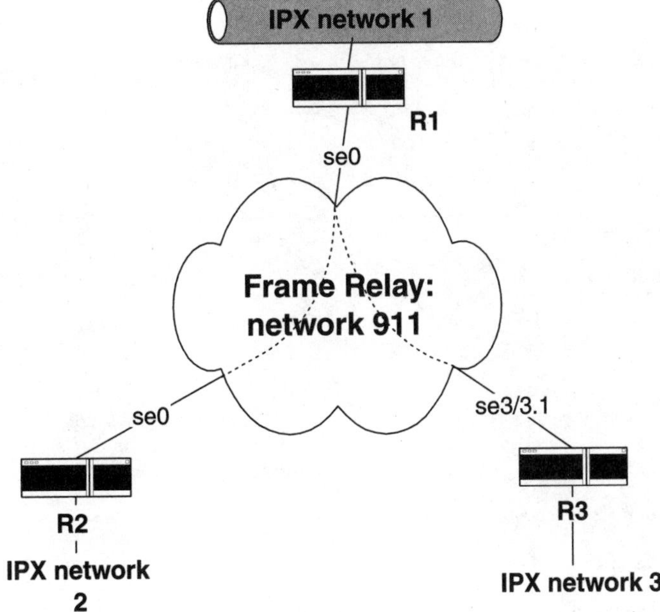

RIP is disabled for this network; this is not essential, but it is good practice (see Listing 9-27).

Split horizon is disabled on serial 0 on the hub router R1 for the IPX EIGRP 1 process. This allows R1 to forward routes that it learns back out this interface. When R3's routing table is checked, IPX network 2 is displayed as an EIGRP-derived route. Likewise, network 3 will be displayed in R2's routing table (see Listing 9-28).

IPX over ISDN

When a Netware LAN environment is extended across a dial-up WAN, there are certain issues that must be addressed carefully to ensure protocol connectivity without incurring prohibitively high dial-up charges. Generally, it is not good design to have an exclusively dial-up WAN backbone supporting a Novell network. The use of ISDN is more appropriate as a backup technology in this case, but some customers still insist on the exclusive use of ISDN in such an environment.

On an IPX RIP network, the following sockets must be filtered using dialer lists to prevent their traffic from unnecessarily bringing up the ISDN line:

```
r3>sh ipx route
Codes: C - Connected primary network,    c - Connected secondary network
       S - Static, F - Floating static, L - Local (internal), W - IPXWAN
       R - RIP, E - EIGRP, N - NLSP, X - External, A - Aggregate
       s - seconds, u - uses

3 Total IPX routes. Up to 1 parallel paths and 16 hops allowed.

No default route known.

C          3 (NOVELL-ETHER),        Ethernet0
C        911 (FRAME-RELAY),    Se3/3.1
R          1 [07/01] via      911.0000.3060.1faa,   10s, Se3/3.1
r3>

r1>sh ipx route
Codes: C - Connected primary network,    c - Connected secondary network
       S - Static, F - Floating static, L - Local (internal), W - IPXWAN
       R - RIP, E - EIGRP, N - NLSP, X - External, s - seconds, u - uses

4 Total IPX routes. Up to 1 parallel paths and 16 hops allowed.

No default route known.

C          1 (UNKNOWN),        Lo0
C        911 (FRAME-RELAY),    Se0
R          2 [07/01] via      911.0000.3020.f8ed,   13s, Se0
R          3 [07/01] via      911.0010.1fc8.9c10,   13s, Se0
r1>
```

Listing 9-26

452: SAP updates

453: IPX RIP updates

457: Netware serialization packets

The IPX watchdog keepalive packets that are exchanged between a server and its logged-on clients also will keep a dial-up line active. Watchdog spoofing for IPX as well as SPX packets should be configured on the ISDN interface to provide a local acknowledgment of these keepalive packets.

The Importance of Dialer Lists Dialing cannot occur if the ISDN BRI interface is not assigned a dialer group. The dialer group is in turn related to a dialer list. The function of the dialer list is to define what type of traffic should cause dialing to be initiated. A typical concern with

Listing 9-27

```
r3#wr t
Building configuration...

Current configuration:
!
version 11.2
!
hostname r3
!
enable password cisco
!
ipx routing 0010.1fc8.9c10
!
interface Ethernet0
 ip address 192.168.33.3 255.255.255.0
 ipx network 3
!
interface Serial3/3
 no ip address
 encapsulation frame-relay
 frame-relay lmi-type ansi
!
interface Serial3/3.1 point-to-point
 ip address 192.168.250.3 255.255.255.0
 ipx network 911
 frame-relay interface-dlci 301
!
router eigrp 1
 network 192.168.250.0
 network 192.168.33.0
!
no ip classless
!
ipx router eigrp 1
 network 911
!
!
ipx router rip
 no network 911
!
```

IPX over ISDN is that the line will be brought up needlessly due to periodic routing or SAP updates. (See Listing 9-29.)

This configuration would prevent IPX SAP, RIP, or Netware serialization packets from causing an ISDN call to be initiated. These IPX packets, however, can flow across the ISDN network while the line is up. Since they are not defined to be "interesting" packets, they do not cause the idle timer to be reset and hence will not needlessly keep the call up. Watchdog spoofing for IPX and SPX packets is also configured. When using IPX over ISDN, it is imperative to have a good understanding of what Novell traffic needs to flow across the WAN. The network and

```
r1#

!
interface Loopback0
 ip address 192.168.111.1 255.255.255.0
 ipx network 1
!
interface Serial0
 ip address 192.168.250.1 255.255.255.0
 encapsulation frame-relay
 no ip split-horizon eigrp 1
 ipx network 911
 no ipx split-horizon eigrp 1
 no fair-queue
 frame-relay lmi-type ansi
 frame-relay map ip 192.168.250.2 102 broadcast
 frame-relay map ip 192.168.250.3 103 broadcast
!
interface Serial1
 no ip address
 shutdown
!
interface TokenRing0
 ip address 130.11.65.1 255.255.255.0
 ring-speed 16
!
interface TokenRing1
 no ip address
 shutdown
!
router eigrp 1
 network 192.168.111.0
 network 192.168.250.0
!
logging buffered
!
!
!
ipx router eigrp 1
 network 911
!
!
ipx router rip
 no network 911
!
!

r1#

r3#sh ipx ro
Codes: C - Connected primary network,    c - Connected secondary network
       S - Static, F - Floating static, L - Local (internal), W - IPXWAN
       R - RIP, E - EIGRP, N - NLSP, X - External, A - Aggregate
       s - seconds, u - uses
```

Listing 9-28

```
4 Total IPX routes. Up to 1 parallel paths and 16 hops allowed.

No default route known.

C          3 (NOVELL-ETHER),         Ethernet0
C        911 (FRAME-RELAY),     Se3/3.1
E          1 [267008000/0] via       911.0000.3060.1faa, age 00:00:12,
                       1u, Se3/3.1
E          2 [267520000/0] via       911.0000.3060.1faa, age 00:00:11,
                       1u, Se3/3.1
r3#
```

Listing 9-28 ***(Cont.)***

router configurations must then be engineered to avoid keeping the ISDN link up for an excessive amount of time.

Snapshot Routing Another alternative is a Cisco feature known as *snapshot routing*. This is designed for chatty protocols such as IPX over dial-up connections. However, it can be applied to other media types such as frame relay or point-to-point HDLC. The idea is that one or more remote sites are configured as snapshot clients, and a designated central site is the snapshot server. The clients connect to the server sites for a period of time known as the *active period*. This can range upward from 5 to 1000 minutes in duration. During this period, routing information and SAP updates are exchanged between the connected sites. At the end of the active period, the *quiet period* begins, and during this interval, which

Listing 9-29

```
!
interface bri0
encapsulation ppp
ipx network 100
dialer map ipx 100.0010.1fc8.9c10 name r5 5551212 broadcast
no ipx route-cache
ipx spx-spoof
ipx watchdog spoof
dialer-group 1
ppp authentication chap
!
access-list 901 deny -1 FFFFFFFF 0 FFFFFFFF 452
access-list 901 deny -1 FFFFFFFF 0 FFFFFFFF 453
access-list 901 deny -1 FFFFFFFF 0 FFFFFFFF 457
access-list 901 permit -1

dialer-list 1 protocol ipx list 901
```

is usually configured to be several orders of magnitude longer than the active period, no dynamic updates are exchanged across the link. Routing and SAP information does not get timed out when snapshot routing is configured, thus eliminating the need for periodic updates.

Snapshot routing is relatively easy to configure, and the sample configuration in Listing 9-30 shows R3 as the snapshot client and R1 as the server. The snapshot relationship in this case is maintained over a serial link rather than ISDN. This problem was investigated because it was noticed on R1 that snapshot calls were occurring too frequently. It is always the client that initiates the snapshot connection, and when R3's configuration is checked, the quiet period is seen to be just 8 minutes. A more realistic value here would be in excess of 24 hours to avoid excessive snapshot connections. This snapshot timer information also can be obtained by using the `show snapshot` command on either router. At this point in time the state was just about to transition from quiet to active, as indicated by the "0 minutes remaining." Snapshot debugging also was written to log on the client in order to demonstrate the messages that are generated when the snapshot routing process transitions between states. Notice also that IPX protocol aging only occurs during the active state; otherwise, the protocol information would timeout during the quiet period.

Multilink PPP When the IPX traffic levels increase above a defined load threshold over ISDN, the second B-channel gets used. Packets can get sent out randomly on either channel. There is, however, no guarantee that traffic across both channels will take an identical path through the public ISDN network; thus there is no guarantee that both channels will experience equal delay while getting to the destination. Hence there is a high probability of packets arriving out of sequence at the destination router. This can cause problems with unreliable protocols or extremely time-sensitive protocols. Even with reliable protocols, a very high number of retransmissions can nullify the effect of using both channels. For example, I have seen instances with IPX where a high percentage of SPX retransmissions meant that the throughput was not significantly greater with two channels than with one.

The solution to this problem is Multilink PPP (MPPP). With this enhancement, a sequencing feature has been added that ensures that data are reassembled in the correct order at layer 2, thus eliminating the need for higher-layer retransmissions. MPPP is negotiated during the LCP setup stage, and both ends of the link must be configured to support

```
r1#

!
interface Serial1
 ip address 172.16.103.1 255.255.255.0
 ipx network 913
 snapshot server 5
 clockrate 56000
!

r3#
!
interface Serial3/3
 ip address 172.16.103.3 255.255.255.0
 ipx network 913
 snapshot client 5 8
!

r3#

r3#sh snapshot
Serial3/3 is up, line protocol is up Snapshot client line state up
  Length of active period:          5 minutes
  Length of quiet period:           8 minutes
  Length of retry period:           8 minutes
    Current state: client post active->quiet, remaining time: 0 minutes
    Updates received this cycle: ipx
r3#

r1#sh snapshot
Serial1 is up, line protocol is up, Snapshot server line state up
  Length of active period:          5 minutes
   For ipx address: 913.0010.1fc8.9c10
    Current state: server post active, remaining time: 0 minutes
r1#
r3#sh debug
Snapshot:
  Snapshot support debugging is on
r3#
*May 31 22:44:48: SNAPSHOT: Serial3/3[0]: moving to active queue
*May 31 22:45:34: SNAPSHOT: Serial3/3[0]: Starting aging of ipx protocol
*May 31 22:50:48: SNAPSHOT: Serial3/3[0]: moving to client post active->quiet queue
*May 31 22:53:48: SNAPSHOT: Serial3/3[0]: moving to quiet queue
*May 31 23:01:48: SNAPSHOT: Serial3/3[0]: Move to active queue (Quiet timer expired)
*May 31 23:01:48: SNAPSHOT: Serial3/3[0]: moving to active queue
*May 31 23:02:34: SNAPSHOT: Serial3/3[0]: Starting aging of ipx protocol
*May 31 23:07:48: SNAPSHOT: Serial3/3[0]: moving to client post active->quiet queue
*May 31 23:10:48: SNAPSHOT: Serial3/3[0]: moving to quiet queue
r3#
```

Listing 9-30

Listing 9-31

```
interface bri0
encapsulation ppp
dialer load-threshold 1
ppp multilink
```

it. The sequencing capability of MPPP allows it to view the two B-channels as a logically aggregated link.

The configuration in Listing 9-31 enables multilink PPP on the BRI0 interface, and both channels will always come up together regardless of interface load. Note that this configuration is at layer 2 and is independent of the IPX traffic on the interface.

More IPX Troubleshooting Scenarios

Consider the network displayed in Figure 9-7. This network is exhibiting several Novell client-server connectivity problems. The configurations for each of the three routers are provided, along with the IPX routing and SAP tables (see Listing 9-32).

After having reviewed this information, it is often a good idea to first check the routing tables to see if all routes have been propagated. The first issue to notice is that neither R1 nor R2 are learning any of R3's routes. When R3 is examined, it is found to have two IPX access lists. Both of these are applied to outgoing EIGRP updates. The network distribute list allows only network 220. Perhaps this is a mistake, and it should be network 320—the Ethernet segment. Also, there is an output SAP filter for EIGRP that denies file services originating from network 320. This explains why the static SAP for FSERV320 does not appear in R1's SAP table. We will remove both these filters, but alternatively, they could have been modified. The correct decision here depends on what type of routing and SAP propagation policy needs to be implemented while solving the problem. (See Listing 9-33.)

FSERV320 now appears in R1's SAP table, and the two local routes from R3 appear in its routing table as EIGRP-derived routes. However, the server advertised by R2 is still absent from R1's SAP table and is also therefore not getting advertised to R3. On examination, R1 is found to

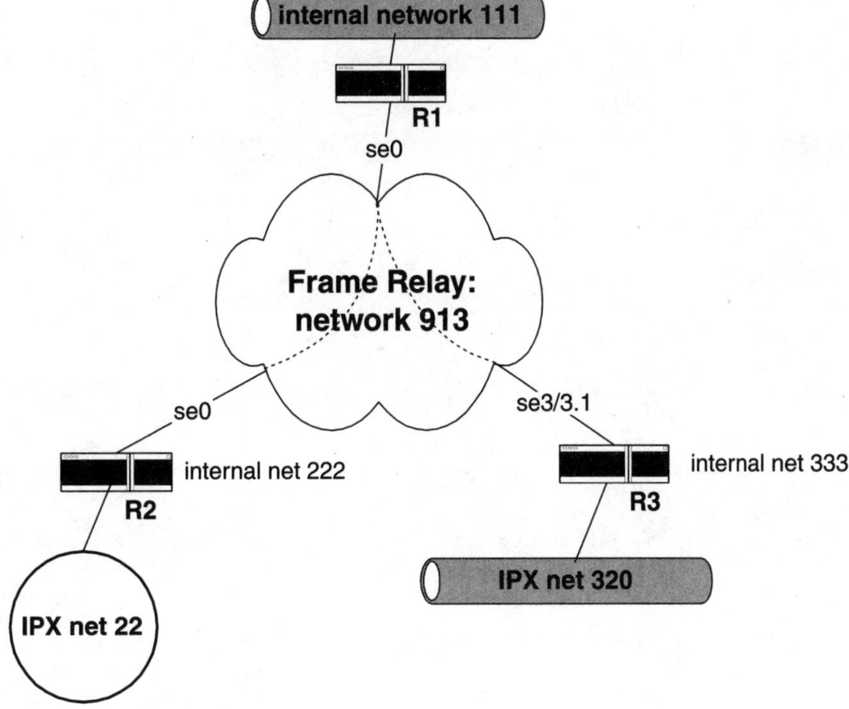

Figure 9-7
IPX RIP/EIGRP troubleshooting scenario.

have an EIGRP route distribute applied to inbound updates on serial 0. This list must be removed because it is blocking updates about network 22. (See Listing 9-34.)

Now R1 is seen to have a full complement of IPX services and routes. This now also appears to be true of R2 and R3. *However, another problem has been reported—that remote clients could not attach to a group of local file servers on R2's token-ring network.* (See Listing 9-35.)

The only local server in R2's SAP table is the static SAP. Access list 1009 is applied as an input SAP filter on the token ring. This filter only allows file services from network 23. Perhaps this is a configuration error. In this case, we will resolve this particular problem by modifying the SAP filter to also allow any services from network 22 and any file server regardless of its network address (see Listing 9-36).

```
r1#sh run

Building configuration...

Current configuration:
!
version 11.0
service udp-small-servers
service tcp-small-servers
!
hostname r1
!
enable password cisco
!
ipx routing 0000.3060.1faa
ipx internal-network 111
!
interface Serial0
 ip address 172.16.103.1 255.255.255.0
 encapsulation frame-relay
 ipx network 913
 no ipx split-horizon eigrp 1
 no fair-queue
 frame-relay lmi-type ansi
 frame-relay map ip 172.16.103.2 102 broadcast
 frame-relay map ip 172.16.103.3 103 broadcast
!
interface TokenRing0
 no ip address
 shutdown
!
interface TokenRing1
 no ip address
 shutdown
!
access-list 801 deny  22
access-list 801 permit FFFFFFFF
!
!
!
ipx router eigrp 1
 distribute-list 801 in Serial0
 network 913
!
!
ipx router rip
 no network 913
!
!
!
!
line con 0
```

Listing 9-32

```
line aux 0
 transport input all
line vty 0 4
 password cisco
 login
!
end

r1#sh ipx server
r1#sh ipx rou
Codes: C - Connected primary network,    c - Connected secondary network
       S - Static, F - Floating static, L - Local (internal), W - IPXWAN
       R - RIP, E - EIGRP, N - NLSP, X - External, s - seconds, u - uses

3 Total IPX routes. Up to 1 parallel paths and 16 hops allowed.

No default route known.

L        111 is the internal network
C        913 (FRAME-RELAY),   Se0
E        222 [267008000/0] via      913.0000.3020.f8ed, age 0:02:22,
                          1u, Se0
r1#

r2#sh run
Building configuration...

Current configuration:
!
version 11.0
service udp-small-servers
service tcp-small-servers
!
hostname r2
!
enable password cisco
!
ipx routing 0000.3020.f8ed
ipx internal-network 222
!
interface Serial0
 ip address 172.16.103.2 255.255.255.0
 encapsulation frame-relay
 ipx network 913
 no fair-queue
 frame-relay lmi-type ansi
 frame-relay map ip 172.16.103.1 201 broadcast
!
interface TokenRing0
 no ip address
 ipx input-sap-filter 1009
 ipx network 22
```

Listing 9-32 (*Cont.*)

```
 ring-speed 16
!
interface TokenRing1
 no ip address
 shutdown
!
access-list 1009 permit 23 4
!
!
!
ipx router eigrp 1
 network 913
!
!
ipx sap 7 PSERV22 22.0000.0c3f.1123 451 1
!
line con 0
line aux 0
 transport input all
line vty 0 4
 password cisco
 login
!
end

r2# sh ipx server
Codes: S - Static, P - Periodic, E - EIGRP, N - NLSP, H - Holddown, + = detail
1 Total IPX Servers

Table ordering is based on routing and server info

   Type Name                      Net     Address    Port     Route Hops Itf
S     7 PSERV22                    22.0000.0c3f.1123:0451      conn    1  To0

r2#sh ipx route
Codes: C - Connected primary network,    c - Connected secondary network
       S - Static, F - Floating static, L - Local (internal), W - IPXWAN
       R - RIP, E - EIGRP, N - NLSP, X - External, s - seconds, u - uses

4 Total IPX routes. Up to 1 parallel paths and 16 hops allowed.

No default route known.

L        222 is the internal network
C         22 (SAP),            To0
C        913 (FRAME-RELAY),   Se0
E        111 [267008000/0] via      913.0000.3060.1faa, age 0:10:18,
                          1u, Se0
r2#

r3#sh run
Building configuration...
```

Listing 9-32 ***(Cont.)***

```
Current configuration:
!
version 11.2
!
hostname r3
!
enable password cisco
!
ipx routing 0010.1fc8.9c10
ipx internal-network 333
!
interface Ethernet2/0
 no ip address
 ipx network 320
!
interface Ethernet2/1
 no ip address
 shutdown
!
!
interface Serial3/3
 no ip address
 encapsulation frame-relay
 frame-relay lmi-type ansi
!
interface Serial3/3.1 point-to-point
 ip address 172.16.103.3 255.255.255.0
 ipx network 913
 frame-relay interface-dlci 301
!
no ip classless
access-list 801 permit 220
access-list 1000 deny 320 4
access-list 1000 permit 320 7
!
!
!
ipx router eigrp 1
 distribute-sap-list 1000 out
 distribute-list 801 out
 network 913
!
!
ipx sap 4 FERV320 320.0000.0323.34c1 451 2
!
!
line con 0
line aux 0
line vty 0 4
 password cisco
 login
!
```

Listing 9-32 (*Cont.*)

```
 end

r3#sh ipx server
Codes: S - Static, P - Periodic, E - EIGRP, N - NLSP, H - Holddown, + = detail
1 Total IPX Servers

Table ordering is based on routing and server info

   Type Name                       Net     Address    Port     Route Hops Itf
S     4 FERV320                    320.0000.0323.34c1:0451      conn   2  Et2/0
r3#sh ipx route
Codes: C - Connected primary network,    c - Connected secondary network
       S - Static, F - Floating static, L - Local (internal), W - IPXWAN
       R - RIP, E - EIGRP, N - NLSP, X - External, A - Aggregate
       s - seconds, u - uses

5 Total IPX routes. Up to 1 parallel paths and 16 hops allowed.

No default route known.

L        333 is the internal network
C        320 (NOVELL-ETHER),  Et2/0
C        913 (FRAME-RELAY),   Se3/3.1
E        111 [267008000/0] via      913.0000.3060.1faa, age 00:03:16,
                       1u, Se3/3.1
E        222 [267520000/0] via      913.0000.3060.1faa, age 00:03:16,
                       1u, Se3/3.1
```

Listing 9-32 (*Cont.*)

```
r3#sh access-list
IPX access list 801
    permit 220
IPX SAP access list 1000
    deny 320 4
    permit 320 7
r3#conf t
Enter configuration commands, one per line.  End with CNTL/Z.
r3(config)#ipx router eigrp 1
r3(config-ipx-router)#no distribute-sap 1000 out
r3#cle ipx route *
r3#
r3#

r1#sh ipx serv
Codes: S - Static, P - Periodic, E - EIGRP, N - NLSP, H - Holddown, + = detail
1 Total IPX Servers

Table ordering is based on routing and server info

   Type Name                       Net     Address    Port     Route Hops Itf
E     4 FERV320                    320.0000.0323.34c1:0451 267008000/01   3  Se0
r1#

r1>sh ipx rou
Codes: C - Connected primary network,    c - Connected secondary network
       S - Static, F - Floating static, L - Local (internal), W - IPXWAN
       R - RIP, E - EIGRP, N - NLSP, X - External, s - seconds, u - uses

5 Total IPX routes. Up to 1 parallel paths and 16 hops allowed.

No default route known.

L        111 is the internal network
C        913 (FRAME-RELAY),   Se0
E        222 [267008000/0] via      913.0000.3020.f8ed, age 0:00:21,
                           1u, Se0
E        320 [267008000/1] via      913.0010.1fc8.9c10, age 0:00:17,
                           1u, Se0
E        333 [267008000/1] via      913.0010.1fc8.9c10, age 0:00:17,
                           1u, Se0
```

Listing 9-33

```
r1>sh access-list
Novell access list 801
    deny  22
    permit FFFFFFFF
r1>en
Password:
r1#conf t
Enter configuration commands, one per line.  End with CNTL/Z.
r1(config)#ipx router eigrp 1
r1(config-ipx-router)#no distribute 801 in ser 0
r1(config-ipx-router)#^Z
r1#cle ipx ro *

r1#sh ipx ro
Codes: C - Connected primary network,    c - Connected secondary network
       S - Static, F - Floating static, L - Local (internal), W - IPXWAN
       R - RIP, E - EIGRP, N - NLSP, X - External, s - seconds, u - uses

6 Total IPX routes. Up to 1 parallel paths and 16 hops allowed.

No default route known.

L        111 is the internal network
C        913 (FRAME-RELAY),   Se0
E         22 [267008000/0] via      913.0000.3020.f8ed, age 0:00:04,
                         3u, Se0
E        222 [267008000/0] via      913.0000.3020.f8ed, age 0:00:04,
                         1u, Se0
E        320 [267008000/1] via      913.0010.1fc8.9c10, age 0:00:01,
                         4u, Se0
E        333 [267008000/1] via      913.0010.1fc8.9c10, age 0:00:01,
                         1u, Se0

r1#sh ipx serv
Codes: S - Static, P - Periodic, E - EIGRP, N - NLSP, H - Holddown, + = detail
2 Total IPX Servers

Table ordering is based on routing and server info

   Type Name                       Net     Address    Port     Route Hops Itf
E     4 FERV320                    320.0000.0323.34c1:0451 267008000/01   3  Se0
E     7 PSERV22                     22.0000.0c3f.1123:0451 267008000/00   2  Se0
r1#
```

Listing 9-34

```
r2>sh ipx ro
Codes: C - Connected primary network,    c - Connected secondary network
       S - Static, F - Floating static, L - Local (internal), W - IPXWAN
       R - RIP, E - EIGRP, N - NLSP, X - External, s - seconds, u - uses

6 Total IPX routes. Up to 1 parallel paths and 16 hops allowed.

No default route known.

L        222 is the internal network
C         22 (SAP),           To0
C        913 (FRAME-RELAY),   Se0
E        111 [267008000/0] via      913.0000.3060.1faa, age 0:00:25,
                          1u, Se0
E        320 [267520000/1] via      913.0000.3060.1faa, age 0:00:24,
                          3u, Se0
E        333 [267520000/1] via      913.0000.3060.1faa, age 0:00:24,
                          1u, Se0
r2>sh ipx server
Codes: S - Static, P - Periodic, E - EIGRP, N - NLSP, H - Holddown, + = detail
2 Total IPX Servers

Table ordering is based on routing and server info

   Type Name                       Net     Address    Port     Route Hops Itf
E     4 FERV320                    320.0000.0323.34c1:0451 267520000/01   2  Se0
S     7 PSERV22                     22.0000.0c3f.1123:0451       conn   1  To0
```

Listing 9-35

Listing 9-36

```
r2>sh access-list
Novell SAP access list 1009
    permit 23 4
r2>en
Password:
r2#conf t
r2(config)#access-l 1009 permit 22
r2(config)#access-l 1009 permit -1 4
r2(config)#^Z
r2#sh access-l 1009
Novell SAP access list 1009
    permit 23 4
    permit 22
    permit FFFFFFFF 4
r2#
```

REVIEW QUESTIONS

1. The default IPX encapsulation on the Ethernet interface of a Cisco router is
   a. ARPA.
   b. SNAP.
   c. SAP.
   d. Novell-Ether.
   e. HDLC.
2. The default update interval for IPX RIP and SAP is
   a. 30 seconds.
   b. 60 seconds.
   c. 90 seconds.
   d. 2 minutes.
   e. incremental, not periodic.
3. An incrementing number of format errors in the output of `show ipx traffic` indicates that
   a. the hop count was exceeded.
   b. CRC errors exist on the LAN.
   c. packets were received with different encapsulations to the router interface.
   d. corrupt packets were received due to collisions.
   e. a remote router is running NLSP.
4. Type the debug command used to study IPX RIP events.
5. Which of the following IPX routing protocols have debug commands that can be confined to a particular IPX network?
   a. RIP
   b. EIGRP
   c. NLSP
   d. b and c
   e. all of the above
6. If a router is running IPX EIGRP on all interfaces, incremental SAPs will be sent by default on

a. all interfaces.

b. LAN interfaces only.

c. WAN interfaces only.

d. the first LAN interface.

e. no interfaces (must be configured).

7. Type the command that enables IPX load balancing on a per-packet basis.

8. Type the command that is also needed to load balance on a per-host basis.

9. If it is required to prevent an FPNW server from being advertised in router GNS replies, use

a. `ipx input-gns-filter`.

b. `ipx output-gns-filter`.

c. `ipx input-sap-filter`.

d. `ipx output-sap-filter`.

e. `ipx output-network-filter`.

10. Which of the following IPX debug commands is likely to place the highest load on a router?

a. `debug ipx nasi events`.

b. `debug ipx spoof`.

c. `debug ipx sap events`.

d. `debug ipx sap activity`.

e. `debug ipx packet`.

11. If router A has a route to a remote server's internal IPX network but does not see its SAPs, which of the following is possible?

a. Remote server is down.

b. Remote router is down.

c. IPX RIP is being filtered by router A.

d. SAPs are being filtered along the path back to router A.

e. Remote router is running split horizon.

12. Type the extended IPX ping option that allows appropriate Novell stations to answer IPX echo requests.

13. If IPX pings are sent to a host on a network that the router does not have a route to, the output will be

a. network unreachable.

b. destination unreachable.

c. request timed out.

d. protocol unreachable.

e. unknown packet type.

14. An incrementing bad hop count in the output of `show ipx traffic` could indicate

a. a routing loop.

b. a backdoor bridge.

c. that split horizon has been turned off.

d. all of the above.

e. a and/or b.

15. The router command that enables servers to share the GNS reply responsibilities is

a. `ipx output-gns-filter.`

b. `ipx input-gns-filter.`

c. `ipx gns-response-delay.`

d. `ipx gns-round-robin.`

e. any of the above.

16. Which Netware routing protocols rely on an internal network number to advertise and accept packets?

a. EIGRP

b. NLSP

c. IPXWAN

d. All of the above

e. b and c

17. Which of the following will *not* help reduce SAP congestion on a serial link?

a. Increasing the SAP interval

b. Increasing the SAP maximum packet size

c. Using EIGRP

d. Enabling split horizon

e. SAP filtering

18. Which of the following will *not* cause a router to drop Novell NetBIOS packets?

a. GNS filter

b. Missing `ipx type-20-propagation` command

c. NetBIOS filter

d. No IPX helper address

19. The Cisco router command that displays the router's SAP table is

a. `display servers`.

b. `S-list`.

c. `show ipx servers`.

d. `show ipx sap`.

e. `show ipx internal`.

20. In order to filter a particular IPX socket, use a

a. standard access list.

b. extended access list.

c. SAP access list.

d. summary address access list.

e. socket access list.

CHAPTER 10

Troubleshooting AppleTalk Connectivity

Introduction

Some fundamental AppleTalk theory will be reviewed at the start of this chapter. As with all desktop protocols, a sound understanding of the client-server connection sequence is essential for the effective troubleshooting of protocol connectivity. However, a very basic knowledge of AppleTalk and how it is configured on Cisco routers is assumed.

The different monitoring and diagnostic tools available for AppleTalk on Cisco routers will be discussed and demonstrated. AppleTalk is quite a user-friendly local-area network (LAN) protocol, but some of the features that contribute to its user-friendliness also can pose challenges for the configuration and troubleshooting of the protocol in a routed environment. Particular attention will be paid to networks that are running AppleTalk in the wide-area network (WAN). This chapter also features a number of troubleshooting scenarios relating to AppleTalk connectivity in the LAN and the WAN.

The objectives of this chapter are to

- Understand the AppleTalk client-server connection sequence.
- Learn how to configure and troubleshoot each of the different types of AppleTalk filters.
- Apply Cisco router `show` and `debug` commands to resolve problems on AppleTalk RTMP and EIGRP networks.
- Overcome the challenges encountered when running AppleTalk over WAN topologies such as ISDN and frame relay.

AppleTalk Client-Server Connection Sequence

The AppleTalk client-server connection sequence must be clearly understood in order to troubleshoot AppleTalk connectivity problems. The AppleTalk Transaction Protocol (ATP) is a connection-oriented transport layer protocol that is used by AppleTalk Filing Protocol (AFP) and the Printer Access Protocol (PAP). ATP is used to provide a reliable client-server connection sequence when a client attempts to attach to an AppleShare server.

This connection sequence for attaching to a remote server is displayed schematically in Figure 10-1 and entails the following:

Figure 10-1 AppleTalk client-server connection sequence.

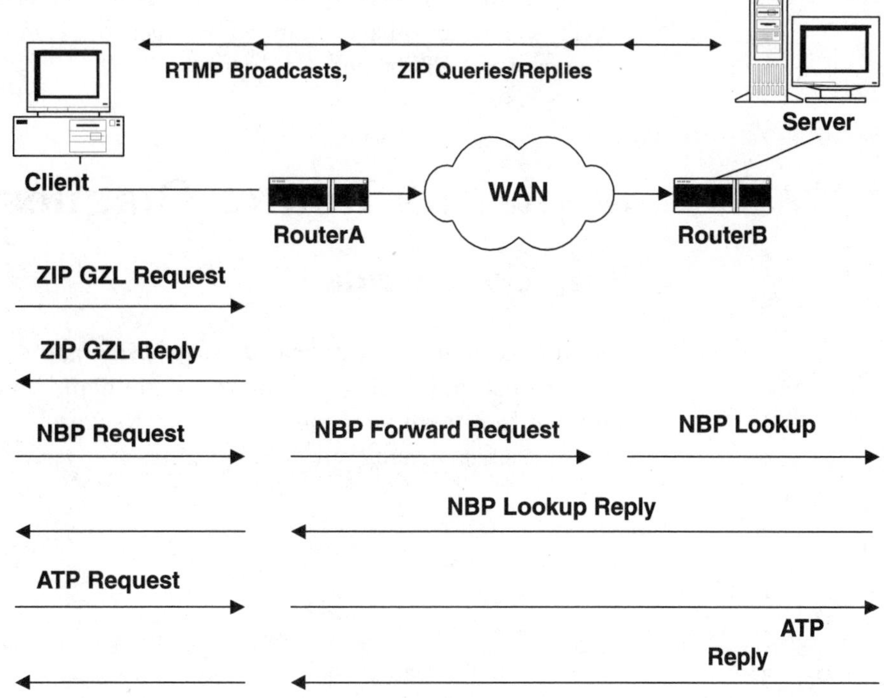

- The Macintosh client opens the Chooser window; this causes a Get Zone List (GZL) request to be generated in order to fill this window.
- The routers on the AppleTalk network have zone tables that are built using the Zone Information Protocol (ZIP), which maps zones against network or cable-range addresses. This enables the local router to answer with a GZL reply allowing the Chooser window to fill with zone names.
- The user then clicks on a zone name and type of service, and the Macintosh sends a Name Binding Protocol (NBP) request to the local router.
- The router then consults its zone information table and forwards the NBP request to all networks that are in the requested zone.
- When the router that is local to the requested zone receives the NBP request, it sends an NBP lookup request out on its local LAN segment. The servers that support the requested service type answer the client machine directly with an NBP lookup reply. This is possible because the NBP messages contain the address of the original client.

- The client then sets up an ATP and AFP connection with the server. ATP echoes are also exchanged between the client and server in order to negotiate ATP timeout values.

AppleTalk Router Diagnostic Tools

Ping Commands

The AppleTalk ping utility was discussed in Chapter 3. Listings 10-1 and 10-2 are examples of a simple and extended AppleTalk ping and are intended to refresh your memory. Table 10-1 provides a summary of the error messages arising out of failed pings.

```
Kildare1_10#ping apple 1000.48

Type escape sequence to abort.
Sending 5, 100-byte AppleTalk Echoes to 1000.48, timeout is 2 seconds:
!!!!!
Success rate is 100 percent (5/5), round-trip min/avg/max = 1/2/4 ms
Kildare1_10#
```

Listing 10-1

```
R3#ping
Protocol [ip]: apple
Target AppleTalk address: 1000.48
Repeat count [5]: 20
Datagram size [100]: 500
Timeout in seconds [2]:
Verbose [n]:
Sweep range of sizes [n]:
Type escape sequence to abort.
Sending 20, 500-byte AppleTalk Echoes to 1000.48, timeout is 2 seconds:
!!!!!!!!!!!!!!!!!!!!
Success rate is 100 percent (20/20), round-trip min/avg/max = 1/2/4 ms
R3#
```

Listing 10-2

TABLE 10-1

Summary of Failed Ping Error Messages

B	A malformed echo was received from the destination.
C	Echo reply failed the DDP checksum.
E	Echo failed to the destination address.
R	No route to the destination network.

NBP Test Commands

The AppleTalk NBP test facility is a feature introduced in Cisco IOS version 11.1, which enables the testing and verification of various NBP objects in the AppleTalk network. Four options are available (see Listing 10-3). The *Confirm* option allows the administrator to check that a particular name is registered to a device that has a specified address and zone. The *Lookup* option can be used to search for a particular NBP entity or set of entities. The *Parameters* option allows for the configuration of NBP timeout values that will be used in subsequent NBP tests. The *Poll* option searches for all NBP entities in all zones, this can generate a lot of traffic on a large network.

The NBP test facility can be used when a zone appears in Chooser, but particular devices in that zone cannot be accessed. If the NBP requests timeout, the corresponding server may be down, or there may be an NBP filter on one of the intermediate routers.

Listing 10-4 is a simple illustration of a router doing a successful NBP lookup for one of its own local entities, its token ring 0 interface.

Note that the fields in AppleTalk names are case sensitive. Also, an equals sign (=) acts as a wildcard for the object and type fields, allowing for a more broad-ranging lookup.

Listing 10-3

```
r2#test appletalk

r2(atalk test)#nbp ?
  confirm      Confirm NBP
  lookup       Send NBP Lookup
  parameters   Set NBP timeouts
  poll         Poll all devices in internet
```

Listing 10-4

```
r2#sh apple nbp
  Net Adr Skt Name                          Type            Zone
   24   2 254 r2.TokenRing0                 ciscoRouter     finance
   99   2 254 r2.Tunnel0                    ciscoRouter     tunnel

r2#test apple
r2(atalk test)#nbp lookup r2.TokenRing0:ciscoRouter@finance
(24n,2a,254s)[1]<-(24.2.2): 'r2.TokenRing0:ciscoRouter@finance'
NBP lookup request completed.
Processed 1 replies, 1 events

r2(atalk test)#end
r2#
```

Show Commands

The `show appletalk route` Command The `show appletalk route` command displays the contents of the AppleTalk routing table. In the example in Listing 10-5, router 3 has three connected networks running AppleTalk. The only remote route is the 3790-3790 cable range, which is one hop away and was learned via the Routing Table Maintenance Protocol (RTMP) from the 1070.145 node. All four routes are in the same AppleTalk zone, i.e., Online.

The `show appletalk zone` Command This command displays all zones of which the router has knowledge. These zones may be associated with locally connected networks or cable ranges that were learned via a dynamic routing protocol. Routers use the Zone Information Protocol

```
Router3>sh apple route
Codes: R - RTMP derived, E - EIGRP derived, C - connected, A - AURP
       S - static  P - proxy
4 routes in internet

The first zone listed for each entry is its default (primary) zone.

C Net 1060-1060 directly connected, Ethernet4/0, zone Online
C Net 1065-1065 directly connected, Ethernet4/1, zone Online
C Net 1070-1070 directly connected, Ethernet4/2, zone Online
R Net 3790-3790 [1/G] via 1070.145, 0 sec, Ethernet4/2, zone Online
Router3>
```

Listing 10-5

(ZIP) to exchange zone information. Note that the router often can maintain ZIP information that is no longer valid in its zone table. For example, if a particular zone or cable range has been decommissioned, it may take the router several hours or possibly even a reload to clear this information from its memory (see Listing 10-6).

The `show appletalk globals` Command The `show appletalk globals` command gives some potentially useful summary information regarding the AppleTalk configuration on the router. This command is best employed when you have something specific to check for rather than just browsing through the various parameter settings. All parameters are at their default settings in this example (Listing 10-7). As you can see, the basic timer intervals for ZIP, RTMP, and AppleTalk ARP are all very short, illustrating what a chatty protocol AppleTalk is. This output confirms that only RTMP is configured on router 3 and that there is just one zone. The line at the bottom of the output is both significant and subtle. The principle that it relates to will be discussed when we are studying AppleTalk access control. For the moment, just keep it as a mental note.

The `show appletalk interface` Command The `show appletalk interface` command is extremely useful. Not only does it display the interface cable range and zone, it also indicates if the interface node address is valid and if the AppleTalk line protocol is up on the interface. This validity of the address confirms that no other node on the network has a conflicting node address, which can be an issue with AppleTalk because of the dynamic nature of node address allocation. On interface Ethernet 2/0, router 3 has formed an AppleTalk neighbor relationship with 1000.243, which has verified the router port configuration (see Listing 10-8).

```
Router3>sh appl zone
Name                                    Network(s)
Online                                  3790-3790 1065-1065 1060-1060 1070-1070

Total of 1 zone
Router3>
```

Listing 10-6

```
Router3>sh apple globals
AppleTalk global information:
  Internet is compatible with older, AT Phase1, routers.
  There are 16 routes in the internet.
  There is 1 zone defined.
  Logging of significant AppleTalk events is disabled.
  ZIP resends queries every 10 seconds.
  RTMP updates are sent every 10 seconds.
  RTMP entries are considered BAD after 20 seconds.
  RTMP entries are discarded after 60 seconds.
  AARP probe retransmit count: 10, interval: 200 msec.
  AARP request retransmit count: 5, interval: 1000 msec.
  DDP datagrams will be checksummed.
  RTMP datagrams will be strictly checked.
  RTMP routes may not be propagated without zones.
  Routes will not be distributed between routing protocols.
  Routing between local devices on an interface will not be performed.
  IPTalk uses the udp base port of 768 (Default).
  AppleTalk EIGRP is not enabled.
  Alternate node address format will not be displayed.
  Access control of any networks of a zone hides the zone.
Router3>
```

Listing 10-7

Listing 10-8

```
Router3>sh appl int e2/0
Ethernet2/0 is up, line protocol is up
  AppleTalk cable range is 1000-1000
  AppleTalk address is 1000.50, Valid
  AppleTalk zone is "Online"
  AppleTalk port configuration verified by 1000.243
  AppleTalk address gleaning is disabled
  AppleTalk route cache is enabled
Router3>
```

The `show appletalk interface` command with no interface specified displays this information for all interfaces on the router that are configured for AppleTalk routing. The `clear appletalk interface` command can be used to reset the interface; the AppleTalk address and zone initialization can then be monitored.

The `show appletalk arp` Command The mapping of AppleTalk node addresses against MAC addresses can be displayed using the `show appletalk arp` command. The node addresses that are of type Hardware are actual router interfaces. The cache has a default timeout

```
Router3>sh appl arp
Address      Age (min)  Type      Hardware Addr         Encap    Interface
1000.50              -  Hardware  00e0.f78a.6d40.0000   SNAP     Ethernet2/0
1005.128             0  Dynamic   0060.b0f3.a503.0000   SNAP     Ethernet2/1
1005.130             3  Dynamic   0060.b078.dbf0.0000   SNAP     Ethernet2/1
1005.131             3  Dynamic   0060.b090.9ac4.0000   SNAP     Ethernet2/1
1005.243             -  Hardware  00e0.f78a.6d41.0000   SNAP     Ethernet2/1
1010.68              -  Hardware  00e0.f78a.6d42.0000   SNAP     Ethernet2/2
1010.128             3  Dynamic   0800.09d7.f2b3.0000   SNAP     Ethernet2/2
```

Listing 10-9

value but can be cleared manually using the `clear appletalk arp` command (see Listing 10-9).

The `show appletalk nbp` Command The `show appletalk nbp` command displays the names of AppleTalk NBP objects that the router has learned about. The AppleTalk node address, zone, and router interface over which the object was learned are also displayed. In Listing 10-10, the only named AppleTalk object that router 3 knows about is itself. It is running AppleTalk on three Ethernet interfaces.

The `show appletalk access-lists` Command This command provides a quick means of checking for AppleTalk access lists that are configured on the router (see Listing 10-11). The configuration should then be checked to see what type of filters these lists represent and to

Listing 10-10

```
Router3#sh appl nbp
  Net Adr Skt Name                      Type           Zone
 1005 243 254 Router3.Ethernet2/1  ciscoRouter     Online
 1010  68 254 Router3.Ethernet2/2  ciscoRouter     Online
 1000  50 254 Router3.Ethernet2/0  ciscoRouter     Online
Router3#
```

Listing 10-11

```
 r2#sh apple access-list
AppleTalk access list 610:
  deny zone development
  permit additional-zones
  permit other-access
r2#
```

what interfaces they are applied. AppleTalk filtering and access control will be discussed in more detail later.

The `show appletalk traffic` Command The `show appletalk traffic` command provides a summary of packets transmitted and received by the router along with error information for each of the protocols in the AppleTalk protocol stack (see Listing 10-12). Similar information on each of the configured AppleTalk routing protocols is also provided. An incrementing *bad hop count* in received packets may indicate a

```
Router3>sh apple traffic
AppleTalk statistics:
  Rcvd:  104395397 total, 0 checksum errors, 0 bad hop count
         8499875 local destination, 0 access denied
         0 for MacIP, 0 bad MacIP, 0 no client
         0 port disabled, 0 no listener
         0 ignored, 0 martians
  Bcast: 759259 received, 22524181 sent
  Sent:  26090201 generated, 181294 forwarded, 94781591 fast forwarded,
    927766 loopback
         0 forwarded from MacIP, 0 MacIP failures
         78 encapsulation failed, 3640 no route, 0 no source
  DDP:   10541633 long, 0 short, 0 macip, 0 bad size
  NBP:   1976840 received, 20 invalid, 0 proxies
         522 replies sent, 2017259 forwards, 1754131 lookups, 293 failures
  RTMP:  4008993 received, 2098 requests, 0 invalid, 0 ignored
         21541945 sent, 0 replies
  AURP: 0 Open Requests, 0 Router Downs
        0 Routing Information sent, 0 Routing Information received
        0 Zone Information sent, 0 Zone Information received
        0 Get Zone Nets sent, 0 Get Zone Nets received
        0 Get Domain Zone List sent, 0 Get Domain Zone List received
        0 bad sequence
  ATP:   0 received
  ZIP:   3444022 received, 3486660 sent, 3443714 netinfo
AppleTalk statistics:
  Echo:  1549 received, 0 discarded, 0 illegal
         67 generated, 1479 replies sent
  Responder:  0 received, 0 illegal, 0 unknown
         0 replies sent, 0 failures
  AARP:  908374 requests, 11566 replies, 52594 probes
         1682 martians, 95 bad encapsulation, 0 unknown
         897623 sent, 0 failures, 11504 delays, 78 drops
  Lost: 0 no buffers
  Unknown: 0 packets
  Discarded: 0 wrong encapsulation, 0 bad SNAP discriminator
Router3>
```

Listing 10-12

backdoor bridge or traffic routed through another device such as a server. The exact meaning of each of the parameters displayed with this command can be researched using the Cisco Command Reference documentation.

Debug Commands

The use of AppleTalk debug commands will now be illustrated. The usual caution should be exercised before employing these tools, and of course, you should have a reasonably clear picture of what you are looking for before turning on any debug commands. The most salient aspects of the output that these commands provide will be described in this section. For an exhaustive reference on the meaning of every element in the debug outputs, the appropriate sections of Cisco's Debug Command Reference should be consulted.

The `debug apple arp` Command The AppleTalk ARP (AARP) process can be monitored using the `debug apple arp` command. This tool can be used when connectivity is failing to a particular node on a local segment. If AARP resolution is seen to be taking place for that node, then the problem is likely to be above layer 2. In the Listing 10-13, the ARP cache is cleared in order to stimulate more activity. The entries are then deleted from the cache. The new entries are then added to the table. Most of the addresses shown in the output belong to router interfaces that had the addresses hard-coded; therefore, there is no change in the AppleTalk node to MAC address mapping. This may not necessarily be the case for many stations on the different LAN segments. The manner in which the AARP protocol searches for duplicates before assigning node addresses also can be observed in this output.

The `debug apple nbp` Command This debug tool can be used to monitor events relating to NBP objects, such as the receipt of NBP lookups by the router. In practice, the NBP test command often proves to be a more useful tool and much less processor-intensive.

The `debug apple events` Command The `debug appletalk events` command provides a useful output of significant AppleTalk events such as the loss or addition of routes or zones and error information. The output in Listing 10-14 was generated after clearing the route to cable range 30-35 from R2's routing table; the zone associated with

```
Router3#debug app arp
AppleTalk ARP debugging is on
Router3#term mon
Router3#cle app arp
Router3#
Dec  2 09:57:27 PST: Ethernet2/0: AARP: Removing entry for 1000.50(00e0.f78a.6d40)
Dec  2 09:57:27 PST: Ethernet2/1: AARP: Removing entry for 1005.128(0060.b0f3.a503)
Dec  2 09:57:27 PST: Ethernet2/1: AARP: Removing entry for 1005.130(0060.b078.dbf0)
Dec  2 09:57:27 PST: Ethernet2/1: AARP: Removing entry for 1005.131(0060.b090.9ac4)
Dec  2 09:57:27 PST: AARP: aarp_insert, entry 6136A3F8 for node
  1000.50(00e0.f78a.6d40) added on Ethernet2/0
Dec  2 09:57:27 PST: AARP: creating entry for Ethernet2/1, 1005.243(00e0.f78a.6d41)
Dec  2 09:57:27 PST: Ethernet2/1: AARP aarp_insert, starting search with 1000.50
  if_number=10
Dec  2 09:57:27 PST: AARP: aarp_insert, entry 6140A794 for node
  1005.243(00e0.f78a.6d41) added on Ethernet2/1
Dec  2 09:57:27 PST: AARP: creating entry for Ethernet2/2, 1010.68(00e0.f78a.6d42)
Dec  2 09:57:27 PST: Ethernet2/2: AARP aarp_insert, starting search with 1000.50
  if_number=10
Dec  2 09:57:27 PST: Ethernet2/2: AARP aarp_insert, continuing search with 1005.243
  if_number=11
```

Listing 10-13

```
r2#debug apple event
AppleTalk Events debugging is on
r2#
AT: RTMP GC complete (0 PDBs freed, 0 PDBs waiting)
AT: EIGRP GC complete (0 PDBs freed, 0 PDBs waiting)
AT: Connected GC complete (0 PDBs freed, 0 PDBs waiting)
%AT-6-PATHDEL: Tunnel0: AppleTalk EIGRP path to 30-35 via 99.3 has been deleted
%AT-6-DELROUTE: AppleTalk network deleted; 30-35 removed from routing table
%AT-6-PATHADD: Tunnel0: AppleTalk EIGRP path to network 30-35 added; via 99.3 (metric
  297270016)
%AT-6-NEWZONE: AppleTalk zone added; zone ether defined
AT: RTMP GC complete (0 PDBs freed, 0 PDBs waiting)
AT: EIGRP GC complete (0 PDBs freed, 0 PDBs waiting)
AT: Connected GC complete (0 PDBs freed, 0 PDBs waiting)
```

Listing 10-14

this cable range is called *Ether*. This is an EIGRP-derived route that is learned over an IP tunnel. EIGRP is then seen immediately replacing the cable range and zone in the routing table.

The `debug apple routing` Command This command can be used to monitor both RTMP and EIGRP. The output in Listing 10-15 displays an RTMP update being sent simultaneously out each of the router interfaces. The updates, which contain 15 routes, are broadcasts on each local cable range. Notice that the last RTMP update was received at 10:06:21 and the route-aging timer restarts at 10:06:22.

On a router that is running RTMP on many interfaces, it may be appropriate to apply this command one interface at a time. This makes the information more readable and reduces the resulting processor load. In this case it is applied to Ethernet 2/0 and Ethernet 2/1 (see Listing 10-16). Two outgoing updates are observed, and notice that they are 10 seconds apart, which is the default update interval for RTMP. The fact that no inbound update was observed during this period could suggest that there are no other routers on these two segments.

```
Router3#deb apple routing
AppleTalk RTMP routing debugging is on
AppleTalk EIGRP routing debugging is on
Router3#
Dec  2 10:06:19 PST: AT: RTMP from 1000.48 (new 0,old 0,bad 0,ign 0, dwn 0)
Dec  2 10:06:21 PST: AT: RTMP from 1070.145 (new 0,old 1,bad 0,ign 1, dwn 0)
Dec  2 10:06:22 PST: AT: src=Ethernet2/0:1000.50, dst=1000-1000, size=100, 15 rtes,
  RTMP pkt sent
Dec  2 10:06:22 PST: AT: src=Ethernet2/1:1005.243, dst=1005-1005, size=100, 15 rtes,
  RTMP pkt sent
Dec  2 10:06:22 PST: AT: src=Ethernet2/2:1010.68, dst=1010-1010, size=100, 15 rtes,
  RTMP pkt sent
Dec  2 10:06:22 PST: AT: src=Ethernet2/3:1015.207, dst=1015-1015, size=100, 15 rtes,
  RTMP pkt sent
Dec  2 10:06:22 PST: AT: src=Ethernet2/4:1020.96, dst=1020-1020, size=100, 15 rtes,
  RTMP pkt sent
Dec  2 10:06:22 PST: AT: src=Ethernet2/5:1025.175, dst=1025-1025, size=100, 15 rtes,
  RTMP pkt sent
Dec  2 10:06:22 PST: AT: Route ager starting on Main AT RoutingTable (16 active
  nodes)
Dec  2 10:06:22 PST: AT: Route ager finished on Main AT RoutingTable (16 active
  nodes)undeb all
All possible debugging has been turned off
Router3#
```

Listing 10-15

```
Router3#deb app routing int e2/0
AppleTalk RTMP routing debugging is on for interface Ethernet2/0
AppleTalk EIGRP routing debugging is on for interface Ethernet2/0
Router3#deb app routing int e2/1
AppleTalk RTMP routing debugging is on for interface Ethernet2/1
AppleTalk EIGRP routing debugging is on for interface Ethernet2/1
Router3#
Dec  2 10:07:12 PST: AT: src=Ethernet2/1:1005.243, dst=1005-1005, size=100, 15 rtes,
  RTMP pkt sent
Dec  2 10:07:12 PST: AT: Route ager starting on Main AT RoutingTable (16 active
  nodes)
Dec  2 10:07:12 PST: AT: Route ager finished on Main AT RoutingTable (16 active
  nodes)
Dec  2 10:07:22 PST: AT: src=Ethernet2/1:1005.243, dst=1005-1005, size=100, 15 rtes,
  RTMP pkt sent
Dec  2 10:07:22 PST: AT: Route ager starting on Main AT RoutingTable (16 active
  nodes)
Dec  2 10:07:22 PST: AT: Route ager finished on Main AT RoutingTable (16 active
  nodes)
Router3#
```

Listing 10-16

The `debug apple zip` Command The `debug apple zip` command can be used to monitor ZIP and GZL requests sent and received by the router. The absence of a particular zone from an update can indicate a filtering issue or other network problem. If update entries are seen with cable-range-to-zone pairings that do not comply with what is configured on the network, then this may indicate corrupted zones or a ZIP storm.

The output in Listing 10-17 relates to the network shown in Figure 10-2. In this case, R2 is seen receiving a ZIP reply from R1 that contains the zone Ether and the network 30 in answer to a ZIP request corresponding to this cable range. R1 has remotely learned cable range 30-35.

This also can be confined to a particular interface or set of interfaces if so desired. In this case, the general command was applied to all AppleTalk interfaces. Here it was unlikely to cause a CPU loading problem because only one zone was configured on this particular router.

The `debug apple packet` Command The `debug apple packet` command provides output on all incoming or outgoing packets that are process switched. It gives information on packet type and encapsulation type, but given the level of output generated, it must be used only with extreme care. If a particular segment needs to be investigated, this command can be confined to the appropriate router interface.

Listing 10-17

```
r2#debug apple zip
AppleTalk ZIP Packets debugging is on

r2#cle apple route 30
r2#
AT: NextNbrZipQuery: [30-35] zoneupdate 0 gw: 12.1 n: 12.1
AT: NextNbrZipQuery: r->rpath.gwptr: 00871DEC, n: 00871DEC
AT: maint_SendNeighborQueries, sending 1 queries to 12.1
AT: 1 query packet sent to neighbor 12.1
AT: maint_SendNeighborQueries, no pending queries
AT: Recvd ZIP cmd 2 from 12.1-6
AT: 1 zones in ZIPreply pkt, src 12.1
AT: net 30, zonelen 5, name ether
```

The `debug apple errors` Command Error information can be monitored using `debug appletalk error`. The sample output in Listing 10-18 was generated after reconfiguring a token-ring interface to have the primary and secondary zones swapped relative to its neighbor on the same segment. The primary zone is determined simply by listing it first in the interface configuration. A resulting error message indicates this condition.

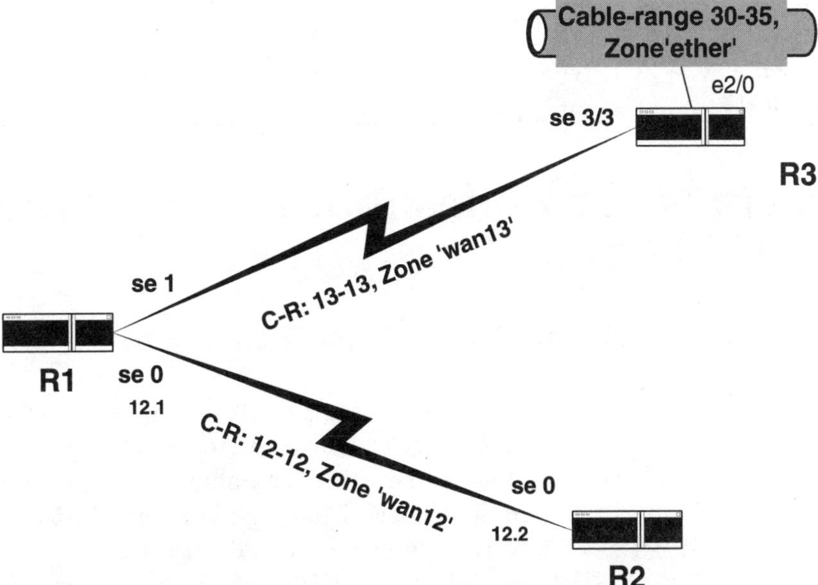

Figure 10-2 AppleTalk ZIP debugging.

```
r2#sh app ro
Codes: R - RTMP derived, E - EIGRP derived, C - connected, A - AURP
       S - static  P - proxy
5 routes in internet

The first zone listed for each entry is its default (primary) zone.

R Net 1-10 [1/G] via 12.1, 6 sec, Serial0, zone legacy
C Net 12-12 directly connected, Serial0, zone wan12
R Net 13-13 [1/G] via 12.1, 6 sec, Serial0, zone wan13
C Net 24-26 directly connected, TokenRing0, zone legacy
            Additional zones: `finance'

r4#sh app in to0
TokenRing0 is up, line protocol is up
  AppleTalk cable range is 24-26
  AppleTalk address is 24.4, Valid
  AppleTalk primary zone is "finance"
  AppleTalk additional zones: "legacy"
  AppleTalk address gleaning is disabled
  AppleTalk route cache is enabled
r4#

r2#sh debug apple packet
AppleTalk packet errors debugging is on
R2#
%AT-5-INTCLEARED: TokenRing0: AppleTalk interface restarting; interface cleared
%AT-6-NBRDELETED: Neighbor entry for 24.4 deleted
%AT-3-DEFZONEERR: TokenRing0: AppleTalk interface warning; default zone differs from
  24.4
%AT-6-CONFIGOK: TokenRing0: AppleTalk interface enabled; verified by 24.4
r2#
```

Listing 10-18

Troubleshooting AppleTalk in the LAN

AppleTalk Phase I and Phase II

The original version of AppleTalk is known as phase I. With this version, each segment only supported a single network, and only one zone could be allocated per network. The maximum number of hosts that can be supported on a phase I network segment is 254, which must be subdivided into 127 end nodes and 127 servers.

With AppleTalk phase II, each physical segment can support multiple networks or what is commonly known as *cable ranges*. This is also termed an *extended AppleTalk network*. Up to 253 devices can be supported on each logical network, which also can belong to multiple zones. The cable ranges must be configured to be identical on every router interface that attaches to a segment. The use of a consistent network address along with "overlapping" cable ranges will not suffice for address verification. For example, Listing 10-19 is a valid configuration for router A and router B that attach to the same AppleTalk segment.

Most networks currently running AppleTalk employ phase II; however, if it is required to integrate the two dissimilar technologies, a cable range of 1 (e.g., cable range 52-52) should be used on the extended or phase II portion of the network.

AppleTalk Discovery Mode AppleTalk also supports a dynamic address allocation feature known as *discovery mode*. When configuring this feature, a single router known as the **seed router** is configured with a static addressing, while all other AppleTalk routers on the segment are placed in discovery mode, where they dynamically discover their cable and end-node addresses.

Discovery mode is supported on both extended and nonextended AppleTalk networks. On an extended network, it is configured as follows on the nonseed routers.

```
interface ethernet0
cable-range 0-0
```

Listing 10-19

```
RouterA#
interface ethernet0
appletalk cable-range 50-55 52.9
appletalk zone engineering

RouterB#
interface ethernet0
appletalk cable-range 50-55 52.10
appletalk zone engineering

While this is invalid, even though the ranges overlap:

RouterA#
interface ethernet0
appletalk cable-range 50-55 52.9
appletalk zone engineering

RouterB#
interface ethernet0
appletalk cable-range 50-52 52.10
appletalk zone engineering
```

Some points to note in relation to discovery mode are that only one router should be configured as seed and also that it does not work over serial links.

AppleTalk Filtering and Access Control

There are a number of different types of AppleTalk access lists, e.g., the GZL filter, ZIP reply filters, AppleTalk route distribute lists, and NBP access filters. It is important to note that these filters act independently of each other. For example, an NBP access-group filter will not have any effect on the propagation of routing updates regardless of its configuration. This is dissimilar to the effect an IP access group would have on IP routing updates.

I will now discuss the different types of AppleTalk filters and how they are configured, since incorrectly configured access lists are frequently at the root of AppleTalk connectivity problems.

GZL Filtering This filter is applied to GZL replies that the router sends to clients on one of its local LAN segments. It can be used to hide certain zones from clients that will not be accessing these zones. If there are multiple routers on the LAN segment, it is important that the GZL filters are consistent; otherwise, clients will see zones disappearing and reappearing from the Chooser window depending on which router answers the GZL request.

The GZL filter in Listing 10-20 denies the zone Legacy from being included in GZL replies from the router to clients on the 40-44 cable range. All other zones are allowed.

ZIP Reply Filtering The ZIP reply filter is used to hide certain zones from downstream routers in order to implement security or other net-

Listing 10-20

```
interface TokenRing1
 no ip address
 appletalk cable-range 40-44 44.4
 appletalk getzonelist-filter 601
 ring-speed 16
!
no ip classless
access-list 601 deny zone legacy
access-list 601 permit additional-zones
access-list 601 permit other-access
```

Listing 10-21

```
R1#

interface Serial0
 appletalk cable-range 12-12 12.1
 appletalk zip-reply-filter 611
 no fair-queue
!
access-list 611 deny zone ether
access-list 611 permit additional-zones
access-list 611 permit other-access
```

working policies. This list is applied to outbound ZIP updates on a router interface.

The configuration in Listing 10-21 would hide the Ether zone from any downstream routers that connect to R1 via serial 0.

RTMP Filtering AppleTalk distribute lists can be used to filter RTMP routing updates. In the example in Listing 10-22, an outbound distribute list on serial 1 denies cable range 1-10. There is also an inbound distribute list that only allows cable range 300-350. As with all filters, it is important to define the default condition for unspecified networks.

In this example, consider the case where the cable range 1-10 is on another part of the network and belongs to zone Bigbyte. If this cable range is filtered from a routing update, then the route filter also will deny any other cable range that belongs to the Bigbyte zone. This is the default condition on Cisco routers. If it is desired to circumvent this feature, the global command `appletalk permit-partial-zones` is used. We will see an example of this in the troubleshooting scenarios later in this chapter.

NOTE: *If it is required to only filter certain cable ranges belonging to a particular zone, the* `appletalk permit-partial-zones` *command must be used.*

By default, the Cisco IOS does not advertise cable ranges that have no associated zones. This is sometimes used as a crude means of preventing the advertisement of certain routes. The feature is intended to prevent ZIP storms due to the propagation of corrupted routes, and it can be disabled using the `no appletalk require-route-zones` global configuration command.

Listing 10-22

```
!
interface Serial1
 appletalk cable-range 13-13 13.1
 appletalk zone wan13
 appletalk access-group 610
 appletalk distribute-list 610 out
 appletalk distribute-list 609 in
!
no ip classless
appletalk permit-partial-zones
access-list 609 permit cable-range 300-350
access-list 609 deny other-access
access-list 610 deny cable-range 1-10
access-list 610 permit other-access
```

NBP Filtering NBP filters can be used to control access to particular zones, service types, or service objects on an AppleTalk network. They are slightly more complex than the other types of AppleTalk access lists because they provide more detail in what services are being controlled and they also include sequence numbers. An important point to remember about NBP filters is that they are applied against inbound traffic when used as an interface access group. However, when used as part of a dialer list, NBP filters are applied against outbound traffic.

For the network in Figure 10-3, an AppleTalk NBP filter is used to deny users on cable range 10-20 access to a particular print server in the zone ServerFarm. The filter on R8 is only effective if applied to the FDDI interface, since NBP filters are applied against inbound traffic in access groups. The sequence number 1 is used to tie the NBP object, type, and zone together. It is also defined that all unspecified objects or traffic types are permitted (see Listing 10-23).

A more inclusive filter could be defined if it is required to block an array of NBP objects. Denying traffic from an entire NBP type or zone can be used to implement such a policy.

Troubleshooting AppleTalk in the WAN

AppleTalk over Frame Relay

A number of key issues must be kept in mind when configuring AppleTalk on a frame-relay network. These issues are equally relevant to any desktop protocol that is being run over frame relay.

Figure 10-3 NBP filtering example.

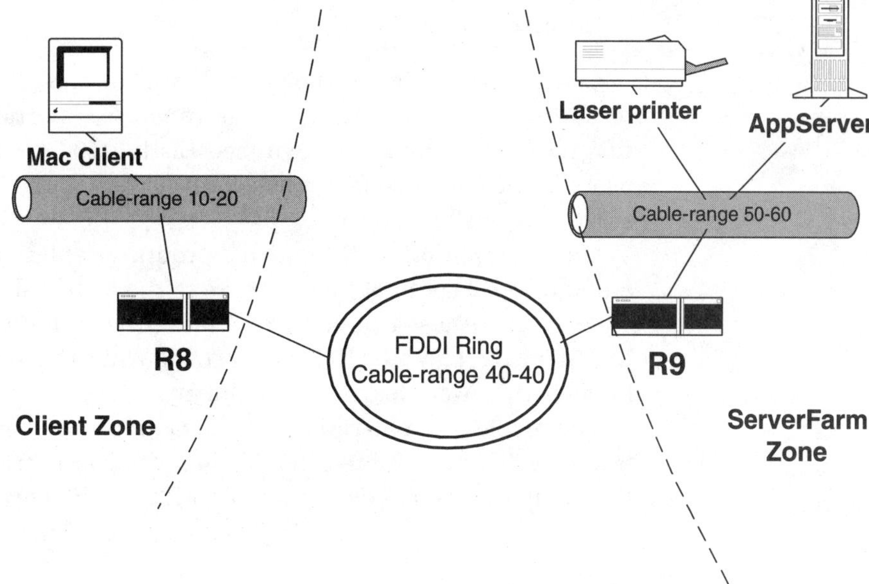

- If a static map is used to relate the AppleTalk next-hop address to the DLCI, then the `broadcast` keyword must be included to ensure that broadcast and multicast traffic is forwarded over the interface. By omitting this keyword, AppleTalk routing updates and other nonunicast traffic will not be forwarded across the NBMA frame-relay medium.
- Split horizon is enabled by default for both RTMP and EIGRP on a frame-relay interface. This may cause routing problems on a network where a hub site is using multipoint frame relay. Split horizon can be disabled manually for each of these protocols to solve any resulting

Listing 10-23

```
R8#

interface Fddi0
 no ip address
 appletalk cable-range 40-40 40.8
 appletalk zone client
 appletalk access-group 650

access-list 650 deny nbp 1 object laser printer
access-list 650 deny nbp 1 type LaserDraw
access-list 650 deny nbp 1 zone ServerFarm
access-list 650 permit other-nbps
access-list 650 permit other-access
```

problems. An example of such a scenario will now be demonstrated in the case of RTMP.

Consider the network shown in Figure 10-4. RTMP is the routing protocol throughout the network. The frame-relay portions of the configuration on R1 and R2 are shown (see Listing 10-24). The problem is that users in the Client zone can attach to servers in the Tok1 zone but not to servers in the Token3 zone.

On examination of R1 and R2's routing tables (Listing 10-25), it is found that R2 does not have a route to the 51-51 cable range that is zone Token3. But it also can be noted that R1 has a route to each of the local LANs on R2 and R3. It is not propagating these routes out serial 0 because they were learned over this interface.

The problem can be resolved by disabling split horizon on R1's serial 0 interface. The two routes should then be cleared from the routing table to stimulate an immediate update to R2 and R3 (see Listing 10-26).

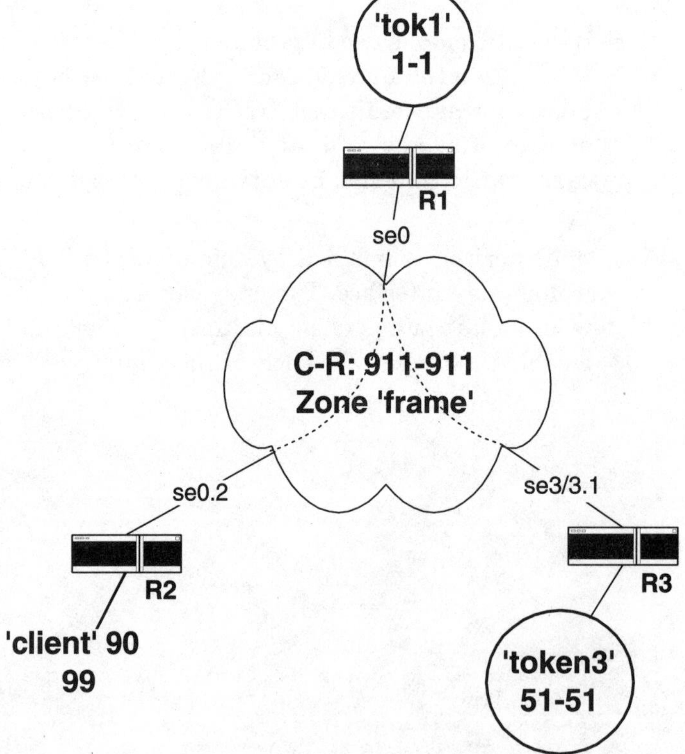

Figure 10-4 AppleTalk over frame relay.

Listing 10-24

```
r1#
!
interface Serial0
 encapsulation frame-relay
 appletalk cable-range 911-911 911.1
 appletalk zone frame
 frame-relay lmi-type ansi
!

r2#
!
interface Serial0
 no ip address
 encapsulation frame-relay
 frame-relay lmi-type ansi
!
interface Serial0.2 point-to-point
 appletalk cable-range 911-911 911.2
 appletalk zone frame
 frame-relay interface-dlci 201
```

```
r2#sh app ro
Codes: R - RTMP derived, E - EIGRP derived, C - connected, A - AURP
       S - static  P - proxy
2 routes in internet

The first zone listed for each entry is its default (primary) zone.

R Net 1-1 [1/G] via 911.1, 3 sec, Serial0.2, zone tok1
C Net 90-99 directly connected, Ethernet0, zone client
C Net 911-911 directly connected, Serial0.2, zone frame
r2#

r1#sh app route
Codes: R - RTMP derived, E - EIGRP derived, C - connected, A - AURP
       S - static  P - proxy
4 routes in internet

The first zone listed for each entry is its default (primary) zone.

C Net 1-1 directly connected, TokenRing0, zone tok1
R Net 51-51 [1/G] via 911.3, 7 sec, Serial0, zone token3
R Net 90-99 [1/G] via 911.2, 7 sec, Serial0, zone client
C Net 911-911 directly connected, Serial0, zone frame
```

Listing 10-25

```
r1#conf t
Enter configuration commands, one per line.  End with CNTL/Z.
r1(config)#in se 0
r1(config-if)#no apple rtmp-split-horizon
r1(config-if)#^Z
r1#clear apple route 90
r1#clear apple route 51
r1#

r2#sh app route
Codes: R - RTMP derived, E - EIGRP derived, C - connected, A - AURP
       S - static  P - proxy
4 routes in internet

The first zone listed for each entry is its default (primary) zone.

R Net 1-1 [1/G] via 911.1, 3 sec, Serial0.2, zone tok1
R Net 51-51 [2/S] via 911.1, 13 sec, Serial0.2, zone token3
C Net 90-99 directly connected, Ethernet0, zone client
C Net 911-911 directly connected, Serial0.2, zone frame
r2#
```

Listing 10-26

Now it can be verified that R2 is able to see R3's local LAN 51-51 in zone Token3. Similarly, R3 will now have a route to R2's client LAN. Note that this issue would not have arisen if subinterfaces were employed on R1's serial 0 interface.

AppleTalk over ISDN

AppleTalk is less than ideal for use over a dial-up WAN given its chatty nature. When used over ISDN, a static route or floating static route is often used to minimize the frequency of ISDN calls generated.

It is important to remember that the ISDN zone must be unique and therefore different from the zone to which the static route relates. In the sample configuration in Listing 10-27, the ISDN network is used to access the 100-110 cable range, and RTMP updates are prevented from passing over the BRI0 interface.

The ISDN debug and show commands discussed in Chapter 6 can be used to determine why calls are not being placed. Equally, if excessive calls are being generated, the `debug dialer` command can be used to find the cause. In order to restrict the type of traffic that causes an ISDN call to be placed, a more stringent dialer list can be defined by applying

Listing 10-27

```
interface BRI0
 no ip mroute-cache
 encapsulation ppp
 appletalk cable-range 98-98 98.1
 appletalk zone DDR
 no appletalk send-rtmps
 dialer map appletalk 98.2 name Router5-pri broadcast 16540134
 dialer-group 1
 ppp authentication chap
!
appletalk static cable-range 100-110 to 98.2 zone MainOffice
!
dialer-list 1 protocol appletalk permit
```

an NBP access list to dialer list 1. For example, an NBP access list 620 could be defined and the dialer list configuration altered appropriately:

```
dialer-list 1 protocol appletalk list 620
```

AppleTalk EIGRP

AppleTalk EIGRP is of course a separate protocol from EIGRP for IP and IPX. It has a separate topology database, and AppleTalk EIGRP routes appear in the AppleTalk routing table. AppleTalk EIGRP does employ most of the same principles as its IP and IPX cousins, such as neighbor formation, incremental updates, and the DUAL algorithm. There is one significant difference in the manner in which AppleTalk EIGRP is configured, in that the concept of a router ID for EIGRP replaces the use of an EIGRP process ID that is associated with the configuration of EIGRP for IP and IPX. In the configuration in Listing 10-28, EIGRP is being used exclusively on the serial link between R2 and R3. The redistribution between RTMP and EIGRP is enabled by default. Note that RTMP is disabled manually on the serial links.

EIGRP Diagnostic Commands The commands used to verify the status of AppleTalk EIGRP neighbor relationships and the topology database are similar to those we have met already in the context of EIGRP for IP and IPX (see Listing 10-29).

The topology database for R2 shows four routes each with a single feasible successor. All routes are in a stable passive state (see Listing 10-30).

Listing 10-28

```
R2#

appletalk routing eigrp 2
appletalk route-redistribution
!
interface Serial0
 no ip address
 appletalk cable-range 99-99 99.2
 appletalk zone wan
 appletalk protocol eigrp
 no appletalk protocol rtmp

R3#

appletalk routing eigrp 3
appletalk route-redistribution
!
interface Serial0
 no ip address
 appletalk cable-range 99-99 99.3
 appletalk zone wan
 appletalk protocol eigrp
 no appletalk protocol rtmp
```

```
r2>sh apple eigrp neig
AT/EIGRP Neighbors for process 1, router id 2
H   Address                  Interface   Hold Uptime    SRTT   RTO  Q  Seq
                                         (sec)          (ms)        Cnt Num
0   99.3                     Se0            11 1d21h      56  5000  0  3
```

Listing 10-29

Listing 10-30

```
r2>sh apple eigrp topology
AT/EIGRP Topology Table for process 1, router id 2

Codes: P - Passive, A - Active, U - Update, Q - Query, R - Reply,
       r - Reply status

P 24-26, 1 successors, FD is 16129
         via Redistributed (16129/0)
P 30-35, 1 successors, FD is 297270016
         via 99.3 (297270016/25601), Serial0
P 40-44, 1 successors, FD is 256540928
         via Redistributed (256540928/0)
P 99-99, 1 successors, FD is 297244416
         via Connected, Serial0
r2>
```

Tunneling in IP

The fact that AppleTalk is a chatty protocol that sometimes can consume an excessive amount of bandwidth poses design challenges when running AppleTalk over the WAN. One frequently used approach is to tunnel the AppleTalk in IP, thereby creating a point-to-point AppleTalk WAN network rather than extensively using AppleTalk on multiple WAN routers. There are a number of tunnel modes and encapsulation types. The default encapsulation on a Cisco router is GRE; this is also the only encapsulation that supports the use of an authentication key. Note that if Cayman tunneling is used to integrate with a GatorBox, then an AppleTalk address cannot be applied to the tunnel interface itself.

The network shown in Figure 10-5 will illustrate the use of an IP tunnel to connect AppleTalk networks that are local to R2 and R3. AppleTalk EIGRP is used as the routing protocol for the tunnel in order to further reduce WAN traffic. The relevant configuration for R2 and R3 is shown in Listing 10-31.

Figure 10-5 AppleTalk tunnel in IP.

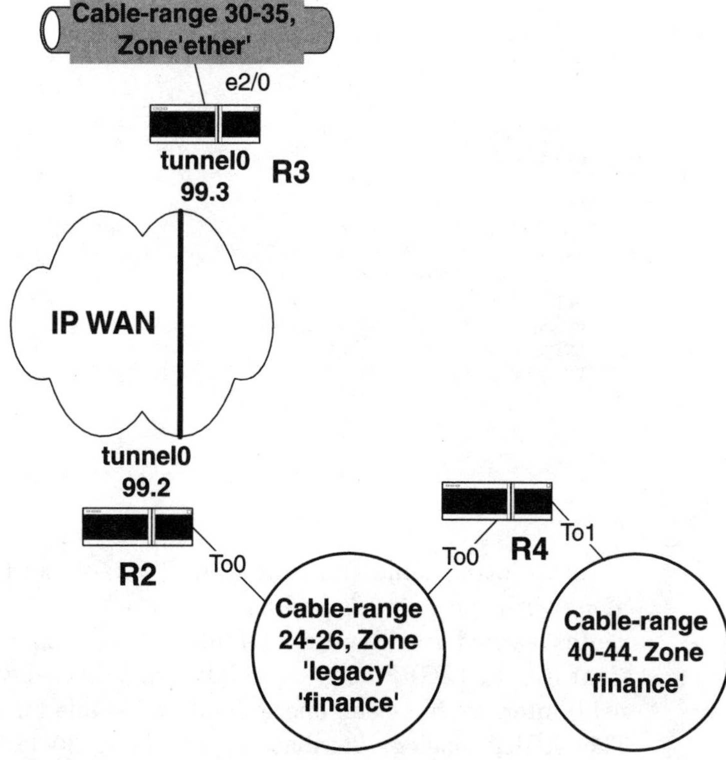

Listing 10-31

```
hostname r2
!
enable password cisco
!
appletalk routing eigrp 2
appletalk route-redistribution
!
interface Tunnel0
 no ip address
 appletalk cable-range 99-99 99.2
 appletalk zone tunnel
 appletalk protocol eigrp
 no appletalk protocol rtmp
 appletalk distribute-list 610 out
 tunnel source 172.16.102.2
 tunnel destination 172.16.100.3
!
interface Serial0
 ip address 172.16.102.2 255.255.255.0
 no fair-queue
!
interface Serial1

r2#

r3#
!
hostname r3
!
enable password cisco
!
appletalk routing eigrp 3
appletalk route-redistribution
!
interface Tunnel0
 no ip address
 appletalk cable-range 99-99 99.3
 appletalk zone tunnel
 appletalk protocol eigrp
 no appletalk protocol rtmp
 tunnel source 172.16.100.3
 tunnel destination 172.16.102.2
!

r3#
```

R3's routing table confirms that the 24-24 and 40-44 cable ranges along with their corresponding zones are displayed as EIGRP-derived routes learned over the tunnel 0 interface (see Listing 10-32).

At R2, the EIGRP neighbor relationship formed with R3 over the tunnel 0 interface has been operational and stable for 1 day and 21 hours. The EIGRP topology database on R2 shows 30-35 learned via R3. The

```
r3#sh app ro
Codes: R - RTMP derived, E - EIGRP derived, C - connected, A - AURP
       S - static  P - proxy
4 routes in internet

The first zone listed for each entry is its default (primary) zone.

E Net 24-26 [1/G] via 99.2, 19385 sec, Tunnel0, zone legacy
                  Additional zones: `finance'
C Net 30-35 directly connected, Ethernet2/0, zone ether
E Net 40-44 [2/G] via 99.2, 19385 sec, Tunnel0, zone finance
C Net 99-99 directly connected, Tunnel0, zone tunnel
r3#
```

Listing 10-32

tunnel network 99-99 is directly connected. The 40-44 cable range has been redistributed from RTMP, which is running on the token ring. For this same reason, 24-26 also shows up as being redistributed into EIGRP, even though it is also connected to R2 (see Listing 10-33).

For the network shown in Figure 10-5, we are going to do things in reverse. Everything is working at the moment, but I will now illustrate how things could go wrong.

A common configuration problem for someone who is unfamiliar with AppleTalk EIGRP is to configure the same "process ID" on each router. When this is attempted on R2, an error message is generated:

```
r2(config)#app routing eigrp 3
r2(config)#
%AT-5-COMPATERR4: AppleTalk EIGRP neighbor incompatibility; 99.3 has
  same router ID (3)
```

Therefore, the EIGRP router ID on R2 must be restored to a unique value. Let us now examine the configuration of the tunnel. The tunnel mode is the Cisco default of GRE/IP at each end and is operating successfully (see Listing 10-34).

A number of different tunnel modes can be applied, but consistency at each end of the tunnel is essential. AURP is applied at the R2 end of the tunnel (see Listing 10-35). This AppleTalk routing protocol is sometimes used for WAN applications because its update interval is 60 seconds, as opposed to RTMP's interval of just 10 seconds.

When this tunnel mode is applied, R3 is seen to lose its AppleTalk neighbor relationship over the tunnel. Note that the line protocol does

```
r2>sh app eigrp neig
AT/EIGRP Neighbors for process 1, router id 2
H   Address                  Interface      Hold Uptime    SRTT    RTO  Q  Seq
                                            (sec)          (ms)         Cnt Num
0   99.3                     Tu0              11 1d21h       56   5000  0  3

r2>sh app eigrp topology
AT/EIGRP Topology Table for process 1, router id 2

Codes: P - Passive, A - Active, U - Update, Q - Query, R - Reply,
       r - Reply status

P 24-26, 1 successors, FD is 16129
         via Redistributed (16129/0)
P 30-35, 1 successors, FD is 297270016
         via 99.3 (297270016/25601), Tunnel0
P 40-44, 1 successors, FD is 256540928
         via Redistributed (256540928/0)
P 99-99, 1 successors, FD is 297244416
         via Connected, Tunnel0
r2>
```

Listing 10-33

```
r2#sh in tun 0
Tunnel0 is up, line protocol is up
  Hardware is Tunnel
  MTU 1514 bytes, BW 9 Kbit, DLY 500000 usec, rely 255/255, load 1/255
  Encapsulation TUNNEL, loopback not set, keepalive set (10 sec)
  Tunnel source 172.16.102.2, destination 172.16.100.3
  Tunnel protocol/transport GRE/IP, key disabled, sequencing disabled
  Checksumming of packets disabled,  fast tunneling enabled
  Last input 00:01:24, output 00:01:23, output hang never
  Last clearing of "show interface" counters never
  Queueing strategy: fifo
  Output queue 0/0, 0 drops; input queue 0/75, 0 drops
  5 minute input rate 0 bits/sec, 0 packets/sec
  5 minute output rate 0 bits/sec, 0 packets/sec
     35502 packets input, 2307380 bytes, 0 no buffer
     Received 0 broadcasts, 0 runts, 0 giants, 0 throttles
     0 input errors, 0 CRC, 0 frame, 0 overrun, 0 ignored, 0 abort
     35538 packets output, 2309695 bytes, 0 underruns
     0 output errors, 0 collisions, 0 interface resets
     0 output buffer failures, 0 output buffers swapped out
```

Listing 10-34

Listing 10-35

```
r2#
r2(config)#in tun 0
r2(config-if)#tunn mode ?
  aurp     AURP TunnelTalk AppleTalk encapsulation
  cayman   Cayman TunnelTalk AppleTalk encapsulation
  dvmrp    DVMRP multicast tunnel
  eon      EON compatible CLNS tunnel
  gre      generic route encapsulation protocol
  ipip     IP over IP encapsulation
  iptalk   Apple IPTalk encapsulation
  nos      IP over IP encapsulation (KA9Q/NOS compatible)

r2(config-if)#tunn mode aurp
r2(config-if)#^Z
r2#
```

remain up because there is tunnel encapsulation at each end and IP connectivity is still available between the two end points. The EIGRP neighbor relationship over the tunnel is also broken (see Listing 10-36).

AppleTalk Troubleshooting Scenarios

The network displayed in Figure 10-6 will be used to illustrate a number of different AppleTalk connectivity problems. The relevant portions of the configurations for routers R1 through R4 are shown in Listing 10-37 along with the AppleTalk routing tables. RTMP is being used exclusively across the network.

The only access restriction policy that should be implemented is that users in the Ether zone should not have access to services on cable range 1-10. As can be observed from the routing tables, no remote connectivity is currently available to any clients on the network.

Therefore, let's start working through this network. At R3, the following message is displayed after the Ethernet 2/0 interface initializes:

```
r3#*Jun 10 03:20:29: %AT-6-ONLYROUTER: Ethernet2/0: AppleTalk port
enabled; no neighbors found
```

This is actually valid because there are no other routers on R3's Ethernet segment. However, the message displayed on R4 (see Listing 10-38) is not okay, because R4 should see R2 as an AppleTalk neighbor on its

```
r3#
%AT-6-ONLYROUTER: Tunnel0: AppleTalk interface enabled; no neighbors found
r3#sh in tun 0
Tunnel0 is up, line protocol is up
  Hardware is Tunnel
  MTU 1500 bytes, BW 9 Kbit, DLY 500000 usec, rely 255/255, load 1/255
  Encapsulation TUNNEL, loopback not set, keepalive set (10 sec)
  Tunnel source 172.16.100.3, destination 172.16.102.2
  Tunnel protocol/transport GRE/IP, key disabled, sequencing disabled
  Checksumming of packets disabled,  fast tunneling enabled
  Last input 00:03:11, output 00:00:03, output hang never
  Last clearing of "show interface" counters never
  Input queue: 0/75/0 (size/max/drops); Total output drops: 0
  5 minute input rate 0 bits/sec, 0 packets/sec
  5 minute output rate 0 bits/sec, 0 packets/sec
     35490 packets input, 2306845 bytes, 0 no buffer
     Received 0 broadcasts, 0 runts, 0 giants
     0 input errors, 0 CRC, 0 frame, 0 overrun, 0 ignored, 0 abort
     35526 packets output, 2308670 bytes, 0 underruns
     0 output errors, 0 collisions, 0 interface resets
     0 output buffer failures, 0 output buffers swapped out
r3#
r2#sh app eig neig
AT/EIGRP Neighbors for process 1, router id 2
r2#
```

Listing 10-36

token-ring 0 interface. When this is investigated, it is seen that R4 sees R2 as a neighbor, but it has an error condition and pings are failing.

The `show appletalk interface` command shows the address as being valid, but significantly, it has not been *verified* by R2. It can be noticed from R2's configuration that the cable range on the segment is 24-26 as opposed to R4's configuration of 26-26; hence 24.2 appears to R4 as being on a different network. One of the interfaces must be readdressed (see Listing 10-39).

Notice that after the cable range was changed on token ring 0, the zones had to be reentered into the configuration. There is one further complication: R2 still sees the old mismatched address for R4, and its neighbor table has to be cleared to speed up the protocol convergence (see Listing 10-40).

R4's original routing table did not show any entry for token ring 1. When the AppleTalk interface status is checked, it is found that no zone has been set. This cable range should be in the Finance zone (see Listing 10-41).

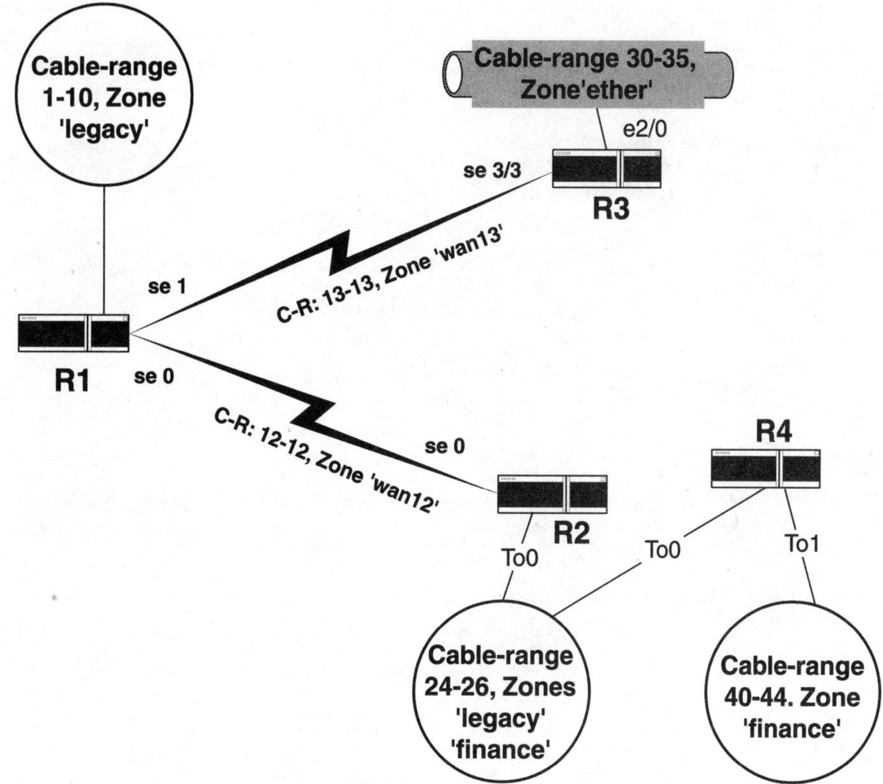

Figure 10-6 AppleTalk trouble - shooting scenarios.

This piece of configuration is performed, and the line protocol subsequently comes up (see Listing 10-42).

One of the problems reported was that users on the 40-44 cable range are required to have full access to the Legacy zone but still could not see the zone in Chooser even after the previous faults were resolved. Before moving further into the network, R4 should be checked for any other issues. On examination of its configuration, the GZL filter 601 on token ring 1 denies access to the Legacy zone. This filter does not block any other zone, so it simply can be removed (see Listing 10-43).

This configuration change, while removing a fault, still does not provide access to the Legacy zone for users on the 40-44 network. Let's explore the network a little more. R1's routing table shows that no remote routes are being learned. In fact, serial 0 is not even in the routing table as a directly connected AppleTalk network. By examining R1's configuration or using `show appletalk interface serial0` it can be noticed that no zone was set. The zone should be Wan12 to match up with R2. When this configuration is applied, the interface comes up, and

```
r3#

appletalk routing
!
interface Ethernet2/0
 ip address 10.129.35.3 255.255.255.0
 appletalk cable-range 30-35 33.23
 appletalk zone ether
!
!
interface Serial3/3
 ip address 172.16.103.3 255.255.255.0
 appletalk cable-range 13-13 13.3
 appletalk zone wan13
!

r3#

r3#sh app ro
Codes: R - RTMP derived, E - EIGRP derived, C - connected, A - AURP
       S - static  P - proxy
2 routes in internet

The first zone listed for each entry is its default (primary) zone.

C Net 13-13 directly connected, Serial3/3, zone wan13
C Net 30-35 directly connected, Ethernet2/0, zone ether
r3#

r1#sh run
Building configuration...

Current configuration:
!
version 11.2
service timestamps debug datetime
service timestamps log datetime
no service password-encryption
service udp-small-servers
service tcp-small-servers
!
hostname r1
!
enable password cisco
!
appletalk routing
!
interface Serial0
 ip address 172.16.102.1 255.255.255.0
 appletalk cable-range 12-12 12.1
 appletalk zip-reply-filter 611
 no fair-queue
```

Listing 10-37

```
 clockrate 56000
!
interface Serial1
 ip address 172.16.103.1 255.255.255.0
 appletalk cable-range 13-13 13.1
 appletalk zone wan13
 appletalk access-group 610
 appletalk distribute-list 610 out
 appletalk distribute-list 609 in
 clockrate 56000
!
interface TokenRing0
 ip address 100.1.1.1 255.255.255.0
 appletalk cable-range 1-10 1.1
 appletalk zone legacy
 ring-speed 16
!
interface TokenRing1
 no ip address
 shutdown
!
no ip classless
access-list 609 permit cable-range 300-350
access-list 609 deny other-access
access-list 610 deny cable-range 1-10
access-list 610 permit other-access
access-list 611 deny zone ether:20
access-list 611 permit additional-zones
access-list 611 permit other-access
!
line con 0
line aux 0
 transport input all
line vty 0 4
 password cisco
 login
!
end

r1#

r1#sh app ro
Codes: R - RTMP derived, E - EIGRP derived, C - connected, A - AURP
       S - static  P - proxy
2 routes in internet

The first zone listed for each entry is its default (primary) zone.

C Net 1-10 directly connected, TokenRing0, zone legacy
C Net 13-13 directly connected, Serial1, zone wan13
r1#
```

Listing 10-37 ***(Cont.)***

```
r2#sh run
Building configuration...

Current configuration:
!
version 11.2
no service password-encryption
service udp-small-servers
service tcp-small-servers
!
hostname r2
!
enable password cisco
!
appletalk routing
!
interface Serial0
 ip address 172.16.102.2 255.255.255.0
 appletalk cable-range 12-12 12.2
 appletalk zone wan12
 no fair-queue
!
interface TokenRing0
 ip address 10.129.32.2 255.255.255.0
 delay 10000000
 appletalk cable-range 24-26 24.2
 appletalk zone legacy
 appletalk zone finance
 ring-speed 16
!
line con 0
line aux 0
 transport input all
line vty 0 4
 password cisco
 login
!
end

r2#

r2#sh app ro
Codes: R - RTMP derived, E - EIGRP derived, C - connected, A - AURP
       S - static  P - proxy
1 route in internet

The first zone listed for each entry is its default (primary) zone.

C Net 24-26 directly connected, TokenRing0, zone legacy
            Additional zones: `finance'
r2#
```

Listing 10-37 *(Cont.)*

```
r4#sh run
Building configuration...

Current configuration:
!
version 11.2
no service password-encryption
no service udp-small-servers
no service tcp-small-servers
!
hostname r4
!
enable password cisco
!
appletalk routing
!
interface TokenRing0
 ip address 10.129.32.4 255.255.255.0
 appletalk cable-range 26-26 26.4
 appletalk zone legacy
 appletalk zone finance
 ring-speed 16
!
interface TokenRing1
 no ip address
 appletalk cable-range 40-44 44.4
 appletalk getzonelist-filter 601
 ring-speed 16
!
no ip classless
access-list 601 deny zone legacy:20
access-list 601 permit additional-zones
access-list 601 permit other-access
!
!
line con 0
line aux 0
line vty 0 4
 password cisco
 login
!
end

r4#sh app ro
Codes: R - RTMP derived, E - EIGRP derived, C - connected, A - AURP
       S - static  P - proxy
1 route in internet

The first zone listed for each entry is its default (primary) zone.

C Net 26-26 directly connected, TokenRing0, zone legacy
            Additional zones: `finance'
r4#
```

Listing 10-37 (*Cont.*)

```
r4#%AT-6-ONLYROUTER: TokenRing0: AppleTalk interface enabled; no neighbors found

r4#sh app neigh
AppleTalk neighbors:
  24.2          TokenRing0, uptime 00:01:18, 8 secs
        Neighbor is reachable as a RTMP peer
        NOTE: Neighbor is not properly configured for cable.
r4#
r4#ping app 24.2

Type escape sequence to abort.
Sending 5, 100-byte AppleTalk Echos to 24.2, timeout is 2 seconds:
RRRRR
Success rate is 0 percent (0/5)
r4#
r4#sh apple in to0
TokenRing0 is up, line protocol is up
  AppleTalk cable range is 26-26
  AppleTalk address is 26.4, Valid
  AppleTalk primary zone is "legacy"
  AppleTalk additional zones: "finance"
  AppleTalk address gleaning is disabled
  AppleTalk route cache is enabled
```

Listing 10-38

Listing 10-39

```
r4(config)#in to0
r4(config-if)#apple cable 24-26 24.4
r4(config-if)#^Z
r4#sh app in to0
TokenRing0 is up, line protocol is up
  AppleTalk node down, Restart port pending
  AppleTalk cable range is 24-26
  AppleTalk address is 24.4, Unknown
  AppleTalk zone is not set.
  AppleTalk address gleaning is disabled
  AppleTalk route cache is disabled, port down
r4#conf t
Enter configuration commands, one per line.  End with CNTL/Z.
r4(config)#in to0
r4(config-if)#appl zone legacy
r4(config-if)#appl zone finance
r4(config-if)#^Z
r4#
```

Listing 10-40

```
r2>sh apple neigh
AppleTalk neighbors:
  26.4          TokenRing0, uptime 00:27:45, 245 secs
        Neighbor is reachable as a RTMP peer
        NOTE: Neighbor is not properly configured for cable.
r2>

r2#cle apple neigh all
```

Listing 10-41

```
r4#sh app in to1
TokenRing1 is up, line protocol is up
  AppleTalk node down, Port configuration error
  AppleTalk cable range is 40-44
  AppleTalk address is 44.4, Invalid
  AppleTalk zone is not set.
  AppleTalk address gleaning is disabled
  AppleTalk route cache is not initialized
r4#
```

Listing 10-42

```
r4#sh app in to1
TokenRing1 is up, line protocol is up
  AppleTalk cable range is 40-44
  AppleTalk address is 44.4, Valid
  AppleTalk zone is "finance"
  AppleTalk address gleaning is disabled
  AppleTalk route cache is enabled
r4#
```

Listing 10-43

```
r4#conf t
Enter configuration commands, one per line.  End with CNTL/Z.
r4(config)#in to1
r4(config-if)#no appl getzonelist-filter 601
r4(config-if)#^Z
r4#
```

the 12.2 node verifies its address. This, of course, is R2's serial interface. (See Listing 10-44.)

R2's routing table is now checked to see what routes are propagating to it after this set of configuration changes. The routes from R4 are being learned correctly. Note that the cable range 1-10 in zone Legacy also appears in R2's routing table. The only route missing is the Ether zone on cable range 30-35. R2 does not have any access lists, so R1 should be

```
r1#sh app rou
Codes: R - RTMP derived, E - EIGRP derived, C - connected, A - AURP
       S - static  P - proxy
2 routes in internet

The first zone listed for each entry is its default (primary) zone.

C Net 1-10 directly connected, TokenRing0, zone legacy
C Net 13-13 directly connected, Serial1, zone wan13
r1#conf t
Enter configuration commands, one per line.  End with CNTL/Z.
r1(config)#in se0
r1(config-if)#appl zone wan12
r1(config-if)#^Z
r1#
r1#sh app int se0
Serial0 is up, line protocol is up
  AppleTalk cable range is 12-12
  AppleTalk address is 12.1, Valid
  AppleTalk zone is "wan12"
  AppleTalk port configuration verified by 12.2
  AppleTalk address gleaning is not supported by hardware
  AppleTalk route cache is enabled
  AppleTalk Zip Reply filter is 611
r1#
```

Listing 10-44

checked again. Here it is observed that there is a ZIP reply filter 611 on serial 0 denying the Ether zone (see Listing 10-45).

After removing the filter, R2 still does not see the zone Ether. When R1's routing table is checked, it can be seen that the reason for this is that R1 does not have a route to cable range 30-35. Thus, even though R1 sees the zone Ether, it does not propagate it because it does not know about its cable range (see Listing 10-46).

All of R1's directly connected networks are active, implying that the absence of a route to the 30-35 cable range is due to a logical rather than a physical issue. R1 and R3 should be checked for routing filters, which may explain why R1 has no route to the 30-35 cable range (see Listing 10-47).

When the inbound distribute list 609 is examined, it is found to only allow the 300-350 cable range. This is possibly a configuration error; in any case, the 30-35 cable range can be added to the list. After this is done, R1 receives the update from R3 about the 30-35 cable range in zone Ether (see Listing 10-48).

```
r2#sh app ro
Codes: R - RTMP derived, E - EIGRP derived, C - connected, A - AURP
       S - static  P - proxy
5 routes in internet

The first zone listed for each entry is its default (primary) zone.

R Net 1-10 [1/G] via 12.1, 6 sec, Serial0, zone legacy
C Net 12-12 directly connected, Serial0, zone wan12
R Net 13-13 [1/G] via 12.1, 6 sec, Serial0, zone wan13
C Net 24-26 directly connected, TokenRing0, zone legacy
            Additional zones: 'finance'
R Net 40-44 [1/G] via 24.4, 3 sec, TokenRing0, zone finance
r2#
r1#sh access-l 611
AppleTalk access list 611:
  deny zone ether
  permit additional-zones
  permit other-access
r1#conf t
Enter configuration commands, one per line.  End with CNTL/Z.
r1(config)#in se0
r1(config-if)#no app zip-reply-fil 611
r1(config-if)#^Z
r1#
```

Listing 10-45

Returning to one of the earlier problems, it can now be verified that R2 receives a ZIP update relating to zone Ether. ZIP debugging is used to illustrate this (see Listing 10-49).

As stated at the outset, it is a network policy that users on Ether should not have access to cable range 1-10 in the Legacy zone, but they are allowed access to all other cable ranges. However, when R3's routing table is examined again, there is one missing route, and that is to the 24-26 cable range (see Listing 10-50). Can you explain this?

It also can be noted that the entire zone Legacy is absent from R3's ZIP table. This should act as a reminder that the `appletalk permit-partial-zones` command should be configured on R1 to allow it to advertise the 24-26 cable range, which also happens to be in zone Legacy (see Listing 10-51).

Now R3 has a route to the 24-26 cable range in zone Legacy but does not have a route to the 1-10 cable range within the same zone. This corrects all the network faults while implementing the required policy.

```
r2#sh app zon
Name                                    Network(s)
legacy                                  1-10 24-26
wan12                                   12-12
wan13                                   13-13
finance                                 40-44 24-26
Total of 4 zones
r2#

r1#sh app ro
Codes: R - RTMP derived, E - EIGRP derived, C - connected, A - AURP
       S - static  P - proxy
5 routes in internet

The first zone listed for each entry is its default (primary) zone.

C Net 1-10 directly connected, TokenRing0, zone legacy
C Net 12-12 directly connected, Serial0, zone wan12
C Net 13-13 directly connected, Serial1, zone wan13
R Net 24-26 [1/G] via 12.2, 5 sec, Serial0, zone legacy
                   Additional zones: 'finance'
R Net 40-44 [2/G] via 12.2, 5 sec, Serial0, zone finance
r1#sh app zone
Name                                    Network(s)
legacy                                  24-26 1-10
ether
wan12                                   12-12
wan13                                   13-13
finance                                 24-26 40-44
Total of 5 zones
r1#
```

Listing 10-46

Listing 10-47

```
r1#
!
interface Serial1
 ip address 172.16.103.1 255.255.255.0
 appletalk cable-range 13-13 13.1
 appletalk zone wan13
 appletalk access-group 610
 appletalk distribute-list 610 out
 appletalk distribute-list 609 in
 clockrate 56000
!
interface TokenRing0
 ip address 100.1.1.1 255.255.255.0
 appletalk cable-range 1-10 1.1
 appletalk zone legacy
 ring-speed 16
!

r1#sh access-l 609
AppleTalk access list 609:
  permit cable-range 300-350
  deny other-access
r1#
```

```
r1#sh access-l
AppleTalk access list 609:
  permit cable-range 30-35
  permit cable-range 300-350
  deny other-access

r1#sh app ro 30
Codes: R - RTMP derived, E - EIGRP derived, C - connected, A - AURP
       S - static  P - proxy
6 routes in internet

The first zone listed for each entry is its default (primary) zone.

R Net 30-35 [1/G] via 13.3, 6 sec, Serial1, zone ether
  Route installed 00:02:16, updated 6 secs ago
  Next hop: 13.3, 1 hop away
  Zone list provided by 13.3
  Valid zones: "ether"
  There is 1 path for this route
* RTMP path, to neighbor 13.3, installed 00:00:06 via Serial1
   Composite metric is 256524800, 1 hop
r1#
```

Listing 10-48

Listing 10-49

```
r2#debug apple zip
AppleTalk ZIP Packets debugging is on

r2#
AT: NextNbrZipQuery: [30-35] zoneupdate 0 gw: 12.1 n: 12.1
AT: NextNbrZipQuery: r->rpath.gwptr: 00871DEC, n: 00871DEC
AT: maint_SendNeighborQueries, sending 1 queries to 12.1
AT: 1 query packet sent to neighbor 12.1
AT: maint_SendNeighborQueries, no pending queries
AT: Recvd ZIP cmd 2 from 12.1-6
AT: 1 zones in ZIPreply pkt, src 12.1
AT: net 30, zonelen 5, name ether
AT: in CancelZoneRequest, cancelling req on 30-35...succeeded
AT: NextNbrZipQuery: [30-35] zoneupdate 0 gw: 12.1 n: 12.1
AT: NextNbrZipQuery: r->rpath.gwptr: 00871DEC, n: 00871DEC
AT: maint_SendNeighborQueries, sending 1 queries to 12.1
AT: 1 query packet sent to neighbor 12.1
AT: maint_SendNeighborQueries, no pending queries
AT: Recvd ZIP cmd 2 from 12.1-6
AT: 1 zones in ZIPreply pkt, src 12.1
AT: net 30, zonelen 5, name ether
```

```
r3>sh app ro
Codes: R - RTMP derived, E - EIGRP derived, C - connected, A - AURP
       S - static  P - proxy
4 routes in internet

The first zone listed for each entry is its default (primary) zone.

R Net 12-12 [1/G] via 13.1, 3 sec, Serial3/3, zone wan12
C Net 13-13 directly connected, Serial3/3, zone wan13
C Net 30-35 directly connected, Ethernet2/0, zone ether
R Net 40-44 [3/G] via 13.1, 3 sec, Serial3/3, zone finance
r3>sh app zon
Name                                Network(s)
ether                               30-35
wan12                               12-12
wan13                               13-13
finance                             40-44
Total of 4 zones
```

Listing 10-50

```
r3>

interface Serial1
 ip address 172.16.103.1 255.255.255.0
 appletalk cable-range 13-13 13.1
 appletalk zone wan13
 appletalk access-group 610
 appletalk distribute-list 610 out
 appletalk distribute-list 609 in
 clockrate 56000
!

r1#sh access-l 610
AppleTalk access list 610:
  permit additional-zones
  deny cable-range 1-10
  permit other-access
r1#conf t
Enter configuration commands, one per line.  End with CNTL/Z.
r1(config)#apple permit-partial-zones
r1(config)#^Z
r1#
r1#cle app rou 24

r3>sh app ro
Codes: R - RTMP derived, E - EIGRP derived, C - connected, A - AURP
       S - static  P - proxy
5 routes in internet

The first zone listed for each entry is its default (primary) zone.

R Net 12-12 [1/G] via 13.1, 7 sec, Serial3/3, zone wan12
C Net 13-13 directly connected, Serial3/3, zone wan13
R Net 24-26 [2/G] via 13.1, 7 sec, Serial3/3, zone legacy
                 Additional zones: `finance'
C Net 30-35 directly connected, Ethernet2/0, zone ether
R Net 40-44 [3/G] via 13.1, 7 sec, Serial3/3, zone finance
r3>sh app zon
Name                                    Network(s)
legacy                                  24-26
ether                                   30-35
wan12                                   12-12
wan13                                   13-13
finance                                 24-26 40-44
Total of 5 zones
r3>
```

Listing 10-51

REVIEW QUESTIONS

For the exercises that are multiple-choice questions, there is only one correct answer unless the question is marked with an asterisk (*). Choose the most suitable answer.

1. How many hosts are available on an AppleTalk phase II segment?
   a. 127
   b. 253
   c. 254
   d. 255
   e. 1024
2. Zones are intended to ensure that broadcasts are confined to their corresponding cable ranges. True or false?
3. An AppleTalk client cannot see a particular zone after opening Chooser. A possible explanation is the presence of a(an)
   a. ZIP reply filter.
   b. GZL filter.
   c. AppleTalk distribute list.
   d. NBP filter.
   e. Any of the above

* 4. A router cannot see a particular zone. A possible explanation is a(an)
   a. ZIP reply filter.
   b. GZL filter.
   c. AppleTalk distribute list.
   d. NBP filter.
   e. Any of the above

5. What is the AppleTalk global command that ensures that the filtering of a particular cable range will not block all cable ranges in the same zone?
6. What type of filter could be preventing access to a particular print server?
   a. ZIP reply filter
   b. GZL filter
   c. AppleTalk distribute list

d. NBP filter

e. Any of the above

7. Which of the following protocols has split horizon disabled by default on a frame-relay interface?

a. RTMP

b. AppleTalk EIGRP

c. Both

d. Neither

8. What is the default IP tunnel encapsulation for AppleTalk on a Cisco router?

a. AURP

b. Cayman

c. GRE

d. DVMRP

e. IPTalk

9. What is the only tunnel encapsulation to support an authentication key?

a. AURP

b. Cayman

c. GRE

d. DVMRP

e. IPTalk

10. Which of the following is *not* an option with the `test appletalk nbp` command?

a. Lookup

b. Poll

c. Object

d. Confirm

e. Parameters

11. What is the most appropriate first-step tool to use for a connectivity problem with a single node on a local segment?

a. `debug apple zip`

b. `debug apple packet`

c. `debug apple routing`

d. `debug apple arp`

e. `debug apple error`

12. When configuring a static route over ISDN, the ISDN zone and the static route zone

a. must match.

b. must be different.

c. It does not matter.

d. A zone should not be applied to ISDN to reduce ZIP traffic.

e. A zone should not be applied to the static route to reduce ZIP traffic.

***13.** When configuring EIGRP on two neighboring routers, the EIGRP ID number

a. refers to the EIGRP process.

b. refers to the router ID.

c. must match on each router.

d. must be different on each router.

e. is entirely arbitrary.

14. By default on a Cisco router, cable ranges that have no associated zones

a. are advertised like any other route.

b. are advertised as unreachable.

c. are not advertised.

d. are advertised with a hop count of 16.

e. are advertised only on the interface over which they were learned.

15. Which of the following is *not* an AppleTalk-related protocol. Explain the function of each of the other four.

a. AFP

b. ATP

c. DDP

d. ASP

e. PAP

CHAPTER 11

Troubleshooting IBM Internetworking

Introduction

Cisco routers feature strong support of IBM internetworking. An array of features is available in the appropriate software suites that support technologies and solutions such as the traditional SDLC, STUN, SDLLC, and Remote Source-Route Bridging (RSRB) and now also the newer technologies such as Data Link Switching (DLSW) and Advanced Peer-to-Peer Networking (APPN). This represents a very broad feature set. This chapter concentrates on the technologies that are currently most prevalent in IBM internetworking solutions and are the least likely to be replaced. The troubleshooting of source-route bridging will be studied because it is fundamental to IBM networking and internetworking technology. RSRB will be discussed because this remains a popular remote networking solution for mainframe connectivity as well as for certain nonroutable protocols such as NetBIOS.

Cisco's enhanced support of DLSW is termed DLSW+, and it is becoming increasingly prevalent in the marketplace, in many cases as a migration strategy from RSRB. The troubleshooting of DLSW+ will be addressed in detail given its growing deployment in the industry.

The use of TCP encapsulation will be the prime focus when discussing RSRB and DLSW peers, since this is by far the most commonly used method for peer definition. Direct encapsulation methods over media such as frame relay also will be visited to a lesser degree.

The objectives of this chapter are to

- Understand the key issues when troubleshooting a remote source-route bridging environment.
- Learn the relevance of NetBIOS name caching and filtering.
- Understand the main issues with DLSW+ in different media, from the basic connection sequence to more advanced features such as peer groups and backup peers.
- Apply Cisco router `show` and `debug` commands to resolve problems in both RSRB and DLSW+ environments.

Remote Source-Route Bridging (RSRB)

Traffic Control with RSRB

Managing Explorers There are two basic kinds of explorers used in source-route bridging. *All-routes explorers* propagate across all routes and all rings searching for the destination MAC address. In redundant topologies, this can result in unnecessarily excessive explorer traffic. Older IBM machines use all-routes explorers, while more modern implementations support the use of *spanning-tree explorers*. A spanning-tree explorer takes a single route path between source and destination. This path can be configured statically or discovered dynamically by the IBM Spanning Tree Protocol.

A static spanning-tree path is configured as follows:

```
interface token ring0
source-bridge 2 3 10
source-bridge spanning
```

The `source-bridge spanning` keyword enables the forwarding of spanning-tree explorers on that router (or in this case bridge) interface. This configuration should be included on any bridge interface that is required to be part of the spanning-tree path.

Another method of implementing a spanning-tree explorer topology is to enable it automatically using the following type of configuration:

```
bridge 1 protocol ibm
!
interface token ring0
source-bridge 2 3 10
source-bridge spanning 1
```

Even spanning-tree explorers can needlessly consume bandwidth, which sometimes adds to the latency experienced by SNA session traffic. This has the potential of causing problems because of the time-sensitive nature of SNA. Explorer storms also can occur in SRB environments that have redundant topologies. An explorer storm can be detected at the router using the `show processor cpu` command. A high utilization in the SRB background field can be indicative of this type of network condition. We will now examine some methods for reducing unnecessary explorer traffic and also the possibility of explorer storms.

The Proxy Explorer function can be enabled on the router interface using the `source-bridge proxy-explorer` interface command. This greatly reduces explorer traffic because the router stores explorer replies in its Routing Information Field (RIF) cache. When end stations generate new explorers, the router examines its RIF cache for an equivalent entry. If it finds an RIF entry, it will then send a directed frame to the destination. If no response is received, the RIF entry will be marked invalid. When the router receives the next explorer for this station, it flushes the invalid entry and forwards the new explorer. It should be noted, however, that proxy explorers cannot be used in conjunction with fast switching; hence it is inefficient to use this feature on, for example, a high-speed LAN segment.

An upper limit can be placed on explorer traffic by specifying a lower maximum rate for fast-switched explorers. This is measured in bytes per interface, and the default is 38,400. This value may need to be reduced in the case of an explorer storm or in a situation where it is suspected that excessive explorer traffic is causing SNA session timeouts. The parameter value is set using the `source-bridge explorer-maxrate` global configuration command.

If the explorers are process switched, a similar effect can be achieved by limiting the size of the explorer queue per interface using the `source-bridge explorerQ-depth` command. Note that explorers are fast switched by default, so for this command to have an effect, the `no source-route explorer-fastswitch` global command also must be employed.

The `source-bridge explorer-dup-ARE-filter` command can be applied globally so that the router will not forward the same all-routes explorer more than once.

If the maximum network diameter for SRB is known to be less than seven hops, then the routers can be configured for this TTL value in order to further reduce any unnecessary explorer forwarding. The `source-bridge max-hops count` command relates to all-routes explorers that are received on a particular interface. The `source-bridge max-in-hops count` and `source-bridge max-out-hops count` commands can control spanning-tree explorers that are received or sent, respectively, from the interface. It is important to be aware of the subtle differences between these source-route bridging commands, particularly those which are used for tuning the service. Otherwise, the configuration change that you make may not have any effect, or it may even cause the problem to escalate.

Static RIFs also can be used to reduce explorer traffic. This is a simple technique that does not have any adverse effect on processor load. As with any static method of managing resources, the network administrator must be mindful of these static entries when managing network changes.

Access Filters Access filters are used frequently in SRB and RSRB environments to reduce unnecessary traffic, optimize performance, and possibly implement security policies. Configuring these types of filters is often a little more tricky than layer 3 access lists, where the engineer may have a greater familiarity. It is important to be very clear about the meaning and consequences of the configuration before actually applying any access list to avoid the risk of unintentional connectivity problems. We will now examine some of the different techniques and options for filtering in a source-route-bridged environment.

The most common method of applying an SRB access list is at the interface with the following type of configuration:

```
Router-1(config-if)#source-bridge ?
  input-address-list   Filter input packets by MAC address
  input-lsap-list      Filter input IEEE 802.5 encapsulated packets
  input-type-list      Filter input packets by type code
  output-address-list  Filter output packets by MAC address
  output-lsap-list     Filter output IEEE 802.5 encapsulated packets
  output-type-list     Filter output packets by type code
```

Filtering traffic based on the MAC address is usually done with the standard 700 series access list. In the example in Listing 11-1, an input address list 701 filters based on source address and will only forward SRB traffic from the following MAC addresses: 0000.0b24.2341, 0000.0c22.1122, and 8000.0c22.1122. Notice that wildcard bits have the

Listing 11-1

```
interface TokenRing1/1
 ring-speed 16
 source-bridge 23 3 200
 source-bridge spanning
 source-bridge input-address-list 701
!

r3#sh access-l 701
Bridge address access list 701
    permit 0000.0b24.2341   0000.0000.0000
    permit 0000.0c22.1122   8000.0000.0000
r3#
```

Listing 11-2

```
interface TokenRing1
 ring-speed 16
 source-bridge 2 1 99
 source-bridge output-type-list 220
!
access-list 220 permit 0x0404 0x0101
access-list 220 permit 0x0004 0x0001
access-list 220 deny   0x0000 0xFFFF
```

exact same meaning as in an IP access list. If no wildcard is specified, the default is a full set of zeros meaning an exact-match only. There is an implicit deny-all for unspecified addresses.

The example in Listing 11-2 shows a type list, which relates to the 200 series access lists in Cisco IOS. Here the router's token ring 1 interface will only forward SRB traffic onto the ring that has an SSAP (source service access point) and DSAP of type 04, which is SNA. The wildcard is 0x0101 to allow for command and response frames to be passed. SNA explorers with a null DSAP are also allowed. The final line is for illustrative purposes only. It is unnecessary because of the implicit deny-all rule.

The LSAP list also uses the 200 series access list. In Listing 11-3, an LSAP list forms part of an access-expression. This type of expression can be used to define one or more conditions for the filter. The example in Listing 11-3 shows an outbound filter that will only forward SAP type F0 (i.e., NetBIOS) traffic that is destined to any MAC address *other than* 4000.0d34.2231. The & symbol indicates that both the specified LSAP and DMAC conditions must be met—similar to a logical AND. A | symbol would denote that meeting either of the conditions would be a successful match to the access expression; in other words, like a logical OR. The ~ character can be used to provide a logical NOT.

Listing 11-3

```
!
interface TokenRing0
 ring-speed 16
 access-expression output (lsap(201) & dmac(770))
 source-bridge 32 2 200
 source-bridge spanning
!
access-list 201 permit 0xf0f0 0x0101
!
access-list 770 deny 4000.0d34.2231 0000.0000.0000
access-list 770 permit 0000.0000.0000 ffff.ffff.ffff
```

Access expressions should be kept as simple as possible to avoid errors. It also should be noted that these expressions cannot be combined with other equivalent filter types on the same interface.

NetBIOS access lists and outbound LSAP lists also can be applied to the RSRB remote peer definition statements.

There is one other important issue to note in relation to potential problems caused by filters. When configuring remote peers based on TCP encapsulation in either an RSRB or DLSW environment, an IP access list configured on the network for a different purpose potentially could prevent the opening of peer relationships. A filter that hinders IP connectivity between the peers sometimes can be overlooked because focus is being placed on layer 2 bridging issues.

NOTE: *Do not forget that existing IP access lists can prevent TCP peer formation.*

Dealing with Session Timeout If the network is characterized by irregular bursts of traffic, it may be prudent to increase the size of the backup queue for TCP-encapsulated RSRB traffic. The appropriate global command is `source-bridge tcp-queue-max`, which can be used to alter the parameter from its default value of 100 packets. If sessions are timing out due to persistently heavy traffic, then it may be better to slightly reduce this queue because, owing to the time-sensitivity of SNA, it is sometimes better to have packets dropped than delayed.

For SNA traffic using LLC2, the LLC2 timing parameters can be tuned to help avoid session timeout. Examples of such parameters are

- *The T1 timer.* This tells the router how long it should wait for an LLC acknowledgment before resending information frames. This could be increased from its default value of 1000 ms using the `llc2 t1-time` interface command.
- *The N2 value.* This is the maximum number of retries before the LLC2 session is terminated. The default number of retries is 8 and can be modified using the `llc2 n2` command in interface mode.

This brief discussion on parameter tuning to reduce the occurrence of SNA session timeouts is really just a scratching of the surface, and it is intended to open your mind to some of the different possible approaches. Doing any such parameter tuning can only be considered on a case-by-case basis depending on the network and the traffic profiles that are present on it. In some cases, a network redesign may be the only suitable option. In all cases when varying TCP and LLC2 parameters in an attempt to tune source-route bridging performance, caution should be exercised. While there may be a certain amount of trial and error involved in this type of approach, parameters should never be altered from their default values without a good understanding of the consequences.

RSRB Troubleshooting Tools

The `show source` Command The `show source` command is a useful means of displaying the current status of the fundamental SRB parameters and obtaining statistical information. From the sample output in Listing 11-4 it can be observed that

- The only local ring that has SRB configured is token ring 0/0. This ring has been configured as 397 for source-route bridging with a bridge number equal to 1 (this is actually the router's token ring 0/0 interface). Statistics for received and transmitted packets across this interface since the counters were last cleared are also provided. The maximum SRB hop count is seven hops. The parameters *r*, *p*, *s*, and *n* refer to the configuration of ring group, proxy explorers, spanning-tree explorers, and NetBIOS name caching. An asterisk indicates that these features are configured on this local interface.
- The figure for drops may or may not be a problem depending on what type of packets are being dropped. Sometimes drops are preferable to delays in an SNA environment given the time-sensitive nature of the protocol. On the other hand, if, for example, session traffic is being discarded due to excessive explorers, then this is an undesirable situation. The section on explorer management dealt with methods for resolving such a problem. While on the subject of explorers, note that specific traffic information is given for all-routes and spanning-tree explorers that are sent and received on each local bridge interface. The maximum explorer rate per interface is at the default value of 38,400 Bps.
- The virtual ring group is 406. The local peer ID is 192.168.202.21, and three remote peers have been defined using TCP encapsulation. All the peers are in the active open state. The peers would be closed if there was a problem with IP connectivity between the RSRB peers or if no SRB traffic was being exchanged between them. Remember that SRB peers will not move to the open state until the first set of explor-

```
Router2>show source

Local Interfaces:                              receive      transmit
           srn bn  trn r p s n  max hops          cnt           cnt          drops
To0/0      397  1  406 * * f *  7  7  7   2285223      15431486        300905

Global RSRB Parameters:
 TCP Queue Length maximum: 100

Ring Group 406:
  This TCP peer: 192.168.202.21
   Maximum output TCP queue length, per peer: 100
  Peers:                   state      bg lv  pkts_rx  pkts_tx  expl_gn    drops TCP
   TCP 192.168.202.21     -               3        0        0        0        0   0
   TCP 10.100.15.254     open            3  1688388  2028655   218369      347   0
   TCP 10.1.3.220        open            3     7585   251415   218369        5   0
   TCP 10.1.1.70         open            3        0   244600   218369        4   0
  Rings:
   bn: 1  rn: 397  local  ma: 400a.f0df.8286 TokenRing0/0       fwd: 1695973
   bn: 7  rn: 1000 remote ma: 4000.3002.0e1e TCP 10.100.15.254   fwd: 12566
   bn: 9  rn: 1406 remote ma: 4000.3002.0ede TCP 10.100.15.254   fwd: 146862
   bn: 1  rn: 170  remote ma: 400a.0af6.1e00 TCP 10.1.1.70        fwd: 2
   bn: 1  rn: 180  remvrt ma: 4000.10b4.2100 TCP 10.1.1.70        fwd: 0
   bn: 3  rn: 226  remote ma: 4008.b01a.1601 TCP 10.1.3.220       fwd: 0

Explorers: ------     input ------              ----- output -----
        spanning  all-rings     total       spanning  all-rings     total
To0/0     216509       1860    218369       13452639     282883  13735522

  Explorer fastswitching enabled
  Local switched: 219670    flushed 0           max Bps 38400

        rings     inputs          bursts         throttles     output drops
        To0/0     219670             561                 0                0

Router2>

Router2#clear source
```

Listing 11-4

ers gets answered between them. The information relating to input and output packets, explorers generated, and drops to each remote peer can be helpful for troubleshooting session connectivity that takes place via these peers.

- Information is provided on remote rings that contain resources accessed using this RSRB process. A significant amount of traffic has been exchanged with rings 1000 and 1406. Both rings are local to the 10.100.15.254 peer.

It is often necessary to clear the source-route bridging statistics and then monitor as they increment. The `clear source` command is used to zero the counters on the output of `show source`. It is important to remember that this is all it does. I have seen people mistakenly think that this command reinitializes the source-route bridging parameters, such as the peers, which is not true.

One of the reasons for managing and monitoring explorer traffic is to guard against the possibility of explorer storms, which particularly can occur in redundant topologies that contain the potential for loops. Thus, how can an explorer storm be detected? Apart from observing excessive explorer traffic on the output of `show source`, the `show processor cpu` command also can be used. A high percentage value in the SRB background field can be indicative of an explorer storm (the sample in Listing 11-5 does *not* indicate such a condition). This is particularly relevant for explorers that are not fast switched.

The `show rif-cache` Command This command is used to examine the contents of the router's RIF cache. The destination MAC address is mapped against the RIF that can be used to source route to that station. In the example in Listing 11-6, all the entries in the RIF cache were learned via the virtual ring group 406. This can be thought of as the next-hop ring for those entries. A physical ring number equally could be present in this column. The idle time since each RIF entry was last accessed is also available. Before I discuss how to analyze the contents of the RIF cache, notice that the two MAC addresses designated by an asterisk are the router interfaces FDDI1/0 and Token Ring 2/0 and hence have no RIF entry, as distinct from stations learned over the virtual ring group 406.

The RIF is not straightforward to interpret. It consists of two basic fields, the Routing Control field and a series of one or more Route Designators (See Figure 11-1).

The Routing Control field has the following components:

- *Type.* This 3-bit field indicates how routing information to this destination is discovered. It can assume the following values:
  - *000.* A specifically routed frame where the source supplies the RIF information for the token-ring frame.
  - *100.* The RIF information is collected using all-routes explorers traversing each ring in the network. The RIF gets built as each bridge appends the number of the ring onto which the frame is about to be forwarded. The first bridge also adds the number of the source ring.

```
Fulton_924>sh process cpu
CPU utilization for five seconds: 15%/4%; one minute: 17%; five minutes: 19%
 PID  Runtime(ms)   Invoked  uSecs     5Sec    1Min    5Min  TTY Process
   1       460184   5380085     85    0.00%   0.00%   0.00%    0 NTP
   2    252749536   2384205 106010    0.00%   2.35%   2.65%    0 Check heaps
   3        28676     12855   2230    0.00%   0.00%   0.00%    0 Pool Manager
   4      3826920  18027652    212    0.00%   0.00%   0.00%    0 Timers
   5       971768    683376   1422    0.00%   0.00%   0.00%    0 ARP Input
   6            0         1      0    0.00%   0.00%   0.00%    0 SERIAL A'detect
   7         1600      3086    518    0.00%   0.00%   0.00%    0 RARP Input
   8     12020508   9837783   1221    0.24%   0.10%   0.08%    0 IP Input
   9       120392   1804348     66    0.00%   0.01%   0.00%    0 TCP Timer
  10          136        61   2229    0.00%   0.00%   0.00%    0 TCP Protocols
  11      2822048   1691386   1668    0.00%   0.01%   0.00%    0 CDP Protocol
  12        79364     23343   3399    0.00%   0.00%   0.00%    0 BOOTP Server
  13     26155236   9135958   2862    0.32%   0.25%   0.22%    0 IP Background
  14       317720    150150   2116    0.00%   0.00%   0.00%    0 IP Cache Ager
  15           52         2  26000    0.00%   0.00%   0.00%    0 Critical Bkgnd
  16         5856      4571   1281    0.00%   0.00%   0.00%    0 Net Background
  17          132        59   2237    0.00%   0.00%   0.00%    0 Logger
  18      2029800   8986220    225    0.00%   0.00%   0.00%    0 TTY Background
  19      1301540   8986278    144    0.00%   0.00%   0.00%    0 Per-Second Jobs
  20      4608976   8986301    512    0.00%   0.02%   0.01%    0 Net Periodic
  21      6566788  16585339    395    0.00%   0.00%   0.00%    0 Net Input
 PID  Runtime(ms)   Invoked  uSecs     5Sec    1Min    5Min  TTY Process
  22      4582304    150150  30518    0.00%   0.02%   0.00%    0 Per-minute Jobs
  32     97862192 220402583    444    0.32%   0.61%   0.60%    0 LanNetMgr Supt
  33            0         9      0    0.00%   0.00%   0.00%    0 CLS Background
  34        16700    901181     18    0.00%   0.00%   0.00%    0 LLC2 Timer
  35            0         2      0    0.00%   0.00%   0.00%    0 VDLC Background
  36     15704404  24690843    636    0.00%   0.02%   0.05%    0 SRB Background
  37      6690020  11356484    589    0.00%   0.01%   0.00%    0 IP-EIGRP Hello
  38          564        82   6878    0.32%   0.50%   0.12%    2 Virtual Exec
  39      4761744    218153  21827    0.00%   0.00%   0.00%    0 IP SNMP
  41          660        23  28695    0.00%   0.00%   0.00%    0 SNMP Traps
  42       215532    150234   1434    0.00%   0.00%   0.00%    0 IP-RT Background
  43     13545760   9536446   1420    0.00%   0.00%   0.00%    0 IP-EIGRP Router
Fulton_924>
```

Listing 11-5

  - *110.* The RIF is built using a spanning-tree explorer that is only forwarded by bridges participating in the spanning-tree topology. The RIF thus gets built as the explorer frame propagates along a single path, therefore reducing explorer traffic.
- *Length.* This 5-bit field indicates the total length of the RIF in bytes. It can have a maximum value of 30 bytes.
- *D bit.* This designates the direction in which the RIF should be read.
  - 0. Left to right
  - 1. Right to left

```
Router2>sh rif
Codes: * interface, - static, + remote

Dst HW Addr     Src HW Addr     How      Idle (min)  Routing Information Field
4000.0306.5114 N/A             rg406           10+  0AB0.51A1.7D16.57E9.1960
0008.b01a.9600 N/A             Fd1/0             *  -
0000.f63a.55a6 N/A             rg406            0+  06B0.57E9.1960
0008.b01a.1601 N/A             To2/0             *  -
0000.f63a.4b85 N/A             rg406            0+  06B0.57E9.1960
4000.0306.5116 N/A             rg406           10+  0AB0.51A1.7D16.57E9.1960
0001.fad4.f5d8 N/A             rg406            6+  0AB0.58D1.7D16.57E9.1960
0010.e37c.51dd N/A             rg406            4+  0AB0.5811.7D54.57E9.1960
0001.fa68.a636 N/A             rg406            9+  0AB0.6A91.7D16.57E9.1960
0000.f63a.4f87 N/A             rg406            0+  0AB0.6A81.7D16.57E9.1960
0001.faf8.2423 N/A             rg406            3+  0AB0.9791.7D54.57E9.1960
0000.f63a.4b82 N/A             rg406            0+  06B0.57E9.1960
0001.c816.4892 N/A             rg406            6+  0AB0.5191.7D16.57E9.1960
0000.f63a.559f N/A             rg406            0+  06B0.57E9.1960
0001.c817.4d95 N/A             rg406            2+  0AB0.5191.7D16.57E9.1960
Router2>
```

Listing 11-6

- *Largest Frame Size*. This 3-bit field indicates the largest frame size in bytes that can be supported along the path. This is set initially by the source and can be reduced by intermediate bridges if the requested frame size cannot be supported. The value is this field is not a direct numerical value for the largest frame size; instead, its value corresponds to a specific largest frame size.

The fields that have been described so far in the Routing Control field total 12 bits; a further 4 bits are stuffed so as to round off to an even 2 bytes.

The Route Designator is a series of one or more ring-bridge pairs that provide the routing information for the destination. It always commences and ends with a ring number. The ring fields are 12 bits and must be unique in the SRB network. The bridge fields are 4 bits and only need to be unique if multiple bridges attach to the same pair of rings.

As an exercise, let us decode the RIF for the entry shown in bold type:

```
0000.f63a.4b85 N/A             rg406           0+  06B0.57E9.1960
```

The Routing Control field is 06B0 in hexadecimal. This corresponds to the following parameter values:

Type. 000, which is a specifically routed nonbroadcast frame where the source supplies the RIF.

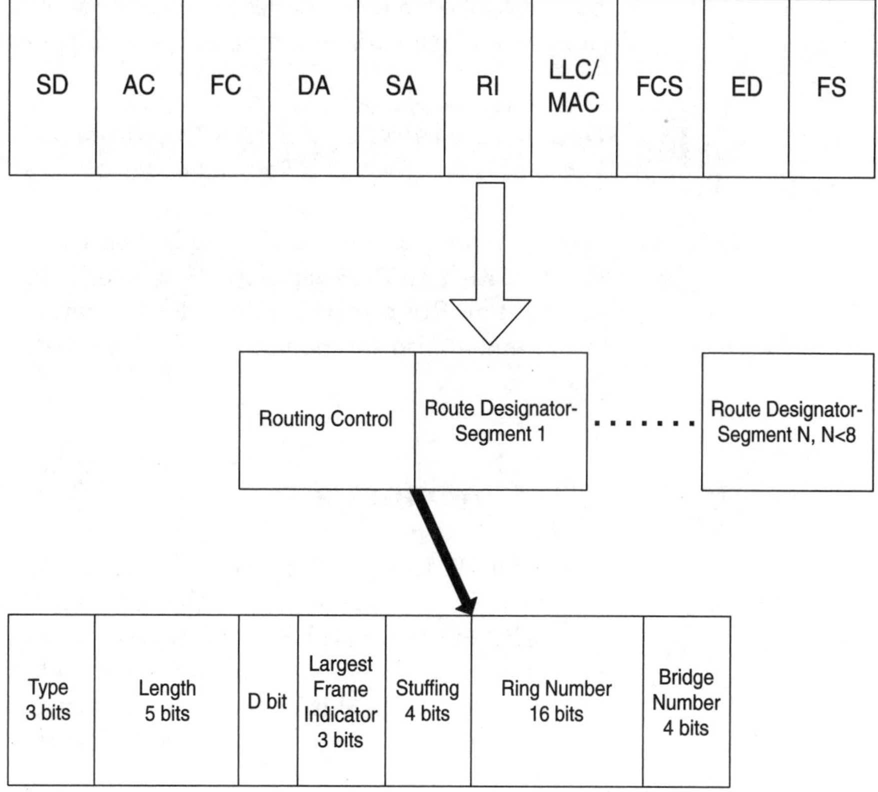

Figure 11-1 The routing information field on an LLC or MAC frame.

Length. 6 bytes, which is seen to be the correct total length of the RIF.

B in hexadecimal is 11 in decimal or 1011 in binary; thus the D-bit is equal to 1, indicating that the RIF should be read from right to left.

The largest frame size is the value that corresponds to 011. As an exercise, this should be looked up in an IBM or Token Ring reference manual.

Now we will examine the Route Designators, reading from right to left. We know that it must begin with a ring; hence the first bridge value is zero. The first ring is 196; this is 406 in decimal, which is the value of the virtual ring group. The next bridge is bridge 9, and the next ring is 57E, or 1406 in decimal. The station 0000.f63a.4b85 thus resides on ring 1406.

If you check back to the sample output for the `show source` command, it can be observed that the 1406 ring and bridge 9 are local to the remote peer 10.100.15.254 that is defined on router 2.

I would like to emphasize a point that was illustrated by decoding the RIF, and this is that the virtual ring *does* count as a hop. This is sometimes overlooked in network design and therefore can result in hop-count limitation and network diameter issues on a live network.

NOTE: When calculating the RSRB network diameter, remember that the virtual ring counts as a hop just as the physical rings do.

The contents of the RIF cache can be cleared using `clear rif`. When troubleshooting an SRB connectivity problem, this is a useful means of checking if an RIF can still be built for the various destination stations. This command also can be used in case the RIF cache has become corrupted.

LNM Commands

Support for IBM's LAN Network Manager (LNM) is enabled by default when source-route bridging is configured on a Cisco router. The `show lnm config` command can be used to verify what information should be configured on an LNM management station that will communicate with the router. Even if LNM is not being used as an SRB management application, this command gives a logical overview of the SRB configuration on the router.

The example in Listing 11-7 relates to the network shown in Figure 11-2. Router R2 has two SRB rings 32 (020 in hex) and 23 (017 in hex) that each bridge to the virtual ring 200 (0C8 in hex).

The `show lnm interface` command can be applied to a specific interface or used without any options (see Listing 11-8). It lists active SRB stations on the ring and is a quick way to find out what station is

Listing 11-7

```
r2#sh lnm config
Bridge(s) currently configured:

    From     ring 020, address 0000.3020.f8ed
    Across bridge 002
    To       ring 0C8, address 4000.3020.f8ed

    From     ring 017, address 0000.3020.f85d
    Across bridge 002
    To       ring 0C8, address 4000.3020.f85d

r2#
```

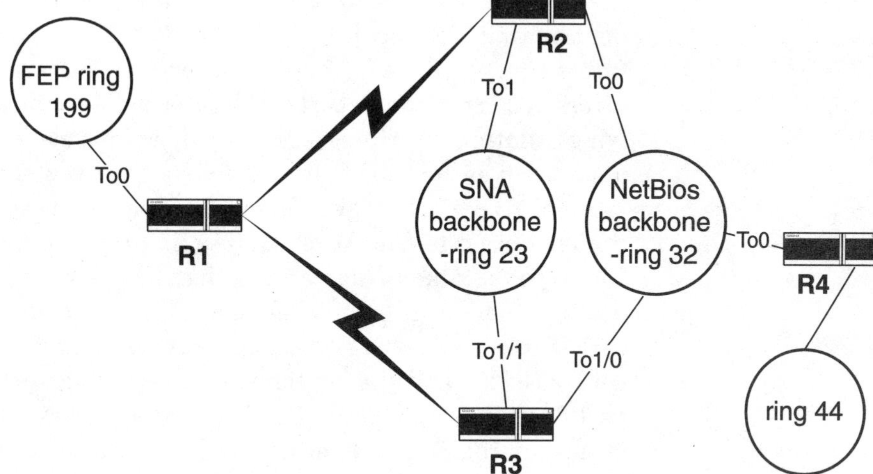

Figure 11-2 RSRB troubleshooting scenarios.

```
r2>sh lnm interface
                                                     nonisolating error counts
interface       ring   Active Monitor    SET     dec  lost  cong.  fc   freq. token

To0             0032   0000.b818.28f0   00200   00001 00000 00000 00000 00000 00000
To1             0023   0000.b84c.60b4   00200   00001 00000 00000 00000 00000 00000

r2>sh lnm interface tok 0
                                                     nonisolating error counts
interface       ring   Active Monitor    SET     dec  lost  cong.  fc   freq. token

To0             0032   0000.b818.28f0   00200   00001 00000 00000 00000 00000 00000
Notification flags: FE00, Ring Intensive: FFFF, Auto Intensive: FFFF
Active Servers: LRM LBS REM RPS CRS

Last NNIN:   never, from 0000.0000.0000.
Last Claim:  never, from 0000.0000.0000.
Last Purge:  never, from 0000.0000.0000.
Last Beacon: never, `none' from 0000.0000.0000.
Last MonErr: never, `none' from 0000.0000.0000.
                                                      isolating error counts
    station        int      ring  loc.     weight     line  inter burst  ac    abort
0000.b818.28f0     To0      0020  0000     00 - N     00000 00000 00000 00000 00000
0000.3020.396a     To0      0020  0000     00 - N     00000 00000 00000 00000 00000
0008.f813.3910     To0      0020  0000     00 - N     00000 00000 00000 00000 00000
0000.3020.f8ed     To0      0020  0001     00 - N     00000 00000 00000 00000 00000
r2>
```

Listing 11-8

the active monitor. Error counting on a variety of different isolating and nonisolating 802.5 error types is also provided, such as congestion errors, frame check, frequency and token errors, line errors, interrupts burst errors, AC errors, and aborts. The interface-specific option, as well as tallying isolating error types, also provides information on the most recent instance of each of the following token-ring events: neighbor notification incomplete (NNIN), token claims, ring purges, beacons, and active monitor error reports. The MAC address that reports the event is also logged. The types of token-ring servers that have ring-management functions are highlighted in bold. They are the LAN reporting manager (LRM), LAN bridge server (LBS), ring error monitor (REM), ring parameter server (RPS), and the configuration reporting server (CRS). The most pertinent of these are the REM, which monitors errors reported by any station on the ring and verifies whether or not the ring is in a functional state. The CRS monitors the current token-ring configuration and reports changes such as the change in the ring's active monitor. The RPS reports to LNM when a new station joins the ring and ensures that all stations agree on parameters such as the ring number. In some cases the RPS causes the router's token-ring interface to go into an administratively down state because another station on the ring has a ring number configured that disagrees with that of the router.

The `show lnm station` command also gives a listing of active stations that are participating in source-route bridging. In Listing 11-9, the command was executed before any live traffic was on R2's token ring 0 and token ring 1 interfaces. Seen here are the addresses of two Cabletron hubs that correspond to rings 23 and 32 along with five Cisco router

```
r2#sh lnm station
                                                  isolating error counts
    station       int     ring  loc.    weight    line  inter burst  ac    abort
0000.b818.28f0    To0     0020  0000    00 - N    00000 00000 00000 00000 00000
0000.3020.396a    To0     0020  0000    00 - N    00000 00000 00000 00000 00000
0008.f813.3910    To0     0020  0000    00 - N    00000 00000 00000 00000 00000
0000.3020.f8ed    To0     0020  0001    00 - N    00000 00000 00000 00000 00000
0000.b818.08d8    To1     0017  0000    00 - N    00000 00000 00000 00000 00000
0008.f813.3990    To1     0017  0000    00 - N    00000 00000 00000 00000 00000
0000.3020.f85d    To1     0017  0000    00 - N    00000 00000 00000 00000 00000
r2#
```

Listing 11-9

ports, which relate to the router interfaces that attach to these rings as seen in Figure 11-2.

SRB Debugging

There are three different Cisco debug tools for source-route bridging. The `debug source event` tool displays significant events such as the formation or loss of peers as well as information error messages. The `debug source error` tool will display all SRB-related errors and error messages.

```
Router-2#deb source ?
  bridge  Source bridging activity
  error   Source bridging errors
  event   A subset of the source-bridge messages
```

The tool that displays the most output, and is therefore the most processor-intensive is `debug source bridge`. Before attempting to employ this tool, use the `show source` command to obtain an understanding of the SRB and RSRB configuration and traffic on the router.

Let us decode the two lines shown in bold in Listing 11-10. The first line states that a packet containing data has been received over the virtual ring 406 from 10.100.105.254 over TCP port 1996, the normal RSRB TCP port. The packet, which is 30 bytes in length, is being placed on the local ring 37. The second boldface line states that a packet containing an explorer frame has been received over the virtual ring 406 from 10.100.105.254 and TCP port 1996. The packet is 4 bytes in length with an offset of 22.

```
Galway#sh debug
General bridging:
  Source Bridge debugging is on
RSRB37: fwd vrn 37 bn 7 trn 1000 to peer 406/10.100.105.254/1996, o=9 v=406 t=6
RSRB: DATA: 406/10.100.105.254/1996 FORWARD, trn 37, vrn 406, off 24581, len 30
RSRB: DATA: 406/10.100.105.254/1996 EXPLORER, trn 24660, vrn 406, off 22, len 4
RSRB: DATA: 406/10.100.105.254/1996 EXPLORER, trn 24660, vrn 406, off 18, len 0
RSRB: DATA: 406/10.100.105.254/1996 EXPLORER, trn 24660, vrn 406, off 18, len 8
RSRB: DATA: 406/10.100.105.254/1996 EXPLORER, trn 24660, vrn 406, off 22, len 9
RSRB: DATA: 406/10.100.105.254/1996 EXPLORER, trn 24660, vrn 406, off 22, len 9
RSRB: DATA: 406/10.100.105.254/1996 EXPLORER, trn 24660, vrn 406, off 22, len 9
```

Listing 11-10

NetBIOS in an SRB Environment

NetBIOS and Bandwidth Consumption

IBM originally adopted NetBIOS for communication in token-ring LAN environments. While in previous chapters we have seen how it can now be run over TCP/IP and IPX, NetBIOS in its purest form is a nonroutable protocol that is not optimized for the wide-area network. It relies extensively on broadcasts and if it is being bridged rather than routed, these broadcasts will propagate throughout the entire broadcast domain. This creates a need for NetBIOS filtering in order to minimize unnecessary traffic in the WAN. NetBIOS name queries can also create unnecessary WAN traffic. Name caching is one solution that can be enabled on the router in order to eliminate any unnecessary name queries in the WAN. Another issue to note in relation to NetBIOS is that it can send data in large chunks of up to 64 bytes. Therefore it should be ensured that any traffic that is interactive, of small packet size, or extremely time sensitive is not "crowded out" when sharing the same WAN resources. This is an important network design issue and can be resolved using a number of different techniques such as protocol prioritization.

Name Caching

NetBIOS name caching is a useful feature that also happens to result in additional router overhead. Therefore it should generally be only used on WAN routers where bandwidth consumption should be spared rather than on busy LAN backbone routers. SRB proxy explorers must be enabled before name caching can be employed. This is demonstrated as follows:

```
R-1(config)#in to1
R-1(config-if)#netbios enable-name-cache
netbios: proxy explorer must be enabled on interface for netbios name
        caching to be used.
R-1(config-if)#source proxy-exp
R-1(config-if)#netbios enable-name-cache
R-1(config-if)#^Z
```

The `show netbios-cache` command displays the contents of the router's NetBIOS name cache (Listing 11-11). This gives a mapping of NetBIOS station names against their MAC addresses. In this example the station names, MAC addresses, the interface over which they were

```
R-1>sh netbios-cache
netbios name-cache timeout 20 minutes

Code: "-" indicates a static entry

    HW Addr      Name                   How       Idle      NetBIOS Packet Savings
0001.fa68.6d7c SARAHWH                  To5/3     2         0
0001.c817.4d6b BARBARA                  To1/2     1         32
0000.f638.e14c MARYOH                   To1/2     3         0
0001.fa68.6d24 ROSALEEN                 To1/2     1         1
0001.fa68.3b8f W305017                  To1/2     3         2
0000.f63a.8ff7 SISD01                   To5/3     2         0
0001.fa68.a68e W3MZ101                  To1/1     3         64
0000.f638.34c9 W3MZ098                  To1/1     1         0
R-1>
```

Listing 11-11

learned, how long they have been idle for, and a tally of packet savings that the cache entries have provided, is also shown. The timeout value shown needs to be manually configured. This command is also a useful means for obtaining a quick estimate of how much NetBIOS traffic is passing through the router and how it is distributed. The cache can be cleared using `clear netbios`.

As stated earlier NetBIOS name caching entails overhead. For example on a busy backbone router that performs a multiplicity of functions, the use of static NetBIOS mappings of name versus MAC address may be more prudent. This can be performed in global configuration mode.

NetBIOS Filtering

The most efficient way to filter NetBIOS traffic is to use a host-based NetBIOS access list (Listing 11-12). It is important to remember that NetBIOS names are case-sensitive. As with all types of access lists care

Listing 11-12

```
netbios access-list host netblock permit Ja*
netbios access-list host netblock permit Fallon*
!
interface TokenRing0
 ring-speed 16
 source-bridge 32 2 200
 source-bridge spanning
 netbios input-access-filter host netblock
!
```

should be exercised as configuration errors on these lists frequently cause connectivity problems. These lists must also be updated if NetBIOS stations are renamed, moved, or if new stations are installed. In the following example only stations that begin with "Ja" or "Fallon" can communicate with hosts outside the Token-Ring 0 LAN segment. There is an implicit deny-all at the end of this list.

NOTE: *NetBios names are case-sensitive. Remember this when dealing with NetBios filters.*

SRB Troubleshooting Scenarios

The network shown in Figure 11-2 uses remote source-route bridging to allow SNA users on rings 23 and 44 to connect to a Front End Processor (FEP) on ring 199. Ring 32 is populated by NetBIOS users requiring remote connectivity. The relevant portions of the router configurations are shown. Currently the network exhibits several serious connectivity problems, which will be explained as we move through the issues. (See Listing 11-13.)

The first problem is that users on R4's rings have no access to the FEP ring. This is because R4 has no IP route to the 172.16.199.1 peer. Upon examination of R4's configuration you will notice an OSPF passive-interface that causes this problem. (See Listing 11-14.)

The next issue that was reported is that users on ring 23 also cannot connect to the FEP.

Let's examine R2 and R3.

```
r3#
!
interface TokenRing1/1
 ip address 172.16.23.3 255.255.255.0
 ring-speed 16
 source-bridge 23 3 200
 source-bridge spanning
 source-bridge input-address-list 701
!

r3#sh access-l 701
Bridge address access list 701
    permit 0000.0b24.2341   0000.0000.0000
    permit 0000.0c22.1122   8000.0000.0000
r3#
```

Listing 11-13

```
r1#sh run
Building configuration...

Current configuration:
!
version 11.2
no service password-encryption
no service udp-small-servers
no service tcp-small-servers
!
hostname r1
!
enable password cisco
!
source-bridge ring-group 200
source-bridge remote-peer 200 tcp 172.16.199.1
source-bridge remote-peer 200 tcp 172.16.23.2
source-bridge remote-peer 200 tcp 172.16.23.3
source-bridge remote-peer 200 tcp 172.16.32.4
!
interface Serial0
 ip address 172.16.102.1 255.255.255.0
 no fair-queue
 clockrate 56000
!
interface Serial1
 ip address 172.16.100.1 255.255.255.0
 clockrate 56000
!
interface TokenRing0
 ip address 172.16.199.1 255.255.255.0
 ring-speed 16
 source-bridge 199 1 200
 source-bridge spanning
!
interface TokenRing1
 no ip address
 shutdown
!
router ospf 1
 network 172.16.0.0 0.0.255.255 area 0
!
no ip classless
!
!
line con 0
line aux 0
line vty 0 4
 password cisco
 login
!
end

r2#
!
hostname r2
!
```

Listing 11-13 (*Cont.*)

```
netbios access-list host Control permit PS*
netbios access-list host Control permit sarah*
enable password cisco
!
source-bridge ring-group 200
source-bridge remote-peer 200 tcp 172.16.199.1
!
interface Serial0
 ip address 172.16.102.2 255.255.255.0
 no fair-queue
!
interface Serial1
 no ip address
 shutdown
!
interface TokenRing0
 ip address 172.16.32.2 255.255.255.0
 ring-speed 16
 access-expression output lsap(201)
 source-bridge 32 2 200
 source-bridge spanning
 netbios input-access-filter host Control
!
interface TokenRing1
 ip address 172.16.23.2 255.255.255.0
 ring-speed 16
!
router ospf 1
 network 172.16.0.0 0.0.255.255 area 0
!
access-list 201 permit 0x0404 0x0101
access-list 201 permit 0x0004 0x0101
access-list 201 deny   0x0000 0xFFFF
!
line con 0
line aux 0
line vty 0 4
 password cisco
 login
!
end

r2#

!
hostname r3
!
netbios access-list host Control permit PS*
netbios access-list host Control permit sarah*
netbios access-list host Control deny *
enable password cisco
!
source-bridge ring-group 200
source-bridge remote-peer 200 tcp 172.16.199.1
source-bridge remote-peer 200 tcp 172.16.23.3
!
interface TokenRing1/0
```

Listing 11-13 (*Cont.*)

```
 ip address 172.16.32.3 255.255.255.0
 ring-speed 16
 source-bridge 32 3 200
 source-bridge spanning
 netbios input-access-filter host Control
!
interface TokenRing1/1
 ip address 172.16.23.3 255.255.255.0
 ring-speed 16
 source-bridge 23 3 200
 source-bridge spanning
 source-bridge input-address-list 701
!

r3#

r4#
!
hostname r4
!
enable password cisco
!
source-bridge ring-group 200
source-bridge remote-peer 200 tcp 172.16.199.1
source-bridge remote-peer 200 tcp 172.16.32.4
!
interface TokenRing0
 ip address 172.16.32.4 255.255.255.0
 ring-speed 16
 source-bridge 32 4 200
!
interface TokenRing1
 no ip address
 ring-speed 16
 source-bridge 44 1 200
!
router ospf 1
 passive-interface TokenRing0
 network 172.16.0.0 0.0.255.255 area 0
!
no ip classless

r4#
```

Access-list 701 was meant to allow traffic only to the FEP 4000.0123.1122:

```
r3#conf t
Enter configuration commands, one per line.  End with CNTL/Z.
r3(config)#access-l 702 per 4000.0123.1122 8000.0000.0000
r3(config)#in to1/1
r3(config-if)#no source-bridge input-address-list 701
r3(config-if)#source-bridge output-address-list 702
r3(config-if)#ex
r3(config)#^Z
r3#
```

```
r4#ping 172.16.199.1

Type escape sequence to abort.
Sending 5, 100-byte ICMP Echos to 172.16.199.1, timeout is 2 seconds:
.....
Success rate is 0 percent (0/5)
r4#sh ip ro 172.16.199.1
% Subnet not in table
r4#conf t
Enter configuration commands, one per line.  End with CNTL/Z.
r4(config)#router ospf 1
r4(config-router)#no passive-inter to0
r4(config-router)#^Z
r4#cle ip ro *
r4#wr
Building configuration...
[OK]
r4#ping 172.16.199.1

Type escape sequence to abort.
Sending 5, 100-byte ICMP Echos to 172.16.199.1, timeout is 2 seconds:
.!!!!
Success rate is 80 percent (4/5), round-trip min/avg/max = 36/36/36 ms
r4#
```

Listing 11-14

Access-list 702 should now allow access to the FEP for Ring 23 via R3. R2's configuration should also be verified. There is likely to be a problem since users on ring 23 should have been able to access the FEP even with the errant filter on R3. It can be seen that bridging has not been enabled on R2's token-ring 1 port. (See Listing 11-15.)

It can also be noticed from R2's configuration that it has no local peer definition for itself. With TCP encapsulation there is no local peer parameter and this must be configured as a remote peer. This is often confusing and is sometimes omitted from the configuration as a result.

```
r2#conf t
Enter configuration commands, one per line.  End with CNTL/Z.
r2(config)#source-bridge remote-peer 200 tcp 172.16.23.2
r2(config)#^Z
r2#
```

R2 seems to have had some basic configuration problems resolved. But NetBIOS users still report connection failures. Machines with the names SARAH and PRINCESS on ring 32 cannot access remote resources. Note that there is a NetBIOS access filter for ring 32 on both R2 and R3.

```
r2>sh lnm interface
                                                  nonisolating error counts
interface      ring   Active Monitor   SET    dec  lost  cong.  fc   freq. token

To0            0032   0000.b818.28f0  00200  00001 00000 00000 00000 00000 00000
To1            0000   0000.b818.08d8  00200  00001 00000 00000 00000 00000 00000
r2>en
Password:
r2#conf t
Enter configuration commands, one per line.  End with CNTL/Z.
r2(config)#in to1
r2(config-if)#source-brid 23 2 200
```

Listing 11-15

```
netbios access-list host Control permit PS*
netbios access-list host Control permit sarah*
netbios access-list host Control deny *
```

Upon examination it is found to only allow names that begin with sarah or PS. NetBIOS name recogition is case-sensitive so neither SARAH nor PRINCESS will be passed. Since there is an unnecessary deny * at the end of the list, this list must be deleted and re-entered in the appropriate form.

After the NetBIOS access list was reconfigured on both R2 and R3, NetBIOS users were still reporting slow response and dropped connections. This started to happen after a router configuration change that took place the previous night.

R2 and R3 should again be examined.

```
r2#sh access-list
Type code access list 201
    permit 0x0404 0x0101
    permit 0x0004 0x0101
    deny   0x0000 0xFFFF
r2#
```

This access list is applied as an outbound access-expression applied on to0 (i.e., ring 32). This only allows SNA traffic and is likely to be a misconfiguration that should have been applied to a ring such as 23, which only has SNA users attached. The result of this filter is that some users are accessing the WAN through R3 and packets that return the same path are successful; however packets that return via R2 will be dropped. This explains the dropped sessions that users are experiencing. It implies that some RIF entries were still cached against the to0 interface, which was valid prior to the "configuration change." Such cache entries should timeout; but you don't want to leave these things to chance in practice. The filter should be reconfigured to allow only NetBIOS traffic to pass:

```
r2#sh access-list 201
Type code access list 201
    permit 0xF0F0 0x0101
    deny   0x0000 0xFFFF
r2#
```

Data-Link Switching

Data-Link Switching (DLSW) is frequently thought of as an enhanced superset of RSRB. One of the areas in which it outstrips RSRB is scalability. Among the more fundamental reasons why DLSW provides superior scalability is that the RIF is terminated at the virtual ring, thus overcoming the traditional hop-count limitation of seven hops with IBM token-ring SRB. The termination of the RIF also opens the door for supporting the Ethernet medium. Ethernet transparent bridge groups can be mapped to the DLSW process in the router's configuration.

Another feature that is added in Cisco's implementation of DLSW (DLSW+) is the ability to configure peer groups. This reduces explorer traffic since explorers will be forwarded only to peers within the same group. Configuration is also reduced since routers only need to be peered with the border peer for that group. DLSW groups communicate via border peers. The promiscuous mode feature, which enables a DLSW router to accept connections from nonconfigured peers can further reduce configuration and network administration.

Peer redundancy can be built into the DLSW design by either configuring backup peers or using equal or unequal cost peers that provide connectivity to the same resources.

The On-Demand Peers feature enables the utilization of DLSW+ in a cost-effective and efficient manner in large networks and also in networks where WAN bandwidth is a constraint. In the sections that follow DLSW can be taken to mean DLSW+.

DLSW supports multiple encapsulation types when defining remote peers: TCP, FST, and direct encapsulation over point-to-point and frame relay. The use of TCP encapsulation will be focused on primarily since it is the most prevalent within the industry.

A Word about RIF Termination

It is important to be clear about what is meant by the RIF termination feature of DLSW. Terminating the RIF at the virtual ring means that each station only retains the RIF information necessary to bridge to the virtual ring. The router that attaches to the virtual ring bridges across that ring and the router at the other end of the virtual ring contains the remaining RIF information that facilitates bridging from the virtual ring to the end-station. For example, consider the network shown in Figure 11-3, in particular stations FEP and CC. If the RIF is passed through rather than being terminated, then the route designator to get to the FEP from CC is R7 B12 R99 B4 R20 B5 R9. Likewise the RIF that FEP uses to bridge to CC is the same read in the opposite direction.

However, with RIF termination the route designator that CC uses to bridge to the FEP is R7 B12 R99. The RIF that FEP bridges to CC with is R9 B5 R20 B4 R99. As you can see, the RIF always terminates with the virtual ring. The two routers that attach to the virtual ring, RA and RB, complete the end-to-end bridging function.

While RIF termination greatly enhances the scalability of DLSW, it can make troubleshooting more difficult since a network analyzer will not be able to detect the full end-to-end RIF.

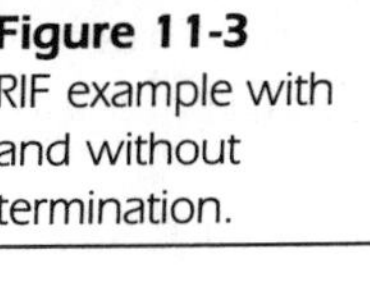

Figure 11-3 RIF example with and without termination.

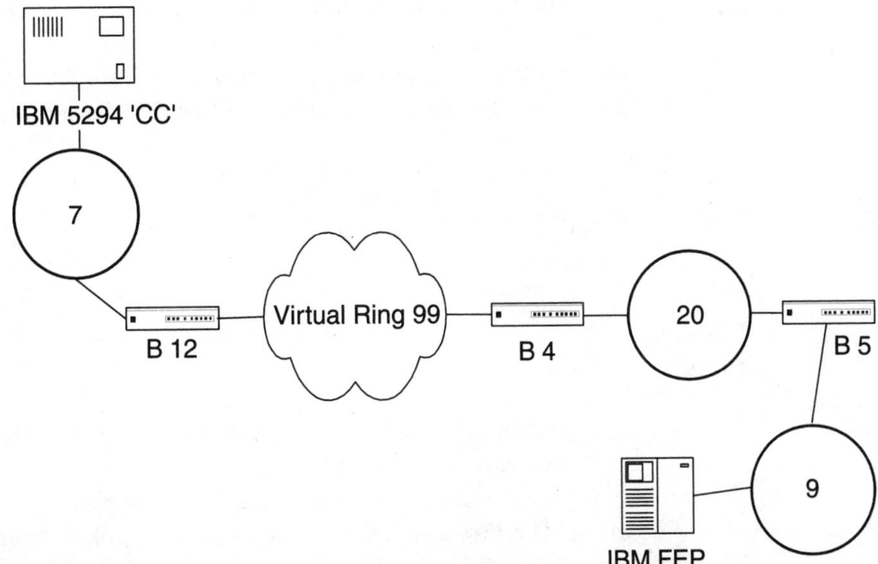

DLSW over Frame Relay

Local-acknowledgment is enabled by default for DLSW when using a TCP-based peer definition. This is unlike the case of RSRB where local-acknowledgment must be manually configured for a remote peer. By having this feature enabled, the responsibility for connection reliability is essentially delegated to the higher-layer TCP protocol, which will provide reliability and sequencing in any case. This is not true when DLSW peers are defined directly over frame relay as in the following configuration:

```
dlsw local-peer peer-id 3.3.3.3
dlsw remote-peer 0 frame-relay interface Serial1 16
```

With this configuration the DLSW peer will never move to the CONNECT state. In order to get the peer to come up; local-acknowledgment must be disabled by including the pass-thru option in the remote peer definition statement.

```
dlsw remote-peer 0 frame-relay interface Serial1 16 pass-thru
```

DLSW and Ethernet

Stations on an Ethernet medium can be integrated into the DLSW protocol, due in part to the fact that the RIF is removed at the end of the virtual ring. The basic configuration step entails mapping an existing transparent bridge group to the DLSW process, for example:

```
dlsw local-peer peer-id 172.16.23.3
dlsw remote-peer 0 tcp 172.16.199.1
dlsw bridge-group 1
!
interface Ethernet2/0
 no ip address
 bridge-group 1
!
bridge 1 protocol ieee
```

In terms of configuration, this is also similar to the way that an SDLC interface can be mapped to DLSW.

A point to note about using DLSW in an Ethernet environment is that all MAC addresses are in noncanonical or token ring format. The DLSW protocol automatically converts the Ethernet MAC addresses, however this must be kept in mind when configuring filters or static resource definitions. The configuration will not work if the MAC address is expressed in canonical form.

NOTE: *Don't forget about MAC address bit-swapping issues when using DLSW in an Ethernet environment.*

Explorer and Traffic Filtering

Limiting Explorers Most of the techniques used in RSRB to curtail any unnecessary explorer traffic have an equivalent in DLSW, and there are also some enhancements. A DLSW explorer is termed a CANUREACH (CUR) message to which a successful response is an ICANREACH (ICR) reply. Static ICR statements can be configured on the router to avoid sending explorers for this particular resource, for example:

```
dlsw icanreach mac-exclusive
dlsw icanreach mac-address 0000.2121.1212 mask ffff.ffff.ffff
```

This configuration places the MAC address 0000.2121.1212 in the router's DLSW reachablility cache. The mask shown is equivalent to an exact match (i.e., it is a mask rather than a wildcard). The `dlsw icanreach mac-exclusive` option tells the router that only statically configured resources are reachable. In this case CUR explorers will never be forwarded to remote peers.

Another technique for limiting the effect of excessive explorers is to reduce the explorer queue size using the `dlsw explorerQ-depth` command. Also when defining a remote peer a destination MAC address can be specified that is exclusively tied to this peer. Only traffic destined for the defined MAC address will be forwarded to that peer. A sample configuration is as follows:

```
dlsw remote-peer 0 tcp 1.1.1.1 dest-mac 0001.0c23.1231
```

DLSW filtering can also be used to control explorer and data traffic, which conveniently brings us onto the next topic.

Traffic Filtering in DLSW Apart from defining layer 2 access lists such as 700-series and 200-series lists and applying them to interfaces in

```
Router-1(config)#dlsw remote-peer 0 tcp 1.1.1.1 ?
  bytes-netbios-out  Configure netbios bytes output filtering for this peer
  dmac-output-list   Filter output destination mac adresses
  host-netbios-out   Configure netbios host output filtering for this peer
  lsap-output-list   Filter output IEEE 802.5 encapsulated packets
```

Listing 11-16

the DLSW network, access control can also be applied when defining the remote peers. (See Listing 11-16.)

In the following example an outbound MAC address list 710 is applied to the remote peer 172.16.23.3 that only allows traffic destined for the two defined MAC addresses to be sent to this peer. Ring list 100 is applied to the 172.16.23.3 and 172.16.23.2 peers. The rings contained in the ring list are rings 199 and 32. Therefore, only traffic that is to or from those rings can be exchanged with the remote peers that contain the ring list 100 in their definition.

```
source-bridge ring-group 200
dlsw local-peer peer-id 172.16.199.1
dlsw ring-list 100 rings 199 32
dlsw remote-peer 100 tcp 172.16.23.3 dmac-output-list 710
dlsw remote-peer 100 tcp 172.16.23.2
!
access-list 710 permit 4000.0123.2234   0000.0000.0000
access-list 710 permit 0000.0213.1210   0000.0000.0000
```

Advanced Features with DLSW

Peer Groups Peer groups can be defined in DLSW+, which further enhances the scalability of the protocol. Each group contains a border peer. Every DLSW router within the group is only required to be capable of forming a peer relationship with the border peer, which in turn forms peer connections with border peers from adjacent groups. Thus, any connectivity can be achieved without the overhead and expense of a full-meshed peer network. For the purposes of troubleshooting, it is important to first understand how the feature is configured.

In the example of Figure 11-4, the routers R3 and R6 are both part of DLSW group 2 with R6 being the border peer. The border peer is configured to be in promiscuous mode. Thus it can accept connections from peers that are not configured on R6 itself. This is often a popular choice

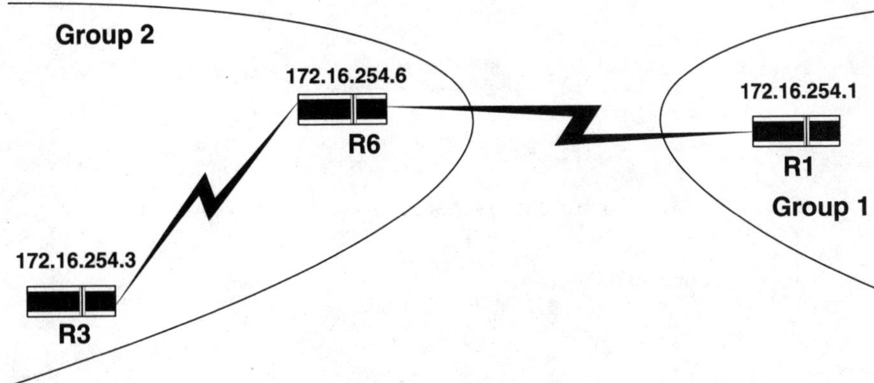

Figure 11-4
DLSW peer groups.

for the border peer of a large group, as all the group members do not then have to be configured on the border peer. R6 has R1 defined as a remote peer; this router is the border peer for group 1. The output of `show dlsw peers` confirms that R1 does not currently have any active peer connections within group 1. See Listing 11-17.

Peer Redundancy: Backup and Cost DLSW provides well-defined peer redundancy features. A backup peer can be defined, which is rather similar to a backup interface. The backup only becomes active if the primary peer moves to a DISCONNECT state. The linger parameter can be used to specify how long the router waits after the primary becomes active before dropping the backup peer connection. The primary peer must be defined first. In the network shown in Figure 11-5, the R3 router is a primary peer that is being backed up by 172.16.23.2, which in the normal stable state will appear as disconnected. For the moment, ignore the cost values that have been assigned. See Listing 11-18.

Peer redundancy can also be achieved by manipulating the peer cost parameter when redundant paths exist. The peer cost can be set at the router that will make the choice or alternatively at each of the remote routers. The central router will learn the cost of each adjacent peer during the DLSW capabilities exchange. Refer again to Figure 11.5. R2 is seen to have a DLSW cost of 20 as opposed to R3, which has a cost of 10. The cost parameter is set when defining the local peer:

```
dlsw local-peer peer-id 172.16.23.3 cost 10
```

If R1 receives ICR reply messages from both R2 and R3, it will favor the R3 path because it is of a lower cost. Remember, however, that using

```
r3#

dlsw local-peer peer-id 172.16.254.3 group 2
dlsw remote-peer 0 tcp 172.16.254.6

r6#

dlsw local-peer peer-id 172.16.254.6 group 2 border promiscuous
dlsw remote-peer 0 tcp 172.16.254.1
!
interface Loopback0
 ip address 172.16.254.6 255.255.255.255
!

r6#sh dls peer
Peers:                  state     pkts_rx   pkts_tx  type  drops ckts TCP   uptime

 TCP 172.16.254.1     CONNECT          2         2  conf      0    0   0  0:00:18

 TCP 172.16.254.3     CONNECT          8         8  prom      0    0   0  0:03:08

r1#

dlsw local-peer peer-id 172.16.254.1 group 1 border promiscuous
dlsw remote-peer 0 tcp 172.16.254.6
!
interface Loopback0
 ip address 172.16.254.1 255.255.255.255

r1#sh dls peer
Peers:                  state     pkts_rx   pkts_tx  type  drops ckts TCP   uptime

 TCP 172.16.254.6     CONNECT          3         3  conf      0    0   0  0:00:56

r1#
```

Listing 11-17

cost rather than backup peers, the less preferable path is still an active peer. R1 may sometimes choose this path, which has a bandwidth of 56k compared to T-1, if R2 happens to answer the CUR message first. This will then be cached in R1's reachablility cache potentially causing future congestion. To avoid this type of problem R1 should be configured with an explorer-wait-time of, say, 2 seconds. This gives R1 up to 2 seconds to wait for R3 to reply with an ICR message, and it will then be chosen as the preferred path.

```
dlsw timer explorer-wait-time 2
```

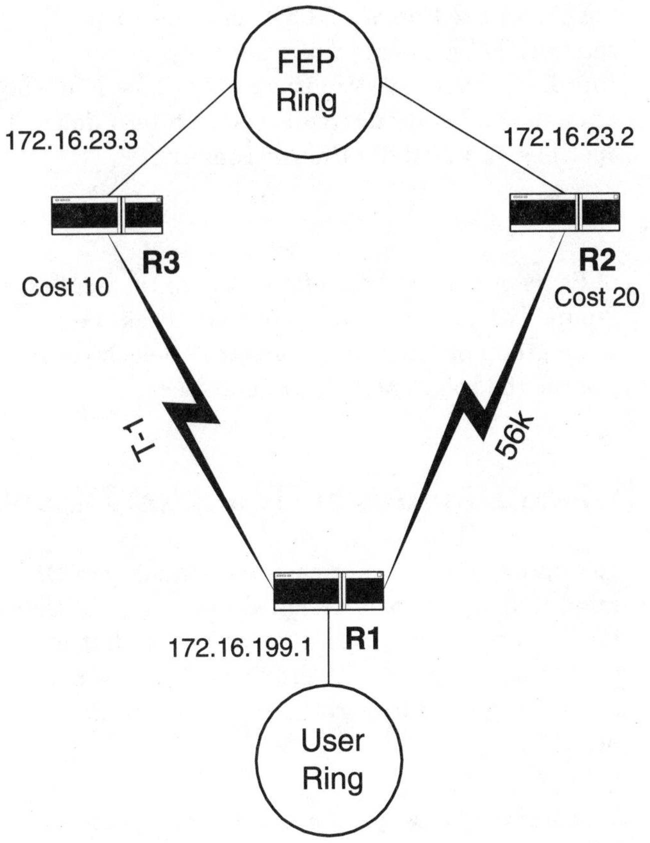

Figure 11-5 Peer redundancy in DLSW.

```
source-bridge ring-group 200
dlsw local-peer peer-id 172.16.199.1
dlsw remote-peer 100 tcp 172.16.23.3
dlsw remote-peer 100 tcp 172.16.23.2 backup-peer 172.16.23.3 linger 1

r1#sh dls peer
Peers:                  state      pkts_rx   pkts_tx  type  drops ckts TCP   uptime
 TCP 172.16.23.3       CONNECT       2125       307  conf      0    0   0 02:34:42
 TCP 172.16.23.2       DISCONN        140       140  conf      0    0   -        -
r1#
```

Listing 11-18

On-Demand Peers DLSW provides a facility for on-demand peers that will not connect until a set of explorers initiates a peer connection. An idle or inactivity timer specifies how long the peer remains active after the end-station circuit has been torn down. The following example specifies an inactivity time of 1 minute.

```
dlsw peer-on-demand-defaults inactivity 1
```

Peers-on-demand are often used on the nonborder peers within a peer group. The feature allows peer formation between remote peers in the same group or different groups where each remote router has its border peer as the sole configured remote peer.

Cisco Diagnostic Tools for DLSW

To improve your theoretical understanding of DLSW, you should bear in mind that DLSW was designed to manage LLC2 connections. Therefore its connection sequence is modeled on that of LLC2. RFC 1795 is an excellent reference that provides a firm grounding in DLSW and the Switch to Switch Protocol (SSP) messages that it uses as part of its connection sequence.

The `show dlsw peers` Command Communication is initiated in DLSW when an end-station sends out a CUR explorer. However before any communication can take place, peer formation must be successfully negotiated between adjacent DLSW routers.

During the successful negotiation of a peer connection, a DLSW peer relationship moves through the following states:

DISCONNECT

CAP_EXG (Capabilities Exchange)

CONNECT

With TCP encapsulation the output of `show dlsw peers` command can potentially display two other states which are informative for troubleshooting an unsuccessful peer connection:

- WAIT_RD: The TCP write port (port 2065) is open and the router is waiting for the remote end to open the read port (port 2067).

- WAN_BUSY: The TCP outbound queue is full. This problem may be rectified by increasing the size of the TCP queue from its default of 200 packets using the `tcp-queue-max` option when defining that remote peer.

The status of all DLSW peer relationships on the router can be examined using `show dlsw peers`. This command will display information on attempted peer connections from nonconfigured peers when the router is in promiscuous mode as well as configured peers. The first sample output (Listing 11-19) shows the R1 router with three configured peers, two of which are in the active CONNECT state. The two peers 172.16.32.4 and 172.16.23.2 were defined using TCP encapsulation and have been up for approximately 1 hour 11 minutes and one-and-a-half minutes, respectively. Information is also available on the number of packets exchanged between R1 and each of its peers along with any dropped packets.

The `ckts` column indicates any active DLSW circuits. That is sessions between end stations, which were brought up using this particular DLSW peer relationship. In this case even for the two active peers no DLSW circuits are active. This illustrates an important point in relation to DLSW peer formation. If configured correctly without any network connectivity problems, a DLSW peer should move to CONNECT even without any end station traffic. This is distinct from RSRB where the peers will not open until the first set of end-station explorers is successfully answered.

In the following example, R4 is running in promiscuous mode and has successfully accepted a peer connection from 172.16.199.1. Apart from a configured or promiscuous peer, a third peer-type can be seen, namely *pod*, corresponding to the peers-on-demand feature (Listing 11-20).

```
r1#sh dlsw peer
Peers:                 state      pkts_rx    pkts_tx   type   drops ckts TCP    uptime
 TCP 172.16.32.4       CONNECT        152        152   conf       0    0    0 01:11:22
 TCP 172.16.23.2       CONNECT        144        144   conf       0    0    0 00:01:28
 TCP 172.16.23.3       DISCONN       2142        310   conf       0    0   -          -
r1#
```

Listing 11-19

```
r4#sh dlsw peer
Peers:                 state     pkts_rx    pkts_tx  type  drops ckts TCP    uptime
 TCP 172.16.199.1     CONNECT          8          8  prom      0    0   0 00:03:29
r4#
```

Listing 11-20

Listing 11-21 shows two more examples of the output of `show dlsw peers` when the peer relationship is not being set up. In the first case, the peer is failing because the remote end has the peer definition of R2 in backup mode. Notice that packets are being sent and received even though the peer connection remains disconnected. In the second case the host 172.16.199.2 does not exist, hence a TCP connection cannot be opened and no packets are being exchanged.

The `show dlsw capabilities` Command While initiating a DLSW peer relationship, the routers will engage in a DLSW capabilities exchange. The information contained in the exchange includes the following:

- DLSW Version and Vendor ID. The example in Listing 11-22 confirms that the two routers are using Cisco's DLSW+.
- Initial Pacing Window.
- Unsupported SAPs as specified by the `dlsw icannotreach` command.
- List of reachable MAC addresses and NetBIOS names, and whether the ICR MAC-exclusive or NetBIOS-exclusive features are configured.

```
r2#sh dlsw peer
Peers:                 state     pkts_rx    pkts_tx  type  drops ckts TCP    uptime
 TCP 172.16.199.1     DISCONN         10         10  conf      0    0  -          -
r2#

r2#sh dlsw peer
Peers:                 state     pkts_rx    pkts_tx  type  drops ckts TCP    uptime
 TCP 172.16.199.2     DISCONN          0          0  conf      0    0  -          -
```

Listing 11-21

- Number of TCP sessions. Two TCP sessions are initially set up. With DLSW+ the second TCP is always torn down after the capabilities exchange.
- The information in Listing 11-22 is appended as part of a DLSW+ capabilities exchange: Cisco version, is the router in a peer group and is it the border peer, peer cost, prioritization configuration, and peer-type (in this case it has been configured)?

It is important to be clear that in the above example the information listed refers to the 172.16.199.1 peer, *not* to R4 itself.

The `show dlsw reachability` Command DLSW explorers are termed CANUREACH (CUR) messages. A successful response to a CUR message is an ICANREACH (ICR). The router places ICR responses in its reachability cache. When the router receives an explorer from a local

```
r4#sh dlsw capab
DLSw: Capabilities for peer 172.16.199.1(2065)
  vendor id (OUI)          : '00C' (cisco)
  version number           : 1
  release number           : 0
  init pacing window       : 20
  unsupported saps         : none
  num of tcp sessions      : 1
  loop prevent support     : no
  icanreach mac-exclusive  : no
  icanreach netbios-excl.  : no
  reachable mac addresses  : none
  reachable netbios names  : none
  cisco version number     : 1
  peer group number        : 0
  border peer capable      : no
  peer cost                : 3
  biu-segment configured   : no
  local-ack configured     : yes
  priority configured      : no
  peer type                : conf
  version string           :

Cisco Internetwork Operating System Software
IOS (tm) 4000 Software (C4000-J-M), Version 11.2(18), RELEASE SOFTWARE (fc1)
Copyright (c) 1986-1999 by cisco Systems, Inc.
Compiled Mon 05-Apr-99 21:09 by jaturner

r4#
```

Listing 11-22

end-station or another DLSW peer, it will check the cache for a corresponding entry. It will only forward an explorer if no such entry is found. The router does not just include successful responses to CUR messages in its reachability cache. Other peers that announce static ICR messages (such as `icanreach mac-exclusive`) will also have entries in the cache. However, these entries will remain in the UNCONFIRM state until DLSW can verify their validity with live traffic that attempts to set up an end-to-end circuit with these stations. There are three such entries in Listing 11-23. Each was configured on the remote peer 172.16.23.3. Another entry has been validated and therefore has a status of FOUND. R1 either learned this entry because one of its local stations sent a CUR message for this MAC address or otherwise it found out about it when doing a capabilities exchange with the 172.16.23.3 peer which has this entry as FOUND in its own reachability cache.

Note that the reachability cache includes local and remote stations along with NetBIOS stations. The RIF is also included when applicable.

Not just reachable entries are placed in the reachability cache. This can be useful for troubleshooting. You can use the command `dlsw timer icannotreach-block-time` to set a nonzero cache life for unreachable resources. In this case unreachable resources will be displayed with a status of NOT_FOUND.

Entries can also appear in the cache while awaiting a response to the CUR message. These entries have the status SEARCHING.

```
r1#sh dls reach
DLSw Local MAC address reachability cache list
Mac Addr        status     Loc.     port                  rif

DLSw Remote MAC address reachability cache list
Mac Addr        status     Loc.     peer
0000.01b2.3020  UNCONFIRM  REMOTE   172.16.23.3(2065)
0000.0c3f.51ef  UNCONFIRM  REMOTE   172.16.23.3(2065)
0000.8160.51ef  FOUND      REMOTE   172.16.23.3(2065)
0001.0b14.1033  UNCONFIRM  REMOTE   172.16.23.3(2065)

DLSw Local NetBIOS Name reachability cache list
NetBIOS Name    status     Loc.     port                  rif

DLSw Remote NetBIOS Name reachability cache list
NetBIOS Name    status     Loc.     peer
```

Listing 11-23

The other value that the status field can take is VERIFY. This occurs when the cache entry has timed out and must again be verified.

The `show dlsw circuits` Command A DLSW circuit is an end-to-end connection between hosts or end-stations. An end-station that wants to establish a connection with another end-system over DLSW first sends a test explorer that is detected by the local DLSW router (RA). RA checks its reachability cache for an entry corresponding to the required destination MAC address. If no entry exists it sends a CUR explorer message to each of its remote peers. Assume that a peer (RB) answers with an ICR explorer response. RA then sends out a test response to the original local device. After receiving a station ID from the local device, RA sends a CUR circuit-setup message to RB, which replies with an ICR circuit setup. After RA sends a reach acknowledgment the circuit will move to the ESTABLISHED state, and the routers can proceed with XID processing. The remainder of the signaling is of the familiar LLC2 format, with SABME, contact, and UA frames being exchanged. The entire connection sequence is shown in Figure 11-6. Note that from the point of the reach acknowledgment onward, the connection frames are tagged with the data link ID and the Origin and Target Circuit IDs. The data link ID is 14 bytes in length and consists of the source and destination station MAC addresses and the source and destination SAPs. The data link IDs are displayed in the output of `show dlsw circuits`. The Origin and Target Circuit ID has the same value at each end after circuit establishment. While the data link ID is only used during circuit setup, the Origin/Target circuit ID is used both during circuit establishment and information transfer between end-stations.

```
R5# show dlsw circuits
Index    local addr(lsap)     remote addr(dsap)    state
45-00    4000.0b03.1234(F0)   1000.0c5a.81cd(F0)   CONNECTED
110-00   1000.3020.5fec(04)   1000.5ac0.140e(08)   CONNECTED
```

The following is a sample output with the `detail` optional keyword included. Note that this also includes the RIF. In recent versions of Cisco IOS, a specific MAC address or circuit ID can be specified with `show dlsw circuits`. This is useful when troubleshooting a large network.

```
R4# show dlsw circuits detail
Index    local addr(lsap)     remote addr(dsap)    state
194-00   1000.0b9b.1111(F0)   1000.5ac1.2222(F0)   CONNECTED
         PCEP: 99B332       UCEP: A50314
         Port: To0/0        peer 172.16.199.1(2065)
```

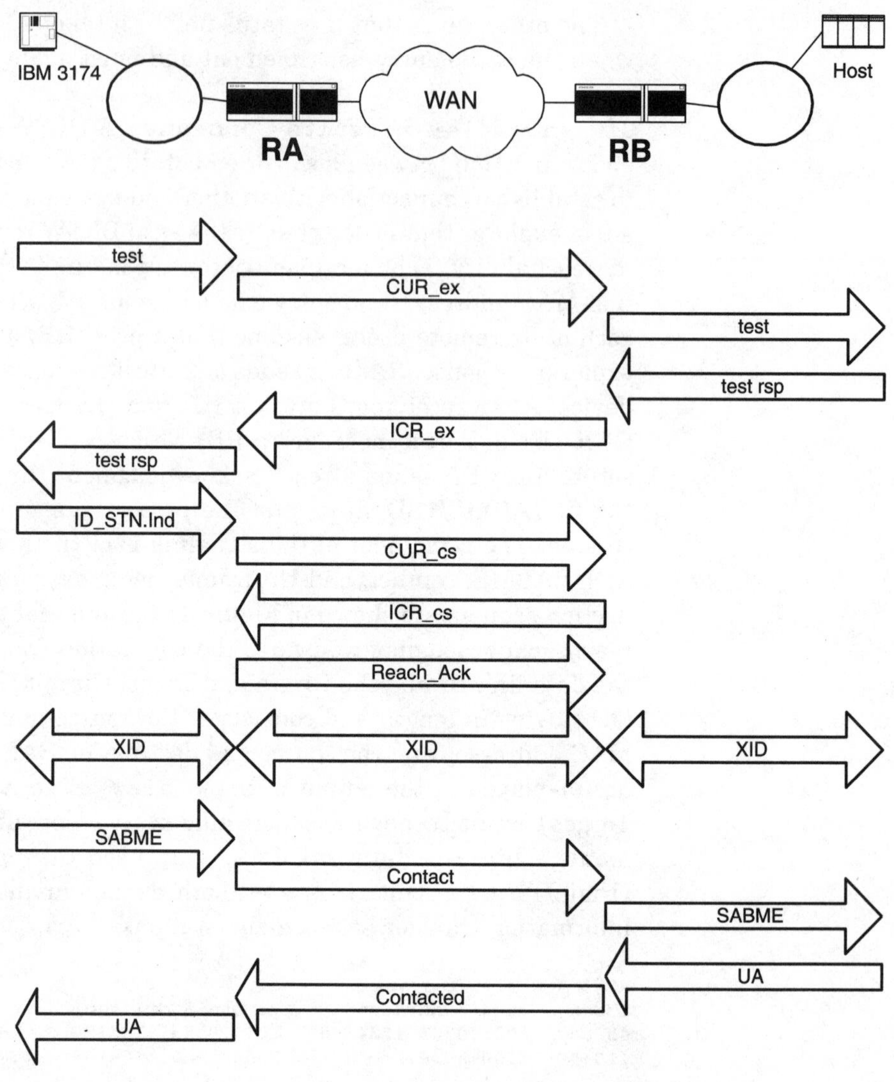

Figure 11-6 DLSW circuit connection sequence.

```
Flow-Control-Tx CW:20, Permitted:28; Rx CW:22, Granted:25
RIF = 0680.0012.0320
```

The DLSW circuit connection sequence for NetBIOS stations is shown in Figure 11-7. The fundamental principles are the same except of course XID processing does not take place on NetBIOS stations.

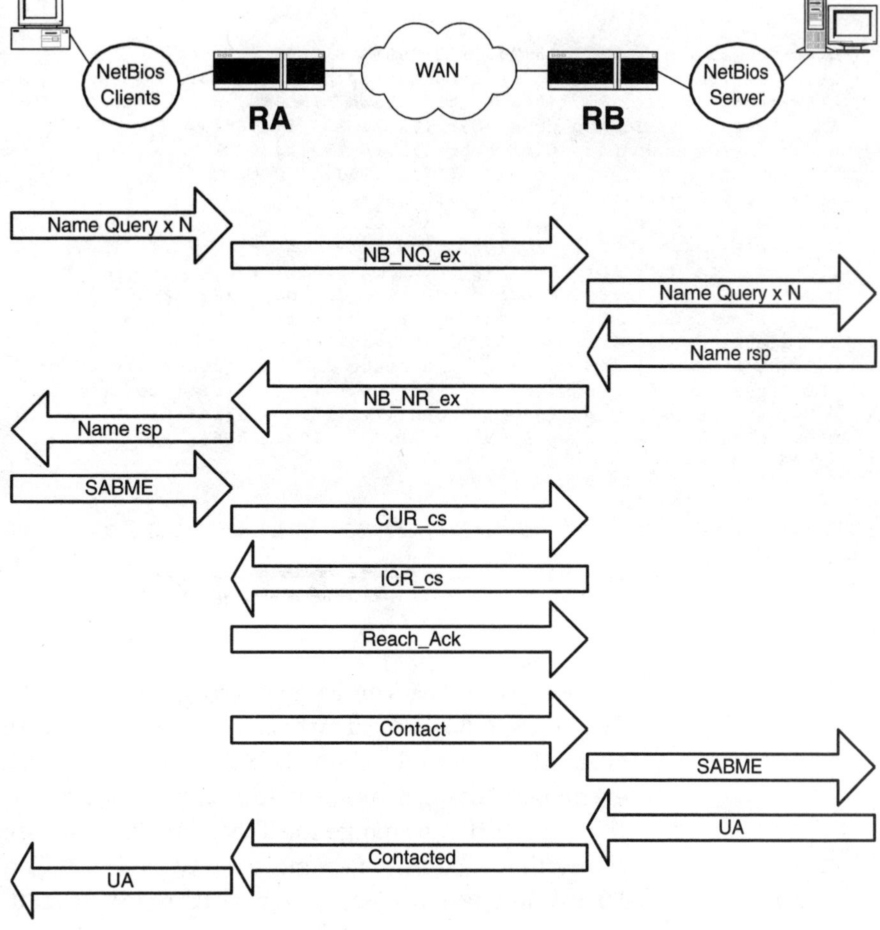

Figure 11-7 DLSW connection sequence for NetBIOS.

The `debug dlsw peers` Command The DLSW debugging options for Cisco IOS version 11.2 is shown below.

```
RouterC#debug dlsw ?
  core            Debug DLSw core
  local-circuit   Debug DLSw local circuit events
  peers           Debug DLSw peer events
  reachability    Debug DLSw reachability (explorer traffic)
  <cr>
```

Listing 11-24 is sample output of `debug dlsw peers` during the successful negotiation of a peer connection using TCP. The first thing to notice is that R4 is engaging in a passive open with 172.16.199.1. This means that R4 is configured as passive (i.e., it cannot initiate a peer con-

```
r4#
DLSw: passive open 172.16.199.1(11095) -> 2065
DLSw: action_b(): opening write pipe for peer 172.16.199.1(2065)
DLSw: peer 172.16.199.1(2065), old state DISCONN, new state CAP_EXG
DLSw: Recv CapExId Msg from peer 172.16.199.1(2065)
DLSw: Pos CapExResp sent to peer 172.16.199.1(2065)
DLSw: CapExId Msg sent to peer 172.16.199.1(2065)
DLSw: action_e(): for peer 172.16.199.1(2065)
DLSw: dlsw_tcpd_fini() for peer 172.16.199.1(2065)
DLSw: dlsw_tcpd_fini() closing write pipe for peer 172.16.199.1
DLSw: action_g(): for peer 172.16.199.1(2065)
DLSw: closing write pipe tcp connection for peer 172.16.199.1(2065)
DLSw: Recv CapExPosRsp Msg from peer 172.16.199.1(2065)
DLSw: action_e(): for peer 172.16.199.1(2065)
DLSw: peer 172.16.199.1(2065), old state CAP_EXG, new state CONNECT
DLSw: peer_act_on_capabilities() for peer 172.16.199.1(2065)
DLSw: Keepalive Request sent to peer 172.16.199.1(2065))
DLSw: Keepalive Response from peer 172.16.199.1(2065)
r4#
```

Listing 11-24

nection) therefore the connection has been initiated by 172.16.199.1. TCP port 2065 is used, which is the write pipe that DLSW uses. The state then changes from DISCONN to CAP_EXG and capabilities exchange messages are sent to and from the remote peer. At the end of the capabilities exchange the TCP write pipe is closed for the second TCP connection. The state now moves to CONNECT. The exchange of periodic DLSW keepalive messages with the 172.16.199.1 peer can then be observed.

This output shows an unsuccessful attempt by router R2 to form a peer with 172.16.199.2, because this peer should be addressed as 172.16.199.1 and therefore a TCP connection cannot be opened.

```
r2#
DLSw: action_a() attempting to connect peer 172.16.199.2(2065)
DLSw: CONN: peer 172.16.199.2 open failed, timed out [10]
DLSw: action_a(): CONN failed - retries 2
DLSw: peer 172.16.199.2(2065), old state DISCONN, new state DISCONN
```

What would happen in the previous scenario if the peer 172.16.199.2 did exist but it did not contain a remote peer statement for R2 (and it is not in promiscuous mode)? The peer state on R2 would move from DISCONN to WAIT_RD and finally to DISCONN again as R2 waits in vain for 172.16.199.2 to open the TCP read port (2067).

The `debug dlsw core reachability` Command When troubleshooting DLSW end-to-end session connectivity, use `debug dlsw core`. The full connection sequence involved in establishing circuits between end-stations can be observed. The messages observed fall into two basic categories; Circuit Setup Messages (CSM) and Common Layer Services Interface (CLSI), which can be thought of as a subset of CSM. CLSI messages are exchanged between the router and the local end-station. An important point to note in relation to CLSI messages is that messages originating from the LAN end-station end with `.Ind`, while messages generated by the router end with `.Rsp`.

The `debug dlsw reachability` command provides output on all explorer-related traffic. Both of these commands must be used with extreme caution in a production environment. The `debug dlsw core` tool can be applied to a single circuit index; however, if you wish to troubleshoot a new circuit being established, this option can obviously not be applied.

DLSW Troubleshooting Scenarios

The network shown in Figure 11-8 uses DLSW to connect SNA users on rings 23 and 44 to a FEP on ring 199. There are NetBIOS clients on ring 32 as well as on R3's Ethernet segment. The relevant parts of the router configurations are shown. The reported problems are listed. Assume full IP connectivty across the network. (See Listing 11-25.)

The problems reported include

1. Users on ring 23 cannot initiate sessions to FEP on ring 199.
2. Users on ring 44 have no connectivity to any remote resources.
3. Ethernet NetBIOS clients (R3 e2/0) cannot access remote servers.
4. Only 2 users on ring 23 could consistently attach to the FEP even before the current problems occurred.
5. R2 is intended to act as a backup peer to R3 (as configured on R1). However when troubleshooting the above problems, it has been noticed that DLSW traffic is being passed over the 56k link between R1 and R2 rather than exclusively over the T-1 between R1 and R3.

Let us begin by checking R1's peers (Listing 11-26).

There are two things to immediately notice in Listing 11-26. First, the peer to R4 is down which relates to the problems on ring 44. Second, the

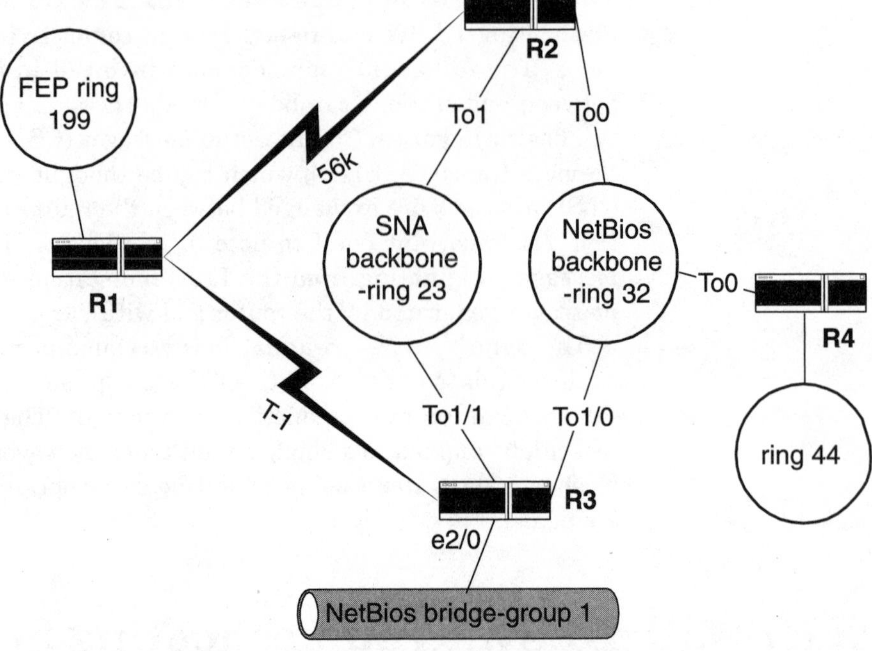

Figure 11-8 DLSW troubleshooting scenarios.

peer to R2 is up, which should not be the case unless the primary peer, R3, is down. We will follow up on the more serious issue of R4 first. (See Listing 11-27.)

There is IP connectivity to the configured peer, so let's telnet to R4 (Listing 11-28).

R4 has no configured peers but is defined to be promiscuous. Therefore it will accept connections from nonconfigured peers. The passive parameter means that it will not initiate a peer connection, which is not relevant in this case since no remote peers are defined.

One other issue to notice is that R4 is using its loopback address as its local peer identifier. This is contrary to the configuration on R1 where R4 is defined by 172.16.32.4, its token ring 0 interface. This may explain why the peer is not coming up. The peer definitions are made consistent by changing the local peer definition on R4. DLSW peer debugging is then enabled and a successful peer initiation from R1 can be observed. (See Listing 11-29.)

So what about the users on ring 23? We know that the peers to R1 are up on the two relevant routers. The fact that there is no connectivity through either R2 or R3 may suggest that R1 should first be checked for a common denominator.

Listing 11-25

```
hostname r1
!
enable password cisco
!
source-bridge ring-group 200
dlsw local-peer peer-id 172.16.199.1
dlsw ring-list 100 rings 199 32
dlsw remote-peer 100 tcp 172.16.23.3 dmac-output-list 710
dlsw remote-peer 100 tcp 172.16.23.2 backup-peer 172.16.23.3
  linger 1
dlsw remote-peer 0 tcp 172.16.32.4
!
interface Serial0
 ip address 172.16.102.1 255.255.255.0
 no fair-queue
 clockrate 56000
!
interface Serial1
 ip address 172.16.100.1 255.255.255.0
 clockrate 56000
!
interface TokenRing0
 ip address 172.16.199.1 255.255.255.0
 ring-speed 16
 source-bridge 199 1 200
 source-bridge spanning
!
interface TokenRing1
 no ip address
 shutdown
!
router ospf 1
 network 172.16.0.0 0.0.255.255 area 0
!
no ip classless
access-list 710 permit 4000.0123.2234   0000.0000.0000
access-list 710 permit 0000.0213.1210   0000.0000.0000
!
hostname r2
!
enable password cisco
!
source-bridge ring-group 200
dlsw local-peer peer-id 172.16.23.2
dlsw remote-peer 0 tcp 172.16.199.1
!
interface Serial0
 ip address 172.16.102.2 255.255.255.0
 no fair-queue
!
interface Serial1
 no ip address
 shutdown
!
interface TokenRing0
 ip address 172.16.32.2 255.255.255.0
```

Listing 11-25 (*Cont.*)

```
 ring-speed 16
 source-bridge 32 2 200
 source-bridge spanning
!
interface TokenRing1
 ip address 172.16.23.2 255.255.255.0
 ring-speed 16
 source-bridge 23 2 200
 source-bridge spanning
!

hostname r3
!
enable password cisco
!
source-bridge ring-group 200
dlsw local-peer peer-id 172.16.23.3
dlsw remote-peer 0 tcp 172.16.199.1
dlsw bridge-group 1
!
interface TokenRing1/0
 ip address 172.16.32.3 255.255.255.0
 ring-speed 16
 source-bridge 32 3 200
 source-bridge spanning
!
interface TokenRing1/1
 ip address 172.16.23.3 255.255.255.0
 ring-speed 16
 source-bridge 23 3 200
 source-bridge spanning
!
!
interface Ethernet2/0
 no ip address
 bridge-group 1
 bridge-group 1 output-type-list 220
!
access-list 220 permit 0x0404 0x0101
access-list 220 permit 0x0004 0x0101
access-list 220 deny   0x0000 0xFFFF
!
bridge 1 protocol ieee
!

hostname r4
!
enable password cisco
!
source-bridge ring-group 200
dlsw local-peer peer-id 172.16.144.4 passive promiscuous
!
interface Loopback0
 ip address 172.16.144.4 255.255.255.0
!
!
```

Listing 11-25 (*Cont.*)

```
interface TokenRing0
 ip address 172.16.32.4 255.255.255.0
 ring-speed 16
 source-bridge 32 4 200
!
interface TokenRing1
 no ip address
 ring-speed 16
 source-bridge 44 1 200
!
```

```
r1>sh dls peer
Peers:                 state     pkts_rx   pkts_tx  type  drops ckts TCP   uptime
 TCP 172.16.23.3       CONNECT       907       133  conf      0    0   0 01:07:40
 TCP 172.16.23.2       CONNECT       112       112  conf      0    0   0 00:56:00
 TCP 172.16.32.4       DISCONN         0         0  conf      0    0   -        -
r1>
```

Listing 11-26

```
r1>ping 172.16.32.4

Type escape sequence to abort.
Sending 5, 100-byte ICMP Echos to 172.16.32.4, timeout is 2 seconds:
!!!!!
Success rate is 100 percent (5/5), round-trip min/avg/max = 32/39/56 ms
r1>
```

Listing 11-27

```
!
source-bridge ring-group 200
dlsw local-peer peer-id 172.16.199.1
dlsw ring-list 100 rings 199 32
dlsw remote-peer 100 tcp 172.16.23.3 dmac-output-list 710
dlsw remote-peer 100 tcp 172.16.23.2 backup-peer 172.16.23.3 linger 1
```

R1's configuration shows a ring list 100 applied against both R2 and R3's remote peer definitions. Ring list 100 does not include ring 23 hence

```
r4#sh dlsw peer
Peers:                  state     pkts_rx   pkts_tx  type  drops ckts TCP   uptime
r4#

hostname r4
!
enable password cisco
!
source-bridge ring-group 200
dlsw local-peer peer-id 172.16.144.4 passive promiscuous
!
interface Loopback0
 ip address 172.16.144.4 255.255.255.0
!
```

Listing 11-28

R1 will not process traffic to or from that ring. Redefining the list to include ring 23 will solve this problem.

```
r1(config)#dlsw ring-list 100 rings 199 32 23
r1(config)#^Z
r1#
```

Telnet to R3 to investigate the NetBIOS problem reported by Ethernet users (Listing 11-30).

An outbound access list is set for bridge-group 1. When this is displayed, it is found to be an obvious configuration error, in that it only allows SNA traffic out Ethernet2/0. This filter must be removed.

```
r3#conf t
Enter configuration commands, one per line.  End with CNTL/Z.
r3(config)#in e2/0
r3(config-if)#no bridge-group 1 output-type-lis 220
r3(config-if)#^Z
r3#
```

Another reported problem that has yet to be addressed is that only two users on ring 23 can attach to the FEP. R1 should again be checked for a common relevant factor since there is a path from both R2 and R3 to the FEP ring.

On examining R1's configuration, an output filter based on destination MAC address is observed in the definition of R3 peer. This list only includes two stations, which explains the problem. The list must be expanded appropriately. The reason other stations were getting intermittent connectivity is because traffic was taking the path over the 56-K link from R1 to R2 and terminating successfully. However, the traffic that returned over the T-1 to R3 was getting dropped. (See Listing 11-31.)

There is one issue still to be resolved and that is the anomolous behavior of the backup peer R2. R1's end is correctly configured, so R2 should also be verified.

```
r4(config)#no dlsw local peer 172.16.144.4 promis pass
r4(config)#dlsw local peer 172.16.32.4 promis pass

r4#sh debug
DLSw:
  DLSw Peer debugging is on
r4#
DLSw: passive open 172.16.199.1(11095) -> 2065
DLSw: action_b(): opening write pipe for peer 172.16.199.1(2065)
DLSw: peer 172.16.199.1(2065), old state DISCONN, new state CAP_EXG
DLSw: Recv CapExId Msg from peer 172.16.199.1(2065)
DLSw: Pos CapExResp sent to peer 172.16.199.1(2065)
DLSw: CapExId Msg sent to peer 172.16.199.1(2065)
DLSw: action_e(): for peer 172.16.199.1(2065)
DLSw: dlsw_tcpd_fini() for peer 172.16.199.1(2065)
DLSw: dlsw_tcpd_fini() closing write pipe for peer 172.16.199.1
DLSw: action_g(): for peer 172.16.199.1(2065)
DLSw: closing write pipe tcp connection for peer 172.16.199.1(2065)
DLSw: Recv CapExPosRsp Msg from peer 172.16.199.1(2065)
DLSw: action_e(): for peer 172.16.199.1(2065)
DLSw: peer 172.16.199.1(2065), old state CAP_EXG, new state CONNECT
DLSw: peer_act_on_capabilities() for peer 172.16.199.1(2065)
DLSw: Keepalive Request sent to peer 172.16.199.1(2065))
DLSw: Keepalive Response from peer 172.16.199.1(2065)
r4#
r4#sh dlsw peer
Peers:               state     pkts_rx   pkts_tx  type  drops ckts TCP   uptime
 TCP 172.16.199.1    CONNECT         8         8  prom      0    0    0 00:03:29
r4#

r4#sh dlsw capab
DLSw: Capabilities for peer 172.16.199.1(2065)
  vendor id (OUI)         : '00C' (cisco)
  version number          : 1
  release number          : 0
  init pacing window      : 20
  unsupported saps        : none
  num of tcp sessions     : 1
  loop prevent support    : no
  icanreach mac-exclusive : no
  icanreach netbios-excl. : no
  reachable mac addresses : none
  reachable netbios names : none
```

Listing 11-29

```
  cisco version number     : 1
  peer group number        : 0
  border peer capable      : no
  peer cost                : 3
  biu-segment configured   : no
  local-ack configured     : yes
  priority configured      : no
  peer type                : conf
  version string           :
Cisco Internetwork Operating System Software
IOS (tm) 4000 Software (C4000-J-M), Version 11.2(18), RELEASE SOFTWARE (fc1)
Copyright (c) 1986-1999 by cisco Systems, Inc.
Compiled Mon 05-Apr-99 21:09 by jaturner

r4#
```

Listing 11-29 *(Cont.)*

```
r2#
!
source-bridge ring-group 200
dlsw local-peer peer-id 172.16.23.2
dlsw remote-peer 0 tcp 172.16.199.1
!
```

The problem here is easy to resolve. If R2 is a backup peer it should be configured to be in promiscousous mode. If a peer definition for R1 is configured as is seen here, this peer may always be up regardless of the status of the primary peer on R1. In fact, it simply comes down to which

```
r3#sh bridge group

Bridge Group 1 is running the IEEE compatible Spanning Tree protocol

   Port 6 (Ethernet2/0) of bridge group 1 is forwarding

      Access list for output filtering on type is set
   Port 21 (DLSw Port0) of bridge group 1 is forwarding

r3#sh access-lis
Type code access list 220
    permit 0x0404 0x0101
    permit 0x0004 0x0101
    deny   0x0000 0xFFFF
r3#
```

Listing 11-30

```
dlsw remote-peer 100 tcp 172.16.23.3 dmac-output-list 710
dlsw remote-peer 100 tcp 172.16.23.2 backup-peer 172.16.23.3 linger 1
dlsw remote-peer 0 tcp 172.16.32.4

r1#sh access-lis 710
Bridge address access list 710
    permit 4000.0123.2234   0000.0000.0000
    permit 0000.0213.1210   0000.0000.0000
r1#
```

Listing 11-31

router is configured first. If DLSW is configured on R2 before R2's statement is placed in R1's configuration, then R2 will initiate a peer relationship with R1. Another solution is to make R2 passive so that it will not initiate a peer relationship.

```
r2#conf t
Enter configuration commands, one per line.  End with CNTL/Z.
r2(config)#no dlsw local peer 172.16.23.2
r2(config)#dlsw local peer 172.16.23.2 promis
r2(config)#^Z
r2#
```

Now R2 is seen as disconnected in R1's peer table. (See Listing 11-32.)

The correct backup mode operation can be verified by shutting down the interface on R3 that is used for its peer definition.

```
r3#conf t
Enter configuration commands, one per line.  End with CNTL/Z.
r3(config)#in to1/1
r3(config-if)#shut
r3(config-if)#^Z
r3#
```

```
r1#sh dls peer
Peers:                state     pkts_rx    pkts_tx  type  drops ckts TCP    uptime
 TCP 172.16.23.3     CONNECT       2125        307  conf      0    0   0 02:34:42
 TCP 172.16.32.4     CONNECT        145        145  conf      0    0   0 01:07:52
 TCP 172.16.23.2     DISCONN        140        140  conf      0    0   -        -
r1#
```

Listing 11-32

```
r1#sh dls peer
Peers:                state     pkts_rx    pkts_tx  type  drops ckts TCP   uptime
 TCP 172.16.32.4      CONNECT       152        152  conf      0    0   0 01:11:22
 TCP 172.16.23.2      CONNECT       144        144  conf      0    0   0 00:01:28
 TCP 172.16.23.3      DISCONN      2142        310  conf      0    0   -        -
r1#
```

Listing 11-33

Now R2 comes up as an active peer when the primary is down. (See Listing 11-33.)

Having both peers up simultaneously was causing traffic congestion on the 56-K link between R1 and R2.

REVIEW QUESTIONS

For the exercises that are multiple-choice questions, there is only one correct answer unless the question is marked with an asterisk (*). Choose the most suitable answer.

1. Which of the following pieces of information cannot be found using the `show source` command?
   a. SRB maximum hop count
   b. Explorer Max Rate
   c. Number of open peer connections
   d. RIF information for RSRB peers
   e. Traffic-count for peers
2. Type the command that displays the contents of the RIF cache.
3. The `clear source` command resets all RSRB peers, true or false?
4. If the IP routing protocol is changed from RIP to IGRP, the RSRB max hop-count changes from 7 to
   a. 15
   b. 100
   c. 13
   d. 7
   e. 9

5. NetBIOS names are not case-sensitive, true or false?
6. NetBIOS name caching will not work unless the following is enabled:
   a. Proxy-explorers
   b. NetBIOS access lists
   c. Source-bridge fast switching
   d. Source-bridge SSE switching
   e. None of the above are required

*7. NetBIOS access list type can be based on
   a. Hostname
   b. Byte-offset
   c. Destination socket
   d. Source socket
   e. All of the above

* 8. Which of the following features are not unique to DLSW?
   a. Peer groups
   b. RIF termination
   c. RIF caching
   d. On-demand peers
   e. Local-ack

9. What command will display whether a remote DLSW peer is using MAC-exclusive?
   a. `show dlsw peers`
   b. `show dlsw capabilities`
   c. `show dlsw statistics`
   d. `show dlsw circuits`
   e. `show dlsw reachability`

10. What command indicates an active end to end-station session over DLSW?
   a. `show dlsw peers`
   b. `show dlsw capabilities`
   c. `show dlsw statistics`
   d. `show dlsw circuits`
   e. `show dlsw reachability`

11. What fields in the output of the `show processor cpu` command should first be examined when checking for an explorer storm?
12. The SRB RIF only counts physical ring-bridge hops when decrementing the time-to-live, true of false?
13. Which of the following filters cannot be applied to RSRB traffic?
    a. Type list
    b. LSAP list
    c. Input-address list
    d. Output-address list
    e. All can be applied
14. Type the command for specifying the local peer ID of 3.3.3.3 in RSRB with TCP encapsulation, and virtual ring 300.
15. Which of the following will be found in a DLSW reachability cache?
    a. Remote MAC addresses
    b. Local MAC addresses
    c. Remote NetBIOS stations
    d. Local NetBIOS stations
    e. All of the above
16. If the local router is waiting for the remote end to open its TCP read pipe, the output of `debug dlsw peers` will show which of these messages?
    a. DISCONN
    b. WAN_BUSY
    c. WAIT_RD
    d. CAP_EXG
    e. None of the above

*17. Which of the following TCP ports does RSRB or DLSW *not* use for peer formation?
    a. 1996
    b. 2065
    c. 2067
    d. 1024
    e. 1406

18. The full-route designator to the IBM host is R2 B4 R10 B11 R3 in an RSRB environment, where the virtual-ring is 10. Write down what it would appear as in running DLSW from the viewpoint of the same end-station.

***19.** Which of the following information pieces is included in a DLSW capabilities exchange?

a. List of reachable MAC addresses

b. List of reachable NetBIOS stations

c. RIF information for reachable stations

d. Peer group number

e. Number of active peers

20. CLSI messages are exchanged between the end-station and the local router. Packets that are sourced by the end-station are identifiable because they end with

a. `.Rsp`

b. `.Req`

c. `.Ind`

d. `_ex`

e. `.CUR`

CHAPTER 12

Troubleshooting Switched Ethernet

Introduction

This chapter discusses Cisco configuration and troubleshooting in a switched local-area network (LAN) environment. The discussion will be confined to Ethernet and Fast Ethernet because these are the most prevalent switching technologies. While Token Ring switching is being deployed, a more popular migration from shared Token Ring is to replace it with a form of Ethernet switching. Most of the concepts and principles that are studied in this chapter apply equally to LAN switching technology other than Ethernet.

The configuration of LAN switches can appear to be deceptively simple. Often a switch will appear to work okay with little more than a default configuration running on it. Sometimes this may well be the case, while in a lot of situations there is the possibility that potentially serious problems are simply being temporarily disguised. The LAN switch environment is inherently different to a routed environment. The switches by their nature contain less intelligence than routers. The network engineer also may find a switched environment more difficult to navigate, since it may not be clearly segmented into different networks and subnetworks. These two factors, while making device configuration easier, ironically can make troubleshooting more difficult.

The first major challenge in the configuration and also the troubleshooting of LAN switches is to have a good understanding of the local LAN environment. The location of the clients and servers and which clients avail of which services need to be understood fully. Partly due to the marketing of LAN switches, many people seem to think that the switch is a type of magic box that dramatically increases LAN bandwidth. I will use an extreme example for the purpose of emphasis. Consider a case where all the servers have to be accessed remotely across the wide-area network (WAN). In this situation, a LAN switch is of limited use because the bottleneck is merely being transferred to the WAN. Thus it is necessary to understand your environment before attempting to troubleshoot an alleged switch problem.

A switch is a less complex device than a router, and a side effect of this is that it provides the network engineer with a narrower range of troubleshooting tools. In this chapter I will focus on the tools available on the Cisco Catalyst 5000 series. This is selected because it is a type of switch that tends to be deployed at the LAN backbone and also because the software that it runs is not full Cisco IOS.

The objectives of this chapter are to

- Learn the different software diagnostic tools on the Cisco Catalyst 5000 series switch.
- Apply these tools to resolve networking problems that are common in a switched LAN environment.
- Understand the design issues and advanced configuration issues that must be mastered for such an environment.

Troubleshooting Tools on the Catalyst 5000/5500

The troubleshooting tools that will be discussed here relate mainly to the software running on the Catalyst 5000 series switch. We will study scenarios arising because the switch has been configured incorrectly or the switched network environment has been designed poorly. You also will learn how the switch can be used as a diagnostic tool for the network that it is part of.

Hardware troubleshooting is only discussed in a limited fashion in this chapter, since most of the pertinent information is available by consulting the manual that is delivered with the product. Also, the resolution of hardware problems on cards is most often just a matter of either reseating or replacing the card itself.

The `ping` Command

In order to check IP connectivity to and from the switch the `ping` command can be used. The console port must be configured with an IP address for this to work. If connectivity is to be tested from another subnet, then the switch must be configured with either a default gateway or an appropriate static route. The IP configuration of the switch along with typical associated problems will be discussed in a later section of this chapter.

Listing 12-1 is a sample output from a simple `ping` along with that of a `ping -s`. The `-s` argument causes a new ping packet to be sent out every second. CONTROL-C is used to quit.

Listing 12-1

```
Console> (enable) ping 172.16.254.254
172.16.254.254 is alive
Console> (enable) ping 172.16.254.1
no answer from 172.16.254.1
Console> (enable)

Console> (enable) ping -s 159.249.100.9
PING 159.249.100.9: 56 data bytes
64 bytes from 159.249.100.9: icmp_seq=0. time=2 ms
64 bytes from 159.249.100.9: icmp_seq=1. time=3 ms
^C
```

The Traceroute facility is also available from the switch. It has the following format and output:

```
5500-A> (enable) traceroute 205.22.5.14
traceroute to 205.22.5.14 (205.22.5.14), 30 hops max, 40 byte packets
 1 209.13.19.3 (209.13.19.3)  3 ms  2 ms  1 ms
 2 205.22.5.14 (205.22.5.14)  2 ms  * 2 ms
5500-A> (enable)
```

Cisco Discovery Protocol (CDP)

You have already briefly met CDP in the context of routers, but this protocol is particularly useful in a Cisco switched environment. Switches provide less intelligence and hence less information than routers. This environment also may be less familiar because it is not clearly segmented into different networks. CDP provides a powerful tool for detecting and identifying other Cisco switches or routers that are attached to switch ports.

CDP is a data link multicast protocol that uses the multicast MAC address 0100.0ccc.cccc. It takes the form of a SNAP type 200 packet and has no layer 3 component. If CDP is enabled on a Cisco router or switch, it is capable of detecting other Cisco devices as neighbors on each device interface. Note that CDP is only intended for detecting directly attached devices. Hence, for example, if two routers are connected together via the same switch, the routers will each see the switch as a CDP neighbor, but they will not see each other. The switch will see each router as a CDP neighbor. This is so because the CDP does not forward frames.

The first example shown here displays a simple CDP neighbors list (Listing 12-2). This is for a Catalyst 5500 switch acting as a collapsed

```
C5500> (enable) sh cdp neigh
Capability Codes: R - Router, T - Trans Bridge, B - Source Route Bridge
                  S - Switch, H - Host, I - IGMP, r - Repeater

Port     Device-ID                Port-ID           Platform        Capability
-------- ------------------------ ----------------- --------------- ----------
 4/1     0050F0440960             A                 cisco 1900           T S
 4/2     0050F0294840             A                 cisco 1900           T S
 4/3     0050F05894C0             A                 cisco 1900           T S
 4/4     0050F0453FB0             A                 cisco 1900           T S
...................................
10/2     008024 668310            1/25              CAT3200              T
10/4     firewall                 Ethernet0         cisco 2500           R
```

Listing 12-2

backbone for a number of wiring closets each containing a Cisco 1900 switch. It also can be seen that there is a Catalyst 3200 switch connecting to port 10/2, and a Cisco 2500 series router is attached to port 10/4. The corresponding ports on the attached devices are shown along with the device capabilities, which basically identifies it as a switch or a router. I have just shown a truncated section of the output, but it is evident how useful this command is especially when the detailed option is employed.

In this example, only the router was given a hostname or device ID. It is a good idea to give all switches and routers an identifiable name for troubleshooting purposes. If further information is required on any of these devices, then the `show cdp neighbor detail` option can be used (see Listing 12-3).

Show and Clear Commands

Let's now look at commands that provide general information on the switch itself, its software and modules, port configuration, and error information, as well as its bridging or switching table. Later on in the relevant sections of this chapter I will discuss commands that give information on IP configuration and routing, virtual LANs (VLANs), spanning-tree parameters, and high-bandwidth features such as Fast Etherchannel.

```
C5500> (enable) sh cdp nei detail 4/2
Device-ID: 0050F0294840
Device Addresses:
  IP Address: 159.24.104.50
Holdtime: 130 sec
Capabilities: TRANSPARENT_BRIDGE SWITCH
Version:
Platform: cisco 1900
Port-ID (Port on Device): A
Port (Our Port): 4/2

C5500> (enable) sh cdp nei detail 10/4
Device-ID: firewall
Device Addresses:
  IP Address: 159.24.105.254
Holdtime: 166 sec
Capabilities: ROUTER
Version:
  Cisco Internetwork Operating System Software
  IOS (tm) 2500 Software (C2500-D-L), Version 11.2(7a), RELEASE SOFTWARE (fc1)
  Copyright (c) 1986-1997 by cisco Systems, Inc.
Platform: cisco 2500
Port-ID (Port on Device): Ethernet0
Port (Our Port): 10/4
C5500> (enable)
```

Listing 12-3

The `show config` Command The `show config` command can be used to display the configuration that is contained in NVRAM just as on a router. With the Catalyst 5000 series, the configuration is written automatically to NVRAM; hence the `write terminal` command displays the same output. The `show running` and `show startup` commands are not applicable to this switch. The configuration can be erased from NVRAM using the `clear config all` command; `clear config` also can be applied to just erase the configuration on a particular module. Listing 12-4 is a sample output for the default configuration on a Catalyst 5513 that has a number of Fast Ethernet, Gigabit Ethernet, and 10/100 modules. A large amount of information is displayed that basically can be divided into the following categories:

- Switch management parameters
- Bridging parameters
- IP configuration
- Virtual LANs

Listing 12-4

```
Console> (enable) show config

begin
set password $1$FMFQ$HfZR5DUszVHIRhrz4h6V70
set enablepass $1$FMFQ$HfZR5DUszVHIRhrz4h6V70
set prompt Console>
set length 24 default
set logout 20
set banner motd ^C^C
!
#system
set system baud  9600
set system modem disable
set system name
set system location
set system contact
!
#snmp
set snmp community read-only      public
set snmp community read-write     private
set snmp community read-write-all secret
set snmp rmon disable
set snmp trap disable module
set snmp trap disable chassis
set snmp trap disable bridge
set snmp trap disable repeater
set snmp trap disable vtp
set snmp trap disable auth
set snmp trap disable ippermit
set snmp trap disable vmps
set snmp trap disable entity
set snmp trap disable config
set snmp trap disable stpx
set snmp extendedrmon vlanmode disable
set snmp extendedrmon vlanagent disable
set snmp extendedrmon enable
!
#ip
set interface sc0 0.0.0.0 0.0.0.0
set interface sc0 up
set interface sl0 0.0.0.0 0.0.0.0
set interface sl0 up
set arp agingtime 1200
set ip redirect   enable
set ip unreachable   enable
set ip fragmentation enable
set ip alias default         0.0.0.0
!
#Command alias
!
#vmps
set vmps server retry 3
set vmps server reconfirminterval 60
set vmps tftpserver 0.0.0.0 vmps-config-database.1
set vmps state disable
```

Listing 12-4 (*Cont.*)

```
!
#dns
set ip dns disable
!
#tacacs+
set tacacs attempts 3
set tacacs directedrequest disable
set tacacs timeout 5
set authentication login tacacs disable
set authentication login local enable
set authentication enable tacacs disable
set authentication enable local enable
!
#bridge
set bridge ipx snaptoether   8023raw
set bridge ipx 8022toether   8023
set bridge ipx 8023rawtofddi snap
!
#vtp
set vtp mode server
set vtp v2 disable
set vtp pruning disable
set vtp pruneeligible 2-1000
clear vtp pruneeligible 1001-1005
!
#spantree
#uplinkfast groups
set spantree uplinkfast disable
#backbonefast
set spantree backbonefast disable
#vlan 1
set spantree enable     1
set spantree fwddelay 15    1
set spantree hello    2     1
set spantree maxage   20    1
set spantree priority 32768 1
#vlan 1003
set spantree enable     1003
set spantree fwddelay 15    1003
set spantree hello    2     1003
set spantree maxage   20    1003
set spantree priority 32768 1003
set spantree portstate 1003 block 0
set spantree portcost 1003 62
set spantree portpri  1003 4
set spantree portfast 1003 disable
#vlan 1005
set spantree disable    1005
set spantree fwddelay 15    1005
set spantree hello    2     1005
set spantree maxage   20    1005
set spantree priority 32768 1005
set spantree multicast-address 1005 ieee
!
#cgmp
set cgmp disable
```

Listing 12-4
(Cont.)

```
set cgmp leave disable
!
#syslog
set logging console enable
set logging server disable
set logging level cdp 2 default
set logging level mcast 2 default
set logging level dtp 5 default
set logging level dvlan 2 default
set logging level earl 2 default
set logging level fddi 2 default
set logging level ip 2 default
set logging level pruning 2 default
set logging level snmp 2 default
set logging level spantree 2 default
set logging level sys 5 default
set logging level tac 2 default
set logging level tcp 2 default
set logging level telnet 2 default
set logging level tftp 2 default
set logging level vtp 2 default
set logging level vmps 2 default
set logging level kernel 2 default
set logging level filesys 2 default
set logging level drip 2 default
set logging level pagp 5 default
set logging level mgmt 5 default
set logging level mls 5 default
set logging level protfilt 2 default
set logging level security 2 default
!
#ntp
set ntp broadcastclient disable
set ntp broadcastdelay 3000
set ntp client disable
clear timezone
set summertime disable
!
#set boot command
set boot config-register 0x102
set boot system flash bootflash:cat5000-sup3.4-3-1a.bin
!
#permit list
set ip permit disable
!
#drip
set tokenring reduction enable
set tokenring distrib-crf disable
!
#igmp
set igmp disable
!
#standby ports
set standbyports disable
!
#module 1 : 2-port 100BaseFX MMF Supervisor
```

Listing 12-4 (*Cont.*)

```
set module name    1
set vlan 1    1/1-2
set port channel 1/1-2 off
set port channel 1/1-2 auto
set port enable      1/1-2
set port level       1/1-2  normal
set port duplex      1/1-2  half
set port trap        1/1-2  disable
set port name        1/1-2
set port security    1/1-2  disable
set port broadcast   1/1-2  100%
set port membership 1/1-2  static
set cdp enable   1/1-2
set cdp interval 1/1-2 60
set trunk 1/1  auto isl 1-1005
set trunk 1/2  auto isl 1-1005
set spantree portfast    1/1-2 disable
set spantree portcost    1/1-2  19
set spantree portpri     1/1-2  32
set spantree portvlanpri 1/1  0
set spantree portvlanpri 1/2  0
set spantree portvlancost 1/1  cost 18
set spantree portvlancost 1/2  cost 18
!
module 2 empty
!
#module 3 : 3-port 1000BaseX Ethernet
set module name    3
set module enable  3
set vlan 1    3/1-3
set port enable      3/1-3
set port level       3/1-3  normal
set port duplex      3/1-3  full
set port trap        3/1-3  disable
set port name        3/1-3
set port security    3/1-3  disable
set port broadcast   3/1-3  100%
set port membership 3/1-3  static
set port negotiation 3/1-3 enable
set port flowcontrol send    3/1-3 desired
set port flowcontrol receive 3/1-3 off
set cdp enable   3/1-3
set cdp interval 3/1-3 60
set trunk 3/1  auto negotiate 1-1005
set trunk 3/2  auto negotiate 1-1005
set trunk 3/3  auto negotiate 1-1005
set spantree portfast    3/1-3 disable
set spantree portcost    3/1-3  4
set spantree portpri     3/1-3  32
set spantree portvlanpri 3/1  0
set spantree portvlanpri 3/2  0
set spantree portvlanpri 3/3  0
set spantree portvlancost 3/1  cost 3
set spantree portvlancost 3/2  cost 3
set spantree portvlancost 3/3  cost 3
!
```

Listing 12-4 (*Cont.*)

```
#module 4 empty
!
#module 5 empty
!
#module 6 empty
!
#module 7 empty
!
#module 8 empty
!
#module 9 empty
!
#module 10 : 12-port 10/100BaseTX Ethernet
set module name     10
set module enable  10
set vlan 1    10/1-12
set port channel 10/1-4 off
set port channel 10/5-8 off
set port channel 10/9-12 off
set port channel 10/1-4 auto
set port channel 10/5-8 auto
set port channel 10/9-12 auto
set port enable      10/1-12
set port level       10/1-12  normal
set port speed       10/1-12  auto
set port trap        10/1-12  disable
set port name        10/1-12
set port security    10/1-12  disable
set port broadcast   10/1-12  0
set port membership 10/1-12  static
set cdp enable   10/1-12
set cdp interval 10/1-12 60
set trunk 10/1  auto isl 1-1005
set trunk 10/2  auto isl 1-1005
set trunk 10/3  auto isl 1-1005
set trunk 10/4  auto isl 1-1005
set trunk 10/5  auto isl 1-1005
set trunk 10/6  auto isl 1-1005
set trunk 10/7  auto isl 1-1005
set trunk 10/8  auto isl 1-1005
set trunk 10/9  auto isl 1-1005
set trunk 10/10 auto isl 1-1005
set trunk 10/11 auto isl 1-1005
set trunk 10/12 auto isl 1-1005
set spantree portfast     10/1-12 disable
set spantree portcost     10/1-12  100
set spantree portpri      10/1-12  32
set spantree portvlanpri 10/1  0
set spantree portvlanpri 10/2  0
set spantree portvlanpri 10/3  0
set spantree portvlanpri 10/4  0
set spantree portvlanpri 10/5  0
set spantree portvlanpri 10/6  0
set spantree portvlanpri 10/7  0
set spantree portvlanpri 10/8  0
set spantree portvlanpri 10/9  0
```

Listing 12-4 (*Cont.*)

```
set spantree portvlanpri 10/10 0
set spantree portvlanpri 10/11 0
set spantree portvlanpri 10/12 0
set spantree portvlancost 10/1  cost 99
set spantree portvlancost 10/2  cost 99
set spantree portvlancost 10/3  cost 99
set spantree portvlancost 10/4  cost 99
set spantree portvlancost 10/5  cost 99
set spantree portvlancost 10/6  cost 99
set spantree portvlancost 10/7  cost 99
set spantree portvlancost 10/8  cost 99
set spantree portvlancost 10/9  cost 99
set spantree portvlancost 10/10 cost 99
set spantree portvlancost 10/11 cost 99
set spantree portvlancost 10/12 cost 99
!
#module 11 empty
!
#module 12 empty
!
#module 13 empty
!
#switch port analyzer
!set span 1 1/1 both inpkts disable
set span disable
!
#cam
set cam agingtime 1,1003,1005 300
end
Console> (enable)
```

- Spanning Tree Protocol configuration
- Module-specific information including port configuration, VLAN membership, trunking, and spanning-tree configuration

It is different from a router configuration, where defaults usually are not displayed. The sample configuration in Listing 12-4 is the default configuration on a Catalyst 5500 switch that contains a Fast Ethernet module, a Gigabit Ethernet module, and a 10/100 module. The subsections that relate to topics that will be examined in this chapter are highlighted in bold. There is no need to get bogged down in its details just yet. Instead, use it as a back reference as we examine the various switch parameters in more detail through the course of this chapter.

The `show cam` Command CAM stands for *content addressable memory*, which is a special type of memory that has a low access time. It is used for storing the bridging or switching table. The `show cam` command is therefore used simply to display the contents of the switching table, which is a listing of destination MAC addresses against the ports from which they were learned. The `dynamic` option is used to just display CAM entries that were learned dynamically by the switch. Sometimes a static CAM entry may be configured on the switch to fix a particular MAC address against a port number. These types of entries can be displayed using the `show cam static` command. The `show cam` command also can be applied to an individual MAC address, a switch port, or a VLAN.

If a problem is suspected whereby the switch may not be learning the MAC address of a particular workstation, it is a good idea to clear the CAM table using `clear cam dynamic` and observe whether the switch again learns the station's MAC address (see Listing 12-5).

Listing 12-5

```
Galway-C5500-1> (enable) sh cam dynamic
VLAN  Destination MAC      Destination Ports or VCs
----  -----------------    ----------------------------
1     00-08-c7-c0-ea-62    5/19
1     08-00-11-08-75-41    5/11
1     00-60-08-e9-d8-f1    6/2
1     00-08-c7-40-ea-e6    7/17
1     00-80-5f-d3-d8-68    7/14
1     00-80-5f-83-05-ff    6/16
1     00-80-5f-bd-43-4d    4/19
1     08-00-20-81-ca-70    3/21
1     00-08-c7-d8-64-51    4/6
1     00-80-5f-93-37-8f    4/4
1     08-00-5a-a3-09-0c    6/17
1     08-00-5a-a3-09-8a    5/18
1     00-08-c7-a0-37-68    4/16
1     00-08-c7-a0-be-9c    4/21
1     00-80-5f-29-30-87    6/20
1     00-80-5f-fd-2a-a0    7/5
1     00-80-5f-a1-4a-0c    7/12
1     00-80-5f-ed-c9-03    7/6
1     00-80-5f-cb-86-b7    4/20
1     00-80-5f-6f-66-cd    3/22
1     08-00-20-8d-41-05    4/22
1     00-08-c7-a0-ef-fb    7/13
1     08-00-20-8d-fc-ec    3/24
Do you wish to continue y/n [n]? y
1     00-c0-f0-22-b5-79    4/13
1     00-80-5f-cb-a6-46    5/1
1     00-80-5f-cb-a6-6c    6/19
1     00-e0-1e-bb-ef-89    4/24
1     00-80-5f-fd-62-c9    5/17
1     00-80-5f-f9-22-b5    6/11
1     00-08-c7-60-37-05    5/4
Total Matching CAM Entries = 30
Galway-C5500-1> (enable)
```

The `show mac` Command The `show mac` command displays information on the number and types of packets that cross each switch port along with the corresponding error information. The command can be used without any options and will give information on every port on the switch. For a heavily loaded switch, this may constitute too much information. In the following example (Listing 12-6) I just looked at module 4.

The output from this command gives a total for unicasts, broadcasts, and multicasts that have been sent and received by each port since the counters were last cleared. A total byte count is also provided for frames sent and received. Error information such as dropped frames and MTU-exceeded and delay-exceeded errors is also displayed on a per-port basis. This information is useful for building up a profile of the type of traffic present on each port, along with its volume and errors that are being reported. In the sample output given, all ports appear clean apart from some delays on port 4/9. This is not one of the busiest ports on the module, but the errors may have been due to some transient event. The counters could be cleared using the `clear counters` command (this also resets the counters on the output of `show port`, which we will discuss shortly); if the errors keep on incrementing, then the device attached to this port should be investigated.

The `show module` Command To display summary information about each of the hardware modules in the switch, use the `show module` command. For each module, the type and number of ports, along with the part name and serial number, are displayed. It is often necessary to ascertain a port's MAC address, e.g., in order to evaluate a LAN analyzer trace. This command provides a summary of the range of the port MAC addresses on each module. The hardware, software, and firmware versions for each module are also provided. The type and status of the supervisor modules are included in the output. In Listing 12-7, the switch has dual supervisor modules, with the supervisor in module 1 being a standby for module 2.

The `show port` Command The `show port` command is a fundamentally useful troubleshooting tool. It gives information on whether a port is connected or not (i.e., is line protocol up?) and the VLAN that the port is in, along with the speed and duplex type. Critical ports that connect to router ports or other switches should be configured with names to ease identification. The information provided by Listing 12-8 includes

- The two supervisor modules are both in standby mode.

```
C5500>sh mac 4
Port                 Rcv-Unicast  Rcv-Multicast            Rcv-Broadcast
-----------------    -----------  --------------------     -------------------
 4/1                     4226701                 19899                  48433
 4/2                     1226099                 16058                  18677
 4/3                     5344824                 20035                 136763
 4/4                     1101003                 13374                 228279
 4/5                     6490947                 15285                  83455
 4/6                      498108                 12078                  21231
 4/7                     1797467                 13888                  42216
 4/8                     6893313                 15482                  99221
 4/9                     1506346                 11834                  24909
 4/10                    1115069                 32884                 102837
 4/11                     368906                 13305                  72806
 4/12                    3831258                 11810                  34883

Port            Xmit-Unicast        Xmit-Multicast         Xmit-Broadcast
----            ---------------     ------------------     ------------------
 4/1                    5752863                1099913                3486720
 4/2                    2098138                1040113                3417419
 4/3                    5974614                1023801                3256590
 4/4                    1709758                 464652                1580980
 4/5                    8661754                 771813                2838349
 4/6                    1322886                 774148                2897789
 4/7                    2758518                 772421                2877065
 4/8                    9080632                 770737                2819823
 4/9                    2351295                 761875                2826347
 4/10                   1793468                 740756                2748365
 4/11                    996671                 759514                2774416
 4/12                   4675005                 675462                2487241

Port       Rcv-Octet              Xmit-Octet
--------   ----------------       ----------------
 4/1             1228940786             4589492259
 4/2              644511750             1451432390
 4/3             3692030825             3903631843
 4/4              221712393             1233581734
 4/5             1542082840             7253672468
 4/6              108505523             1322306749
 4/7              580749662             2296000801
 4/8             1354508871             6728566301
 4/9              643731771             2117483939
 4/10             294074951             1303635639
 4/11             107240153              818458709
 4/12            1401237527             3244595170

MAC      Dely-Exced MTU-Exced  In-Discard Lrn-Discrd In-Lost    Out-Lost
---      ---------- ---------- ---------- ---------- ---------- ----------
 4/1              0         0          0          0          0          0
 4/2              0         0          0          0          0          0
 4/3              0         0          0          0          0          0
 4/4              0         0          0          0          0          0
```

Listing 12-6

```
 4/5             0        0        0        0        0        0
 4/6             0        0        0        0        0        0
 4/7             0        0        0        0        0        0
 4/8             0        0        0        0        0        0
 4/9           215        0        0        0        0        0
 4/10            0        0        0        0        0        0
 4/11            0        0        0        0        0        0
 4/12            0        0        0        0        0        0

Last-Time-Cleared
-----------------
Sat May 15 1999, 10:37:48
C5500>
```

Listing 12-6 (*Cont.*)

```
Galway-C5500-1> (enable) sh module
Mod Module-Name         Ports Module-Type           Model    Serial-Num Status
--- ------------------- ----- --------------------- ------- ------------------
1                       2     100BaseTX Supervisor  WS-X5509  007481469 standby
2                       2     100BaseTX Supervisor  WS-X5509  007482013 ok
3                       24    10/100BaseTX Ethernet WS-X5224  007479316 ok
4                       24    10BaseT Ethernet      WS-X5013  006813622 ok
5                       24    10BaseT Ethernet      WS-X5013  006813615 ok
6                       24    10BaseT Ethernet      WS-X5013  006774069 ok
7                       24    10BaseT Ethernet      WS-X5013  006774257 ok

Mod MAC-Address(es)                           Hw     Fw      Sw
--- ---------------------------------------- ------ ------ --------
1   00-10-0d-35-37-00 thru 00-10-0d-35-3a-ff  2.1    2.4(1)  2.4(4)
2   00-10-0d-35-37-00 thru 00-10-0d-35-3a-ff  2.1    2.4(1)  2.4(4)
3   00-e0-1e-fa-91-00 thru 00-e0-1e-fa-91-17  1.3    3.1(1)  2.4(4)
4   00-e0-1e-90-35-e0 thru 00-e0-1e-90-35-f7  1.1    2.3(1)  2.4(4)
5   00-10-54-86-37-38 thru 00-10-54-86-37-4f  1.1    2.3(1)  2.4(4)
6   00-10-54-86-35-88 thru 00-10-54-86-35-9f  1.1    2.3(1)  2.4(4)
7   00-10-54-86-36-90 thru 00-10-54-86-36-a7  1.1    2.3(1)  2.4(4)

Mod Sub-Type Sub-Model Sub-Serial Sub-Hw
--- -------- --------- ---------- ------
1   EARL 1+  WS-F5511  0007471869 1.0
2   EARL 1+  WS-F5511  0006807582 1.0
Galway-C5500-1> (enable)
```

Listing 12-7

```
Galway-C5500-1> (enable) sh port
Port  Name               Status     Vlan       Level  Duplex Speed Type
----------               ---------- ----       ------ ------ ----- ------------
 1/1                     standby    1          normal   full   100 100BaseTX
 1/2                     standby    1          normal   full   100 100BaseTX
 2/1                     notconnect 1          normal   full   100 100BaseTX
 2/2                     notconnect 1          normal   full   100 100BaseTX
 3/1                     connected  1          normal a-full  a-100 10/100BaseTX
 3/2       7513Router    connected  1          normal a-half a-10 10/100BaseTX
 3/3                     notconnect 1          normal   auto  auto 10/100BaseTX
 3/4                     connected  1          normal a-half  a-10 10/100BaseTX
 3/5                     notconnect 1          normal   auto  auto 10/100BaseTX
 3/6                     notconnect 1          normal   auto  auto 10/100BaseTX
 3/7                     notconnect 1          normal   auto  auto 10/100BaseTX
 3/8                     notconnect 1          normal   auto  auto 10/100BaseTX
 3/9                     notconnect 1          normal   auto  auto 10/100BaseTX
 3/10                    notconnect 1          normal   auto  auto 10/100BaseTX
 3/11                    notconnect 1          normal   auto  auto 10/100BaseTX
 3/12                    connected  1          normal a-full a-100 10/100BaseTX
Galway-C5500-1> (enable)
```

Listing 12-8

- Just four of the twelve ports in module 3 have stations connected, one of which is the router port (port 3/2).
- All the ports in module 3 are in autonegotiation mode for speed and duplex type. The two half-duplex ports are running at 10 Mbps, while the two full-duplex ports are each running at 100 Mbps. Note that these pairings for speed and duplex are not necessarily synonymous.
- The port level is at the default setting of normal for all ports. The *Level* parameter relates to a priority level for access to the switching backplane. It is a parameter that rarely needs modification from its default setting. I also would like to emphasize that this has nothing to do with spanning-tree priorities.

You can get more detail on any port by applying the command solely to that port (see Listing 12-9). Let us look a little closer at the port that connects to the router. It can be seen that port security is disabled (I will talk more about this later); SNMP traps are not generated when this port changes state. There is percentage limit on what bandwidth broadcasts can consume on this port. The port has been free of physical layer errors or late collisions since the counters were last cleared.

```
Galway-C5500-1> (enable) sh port 3/2
Port  Name               Status     Vlan       Level  Duplex Speed Type
----  ------------  ------------  ----  --------------------------------
 3/2  7513Router     connected  1         normal a-half  a-10 10/100BaseTX

Port    Security  Secure-Src-Addr    Last-Src-Addr      Shutdown  Trap
----    --------  -----------------  -------------      --------  ---------
 3/2    disabled                                         No        disabled

Port      Broadcast-Limit Broadcast-Drop
----      ----------------------------
 3/2                   -              0

Port  Align-Err  FCS-Err    Xmit-Err   Rcv-Err    UnderSize
----  ---------  ---------  ---------  ---------  ---------
 3/2          0          0          0          0          0

Port  Single-Col Multi-Coll Late-Coll  Excess-Col Carri-Sen Runts     Giants
----  -----------------------------  ---------- --------- --------  ------
 3/2         338        603          0          0         0        0       0

Last-Time-Cleared
-------------------------
Thu Jun 11 1998, 16:06:08
Galway-C5500-1> (enable)
```

Listing 12-9

If an ordinary workstation connects to a switch port, then it is usually a good idea to leave the up/down trap in its default disable state. This prevents traps from being generated each time the station is powered on or off. However, for ports that connect to a router or an important server, you may want to enable this feature. In this case, it is disabled. There is another query that I would raise about port 3/2. Why is the port that attaches to a 7513 router not full duplex? The fact that it is half duplex after autonegotiation implies that the router port itself is not configured as full duplex. It is generally not considered good practice to allow autonegotiation to control the speed and duplex parameters where possible. I will also talk more about this later.

A final point to notice is that if this were a full-duplex port, the collisions tally would be zero. Can you explain why this would be so? If not, then simply read on.

The `show system` Command To obtain the status of environmental parameters such as power, use the `show system` command. As well as the status of the power supplies, information on system uptime, peak

```
Galway-C5500-1> (enable) show system
PS1-Status PS2-Status Fan-Status Temp-Alarm Sys-Status Uptime d,h:m:s Logout
---------- ---------- ---------- ---------- ---------- -------------- ------
ok         ok         ok         off        ok         167,01:31:02   20 min

PS1-Type   PS2-Type   Modem   Baud  Traffic Peak Peak-Time
--------   --------   ------- ----  ------- ----------------------------
WS-C5508   WS-C5508   disable 9600   0%      10% Fri Nov 6 1998, 10:03:01

System Name             System Location          System Contact
----------------------- ------------------------ -----------------------
Cat5000 NER 11th Floor  2 40 Maunsells Pk Galway  Cormac Long 491-7521661
Galway-C5500-1> (enable)

#system
set system baud  9600
set system modem disable
set system name  cgate-ner4
set system location city gate ner4 cab-10
set system contact cormac long
!
```

Listing 12-10

traffic loading, and out-of-band management, along with configured contact information, is also provided (see Listing 12-10).

The `show version` Command The particular information that is provided by the `show version` command is the system bootstrap version, the amount of DRAM, Flash, and NVRAM (free and used). The other information that is provided by this command also could be obtained using the `show module` and `show system` commands. (See Listing 12-11.)

Logging

The Syslog defaults on the Catalyst 5000 series can be viewed in the default configuration or using the `show logging` command. In Listing 12-12, Syslog messages are being sent to the server with IP address 172.16.101.19. Logging to the console and the internal buffer is enabled by default. The Syslog parameters are similar to those discussed in relation to routers in Chapter 3. The severity level for each of the facilities can be changed from its default setting. Both the default and current severity level for each facility is shown in the output of `show logging`

```
Galway-C5500-1> (enable) sh version
WS-C5500 Software, Version McpSW: 2.4(4) NmpSW: 2.4(4)
Copyright (c) 1995-1997 by Cisco Systems
NMP S/W compiled on Jan 23 1998, 11:54:52
MCP S/W compiled on Jan 23 1998, 12:12:25

System Bootstrap Version: 2.4(1)

Hardware Version: 1.3  Model: WS-C5500  Serial #: 069022065

Module Ports Model      Serial # Hw     Fw       Fw1      Sw
------ ----- --------   --------- ---   ------   -----    -----------
1      2     WS-X5509   007481469 2.1   2.4(1)   2.4(1)   2.4(4)
2      2     WS-X5509   007482013 2.1   2.4(1)   2.4(1)   2.4(4)
3      24    WS-X5224   007479316 1.3   3.1(1)            2.4(4)
4      24    WS-X5013   006813622 1.1   2.3(1)            2.4(4)
5      24    WS-X5013   006813615 1.1   2.3(1)            2.4(4)
6      24    WS-X5013   006774069 1.1   2.3(1)            2.4(4)
7      24    WS-X5013   006774257 1.1   2.3(1)            2.4(4)

Module DRAM     FLASH   NVRAM   Used    Available
------ -------  -----   -----   ----    ---------
1       16384K   8192K   256K     97K       159K

Uptime is 167 days, 1 hour, 31 minutes
Galway-C5500-1> (enable)
```

Listing 12-11

along with an explanation of the different severity levels. I have included a description for facilities whose acronyms are not self-explanatory. The severity level means the same as on a router, for example, spanning tree has severity level 2 means that critical alerts and emergency messages will be reported for the spanning-tree facility.

The contents of the switch's internal buffer can be examined using the `show logging buffer` command. Listing 12-13 shows a series of notifications about different bridge ports that are changing status. This most likely means that the line protocol is transitioning on those ports, which could simply be due to the corresponding workstations being powered on and off.

SPAN Analyzer Port

The *switch port analyzer* (SPAN) feature provides a powerful troubleshooting tool on the Catalyst 5000 series switch. This feature allows

```
C5508> (enable) sh logging

Logging console:              enabled
Logging server:               enabled
{172.16.101.19}
Current Logging Session:      enabled

Facility            Server/Default Severity  Current Session Severity
--------            -----------------------  ------------------------
cdp                 2                        2
mcast               2                        2
dtp                 5                        5 Dynamic Trunking Protocol
dvlan               2                        2
earl                2                        2
fddi                2                        2
ip                  2                        2 ip permit list
pruning             2                        2
snmp                2                        2
spantree            2                        2
sys                 5                        5 system
tac                 2                        2
tcp                 2                        2
telnet              2                        2
tftp                2                        2
vtp                 2                        2
vmps                2                        2
kernel              2                        2
filesys             2                        2 Flash file system
drip                2                        2 Dual Ring Protocol
pagp                5                        5 Port Aggregation Protocol
mgmt                5                        5
mls                 5                        5
protfilt            2                        2
security            2                        2

0(emergencies)        1(alerts)             2(critical)
3(errors)             4(warnings)           5(notifications)
6(information)        7(debugging)
C5508> (enable)
```

Listing 12-12

the copying of traffic passing on the port under investigation to the SPAN port. SPAN is disabled by default and needs to be configured. In the following example (Listing 12-14), there is a problem on the station that connects to port 6/9. The traffic on this port is copied to port 10/1, which is being used as the analyzer port. A LAN analyzer could be connected to port 10/1 to troubleshoot the problem without interrupting current traffic flow.

```
C5508>sh loggin buffer
05/07/1999,14:27:32:PAGP-5:Port 6/3 joined bridge port 6/3.
05/07/1999,14:29:49:PAGP-5:Port 6/2 joined bridge port 6/2.
05/07/1999,16:53:16:PAGP-5:Port 4/11 left bridge port 4/11.
05/07/1999,16:53:38:PAGP-5:Port 4/11 joined bridge port 4/11.
05/07/1999,16:54:05:PAGP-5:Port 5/2 joined bridge port 5/2.
05/07/1999,19:12:26:PAGP-5:Port 10/4 joined bridge port 10/4.
05/07/1999,19:17:59:PAGP-5:Port 11/12 joined bridge port 11/12.
05/07/1999,19:28:19:PAGP-5:Port 11/12 left bridge port 11/12.
05/07/1999,19:33:54:PAGP-5:Port 11/12 joined bridge port 11/12.
05/07/1999,20:46:27:PAGP-5:Port 10/2 left bridge port 10/2.
05/07/1999,20:46:47:PAGP-5:Port 10/2 joined bridge port 10/2.
05/07/1999,20:59:05:PAGP-5:Port 4/12 left bridge port 4/12.
05/07/1999,20:59:25:PAGP-5:Port 4/12 joined bridge port 4/12.
05/08/1999,17:04:26:PAGP-5:Port 6/8 joined bridge port 6/8.
05/08/1999,17:05:57:PAGP-5:Port 6/8 left bridge port 6/8.
C5508>
```

Listing 12-13

```
C5508> (enable) set span enable
C5508> (enable) set span 6/9 10/1
Enabled monitoring of Port 6/9 transmit/receive traffic by Port 10/1

C5508> (enable) sh span
Status           : enabled
Admin Source     : Port 6/9
Oper Source      : Port 6/9
Destination      : Port 10/1
Direction        : transmit/receive
Incoming Packets: disabled
C5508> (enable)
```

Listing 12-14

Traffic on more than one port can be monitored. In addition, traffic from an entire VLAN can be mirrored to the destination SPAN port. The option also exists to mirror only transmit or only receive traffic. The incoming packets disabled statement means that normal packets destined for the SPAN port are not allowed, as is the default.

The following example (Listing 12-15) mirrors only transmit frames from VLAN 2 to the 10/1 SPAN port. Ports 11/7-9 are in VLAN 2, so the same effect could be accomplished by specifying 11/7-9 as the source ports.

The are some issues to be mindful of when configuring and using SPAN:

Listing 12-15

```
C5508> (enable) set span 2 10/1 tx
Enabled monitoring of VLAN 2 transmit traffic by Port 10/1
C5508> (enable) sh span
Status            : enabled
Admin Source      : VLAN 2
Oper Source       : Port 11/7-9
Destination       : Port 10/1
Direction         : transmit
Incoming Packets: disabled
C5508> (enable)
```

- Remember that, as distinct from a hub, each switch port is its own bridged collision domain. Hence, by copying a port or group of ports to the SPAN port, you cannot simply "listen" to the wire. The SPAN port will only pick up frames transmitted by the source port destined for other segments or frames switched to this port from other segments, including broadcasts. The rules of transparent bridging apply here. If, for example, a concentrator attaches to the source port, packets sent between two stations on this concentrator will not be mirrored to the SPAN port because they did not cross the source switch port.
- The SPAN port can be part of a normal active VLAN, but this is not advisable because this port does not participate in spanning tree. Remember that by default this port will be in VLAN 1, just like all other ports. To avoid the possibility of loops, assign the SPAN destination port to its own VLAN.
- When mirroring a port on the Gigabit Etherchannel module, traffic in both directions must be monitored. Another constraint currently with this module is that the source and destination SPAN ports must reside on the same card.
- Note also that the SPAN cannot be configured on a Catalyst 5000 series FDDI module.

SNMP on the Catalyst 5000

The SNMP configuration on the Catalyst 5000 series also bears a striking resemblance to that of the router's IOS. The default SNMP settings are displayed in the sample default configuration seen at the start of the chapter. The password strings for each of the three community-access types can be set. Along with the read-only and read-write communities,

Listing 12-16

```
#snmp
set snmp community read-only      sam98
set snmp community read-write     maguire
set snmp community read-write-all secret
set snmp rmon enable
set snmp trap enable  module
set snmp trap enable  chassis
set snmp trap disable bridge
set snmp trap disable repeater
set snmp trap disable vtp
set snmp trap disable auth
set snmp trap disable ippermit
set snmp trap 133.1.12.19   sam98

Galway-C5500-1> (enable) sh snmp
RMON: Enabled
Traps Enabled: Module,Chassis
Port Traps Enabled: None

Community-Access     Community-String
----------------     --------------------
read-only              sam98
read-write           maguire
read-write-all       secret

Trap-Rec-Address                            Trap-Rec-Community
----------------------------------------    ------------------
133.1.12.19                                     sam98
Galway-C5500-1> (enable)
```

there is a read-write-all community that has the power to modify the actual SNMP parameter settings. In this example (Listing 12-16), module and chassis traps are being sent to the SNMP server at 133.1.12.19 as part of the read-only community. Port traps are not enabled by default; this is to prevent the SNMP server or monitoring station from being overloaded with traps simply due to stations being powered on and off.

RMON is also enabled, although it must be noted that for extended RMON to be availed of, the appropriate extended RMON module must be present on the switch.

Problems with VLANs

The virtual LAN is an extremely useful feature of LAN switching. VLANs provide broadcast containment, enhanced security, the possibility for protocol filtering, and the ability to isolate autonomous workgroups within an organization.

VLANs generally are easy to configure, but the motivation behind the creation of a VLAN must be clearly understood along with the consequences of having that particular VLAN in the network. Problems frequently occur on live networks because insufficient thought was given to what VLANs really are and, in particular, how different VLANs communicate with each other. For much of the remainder of this chapter I will discuss VLAN configuration and troubleshooting, along with working through some troubleshooting scenarios.

The Default VLAN

By default, all Ethernet ports on Catalyst 5000 series switches are in VLAN 1. This includes all switching ports, ports on the supervisor module, and the in-band management console port. This is a point worth emphasizing, and just to illustrate this, consider the following scenario: A switch has all ports configured to be in VLAN 2. A new card is added to the switch to facilitate additional users on the workgroup that the switch and VLAN 2 services. When the switch is powered back up, no communication is available between users on the new module and the already incumbent modules. The cause of the problem is that the new card is in VLAN 1 not VLAN 2; hence the switch must have the new ports configured manually to be in VLAN 2. This task is straightforward. For example, if a 24-port card was placed in module 4, the configuration would be

```
set vlan 2 4/1-24
```

Routing between the VLANs also could have restored communication, but in this case we wanted all ports to be in VLAN 2.

This point about VLAN 1 may seem obvious, but having said this, I did see this problem occur on a very large corporate network.

CAUTION: *All ports on the switch are in VLAN 1 by default. This should particularly be remembered when adding new modules.*

The `show vlan` Command To check what VLANs have been configured on the switch, use the `show vlan` command (see Listing 12-17). VLAN 1 is the default VLAN for all the different flavors of Ethernet.

```
cgate-4> (enable) sh vlan
VLAN Name                             Status    Mod/Ports, Vlans
---- -------------------------------- --------- ----------------------------
1    default                          active    1/1-2
                                                4/5-12
                                                5/3-24
                                                6/1-24
3    VLAN0003                         active    5/1-2
10   VLAN0010                         active
11   VLAN0011                         active
1002 fddi-default                     active
1003 token-ring-default               active
1004 fddinet-default                  active
1005 trnet-default                    active

VLAN Type  SAID       MTU   Parent RingNo BrdgNo Stp  BrdgMode Trans1 Trans2
---- ----- ---------- ----- ------ ------ --- -- ---- -------- ------ --------
1    enet  100001     1500  -      -      -      -    -        0      0
3    enet  100003     1500  -      -      -      -    -        0      0
10   enet  100010     1500  -      -      -      -    -        0      0
11   enet  100011     1500  -      -      -      -    -        0      0
1002 fddi  101002     1500  -      0x0    -      -    -        0      0
1003 trcrf 101003     1500  0      0x0    -      -    -        0      0
1004 fdnet 101004     1500  -      -      0x0    ieee -        0      0
1005 trbrf 101005     1500  -      -      0x0    ibm  -        0      0

VLAN AREHops STEHops Backup CRF
---- ------- ------- ----------
1003 7       7       off
cgate-4> (enable)
```

Listing 12-17

Default VLANs are also defined for Token Ring and FDDI. On the switch named cgate-4, VLANs 3, 10, and 11 also have been defined. However, notice that only VLAN 3 has been assigned to any ports. VLANs 10 and 11 may have been configured without having yet been assigned to any ports, or alternatively, these VLANs may have been learned over a trunk from another switch. The VLAN remains active until the `clear vlan` command is issued, even if it does not relate to any ports on the switch.

Looking farther through the output of `show vlan`, the *Security Association ID* (SAID) is a unique VLAN identifier assigned by the switch based on the VLAN number. Information is also provided on VLAN MTU, spanning-tree type, translational bridging, and Token Ring hop count.

A point to note about the `clear vlan` command is that all ports that were in the deleted VLAN will then get disabled. They will not be reen-

```
Galway-C5500-1> (enable) sh vtp domain
Domain Name                      Domain Index VTP Version Local Mode  Password
-----------                      ------------ ----------- ----------  --------
CORMAC                               1             1          server      -

Vlan-count Max-vlan-storage Config Revision Notifications
---------- ---------------- --------------- -------------
5          1023             2               disabled

Last Updater     Pruning  PruneEligible on Vlans
------------     -------  ----------------------
171.133.208.254 disabled 2-1000
Galway-C5500-1> (enable)
```

Listing 12-18

abled until they are assigned to another VLAN. Simply reassigning them to VLAN 1 would activate the ports.

The `show vtp` Command The VLAN Trunk Protocol (VTP) is a dynamic means of propagating new VLANs throughout a switched environment. By default, each Catalyst 5000 is a VTP server. Switches that connect to a VTP server switch can be configured as VTP clients. This allows VLANs configured on the server to automatically propagate to the client switches. VLANs cannot be configured or deleted on switches that are set as VTP clients. For VTP to work, each participating switch must belong to the same VTP domain. In the case of the Galway-C5500-1 switch, one or more other switches could be configured as VTP clients in VTP domain CORMAC. (See Listing 12-18.)

It is a judgment call whether or not to use VTP on your network. While it reduces configuration, it can create problems if not administered properly. Setting the VTP mode to transparent can disable VTP:

```
set vtp mode transparent
```

VTP also can cause problems if its configuration is not understood properly. For example, if two switches that connect are configured to be in the same VTP domain but both are left at the default server setting, a VTP message loop will be created.

Another issue to note is that all switches must be running the same VTP version, 1 or 2. Token Ring modules require version 2. The VTP version can be configured manually.

CAUTION: Having two connected switches in the same VTP domain, both configured as servers, can create Loops.

NOTE: All switches in a VTP domain must be running the same VTP version.

Trunking

A *trunk* is, most basically, a point-to-point connection between two switches that allows the exchange of VLAN information. Trunking allows VLANs to be extended across multiple switches in the network. Multiple connections can trunk between the same two switches, and trunks can be combined in a set of two or four links to provide a high-bandwidth channel.

Here are some guidelines to ensure that trunking operates correctly:

- There are two trunk encapsulation types for high-speed Ethernet: ISL (Cisco proprietary) and the standards-based 802.1Q. Obviously, these encapsulations must match at each end of the trunk. The 802.1Q or dot1Q encapsulation is only supported in software versions 4.1 and later.
- Each trunk port must have a trunking mode. The mode at each end of the link does not have to agree exactly but must be compatible for the trunk to come up. The trunk mode can be set to one of the following:
  - *On*. The port is permanently in trunking mode.
  - *Off*. The port is nontrunking, even if the neighbor at the other end of the link is set to trunk.
  - *Desirable*. This type of port will become a trunk if the other end is set to *Auto* or *On*.
  - *Auto*. An autonegotiating port will form a trunk if the other end is set to *On* or *Desirable*. This is the default setting for Fast Ethernet and Gigabit Ethernet ports.
  - *Nonnegotiate*. This puts the port in permanent trunking mode but prevents it from generating any Dynamic Trunking Protocol (DTP) updates. A trunk is formed if the other end of the link is manually configured to trunk.

The `show trunk` **Command** Use the `show trunk` command to verify the status of trunks on the switch. In the case of cgate-4, it can be observed that five ports are trunking, all using ISL encapsulation. All trunk ports have been set to on and are themselves in VLAN 1. A trunk port must be in the same native VLAN at each end of the link.

Port 3/1 allows all VLANs to trunk across it, which is the default for a trunk port. However, ports 4/1-4 only trunk for VLANs 1, 10, and 11. In this instance, it can seen that these designated VLANs are the only active VLANs on the switch, so the configuration of the allowed VLANs happens to have no effect at the moment. Finally, you will notice that ports 4/1 and 4/2 are in blocking mode as per the spanning-tree protocol. If multiple trunks are configured between the same two switches, then only one trunk can be in a forwarding state for each VLAN. (See Listing 12-19.)

The `show trunk` command also can be applied to an individual port (see Listing 12-20).

Listing 12-19

```
cgate-4> (enable) sh trunk
Port      Mode         Encapsulation  Status        Native vlan
--------  ----         -------------  ------------  -----------
 3/1      on           isl            trunking      1
 4/1      on           isl            trunking      1
 4/2      on           isl            trunking      1
 4/3      on           isl            trunking      1
 4/4      on           isl            trunking      1

Port      Vlans allowed on trunk
--------  ----------------------
 3/1      1-1005
 4/1      1,10-11
 4/2      1,10-11
 4/3      1,10-11
 4/4      1,10-11

Port      Vlans allowed and active in management domain
--------  ---------------------------------------------------
 3/1      3,10-11
 4/1      1,10-11
 4/2      1,10-11
 4/3      1,10-11
 4/4      1,10-11

Port      Vlans in spanning tree forwarding state and not pruned
--------  ------------------------------------------------------
 3/1      3,10-11
 4/1
 4/2
 4/3      1,10-11
 4/4      1,10-11
cgate-4> (enable)
```

Listing 12-20

```
5500-A> (enable) sh trunk 1/1
Port      Mode         Encapsulation  Status        Native vlan
--------  -----------  -------------  ------------  -----------
 1/1      on           isl            trunking      1

Port      Vlans allowed on trunk
--------  ---------------------------------------------------------
 1/1      1-2,10,20-1005

Port      Vlans allowed and active in management domain
--------  ---------------------------------------------------------
 1/1      1-2,10,20-67

Port      Vlans in spanning tree forwarding state and not pruned
--------  ---------------------------------------------------------
 1/1      1-2,10,20-67,1003,1005
```

If it was decided for the following example to allow port 1/1 to act as a trunk for VLAN 11 but not for VLAN 10 and to change the mode to auto, then this could be accomplished as shown (see Listing 12-21).

Inter-VLAN Communication

Traffic that crosses between VLANs must be routed. The two fundamental methods for routing between VLANs are

- The use of an external router that either has a physical interface in each VLAN or uses a single physical connection to the switch with multiple logical subinterfaces that each relate to a different VLAN. Figure 12-1 shows a sample topology for this type of solution.

```
5500-A> (enable) clear trunk 1/1 10
Removing Vlan(s) 10 from allowed list.
Port 1/1 allowed vlans modified to 1-9,11-1005.
5500-A> (enable)

5500-A> (enable) set trunk 1/1 auto 11
Adding vlans 11 to allowed list.
Please use the 'clear trunk' command to remove vlans from allowed list.
Port(s) 1/1 allowed vlans modified to 1-9,11,20-1005.
Port(s) 1/1 trunk mode set to auto.
5500-A> (enable)
```

Listing 12-21

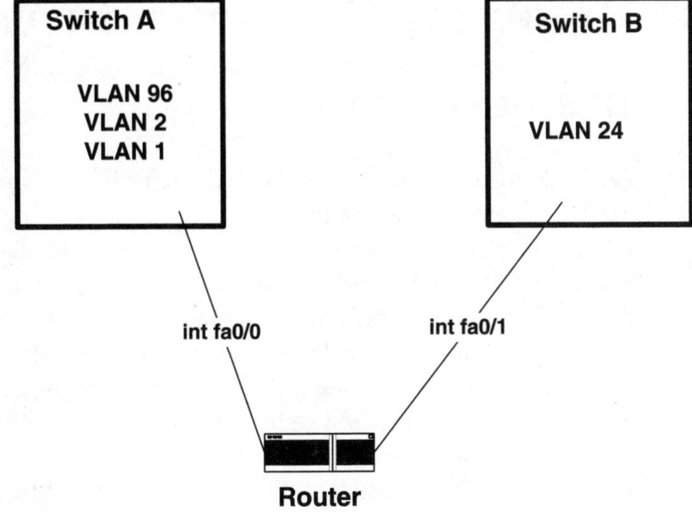

Figure 12-1 Inter-VLAN routing using an external router.

- The inclusion of a route-switch module (RSM) in the Catalyst 5000 series switch. This card is effectively a logical router that can route between the different VLANs on the switch. It also supports dynamic routing protocols; hence RSMs can be used exactly like physical routers to route between all VLANs on an enterprise network. A logical diagram demonstrating the use of RSMs for inter-VLAN routing is shown in Figure 12-2.

Inter-VLAN routing will be discussed in more detail when we examine the Catalyst 5000 series in an IP environment.

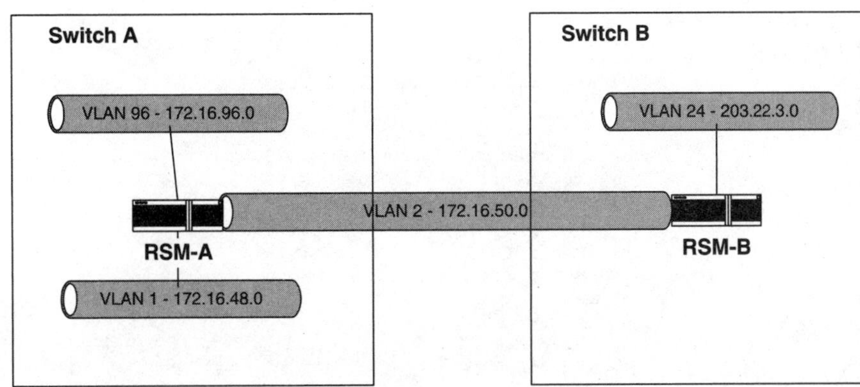

Figure 12-2 Inter-VLAN routing using RSMs.

Resolving IP-Related Problems

IP Switch Configuration

An IP address is put on the switch usually for management purposes. Management can be accomplished out of band using the SLIP or the sl0 port. For in-band management, the console or sc0 port is used. The switch is not a router and therefore does not support any dynamic routing. The switch can only route using static routes or a default gateway. By default, the sc0 interface has 0.0.0.0 as its IP address. In this scenario, the switch will issue a BOOTP or DHCP request for an IP address. This is usually undesirable, since the switch's IP address should be hardcoded. In the following example (Listing 12-22), the sc0 port is given an IP address of 165.8.208.254/25. The broadcast address is included in the configuration by default. Notice that the console port has been placed in VLAN 3 instead of the default VLAN. A default gateway to a router port at 165.8.208.129 has been configured with a default metric of 1. This router port also must be in VLAN 3.

The `show interface` Command The addressing and VLAN membership of sc0 and sl0 can be checked using the `show interface` command. Listing 12-23 shows sl0 not being used. The console port has an IP address of 171.33.208.254/24 and is in VLAN 1.

The `show ip route` Command The `show ip route` command displays the contents of the routing table, just as on a router. In the case of the switch, this command will display the IP address of the sc0 port, along with any configured default gateway or static routes. In Listing

Listing 12-22

```
#ip
set interface sc0 3 165.8.208.254 255.255.255.128 165.48.208.255

set interface sc0 up
set interface sl0 0.0.0.0 0.0.0.0
set interface sl0 up
set arp agingtime 1200
set ip redirect   enable
set ip unreachable   enable
set ip fragmentation enable
set ip route 0.0.0.0          165.8.208.129  1
set ip alias default          0.0.0.0
!
```

```
Galway-C5500-1> (enable) sh interface
sl0: flags=51<UP,POINTOPOINT,RUNNING>
       slip 0.0.0.0 dest 0.0.0.0
sc0: flags=63<UP,BROADCAST,RUNNING>
       vlan 1 inet 171.33.208.254 netmask 255.255.255.0 broadcast 171.33.208.255
Galway-C5500-1> (enable)
```

Listing 12-23

12-24, the sc0 port is 171.33.208.254, and the default gateway is the address of the local router port 172.33.208.1.

The `show arp` Command Having an IP address on the switch also enables you to use the switch as an IP troubleshooting tool. IP connectivity can be tested for all stations that are in the same VLAN as the sc0 port. The switch holds an ARP table that can be examined using `show arp` (see Listing 12-25).

```
Galway-C5500-1> sh ip route
Fragmentation   Redirect   Unreachable
-------------   --------   -----------
enabled         enabled    enabled

The primary gateway: 171.33.208.1
Destination           Gateway               Flags   Use          Interface
--------------------  --------------------  ------  ----------   ---------
171.33.208.0          171.33.208.254          U       7475         sc0
default               171.33.208.1            UG      380426       sc0
default               default                 UH           0       sl0
```

Listing 12-24

Listing 12-25

```
Galway-C5500-1> (enable) sh arp
ARP Aging time = 1200 sec
171.33.208.229                              at 08-00-09-0d-f3-4d
171.33.208.27                               at 08-00-09-1e-4d-1e
171.33.208.141                              at 00-60-b0-cc-3d-95
171.33.208.158                              at 00-60-b0-cc-2d-07
171.33.208.169                              at 00-60-b0-cc-3d-68
171.33.208.167                              at 00-60-b0-cc-2d-05
171.33.208.18                               at 02-60-8c-2d-a3-70
Galway-C5500-1> (enable)
```

Let's now consider a troubleshooting scenario: For a particular switch, it was decided to place the first six ports on card 4 in VLAN 24. Prior to this, the switch was only using the default VLAN. Immediately after the new VLAN was configured, the main network management declared that the entire switch was down. (See Listing 12-26.)

By attaching a terminal to the console port on the switch, it is verified that VLAN 24 was configured successfully. It is further observed that the switch can ping its own console port but cannot ping its router gateway. This explains why the management station sees the switch as being down. (See Listing 12-27.)

When the router is examined, it is found that the router cannot ping the sc0 port on the switch and does not receive an ARP reply for the switch's IP address. This could imply that broadcasts are not propagating between the router and the switch. This should remind you of VLANs and the fact that the sc0 port is in VLAN 1. It was confirmed from the CAM table that the router's MAC address was learned over port 4/1; hence it is now in VLAN 24. This explains the cause of the problem, which could be solved by either moving port 4/1 to VLAN 1 or moving sc0 to VLAN 24. (See Listing 12-28.)

Let's solve the problem by putting interface sc0 in VLAN 24, and now the switch can ping the router port (see Listing 12-29).

There is an issue here that deserves further emphasis. The stations on VLAN 1 must have some way to route to other VLANs now that the port that connects to the router is in VLAN 24. This can be done using an RSM module in the Catalyst 5000 or by configuring Fast Ethernet subinterfaces on the route with ISL encapsulation.

For the sake of illustrating a further point, suppose you solved the problem by reassigning port 4/1-6 back to VLAN 1 (see Listing 12-30).

```
Console> (enable) set vlan 24 4/1-6
VLAN 24 modified.
VLAN 1 modified.
VLAN  Mod/Ports
----  ----------------
24    4/1-6

Vlan 24 is not active.
Console> (enable) 04/26/2000,17:06:50:PAGP-5:Port 4/1 left bridge port 4/1.
```

Listing 12-26

```
Console> (enable) sh vlan
VLAN Name                             Status    IfIndex Mod/Ports, Vlans
---- -------------------------------- --------- ------- ------------------------
1    default                          active    5       1/1-2
                                                        3/1-3
                                                        4/7-12
                                                        5/1-12
                                                        6/1-12
                                                        7/1-12
                                                        10/1-12
                                                        11/1-12
24   VLAN0024                         active    111     4/1-6
1002 fddi-default                     active    6
1003 token-ring-default               active    9
1004 fddinet-default                  active    7
1005 trnet-default                    active    8

VLAN Type  SAID       MTU   Parent RingNo BrdgNo Stp  BrdgMode Trans1 Trans2
---- ----- ---------- ----- ------ ------ ------ ---- -------- ------ ------
1    enet  100001     1500  -      -      -      -    -        0      0
24   enet  100024     1500  -      -      -      -    -        0      0
1002 fddi  101002     1500  -      -      -      -    -        0      0
1003 trcrf 101003     1500  0      0x0    -      -    -        0      0
1004 fdnet 101004     1500  -      -      0x0    ieee -        0      0
1005 trbrf 101005     1500  -      -      0x0    ibm  -        0      0

VLAN AREHops STEHops Backup CRF
---- ------- ------- ----------
1003 7       7       off

Console> (enable) ping 172.16.254.254
172.16.254.254 is alive
Console> (enable) ping 172.16.254.1
no answer from 172.16.254.1
Console> (enable)
```

Listing 12-27

Unexpectedly, pings are still failing to the router port. The reason for this can be found by checking the VLAN table. VLAN 24 is still there. It must be cleared manually using the `clear vlan` command. After this is done, the router can be pinged successfully (see Listing 12-31).

Note the warning that is provided before using the `clear vlan` command. If there were any other ports in VLAN 24, they would have to be reenabled before again becoming usable.

```
Router#ping 172.16.254.254

Type escape sequence to abort.
Sending 5, 100-byte ICMP Echos to 172.16.254.254, timeout is 2 seconds:
.....
Success rate is 0 percent (0/5)
Router#

Router#sh arp
Protocol  Address          Age (min)  Hardware Addr   Type   Interface
Internet  172.16.254.1            -   0050.0b74.e8c0  ARPA   FastEthernet6/0/0
Internet  172.16.254.254          0   Incomplete      ARPA
Router#
```

Listing 12-28

```
Console> (enable) set in sc0 24
Interface sc0 vlan set.
Console> (enable) sh int sc0
Usage: show interface
Console> (enable) sh int
sl0: flags=51<UP,POINTOPOINT,RUNNING>
        slip 0.0.0.0 dest 0.0.0.0
sc0: flags=63<UP,BROADCAST,RUNNING>
        vlan 24 inet 172.16.254.254 netmask 255.255.255.0 broadcast 172.16.254.2
55
Console> (enable) ping 172.16.254.254
172.16.254.254 is alive
Console> (enable) ping 172.16.254.1
172.16.254.1 is alive
Console> (enable)
```

Listing 12-29

Routing and the RSM Module

It is important to be clear on how traffic is routed between VLANs. This topic frequently creates confusion due to the fact that VLANs are still a relatively new concept for practical use and do not relate directly to physical segments. This confusion, in turn, is often the source of configuration errors on the switches, routers, and RSM modules.

Listing 12-30

```
Console> (enable) set vlan 1 4/1-6
VLAN 1 modified.
VLAN 24 modified.
VLAN  Mod/Ports
----  ----------------------
1     1/1-2
      3/1-3
      4/1-12
      5/1-12
      6/1-12
      7/1-12
      10/1-12
      11/1-12

Console> (enable) ping 172.16.254.1
no answer from 172.16.254.1
Console> (enable) ping 172.16.254.1
```

There are two basic methods for routing between VLANs that reside on the same switch or on multiple switches. This is the use of an external router or an RSM module within the Catalyst 5000 series switch. Schematic diagrams for the two solutions are provided in Figures 12-1 and 12-2, respectively.

Listing 12-32 is a sample router configuration that would enable the routing of IP and IPX between the VLANs shown. ISL encapsulation is used on the Fast Ethernet router interfaces and the trunk ports on the two switches. The use of subinterfaces provides a logical connection from the router to each VLAN on the switch.

An RSM module also can be used to route between local and remote VLANs. The configuration is very similar to that of a router. The interfaces are logical rather than physical, and each applies to an individual VLAN. The same rules for dynamic routing apply as with a physical router box, and all the same Cisco IOS features are supported. The RSM should be thought of as a router within the switch that logically routes between VLANs, as demonstrated in Figure 12-2. To connect to the RSM from the switch, open a session to the appropriate module. In the case of switch A, the RSM is in module 3 (see Listing 12-33).

It can be verified that the RSM sees the switch as a CDP neighbor (see Listing 12-34).

```
Console> (enable)
Console> (enable) sh vlan
VLAN Name                              Status    IfIndex Mod/Ports, Vlans
---- -------                           ------    ------- ----------------
----
1    default                           active    5        1/1-2
                                                          3/1-3
                                                          4/1-12
                                                          5/1-12
                                                          6/1-12
                                                          7/1-12
                                                          10/1-12
                                                          11/1-12
24   VLAN0024                          active    111
1002 fddi-default                      active    6
1003 token-ring-default                active    9
1004 fddinet-default                   active    7
1005 trnet-default                     active    8

VLAN Type  SAID       MTU   Parent RingNo BrdgNo Stp  BrdgMode Trans1 Trans2
---- ----- ------     ----  ------ ------ ------ ---  -------- ------ ------
1    enet  100001     1500  -      -      -      -    -        0      0
24   enet  100024     1500  -      -      -      -    -        0      0
1002 fddi  101002     1500  -      -      -      -    -        0      0
1003 trcrf 101003     1500  0      0x0    -      -    -        0      0
1004 fdnet 101004     1500  -      -      0x0    ieee -        0 0
1005 trbrf 101005     1500  -      -      0x0    ibm  -        0      0

VLAN AREHops STEHops Backup CRF
---- ------- ------- ----------
1003 7       7       off
Console> (enable) clear vlan 24
This command will deactivate all ports on vlan 24
in the entire management domain
Do you want to continue(y/n) [n]?y
Vlan 24 deleted
Console> (enable) ping 172.16.254.1
172.16.254.1 is alive
Console> (enable)
```

Listing 12-31

Issues with Spanning-Tree Protocol

Configuring the Spanning-Tree Parameters

All ports on the switch automatically participate in the Spanning-Tree Protocol (STP). In a network with multiple switches, the convergence of the STP in each VLAN results in the following:

Listing 12-32

```
Router#

ipx routing 0050.0b74.e8c0
!
interface fastethernet 0/0.1
encapsulation isl 1
ip address 172.16.48.2 255.255.255.0
ipx network ab1
!
interface fastethernet 0/0.2
encapsulation isl 2
ip address 172.16.50.2 255.255.255.0
ipx network ab2
!
interface fastethernet 0/0.96
encapsulation isl 96
ip address 172.16.96.2 255.255.255.0
ipx network ab96
!
interface fastethernet 0/1.24
encapsulation isl 24
ip address 203.22.3.1 255.255.255.0
ipx network cd24
!
router igrp 1
network 172.16.0.0
network 203.22.3.0
```

- The election of a root switch for each VLAN across the switched network. The root switch is the switch with the lowest MAC address on the VLAN if all spanning-tree parameters are left at their default settings. It should be ensured through careful design that switches on or close to the network backbone become the root switches. Therefore, it is not a good idea to allow MAC addresses to determine what switch becomes root. More control can be exercised using the *Switch priority* parameter. In this case, the switch with the lowest priority becomes root.
- The election of a designated switch for each switched LAN segment. This is usually the switch closest to the root. Other switches use the designated switch to forward their frames to the root switch.
- The port with the shortest distance to the root switch is calculated for each switch. This is based on cost.
- In cases of redundant parallel links, all but the least-cost port are placed in blocking mode to ensure a loop-free topology.

The `show spantree` Command To obtain information on the spanning-tree parameters for each VLAN, use the `show spantree` com-

Listing 12-33

```
5500-SwitchA> (enable) session 3
Trying Router-3...
Connected to Router-3.
Escape character is '^]'.

User Access Verification

Password:
5500-RSM>en
Password:
5500-RSM#
5500-RSM#wr t
Building configuration...

Current configuration:
!
version 11.3
service timestamps debug uptime
service timestamps log uptime
service password-encryption
!
hostname 5500-RSM
!
boot system flash
enable password 7 00071A150754

ipx routing 0050.0b72.e110
!
interface Vlan1
 ip address 172.16.48.2 255.255.255.0
 ipx network ab1
!
interface Vlan2
 ip address 172.16.50.2 255.255.255.0
 ipx network ab2
!
interface Vlan96
 ip address 172.16.96.2 255.255.255.0
 ipx network ab96
!
router igrp 1
 network 172.16.0.0
!
ip classless
!
line con 0
line aux 0
line vty 0 4
 password 7 060506324F41
 login
!
end
```

```
5500-RSM#sh cdp neig
Capability Codes: R - Router, T - Trans Bridge, B - Source Route Bridge
                  S - Switch, H - Host, I - IGMP, r - Repeater

Device ID         Local Intrfce       Holdtme     Capability  Platform  Port ID
5500-SwitchA                           119          T B S      WS-C5500  3/1
5500-RSM#
```

Listing 12-34

mand. In this example (Listing 12-35), the spanning-tree information for VLAN 2 is investigated. The most relevant points that can be seen from this output are

- The IEEE Spanning-Tree Protocol has not elected switch 5500-B as the root for VLAN 2. The root switch has a priority of 8191, which is approximately one-quarter of the default setting. This switch's priority of 16384 for VLAN 2 is about one-half the default. This indicates that switch priorities were configured to influence the root switch election for VLAN 2.
- The designated root cost of 3004 is the least-cost path to the root switch from this particular switch. This has been used to elect port 1/1 as the designated root port, although other ports happen to have the same path cost to the root switch.
- Fundamental STP parameters such as *Hello interval, Max age*, and *Forward delay* are all at their default values for VLAN 2. The *Max age* is the duration after which Spanning-Tree Protocol information gets aged out by the switch. The *Forward delay* is the time that each switch port remains in listening and learning state before moving to a forwarding state.
- The bridge ID MAC address is different for each VLAN that is configured on the switch. It is important to be mindful of this, particularly when troubleshooting.
- The output from `show spantree 2` also lists all ports in VLAN 2, indicating which are in a forwarding and which are in a blocking state. Notice that the higher-cost ports tend to be in blocking mode. The default port cost for Spanning Tree varies depending on the port speed; e.g., Gigabit Ethernet has a lower cost than Fast Ethernet. In this case, the port costs have been configured manually. The default port priority is 32 regardless of port speed.

```
5500-B> sh spantree 2
VLAN 2
Spanning tree enabled
Spanning tree type          ieee

Designated Root             00-90-6f-bd-c8-01
Designated Root Priority    8191
Designated Root Cost        3004
Designated Root Port        1/1
Root Max Age   20 sec    Hello Time 2  sec   Forward Delay 15 sec

Bridge ID MAC ADDR          00-50-50-9b-9c-01
Bridge ID Priority          16384
Bridge Max Age 20 sec    Hello Time 2  sec   Forward Delay 15 sec

Port      Vlan  Port-State    Cost   Priority  Fast-Start  Group-Method
----      ----  ----------    -----  --------  ----------  ------------
 1/1      2     forwarding     3004        32   disabled
 1/2      2     blocking       3004        32   disabled
 2/1-2    2     blocking       3019        32   disabled    redundancy
 5/1      2     blocking       3004        32   disabled
 5/2      2     forwarding     3004        32   disabled
 5/3      2     forwarding     3004        32   disabled
 5/4      2     forwarding     3004        32   disabled
 5/5      2     forwarding     3004        32   disabled
 5/6      2     forwarding     3004        32   disabled
 6/1      2     blocking       3019        32   disabled
 6/2      2     blocking       3019        32   disabled
 6/3      2     blocking       3019        32   disabled
 6/4      2     blocking       3019        32   disabled
 6/5      2     blocking       3019        32   disabled
 6/7      2     blocking       3019        32   disabled
 6/8      2     blocking       3019        32   disabled
 6/9      2     blocking       3019        32   disabled
 6/10     2     blocking       3019        32   disabled
 6/11     2     blocking       3019        32   disabled
 6/12     2     blocking       3019        32   disabled
```

Listing 12-35

- The *Portfast* feature, which we will discuss shortly, is in its default state of being disabled for all ports in VLAN 2.

More About the Root Switch As mentioned previously, it is critical to ensure that an appropriate backbone switch is elected as root. The root switch should have high-speed port access and should reside in a section of the network that has high redundancy. If a root switch crashes, the Spanning-Tree Protocol sometimes can be cumbersome in converging to the election of a successor.

The potential for such a problem occurring can be reduced by manipulating the switch priorities. This also will protect against a scenario whereby a new switch with a lower MAC address than the root switch is added to the VLAN and then becomes root. Such a situation can be very serious first because it is totally unforeseen and second because the new switch may have a low port speed and be located at a stub point of the network.

In the following scenario (Listing 12-36), it is desired to ensure that the switch in question will always be the root switch for VLAN 24 even if other switches are added.

The `set spantree root` command is used to reduce this switch's priority on VLAN 24 to 8192 from the default of 32768. To ensure that another preassigned switch becomes root in the event of this switch failing, the `set spantree root secondary` command could be used to set the priority on that switch to 16384. (See Listing 12-37.)

```
Console> (enable) sh vlan
VLAN Name                             Status    IfIndex Mod/Ports, Vlans
---- -------------------------------- --------- ------- --------------------
----
1    default                          active    5       1/1-2
                                                        3/1-3
                                                        4/7-12
                                                        5/1-12
                                                        6/1-12
                                                        7/1-12
                                                        10/1-12
                                                        11/1-12
24   VLAN0024                         active    112     4/1-6
1002 fddi-default                     active    6
1003 token-ring-default               active    9
1004 fddinet-default                  active    7
1005 trnet-default                    active    8

VLAN Type  SAID       MTU   Parent RingNo BrdgNo Stp  BrdgMode Trans1 Trans2
---- ----- ---------- ----- ------ ------ ------ ---- -------- ------ ------
1    enet  100001     1500  -      -      -      -    -        0      0
24   enet  100024     1500  -      -      -      -    -        0      0
1002 fddi  101002     1500  -      -      -      -    -        0      0
1003 trcrf 101003     1500  0      0x0    -      -    -        0      0
1004 fdnet 101004     1500  -      -      0x0    ieee -        0      0
1005 trbrf 101005     1500  -      -      0x0    ibm  -        0      0

VLAN AREHops STEHops Backup CRF
---- ------- ------- ----------
1003 7       7       off
```

Listing 12-36

```
Console> (enable) set spantree root ?
Usage: set spantree root [secondary] <vlans> [dia <network_diameter>]
                         [hello <hello_time>]
       (vlans = 1..1005, network_diameter = 2..7, hello_time = 1..10)

Console> (enable) set spantree root 24
VLAN 24 bridge priority set to 8192.
VLAN 24 bridge max aging time set to 20.
VLAN 24 bridge hello time set to 2.
VLAN 24 bridge forward delay set to 15.
Switch is now the root switch for active VLAN 24.
```

Listing 12-37

It can be verified that this switch is now the root for VLAN 24. Notice that, as expected, the root cost is 0 on the root switch itself. (See Listing 12-38.)

Okay, this is all very well, but what if another switch was mistakenly configured with a spanning-tree priority of 1000 for VLAN 24? That switch would then become the root after spanning-tree converged. The

```
Console> (enable) sh spantree 24
VLAN 24
Spanning tree enabled
Spanning tree type           ieee

Designated Root              00-50-3e-89-90-17
Designated Root Priority     8192
Designated Root Cost         0
Designated Root Port         1/0
Root Max Age   20 sec    Hello Time 2  sec   Forward Delay 15 sec

Bridge ID MAC ADDR           00-50-3e-89-90-17
Bridge ID Priority           8192
Bridge Max Age 20 sec    Hello Time 2  sec   Forward Delay 15 sec

Port      Vlan  Port-State       Cost   Priority  Fast-Start  Group-Method
--------  ----  -------------    ----   --------  ----------  ------------
 4/1      24    forwarding        19        32     disabled
 4/2      24    not-connected     19        32     disabled
 4/3      24    not-connected     19        32     disabled
 4/4      24    not-connected     19        32     disabled
 4/5      24    not-connected     19        32     disabled
 4/6      24    not-connected     19        32     disabled
Console> (enable)
```

Listing 12-38

only way to completely guarantee that this switch will always be the root on VLAN 24 is to set the priority to zero (see Listing 12-39).

The *Portfast* Option

There is a feature known as Spanning Tree *Portfast*, or *Fast-Start*, that you will have noticed has been disabled on all the ports studied so far. This feature causes a port to move directly to the forwarding state without going through the listening and learning states. It is like setting the forward-delay timer to zero for an individual port (which you cannot do, and do you know why?). Enabling Portfast effectively stops that port from participating in Spanning Tree. For this reason, Portfast only should be enabled on ports that connect to individual stations and not on ports that connect to other switches.

The reason Portfast is ever enabled is that some applications can fail at the outset because the port to which the station connects is still in

```
Console> (enable) set spantree priority 0 24
Spantree 24 bridge priority set to 0.
Console> (enable) sh spantree 24
VLAN 24
Spanning tree enabled
Spanning tree type          ieee

Designated Root             00-50-3e-89-90-17
Designated Root Priority    0
Designated Root Cost        0
Designated Root Port        1/0
Root Max Age   20 sec    Hello Time 2  sec   Forward Delay 15 sec

Bridge ID MAC ADDR          00-50-3e-89-90-17
Bridge ID Priority          0
Bridge Max Age 20 sec    Hello Time 2  sec   Forward Delay 15 sec

Port      Vlan  Port-State     Cost   Priority  Fast-Start  Group-Method
----      ----  -------------  ----   --------  ----------  ------------
 4/1      24    forwarding        19        32    disabled
 4/2      24    not-connected     19        32    disabled
 4/3      24    not-connected     19        32    disabled
 4/4      24    not-connected     19        32    disabled
 4/5      24    not-connected     19        32    disabled
 4/6      24    not-connected     19        32    disabled
Console> (enable)
```

Listing 12-39

blocking mode. Another example of its use could be to ensure that a redundant LAN port on a server becomes active without having to wait for Spanning Tree to converge.

CAUTION: *The Spanning Tree Portfast feature only should be enabled on ports that connect to individual workstations or servers.*

High-Bandwidth Features

Full-Duplex Transmission

On a shared Ethernet segment, a station will listen to the wire and only transmit if no other transmitting stations are detected. This is an example of *half-duplex transmission*, whereby stations cannot transmit and receive simultaneously. Shared Ethernet must operate in half-duplex mode to minimize collisions.

Now consider a switched segment that only has one station connecting to the switch port. This forms a point-to-point bridged (or switched) collision domain. Collisions cannot occur because only two stations are transmitting on the segment. Therefore, each of the stations can stop listening for collisions and transmit regardless of the status of the wire. This is known as *full-duplex transmission*.

Switch ports are half duplex by default on nonautonegotiated Fast Ethernet ports. Full-duplex mode should only be enabled on ports that connect to a single station; otherwise, undetected collisions will cause the dropping of packets. For example, a switch port that acts as an uplink from a shared concentrator should not be configured as full duplex. If this type of switch port were full duplex, it would transmit packets into the shared collision domain, which possibly contains several end stations, without listening for collisions.

A switch port that connects to another switch, a router, a server, or a workstation can be configured as full duplex as long as the other end is also full duplex. The duplex mode can be configured manually or set through autonegotiation. It is usually better to set the duplex mode manually. While the autonegotiation of speed can be unreliable, setting the duplex mode in this manner is even less reliable. I always prefer to set both the speed and duplex parameters manually.

So what happens if there is a duplex mismatch between the two ends of a point-to-point segment? The line protocol will stay up, and the port will appear as "connected" in the output of the `show port` command. This is distinct from a speed mismatch; if, for example, one end was set at 10 Mbps and the other at 100 Mbps, the line protocol would not come up, and the port would show as a "not connect" at the switch. In the case of a duplex mismatch, one end of the link listens for collisions, while the other does not. The end of the link set to half duplex may unnecessarily refrain from transmitting when the other end is transmitting. This can cause packet loss, particularly if the full-duplex end is sending large packets. This can be demonstrated by configuring a router port as full duplex and the switch port to which it attaches as half duplex. Pings will still be successful between the router and the switch. However, if an extended ping is done with a larger datagram size, packet loss eventually will be observed.

NOTE:

- *Only ports on a point-to-point switched segment should be configured as full duplex.*
- *The duplex mode should be configured manually rather than autonegotiated.*
- *A duplex mismatch (unlike a speed mismatch) will not cause a loss of line protocol, but it may cause packet loss.*

Let's now look at an example where it was decided to make port 10/1 full duplex because it is attached to a server that can autonegotiate 10/100 and duplex mode (see Listing 12-40). The switch port is currently in autonegotiation mode for speed and duplex type.

The switch will not allow us to manually set the port to full duplex while it is in autonegotiation mode. It is taken out of autonegotiation mode by manually setting the speed to 100 Mbps. The port can then be configured as full duplex (see Listing 12-41).

Fast Etherchannel and Gigabit Etherchannel

Ports that support this feature can be grouped into sets of two or four ports to provide a high-speed Etherchannel (FEC). Using Fast Ethernet ports, this feature can create a high-bandwidth pipe of up to 800 Mpbs

```
C5508> (enable) sh port 10/1
Port  Name                Status     Vlan       Level  Duplex Speed Type
---- ----------------- --------- --------- ------ -------------------------
----
10/1                      connected  1          normal   auto  auto 10/100BaseTX

Port  Security Secure-Src-Addr   Last-Src-Addr     Shutdown Trap      IfIndex
----  ------------------------  ----------------  ----------------- --------
10/1  disabled                                     No       disabled 51

Port     Broadcast-Limit Broadcast-Drop
-------  --------------------------------
10/1                   -              0

Port  Status      Channel   Channel     Neighbor                  Neighbor
                  mode      status      device                    port
----  ----------- --------- ----------- ------------------------ --------
10/1  notconnect auto      not channel

Port  Align-Err  FCS-Err    Xmit-Err  Rcv-Err    UnderSize
----  ---------  ---------  ---------  ---------  ----------
10/1          0          0          0          0          0
Port  Single-Col Multi-Coll Late-Coll  Excess-Col Carri-Sen Runts    Giants
------ --------- --------- ---------  --------------------------------------
------
10/1           1          2          0          0          0          1          0

Last-Time-Cleared
-------------------------
Sat May 15 1999, 10:37:48

C5508> (enable) set port duplex 10/1 full
Port 10/1 is in auto-sensing mode.
C5508> (enable) set port speed 10/1 100
Port(s) 10/1 speed set to 100Mbps.
C5508> (enable) set port duplex 10/1 full
Port(s) 10/1 set to full-duplex.
C5508> (enable)
```

Listing 12-40

(four Fast Ethernet ports in full-duplex mode), and similarly with Gigabit Ethernet, up to 8 Gbps can be achieved. A typical application for this feature is to create a high-speed interswitch backbone. The *Port Aggregation Protocol* (PAgP) arranges the ports as a single logical link after the appropriate configuration has been entered.

The configuration of Etherchannel, like many switching features, is itself quite straightforward; however, there are points to be noted to ensure that the creation of an Etherchannel does not entail latent problems.

```
C5508> (enable) sh port 10/1
Port  Name               Status     Vlan       Level  Duplex Speed Type
----  ----------------- ---------  ---------  ------ ------------------------
----
10/1                     connected  1          normal   full   100 10/100BaseTX

Port  Security Secure-Src-Addr   Last-Src-Addr     Shutdown Trap      IfIndex
----  ------------------------  -----------------  ---------------- ----------
10/1  disabled                                     No       disabled 51

Port     Broadcast-Limit Broadcast-Drop
-------  ------------------------------
10/1                   -              0

Port  Status      Channel    Channel     Neighbor                  Neighbor
                  mode       status      device                    port
----  ---------   --------   ----------- ------------------------- ----------
10/1  notconnect  auto       not channel

Port  Align-Err  FCS-Err    Xmit-Err   Rcv-Err    UnderSize
----  ---------  ---------  ---------  ---------  ---------
10/1          0          0          0          0          0

Port  Single-Col Multi-Coll Late-Coll  Excess-Col Carri-Sen Runts     Giants
----  -------------------------------  -----------------------------  ------
----
C5508> (enable)
```

Listing 12-41

- A channel mode needs to be defined similar to the configuration of a trunk. However, the compatibility constraints are more stringent.
  - *On*. A port in the *On* channel mode does not use the PAgP and will only form a channel successfully with another *On* port.
  - *Auto*. This mode will only form a channel with a port in *Desirable* mode through the use of PAgP negotiation.
  - *Desirable*. This mode will only form a channel with a port in *Auto* or *Desirable* mode.
  - *Off*. No channel can be formed, and PAgP is disabled.
- The ports designated for channeling should be a contiguous set of two or four ports that are channel capable. Whether or not a port can support this feature is verified using the `show port capability` command (see Listing 12-42). Possible configuration syntax could be

```
set port channel 5/1-4 auto
```

- Each of the channel ports should have the same speed and duplex settings as each other and at each end of the link.

```
5500-A> sh port capabil 5/1
Model                    WS-X5410
Port                     5/1
Type                     1000-LX/LH
Speed                    1000
Duplex                   full
Trunk encap type         802.1Q
Trunk mode               on,off,desirable,auto,nonegotiate
Channel                  5/1-2,5/1-4
Broadcast suppression    percentage(0-100)
Flow control             receive-(off,on,desired),send-(off,on,desired)
Security                 yes
Membership               static,dynamic
Fast start               yes
Rewrite                  no
5500-A>
```

Listing 12-42

- All ports in the channel should be in the same VLAN or else configured as trunks. If the channel ports are configured as trunks, ensure that the identical trunk mode is configured on all ports at both ends.
- For trunk ports, also ensure that the same range of VLANs is allowed to propagate across each channel port. Otherwise, packets may be dropped going to or from a VLAN that is not allowed on all ports in the channel.
- It is imperative that port security is not enabled on any port in the channel. A port would get disabled if a packet were received from a nonsecure MAC address.
- PAgP groups the channel ports as a single logical link for the purposes of Spanning Tree. If it is desired to disable the channel feature, it must first be ensured that Spanning Tree is enabled. Consider, for example, a situation where *Fast-Start* had been enabled on some of the individual ports that were later configured as a channel. This effectively disables Spanning Tree. Therefore, if this had gone unnoticed, the removal of the channel would cause immediate spanning-tree loops. And in case you are thinking that this would never happen to you, I will mention that I have seen this actually happen on a mission-critical network.

Switch Security

Here I will discuss two aspects of switch security: port security and telnet restriction for access to the switch itself. I will discuss how these features should be configured to ensure correct operation, as well as scenarios showing what can go wrong.

Port Security

In this example (Listing 12-43), users on a switched segment cannot communicate with a particular server that attaches to port 4/1 on the switch. When the switch is examined, port 4/1 is seen as shut down. A port gets shut down automatically after a security violation. The port is seen to have security enabled, and there is a mismatch between the secure address and the last source address, which, of course, is the server's MAC address.

The problem can be solved by first disabling port security on port 4/1 in order to bring up the line protocol (see Listing 12-44).

Specifying the MAC address of the server can then correctly enable port security. IP connectivity is then verified by pinging the server's IP address (see Listing 12-45).

Telnet Restrictions

In the network shown in Figure 12-3, each router can ping the switch; however, telnet is being denied from R7 but not from R6. This is the opposite of the intended policy for allowing telnet access to the switch (see Listing 12-46).

The "access not permitted" message implies that there is an IP permit list configured on the switch that does not include R7's source address. Note, however, that the restriction is only applied to telnet; the ICMP echoes were replied to. We can verify this by gaining access to the switch through R6 (see Listing 12-47).

The IP permit list is modified *after* disabling the IP permit feature (see Listing 12-48). You must be careful to do this in the correct order by specifying the permitted IP address *before* enabling the IP permit feature; otherwise, you will lose the telnet session.

```
Console> (enable) sh port 4/1
Port  Name               Status     Vlan       Level  Duplex Speed Type
----  ------------------ ---------- ---------- ------ ------ ------------------
 4/1                     shutdown   1          normal   full   100 100BaseFX MM

Port  Security Secure-Src-Addr    Last-Src-Addr     Shutdown Trap       IfIndex
----  -------- -----------------  ----------------  ----------------  --------
 4/1  enabled  00-00-0c-3f-12-34 00-50-0b-74-e8-c0 Yes      disabled 27

Port      Broadcast-Limit Broadcast-Drop
----      ------------------------------
 4/1                    -             0

Port   Send FlowControl    Receive FlowControl   RxPause TxPause Unsupported
       admin    oper       admin    oper                         opcodes
-----  ----- ------------  ------- ------------- ------- ------- -----------
 4/1   off      off        on       on           0       0       0

Port  Status     Channel    Channel     Neighbor                     Neighbor
                 mode       status      device                       port
----  ---------- ---------  ----------  ------------------------   --------
 4/1  shutdown   auto       not channel

Port  Align-Err  FCS-Err    Xmit-Err   Rcv-Err    UnderSize
----  ---------  -------    ---------  -------    ---------
 4/1          0     5590            0        0            0

Port  Single-Col Multi-Coll Late-Coll  Excess-Col Carri-Sen Runts     Giants
----  ---------- ---------- ---------  ---------- --------- --------- -------
 4/1           0          0         0           0         0         0        0
Last-Time-Cleared
-----------------
Fri Apr 21 2000, 13:59:31
Console> (enable)
```

Listing 12-43

More Switched Ethernet Troubleshooting Scenarios

Problem Definition

The 100-Mbps server FSERV connects to a port on switch CatA. No clients on the CatB switch can attach to this server, while clients on CatA experience very slow response. FSERV's MAC address is 00-e0-1e-60-2a-bf. Please note that while a schematic diagram for the two

```
Console> (enable) set port security 4/1 disable
Port 4/1 port security disabled.
Console> (enable) sh port 4/1
Port  Name                Status     Vlan       Level  Duplex Speed Type
----  ------------------  ---------  ---------- ------ ------ ----------------
 4/1                      connected  1          normal   full   100 100BaseFX MM

Port  Security Secure-Src-Addr    Last-Src-Addr     Shutdown Trap     IfIndex
----  -------- -----------------  -------------     -------- -------- -------
 4/1  disabled                                      No       disabled 27

Port     Broadcast-Limit Broadcast-Drop
----     --------------------------------
 4/1                   -              0

Port   Send FlowControl    Receive FlowControl   RxPause TxPause Unsupported
       admin   oper        admin    oper                          opcodes
-----  ----- ----------    -------- ----------   ------- ------- -----------
 4/1   off     off         on       on           0       0       0

Port  Status     Channel   Channel     Neighbor                   Neighbor
                 mode      status      device                     port
----  ---------  -------   ----------- -------                    --------
 4/1  connected  auto      not channel

Port  Align-Err  FCS-Err    Xmit-Err   Rcv-Err    UnderSize
----  ---------  -------    --------   -------    ---------
 4/1          0     5592           0          0           0

Port  Single-Col Multi-Coll Late-Coll  Excess-Col Carri-Sen Runts     Giants
----  ---------- ---------- ---------  ---------- ----------------- ------
 4/1           0          0          0          0         0      0         0
Last-Time-Cleared
-----------------
Fri Apr 21 2000, 13:59:31
Console> (enable) 04/26/2000,16:19:14:PAGP-5:Port 4/1 joined bridge port 4/1.
```

Listing 12-44

```
Console> (enable) set port security 4/1 enable 00-50-0b-74-e8-c0
Port 4/1 port security enabled with 00-50-0b-74-e8-c0 as the secure mac address
Console> (enable) ping 172.16.254.11
172.16.254.11 is alive
Console>
```

Listing 12-45

```
R7>ping 172.16.254.254

Type escape sequence to abort.
Sending 5, 100-byte ICMP Echos to 172.16.254.254, timeout is 2 seconds:
!!!!!
Success rate is 100 percent (5/5), round-trip min/avg/max = 1/1/4 ms
R7>telnet 172.16.254.254
Trying 172.16.254.254 ... Open
Access not permitted. Closing connection...

[Connection to 172.16.254.254 closed by foreign host]
R7>
```

Listing 12-46

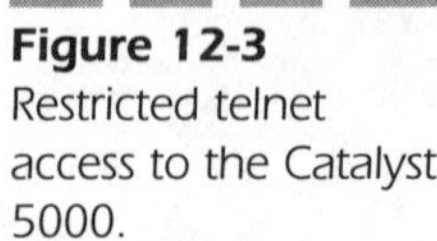

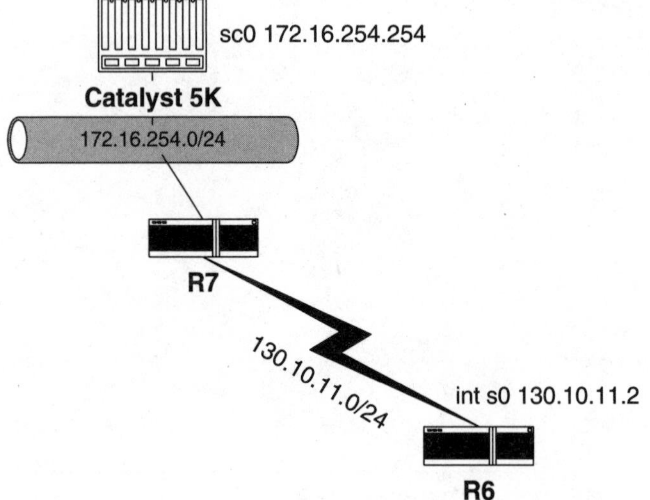

Figure 12-3 Restricted telnet access to the Catalyst 5000.

switches is shown in Figure 12-4, it is an important troubleshooting skill to be capable of constructing your own diagram using the tools on the routers and switches. In the real world, an accurate network diagram is not always at hand!

The most pressing problem is the inability of any users on CatB to attach to the server, so let's attempt to solve that first. A good starting point is to check the trunking between the two switches (see Listing 12-49).

```
r6#ping 172.16.254.254
Type escape sequence to abort.
Sending 5, 100-byte ICMP Echos to 172.16.254.254, timeout is 2 seconds:
!!!!!
Success rate is 100 percent (5/5), round-trip min/avg/max = 40/44/64 ms
r6#telnet 172.16.254.254
Trying 172.16.254.254 ... Open

Cisco Systems Console

Enter password:
-Console> en
Enter password:
Console> (enable)
```

Listing 12-47

Listing 12-48

```
Console> (enable) set ip permit 130.10.11.2
130.10.11.2 added to IP permit list.
Console> (enable) set ip permit enable
IP permit list enabled.
Console> (enable)

Console> (enable) sh ip permit
IP permit list feature enabled.
Permit List         Mask
----------------    ----
130.10.11.2

Denied IP Address   Last Accessed Time    Type
-----------------   ------------------    ----
Console> (enable)
```

The trunk configuration on CatB appears normal. Now let us check CatA (see Listing 12-50).

What is noticeable here is that there is a VLAN 99 active that is not allowed on the trunk to the CatB switch. We see that ports 10/1-6 are in VLAN 99 on the CatA switch. The next question is whether the FSERV server is one of these ports (see Listing 12-51).

Using the `show cam` command for FSERV's MAC address, it can be seen that this server is attached to port 10/4 and hence is in VLAN 99. This should explain the connectivity problem from CatB. (See Listing 12-52.)

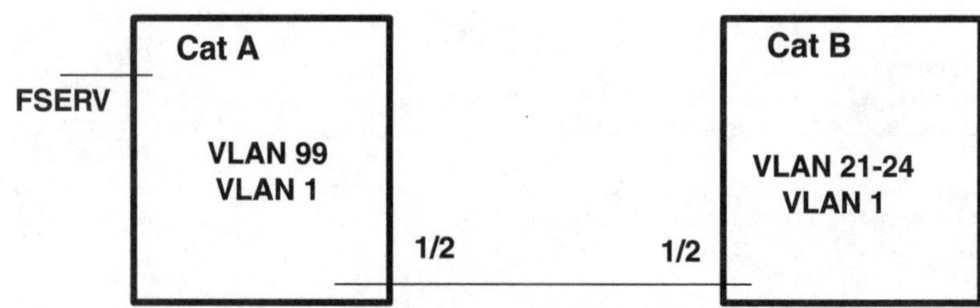

Figure 12-4 Interswitch troubleshooting scenario.

Listing 12-49

```
CatB> (enable) show trunk 1/2
Port      Mode         Encapsulation  Status        Native vlan
--------  -----------  -------------  ------------  -----------
 1/2      desirable    isl            trunking      1
Port      Vlans allowed on trunk
--------  ---------------------
 1/2      1-1005
Port      Vlans allowed and active in management domain
--------  -------------------------------------------------------
 1/2      1,21-24
Port      Vlans in spanning tree forwarding state and not pruned
--------  -------------------------------------------------------
 1/2      1,21-24
CatB> (enable)
```

Listing 12-50

```
CatA> (enable) show trunk 1/2
Port      Mode         Encapsulation  Status        Native vlan
--------  ---------    -------------  --------      -----------
 1/2      desirable    isl            trunking      1
Port      Vlans allowed on trunk
--------  ---------------------
 1/2      1-25
Port      Vlans allowed and active in management domain
--------  -------------------------------------------------------
 1/2      1,99,21-24
Port      Vlans in spanning tree forwarding state and not pruned
--------  -------------------------------------------------------
 1/2      1,21-24
CatA> (enable)
```

By adding VLAN 99 to the allowed list for the trunk between CatA and CatB, it should now appear in CatB's VLAN table. What command would you use on CatB to verify this?

Now let's investigate the slow-response problem experienced by local clients on CatA. Let's look at the switch port that the server connects to for more clues (see Listing 12-53).

```
CatA> (enable) sh vlan 99
VLAN Name                             Status    IfIndex Mod/Ports, Vlans
---- -------------------------------- --------- ------- --------------------
----
99   VLAN0099                         active    92      10/1-6

VLAN Type  SAID       MTU   Parent RingNo BrdgNo Stp  BrdgMode Trans1 Trans2
---- ----- ---------- ----- ------ ------ ------ ---- -------- ------ ------
99   enet  100099     1500  -      -      -      -    -        0      0

VLAN AREHops STEHops Backup CRF
---- ------- ------- ----------
CatA> (enable)
```

Listing 12-51

```
CatA> (enable) sh cam 00-e0-1e-60-2a-bf
* = Static Entry. + = Permanent Entry. # = System Entry. R = Router Entry. X = P
ort Security Entry

VLAN  Dest MAC/Route Des  Destination Ports or VCs / [Protocol Type]
----  ------------------  ----------------------------------------
----
1     00-e0-1e-60-2a-bf   10/4 [ALL]
Total Matching CAM Entries Displayed = 1

CatA> (enable) set trunk 1/2 99
Adding vlans 99 to allowed list.
Port(s) 1/2 allowed vlans modified to 1-25,99.
CatA> (enable)
```

Listing 12-52

The server, when checked, is seen to be configured for full duplex. The autonegotiation between the switch port and the server therefore has not worked properly. Also, the speed has been autonegotiated to 10 Mbps, whereas both the server and the switch can support 100 Mbps. This reduced speed, along with the duplex mismatch, would both contribute to slow response times from the server (see Listing 12-54).

When configuring the port for full duplex, remember to first set the speed to 100 in order to bring the port out of autosensing mode.

```
CatA> (enable) sh port 10/4
Port  Name               Status     Vlan       Level  Duplex Speed Type
----  ------------------ ---------  ---------  ------------------------------
----
10/4                     connected  1          normal a-half  a-10 10/100BaseTX

Port  Security Secure-Src-Addr   Last-Src-Addr     Shutdown Trap      IfIndex
----  ------------------------   ----------------  -------------      -------
10/4  disabled                                     No       disabled  54

Port     Broadcast-Limit Broadcast-Drop
-------  ------------------------------
10/4                   -              0

Port  Status     Channel   Channel     Neighbor                   Neighbor
                 mode      status      device                     port
----  ---------  --------  ----------  -------------------------  -----------
10/4  connected  auto      not channel

Port  Align-Err  FCS-Err    Xmit-Err   Rcv-Err    UnderSize
----  ---------  -------    --------   -------    ---------
10/4          9        0           0         0            0

Port  Single-Col Multi-Coll Late-Coll  Excess-Col Carri-Sen Runts     Giants
----  ---------- ---------- ---------  ---------- --------- --------  ------
----
10/4      148908      81064       911           0         0        3       0

Last-Time-Cleared
-----------------
Tue May 11 1999, 12:14:59
CatA> (enable)
```

Listing 12-53

Listing 12-54

```
CatA> (enable) set port duplex 10/4 full
Port 10/4 is in auto-sensing mode.
CatA> (enable) set port speed 10/4 100
Port(s) 10/4 speed set to 100Mbps.
CatA> (enable) set port duplex 10/4 full
Port(s) 10/4 set to full-duplex.
CatA> (enable)
```

REVIEW QUESTIONS

For the exercises that are multiple-choice questions, there is only one correct answer unless the question is marked with an asterisk (*). Choose the most suitable answer.

1. A switch port provides
   a. separate collision domains.
   b. separate broadcast domains.
   c. separate subnets.
   d. a, b, and c.
   e. none of the above.
2. A VLAN provides
   a. separate collision domains.
   b. separate broadcast domains.
   c. separate subnets.
   d. a, b, and c.
   e. b and c.
3. Traffic passing between VLANs must be
   a. bridged.
   b. switched.
   c. routed.
   d. filtered.
4. Which of the following commands disables VTP?
   a. `set vtp disable`
   b. `set vtp domain cisco disable`
   c. `set vtp domain cisco mode client`
   d. `set vtp domain cisco mode transparent`
   e. `clear vtp domain cisco mode server`
5. Type the configuration that enables port 6/1 to mirror traffic switched through ports 4/6 and 4/7.
6. A trunk that is set to *Auto* will form a trunk with a corresponding port that is set to
   a. *Auto*.
   b. *Desirable*.

c. *On*.

d. *On/Desirable*.

e. *On/Desirable/Auto*.

7. A channel port that is set to *Auto* will form a channel with a corresponding port that is set to

a. *Auto*.

b. *Desirable*.

c. *On*.

d. *On/Desirable*.

e. *On/Desirable/Auto*.

8. Type an appropriate configuration that allows all VLANs except VLAN 30 to be extended across ISL trunk port 1/1.

9. Type the command that will ensure that the switch is the spanning-tree root for VLAN 21.

10. A new switch is connected on a segment that includes a DHCP server. How can the switch be configured to prevent it from dynamically obtaining an IP address?

11. What error will be indicated if the following configuration is attempted?

```
Set vtp domain cisco mode client
Set vlan 2 4/1-6
```

12. A switch that does not contain an RSM can support the following types of routing.

a. Default gateway

b. Static routes

c. EIGRP and OSPF

d. a, b, and c

e. a and b

13. A switch that does contain an RSM can support the following types of routing.

a. Default gateway

b. Static routes

c. EIGRP and OSPF

d. a, b, and c

e. a and b

14. A duplex mismatch will cause

a. loss of line protocol.

b. dropped packets.

c. excessive collisions.

d. a, b, and c.

e. b and c.

15. An Ethernet speed mismatch will cause

a. loss of line protocol.

b. dropped packets.

c. excessive collisions.

d. a, b, and c.

e. b and c.

***16.** Which of the following commands will verify if line protocol is up on port 5/2?

a. `show interface 5/2`

b. `show port 5/2`

c. `show port`

d. `show port capabilities 5/2`

e. `show interface`

17. What command will indicate how much Flash memory, DRAM, and NVRAM are loaded on the Catalyst 5000?

a. `show memory`

b. `show system`

c. `show module`

d. `show version`

e. All of the above

***18.** The Cisco TAC is requesting the serial number of a supervisor module in order to issue a replacement. Which command can you use?

a. `show memory`

b. `show system`

c. `show module`

d. `show version`

e. All of the above

19. A particular station is exhibiting very slow response. You know the station's MAC address, but you need to find out the switch port to which it connects. Which command do you use?

a. `show port`

b. `show mac`

c. `show cam dynamic`

d. `show cam static`

e. `show interface`

***20.** You find that the station connects to port 4/5. You now want to check that port for activity and error information. Which commands do you use?

a. `show port 4/5`

b. `show mac 4/5`

c. `show test 4/5`

d. `show interface`

e. `show netstat 4/5`

CHAPTER 13

Laboratory Exercises

Introduction

For each of the troubleshooting scenarios in this chapter, build an equivalent network using your own laboratory facilities. Load the given configurations (which have faults inserted) for each of the routers. Then begin the troubleshooting process based on the information relayed at the start of each exercise. To obtain the best benefit from these exercises, use as many router diagnostic tools as possible and only look at the configurations when you feel that you have no other choice. If limitations on your laboratory facilities mean that the network cannot be replicated exactly, then try to improvise to create a network that is close in principle. In the absence of any laboratory facilities, you can work through the configurations and attempt to spot faults. Although this is a very useful exercise, obviously it will not provide the benefits of a hands-on approach.

The objectives of this chapter are to

- Allow you to practice troubleshooting for some of the main technologies studied in this book.
- Enable you to gauge the level of your present skill set.

Exercise 1: Router Disaster Recovery

While troubleshooting a reported network fault, the router R4 was indicating a problem. From the output of `show version` and `show flash` (see Listing 13-1) diagnose the problem. Ideally, you should attempt to replicate the problem and solution in a laboratory.

There is a TFTP server on the token-ring 0 segment to which R4 attaches. The token-ring 1 interface has now been shut down, along with R4's serial interfaces. The server contains the image "c4000-j-mz.112-18.bin." How can it be used to solve the problem?

As an additional exercise, research how a Cisco router can be used as a TFTP server, and use this feature in your laboratory to restore R4's image.

```
r4(boot)#sh ver
4000 Bootstrap Software (XX-RXBOOT), Version 9.14(9), RELEASE SOFTWARE (fc1)
Patchlevel = 9.1(12.6)
Copyright (c) 1986-1994 by cisco Systems, Inc.
Compiled Wed 28-Sep-94 14:28 by chansen

System Bootstrap, Version 4.14(9), SOFTWARE

r4 uptime is 0 minutes
System restarted by reload
Running default software

cisco 4000 (68030) processor (revision 0xA0) with 16384K/4096K bytes of memory.
Processor ID 5011111
DDN X.25 software, Version 2.0, NET2 and BFE compliant.
2 Token Ring/IEEE 802.5 interfaces.
4 Serial network interfaces.
128K bytes of non-volatile configuration memory.

4096K bytes of processor board System flash (Read/Write)
Configuration register is 0x2101

r4(boot)#sh flas

No files on System flash
[0 bytes used, 4194304 available, 4194304 total]
4096K bytes of processor board System flash (Read/Write)

r4(boot)#
```

Listing 13-1

Exercise 2: IGRP/EIGRP Routing Problem Scenario

On the network shown in Figure 13-1, the following policies are to be implemented:

- Traffic crossing between the IGRP and EIGRP domains should prefer R2 instead of R3 in both directions.
- The 100.0.0.0 should get summarized as a single external route within the EIGRP domain.
- Security policy dictates that 10.129.17.0 and 10.129.18.0 should appear as explicit networks in order to have different policies applied to them.

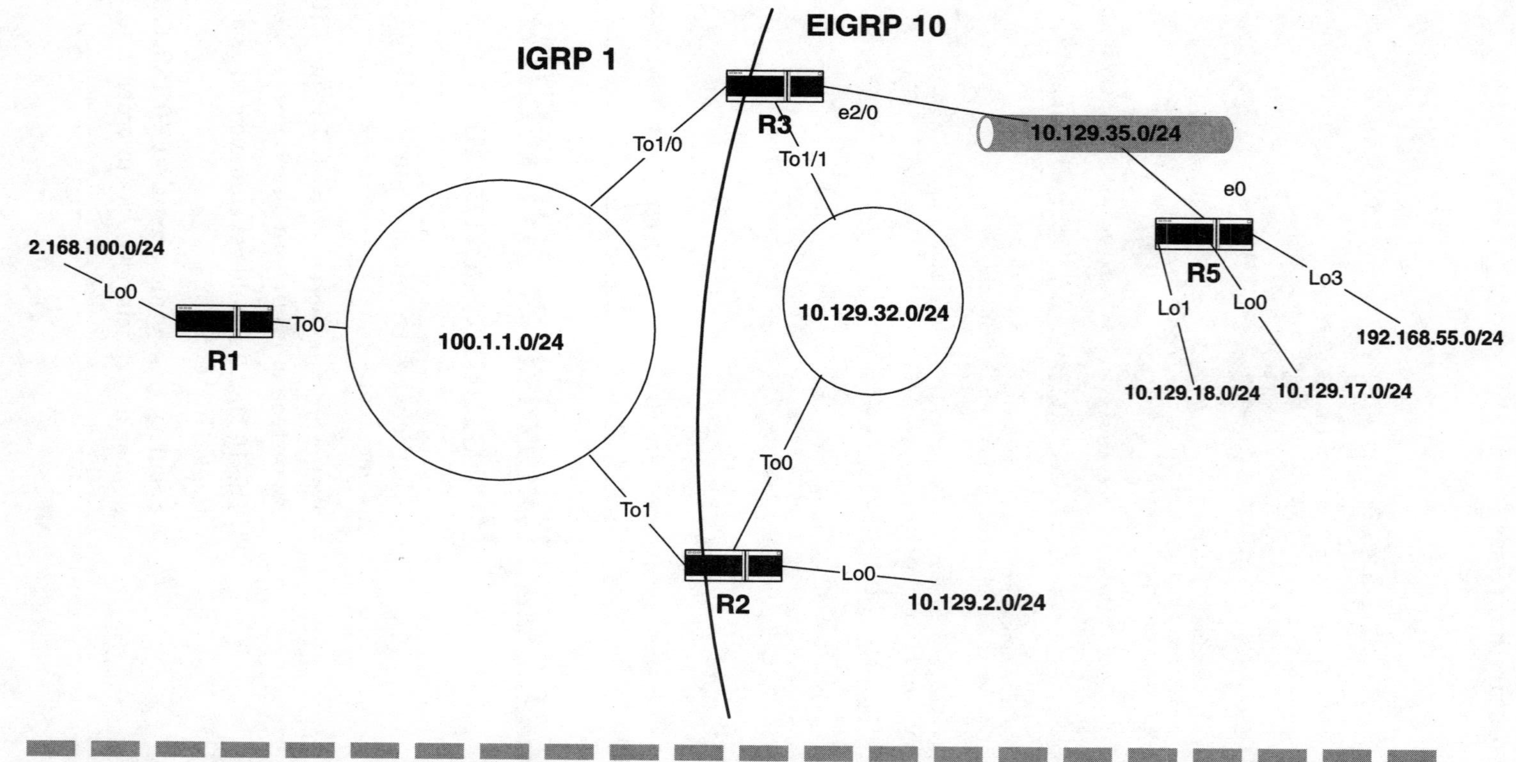

Figure 13.1 IGRP/EIGRP network for Exercise 2.

Build the network with the configurations shown in Listings 13-2 through 13-4 and see if these policies are being satisfied.

For this network, since some of the routing issues are quite involved, I also will display the routing tables (Listings 13-5 through 13-8) that you should see with the preceding configurations.

```
r1#sh run
Building configuration...

Current configuration:
!
version 11.0
service timestamps debug datetime
service timestamps log datetime
service udp-small-servers
service tcp-small-servers
!
hostname r1
!
enable password cisco
!
interface Loopback0
 ip address 192.168.100.1 255.255.255.0
!
interface Loopback1
 ip address 100.2.2.1 255.255.255.0
!
interface TokenRing0
 ip address 100.1.1.1 255.255.255.0
 ring-speed 16
!
interface TokenRing1
 no ip address
 shutdown
!
router igrp 1
 network 100.0.0.0
 network 192.168.100.0
!
logging buffered
!
line con 0
line aux 0
 transport input all
line vty 0 4
 password cisco
 login
!
end
```

Listing 13-2

```
r2#sh run
Building configuration...

Current configuration:
!
version 11.0
service udp-small-servers
service tcp-small-servers
!
hostname r2
!
enable password cisco
!
interface Loopback0
 ip address 10.129.2.2 255.255.255.0
!
interface Serial1
 no ip address
 shutdown
!
interface TokenRing0
 ip address 10.129.32.2 255.255.255.0
 ring-speed 16
!
interface TokenRing1
 ip address 100.1.1.2 255.255.255.0
 ring-speed 16
!
router eigrp 10
 redistribute igrp 1 metric 100 100000 255 1 1500
 network 10.0.0.0
!
router igrp 1
 redistribute eigrp 10 metric 100 100000 255 1 1500
 network 100.0.0.0
 distance 210
!
logging buffered
!
!
line con 0
line aux 0
 transport input all
line vty 0 4
 password cisco
 login
!
end
r3#sh run
Building configuration...

Current configuration:
!
```

Listing 13-3

```
version 11.2
service timestamps debug datetime
service timestamps log datetime
!
hostname r3
!
enable password cisco
!
!
interface TokenRing1/0
 ip address 100.1.1.3 255.255.255.0
 ring-speed 16
!
interface TokenRing1/1
 ip address 10.129.32.3 255.255.255.0
 ring-speed 16
!
interface TokenRing1/2
 no ip address
 shutdown
 ring-speed 16
!
interface TokenRing1/3
 no ip address
 shutdown
 ring-speed 16
!
interface Ethernet2/0
 ip address 10.129.35.3 255.255.255.0
!
router eigrp 10
 redistribute igrp 1 metric 10000 100 255 1 1500
 network 10.0.0.0
!
router igrp 1
 redistribute eigrp 10 metric 10000 100 255 1 1500
 network 100.0.0.0
!
no ip classless
!
line con 0
line aux 0
line vty 0 4
 password cisco
 login
!
end
```

Listing 13-3 ***(Cont.)***

```
r5#sh run
Building configuration...

Current configuration:
!
version 11.0
service udp-small-servers
service tcp-small-servers
!
hostname r5
!
enable password cisco
!
interface Loopback0
 ip address 10.129.17.5 255.255.255.0
!
interface Loopback1
 ip address 10.129.18.5 255.255.255.0
!
interface Loopback3
 ip address 192.168.55.5 255.255.255.0
!
interface Ethernet0
 ip address 10.129.35.5 255.255.255.0
 ip summary-address eigrp 10 10.129.16.0 255.255.248.0
 media-type 10BaseT
!
interface Ethernet1
 no ip address
 shutdown
!
router eigrp 10
 network 10.0.0.0
 network 192.168.55.0
!
logging buffered
!
!
!
!
!
line con 0
line aux 0
 transport input all
line vty 0 4
 password cisco
 login
!
end
```

Listing 13-4

```
r1#sh ip route
Codes: C - connected, S - static, I - IGRP, R - RIP, M - mobile, B - BGP
       D - EIGRP, EX - EIGRP external, O - OSPF, IA - OSPF inter area
       E1 - OSPF external type 1, E2 - OSPF external type 2, E - EGP
       i - IS-IS, L1 - IS-IS level-1, L2 - IS-IS level-2, * - candidate default

Gateway of last resort is not set

I    10.0.0.0 [100/751] via 100.1.1.3, 00:00:26, TokenRing0
C    192.168.100.0 is directly connected, Loopback0
I    192.168.55.0 [100/1663] via 100.1.1.3, 00:00:26, TokenRing0
     100.0.0.0 255.255.255.0 is subnetted, 2 subnets
C       100.1.1.0 is directly connected, TokenRing0
C       100.2.2.0 is directly connected, Loopback1
r1#
```

Listing 13-5

```
r2#sh ip rou
Codes: C - connected, S - static, I - IGRP, R - RIP, M - mobile, B - BGP
       D - EIGRP, EX - EIGRP external, O - OSPF, IA - OSPF inter area
       E1 - OSPF external type 1, E2 - OSPF external type 2, E - EGP
       i - IS-IS, L1 - IS-IS level-1, L2 - IS-IS level-2, * - candidate default

Gateway of last resort is not set

     10.0.0.0 is variably subnetted, 5 subnets, 3 masks
D EX    10.0.0.0 255.0.0.0 [170/320256] via 10.129.32.3, 01:35:12, TokenRing0
C       10.129.2.0 255.255.255.0 is directly connected, Loopback0
D       10.129.16.0 255.255.248.0
           [90/425728] via 10.129.32.3, 00:05:12, TokenRing0
D      10.129.35.0 255.255.255.0
           [90/297728] via 10.129.32.3, 01:35:12, TokenRing0
C       10.129.32.0 255.255.255.0 is directly connected, TokenRing0
D EX 192.168.100.0 [170/320256] via 10.129.32.3, 01:35:12, TokenRing0
D    192.168.55.0 [90/425728] via 10.129.32.3, 00:05:12, TokenRing0
     100.0.0.0 255.255.255.0 is subnetted, 2 subnets
D EX    100.2.2.0 [170/320256] via 10.129.32.3, 00:07:38, TokenRing0
C       100.1.1.0 is directly connected, TokenRing1
r2#
```

Listing 13-6

```
r3#sh ip rou
Codes: C - connected, S - static, I - IGRP, R - RIP, M - mobile, B - BGP
       D - EIGRP, EX - EIGRP external, O - OSPF, IA - OSPF inter area
       N1 - OSPF NSSA external type 1, N2 - OSPF NSSA external type 2
       E1 - OSPF external type 1, E2 - OSPF external type 2, E - EGP
       i - IS-IS, L1 - IS-IS level-1, L2 - IS-IS level-2, * - candidate default
       U - per-user static route, o - ODR

Gateway of last resort is not set

     10.0.0.0/8 is variably subnetted, 5 subnets, 3 masks
I       10.0.0.0/8 [100/1188] via 100.1.1.2, 00:00:04, TokenRing1/0
D       10.129.2.0/24 [90/304128] via 10.129.32.2, 00:05:59, TokenRing1/1
D       10.129.16.0/21 [90/409600] via 10.129.35.5, 00:05:59, Ethernet2/0
C       10.129.35.0/24 is directly connected, Ethernet2/0
C       10.129.32.0/24 is directly connected, TokenRing1/1
I    192.168.100.0/24 [100/1188] via 100.1.1.1, 00:00:44, TokenRing1/0
D    192.168.55.0/24 [90/409600] via 10.129.35.5, 00:05:59, Ethernet2/0
     100.0.0.0/24 is subnetted, 2 subnets
I       100.2.2.0 [100/1188] via 100.1.1.1, 00:00:44, TokenRing1/0
C       100.1.1.0 is directly connected, TokenRing1/0
r3#
```

Listing 13-7

```
r5#sh ip ro
Codes: C - connected, S - static, I - IGRP, R - RIP, M - mobile, B - BGP
       D - EIGRP, EX - EIGRP external, O - OSPF, IA - OSPF inter area
       E1 - OSPF external type 1, E2 - OSPF external type 2, E - EGP
       i - IS-IS, L1 - IS-IS level-1, L2 - IS-IS level-2, * - candidate default

Gateway of last resort is not set

     10.0.0.0 is variably subnetted, 7 subnets, 3 masks
D       10.0.0.0 255.0.0.0 is a summary, 00:06:44, Null0
D       10.129.2.0 255.255.255.0
           [90/425728] via 10.129.35.3, 00:06:44, Ethernet0
C       10.129.18.0 255.255.255.0 is directly connected, Loopback1
C       10.129.17.0 255.255.255.0 is directly connected, Loopback0
D       10.129.16.0 255.255.248.0 is a summary, 00:06:44, Null0
C       10.129.35.0 255.255.255.0 is directly connected, Ethernet0
D       10.129.32.0 255.255.255.0
           [90/297728] via 10.129.35.3, 00:06:44, Ethernet0
D EX 192.168.100.0 [170/425728] via 10.129.35.3, 00:06:44, Ethernet0
C    192.168.55.0 is directly connected, Loopback3
     100.0.0.0 255.255.255.0 is subnetted, 2 subnets
D EX    100.1.1.0 [170/281600] via 10.129.35.3, 00:06:44, Ethernet0
D EX    100.2.2.0 [170/425728] via 10.129.35.3, 00:06:44, Ethernet0
r5#
```

Listing 13-8

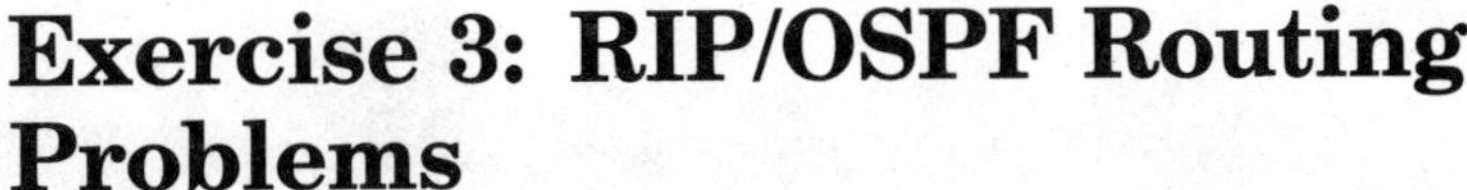

Exercise 3: RIP/OSPF Routing Problems

Build the network shown in Figure 13-2. Use the four sets of configurations given (Listings 13-9 through 13-12). On this network, all routes should be redistributed across the routers in the OSPF 10 and RIP domains. All RIP-originating routes should be visible to each of the OSPF routers. Conversely, all OSPF routes should be available within the RIP domain. From any router you should be able to ping each interface on all the other three routers. You also should be able to telnet into each of the routers using the in-band network connectivity.

After configuring the routers with the given configurations, diagnose and resolve 10 network faults.

Note also that if you are not already familiar with how to configure a router as a frame-relay switch, you will have to research this in the Cisco IOS configuration guide.

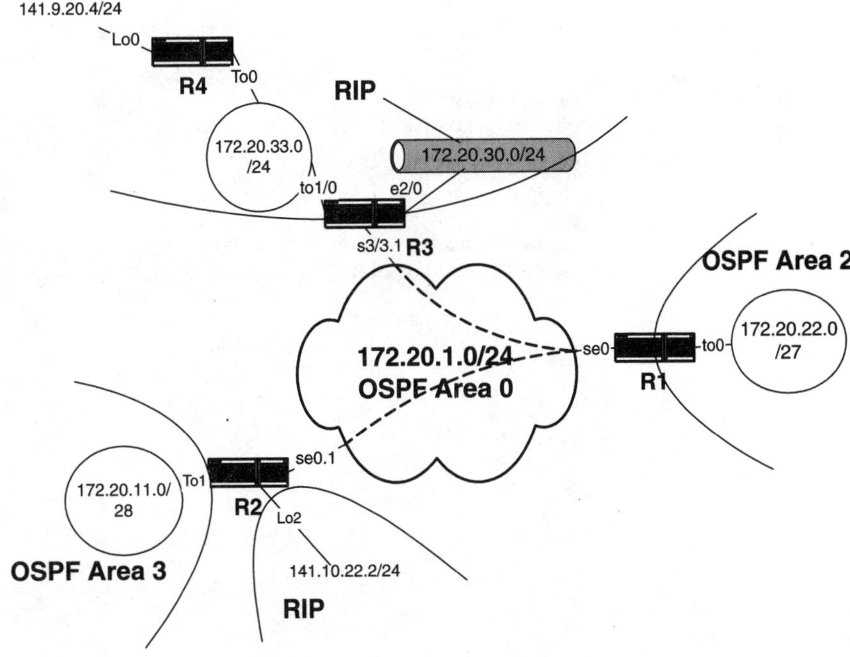

Figure 13-2 RIP/OSPF network for Exercise 3.

Listing 13-9

```
r1#sh run
Building configuration...

Current configuration:
!
version 11.2
no service password-encryption
no service udp-small-servers
no service tcp-small-servers
!
hostname r1
!
enable password cisco
!
!
interface Serial0
 ip address 172.20.1.1 255.255.255.0
 encapsulation frame-relay
 ip ospf message-digest-key 1 md5 ospf
 ip ospf network broadcast
 ip ospf priority 100
 no fair-queue
 frame-relay map ip 172.20.1.2 102 broadcast
 frame-relay map ip 172.20.1.3 103 broadcast
 frame-relay lmi-type ansi
!
interface Serial1
 no ip address
 shutdown
!
interface TokenRing0
 ip address 172.20.22.1 255.255.255.224
 ring-speed 16
!
interface TokenRing1
 no ip address
 shutdown
!
router ospf 10
 network 172.20.1.0 0.0.0.255 area 0
 network 172.20.22.0 0.0.0.255 area 2
 area 0 authentication message-digest
!
no ip classless
!
!
line con 0
line aux 0
line vty 0 4
 password cisco
 login
!
end
```

Listing 13-10

```
r2#sh run
Building configuration...

Current configuration:
!
version 11.2
no service password-encryption
no service udp-small-servers
no service tcp-small-servers
!
hostname r2
!
enable password cisco
!
!
interface Loopback2
 ip address 141.10.22.2 255.255.255.0
!
interface Serial0
 no ip address
 encapsulation frame-relay
 no fair-queue
 frame-relay lmi-type ansi
!
interface Serial0.1 point-to-point
 ip address 172.20.1.2 255.255.255.0
 ip ospf message-digest-key 1 md5 cisco
 ip ospf network point-to-multipoint
 frame-relay interface-dlci 201
!
interface Serial1
 no ip address
 shutdown
!

 no ip address
 shutdown
!
interface TokenRing1
 ip address 172.20.11.2 255.255.255.240
 ring-speed 16
!
router ospf 10
 summary-address 141.8.0.0 255.248.0.0
 redistribute rip metric 50 subnets
 network 172.20.1.0 0.0.0.255 area 0
 network 172.20.11.0 0.0.0.255 area 3
 area 0 authentication message-digest
 area 3 range 172.20.11.0 255.255.255.192
!

 router rip
 network 141.10.0.0
!
```

Listing 13-10 (Cont.)

```
no ip classless
!
!
line con 0
line aux 0
line vty 0 4
 password cisco
 login
!
end

r2#
```

Listing 13-11

```
r3#sh run
Building configuration...

Current configuration:
!
version 11.2
!
hostname r3
!
enable password cisco
!
!
interface TokenRing1/0
 ip address 172.20.33.3 255.255.255.0
 ring-speed 16
!
interface Ethernet2/0
 ip address 172.20.30.3 255.255.255.0
!
interface Serial3/3
 no ip address
 encapsulation frame-relay
 frame-relay lmi-type ansi
!
interface Serial3/3.1 point-to-point
 ip address 172.20.1.3 255.255.255.0
 ip ospf message-digest-key 1 md5 cisco
 ip ospf network broadcast
 ip ospf hello-interval 4
 ip ospf priority 250
 frame-relay interface-dlci 301
!
router ospf 10
 summary-address 141.8.0.0 255.248.0.0
 redistribute rip metric 100 route-map rip-os
 network 172.20.1.0 0.0.0.255 area 0
 area 0 authentication message-digest
!
```

Listing 13-11 (*Cont.*)

```
router rip
 version 2
 redistribute ospf 10 route-map os-rip
 network 172.20.0.0
 default-metric 2
!
no ip classless
access-list 1 permit 141.8.0.0 0.0.0.255
access-list 2 permit any
access-list 3 permit 172.20.33.0 0.0.0.255
route-map os-rip deny 10
 match ip address 1
!
route-map os-rip permit 20
 match ip address 2
!
route-map rip-os permit 27
 match ip address 1
!
route-map rip-os permit 28
 match ip address 3
!
!
!
line con 0
line aux 0
line vty 0
 exec-timeout 0 1
 password cisco
 login
 length 0
line vty 1 4
 exec-timeout 0 1
 password cisco
 login
!
end
```

Listing 13-12

```
r4#sh run
Building configuration...

Current configuration:
!
version 11.2
service password-encryption
no service udp-small-servers
no service tcp-small-servers
!
hostname r4
!
enable password 7 060506324F41
!
!
interface Loopback0
 ip address 141.9.20.4 255.255.255.0
!
interface TokenRing0
 ip address 172.20.33.4 255.255.255.0
 ip rip receive version 1
 ring-speed 16
!
router rip
 version 2
 network 172.20.0.0
 network 141.9.0.0
!
no ip classless
!
!
line con 0
line aux 0
line vty 0 4
 password 7 045802150C2E
 login
!
end
r4#
```

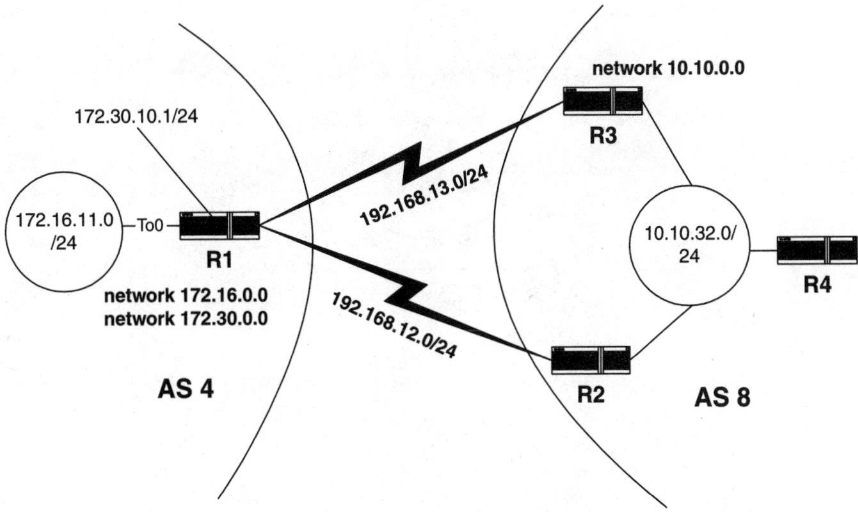

Figure 13-3 BGP network for Exercise 4.

Exercise 4: BGP Routing Problem Scenario

The network shown in Figure 13-3 has the following requirements and policies for BGP routing:

1. R3 and R2 are not to be peered together.
2. Traffic leaving AS8 destined for 172.x.y.0 should do so via R3.
3. Traffic entering AS8 from AS4 should do so via R2.
4. R1 is distributing 172.16.0.0 and 172.30.10.0 into BGP4. R3 is distributing 10.10.0.0 into BGP 8. These routes should appear in the IP routing table of all four routers.
5. It is *not* required to distribute the 192.168.x.0 networks into BGP.

Set up the network using the configurations given (Listings 13-13 through 13-16). Then diagnose and resolve 10 faults relating to BGP routing, connectivity, and policy.

Listing 13-13

```
r1#

sh run
Building configuration...

Current configuration:
!
version 11.2
service password-encryption
no service udp-small-servers
no service tcp-small-servers
!
hostname r1
!
enable password 7 045802150C2E
!
!
interface Loopback0
 ip address 172.30.10.1 255.255.255.0
!
interface Serial0
 ip address 192.168.12.1 255.255.255.0
 no fair-queue
 clockrate 56000
!
interface Serial1
 ip address 192.168.13.1 255.255.255.0
 clockrate 56000
!
interface TokenRing0
 ip address 172.16.11.1 255.255.255.0
 ring-speed 16
!
interface TokenRing1
 no ip address
 shutdown
!
router rip
 network 172.30.0.0
!
router bgp 4
 network 172.16.0.0
 network 172.30.10.0 mask 255.255.255.0
 neighbor 10.10.32.2 remote-as 8
 neighbor 192.168.13.3 remote-as 8
 neighbor 192.168.13.3 distribute-list 1 out
!
no ip classless
access-list 1 permit 172.16.0.0 0.0.255.255
!
line con 0
line aux 0
line vty 0 4
 password 7 01100F175804
 login
!
end
```

Listing 13-14

```
r2#sh run
Building configuration...

Current configuration:
!
version 11.2
service password-encryption
no service udp-small-servers
no service tcp-small-servers
!
hostname r2
!
enable password 7 00071A150754
!
!
interface Serial0
 ip address 192.168.12.2 255.255.255.0
 no fair-queue
!
interface Serial1
 no ip address
 shutdown
!
interface TokenRing0
 ip address 10.10.32.2 255.255.255.0
 ring-speed 16
!
interface TokenRing1
 no ip address
 shutdown
!
router bgp 8
 neighbor 10.10.32.4 remote-as 8
 neighbor 192.168.12.1 remote-as 4
 neighbor 192.168.12.1 route-map setloc in
 neighbor 192.168.12.1 route-map setmetric out
 neighbor 192.168.12.1 filter-list 9 out
!
no ip classless
ip as-path access-list 9 deny ^$
ip as-path access-list 9 permit .*
access-list 2 permit 10.0.0.0 0.255.255.255
route-map setloc permit 192
 set local-preference 150
!
route-map setmetric permit 10
 match ip address 2
 set metric 20
!
!
!
line con 0
line aux 0
line vty 0 4
 password 7 14141B180F0B
 login
!
end
```

Listing 13-15

```
r3#sh run
Building configuration...

Current configuration:
!
version 11.2
service password-encryption
!
hostname r3
!
enable password 7 14141B180F0B
!
!
interface TokenRing1/0
 ip address 10.10.32.3 255.255.255.0
 ring-speed 16
!
interface Serial3/3
 ip address 192.168.13.3 255.255.255.0
!
router bgp 8
 network 10.10.0.0
 neighbor 10.10.32.4 remote-as 8
 neighbor 192.168.13.1 remote-as 4
 neighbor 192.168.13.1 route-map setlocal in
!
no ip classless
route-map setlocal permit 10
 set local-preference 50
!
!
!
line con 0
 exec-timeout 0 0
line aux 0
line vty 0 4
 password 7 14141B180F0B
 login
!
end
```

Listing 13-16

```
r4#sh run
Building configuration...

Current configuration:
!
version 11.2
service password-encryption
no service udp-small-servers
no service tcp-small-servers
!
hostname r4
!
enable password 7 030752180500
!
interface TokenRing0
 ip address 10.10.32.4 255.255.255.0
 ring-speed 4
!
interface TokenRing1
 no ip address
 shutdown
!
router bgp 8
 neighbor 10.10.32.2 remote-as 8
 neighbor 10.10.32.3 remote-as 8
!
no ip classless
!
!
line con 0
line aux 0
line vty 0 4
 password 7 030752180500
 login
!
end

r4#
```

Exercise 5: DLSW+ Fault Scenarios

The network shown in Figure 13-4 is intended to implement two DLSW peer groups, 1 and 2. Only R4 is in peer group 2 on the section of the network that is shown. All rings require SNA connectivity, and the Ethernet segment should only pass NetBIOS traffic. NetBIOS traffic should be prevented from propagating onto ring 2. R1 should only forward DLSW traffic to R4 if it is destined for the locally administered MAC address, 4000.0111.1c11, of the FEP.

Build the network topology shown in Figure 13-4 with the configuration information given (Listings 13-17 through 13-20). Diagnose and resolve 10 faults.

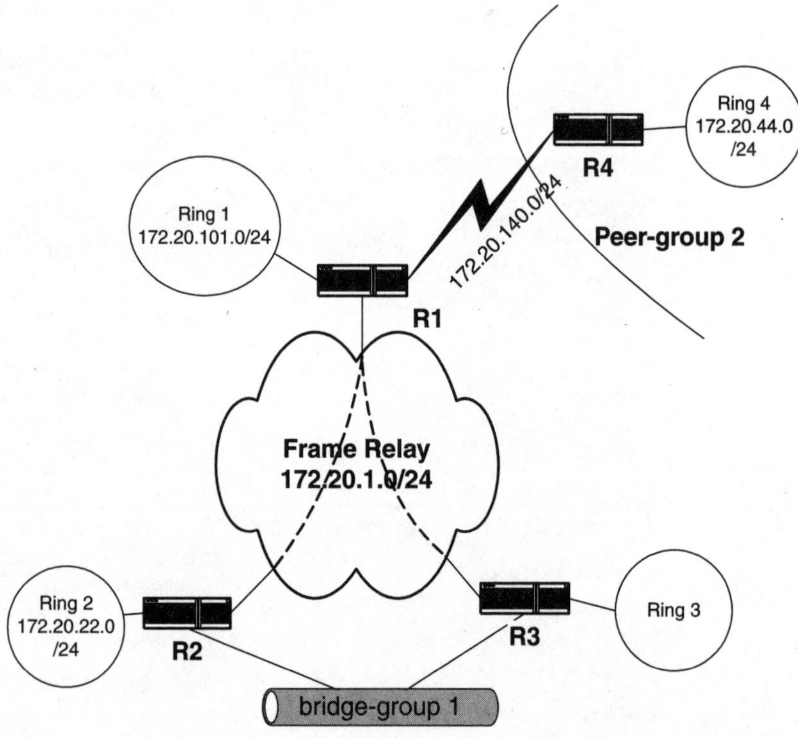

Figure 13-4 DLSW+ network for Exercise 5.

Listing 13-17

```
r1#sh run
Building configuration...

Current configuration:
!
version 11.2
no service password-encryption
no service udp-small-servers
no service tcp-small-servers
!
hostname r1
!
enable password cisco
!
source-bridge ring-group 100
dlsw local-peer peer-id 172.20.101.1 group 1 passive
dlsw remote-peer 0 tcp 172.20.140.4 dmac-output-list 720
!
interface Serial0
 ip address 172.20.1.1 255.255.255.0
 encapsulation frame-relay
 no ip split-horizon eigrp 10
 frame-relay map ip 172.20.1.2 102 broadcast
 frame-relay map ip 172.20.1.3 103 broadcast
 frame-relay lmi-type ansi
!
interface Serial1
 ip address 172.20.140.1 255.255.255.0
 ip access-group 10 in
!
interface TokenRing0
 ip address 172.20.101.1 255.255.255.0
 ring-speed 16
 source-bridge 1 1 100
 source-bridge spanning
!
interface TokenRing1
 no ip address
 shutdown
!
router eigrp 10
 network 172.20.0.0
!
no ip classless
access-list 10 permit 172.20.128.0 0.0.127.255
access-list 720 deny   4000.0111.1c11   0000.0000.0000
access-list 720 permit 0000.0000.0000   ffff.ffff.ffff
!
!
line con 0
line aux 0
line vty 0 4
 password cisco
 login
!
end
```

Listing 13-18

```
r2#sh run
Building configuration...

Current configuration:
!
version 11.2
no service password-encryption
no service udp-small-servers
no service tcp-small-servers
!
hostname r2
!
enable password cisco
!
source-bridge ring-group 100
dlsw local-peer peer-id 172.20.22.2 group 1
dlsw ring-list 1 rings 2 4
dlsw remote-peer 1 tcp 172.20.101.1
dlsw bridge-group 1
!
interface Serial0
 no ip address
 encapsulation frame-relay
 frame-relay lmi-type ansi
!
interface Serial0.1 point-to-point
 ip address 172.20.1.2 255.255.255.0
 frame-relay interface-dlci 201
!
interface Serial1
 no ip address
 shutdown
!
interface Ethernet0
 ip address 172.20.33.2 255.255.255.0
 bridge-group 1
 bridge-group 1 output-lsap-list 210
!
interface TokenRing1
 ip address 172.20.22.2 255.255.255.0
 ring-speed 16
 source-bridge 2 1 100
 source-bridge spanning
 source-bridge output-lsap-list 201
!
router eigrp 10
 network 172.20.0.0
!
no ip classless
access-list 201 permit 0x0404 0x0000
access-list 201 deny   0x0000 0xFFFF
access-list 210 permit 0x0404 0x0101
access-list 210 permit 0x0004 0x0101
!
bridge 1 protocol ieee
!
```

Listing 13-18 (*Cont.*)

```
line con 0
line aux 0
line vty 0 4
 password cisco
 login
!
end
```

Listing 13-19 (*Cont.*)

```
r3#sh run
Building configuration...

Current configuration:
!
version 11.2
!
hostname r3
!
enable password cisco
!
source-bridge ring-group 100
dlsw local-peer peer-id 172.20.1.3 group 1 border
dlsw remote-peer 0 tcp 172.20.1.1 lsap-output-list 250
dlsw bridge-group 1
!
interface TokenRing1/0
 no ip address
 ring-speed 16
 source-bridge 3 1 100
 source-bridge spanning
!
interface Ethernet2/0
 ip address 172.20.33.3 255.255.255.0
 bridge-group 1
 bridge-group 1 output-lsap-list 210
!
interface Serial3/3
 no ip address
 encapsulation frame-relay
 frame-relay lmi-type ansi
!
interface Serial3/3.1 point-to-point
 ip address 172.20.1.3 255.255.255.0
 frame-relay interface-dlci 301
!
router eigrp 10
 network 172.20.0.0
!
no ip classless
access-list 210 permit 0x0404 0x0101
access-list 210 permit 0x0004 0x0101
access-list 250 permit 0xF0F0 0x0101
!
```

Listing 13-19 (*Cont.*)

```
bridge 1 protocol ieee
!
line con 0
line aux 0
line vty 0
 password cisco
 login
line vty 1
 password cisco
 login
 length 0
line vty 2 4
 password cisco
 login
!
end
```

Listing 13-20

```
r4#sh run
Building configuration...

Current configuration:
!
version 11.2
service password-encryption
no service udp-small-servers
no service tcp-small-servers
!
hostname r4
!
enable password 7 060506324F41
!
source-bridge ring-group 200
dlsw local-peer peer-id 172.20.44.4 group 2 border
dlsw remote-peer 0 tcp 172.20.101.1
!
interface TokenRing0
 ip address 172.20.44.4 255.255.255.0
 ring-speed 16
 source-bridge 4 1 200
 source-bridge spanning
!
interface Serial0
 ip address 172.20.140.4 255.255.255.0
 no fair-queue
 clockrate 56000
!
router eigrp 10
 network 172.20.0.0
!
no ip classless
!
!
line con 0
```

Listing 13-20 *(Cont.)*

```
line aux 0
line vty 0 4
 password 7 045802150C2E
 login
!
end

r4#
```

Exercise 6: IPX RIP/EIGRP Fault Scenario

On the IPX network shown in Figure 13-5, all routers should be able to see all IPX routes. Each router also should see the SAPs for FSERV and PSERV. IPX RIP should run on each LAN, and IPX EIGRP should be the only protocol running on the WAN. Build the network with the configurations given (Listings 13-21 through 13-24) and then diagnose and resolve at least 10 network faults. Access lists can be modified but not deleted.

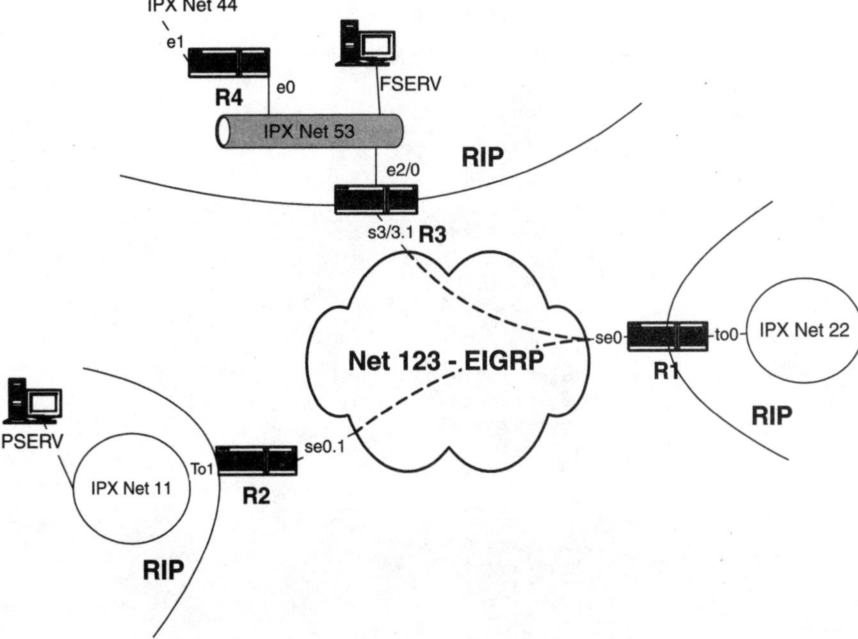

Figure 13-5 IPX RIP/EIGRP network for Exercise 6.

Listing 13-21

```
r1#sh run
Building configuration...

Current configuration:
!
version 11.2
no service password-encryption
no service udp-small-servers
no service tcp-small-servers
!
hostname r1
!
enable password cisco
!
ipx routing 0000.3060.1faa
!
interface Serial0
 ip address 172.20.1.1 255.255.255.0
 encapsulation frame-relay
 ipx network 123
 frame-relay map ip 172.20.1.2 102 broadcast
 frame-relay map ip 172.20.1.3 103 broadcast
 frame-relay lmi-type ansi
!
interface Serial1
 no ip address
 shutdown
!
interface TokenRing0
 no ip address
 ipx network 22
 ring-speed 16
!
interface TokenRing1
 no ip address
 shutdown
!
no ip classless
access-list 801 permit 20
access-list 1001 permit FFFFFFFF 7
access-list 1001 permit 11 4
!
!
ipx route 11 123.0010.1fc8.9c10
!
ipx router eigrp 10
 distribute-sap-list 1001 out
 distribute-list 801 out Serial0
 network 123
!
!
!
!
line con 0
line aux 0
```

Listing 13-21 (*Cont.*)

```
line vty 0 4
 password cisco
 login
!
end
```

Listing 13-22

```
r2#sh run

Building configuration...

Current configuration:
!
version 11.2
no service password-encryption
no service udp-small-servers
no service tcp-small-servers
!
hostname r2
!
enable password cisco
!
ipx routing 0000.3020.f8ed
!
interface Serial0
 no ip address
 encapsulation frame-relay
 frame-relay lmi-type ansi
!
interface Serial0.1 point-to-point
 ip address 172.20.1.2 255.255.255.0
 ipx network 129
 frame-relay interface-dlci 201
!
interface Serial1
 no ip address
 shutdown
!
interface TokenRing0
 no ip address
 shutdown
 ring-speed 16
!
interface TokenRing1
 no ip address
 ipx network 11
 ring-speed 16
!
no ip classless
access-list 1010 permit FFFFFFFF 7
!
!
```

Listing 13-22 (*Cont.*)

```
!
ipx router eigrp 10
 no redistribute rip
 distribute-sap-list 1010 in Serial0.1
 network 123
!
ipx router rip
 no network 123
!
ipx sap 7 PSERV 11.0000.0234.2213 451 1
!
!
line con 0
line aux 0
line vty 0 4
 password cisco
 login
!
end
```

Listing 13-23

```
r3#sh run
Building configuration...

Current configuration:
!
version 11.2
!
hostname r3
!
enable password cisco
!
ipx routing 0010.1fc8.9c10
!
interface Ethernet2/0
 no ip address
 ipx encapsulation SAP
 ipx network 53
 ipx output-sap-filter 1009
!
interface Serial3/3
 no ip address
 encapsulation frame-relay
 frame-relay lmi-type ansi
!
interface Serial3/3.1 point-to-point
 ip address 172.20.1.3 255.255.255.0
 ipx network 123
 frame-relay interface-dlci 301
!
no ip classless
access-list 1009 permit 11 4
access-list 1009 permit 22 4
!
```

Listing 13-23 (*Cont.*)

```
!
!
ipx router eigrp 10
 network 53
!
!
ipx sap 4 FSERV 53.0000.02f2.1ce2 451 1
!
!
line con 0
line aux 0
line vty 0
 password cisco
 login
 length 0
line vty 1 4
 password cisco
 login
!
end
```

Listing 13-24

```
r3#

r4#sh run
Building configuration...

Current configuration:
!
version 11.2
no service password-encryption
no service udp-small-servers
no service tcp-small-servers
!
hostname r4
!
enable password cisco
!
ipx routing 0010.1fc8.3c01
!
interface Ethernet0
 no ip address
 ipx network 53
!
interface Ethernet1
 no ip address
 ipx network 44
!
no ip classless
!
line con 0
line aux 0
```

Listing 13-24 (*Cont.*)

```
line vty 0 4
 password cisco
 login
!
end
```

APPENDIX

Answers to Chapter Review Questions

Chapter 2

1. Attenuation, noise, crosstalk
2. 10^{8}
3. 10^{-9}
4. False. They are tested “on the reel” prior to installation.
5. False. The principle is equally applicable to copper cable.
6. Fault, Configuration, Accounting, Performance, Security
7. Managed devices, Agent, MIB, NMS
8. Reads, Writes, Traps, Traversal Operations
12. Using a capture filter.
13. False, transport layer up to application layer can also be analyzed.

Chapter 3

1. b
2. d
3. e
4. d
5. e

6. e
7. a
8. a
9. a
10. b
11. c
12. e
13. c
14. c, e, a, b, d
15. a, e, b, c, d
16. c
17. c
18. c, a, b, d, e
19. d
20. Show controllers token ring 0

Chapter 4

1. a
2. c
3. e
4. b and d
5. False
6. b
7. False
8. Broadcast
9. Show line
10. e
11. b
12. b
13. d
14. d
15. a and d

Chapter 5

1. b and c
2. b
3. c
4. c
5. b
6. a
7. False. Broadcasts and multicasts will be dropped.
8. a
9. c
10. c
11. c and d
12. d
13. b and d
14. Frame-relay broadcast queuing
15. b

Chapter 6

1. b
2. a
3. a
4. debug dialer
5. b
6. debug isdn q931
7. c
8. dialer idle-timeout 300
9. a
10. show dialer
11. d
12. e
13. PPP multilink

14. IP OSPF demand-circuit
15. a

Chapters 7 and 8

1. e
2. c
3. e
4. `passive-interface ethernet0`
5. a
6. `show ip protocols`
7. e
8. `access-list 1 permit 172.16.0.0`
   `access-list 1 deny 172.16.0.0 0.0.255.255`
9. e
10. a
11. e
12. `no ip route-cache`
13. a
14. d
15. c, d, a, b
16. d
17. a
18. The DF bit
19. `clear ip route *`
20. b
21. `ip summary-address EIGRP 21` *`network mask`*
22. a
23. c and e
24. c, d, and e
25. An increasing number of route queries have not been replied to by the neighbor in question.
26. c and d

27. c
28. b
29. Area-Border Router (ABR)
30. `ospf demand-circuit`
31. c and d
32. a
33. `subnets`
34. d
35. c and d
36. `timers basic`
37. d, c, b, e, a
38. b
39. b
40. b, d, e, a, c

Chapter 9

1. d
2. b
3. c
4. `debug ipx routing events`
5. d
6. c
7. `ipx maximum-paths`
8. `ipx per-host-load-share`
9. b
10. e
11. d
12. `Novell standard echo`
13. c
14. e
15. d
16. e

17. d
18. a
19. c
20. b

Chapter 10

1. b
2. False. Zones can be extended across multiple cable-ranges.
3. e
4. a and c
5. `Appletalk permit-partial-zones`
6. d
7. d
8. c
9. c
10. c
11. d
12. b
13. b and d
14. c
15. d

Chapter 11

1. d
2. `show rif`
3. False. It only resets the SRB statistical counters.
4. d
5. False
6. a
7. a and b
8. c and e

9. b
10. d
11. SRB background
12. False. The virtual-ring counts also.
13. e
14. `source-bridge remote-peer 300 tcp 3.3.3.3`
15. e
16. c
17. d and e
18. R2 B4 R10
19. a, b, and d
20. c

Chapter 12

1. a
2. e
3. c
4. d
5. ```
   set span enable
   set span 4/6-7 6/1
   ```
6. d
7. b
8. ```
   set trunk 1/1 on isl
   clear trunk 1/1 30
   ```
9. `set spantree priority 0 21`
10. `set interface sc0 <ip address mask>` to set a static ip address.
11. Cannot configure VLANs on a VTP client
12. e
13. d
14. e
15. a

16. b and c

17. d

18. c and d

19. c

20. a and b

Chapter 13

Exercise 1

```
r4(boot)#copy tftp flash

No files on System flash
[0 bytes used, 4194304 available, 4194304 total]

Address or name of remote host [255.255.255.255]?
Source file name? c4000-j-mz.112-18.bin
Destination file name [default = source name]?
Accessing file 'c4000-j-mz.112-18.bin' on 255.255.255.255...
Loading from 10.10.32.2:
Device needs erasure before copying new file
Erase flash device before writing? [confirm]
Copy `c4000-j-mz.112-18.bin' from TFTP server
as `c4000-j-mz.112-18.bin' into Flash WITH erase ? y
Erasing device...  ... erased
Loading from 10.10.32.2:
!!!!!!!!!!!!!!!!!!!!!!!!!!!!!!!!!!!!!!!!!!!!!!!!!!!!!!!!
!!!!!!!!!!!!!!!!!!!!!!!!!!!!!!!!!!!!!!!!!!!!!!!!!!!!!!!!!!!!!!!!!!!!!!
!!!!!!!!!!
!!!!!!!!!!!!!!!!!!!!!!!!!!!!!!!!!!!!!!!!!!!!!!!!!!!!!!!!!!!!!!!!!!!!!!
!!!!!!!!!!
!!!!!!!!!!! [OK - 3707389/4194304 bytes]

Verifying checksum...  OK (0xCFF8)
Flash copy took 72640 msecs
r4(boot)#sh flash

System flash directory:
File  Length   Name/status
  1   3707389  c4000-j-mz.112-18.bin
[3707456 bytes used, 486848 available, 4194304 total]
4096K bytes of processor board System flash (Read/Write)

r4(boot)#sh version
4000 Bootstrap Software (XX-RXBOOT), Version 9.14(9), RELEASE SOFTWARE
  (fc1)
Patchlevel = 9.1(12.6)
Copyright (c) 1986-1994 by cisco Systems, Inc.
Compiled Wed 28-Sep-94 14:28 by chansen
```

```
System Bootstrap, Version 4.14(9), SOFTWARE

r4 uptime is 4 minutes
System restarted by reload
Running default software

cisco 4000 (68030) processor (revision 0xA0) with 16384K/4096K bytes of
  memory.
Processor ID 5011111
DDN X.25 software, Version 2.0, NET2 and BFE compliant.
2 Token Ring/IEEE 802.5 interfaces.
4 Serial network interfaces.
128K bytes of non-volatile configuration memory.

4096K bytes of processor board System flash (Read/Write)
Configuration register is 0x2101
r4(boot)#conf t

Enter configuration commands, one per line.
Edit with DELETE, CTRL/W, and CTRL/U; end with CTRL/Z
config-reg 0x2102
^Z

r4(boot)#sh ver
4000 Bootstrap Software (XX-RXBOOT), Version 9.14(9),
  RELEASE SOFTWARE (fc1)
Patchlevel = 9.1(12.6)
Copyright (c) 1986-1994 by cisco Systems, Inc.
Compiled Wed 28-Sep-94 14:28 by chansen

System Bootstrap, Version 4.14(9), SOFTWARE

r4 uptime is 5 minutes
System restarted by reload
Running default software

cisco 4000 (68030) processor (revision 0xA0) with 16384K/4096K bytes of
  memory.
Processor ID 5011111
DDN X.25 software, Version 2.0, NET2 and BFE compliant.
2 Token Ring/IEEE 802.5 interfaces.
4 Serial network interfaces.
128K bytes of non-volatile configuration memory.

4096K bytes of processor board System flash (Read/Write)
Configuration register is 0x2101 (will be 0x2102 at next reload)

r4(boot)# reload
[confirm]

r4#sh ver
Cisco Internetwork Operating System Software
IOS (tm) 4000 Software (C4000-J-M), Version 11.2(18),
  RELEASE SOFTWARE (fc1)
Copyright (c) 1986-1999 by cisco Systems, Inc.
Compiled Mon 05-Apr-99 21:09 by jaturner
```

```
Image text-base: 0x00012000, data-base: 0x007742AC

ROM: System Bootstrap, Version 4.14(9), SOFTWARE

r4 uptime is 1 minute
System restarted by reload
System image file is "c4000-j-mz.112-18.bin", booted via flash

cisco 4000 (68030) processor (revision 0xA0) with 16384K/4096K bytes of
  memory.
Processor board ID 5011111
G.703/E1 software, Version 1.0.
Bridging software.
SuperLAT software copyright 1990 by Meridian Technology Corp).
X.25 software, Version 2.0, NET2, BFE and GOSIP compliant.
TN3270 Emulation software.
2 Token Ring/IEEE 802.5 interface(s)
4 Serial network interface(s)
128K bytes of non-volatile configuration memory.
4096K bytes of processor board System flash (Read/Write)

Configuration register is 0x2102

r4#
```

NOTE:

1. *Since the TFTP server was on a broadcast segment, it was not required to know its IP address.*
2. *The other problem was that the configuration register was set to 0x2101, forcing the router to boot from ROM instead of from Flash.*

Exercise 2

Faults:

1. Traffic from IGRP to EIGRP is going via R3, when R2 is supposed to be the preferred path. The redistribution metric should be made more favorable on R2 than R3.
2. Likewise EIGRP to IGRP traffic is going via R3 rather than R2.
3. The 100.0.0.0 class A network is not getting summarized even when it crosses a major network boundary, resulting in larger routing tables downstream in the EIGRP domain. Summarization must be manually configured because EIGRP does not automatically summarize external routes. Use the `ip summary-address eigrp 10 100.0.0.0 255.0.0.0` interface command.

4. The 10.129.17.0 and 10.129.18.0 routes are appearing only as summary and not as explicit routes. This is due to the manually configured summary route: 10.129.16.0/21. In implementing the correct policy, remove this manual summarization and also disable EIGRP autosummary, so that R1 will also see explicit routes.
5. Can you spot any potential for a routing loop? A loop can be created due to the two points of mutual redistribution between IGRP and EIGRP, as routes that originate in one domain get redistributed back into that domain. Research the topic of mutual redistribution, and then play with this network in your lab.

Exercise 3

Faults:

1. There is a mismatch of OSPF network types on the three frame-relay interfaces for R1, R2, and R3.
2. If this problem is resolved by making them all broadcast networks, then R1 not R3 should have the highest OSPF priority so that it will become the designated router. R3 cannot be the DR because it does not have a PVC to R2.
3. The hello interval on R3's frame-relay interface does not match with R1; therefore neighbors cannot be formed.
4. R1's MD5 password for OSPF area 0 does not match that of R2 and R3.
5. 172.20.22.0/27 is not visible within RIP. R1 must summarize this as a 24-bit subnet mask.
6. 172.20.11.0/28 is not visible with RIP because R2 has it summarized as a 26-bit mask. It should be a 24-bit mask.
7. There is a missing `subnets` keyword on R3 when redistributing from RIP to OSPF.
8. R4 cannot see R3's RIP routes because of the mismatch between RIP versions 1 and 2. Either R3 should send version 1 or R5 should be configured for version 2.
9. The route maps on R3 are incorrect. For example, access-list 1 permits only a specific match of 141.8.0.x, along with 172.20.33.0. Hence the 141.9.20.0 and 172.20.30.0 routes will not be redistributed into OSPF. A correct solution is:

```
access-list 1 permit 141.9.0.0 0.0.255.255
access-list 2 permit any
access-list 3 permit 172.20.0.0 0.0.63.255
route-map os-rip deny 10
 match ip address 1
!
route-map os-rip permit 20
 match ip address 2
!
route-map rip-os permit 27
 match ip address 1
!
route-map rip-os permit 28
 match ip address 3
```

10. The summary route 141.8.0.0/13 is configured on both R2 and R3. From R1's perspective this creates a discontiguous network for this route. R1 will be able to ping 141.10.22.2 but not 141.9.20.4. This is because RIP routes are redistributed into OSPF with a lower metric on R2 than R3 (50 compared to 100). This summarization must be changed on R2 or R3 so that the advertised summary routes don't have overlapping prefixes for 141.x.0.0. Summarizing the routes as 141.9.0.0/16 and 141.10.0.0/16 respectively could solve the problem.
11. The `vty 0 4 exec-timeout` on R3 is just 1 second. It should be returned to its default value so that you can successfully telnet into R3.

Exercise 4

Faults:

1. The local preference for 172.16.0.0 and 172.30.0.0 should be higher on R3 than on R2.
2. The metric advertised into AS4 for 10.0.0.0 routes should be lower from R2 than from R3.
3. Synchronization should be disabled on R2, R3, and R4, so that all routes will appear in IP routing tables.
4. R4 should have R2 as a route-reflector client so that R2 will see the 10.10.0.0 network in BGP.
5. R1 is using R2's token-ring address to define neighbor relationship; it should use a directly connected serial link for EBGP.
6. R3 needs a mask statement to distribute 10.10.0.0 into BGP.
7. R2 and R3 should use the next-hop-self attribute in relation to R4, since R4 has no route to the 192.168.12/13.x next-hop.

8. R4 token ring 0 has ring speed = 4.
9. Distribute-list 1 out on R1 prevents it from advertising 172.30.0.0 to R3.
10. Filter-list 9 on R2 prevents it from advertising any routes to R1 that originate in AS8.

Exercise 5

Faults:

1. The ring list on R2 prevents communication with ring 1.
2. R3 is the border peer for group 1; it should be R1.
3. R1 should be the border peer and in promiscuous mode. In passive mode it cannot initiate peer connections.
4. R3 has an inconsistent peer definition for R1. It uses 172.20.1.1 instead of 172.20.101.1, which R1 uses in its local peer definition.
5. The IP access-group 10 on R1 serial 1 prevents it from forming a peer with R4.
6. The `dmac-output-list` 720 on R1 applied to the R4 peer definition is the opposite from what is required. Traffic to 4000.0111.1c11 is blocked, the following simpler configuration would suffice:

```
dlsw remote-peer 0 tcp 172.20.44.4 dest-mac 4000.0111.1c11
```

7. The LSAP-list 250 applied on R3 to its peer definition for R1 permits only NetBIOS traffic. This will cause a problem for ring 3 users.
8. The LSAP-list 210 applied to the Ethernet on R2 and R3 permits only SNA! This access list should be like access-list 250 on R3.
9. On R2 access-list 201 should be modified to the following to allow for Command and Response and the Null SAP:

```
Access-list 201 permit 0x0404 0x0101
Access-list 201 permit 0x0004 0x0101
```

10. DLSW should not be enabled on the Ethernet interfaces of both R2 and R3. The reason is that CUR messages from this segment will receive ICR replies that propagate onto the Ethernet from each router port. This can cause loops since there is no RIF to dis-

tinguish between the ICR messages. Disable DLSW on one of these interfaces.

Exercise 6

Faults:

1. EIGRP split-horizon must be disabled on R1 serial0.
2. Different IPX Ethernet encapsulations on R3 (SAP) and R4 (Novell_Ether).
3. Incorrect IPX address on R2 se0.1 (129).
4. Distribute-list 801 on R1 permits only network 20 to be advertised out serial 0. It should include all IPX networks.
5. R2 has `no redistribute rip` in its EIGRP configuration. This should be removed. However if you test this you may find that connected routes continue to be redistributed into EIGRP.
6. Static route on R1 that incorrectly points to R3 as the next-hop for network 11.
7. R3 Ethernet0 has an `ipx-output-sap` filter that only allows type 4 SAPs from networks 11 and 22. Thus R4 cannot see the type 7 SAP from network 11.
8. R2 has an inbound SAP filter 1010 that only allows type 7 SAPs.
9. On R3, network 53 has been placed in the EIGRP process rather than the frame-relay network.
10. R1 has an outbound SAP filter in EIGRP that blocks the file service (SAP type 4) from network 53.
11. IPX RIP has not been disabled on the PVC between R1 and R3.

INDEX

C

D

E

K

L

M

N

O

P

Q

R

T

U

V

W

X

Z

ABOUT THE AUTHOR

Cormac S. Long (MSEE, CCNP™; CCNA™) has more than 12 years' experience as a network administrator, and is currently a network design consultant with MCI. He has designed and installed Cisco-based networks for such clients as the Bank of America, Pacific Bell, and Telecom Ireland. He holds a master's degree in engineering.

ABOUT THE REVIEWERS

As the leading publisher of technical books for more than 100 years, McGraw-Hill prides itself on bringing you the most authoritative and up-to-date information available. To ensure that our books meet the highest standards of accuracy, we have asked top professionals and technical experts to review the accuracy of the material you are about to read.

We take great pleasure in thanking the following technical reviewers for their insights:

John L. Mairs, CCNA, has worked in the computing and information systems field for more than 14 years. Currently, he is President of Analogix (San Carlos, CA). He has held positions at Lincoln Electric, Executive Systems Controlling, and Professional Data Systems, which he founded.

Jonathan R. Worthington is President of American International Business Planning Inc., a systems consulting concern that operates primarily in New York City, New Jersey, and Connecticut. The company specializes in providing project management, systems integration, and systems design services for large corporations and New York City government agencies. Product specialties are Cisco, Bay and Fore, IBM, VTAM, NCP. The company has been in existence since 1994.

Mr. Worthington is a graduate of Fordham University, CLC with a BA in Economics. He has been employed for the past eighteen years in the technology industry, working with LAN and WAN technologies for several companies, designing and implementing IBM SNA, IP, Frame Relay, ATM, VPN, as well as Ethernet and Token Ring switching networks.